concepts in strategic management

canadian edition

concepts in **strategic** management

thomas l. wheelen
UNIVERSITY OF SOUTH FLORIDA

j. david hunger
IOWA STATE UNIVERSITY

david wicks
ST. MARY'S UNIVERSITY

PEARSON
Prentice
Hall

Toronto

National Library of Canada Cataloguing in Publication

Wheelen, Thomas L.
   Concepts in strategic management / Thomas L. Wheelen, J. David Hunger, David Wicks.—Canadian ed.

Includes index.
ISBN 0-13-121497-7

   1. Strategic planning. I. Hunger, J. David, 1941– II. Wicks, David, 1964– III. Title.

HD30.28.W46 2005   658.4'012   C2003-905584-1

0-13-121497-7

Vice President, Editorial Director: Michael J. Young
Acquisitions Editor: James Bosma
Marketing Manager: Bill Todd
Developmental Editor: Meaghan Eley
Production Editor: Jennifer Handel
Copy Editor: Martin Townsend
Proofreader: Dawn Hunter
Production Coordinator: Andrea Falkenberg
Page Layout: Bill Renaud
Art Director: Julia Hall
Interior and Cover Design: Gillian Tsintziras
Cover Image: Photonica

Statistics Canada information is used with the permission of the Minister of Industry, as Minister responsible for Statistics Canada. Information on the availability of the wide range of data from Statistics Canada can be obtained from Statistics Canada's Regional Offices, its World Wide Web site at http://www.statcan.ca, and its toll-free access number 1-800-263-1136. The Statistics Canada CANSIM II database can be accessed at http://cansim2.statcan.ca/cgi-win/CNSMCGI.EXE.

1 2 3 4 5   09 08 07 06 05

Printed and bound in Canada.

Brief Contents

Contents

Preface

Concepts in Strategic Management was written to introduce you to strategic management—a field of inquiry that focuses on the organization as a whole and its interactions with its environment. The business world is in the process of transformation driven by information technology (in particular the internet) and globalization. Strategic management takes a panoramic view of this changing terrain and attempts to show how large and small organizations can be more effective and efficient not only in today's world, but in tomorrow's as well.

This text contains the latest theory and research currently available in strategic management. We sifted through recent articles from the following academic and business publications: *Academy of Management Journal, Strategic Management Journal, Academy of Management Review, Administrative Science Quarterly, Journal of Management, Long Range Planning, Organization Science, Academy of Management Executive, Organization Dynamics, Journal of Business Strategy, SAM Advanced Management Journal, Journal of Business Strategies, Strategy and Leadership* (previously *Planning Review*), *Strategy and Business, Competitive Intelligence, Journal of Business Venturing, Entrepreneurship Theory and Practice, Harvard Business Review, Business Week,* and *The Economist.*

The concepts and exercises concluding each chapter have been class-tested in strategy courses and revised based on feedback from students and instructors. The first 10 chapters are organized around a strategic management model that prefaces each chapter and provides a structure for both content and case analysis. We emphasize those concepts that have proven to be most useful in understanding strategic decision making and in conducting case analysis. Our goal was to make the text as comprehensive as possible without getting bogged down in any one area. Endnote references are provided for those who want to learn more about any particular topic. As an aid to case analysis, we propose the strategic audit as an analytical technique.

OBJECTIVES

This book focuses on the following objectives, typically found in most strategic management and business policy courses:

- To develop an understanding of strategic concepts, research, and theories
- To develop a framework of analysis to enable a student to identify central issues and problems in complex, comprehensive cases; to suggest alternative courses of action; and to present well-supported recommendations for future action
- To develop conceptual skills so that a student is able to integrate previously learned aspects of organizations
- To develop an understanding of the global economy and the internet and their current and potential impact on business activities in any location
- To develop an understanding of the role of corporate governance in strategic management
- To develop the ability to analyze and evaluate, both quantitatively and qualitatively, the performance of the people responsible for strategic decisions

- To bridge the gap between theory and practice by developing an understanding of when and how to apply concepts and techniques learned in earlier courses on marketing, accounting, finance, management, production, and information systems

- To improve research capabilities necessary to gather and interpret key environmental data

- To develop a better understanding of the present and future environments in which organizations must function

- To develop analytical and decision-making skills for dealing with complex conceptual problems in an ethical and socially responsible manner

This book achieves these objectives by presenting and explaining concepts and theories useful in understanding the strategic management process. It critically analyzes studies in the field of strategy to acquaint the student with the literature of this area and to help develop the student's research capabilities. It also suggests a model of strategic management. It recommends the strategic audit as one approach to the systematic analysis of complex organization-wide issues. Through a series of special issue and comprehensive cases (available in the cases text that accompanies this book), it provides the student with an opportunity to apply concepts, skills, and techniques to real-world business problems. The book focuses on the business organization because of its crucial position in the economic system of the world and in the material development of any society.

TIME-TESTED FEATURES

This edition contains many of the same features and content that helped make previous editions successful. Some of the features are the following:

- A strategic management model runs throughout the first 10 chapters as a unifying concept (explained in Chapter 1).

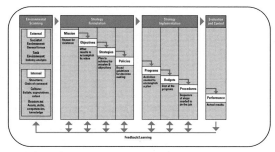

- Social responsibility and managerial ethics are examined in detail in terms of how they affect decision making. This chapter now contains an expanded discussion of a culture of ethics within organizations (Chapter 2).

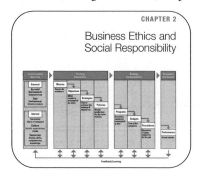

- Equal emphasis is placed on environmental scanning of the social environment as well as on the task environment. Topics include forecasting, the competitive advantage of nations, and industry competitive analysis (Chapter 3).

- Core and distinctive competencies are examined within the framework of the resource-based view of the firm (Chapter 4).

- Lean manufacturing, which emphasizes the elimination of waste throughout a production process, is discussed as a new operations strategy (Chapter 7).

- Two chapters deal with issues in strategy implementation, such as organizational and job design plus strategy-manager fit, action planning, and organizational culture (Chapters 8 and 9).

- A separate chapter on evaluation and control explains the importance of measurement and incentives to organizational performance. Corporate governance is examined in terms of the roles, responsibilities, and interactions of top management and the board of directors in the context of monitoring the organization's behaviour and ensuring the interests of shareholders are safeguarded (Chapter 10).

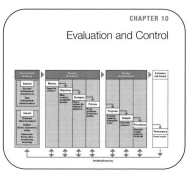

- A chapter dedicated to the strategic issues in managing not-for-profit organizations, issues that are often ignored by other strategy textbooks (Chapter 11).

- Suggestions for in-depth case analysis provide a complete listing of financial ratios, recommendations for oral and written analysis, and ideas for further research (Appendix).

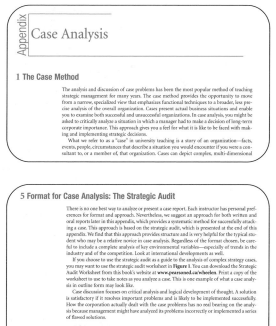

- The strategic audit, a way to operationalize the strategic decision-making process, provides a tested methodology in case analysis (Appendix).

- The Strategic Audit Worksheet is based on the time-tested strategic audit and is designed to help students organize and structure daily case preparation in a brief period of time. The worksheet works exceedingly well for checking the level of daily student case preparation—especially for open class discussions on cases (Appendix).

Figure 1 Strategic Audit Worksheet

Strategic Audit Heading	Analysis		
	(+) Factors	(−) Factors	Comments
I. Current Situation			
A. Past Corporate Performance Indexes			
B. Strategic Posture: Current Mission Current Objectives Current Strategies Current Policies			
SWOT Analysis Begins:			
II. Corporate Governance			
A. Board of Directors			
B. Top Management			
III. External Environment (EFAS): Opportunities and Threats (SWOT)			
A. Societal Environment			
B. Task Environment (Industry Analysis)			
IV. Internal Environment (IFAS): Strengths and Weaknesses (SWOT)			
A. Corporate Structure			
B. Corporate Culture			

- Theory As It Applies capsules in various chapters explain key theories and underlying strategic management. This feature adds emphasis to the theories but does not interrupt the flow of the text material.

Theory As It Applies
Transaction Cost Economics Analyzes Vertical Growth Strategy

- An experiential exercise focusing on the material covered in each chapter helps the reader to apply strategic concepts to an actual situation.

FEATURES NEW TO THIS CANADIAN EDITION

Eleven Revised and Updated Chapters of Text

- At the beginning of each chapter is a short description of a Canadian company's recent activities, discussed in the context of the material presented in the chapter.

- A series of margin definitions enable the reader to find and concisely define important concepts as they are introduced in each chapter.

- Each chapter contains a major section dealing with the impact of the internet on the content in that chapter as well as a boxed insert providing an illustration of how the Internet is affecting strategic management.

- A new section on theories of organizational adaptation has been added to Chapter 1, along with a discussion of organizational success and failure.

- Chapter 3 contains a new section on the determinants of national advantage as well as one on using key success factors to create an industry matrix.

- Organizational stakeholders are also discussed in Chapter 3 but separately from other competitive forces, with their needs and priorities incorporated into the strategy formulation process.

- Chapter 3 now includes a categorization of international industries as a function of pressure for coordination and pressure for local responsiveness.

- The resource-based view of the firm is discussed in detail in Chapter 4. Expanding this discussion from the previous edition allows us to include an activity system map as a means for displaying and understanding the complexities of competitive advantage in organizations.

- Chapter 6 contains an expanded section on horizontal corporate strategy and multipoint competition.

- Real options are discussed in Chapter 7 as a way of evaluating strategic alternatives in a turbulent environment.

- Strategy implementation in Chapter 8 now includes a section on the cellular organization, a new type of structure, which goes beyond the network structure.

- Chapter 10 includes a new section dealing with enterprise resource planning as a part of strategic information systems.

- The corporate governance theory capsule in Chapter 10 compares agency theory with stewardship theory.

- Chapter 11 describes the non-profit sector in Canada and identifies the unique strategies required by these firms to generate the resources necessary to achieve their mission.

SUPPLEMENTS

Many supplemental materials are available to the instructor and student, including an Instructor's Resource CD-ROM containing the Instructor's Manual, Computerized Test Item File, and PowerPoint Electronic Transparencies; and New Part-Ending Videos.

Instructor's Resource CD-ROM

The Instructor's Resource CD-ROM includes the electronic Instructor's Manual, Computerized Test Item File (TestGen-EQ software), and PowerPoint Electronic Transparencies.

Instructor's Manual

- To aid in discussing the 11 chapters dealing with strategic management concepts, the Instructor's Manual includes summaries of each chapter, suggested answers to discussion questions, suggestions for using end-of-chapter cases and exercises, and additional discussion questions (with answers) and lecture modules.

Computerized Test Item File

- The TestGen-EQ test-generating software allows instructors to custom design, save, and generate classroom tests. The test program permits instructors to edit, add, or delete questions from the test banks; edit existing graphics and create new graphics; analyze test results; and organize a database of tests and student results. This new software allows for greater flexibility and ease of use.

PowerPoints

- The PowerPoint transparencies, a comprehensive package of text outlines and figures corresponding to the text, are designed to aid the educator and supplement in-class lectures.

CBC Video Segments

Current information from the CBC series *Venture* complements the text and enhances learning by bringing to life practical applications and issues. With the latest news and information, these videos provide an excellent vehicle for launching lectures, showing additional examples, and sparking classroom discussion. Accompanying case information can be found at the end of the four parts in the text.

ACKNOWLEDGEMENTS

I would like to thank the many people at Pearson Education Canada who helped make this edition possible. I am especially grateful to my editors: James Bosma, who got the project off the ground in the first place; Meaghan Eley, who worked tirelessly and patiently throughout the development stage; Martin Townsend, whose copy editing improved the readability of the text greatly; and Jennifer Handel and Andrea Falkenberg, who oversaw the production of the text and accompanying supplements.

I am also grateful to Lee Whitmore and Charlene Hercules, both MBA students at Saint Mary's University, for their technical expertise in preparing this manuscript and the accompanying PowerPoint slides.

Lastly, to the many strategy/policy instructors and students who have expressed their problems with the strategy/policy course: I have tried to respond to your concerns as best as possible by providing a comprehensive yet usable text coupled with recent and complex cases. To you, the people who work hard in the strategy/policy trenches, I acknowledge my debt. This book is yours.

D.W.
Halifax, Nova Scotia

CHAPTER 1

Basic Concepts of Strategic Management

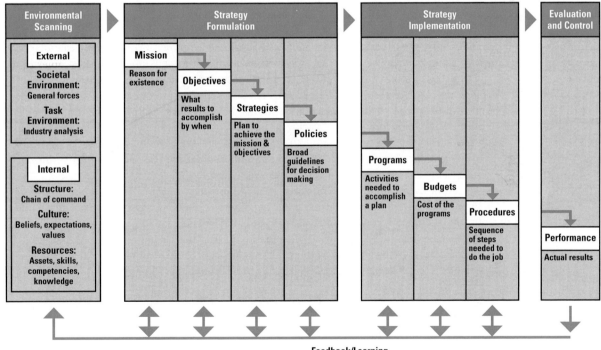

Learning Objectives

After reading this chapter you should be able to

Understand the benefits of strategic thinking to a variety of organizations

Explain how globalization and electronic commerce have influenced strategic management

Recognize the importance of strategic flexibility and organizational learning in today's highly competitive environment

Define the four elements of strategic management

Identify some common triggering events that act as stimuli for strategic change

How does a company become successful and stay successful? By making wise strategic choices and then following them up by creating an organization capable of implementing them. History has shown us that successful organizations in a wide variety of industries can be managed in many different styles, pursuing one strategy or a combination of strategies. So although different organizations have become successful by doing many things differently, what they share is an attention to the foundation of successful strategies and to the decisions that need to be made in order to implement them.

Bombardier is one of Canada's best-known companies. Founded in 1942 by Joseph-Armand Bombardier, this once-small organization has turned into a large, diversified, multinational manufacturing and services company. It is currently a world-leading manufacturer of business jets, regional aircraft, rail transportation equipment, and motorized recreational products. It also provides financial services and asset management in business areas aligned with its core products. The tremendous success of Bombardier is due in large part to its growth through carefully selected acquisitions. Bombardier's vision is to be the leader in all markets in which it operates. To achieve this leadership position, it seeks to exceed customer expectations with innovative products and services. At the heart of its strategy to realize this vision is the company's expertise in developing and commercializing innovative products, such as the Ski-Doo that Bombardier's founder invented.

From its beginning, this combination of acquisitions and initiatives has led Bombardier to invest in certain industries while avoiding others. In other words, it has followed a strategy involving targeted growth into areas where it had particular expertise. Throughout all of this, Bombardier had to be adaptive. For example, during the energy crisis and recession of the 1970s, sales of recreational products slowed, so the company made product changes to enhance fuel efficiency and lower costs. In 1974 Bombardier diversified into transit equipment with a contract to build rolling stock for the City of Montreal's subway system. It followed this up with a number of related acquisitions that provided it with a large customer base, significant production capacity, and skilled management. In 1986 it diversified into the aerospace industry through its acquisition of Canadair. Again this first step was followed by acquisitions that solidified its position in this industry, allowing the company to achieve its goal of being a market leader in every market in which it operates.

This type of strategy might not be right for all firms, but it was successful for Bombardier throughout the 1980s and 1990s. The company's strategic investment in new markets not only provided a basis for future sales growth but also diversified its portfolio of businesses to mitigate weaknesses in any given market. But perhaps more important, its choice to be a big player in a small number of markets allowed it to create a critical mass in all of its markets. This permitted Bombardier to offer expanded product lines and engage in the development of new technologies to keep it ahead of its rivals.

Supporting all activities at Bombardier is a Six Sigma concept,[1] a goal of generating fewer than four defects over one million operations. This performance improvement strategy was adopted by Bombardier in 1997 to increase both the speed and the accuracy of its business activities. Implementing Six Sigma required extensive training and a lot of process redesign, but the results have been tremendous. In fact Six Sigma's tools and principles have become a crucial part of Bombardier's highly successful overall business strategy.[2]

Even strategies such as these are not without risk. The events of September 11, 2001, have harmed virtually every business associated with airplanes and tourism. As a result, thousands of Bombardier workers worldwide have been laid off, a significant portion of them Canadians. Bombardier CEO Paul Tellier has responded to this by adjusting the organization's strategy. To create a healthy organization that can successfully compete in a small number of large markets, he is trying to spin off the recreational products division and raise $1.5 billion in doing so. Because this division is mature and foreign competition is fierce, it represents a drain on corporate resources that Tellier wants to use to improve the company's core businesses: planes and trains.[3]

1.1 The Study of Strategic Management

strategic management
the set of decisions, actions, and investments that determine an organization's performance

Strategic management is the set of managerial decisions, and the actions and investments that follow, that determine the long-run performance of an organization. It includes environmental scanning (both external and internal), strategy formulation (strategic or long-range planning), strategy implementation, and evaluation and control. The study of strategic management, therefore, emphasizes the monitoring and evaluating of external opportunities and threats in light of an organization's capabilities. As a discipline, strategic management is thus concerned with the choices that organizations and their members make to improve performance. In profit-seeking firms it focuses on how profitable growth can be achieved, how the chances of survival can be enhanced, and how competition can be withstood. In non-profit organizations it is concerned with securing the financial resources necessary for achieving the organization's purpose, monitoring the effectiveness of service delivery, and understanding threats to the organization's survival.

EVOLUTION OF STRATEGIC MANAGEMENT

Many of the concepts and techniques dealing with strategic management have been developed and used successfully by business organizations such as General Electric and the Boston Consulting Group. Over time, business practitioners and academic researchers have expanded and refined these concepts. Initially, strategic management was of most use to larger organizations operating in multiple industries. Increasing risks of error, costly mistakes, and even economic ruin are causing today's professional managers in all organizations to take strategic management seriously in order to keep their companies competitive in an increasingly volatile environment.

As managers attempt to deal better with their changing world, their firms generally evolve through the following four phases of strategic management.[4]

Phase 1. *Basic financial planning:* Managers initiate serious planning when they are requested to propose next year's budget. Projects are proposed on the basis of very little analysis, with most information coming from within the firm. The sales force usually provides the small amount of environmental information. Such simplistic operational planning only pretends to be strategic management, yet it is quite time-consuming. Normal company activities are often suspended for weeks while managers try to cram ideas into the proposed budget. The time horizon of this type of planning is usually just one year.

Phase 2.   *Forecast-based planning:* As annual budgets become less useful at stimulating long-term planning, managers attempt to propose five-year plans. They now consider projects that may take more than one year. In addition to internal information, managers gather any available environmental data—usually on an ad hoc basis—and extrapolate current trends five years into the future. This phase is also time-consuming, often involving a full month of managerial activity to make sure all the proposed budgets fit together. The process gets very political as managers compete for larger shares of funds. Endless meetings take place to evaluate proposals and justify assumptions. The time horizon is usually three to five years.

Phase 3.   *Externally oriented planning (strategic planning):* Frustrated with highly political yet ineffectual five-year plans, top management takes control of the planning process by initiating strategic planning. The company seeks to increase its responsiveness to changing markets and competition by thinking strategically. Planning is taken out of the hands of lower level managers and concentrated in a planning staff whose task is to develop strategic plans for the organization. Consultants often provide the sophisticated and innovative techniques that the planning staff use to gather information and forecast future trends. Ex-military experts develop competitive intelligence units. Upper level managers meet once a year at a resort "retreat" led by key members of the planning staff to evaluate and update the current strategic plan. Such top-down planning emphasizes formal strategy formulation and leaves the implementation issues to lower management levels. Top management typically develops five-year plans with help from consultants but with minimal input from lower levels.

Phase 4.   *Advanced strategic management:* Realizing that even the best strategic plans are worthless without the input and commitment of lower level managers, top management forms planning groups of managers and key employees at many levels from various departments and work groups. They develop and integrate a series of strategic plans aimed at achieving the company's primary objectives. Strategic plans now detail the implementation, evaluation, and control issues. Rather than attempting to perfectly forecast the future, the plans emphasize probable scenarios and contingency strategies. The sophisticated annual five-year strategic plan is replaced with strategic thinking at all levels of the organization throughout the year. Strategic information, previously available only centrally to top management, is available via local area networks and intranets to people throughout the organization. Instead of a large centralized planning staff, internal and external planning consultants are available to help guide group strategy discussions. Although top management may still initiate the strategic planning process, the resulting strategies may come from anywhere in the organization. Planning is typically interactive across levels and is no longer top-down. People at all levels are now involved, and cross-functional work teams are increasingly popular.

BENEFITS OF STRATEGIC THINKING

Research has revealed that organizations that engage in strategic management generally outperform those that do not.[5] The attainment of an appropriate match or "fit" between an organization's environment and its strategy, structure, and processes has positive effects on the organization's performance.[6] For example, a study of the impact of deregulation on US railroads found that those railroads that changed their strategy as their environment changed outperformed those that did not change their strategy.[7] Studies of the deregulation of the US airline and trucking industries showed that strategic persistence (that is, a failure to change strategy in light of environmental changes) led to performance declines.[8]

A survey of organizations in a variety of countries and industries found these to be the three most highly rated benefits of strategic management:

- Clearer sense of strategic vision for the firm
- Sharper focus on what is strategically important
- Improved understanding of a rapidly changing environment[9]

To be effective, however, strategic management need not always be a formal process. It can begin with a few simple questions:

1. Where is the organization now? (Not where do we *hope* it is!)

2. If no changes are made, where will the organization be in one year? Two years? Five years? Ten years? Are the answers acceptable?

3. If the answers are not acceptable, what specific actions should management undertake? What are the risks and payoffs involved?

A survey by Bain & Company revealed the most popular management tools to be strategic planning and developing mission and vision statements—essential parts of strategic management.[10] Studies of the planning practices of actual organizations suggest that the real value of strategic planning may be more in the future-oriented nature of the planning process itself than in any written strategic plan. Small companies, in particular, may plan informally and irregularly. Nevertheless, studies of small businesses reveal that even though the degree of formality in strategic planning may have only a small to moderate impact on a firm's profitability, formal planners have significantly greater growth in sales than do informal planners.[11]

Planning the strategy of large, multidivisional organizations can become complex and time-consuming. It often takes slightly more than a year for a large company to move from situation assessment to a final decision agreement. Because of the relatively large number of people affected by a strategic decision in such a firm, a more sophisticated, formalized system is needed to ensure that strategic planning leads to successful performance. Otherwise, top management becomes isolated from developments in the business units, and lower level managers lose sight of the organizational mission and objectives.

WHAT MAKES ORGANIZATIONS SUCCESSFUL?

Strategic management is concerned with understanding how organizations can become and remain successful. But what do we mean by "success" and how can we tell when it has been achieved? These are by no means simple questions. What must be considered are the types of criteria of effectiveness that different constituencies use and what impact these have on the organization.

How well an organization is doing, and how this is assessed, can be understood in a number of ways.[12] First, organizations can be viewed as goal-achieving entities, and as such they become "successful" by efficiently and effectively achieving their stated goals and purposes. By measuring production levels, quality, productivity, and efficient use of resources, organizations view success in their own terms, that is, in relation to the goals and objectives they define in their strategies. Second, organizations will additionally engage in activities to create the supports necessary to achieve their primary goals. Examples of these supports include high levels of management skill and employee satisfaction and morale, and low levels of staff absenteeism and turnover. All of these indicate the success of an organization's efforts to create a collection of people and processes that will support the accomplishment of organizational goals. Finally, organizations need to be skilled in activities such as information acquisition and processing, especially in terms of environmental scanning and forecasting. An organization's survival is increasingly tied to its ability to detect and respond to changes in its environment. Organizations also need to be able to provide value to consumers, which requires effective market sensing and research.

In addition to these different facets of success, organizations need to be mindful of the different constituents (or stakeholders) that shape the views and definitions of organizational performance. It is often the case that different stakeholders have different goals and as such might view an organization's activities in very different ways. For example, workers might view their employer's investment in training and development and above-average wages as indicators of success. On the other hand, the community in which the organization operates might view philanthropy and environmental responsibility as primary indicators. Any organization will face a variety of constituencies that will set criteria for assessing organizational performance. Unfortunately these criteria sometimes conflict. The criteria important to each constituent are usually based on self-interest. Customers want superior value, suppliers want top dollar for their products and predictable sales. In other words, we should expect stakeholders to evaluate firm performance in terms of criteria that benefit them.

What does this mean for organizations? It means that success can take many shapes and must be understood in context: success at doing what, and success according to whom? Throughout the process of strategic development, it is important to keep these questions in mind. Doing so will ensure that the interests of a diverse group of stakeholders are considered. It will also encourage managers to think about the types of measures that would best indicate success. Usually this will involve examining outcomes, processes, and capabilities.

- *Outcomes*. These indicators focus on factors such as employee knowledge, workplace attitudes, and product quality. They are the most frequently used measures of effectiveness. But because these measures can be influenced by factors beyond the organization's control, they are never pure indicators of success.

- *Processes*. These indicators focus on an organization's activities. They encompass effort and how a job is done, assuming it is known what activities are required to ensure effectiveness. This emphasis is not well-suited for non-standard tasks or customized products or services, but organizations are more likely to gather data on processes than on outcomes.

- *Capabilities*. Structural properties indicate an organization's capacity for effective performance. In other words, do an organization's structures and processes provide the capability for high performance now and into the future? This can be judged by examining capital equipment, facilities, technological know-how, education levels, and adaptability. In other words, by demonstrating the capacity to perform work, these aspects of success indicate an organization's potential to be successful in the future. What is required, however, is the ability to turn capabilities into process, and in turn into results.

Consideration of as many dimensions of success as possible allows organizations to be more aware of the consequences of the strategic decisions they make. It also provides the basis for sound strategic control systems (discussed in more detail in **Chapter 10**).

CAUSES OF ORGANIZATIONAL SUCCESS AND FAILURE

One of the benefits of strategic thinking is improved firm performance. In other words, firms that actively engage in the four phases of strategic management should outperform those that do not. But is a well-planned and carefully executed strategy all that an organization needs to be concerned with? What other factors might affect an organization's bottom line, either in favourable or unfavourable ways?

Overall Industry Growth   When demand for a product is growing rapidly, as it does in the rapid growth phase of the product life cycle, most producing firms enjoy a certain amount of success, even if their products are not superior or if their operations are not particularly efficient. For example, during the late 1980s there was rapid growth in the facsimile-machine market, which created a situation where production was unable to keep up with demand. For several years, the rapid adoption of fax technology and its replacement of the telex saw a large number of office equipment manufacturers achieving huge sales growth. This situation was short-lived, however. Once the leading manufacturers (Canon and Ricoh) were able to expand their capacity to meet the burgeoning demand, they took away sales from firms with less sophisticated products and used their large size to achieve economies of scale and put downward pressure on prices.

Organizational Resources and Capabilities   Not all organizations possess the same resources and capabilities: the people, equipment, money, and knowledge to develop and profitably sell a product. So although a number of firms in the same industry might be pursuing the same strategy, they will not necessarily be able to implement these equally well. Because different firms have the ability to do different things relatively well, we can expect to see differing rates of profitability between firms as a result of the resources and capabilities they possess. For example, Zellers and Wal-Mart use similar "every day low price" strategies in department store retailing. Wal-Mart, however, has tremendous strength (partly due to its size) in buying power, supply chain management, and computerized inventory management systems. As a result, Wal-Mart has been able to outperform Zellers in many areas, especially in terms of broad product lines and low prices. Wal-Mart is already one of the world's largest and most efficient retailers, and it continues to grow. It can therefore strengthen its position as a discount retailer and use its distinctive competencies to widen the gap between itself and its rivals.

Strategic Inertia   When firms continue with strategies that should be abandoned or changed, they display what is called strategic inertia. This occurs when a once-successful strategy somehow fails to deliver the results it once did. One reason this can occur is because of strategic drift, the gradual misalignment of a firm's strategy and its environment. As environments change (for example, when they become deregulated or attract new entrants), a strategy that was once successful becomes suboptimal.

   Why does strategic inertia occur? It can be a result of a natural human tendency to resist change, something most people can relate to. As the discussion of triggering events later in this chapter will indicate, often it takes a severe shock to an organization's survival to trigger reassessment of current strategies. Strategic inertia can also be the result of cognitive biases inherent in all people. This has been referred to as the paradox of success, the result of a firm's inability or unwillingness to change its strategy in light of evidence that calls its effectiveness into question.[13] Because decision makers have been successful pursuing a particular strategy, it often takes an overwhelming amount of evidence to call its effectiveness into question. There is a political element to this as well: it can be very hard to admit that past strategic decisions were somehow wrong. The result is often an escalation of commitment to a failing course of action and a tendency to find ways to justify continuing to use existing strategies rather than developing new ones.[14]

   In conclusion, the study of strategic management is concerned with the nature of the managerial decisions made to improve the long-run performance of an organization, and the processes by which they are made. One way to gauge an organization's ability to manage its strategy effectively is to look at its results—this is the true test of how good a strategy is. Each of the remaining chapters deals with one aspect of the strategic management process. The better these various aspects are handled, the more likely an organization will be to benefit from thinking strategically.

1.2 Globalization and Electronic Commerce: Challenges to Strategic Management

Not too long ago, a business organization could be successful by focusing only on making and selling goods and services within its national boundaries. International considerations were minimal. Profits earned from exporting products to foreign lands were considered frosting on the cake but not really essential to organizational success. During the 1960s, for example, most large companies organized themselves around a number of product divisions that made and sold goods domestically. International manufacturing and sales were typically managed through a separate division. An international assignment was usually considered a message that the person was no longer promotable and should be looking for another job.

Similarly, until the mid-1990s, a business could be very successful without using the internet for anything more than a public relations website. Most business was done through a sales force and a network of distributors, with the eventual sale to the consumer being made through retail outlets. Few executives used a personal computer, let alone "surfed" the World Wide Web. The internet may have been useful for research, but until recently it was not seriously viewed as a means to actually conduct normal business transactions.

IMPACT OF GLOBALIZATION

globalization awareness of the influence of international activities on firm performance and increased transactions across national borders

Today, many things have changed. **Globalization**, the internationalization of markets and organizations, has changed the way modern organizations do business. To reach the economies of scale necessary to achieve the low costs, and thus the low prices, that are needed to be competitive, companies are now thinking in terms of a global (worldwide) market instead of a national market. Nike and Reebok, for example, manufacture their athletic shoes in various countries throughout Asia for sale on every continent. Instead of using one international division to manage everything outside the home country, large organizations are now using structures in which product units are interwoven with country or regional units. International assignments are now considered key for anyone interested in reaching top management.

As more industries become global, strategic management is becoming an increasingly important way to keep track of international developments and to position companies for long-term competitive advantage. For example, Maytag Corporation purchased Hoover not so much for its vacuum cleaner business as for its European laundry, cooking, and refrigeration business. Maytag's management realized that a company without a manufacturing presence in the European Union would be at a competitive disadvantage in the changing major home appliance industry. Similar international considerations have led to the Star Alliance (including Air Canada, Lufthansa, Scandinavian Airlines, and United), now the world's largest airline network; the merger between Daimler-Benz and Chrysler Corporation; and Bombardier's acquisition of Shorts Brothers in Ireland and DaimlerChrysler Rail Systems in Germany. See the **Global Issue** feature to learn how regional trade associations are changing the way that international business is conducted.

Global Issue
Regional Trade Associations Replace National Trade Barriers

Previously known as the Common Market and the European Community, the European Union (EU) is the most significant trade association in the world. The goal of the EU is the complete economic integration of its 15 member countries—Austria, Belgium, Denmark, Finland, France, Germany, Greece, Ireland, Italy, Luxembourg, the Netherlands, Portugal, Spain, Sweden, and the United Kingdom—so that goods made in one part of Europe can move freely to another without ever stopping for a customs inspection. One currency, the euro, is being used throughout the region as members integrate their monetary systems. The steady elimination of barriers to free trade is providing the impetus for a series of mergers, acquisitions, and joint ventures among business organizations. The EU's requirement of at least 60% local content to avoid tariffs has forced many American and Asian companies to abandon exporting in favour of a strong local presence in Europe. The EU has agreed to expand its membership to include the Czech Republic, Hungary, Estonia, Poland, Malta, Cyprus, and Slovenia by 2004; Latvia, Lithuania, and Slovakia by 2006; and Bulgaria and Romania by 2010. Turkey is being considered for admission in 2011.

Canada, the United States, and Mexico are affiliated economically under the North American Free Trade Agreement (NAFTA). The goal of NAFTA is improved trade among the three member countries rather than complete economic integration. Launched in 1994, the agreement requires the three members to remove all tariffs among themselves over 15 years, but they are allowed to have their own tariff arrangements with non-member countries. Cars and trucks must have 62.5% North American content to qualify for duty-free status. Transportation restrictions and other regulations are being significantly reduced. Some Asian and European organizations are locating operations in one of the countries to obtain access to the entire North American region. Vicente Fox, president of Mexico, is proposing that NAFTA become more like the European Union in allowing the free movement of people and goods across borders from Mexico to Canada. In addition, there have been some discussions of extending NAFTA southward to include Chile, but thus far nothing formal has been proposed.

South American countries are also working to harmonize their trading relationships with each other and to form trade associations. The establishment of the Mercosur (Mercosul in Portuguese) free-trade area among Argentina, Brazil, Uruguay, and Paraguay means that a manufacturing presence within these countries is becoming essential for non-member countries in order for them to avoid tariffs. Claiming to be NAFTA's southern counterpart, Mercosur has extended free-trade agreements to Bolivia and Venezuela. With Chile and Argentina co-operating to build a tunnel through the Andes to connect the two countries, it is likely that Chile may soon form some economic relationship with Mercosur.

Asia currently has no comparable regional trade association to match the potential economic power of either NAFTA or the EU. Japan, South Korea, China, and India generally operate as independent economic powers. Nevertheless, the Association of South East Asian Nations (ASEAN)—comprising Brunei, Indonesia, Malaysia, the Philippines, Singapore, Thailand, and Vietnam—is attempting to link its members into a borderless economic zone. Increasingly referred to as ASEAN+3, it is already including China, Japan, and South Korea in its annual summit meetings. The ASEAN nations are negotiating the linkage of the ASEAN Free-Trade Area (AFTA) with the existing FTA of Australia and New Zealand. With the EU extending eastward and NAFTA extending southward to someday connect with Mercosur, pressure is already building on the independent Asian nations to soon form an expanded version of ASEAN.

IMPACT OF ELECTRONIC COMMERCE

electronic commerce business transactions conducted across the internet

Electronic commerce refers to the use of the internet to conduct business transactions. A 1999 survey of more than 525 top executives from a wide range of industries revealed that the internet is reshaping the global marketplace and that it will continue to do so for many years. More than 90% of the executives believed that the internet would transform or have a major impact on their organizational strategy within two years. According to Matthew Barrett, former chairman and CEO of the Bank of Montreal, "We are only standing at the threshold of a New World. It is as if we had just invented printing or the steam engine."[15] Not only is the internet changing the way customers, suppliers, and companies interact, but it is also changing the way companies work internally.

In just the few years since its introduction, the internet has profoundly affected the basis of competition in many industries. Instead of the traditional focus on product features and costs, the internet is shifting the basis for competition to a more strategic level in which the traditional value chain of an industry is drastically altered. A 1999 report by AMR Research indicated that industry leaders are in the process of moving 60% to 100% of their business-to-business (B2B) transactions to the internet. The net B2B marketplace includes (a) trading exchange platforms like VerticalNet and i2 Technologies' TradeMatrix, which support trading communities in multiple markets; (b) industry-sponsored exchanges, such as the one being built by major automakers; and (c) net market makers, like e-Steel, NECX, and BuildPoint, which focus on a specific industry's value chain or business processes to mediate multiple transactions among businesses. The Garner Group predicts that the worldwide B2B market will grow from $145 billion in 1999 to $7.29 trillion in 2004, at which time it will represent 7% of total global sales transactions.[16]

The previously mentioned survey of top executives identified the following seven trends, each due at least in part to the rise of the internet:[17]

1. The internet is forcing companies to transform themselves. The concept of electronically networking customers, suppliers, and partners is now a reality.

2. New channels are changing market access and branding, causing the disintermediation (breaking down of the intermediary role) of traditional distribution channels. By working directly with customers, companies are able to avoid the usual distributors, thus forming closer relationships with the end users, improving service, and reducing costs.

3. The balance of power is shifting to the consumer. Now having unlimited access to information on the internet, customers are much more demanding than their "non-wired" predecessors.

4. Competition is changing. New technology-driven firms and older traditional competitors are exploiting the internet to become more innovative and efficient.

5. The pace of business is increasing drastically. Planning horizons, information needs, and customer and supplier expectations are reflecting the immediacy of the internet. Because of this turbulent environment, time is compressed into "dog years" in which one year feels like seven years.

6. The internet is pushing organizations out of their traditional boundaries. The traditional separation among suppliers, manufacturers, and customers is becoming blurred with the development and expansion of extranets, in which co-operating firms have access to each other's internal operating plans and processes. For example, Lockheed Martin, the aerospace company, has an extranet linking Lockheed to Boeing, a project partner, and to the US defence department, a key customer.

7. Knowledge is becoming a key asset and a source of competitive advantage. For example, physical assets accounted for 62.8% of the total market value of US manufacturing firms in 1980 but only 37.9% in 1991. The remainder of the market value comprises intangible assets, primarily intellectual capital.[18]

In summary, the internet has fundamentally changed the way organizations function and compete. Traditionally, businesses competed within a geographically defined market. The internet, however, is making boundaries between markets almost meaningless. Fast and inexpensive technologies now make it possible for organizations and their customers to be physically far apart and perhaps never meet face to face. This means that organizations that were market leaders in a particular geographical area will now face new competition from market leaders in other areas. Electronic commerce has, especially in industries like consumer electronics, books, and music, both increased the amount of competition organizations face and increased the market for their products. In other words, both opportunities and threats are associated with these technological trends.

But to what extent has the internet changed everything? Michael Porter argues that although businesses have undergone many changes as a result of increased internet use, many things have remained the same.[19] In fact, many organizations (dot-coms and traditional firms) have made bad decisions based on the assumption that the internet and electronic commerce would revolutionize the way business is done. In reality, however, these changes have not been as significant as anticipated, and organizations have not been able to use internet technologies to create economic value. Porter identified an interesting paradox about the internet: its very benefits (making information widely available; reducing difficulty in purchasing, marketing, and distributing; allowing buyers and sellers to find each other more easily) also make it harder for organizations to earn profits. The most successful organizations are ones that use internet technologies to build a competitive advantage and create a unique strategic positioning for themselves (these concepts are discussed in detail in **Chapter 4**). Unfortunately for many organizations, the internet has made this harder to do, not easier.

1.3 Creating a Learning Organization

Strategic management has now evolved to the point that its primary value is in helping the organization operate successfully in a dynamic, complex environment. Inland Steel Company, for example, uses strategic planning as a tool to drive organizational change. Managers at all levels are expected to continually analyze the changing steel industry in order to create or modify strategic plans throughout the year.[20] To be competitive in dynamic environments, organizations are having to become less bureaucratic and more flexible. In stable environments, such as those that existed in years past, a competitive strategy simply involved defining a competitive position and then defending it. As it takes less and less time for one product or technology to replace another, companies are finding that there is no such thing as a permanent competitive advantage. Many agree with Richard D'Aveni (the author of the book *Hypercompetition*) that any sustainable competitive advantage lies not in doggedly following a centrally managed five-year plan, but in stringing together a series of strategic short-term thrusts (as Intel does by cutting into the sales of its own offerings with periodic introductions of new products).[21] This means that organizations must develop strategic flexibility—the ability to shift from one dominant strategy to another.[22]

learning organization
an organization skilled at changing in response to new knowledge and insights obtained from the environment, and at nurturing of new ways of thinking

Strategic flexibility demands a long-term commitment to the development and nurturing of critical resources. It also demands that the company become a **learning organization**—an organization skilled at creating, acquiring, and transferring knowledge, and at modifying its behaviour to reflect new knowledge and insights. Organizational learning is a critical component of competitiveness in a dynamic environment. It is particularly important to innovation and new product development.[23] For example, Hewlett-Packard uses an extensive network of informal committees to transfer knowledge among its cross-functional teams and to help spread new sources of knowledge quickly.[24] Learning organizations are skilled at four main activities:

- Solving problems systematically
- Experimenting with new approaches
- Learning from their own experiences and past history as well as from the experiences of others
- Transferring knowledge quickly and efficiently throughout the organization[25]

Learning organizations avoid stagnation through continual self-examination and experimentation. People at all levels, not just top management, need to be involved in strategic management, helping to scan the environment for critical information; suggesting changes to strategies and programs to take advantage of environmental shifts; and working with others to continually improve work methods, procedures, and evaluation techniques. Motorola, for example, developed an action learning format in which people from marketing, product development, and manufacturing meet to argue and reach agreement about the needs of the market, the best new product, and the schedules of each group producing it. This action learning approach overcame the problems that arose previously when the three departments met and formally agreed on plans but continued with their work as if nothing had happened.[26]

Organizations that are willing to experiment and able to learn from their experiences are more successful than those that are not. For example, in a study of manufacturers of diagnostic imaging equipment, the most successful firms were those that improved products sold domestically by incorporating some of what they had learned from their manufacturing and sales experiences in other nations. Less successful firms used the foreign operations primarily as sales outlets, not as important sources of technical knowledge.[27] In other words, more successful organizations are able to build on people's inherent commitment and capacity to learn. Peter Senge, author of *The Fifth Discipline*, identifies five disciplines that characterize the learning organization:[28]

1. *Systems Thinking.* Organizations should be viewed as systems, with each part having an influence on the others. Rather than focus on what is easy to observe, or what is directly under our control, systems thinking encourages managers to examine whole patterns of change, especially what might be hidden from view.

2. *Personal Mastery.* By continually clarifying and deepening personal vision, focusing energies, developing patience, and seeing reality more objectively, people become committed to lifelong learning. As a result, the organizations they work for benefit.

3. *Mental Models.* These are deeply held assumptions, generalizations or world views that influence how we understand the world around us. Learning comes from discovering our individual mental models and holding them up to scrutiny.

4. *Building Shared Vision.* A sign of good leadership is to create goals, values, and missions that are shared throughout the organization. Where there is a genuine vision, people excel and learn of their own volition.

5. *Team Learning.* All organizations require successful groups and teams to carry out complex tasks. Unfortunately many teams fail to benefit from the knowledge and skills of their members. By learning to think together—allowing individual beliefs to be challenged by others—and by identifying the factors that undermine learning, organizations can more effectively use teams.

1.4 Basic Model of Strategic Management

Strategic management consists of four basic elements:

- Environmental scanning
- Strategy formulation
- Strategy implementation
- Evaluation and control

Figure 1–1 shows simply how these elements interact; **Figure 1–2** expands each of these

Figure 1–1 Basic Elements of the Strategic Management Process

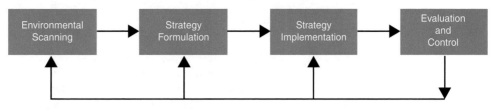

elements and serves as the model for this book.[29] The terms used in **Figure 1–2** are explained in the following pages.

ENVIRONMENTAL SCANNING

SWOT analysis an organizing framework for organizational strengths, and weaknesses, and environmental opportunities and threats

Environmental scanning is the monitoring, evaluating, and disseminating of information from the external and internal environments to key people within the organization. Its purpose is to identify strategic factors—those external and internal elements that will determine the future of the organization. The simplest way to conduct environmental scanning is through **SWOT analysis**. "SWOT" is an acronym used to describe those particular **S**trengths, **W**eaknesses, **O**pportunities, and **T**hreats that are strategic factors for a specific company. The external environment consists of variables (**O**pportunities and **T**hreats) that are outside the organization and not typically within the short-run control of top management. These variables form the context within which the organization exists. **Figure 1–3** depicts key environmental variables. They may be general forces and trends within the overall societal environment or specific factors that operate within an organization's specific task

Figure 1–2 Strategic Management Model

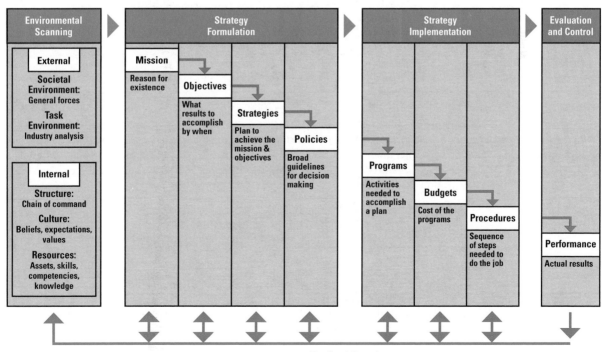

Figure 1–3 Environmental Variables

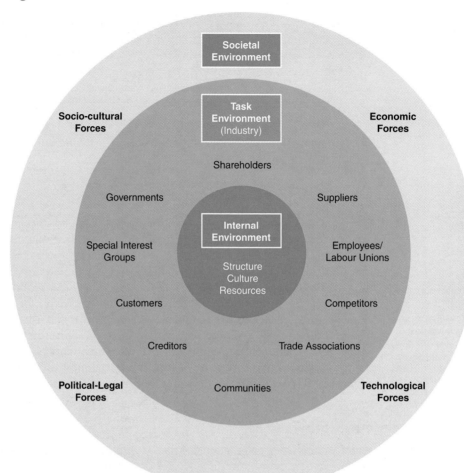

environment—often called its industry. (These external variables are defined and discussed in more detail in **Chapter 3**).

The internal environment of an organization consists of variables (**S**trengths and **W**eaknesses) that are within the organization itself but usually outside the short-run control of top management. These variables form the context in which work is done. They include the organization's structure, culture, and resources. Key strengths form a set of core competencies that the organization can use to gain competitive advantage. (These internal variables and core competencies are defined and discussed in more detail in **Chapter 4**).

STRATEGY FORMULATION

Strategy formulation is the development of short- and long-range plans for the effective management of environmental opportunities and threats, in light of organizational strengths and weaknesses. It includes defining the organizational mission, specifying achievable objectives, developing strategies, and setting policy guidelines.

Mission

mission an organization's statement of purpose, communicating its basic goals and guiding philosophies

An organization's **mission** is the purpose or reason for its existence. It tells what the company is providing to society: either a service like housecleaning or a product like automobiles. A well-conceived mission statement defines the fundamental, unique purpose that sets a company apart from other firms of its type and identifies the scope of the company's operations in terms of products (including services) offered and markets served. It may also include the firm's philosophy about how it does business and treats its employees. It puts into words not only what the company is now, but also what it wants to become—management's strategic vision of the firm's future. (Some people like to consider vision and mission as two different concepts, with a mission statement describing what the organization is now and a vision statement describing what the organization would like to become. We prefer to combine these ideas into a single mission statement.)[30] The mission statement promotes a sense of shared expectations in employees and communicates a public image to important stakeholder groups in the company's task environment. *It tells who we are and what we do as well as what we'd like to become.*

One example of a mission statement is that of Mountain Equipment Co-op (MEC):

MEC is a member-owned and directed retail consumer co-operative which provides products and services for self-propelled wilderness oriented recreational activities... at the lowest reasonable price in an informative, helpful and environmentally responsible manner.[31]

Another classic example is that etched in bronze at Newport News Shipbuilding, unchanged since its founding in 1886:

We shall build good ships here—at a profit if we can—at a loss if we must—but always good ships.[32]

A mission may be defined narrowly or broadly. An example of a broad mission statement is that used by many organizations: to serve the best interests of shareholders, customers, and employees. A broadly defined mission statement such as this keeps the company from restricting itself to one field or product line, but it fails to clearly identify either what it makes or which product and markets it plans to emphasize. Because this broad statement is so general, a narrow mission statement, such as the preceding one by Mountain Equipment Co-op, is more useful. A narrow mission very clearly states the organization's primary business, but it may limit the scope of the firm's activities in terms of the product or service offered, the technology used, and the market served. Instead of just stating it is a "railroad," a company might be better calling itself a "transportation company."

Objectives

objectives specific, quantifiable performance targets expected from fulfilling the organization's mission

Objectives are the end results of planned activity. They state what is to be accomplished by when and should be quantified if possible. The achievement of organizational objectives should result in the fulfillment of an organization's mission. In effect, this is what society gives back to the organization when it does a good job of fulfilling its mission. For example, Bombardier is committed to being a market leader in all its markets. This rather ambitious objective shows the priority the organization places on excelling in a small number of markets rather than spreading itself thinly. And to achieve this market dominance, Bombardier created a set of goals relating to profit targets, customer service levels, product innovation, and a culture that fosters entrepreneurship.

goal a loosely defined statement of what an organization hopes to accomplish

The term "goal" is often used interchangeably with the term "objective." In this book, we prefer to differentiate the two terms. In contrast to an objective, we consider a **goal** as what one wants to accomplish, expressed in an open-ended statement with no quantification of what is to be achieved and no specified time for completion. For example, committing to "increased profitability" is thus stating a goal, not an objective, because the stated goal does not specify how much profit the firm wants to make over what period of time. An objective would say something like "increase profits 10% over last year."

Here are some of the areas in which an organization might establish its goals and objectives:

- Profitability (net profits)
- Efficiency (low costs, etc.)
- Growth (increase in total assets, sales, etc.)
- Shareholder wealth (dividends plus stock price appreciation)
- Utilization of resources (return on investment or equity)
- Reputation (being considered a "top" firm)
- Contributions to employees (employment security, wages, diversity)
- Contributions to society (taxes paid, participation in charities, providing a needed product or service)
- Market leadership (market share)
- Technological leadership (innovations, creativity)
- Survival (avoiding bankruptcy)
- Personal needs of top management (using the firm for personal purposes, such as providing jobs for relatives)

Strategies

strategy a plan of how an organization's objectives, and therefore mission, will be achieved

A **strategy** of an organization forms a comprehensive master plan stating how the organization will achieve its mission and objectives. It maximizes competitive advantage and minimizes competitive disadvantage. For example, Bombardier continued to strengthen its position in the aerospace industry by acquiring Shorts Brothers and Learjet. These acquisitions allowed it to develop strength in regional and business jets, now the cornerstone of its aerospace division. It also solidified its leadership position in rail transportation equipment through its biggest acquisition yet, DaimlerChrysler Rail Systems GmbH (Adtranz), based in Berlin, Germany. These acquisitions were both in areas that management felt had a strong strategic fit with current operations and tremendous opportunities for growth.

The typical business firm usually considers three types of strategy: corporate, business, and functional.

corporate strategy the general direction of an organization's entry into or exit from different businesses and markets

1. **Corporate strategy** describes a company's overall direction in terms of its general attitude toward growth and the management of its various businesses and product lines. Corporate strategies typically fit within the three main categories of stability, growth, and retrenchment. For example, Bombardier followed a corporate growth strategy by acquiring other companies in selected industries in order to have a critical mass in each market that would allow them to deliver the highest-quality products and generate future innovations.

business strategy the choices an organization makes in a product market to improve long-run performance

2. **Business strategy** usually occurs at the business unit or product level, and it emphasizes improvement of the competitive position of an organization's products or services in the specific industry or market segment served by that business unit. Business strategies may fit within the two categories of *competitive* or *co-operative* strategies. For example, Apple Computer uses a differentiation competitive strategy that emphasizes innovative products with creative design. The distinctive design and colours of its iMac line of

personal computers (when contrasted with the usual beige of competitors' products) successfully boosted the company's market share and profits. In contrast, Air Canada followed a co-operative strategy by entering into the Star Alliance to provide global service.

functional strategy
how each functional area of the organization achieves its unit objectives and thus contributes to the achievement of an organization's mission

3. **Functional strategy** is the approach taken by a functional area to achieve organizational and business unit objectives and strategies by maximizing resource productivity. It is concerned with developing and nurturing a *distinctive competence* (see **Chapter 4**) to provide a company or business unit with a competitive advantage. Examples of R & D functional strategies are technological followership (imitate the products of other companies) and technological leadership (pioneer an innovation). For years, Magic Chef had been a successful appliance maker by spending little on R & D but quickly imitating the innovations of other competitors. This helped the company to keep its costs lower than those of its competitors and consequently to compete on the basis of lower prices. In terms of marketing functional strategies, Pfizer Canada is a model innovator, spending huge amounts on R & D and advertising to develop and test new pharmaceutical products and create customer demand. This supports Pfizer's competitive strategy of differentiating its products from those of its competitors with revolutionary pharmaceutical innovations.

Business firms use all three types of strategy simultaneously. A hierarchy of strategy is the grouping of strategy types by level in the organization. This hierarchy of strategy is a nesting of one strategy within another so that they complement and support one another (see **Figure 1–4**). Functional strategies support business strategies, which, in turn, support the organizational strategy (or strategies).

Just as many firms often have no formally stated objectives, many firms have unstated, incremental, or intuitive strategies that have never been articulated or analyzed. Often the only way to spot an organization's implicit strategies is to look not at what management says, but at what it does. Implicit strategies can be derived from organizational policies, programs approved (and disapproved), and authorized budgets. Programs and divisions favoured by budget increases and staffed by managers who are considered to be on the fast promotion track reveal where the organization is putting its money and its energy.

Figure 1–4 Hierarchy of Strategy

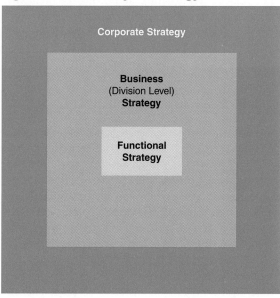

Corporate Strategy

Business
(Division Level)
Strategy

Functional
Strategy

Policies

A **policy** is a broad guideline for decision making that links the formulation of strategy with its implementation. Companies use policies to make sure that employees throughout the firm make decisions and take actions that support the organization's mission, objectives, and strategies. In other words, policies reflect the core values of an organization. For example, consider the following company policies:

- **Maytag:** Maytag will not approve any cost reduction proposal if it reduces product quality in any way. (This policy supports Maytag's strategy for Maytag brands to compete on quality rather than on price.)

- **Molson Inc.:** Molson is pursuing a cost-cutting strategy to save $100 million over a three-year period. A major area of saving is workforce reductions, so to get its employees to buy into the strategy, Molson has created higher-level and more secure jobs for those who remain. The company is empowering production workers to run production lines in ways that will increase efficiencies and reduce costs. These workers will also play an important role in the redesign of production lines.

- **3M:** Researchers should spend 15% of their time working on something other than their primary project. (This supports 3M's strong product development strategy.)

- **Intel:** Cannibalize your product line (undercut the sales of your current products) with better products before a competitor does it to you. (This supports Intel's objective of market leadership.)

- **Sears:** A "no questions asked" merchandise return policy, because the customer is always right. (This supports its competitive strategy of differentiation through excellent service.)

Policies like these provide clear guidance to managers throughout the organization. (Strategy formulation is discussed in greater detail in **Chapters 5, 6**, and **7**).

STRATEGY IMPLEMENTATION

Strategy implementation is the process by which strategies and policies are put into action through the development of programs, budgets, and procedures. This process might involve changes within the overall culture, structure, and/or management system of the entire organization. Except when such drastic organization-wide changes are needed, however, the implementation of strategy is typically conducted by middle- and lower-level managers with review by top management. Sometimes referred to as operational planning, strategy implementation often involves day-to-day decisions in resource allocation.

Programs

A **program** is a statement of the activities or steps needed to accomplish a single-use plan. It makes the strategy action-oriented. It may involve restructuring the organization, changing the company's internal culture, or beginning a new research effort. For example, consider Intel Corporation, the microprocessor manufacturer. Realizing that Intel would not be able to continue its organizational growth strategy without the continual development of new generations of microprocessors, management decided to implement a series of programs. They formed an alliance with Hewlett-Packard to develop the successor to the Pentium Pro chip and assembled an elite team of engineers and scientists to do long-term research into computer chip design. Another example is Purolator Courier's program to install a sophisticated information system to enable its customers to order supplies, schedule pickups, and track their shipments at any time. Real-time data on customer accounts and delivery status were made accessible via the internet, and proprietary software was provided to permit shippers to label many of their own packages. This not only built in some switching costs (discussed in more detail in **Chapter 3**) but also reduced errors and sped up package pickups.

Budgets

budget a statement of the estimated costs of an organization's programs

A **budget** states an organization's programs in terms of dollars. Used in planning and control, a budget lists the detailed cost of each program. Many organizations demand a certain percentage return on investment, often called a "hurdle rate," before management will approve a new program. This ensures that the new program will significantly add to the organization's profit performance and thus build shareholder value. The budget thus not only serves as a detailed plan of the new strategy in action, but also specifies through pro forma financial statements the expected impact on the firm's financial future. For example, at Aliant Telecom, new business products are assessed on their payback period in addition to their contribution to profit. Because the telecommunications industry is changing so quickly, a project that cannot pay back start-up costs and contribute to the organization's profitability within two years will not be pursued.

Procedures

procedure a standardized approach to performing a task

Procedures, sometimes termed standard operating procedures (SOPs), are a system of sequential steps or techniques that describe in detail how a particular task or job is to be done. They typically detail the various activities that must be carried out to complete the organization's programs. For example, Hermes Electronics, a producer of underwater surveillance equipment, used various procedures to cut costs in order to strengthen its position in a mature industry. It did this by mapping current- and future-state value streams and implementing continuous flow production cells to eliminate waste at various stages of production. These changes were made as part of an organization-wide effort to reduce cycle times, which had caused excess work-in-process inventories and production bottlenecks. (Strategy implementation is discussed more fully in **Chapters 8** and **9**.)

EVALUATION AND CONTROL

evaluation and control a system of monitoring and feedback of actual versus desired performance

Evaluation and control is the process in which organizational activities and performance results are monitored so that actual performance can be compared with desired performance. Managers at all levels use the resulting information to take corrective action and resolve problems. Although evaluation and control is the final major element of strategic management, it can also pinpoint weaknesses in previously implemented strategic plans and thus stimulate the entire process to begin again.

An organization's performance is the end result of its activities.[33] It includes the actual outcomes of the strategic management process. The practice of strategic management is justified in terms of its ability to improve an organization's performance, typically measured in terms of profits and return on investment. For evaluation and control to be effective, managers must obtain clear, prompt, and unbiased information from the people below them in the organization's hierarchy. Using this information, managers compare what is actually happening with what was originally planned in the formulation stage. For example, WestJet's strategy of having restricted routes and limited schedules combined with low prices offers consumers an alternative to larger, conventional airlines. To assess how successful this strategy is, management requires details on passenger load factors (how full their planes are), the proportion of labour costs in total operating costs, and revenue yields. A combination of these three measurements allows WestJet to evaluate its performance and determine the extent to which it can profit from this strategy, in addition to signalling the direction and pace of future growth.

The evaluation and control of performance completes the strategic management model. Based on performance results, management may need to make adjustments in its strategy formulation, in implementation, or in both. (Evaluation and control is discussed in more detail in **Chapter 10**.)

FEEDBACK/LEARNING PROCESS

Note that the strategic management model depicted in **Figure 1–2** includes a feedback/learning process. Arrows are drawn coming out of each part of the model and taking information to each of the previous parts of the model. As a firm or business unit develops strategies, programs, and the like, it often must go back to revise or correct decisions made earlier in the model. For example, poor performance (as measured in evaluation and control) usually indicates that something has gone wrong with either strategy formulation or implementation. It could mean that a key variable, such as a new competitor, was ignored during environmental scanning and assessment (an error in formulation). It could also mean that organizational changes designed to improve efficiency or responsiveness were met with resistance and as such were too costly and/or slow to bring about the desired performance changes (an error in implementation).

1.5 Initiation of Strategy: Triggering Events

After much research, the Canadian strategist Henry Mintzberg discovered that strategy formulation is typically not a regular, continuous process: "It is most often an irregular, discontinuous process, proceeding in fits and starts. There are periods of stability in strategy development, but also there are periods of flux, of groping, of piecemeal change, and of global change."[34] This view of strategy formulation as an irregular process can be explained by the very human tendency to continue on a particular course of action until something goes wrong or one is forced to question one's actions. This period of "strategic drift" may result from inertia on the part of the organization or may simply reflect management's belief that the current strategy is still appropriate and needs only fine tuning. Often it is some sort of shock to the system that motivates management to seriously reassess the organization's situation. So in other words, organizations are more amenable to change at certain times than at others. When a firm is near crisis, change is unavoidable, and moving quickly is crucial.[35] Unfortunately many firms fail to see the need for change in the absence of a crisis or some triggering event that begins to erode business performance.

triggering event something that acts as a stimulus for strategic change

A **triggering event** is something that acts as a stimulus for a change in strategy. Here are a few possible triggering events:

- **New CEO:** By asking a series of embarrassing questions, the new CEO cuts through the veil of complacency and forces people to question the very reason for the organization's existence.
- **External Intervention:** The firm's bank refuses to approve a new loan or suddenly demands payment in full on an old one. A customer complains about a serious product defect.
- **Threat of a Change in Ownership:** Another firm may initiate a takeover by buying the company's common stock.
- **Performance Gap:** A performance gap exists when performance does not meet expectations. Sales and profits are no longer increasing or may even be falling.

Indigo Books and Music is an example of one company in which a triggering event forced its management to seriously rethink what it was doing. See the **Internet Issue** feature to learn how the success of Amazon.ca and the performance gap it has created have stimulated a restructuring plan at Indigo.

Internet Issue

Triggering Event at Indigo Books and Music

Indigo Books and Music's CEO, Heather Reisman, recently reported a $48 million loss in her 2002 annual report to shareholders. Indigo grew into a nationwide retailer as a result of its 2001 hostile takeover of Chapters Inc. In doing this it acquired more than 300 locations and removed a strong competitor. Since the takeover, Reisman has been trying to reposition Indigo by increasing its gift section and promoting "Heather's Picks" in stores and on the radio. The problem is that Indigo's financial results since acquiring Chapters have been anything but good. Part of the reason is that Riesman acquired many of the problems of Chapters at the same time as she acquired its locations: an inefficient computer network, a huge inventory of unpopular books, and a money-losing online operation.

The large losses experienced by Indigo (caused by higher-than-anticipated expenses) demonstrate a performance gap that can act as a triggering event. Most of Indigo's problems stem from its costly acquisition of Chapters and the costs of integrating it into Indigo's existing operations. But as if those problems were not significant enough, Canadian Heritage has approved the establishment of Amazon.ca, a division of the successful American online firm Amazon.com Inc. This new level of competition has made Reisman consider restructuring Indigo in order to be able to offer competitive pricing to consumers. Amazon.ca commenced its operations in June 2002, offering customers 30% discounts off the list prices of best-sellers and free shipping on orders above $75. As the Christmas season approached, this discount increased to 40%, and the free shipping cut-off decreased to $39. Reisman matched these rates but cut profit margins so far that they pushed Indigo's bottom line into the red. In view of Indigo's inability to remain cost-competitive with Amazon.ca's products, Reisman will be forced to re-evaluate Indigo's strategy to increase margins in its online business, or perhaps consider withdrawing from the head-to-head competition with Amazon.ca altogether. In all likelihood, Amazon.ca is going to be operating in Canada for a fairly long time, and given how strong its supply-chain and inventory management systems are, the competitive threat it poses cannot be ignored by Indigo.

Mintzberg has also been influential in shaping the way we define strategy, especially in terms of the way formally planned strategies can change over time. The previous discussion of triggering events is one example of this. But under what other circumstances do strategies change, and what causes them to do so? Mintzberg suggests that a strategy usually starts out as a *plan*, a consciously chosen course of action made with the object of improving organizational performance. This mode of strategic decision making is characterized by conscious and purposeful decisions being made in advance of taking action. On the other hand, many organizations end up pursuing strategies other than the ones they intended to pursue. Viewing strategy as a *pattern*, Mintzberg shows how the activities that are performed over time accumulate into a strategy. Rather than being planned in advance, strategy reflects an accumulation of behaviours and decisions. Strategy is therefore characterized by a consistent set of behaviours, whether or not it is intentional or formally planned.

An interesting feature of these different views of strategy is that the *plan* and the *pattern* can be independent of each other. Plans may go unrealized and patterns can result without any planning. This is illustrated in **Figure 1–5** on page 22. The top-down planning process results in an intended strategy. Emergent strategies on the other hand result from patterns developed in the absence of intentions. This means that a portion of any strategy is realized, and often another portion is not. Why does this occur? Usually because no strategist, no matter how skilled, can consistently plan a strategy that is 100% successful. Obtaining

Figure 1–5 Forms of Strategy

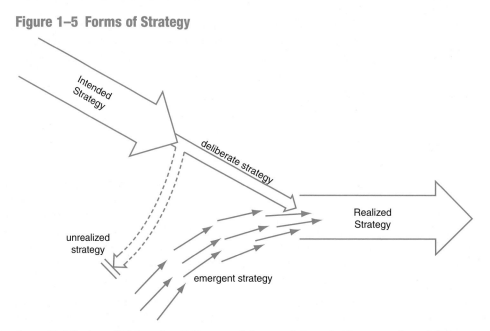

Source: H. Mintzberg, "Of Strategies: Deliberate and Emergent," *Strategic Management Journal* (Vol. 6, 1985), pp. 257–272.

information is time-consuming and costly, which means that strategic decisions are made in the context of incomplete information. Beyond this, there are many situations beyond the control of the organization that can affect its performance. Some of these factors were discussed earlier in this chapter. Competitors can be unpredictable. Government regulations or consumer tastes can change. New management practices are developed that allow organizations to improve their products and their processes. How strategies emerge is therefore important to understand, although the focus of this book is on planning. A theme throughout this book is that continuous monitoring and feedback will allow management to determine the effectiveness and suitability of its intended strategy while being alert to the external influences that may indicate the need for strategic change.

1.6 Strategic Decision Making

The distinguishing characteristic of strategic management is its emphasis on strategic decision making. As organizations grow larger and more complex in more uncertain environments, decisions become increasingly complicated and difficult to make. In agreement with the strategic choice perspective mentioned earlier, this book proposes a strategic decision-making framework that can help people make these decisions regardless of their level and function in the organization.

WHAT MAKES A DECISION STRATEGIC

strategic decision a decision affecting the mission and/or objectives of an organization and consequently its position in the long run

Unlike many other decisions, **strategic decisions** deal with the long-run future of the entire organization and have three characteristics:

1.   **Rare:** Strategic decisions are unusual and typically have no precedent to follow.

2. **Consequential:** Strategic decisions commit substantial resources and demand a great deal of commitment from people at all levels.

3. **Directive:** Strategic decisions set precedents for lesser decisions and future actions throughout the organization.[36]

One example of a strategic decision was that made by Nortel to become an internet company rather than a telephone company.

MINTZBERG'S MODES OF STRATEGIC DECISION MAKING

Some strategic decisions are made in a flash by one person (often an entrepreneur or a powerful chief executive officer) who has a brilliant insight and is quickly able to convince others to adopt his or her idea. Other strategic decisions seem to develop out of a series of small incremental choices that over time push the organization more in one direction than another. According to Henry Mintzberg, the three most typical approaches, or modes, of strategic decision making are entrepreneurial, adaptive, and planning.[37] A fourth mode, logical incrementalism, was added later by Quinn.

1. **Entrepreneurial Mode:** Strategy is made by one powerful individual. The focus is on opportunities; problems are secondary. Strategy is guided by the founder's own vision of direction and is exemplified by large, bold decisions. The dominant goal is growth of the organization. America Online, founded by Steve Case, is an example of this mode of strategic decision making. The company reflects his vision of the internet provider industry. Although AOL's clear growth strategy is certainly an advantage of the entrepreneurial mode, its tendency to market its products before the company is able to support them is a significant disadvantage.

2. **Adaptive Mode:** Sometimes referred to as "muddling through," this decision-making mode is characterized by reactive solutions to existing problems, rather than a proactive search for new opportunities. Much bargaining goes on concerning priorities of objectives. Strategy is fragmented and is developed to move the organization forward incrementally. This mode is typical of most universities, many large hospitals, a large number of governmental agencies, and a surprising number of large organizations. The Bay and Zellers operated successfully for many years in this mode. They continued to rely on their strong Canadian image and their regularly occurring sales to firmly establish themselves in the market. But as the economy weakened and big-box retailers proliferated, changes to product lines and pricing strategies were made to position these stores more favourably in an increasingly competitive industry.

3. **Planning Mode:** This decision-making mode involves the systematic gathering of appropriate information for situation analysis, the generation of feasible alternative strategies, and the rational selection of the most appropriate strategy. It includes both the proactive search for new opportunities and the reactive solution of existing problems. Bombardier is an example of an organization in the planning mode. After a careful study of trends in the transportation industries, management noted that the company needed to stop thinking of itself as a snowmobile company. Diversifying its operations into different product markets would reduce its dependence on a single market and provide opportunities for future growth. The company got into passenger trains in the 1970s and aerospace in the 1980s, both via acquisition.

4. **Logical Incrementalism:** A fourth decision-making mode, which can be viewed as a synthesis of the planning, adaptive, and, to a lesser extent, the entrepreneurial modes, was proposed by Quinn. In this mode, top management has a reasonably clear idea of the

organization's mission and objectives, but, in its development of strategies, it chooses to use "an interactive process in which the organization probes the future, experiments and learns from a series of partial (incremental) commitments rather than through global formulations of total strategies."[38] Thus, although the mission and objectives are set, the strategy is allowed to emerge out of debate, discussion, and experimentation. This approach appears to be useful when the environment is changing rapidly and when it is important to build consensus and develop needed resources before committing the entire organization to a specific strategy.

STRATEGIC DECISION-MAKING PROCESS: AID TO BETTER DECISIONS

Good arguments can be made for using either the entrepreneurial or adaptive modes (or logical incrementalism) in certain situations. This book proposes, however, that in most situations the planning mode, which includes the basic elements of the strategic management process, is a more rational, and thus better, way of making strategic decisions. Research indicates that the planning mode is not only more analytical and less political than the other modes, but it is also more appropriate for dealing with complex, changing environments.[39]

We therefore propose the following eight-step strategic decision-making process to improve the making of strategic decisions (see **Figure 1–6**):

Figure 1–6 Strategic Decision-Making Process

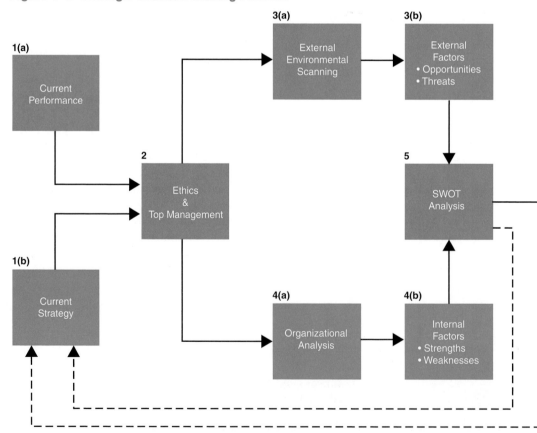

Source: Adapted from T.L. Wheelen and J.D. Hunger, "Strategic Decision-Making Process," Copyright © 1994 and 1997 by Wheelen and Hunger Associates. Reprinted by permission.

1. **Evaluate current performance results** in terms of (a) return on investment, profitability, and so forth, and (b) the current mission, objectives, strategies, and policies.

2. **Review ethics and top management**, that is, the performance of the firm's board of directors and top management, code of ethics, and social responsibilities.

3. **Scan and assess the external environment** to determine the strategic factors that pose **O**pportunities and **T**hreats.

4. **Scan and assess the internal organizational environment** to determine the strategic factors that are **S**trengths (especially core competencies) and **W**eaknesses.

5. **Analyze strategic (SWOT) factors** to (a) pinpoint problem areas, and (b) review and revise the organizational mission and objectives as necessary.

6. **Generate, evaluate, and select the best alternative strategy** in light of the analysis conducted in Step 5.

7. **Implement selected strategies** via programs, budgets, and procedures.

8. **Evaluate and control implemented strategies** via monitoring and feedback systems to ensure minimum deviation from plans and to allow for timely corrective action.

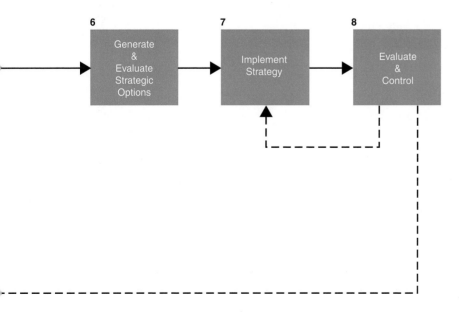

1.7 Impact of the Internet on Strategic Management

Few innovations in history provide as many potential benefits to the strategic management of an organization as electronic commerce (ecommerce) via the internet. The global nature of the technology, its low cost, the opportunity it provides to reach millions of people, its interactive nature, and its variety of possibilities result in many potential benefits to strategic managers. Ecommerce provides the following benefits to the strategic management of organizations:

- Expands the marketplace to national and international markets. All anyone now needs to connect buyers and sellers is a computer.
- Decreases the cost of creating, processing, distributing, storing, and retrieving information. The cost of electronic payment is a small fraction of the cost of a paper cheque.
- Enables people to create new, highly specialized business ventures. Very narrow market niches can now be reached via special interest chat rooms and internet search engines.
- Allows smaller inventories, just-in-time manufacturing, and fewer overhead expenses by facilitating pull-type supply chain management. Dell, the computer company, orders the parts it needs as soon as it receives an order from a customer.
- Enables the customization of products and services to better suit customer needs. Customers are encouraged to select options and styles for the auto of their choice on the BMW website.
- Allows clients of large organizations to use more cost-effective means of interfacing with business. The growth of internet banking has allowed large Canadian banks to reduce the number of branch staff, locations, and hours as more customers engage in a variety of their banking transactions online.
- Provides the stimulus to rethink a firm's strategy and to initiate re-engineering projects. The success of Amazon.com forced Indigo Books & Music Inc. to rethink its pure "bricks and mortar" strategy of retail bookstores and to begin selling books over its own website.
- Increases flexibility, compresses cycle and delivery time, and provides easy access to information on customers, suppliers, and competitors.[40]

Discussion Questions

1. Why has strategic management become so important to today's organizations?

2. How does strategic management typically evolve in an organization?

3. What is a learning organization? In what ways could an organization's strategic management process be improved by becoming one?

4. How are strategic decisions different from other kinds of decisions?

5. When is the planning mode of strategic decision making superior to the entrepreneurial and adaptive modes?

Strategic Practice Exercise

Mission statements vary widely from one company to another. Why is one mission statement better than another? Develop some criteria for evaluating a mission statement. Then, do one or both of the following exercises.

1. Evaluate the following vision and mission statements of the Canadian Wheat Board (CWB):

   Vision: To create value for Prairie farmers by being an innovative world leader in marketing grain.

Mission: The CWB markets quality products and services to maximize returns to western Canadian grain producers.

2. Using the internet, find the mission statements of two different organizations in the same industry (they can be businesses or non-profits). Which mission statement is best? Why?

Notes

1. T. Pyzdek, *The Six Sigma Handbook: A Complete Guide for Greenbelts, Blackbelts, and Managers at All Levels* (New York: Prentice-Hall, 2001). The Six Sigma concept grew out of General Electric's performance improvement strategy. Its goal is to do business more effectively and efficiently by reducing defects. The building blocks of a Six Sigma program are recognizing, defining, measuring, analyzing, designing and improving, validating and controlling, realizing, standardizing, and integrating.
2. Bombardier Inc., *2001 Annual Report* and company website, **www.bombardier.com** (accessed February 28, 2003).
3. "Bombardier Is Moving into a New Era," *The Globe and Mail* (April 4, 2003), p. B4.
4. F.W. Gluck, S.P. Kaufman, and A.S. Walleck, "The Four Phases of Strategic Management," *Journal of Business Strategy* (Winter 1982), pp. 9–21.
5. T.J. Andersen, "Strategic Planning, Autonomous Actions and Corporate Performance," *Long Range Planning* (April 2000), pp. 184–200; C.C. Miller and L.B. Cardinal, "Strategic Planning and Firm Performance: A Synthesis of More Than Two Decades of Research," *Academy of Management Journal* (December 1994), pp. 1649–1665; P. Pekar Jr. and S. Abraham, "Is Strategic Management Living Up to Its Promise?" *Long Range Planning* (October 1995), pp. 32–44.
6. E.J. Zajac, M.S. Kraatz, and R.F. Bresser, "Modeling the Dynamics of Strategic Fit: A Normative Approach to Strategic Change," *Strategic Management Journal* (April 2000), pp. 429–453.
7. K.G. Smith and C.M. Grimm, "Environmental Variation, Strategic Change and Firm Performance: A Study of Railroad Deregulation," *Strategic Management Journal* (July–August 1987), pp. 363–376.
8. P.G. Audia, E.A. Locke, and K.G. Smith, "The Paradox of Success: An Archival and a Laboratory Study of Strategic Persistence Following Radical Environmental Change," *Academy of Management Journal*, Vol. 43, No. 5 (2000), pp. 837–853.
9. I. Wilson, "Strategic Planning Isn't Dead—It Changed," *Long Range Planning* (August 1994), p. 20.
10. R.M. Grant, "Transforming Uncertainty into Success: Strategic Leadership Forum 1999," *Strategy & Leadership* (July/August/ September 1999), p. 33.
11. L.W. Rue and N.A. Ibrahim, "The Relationship between Planning Sophistication and Performance in Small Businesses," *Journal of Small Business Management* (October 1998), pp. 24–32; M.A. Lyles, I.S. Baird, J.B. Orris, and D.F. Kuratko, "Formalized Planning in Small Business: Increasing Strategic Choices," *Journal of Small Business Management* (April 1993), pp. 38–50.
12. W.R. Scott, *Organizations: Rational, Natural and Open Systems*, 3rd edition (Englewood Cliffs: Prentice Hall, 1992). Scott discusses different notions of "effectiveness" based on different views of organizations themselves. See pp. 342–362.
13. P.G. Audia, E.A. Locke, and K.G. Smith, "The Paradox of Success: An Archival and a Laboratory Study of Strategic Persistence Following Radical Environmental Change," *Academy of Management Journal*, Vol. 43, No. 5 (2000), pp. 837–853.
14. J. Brockner, "The Escalation of Commitment to a Failing Course of Action: Toward Theoretical Progress," *Academy of Management Review*, Vol. 17 (1992), pp. 39–61. The notion of escalation of commitment was first introduced by Barry Staw in his article "The Escalation of Commitment to a Course of Action," *Academy of Management Review*, Vol. 6 (1981), pp. 577–587. This phenomenon is characterized by repeated decision making in the face of negative feedback and uncertainty of success.
15. C.V. Callahan and B.A. Pasternack, "Corporate Strategy in the Digital Age," *Strategy and Business*, Issue 15 (2nd Quarter 1999), pp. 2–6.
16. J. Bowles, "How Digital Marketplaces Are Shaping the Future of B2B Commerce," Special Advertising Section on e Marketmakers, *Forbes* (July 23, 2000).
17. C.V. Callahan and B.A. Pasternack, "Corporate Strategy in the Digital Age," *Strategy & Business*, Issue 15 (2nd Quarter 1999), p. 3.
18. R.M. Kanter, "Managing the Extended Enterprise in a Globally Connected World," *Organizational Dynamics* (Summer 1999), pp. 7–23; C. Havens and E. Knapp, "Easing into Knowledge Management," *Strategy & Leadership* (March/April 1999), pp. 4–9.
19. M.E. Porter (2001). "Strategy and the Internet," *Harvard Business Review* (March 2001), pp. 63–78.
20. C. Gebelein, "Strategic Planning: The Engine of Change," *Planning Review* (September/October 1993), pp. 17–19.
21. R.A. D'Aveni, *Hypercompetition* (New York: Free Press, 1994). Hypercompetition is discussed in detail in Chapters 3 and 5.
22. R.S.M. Lau, "Strategic Flexibility: A New Reality for World-Class Manufacturing," *SAM Advanced Management Journal* (Spring 1996), pp. 11–15.
23. M.A. Hitt, B.W. Keats, and S.M. DeMarie, "Navigating in the New Competitive Landscape: Building Strategic Flexibility and Competitive Advantage in the 21st Century," *Academy of Management Executive* (November 1998), pp. 22–42.
24. D. Lei, J.W. Slocum, and R.A. Pitts, "Designing Organizations for Competitive Advantage: The Power of Unlearning and Learning," *Organizational Dynamics* (Winter 1999), pp. 24–38.
25. D.A. Garvin, "Building a Learning Organization," *Harvard Business Review* (July/August 1993), p. 80. See also P.M. Senge, *The Fifth Discipline: The Art and Practice of the Learning Organization* (New York: Doubleday, 1990).
26. T.T. Baldwin, C. Danielson, and W. Wiggenhorn, "The Evolution of Learning Strategies in Organizations: From Employee Development to Business Redefinition," *Academy of Management Executive* (November 1997), pp. 47–58.
27. W. Mitchell, J.M. Shaver, and B. Yeung, "Getting There in a Global Industry: Impacts on Performance of Changing International Presence," *Strategic Management Journal* (September 1992), pp. 419–432.
28. P.M. Senge, *The Fifth Discipline: The Art and Practice of the Learning Organization* (New York: Durrency Doubleday, 1990).
29. Research supports the use of this model in examining firm strategies. See J.A. Smith, "Strategies for Start-Ups," *Long Range Planning* (December 1998), pp. 857–872.
30. See A. Campbell and S. Yeung, "Brief Case: Mission, Vision, and Strategic Intent," *Long Range Planning* (August 1991), pp. 145–147; S. Cummings and J. Davies, "Mission, Vision, Fusion," *Long Range Planning* (December 1994), pp. 147–150.
31. Mountain Equipment Co-op, *Election Information and Annual Reports 1998*.
32. J. Cosco, "Down to the Sea in Ships," *Journal of Business Strategy* (November/December 1995), p. 48.

33. H.A. Simon, *Administrative Behavior,* 2nd edition (New York: Free Press, 1957), p. 231.

34. H. Mintzberg, "Planning on the Left Side and Managing on the Right," *Harvard Business Review* (July–August 1976), p. 56.

35. J.N. Fry and J. Peter Killing, *Strategic Analysis and Action,* 4th edition (Scarborough, Ont.: Prentice-Hall, 1998). It is useful to link the urgency of change to the likelihood of change being successfully implemented. Triggering events, if they do not create a crisis for a firm, put them into a reactive mode as the firm tries to restore performance.

36. D.J. Hickson, R. J. Butler, D. Cray, G. R. Mallory, and D. C. Wilson, *Top Decisions: Strategic Decision-Making in Organizations* (San Francisco: Jossey-Bass, 1986), pp. 26–42.

37. H. Mintzberg, "Strategy-Making in Three Modes," *California Management Review* (Winter 1973), pp. 44–53.

38. J.B. Quinn, *Strategies for Change: Logical Incrementalism* (Homewood, Ill.: Irwin, 1980), p. 58.

39. I. Gold and A.M.A. Rasheed, "Rational Decision-Making and Firm Performance: The Moderating Role of the Environment," *Strategic Management Journal* (August 1997), pp. 583–591; R.L. Priem, A.M.A. Rasheed, and A.G. Kotulic, "Rationality in Strategic Decision Processes, Environmental Dynamism and Firm Performance," *Journal of Management,* Vol. 21, No. 5 (1995), pp. 913–929; J.W. Dean, Jr., and M.P. Sharfman, "Does Decision Process Matter? A Study of Strategic Decision-Making Effectiveness," *Academy of Management Journal* (April 1996), pp. 368–396.

40. E. Turban, J. Lee, D. King, and H.M. Chung, *Electronic Commerce: A Managerial Perspective* (Upper Saddle River, NJ: Prentice Hall, 2000), p. 15. See also M.J. Shaw, "Electronic Commerce: State of the Art," in M.J. Shaw, R. Blanning, T. Strader, and A. Whinston (eds.), *Handbook on Electronic Commerce* (Berlin: Springer, 2000), pp. 3–24.

CHAPTER 2

Business Ethics and Social Responsibility

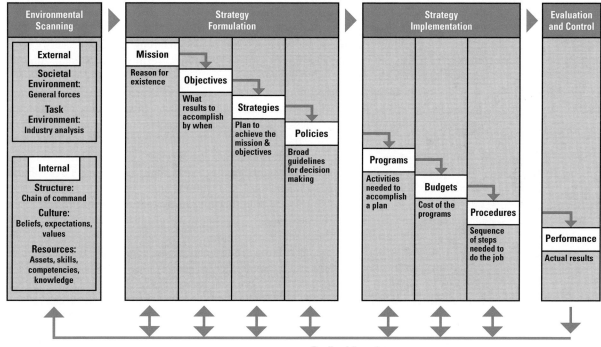

Learning Objectives

After reading this chapter you should be able to

Demonstrate a sound knowledge of business ethics and the pressures toward acting ethically

Utilize different approaches to making ethical decisions

Identify the basis of unethical behaviour

Explain top management's role in shaping an organization's stance toward social responsibility and ethics

Enumerate the different responsibilities of business

Identify organizational stakeholders and their influence in firm behaviour

TransFair is an independent Canadian certification organization for fair-trade coffee, tea, cocoa, and sugar. It awards a certification logo to organizations that adhere to certain criteria and standards established by Fairtrade Labelling Organizations International (FLO). When the FLO logo is displayed on a product, it acts as a guarantee that the product originates from FLO-affiliated producers. Canadian distributors pay a set minimum price that covers production costs; they advance payments or extend credit to producers to finance the next year's production; and they agree to long-term trading relationships to provide producers with added security. There are almost 100 licensees in Canada, including Aroma Specialty Coffee Roaster in British Columbia, Beans Etc. in Ontario, Custom Gourmet Coffee Ltd. in Alberta, and Just Us! Coffee Roasters Co-Op in Nova Scotia.

Consumers are increasingly concerned with the circumstances under which products are made. This has created the need for organizations like the FLO, whose purpose is to ensure a "fair" price so that farmers, regardless of their location and economic circumstances, make a minimal living wage. Part of their strategy is to organize small-scale farmers as co-ops, providing them some of the benefits of being small without depriving them of their autonomy. Products certified by FLO are also grown with sustainability in mind, in terms of a livelihood for farmers, the physical environment, and the communities in which they operate. International coffee prices are now so low that they do not cover the costs of production in many coffee-growing areas of the world, meaning that many producers are not able to provide the most basic needs for their families. Fairtrade-certified coffee, however, ensures a fair price for FLO's coffee producers. This allows producers not only to have a better standard of living, but also to make investments in infrastructure, production facilities, and the local community. The growth and success of FLO licensees is evidence of the viability of a strategy that is fundamentally based on being socially responsible. It proves that a business can be successful and pay decent prices to its suppliers. So in the context of an increasingly globalized world where developing countries are used as production sites for more affluent markets, organizations like TransFair help minimize the negative impact of globalization. TransFair offers a product for conscientious consumers, who are increasingly pressuring organizations to become more responsible.[1]

2.1 Business Ethics

business ethics beliefs concerning acceptable business conduct

Business ethics is concerned with the beliefs that determine what is acceptable (and what is not) in business. What is considered acceptable is, however, something that is determined by people—decision makers themselves, consumers, competitors, community members, and investors. Because the field of ethics is concerned with defining "acceptability," it is strongly influenced by the values and morals contained in the business environment. These help determine what goals should be pursued and what strategies are used to pursue them. The emergence of fair-trade organizations like those discussed earlier indicates that the social implications of business activity matter to consumers and that organizations are gradually becoming expected to be good corporate citizens in their pursuit of profit.

More and more we are seeing organizations emphasizing values in their mission, stating concern with employees, customers, ethics, integrity, and sustainability. But is this talk of ethics and social responsibility anything more than just talk? Recent evidence suggests that not only is the talk about ethics and integrity becoming more accepted in business, but it is also becoming necessary for success.[2] Consumers are beginning to reward ethical organizations by giving them more business. In a recent survey, almost 50% of consumers said they would be much more likely to buy from a socially responsible company if its products were on par with those of rivals. More than two thirds said they would not do business with a firm that was not socially responsible, at any price. In other words, good ethics and good business are one and the same.

For a long time "business ethics" was said to be an oxymoron. The scandals of Bre-X, WorldCom, and Enron have done nothing to change this view. But a long time before such large-scale corporate wrongdoing, there was a widely held view that business had a fiduciary responsibility to shareholders only. Any sort of philanthropy was seen as a breach of management by economists like Milton Friedman, who viewed management solely as an agent's service to a principal.[3] Doing anything other than maximizing profit was considered to be neither legally nor morally permitted. But today, focusing exclusively on maximizing profit is not what most businesses do, partly because it might violate their own values, and partly because it is no longer socially acceptable to do so. As the discussion in **Chapter 3** will indicate, any organization is dependent on its environment for survival. Ignoring society's interests is something no organization can do, and increasingly we are seeing organizations respond to society's demands for more ethical and accountable business practices.

There are therefore two pressures that businesses experience that encourage them to act ethically and responsibly. The first influence is based on values and morals. In other words, many organizational decision makers desire to do the right thing, regardless of any pressure or obligation to do so. Businesses can make these types of choices without being coerced by public interest groups or government regulation. FairTrade organizations pay a higher price for coffee beans than they would in a commodity market because they value building sustainable relationships between themselves and growers in developing regions. Similarly, many organizations give a range of benefits (holidays, insurance coverage) far exceeding what is required by law. Because organizations feel an obligation to do the right thing, they are usually willing to pay a certain price to do so, even though it means giving up something in terms of shareholder value.

The second influence is based on economics. In other words, firms will act ethically if it makes good business sense to do so. So rather than actually being ethical in its decision-making, a firm calculates the costs of acting unethically and weighs them against the associated gains. In these cases, organizations are concerned with *appearing* proper, because this perception can turn into increased sales and a better reputation in the market. Advertising and public relations are often used to convince stakeholders that the organization is doing the right thing.

In reality, most organizations are probably somewhere in between these extreme positions. Ultimately it might not matter to stakeholders what an organization's motives are, as long as it ends up acting in ethically and socially responsible ways.

MAKING ETHICAL DECISIONS

Business ethics is discussed in this chapter not to teach a particular definition of acceptable business conduct, but rather to provide a systematic way of assessing the impact of organizational decisions on organizational stakeholders. An important first step is being able to identify ethical elements of an issue. There are situations where decisions are made that could be considered right or wrong, ethical or unethical. When in these situations, decision makers need to determine the benefits and harms associated with any given decision in order to assess its impact on organizational stakeholders. Any time the ethics of a situation come into question, there is always a subjective dimension to assessing organizational behaviour.

How do we arrive at a comprehensive statement of ethics to use in making decisions in a specific occupation, trade, or profession? A starting point for a code of ethics is to consider the three basic approaches to ethical behaviour:[4]

utilitarian approach decisions are judged by their harms and benefits to society as a whole

1. **Utilitarian Approach**: This approach proposes that actions and plans should be judged by their consequences. People should therefore behave in such a way that will produce the greatest benefit to society with the least harm or the lowest cost. A problem with this approach is the difficulty in recognizing all the benefits and the costs of any particular decision. Research reveals that only the stakeholders having the most *power* (ability to affect the company), *legitimacy* (legal or moral claim on company resources), and *urgency* (demand for immediate attention) are given priority by CEOs.[5] It is therefore likely that only the most obvious stakeholders will be considered, while others are ignored.

individual rights approach decisions are judged by their interference with the rights of others

2. **Individual Rights Approach**: This approach proposes that human beings have certain fundamental rights that should be respected in all decisions. A particular decision or behaviour should be avoided if it interferes with the rights of others. A problem with this approach is in defining "fundamental rights." The protections offered in the Canadian Charter of Rights and Freedoms may or may not be accepted throughout the world. The approach can also encourage selfish behaviour when a person defines a personal need or want as a right.

justice approach decisions are judged by the fairness of the process by which they are made

3. **Justice Approach**: This approach proposes that decision makers are equitable, fair, and impartial in the distribution of costs and benefits to individuals and groups. It follows the principles of distributive justice (people who are similar in relevant dimensions such as job seniority should be treated in the same way) and fairness (liberty should be equal for all persons). The justice approach can also include the concepts of retributive justice (punishment should be proportional to the crime) and compensatory justice (wrongs should be compensated in proportion to the offence). Employment equity issues such as reverse discrimination are examples of conflicts between distributive and compensatory justice.

Ethical problems can be solved by asking the following three questions regarding an act or decision:

1. **Utility:** Does it optimize the satisfaction of all stakeholders?

2. **Rights:** Does it respect the rights of the individuals involved?

3. **Justice:** Is it consistent with the canons of justice?

For example, is padding an expense account ethical or not? Using the utility criterion, this action increases the company's costs and thus does not optimize benefits to shareholders or customers. Using the rights approach, a person has no right to the money. Using the justice criterion, salary and commissions constitute ordinary compensation, but expense accounts only compensate a person for expenses incurred in doing his or her job—expenses that the person would not normally incur except in doing this job.[6]

Another approach to resolving ethical dilemmas is by applying the logic of the philosopher Immanuel Kant. Kant presents two principles—called **categorical imperatives**—to guide our actions:

categorical imperatives Immanuel Kant's idea of the two ways in which people resolve ethical dilemmas: the golden rule and not treating people as a means to an end

1.   A person's action is ethical only if that person is willing for that same action to be taken by everyone who is in a similar situation. This is a restatement of the familiar golden rule: Treat others as you would like them to treat you. For example, padding an expense account would be considered ethical if the person were also willing for everyone to do the same if he or she were the boss. Because it is very doubtful that any manager would be pleased with expense account padding by his or her employees, the action must be considered unethical.

2.   A person should never treat another human being simply as a means but always as an end. This principle indicates that an action is morally wrong for a person if that person uses others merely as a way of advancing his or her own interests. To be moral, the act should not restrict other people's actions so that they are left disadvantaged in some way.[7]

Organizations try to encourage ethical behaviour for a variety of reasons and in a number of different ways. At a minimum, firms establish codes of conduct that articulate their ethical position to both employees and the public. But in addition to a written code, the support and action of management is necessary if these codes are to be taken seriously and not viewed simply as meaningless phrases. Organizations that both develop formal codes of ethics and act in accordance with them send clear signals to all stakeholders that they act in principled ways and actively discourage ethically dubious behaviour. In other words, there needs to be both a policy of ethical behaviour and an organizational culture to underlie it:

code of ethics a formal statement of an organization's position on its ethical behaviour

1.   *Codes of Ethics.* A professional **code of ethics** is a formal statement of how an organization will conduct its affairs. **Figure 2–1** on page 34 shows the code of ethics for the Nova Scotia Home Builders' Association. In this code we see a commitment to a range of stakeholders and a clear willingness to adhere to a higher standard of accountability than is prescribed by law. A code of ethics, therefore, prescribes certain behaviours for organizational members and sends a signal of confidence and trustworthiness to the market. Because more and more consumers are demanding that organizations be accountable for their actions, statements like these can be used to improve attitudes toward an organization's activities, creating a widespread perception of the organization's concern with consumer satisfaction and the well-being of the entire industry.

2.   *A Culture of Ethics.* Because formal policies are rarely sufficient to guide individual behaviour, an ethical culture is necessary to create the expectation of ethical behaviour among workers and to promote the active discouragement of unethical behaviour. This can occur through training programs where individuals learn to recognize ethical dilemmas and to appreciate the impact their decisions have on a wide range of stakeholders. Ethics training is an ideal context in which to communicate an organization's code of ethics and encourage employees to act in accordance with it. This means that even if it disrupts the status quo, slows down the decision-making process, and increases costs, individuals should still act responsibly and ethically. It also means that workers need to know ethical wrongdoing is not permitted and will be treated severely. Most organizations adopting this stance would prefer to deal with illegal or unethical behaviour internally rather than have their actions exposed publicly by a whistle-blower or an investigative journalist. So to support a code of ethics, a strong ethical culture is necessary, one that makes ethics and accountability core organizational values.

Figure 2–1 Nova Scotia Home Builders' Association Code of Ethics

Members shall comply with the National Building Code of Canada as a minimum standard for construction and work towards its improvement in the interests of structural sufficiency, safety, and health.

Members shall plan their sites and homes to conform to the principles of good community planning.

Members shall deal honestly and fairly with their customers.

Members shall co-operate to extend the effectiveness of the Association by exchanging information and experience and techniques in order to provide the best value for their customers.

Members shall uphold the principle of appropriate and adequate compensation for the services which they render.

Members shall avoid all conduct or practice detrimental to the house building industry, to the Association, to the good name or reputation of any of its members, or to customers.

Source: NSHBA Code of Ethics, www.nshba.ns.ca/code_of_ethics.html (accessed March 15, 2003), Canadian Homebuilders' Association.

An increasing number of companies are developing codes of ethics and implementing ethics training workshops and seminars to create ethical cultures. Research indicates, however, that when faced with a question of ethics, managers often ignore codes of ethics and try to solve their dilemmas on their own.[8] To combat this tendency, the management of a company that wants to improve its employees' ethical behaviour should not only develop a comprehensive code of ethics, but also communicate the code in its training programs, through its performance appraisal system, in policies and procedures, and through its own actions. It may also want to do the same for those companies with which it does business. For example, Reebok International has developed a set of human rights production standards for the manufacturers that supply the company with its athletic shoes on a contract basis. Reebok requires the following of its suppliers:

- That they do not discriminate on the grounds of race, colour, national origin, gender, religion, or political opinion
- That they do not normally require more than a 60-hour work week
- That they do not use forced labour
- That they provide fair wages and benefits
- That they do not employ children
- That they provide a safe and healthy workplace

In response to a report commissioned by Reebok that found health and safety problems at two subcontractor plants in Indonesia, the two suppliers were forced to spend $500 000 in factory improvements in order to keep Reebok's business.[9]

SOME REASONS FOR UNETHICAL BEHAVIOUR

Why are many business people perceived to be acting unethically? It may be that the people involved are not even aware that they are doing something questionable. There is no worldwide standard of conduct for business people. Cultural norms and values vary between countries and even between different geographic regions and ethnic groups within a country. For example, what is considered in one country to be a bribe to expedite service is sometimes considered in another country to be normal business practice.

values belief in the acceptability of certain conditions or decisions, usually judged in comparison with some other conditions or decisions

Another possible reason for what is often perceived to be unethical behaviour lies in differences in **values** between business people and key stakeholders. Some business people may believe profit maximization is the key goal of their firm, whereas concerned interest groups may have other priorities, such as the hiring of minorities and women or the safety of their neighbourhoods. Of the six values measured by the Allport-Vernon-Lindzey Study of Values test (*aesthetic, economic, political, religious, social,* and *theoretical*), both American and British executives consistently score highest on economic and political values and lowest on social and religious ones. This is similar to the value profile of managers from Japan, Korea, India, and Australia, as well as those of American business school students. American Protestant ministers, in contrast, score highest on religious and social values and very low on economic values.[10]

This difference in values can make it difficult for one group of people to understand another's actions. For example, even though some people feel that the advertising of cigarettes (especially to youth) is unethical, the people managing these companies respond that they are simply offering a product. "Let the buyer beware" (*caveat emptor*) is a traditional saying among free-market capitalists. They argue that customers in a free-market democracy have the right to choose how they spend their money and live their lives. Social progressives may contend that business people working in such industries as tobacco, alcoholic beverages, and gambling are acting unethically by making and advertising products with potentially dangerous and expensive side effects, such as cancer, alcoholism, and addiction. People working in these industries could respond by asking whether it is ethical for people who don't smoke, drink, or gamble to reject another person's right to do so.

Moral Relativism

Some people justify their seemingly unethical positions by arguing that there is no one absolute code of ethics and that morality is relative. Simply put, moral relativism claims that morality is relative to some personal, social, or cultural standard and that there is no method for deciding whether one decision is better than another.

moral relativism the belief that morality is solely individually based and subjective

Adherents of **moral relativism** may believe that all moral decisions are deeply personal and that individuals have the right to run their own lives; each person should be allowed to interpret situations and act on his or her own moral values. They may also argue that social roles carry with them certain obligations to those roles only. A manager in charge of a department, for example, must put aside his or her personal beliefs and instead do what the role requires, that is, act in the best interests of the department. They could also argue that a decision is legitimate if it is common practice regardless of other considerations ("Everyone's doing it"). Some propose that morality itself is relative to a particular culture, society, or community. People should therefore understand the practices of other countries but not judge them. If the citizens of another country share certain norms and customs, what right does an outsider have to criticize them?

Although these arguments make some sense, moral relativism could enable a person to justify almost any sort of decision or action, as long as it is not declared illegal.

Kohlberg's Levels of Moral Development

Another reason why some business people might be seen as unethical is that they may have no well-developed personal sense of ethics. A person's ethical behaviour will be affected by his or her level of moral development, certain personality variables, and such situational factors as the job itself, the supervisor, and the organizational culture.[11] Kohlberg proposes that a person progresses through three levels of moral development.[12] Individuals move from total self-centredness to a concern for universal values. Kohlberg's three levels are as follows:

1. **The preconventional level** is characterized by a concern for self. Small children and others who have not progressed beyond this stage evaluate behaviours on the basis of personal interest—maximizing gain while avoiding punishment.
2. **The conventional level** is characterized by considerations of society's laws and norms. Actions are justified by an external code of conduct.
3. **The principled level** is characterized by a person's adherence to an internal moral code. The individual at this level looks beyond norms or laws to find universal values or principles.

Kohlberg places most people in the conventional level, with fewer than 20% of adults in the principled level of development.[13]

2.2 The Role of Top Management

The top management function is usually conducted by the CEO of the organization in co-ordination with the COO (chief operating officer) or president, the executive vice-president, and the vice-presidents of divisions and functional areas. Even though strategic management involves everyone in the organization, top management and its board of directors hold top management primarily responsible for the strategic management of the firm.[14] Top management is especially important in forming an organization's ethical culture and its stance on social responsibility.

RESPONSIBILITIES OF TOP MANAGEMENT

Top management's responsibilities, especially those of the CEO, involve getting things accomplished through and with others to meet organizational objectives. Top management's job is thus multidimensional and oriented toward the welfare of the total organization. Specific top management tasks vary from firm to firm and are developed from an analysis of the mission, objectives, strategies, and key activities of the organization. Tasks are typically divided among the members of the top management team. A diversity of skills can thus be very important. Research indicates that top management teams with a diversity of functional and educational backgrounds and length of time with the company tend to be significantly related to improvements in market share and profitability.[15] Nevertheless, the CEO, with the support of the rest of the top management team, must successfully handle two primary responsibilities crucial to the effective strategic management of the organization: (1) provide executive leadership and a strategic vision, and (2) manage the strategic planning process.

Executive Leadership and Strategic Vision

executive leadership the process of directing the activities of organizational members toward the achievement of the organization's purpose

strategic vision a statement of what an organization desires to be and is capable of becoming

Executive leadership is the directing of activities toward the accomplishment of organizational objectives. Executive leadership is important because it sets the tone for the entire organization. A **strategic vision** is a description of what the company is capable of becoming. People in an organization want to have a sense of mission, but only top management is in the position to specify and communicate this strategic vision to the general workforce. Top management's enthusiasm (or lack of it) about the organization tends to be contagious. Entrepreneurs are noted for having a strong passion for their company and for their ability to communicate it to others. The importance of executive leadership is illustrated by John Welch Jr., the successful chairman and CEO of General Electric Company (GE). According to Welch: "Good business leaders create a vision, articulate the vision, and relentlessly drive it to completion."[16]

Chief executive officers with a clear strategic vision are often perceived as dynamic and charismatic leaders. For instance, the positive attitude characterizing many well-known industrial leaders of recent years—such as Bill Gates at Microsoft, Anita Roddick at The Body Shop, Ted Turner at CNN, Steve Jobs at Apple Computer, Herb Kelleher at Southwest Airlines, and Andy Grove at Intel—has energized their organizations. Leaders like these are able to command respect and influence strategy formulation and implementation because they tend to have three key characteristics:

1. **The CEO articulates a strategic vision** for the organization. The CEO envisions the company not as it currently is, but as it can become. The new perspective that the CEO's vision brings to activities and conflicts gives renewed meaning to everyone's work and enables employees to see beyond the details of their own jobs to the functioning of the total organization. In a recent survey of 1500 senior executives from 20 different countries, when asked the most important behavioural trait a CEO must have, 98% responded that the CEO must convey "a strong sense of vision."[17]

2. **The CEO presents a role** for others to identify with and to follow. The leader sets an example in terms of behaviour and dress. The CEO's attitudes and values concerning the organization's purpose and activities are clear-cut and constantly communicated in words and deeds. People know what to expect from, and have trust in, their CEO. Research indicates that those businesses in which the general manager has the trust of the employees have higher sales and profits with lower turnover than do businesses in which there is less trust.[18]

3. **The CEO communicates high performance standards and also shows confidence in the followers' abilities** to meet these standards. No leader ever improved performance by setting easily attainable goals that provided no challenge. The CEO must be willing to follow through by coaching people. Selected the "Best CEO" of 2000, John Chambers of Cisco Systems has this characteristic. According to his subordinates, "John treats us like peers.... He asks our advice. He gives us power and resources, then sets the sales targets incredibly high, which keeps us challenged. He is an adhesive force keeping us working together and not flying apart."[19]

Developing Strategic Vision

The previous section discussed the role of executive leadership in articulating and communicating strategic vision. But what makes a good strategic vision and why is it important for the organization? Vision is important because it provides a focus on the future. Without a vision of *where* the organization needs to go, it is difficult to make decisions about *how* to get there. In other words, strategy formulation needs to be made in the context of where the organization wants to head, what needs it is trying to satisfy in the market, and what goals it wants to achieve.

Mission statements were discussed in **Chapter 1** as statements of the organization's purpose. As a starting point in creating strategic vision, mission statements define the organization in terms of the products it provides to the market and how it will profitably provide them. The organization's mission, therefore, focuses on what the organization is currently doing and what makes it different from its competitors. Strategic vision, on the other hand, takes a forward-looking approach to decide what an organization's priorities should be in the future and to create the plans and strategies necessary to accomplish them. This requires strategic decision makers to consider and forecast changes in the organization's environment that will affect its performance.

A range of analytical techniques are presented in **Chapter 3**. In preparing an organization for the future, a systematic analysis of the organization's past, its current performance, and the anticipated changes around it will be necessary. Without a clear understanding of these, organizations will have a difficult time in preparing themselves for the future. See the illustration of how a new strategic vision was developed for Choice Hotels.

A New Strategic Vision at Choice Hotels Canada

Choice Hotels Canada Inc. is the largest hotel chain in Canada, with more than 250 properties. Its brands include Comfort, Quality, Sleep Inn, Clarion, Econo Lodge, and MainStay Suites. President and CEO Gary Decatur led a management team in developing a strategic vision based on five focus points:

1. **Strategic Growth**: Continued growth in a responsible and strategic manner is directed toward conversion opportunities at Econo Lodge and new construction at Sleep Inn.

2. **Operational Services**: To enhance operational services, an innovative preventive maintenance program has been developed to assist licensees in planning and budgeting for capital improvements.

3. **Sales**: A sales strategy to drive business into hotels from local, national, and international sources has also been introduced.

4. **Marketing**: New initiatives include a reward component added to its existing guest recognition program, increased funding for regional marketing, and an upgraded website.

5. **Communication**: Communication between the corporation and its licensees is key. Regular town hall meetings, newsletters, and training programs have now been instituted.

Source: www.airhighways.com/hotels_choice.htm (accessed July 10, 2003).

Manage the Strategic Planning Process

As business organizations adopt more of the characteristics of the learning organization, strategic planning initiatives can now come from any part of an organization. Many large organizations first propose at the subsidiary or division level and then send to headquarters for approval.[20] However, unless top management encourages and supports the planning process, strategic management is not likely to result. In most organizations, top management must initiate and manage the strategic planning process. It may do so by first asking business units and functional areas to propose strategic plans for themselves, or it may begin by drafting an overall organizational plan within which the units can then build their own plans. Research suggests that bottom-up strategic planning may be most appropriate in multidivisional organizations operating in relatively stable environments, but that top-down strategic planning may be most appropriate for firms operating in turbulent environments.[21] Other organizations engage in concurrent strategic planning in which all the organization's units draft plans for themselves after they have been provided with the organization's overall mission and objectives.

Regardless of the approach taken, top management must manage the overall strategic planning process so that the plans of all the units and functional areas fit together into an overall organizational plan. Top management's job, therefore, includes the tasks of evaluating unit plans and providing feedback. To do this, it may require each unit to justify its proposed objectives, strategies, and programs in terms of how well they satisfy the organization's overall objectives in light of available resources.[22]

Many large organizations have a strategic planning staff charged with supporting both top management and the business units in the strategic planning process. This planning staff typically consists of fewer than 10 people, headed by a senior vice-president or director of corporate planning. The staff's major responsibilities are as follows:

1. Identify and analyze company-wide strategic issues, and suggest strategic alternatives to top management

2. Work as facilitators with business units to guide them through the strategic planning process

2.3 Social Responsibilities of Strategic Decision Makers

Should strategic decision makers be responsible only to shareholders, or do they have broader responsibilities? The concept of social responsibility proposes that a private organization has responsibilities to society that extend beyond making a profit. Strategic decisions often affect more than just the organization. A decision to retrench by closing some plants and discontinuing product lines, for example, affects not only the firm's workforce, but also the communities where the plants are located and the customers with no other source of the discontinued product. Such situations raise questions of the appropriateness of certain missions, objectives, and strategies of business organizations. Managers must be able to deal with these conflicting interests in an ethical manner to formulate a viable strategic plan.

RESPONSIBILITIES OF A BUSINESS FIRM

What are the responsibilities of a business firm, and to what extent must they be fulfilled? Milton Friedman and Archie Carroll offer two contrasting views of the responsibilities of business firms to society.

Friedman's Traditional View of Business Responsibility

Urging a return to a laissez-faire worldwide economy with a minimum of government regulation, Milton Friedman argues against the concept of social responsibility. A business person who acts "responsibly" by cutting the price of the firm's product to prevent inflation, or by making expenditures to reduce pollution, or by hiring the hard-core unemployed, according to Friedman, is spending the shareholders' money for a general social interest. Even if the business person has shareholder permission or encouragement to do so, he or she is still acting from non-economic motives and may, in the long run, harm the very society the firm is trying to help. By taking on the burden of these social costs, the business becomes less efficient—either prices go up to pay for the increased costs or investment in new activities and research is postponed. These results negatively affect—perhaps fatally—the long-term efficiency of a business. Friedman thus referred to the social responsibility of business as a "fundamentally subversive doctrine" and stated:

> There is one and only one social responsibility of business—to use its resources and engage in activities designed to increase its profits so long as it stays within the rules of the game, which is to say, engages in open and free competition without deception or fraud.[23]

Carroll's Four Responsibilities of Business

As shown in **Figure 2–2**, Archie Carroll proposes that the managers of business organizations have four responsibilities: economic, legal, ethical, and discretionary.[24]

1. **Economic** responsibilities of a business organization's management are to produce goods and services of value to society so that the firm may repay its creditors and shareholders.

2. **Legal** responsibilities are defined by governments in laws that management is expected to obey. For example, business firms are required to hire and promote people based on their credentials rather than discriminate on non-job-related characteristics such as race, gender, or religion.

3. **Ethical** responsibilities of an organization's management are to follow the generally held beliefs about appropriate behaviour in a society. For example, society generally expects firms to work with the employees and the community in planning for layoffs, even though no law may require this. The affected people can get very upset if an organization's management fails to act according to generally prevailing ethical values.

4. **Discretionary** responsibilities are the purely voluntary obligations an organization assumes. Examples are philanthropic contributions, training the hard-core unemployed, and providing daycare centres. The difference between ethical and discretionary responsibilities is that few people expect an organization to fulfill discretionary responsibilities, whereas many expect an organization to fulfill ethical ones.[25]

Figure 2–2 Responsibilities of Business

Voluntary Responsibilities
being a "good corporate citizen"; contributing to the community and quality of life

Ethical Responsibilities
being ethical; doing what is right, just, and fair; avoiding harm

Legal Responsibilities
obeying the law (society's codification of right and wrong); playing by the rules of the game

Economic Responsibilities
being profitable

Source: Adapted from A.B. Carroll, "A Three Dimensional Conceptual Model of Corporate Performance," *Academy of Management Review* (October 1979), p. 499. Reprinted with permission.

Carroll lists these four responsibilities *in order of priority*. A business firm must first make a profit to satisfy its economic responsibilities. To continue in existence, the firm must follow the laws, thus fulfilling its legal responsibilities. There is evidence that companies found guilty of violating laws have lower profits and sales growth after conviction.[26] On this point Carroll and Friedman are in agreement. Carroll, however, goes further by arguing that business managers have responsibilities beyond the economic and legal ones.

Having satisfied the two basic responsibilities, according to Carroll, the firm should look to fulfilling its social responsibilities. **Social responsibility**, therefore, *includes both ethical and discretionary but not economic and legal responsibilities*. A firm can fulfill its ethical responsibilities by taking actions that society tends to value but has not yet put into law. When ethical responsibilities are satisfied, a firm can focus on discretionary responsibilities—purely voluntary actions that society has not yet decided are important.

The discretionary responsibilities of today may become the ethical responsibilities of tomorrow. The provision of daycare facilities is, for example, moving rapidly from a discretionary to an ethical responsibility. Carroll suggests that to the extent that business organizations fail to acknowledge discretionary or ethical responsibilities, society, through government, will act, making them legal responsibilities. Government may do this, moreover, without regard to an organization's economic responsibilities. As a result, the organization may have greater difficulty in earning a profit than it would have had if it had voluntarily assumed some ethical and discretionary responsibilities.

Both Friedman and Carroll argue their positions based on the impact of socially responsible actions on a firm's profits. Friedman says that socially responsible actions hurt a firm's efficiency. Carroll proposes that a lack of social responsibility results in increased government regulations, which reduce a firm's efficiency.

Research is mixed regarding the effect of social responsibility on a firm's financial performance. Although a number of research studies find no significant relationship,[27] an increasing number are finding a positive relationship.[28]

On the other hand, refusing to live up to the expectations of society can sometimes pay off. For example, three firms that remained in racially segregated South Africa during the economic sanctions of the 1980s—Colgate-Palmolive, Johnson & Johnson, and 3M—were damned in shareholder resolutions, college demonstrations, and informal boycotts of their products. They were, however, able to expand their base quickly once apartheid ended and now dominate their South African markets. Firms that lived up to society's expectations by leaving found it very difficult to return to South Africa because they were at a competitive disadvantage. McDonald's, which pulled its operations out of South Africa during apartheid, lost the right to its trademark during the firm's absence.

In contrast, firms that are known to be ethical and socially responsible often enjoy some benefits that may even give them a competitive advantage. For example, companies that take the lead in being environmentally friendly, for instance by using recycled materials, pre-empt attacks from environmental groups and enhance their organizational image. Programs to reduce pollution, for example, can actually reduce waste and maximize resource productivity. One study examining ecological initiatives found the average payback period to be only 18 months.[29] Here are other examples of benefits to companies from being socially responsible:

- Their environmental concerns may enable them to charge premium prices and gain brand loyalty (as with Ben & Jerry's Ice Cream).

- Their trustworthiness may help them generate enduring relationships with suppliers and distributors without needing to spend a lot of time and money policing contracts (Maytag).

- They can attract outstanding employees who prefer working for a responsible firm (Procter & Gamble).

social responsibility
ethical and discretionary responsibilities that reflect voluntary efforts to fulfill more than the most basic responsibilities

- They are more likely to be welcomed into a foreign country (Levi Strauss).
- They can utilize the goodwill of public officials for support in difficult times (Minnesota supported Dayton-Hudson's fight to avoid being acquired by Dart Industries of Maryland).
- They are more likely to attract capital infusions from investors who view reputable companies as desirable long-term investments (Rubbermaid).[30]

ORGANIZATIONAL STAKEHOLDERS

organizational stake-holders groups that can affect or be affected by a firm's behaviour

The concept that business must be socially responsible sounds appealing until we ask, "Responsible to whom?" An organization's task environment includes a large number of groups with interest in a firm's activities. These groups are referred to as **organizational stakeholders** because they affect or are affected by the achievement of the firm's objectives.[31] Should an organization be responsible only to some of these groups, or does business have an equal responsibility to all of them? See the **Global Issue** feature showing how the community in which business operates is becoming increasingly global.

Global Issue

Responsibility and the "Community"

A recent study of two global mining companies shows a change in how they attempted to act in socially responsible ways when operating in developing countries. Mining companies of all types have had rather questionable track records of social responsibility, due in large part to the nature of their business. Extracting minerals from the ground usually involves a certain amount of environmental destruction, in addition to whatever damage might be caused by the refining or producing processes necessary after extraction. How do firms like these act in ways that are responsive to the local communities in which they operate?

In developed countries, organizations have paid the most attention to the concerns of local communities where pressures to be a "good neighbour" are strongest. When communities are in the position to impose costs on an organization, they are seldom neglected. The reality is, however, that not all communities have the resources to effectively lobby against destructive firm behaviour, and the individuals opposed to the behaviour often have no effective way to organize so their voices can be heard collectively. Both factors lead to a relatively powerless community, which in turns leads to their concerns being neglected.

Nowhere has this been more noticeable than in developing nations, whose economies often so strongly depend on the extraction of natural resources. There is no shortage of examples of this: "conflict diamonds" from Sierra Leone, cocoa from the Ivory Coast, and oil from Nigeria. Deplorable working conditions and dubious business practices seem anything but socially responsible. Gradually, however, as globalization has encouraged firms to shift their production to lower-cost regions, they are now faced with new communities to deal with and new-found opposition. Environmental and corporate watchdog groups have also globalized, increasing their power by collaborating with local community groups in developing nations. This makes the overseas operations of a wide range of companies more subject to inspection and criticism. Over time there has been increasing pressure for global mining companies to adopt a more socially responsible stance in *all* of their markets. The fact that many organizational responses to this sort of pressure have occurred as a result of bad publicity, sabotage, and interest group pressure suggests that most natural resource firms display a strong utilitarian basis of ethics and responsibility. Nothing makes this more clear than organizations trying to hide their wrongdoing from scrutiny, justifying offences in terms of the economic benefit to an otherwise poor economy, or discrediting the concerns of a small local community in order to *appear* ethical in its behaviours.

Sources: C. Driscoll and A. Crombie, "Stakeholder Legitimacy Management and the Qualified Good Neighbour: The Case of Nova Nada and JDI," *Business & Society* (Vol. 40, 2001), pp. 442–471; P. Kapelus, "Mining, Corporate Social Responsibility and the 'Community': The Case of Rio Tinto, Richards Bay Minerals and the Mbonambi," *Journal of Business Ethics* (Vol. 39, 2002), pp. 275–296.

Recent surveys suggest that the general public believes that business is becoming too concerned with profits. A recent survey conducted by Harris Poll found that 66% either strongly or somewhat agreed that large profits are more important to big business than developing safe, reliable, quality products for consumers. Recent revelations of tainted milk in Japan (Snow Brand), flawed child strollers in the United States (Cosco), and unsafe tires globally (Firestone) only add to the public concern that business is ignoring its stakeholders and may be operating unethically or even illegally. Executive compensation has been a controversial matter for years, especially in North America, where the gap between the wages of CEOs and workers is more pronounced and executive compensation appears to bear no relation to firm performance. Public opinion is increasingly showing a feeling that organizations owe something to their workers and the communities in which they operate. As discussed earlier, it is no longer socially acceptable for an organization to maximize profit at any cost. Rather, society is now showing a belief that business should sometimes sacrifice some profit for the sake of making things better for their workers and communities.[32]

In any strategic decision, the interests of one stakeholder group can conflict with another's. For example, a business firm's decision to use only recycled materials in its manufacturing process may have a positive effect on environmental groups but a negative effect on shareholder dividends. In another example, Nortel's top management decided to move a tremendous amount of production out of Canada to a lower-wage location in Asia. On the one hand, shareholders were generally pleased with the decision because it lowered costs. On the other hand, the local community was very unhappy at what they called "community cannibalism." Which group's interests should have priority?

Given the wide range of interests and concerns present in any organization's task environment, one or more groups, at any one time, probably will be dissatisfied with an organization's activities—even if management is trying to be socially responsible. A company may have some stakeholders of which it is only marginally aware. Therefore, before making a strategic decision, strategic managers should consider how each alternative would affect various stakeholder groups. What seems at first to be the best decision because it appears to be the most profitable may actually result in the worst set of consequences to the organization.

2.4 Impact of the Internet on Social Responsibility

Electronic commerce is offering many benefits, but it is also raising a number of issues relating to social responsibility and stakeholders. Thus far, the internet is generally unregulated by governments. To the extent that groups of people find the internet to have negative effects, government will be called upon eventually to intervene. Europeans are concerned about the user's privacy. Middle Easterners are concerned about decency standards. Americans are concerned about con artists using websites and email to take money without providing a service.

In Russia, for example, a recently passed law allows the Federal Security Bureau (FSB) to monitor all internet, cellular telephone, and pager communication traffic. Directives require all Russian ISPs (internet service providers) to equip their networks with an FSB monitor and connect them with a high-speed fibre-optic link to FSB headquarters. "This is an end to all email privacy," protested Anatoly Levanchuk, an internet and free speech advocate.[33]

A number of problems may make it difficult to keep the internet unregulated. Among them are these:

- **Cybersquatting:** This occurs when a private speculator purchases the right to a valuable corporate brand name domain, such as **businessweek.com**, and then sells it to the company at an exorbitant price. Because web addresses are critical to online branding, companies want to establish a rule that they are entitled to any domain name using their trademark. In response, consumer advocates say that such a rule would unfairly restrict the rights of schools, museums, religions, and clubs. They argue that an astronomy club should be able to register **saturn.com** if the domain is available—and not later lose it to a car company.[34]

■ **Fraud:** The internet is an excellent source of information—information that can be used to defraud innocent people by temporarily stealing their identity. Thanks to personal websites and other publicly available information, the internet can provide all that is needed to charge purchases to someone else's credit cards and to transfer funds out of their bank accounts.

■ **Taxation:** In international trade, goods tend to be subject to tariffs while services are not. The internet is making this distinction difficult. For example, a compact disc (CD) sent from one country to another is a good and thus incurs a tariff as it crosses a border. But what if the music on the CD is sent electronically from a computer in one country to a computer in another country? Since customized data and software, which can also be put on a CD, are usually treated as services, is the music a good or a service?[35]

■ **Public Interest:** Since most societies have some sort of restrictions on children's access to pornography, should pornographic websites also be restricted? If so, by whom? Given that government is often expected to protect its citizens from fraudulent investment schemes and quack medical treatments, what should it do when these things are offered on the internet? Governments could impose trade restrictions requiring that financial firms selling on the internet to residents of that country must also have an office in the country. See the **Internet Issue** feature for examples of governmental attempts to regulate the internet.

In addition, the internet is providing a fast way to communicate a company's mistakes and any unethical or illegal actions to interested people throughout the world. This is making it increasingly difficult for companies undertaking questionable activities to keep things quiet while they cover up the problem with a public relations campaign. Fuelled by passion and technical expertise, activists of all kinds have launched sophisticated websites that attack individual companies regarding their environmental or labour practices and other issues. For example, the Corporate Watch website (**www.corporatewatch.org.uk**) contains articles on the risks of genetic modification of plants, with case studies targeting leading biotech companies. Interestingly, some companies are beginning to respond by upgrading their websites to reflect their shift to a more open dialogue with a wide range of stakeholders. In response to Greenpeace's Shareholders Against New Exploration (SANE) campaign, BP Amoco has added website links to environmental information and an animated explanation of its solar energy research.[36]

Internet Issue

Governments Act to Protect Society by Regulating the Internet

On November 20, 2000, a French court ordered Yahoo! to find some way of banning French users from seeing the Nazi memorabilia posted on its US websites or face a daily fine of 100 000 francs. Although Yahoo! appealed the court's decision, it stopped listing sales of Nazi memorabilia on any of its websites. France is not alone in regulating the internet. Myanmar (formerly known as Burma) bans access to the internet. South Korea outlawed access to gambling websites. The United States passed a law requiring schools and libraries that received federal funds for internet connections to install software on their computers to block material deemed harmful to children. Under a new European Union (EU) law, European consumers may now sue EU-based internet sites in their own countries. There is some pressure to extend the rule internationally. The United States has endorsed the Council of Europe's cybercrime treaty, which aims to harmonize international laws against hacking, internet fraud, and child pornography.

Two tools that can be used to limit the freedom of internet

users are filtering and internet provider (IP) address identification software. Filtering software can be installed on a computer, an internet provider's servers, or gateways linking one country with another. This software acts to block access to certain websites. China, for example, has installed this software nationwide to block access to internet sites with unwanted content. China has also passed laws requiring internet companies to apply for a licence and holding them accountable for illegal content carried on their websites. Websites can also block users by tracking an internet server's IP address, the

number that identifies computers on the internet and often reveals where a user is located. A controversial feature, called IPV6, was designed by the Internet Engineering Task Force (IETF) to expand the IP address to include the unique serial number of each computer's network connection software. Every data packet would thus contain a user's electronic "fingerprints."

Source: "Stop Signs on the Web," *The Economist* (January 13, 2001), pp. 21–25.

Discussion Questions

1. What is the relationship between business ethics and social responsibility?

2. What is your opinion of Reebok's production standards of human rights for its suppliers? What would Milton Friedman say? Contrast his view with Archie Carroll's view.

3. Does a company have to act selflessly to be considered socially responsible? For example, when building a new plant, an organization voluntarily invested in additional equipment enabling it to reduce its pollution emissions beyond any current laws. Knowing that it would be very expensive for its competitors to do the same, the firm lobbied the government to make pollution regulations more restrictive on the entire industry. Is this company socially responsible? Were its managers acting ethically?

Strategic Practice Exercise

How far should people in a business firm go in gathering competitive intelligence? Where do you draw the line?

Evaluate each of the following approaches that a business firm could use to gather information about competition. For each approach, mark your feeling about its appropriateness: 1 (definitely not appropriate), 2 (probably not appropriate), 3 (undecided), 4 (probably appropriate), or 5 (definitely appropriate).

The business firm should try to get useful information about competitors by:

_____ Careful study of trade journals
_____ Wiretapping the telephones of competitors
_____ Posing as a potential customer to competitors
_____ Getting loyal customers to put out a phony "request for proposal" soliciting competitors' bids
_____ Buying competitors' products and taking them apart
_____ Hiring management consultants who have worked for competitors
_____ Rewarding competitors' employees for useful "tips"
_____ Questioning competitors' customers or suppliers
_____ Buying and analyzing competitors' garbage
_____ Advertising and interviewing for non-existent jobs
_____ Taking public tours of competitors' facilities

_____ Releasing false information about the company to confuse competitors
_____ Questioning competitors' technical people at trade shows and conferences
_____ Hiring key people away from competitors
_____ Analyzing competitors' labour union contracts
_____ Having employees date persons who work for competitors
_____ Studying aerial photographs of competitors' facilities

After marking each of the preceding approaches, compare your responses with those of other people in your class. For each approach, the people marking 4 or 5 should say why they thought this particular act would be appropriate. Those who marked 1 or 2 should then state why they thought this act would be inappropriate.

What does this exercise tell us about ethics and socially responsible behaviour?

Source: Developed from W.A. Jones Jr. and N.B. Bryan Jr., "Business Ethics and Business Intelligence: An Empirical Study of Information-Gathering Alternatives," *International Journal of Management* (June 1995), pp. 204–208. For actual examples of some of these activities, see J. Kerstetter, P. Burrows, J. Greene, G. Smith, and M. Conlin, "The Dark Side of the Valley," *Business Week* (July 17, 2000), pp. 42–43.

Notes

1. www.fairtrade.com (accessed March 15, 2003); www.justuscoffee.ca (accessed March 15, 2003).
2. G.S. Stodder, "Goodwill Hunting," *Entrepreneur* (July 1998), pp. 118–121.
3. M. Friedman, *Capitalism and Freedom* (Chicago: University of Chicago Press, 1962).
4. G.F. Cavanagh, *American Business Values*, 3rd edition (Upper Saddle River, NJ: Prentice Hall, 1990), pp. 186–199.
5. B.R. Agle, R.K. Mitchell, and J.A. Sonnenfeld, "Who Matters Most to CEOs? An Investigation of Stakeholder Attributes and Salience, Corporate Performance, and CEO Values," *Academy of Management Journal* (October 1999), pp. 507–525.
6. G.F. Cavanagh, *American Business Values*, 3rd edition (Upper Saddle River, NJ: Prentice Hall, 1990), pp. 186–199.
7. I. Kant, "The Foundations of the Metaphysic of Morals," in *Ethical Theory: Classical and Contemporary Readings*, 2nd edition, by L.P. Pojman (Belmont, CA: Wadsworth Publishing, 1995), pp. 255–279.
8. G.F. Kohut and S.E. Corriher, "The Relationship of Age, Gender, Experience and Awareness of Written Ethics Policies to Business Decision Making," *SAM Advanced Management Journal* (Winter 1994), pp. 32–39.
9. "Reebok Finds Bad Conditions in Two Factories," *Des Moines Register* (October 19, 1999), p. 85.
10. K. Kumar, "Ethical Orientation of Future American Executives: What the Value Profiles of Business School Students Portend," *SAM Advanced Management Journal* (Autumn 1995), pp. 32–36, 47; M. Gable and P. Arlow, "A Comparative Examination of the Value Orientations of British and American Executives," *International Journal of Management* (September 1986), pp. 97–106; W.D. Guth and R. Tagiuri, "Personal Values and Corporate Strategy," *Harvard Business Review* (September–October 1965), pp. 126–127; G.W. England, "Managers and Their Value Systems: A Five Country Comparative Study," *Columbia Journal of World Business* (Summer 1978), p. 35.
11. L.K. Trevino, "Ethical Decision Making in Organizations: A Person-Situation Interactionist Model," *Academy of Management Review* (July 1986), pp. 601–617.
12. L. Kohlberg, "Moral Stage and Moralization: The Cognitive-Development Approach," in *Moral Development and Behavior*, edited by T. Lickona (New York: Holt, Rinehart & Winston, 1976).
13. Trevino, p. 606.
14. S. Finkelstein and D.C. Hambrick, *Strategic Leadership: Top Executives and Their Impact on Organizations* (St. Louis: West, 1996).
15. D.C. Hambrick, T.S. Cho, and M.J. Chen, "The Influence of Top Management Team Heterogeneity on Firms' Competitive Moves," *Administrative Science Quarterly* (December 1996), pp. 659–684.
16. N. Tichy and R. Charan, "Speed, Simplicity, Self-Confidence: An Interview with Jack Welch," *Harvard Business Review* (September–October 1989), p. 113.
17. M. Lipton, "Demystifying the Development of an Organizational Vision," *Sloan Management Review* (Summer 1996), p. 84.
18. J.H. David, F.D. Schoorman, R. Mayer, and H.H. Tan, "The Trusted General Manager and Business Unit Performance: Empirical Evidence of a Competitive Advantage," *Strategic Management Journal* (May 2000), pp. 563–576.
19. R.X. Cringely, "The Best CEOs," *Worth* (May 2000), p. 128.
20. M.S. Chae and J.S. Hill, "The Hazards of Strategic Planning for Global Markets," *Long Range Planning* (December 1996), pp. 880–891.
21. T.R. Eisenmann and J.L. Bower, "The Entrepreneurial M-Form: Strategic Integration in Global Media Firms," *Organization Science* (May–June 2000), pp. 348–355.
22. For an in-depth guide to conducting the strategic planning process, see C.D. Fogg, *Team-Based Strategic Planning* (New York: AMACOM, 1994).
23. M. Friedman, "The Social Responsibility of Business Is to Increase Its Profits," *New York Times Magazine* (September 13, 1970), pp. 30, 126–127; and *Capitalism and Freedom* (Chicago: University of Chicago Press, 1963), p. 133.
24. A.B. Carroll, "A Three-Dimensional Conceptual Model of Corporate Performance," *Academy of Management Review* (October 1979), pp. 497–505.
25. Carroll refers to discretionary responsibilities as philanthropic responsibilities in A.B. Carroll, "The Pyramid of Corporate Social Responsibility: Toward the Moral Management of Organizational Stakeholders," *Business Horizons* (July–August 1991), pp. 39–48.
26. M.S. Baucus and D.A. Baucus, "Paying the Piper: An Empirical Examination of Longer-Term Financial Consequences of Illegal Corporate Behavior," *Academy of Management Journal* (February 1997), pp. 129–151.
27. A. McWilliams and D. Siegel, "Corporate Social Responsibility and Financial Performance: Correlation or Misspecification?" *Strategic Management Journal* (May 2000), pp. 603–609; P. Rechner and K. Roth, "Social Responsibility and Financial Performance: A Structural Equation Methodology," *International Journal of Management* (December 1990), pp. 382–391; K.E. Aupperle, A.B. Carroll, and J.D. Hatfield, "An Empirical Examination of the Relationship between Corporate Social Responsibility and Profitability," *Academy of Management Journal* (June 1985), p. 459.
28. S.A. Waddock and S.B. Graves, "The Corporate Social Performance—Financial Performance Link," *Strategic Management Journal* (April 1997), pp. 303–319; M.V. Russo and P.A. Fouts, *Academy of Management Journal* (July 1997), pp. 534–559; H. Meyer, "The Greening of Corporate America," *Journal of Business Strategy* (January/February 2000), pp. 38–43.
29. C.L. Harman and E.R. Stafford, "Green Alliances: Building New Business with Environmental Groups," *Long Range Planning* (April 1997), pp. 184–196.
30. D.B. Turner and D.W. Greening, "Corporate Social Performance and Organizational Attractiveness to Prospective Employees," *Academy of Management Journal* (July 1997), pp. 658–672; S. Preece, C. Fleisher, and J. Toccacelli, "Building a Reputation along the Value Chain at Levi Strauss," *Long Range Planning* (December 1995), pp. 88–98; J.B. Barney and M.H. Hansen, "Trustworthiness as a Source of Competitive Advantage," *Strategic Management Journal* (Special Winter Issue, 1994), pp. 175–190.
31. R.E. Freeman and D.R. Gilbert, *Corporate Strategy and the Search for Ethics* (Upper Saddle River, NJ: Prentice Hall, 1988), p. 6.
32. M. Arndt, W. Zellner, and P. Coy, "Too Much Corporate Power?" *Business Week* (September 11, 2000), pp. 144–158.
33. M. Coker, "Russia's Stealth Monitoring of Web Traffic," *Daily Tribune* (Ames, Iowa; September 11, 2000), p. C8.
34. M. France, "The Net: How to Head Off Big-Time Regulation," *Business Week* (May 10, 1999), p. 89.
35. "The Wired Trade Organization," *The Economist: Survey of World Trade* (October 3, 1998), p. 16.
36. S. Berkeley, "Web Attack," *Harvard Business Review* (September–October 2000), p. 20.

Clodhoppers

Chris Emery and Larry Finnson, both from Winnipeg, started Krave's Candy Co. in 1996. The enthusiasm of these young entrepreneurs was sparked by their college roommate's love for a white chocolate and cashew candy made by Emery's grandmother. They hoped the product, Clodhoppers, would compete head-to-head with national brands like Pot of Gold or Turtles based on the positive results of informal focus groups. But by 1977 it was apparent that the product wasn't coming close to making inroads into the market. First year sales were only $57 000.

In order to address this shortcoming in sales, Emery and Finnson knew they needed to make some changes. One change they decided to make was in their packaging, transforming their simple box into an attention-getting box featuring caricatures of Emery and Finnson. Something seemingly as unimportant as packaging turned out to make a big difference to consumers when faced with shelves and shelves of candy fighting for attention. The original Clodhopper packaging was a clear plastic jar with a black lid. Over time, the pieces of candy would smudge the jar's walls and settle within the jar, giving consumers the impression that they were getting very little for their money. The black lid attracted dust, making the jars look like they had been sitting in a warehouse or on a shelf for a long time, and therefore stale. The gold, red, and black label looked good on paper, but looked flat and dull in the poor lighting of many grocers and department stores. Given that Clodhoppers sold more during the holiday season than any other time of year, it was also important that the packaging looked good enough to give as a gift. Some additional market research and a few simple design changes improved Krave's results tremendously. By 1998, their product was stocked in Wal-Mart Canada and the British grocer Sainsbury's. Thanks to these new orders, sales quickly rose to $700 000.

Gaining Wal-Mart Canada's business was an important milestone for Krave's, not only because it represented a $250 000 order, but also because it came after two rejections from Wal-Mart. Discarding the ugly jar in favour of an attention-getting, elegant black box with foil-embossed lettering was something that impressed the Wal-Mart buyers. Securing this order was not without its problems. It put a tremendous cash drain on the organization because it very quickly needed to produce a large batch of product and get it to Wal-Mart's shelves in time for the Christmas rush. Their initial successes in getting Clodhoppers on the shelves of a national retailer like Wal-Mart has helped get their product in Canadian Tire and Safeway, as well as getting it chosen as an ingredient in Dairy Queen Blizzard desserts.

As highlighted in the video, Krave's is past its major cash shortages that many new and small organizations face. Especially in an industry that is highly seasonal, large amounts of cash are required in order to build inventories for the holiday buying season, and the high-risk nature of a new, entrepreneurial firm make many lending institutions nervous. Now that Krave's can finance more of its operations from internally generated funds, they are looking at ways to increase sales growth and capitalize on their successes in Canada. In 2002, Clodhoppers was tested in 400 American Wal-Mart stores. Initial sales were moving very slowly, which caused concern for Emery and Finnson. Not only was there a huge investment in inventory to fill the Wal-Mart order, but the success of this test could open the door for distribution in all 2600 Wal-Mart sites in the United States. With an increasing awareness of the Clodhoppers brand, entry into the 6000 American Dairy Queen locations also appeared within reach.

Concepts Illustrated in the Video

The learning organization

Theories of organizational adaptation

Causes of organizational success and failure

Modes of strategic decision making

Strategic decision-making process

Strategic vision

Study Questions

1. How is Clodhoppers an example of a learning organization?

2. What explains the past performance levels of Clodhoppers? What are the major challenges to continued success?

3. What do you think might be the company's (a) current mission or vision, (b) objectives, and (c) strategies? Give an example of each from the video.

4. Clodhoppers illustrates what mode of strategic decision making? Is it appropriate? Discuss alternative modes and how they could be implemented to improve future firm performance.

Video Resource: "Clodhoppers Update II," *Venture* #804, December 2, 2001.

CHAPTER 3

Environmental Scanning
and Industry Analysis

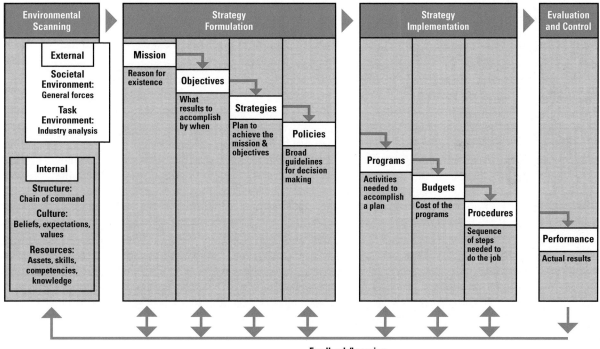

Learning Objectives

After reading this chapter you should be able to

Recognize aspects of an organization's environment that can influence its long-run decisions

Identify the aspects of an organization's environment that are most strategically important

Conduct an industry analysis to understand the competitive forces that influence the intensity of rivalry within an industry

Identify the range of stakeholders that can affect an organization's activities or be affected by them

Understand how industry maturity affects industry competitive forces

Categorize international industries based on their pressures for coordination and localization

Construct strategic group maps to assess the competitive positions of firms in an industry

Identify key success factors for industries and strategic groups

Use publicly available information to conduct competitive intelligence

Use a range of forecasting techniques to predict future firm performance

Understand the most significant environmental forces to which an organization must respond in order to enhance its long-term prospects of profitability and survival

In the past several years, Nortel Networks has made headlines with its impact on the Canadian economy and society. Nortel has gone from being Canada's largest firm to its biggest downsizer, from the nation's largest market capitalization firm to its biggest money loser, from the pillar of the Toronto Stock Exchange to its most significant drain. The performance of no other corporation in Canada's history has had such a profound effect, in terms of both employment and investments. From its summer 2000 high of $124.50 per share, the price of Nortel stock has fallen as low as $0.73 and come close to being delisted from the New York Stock Exchange, nearing penny-stock status.

To understand Nortel's financial difficulties, one must be able to identify and evaluate the trends in the company's environment—factors outside the control of any organization—that have affected its performance. Nortel's roots were in manufacturing traditional telephone equipment, as part of Bell Telephone. Nortel grew rapidly as it moved toward becoming an internet company, as technological changes occurred that it was well-positioned to exploit. During the 1990s tremendous growth in internet usage created a new market for telecommunications hardware, and manufacturers had a difficult time keeping up with demand. Nortel's challenge was to speed up product development and manufacturing processes to keep one step ahead of the quickly changing world of internet technology. What resulted was a significant investment in internal capacity expansion and acquisition of smaller firms.

By 2001 Nortel was faced with a much smaller demand for its products, brought about largely by changes in the global telecommunications industry. Nortel's buyers experienced lower sales because of a lagging economy and excess capacity, the latter resulting from capital expansions that had exceeded the pace of business growth. Consequently, Nortel was forced to both forecast negative earnings and engage in massive cost-cutting. It did so through huge layoffs and by selling off non-core business units. In efforts to return to profitability amid a bleak forecast for the economy and investment in telecommunications infrastructure, Nortel is making changes in its leadership and structure. It hopes to streamline its operations and create greater customer value and satisfaction. Yet as this announcement is being made, Nortel continues to lower its revenue forecast based on continued decreases in spending on network hardware.

The lesson is a simple one: To be successful over time, an organization needs to be in tune with its external environment and how it is changing. There must be a strategic fit between what the market wants and the opportunities it creates, and what the organization has the ability to do. If current trends continue, the environment for all organizations will become even more uncertain and continually change with every passing year. What is **environmental uncertainty**? It is the *degree of complexity* plus the *speed of change* existing in an organization's external environment. As more and more markets become global and intensely competitive, the number of factors an organization must consider in any decision becomes huge. With new technologies being discovered every year, markets change, products must change with them, and organizations must also change to survive.

Uncertain environments are always more difficult to understand than simple, static ones. Environmental uncertainty is a threat to strategic managers because it hampers their ability to develop long-range plans and to make strategic decisions to keep the organization in equilibrium with its external environment. On the other hand, environmental uncertainty creates opportunities because it creates a new playing field in which creativity and innovation can have a major part in strategic decisions.

> **environmental uncertainty** the degree of complexity plus the degree of change existing in an organization's external environment

3.1 External Environmental Scanning

> **environmental scanning** the monitoring and evaluating of information from the external and internal environments for use in strategic decision making

Before an organization can begin strategy formulation, it must scan the external environment to identify possible opportunities and threats. **Environmental scanning** is the monitoring and evaluating of information from the external and internal environments for input into strategic decision making. An organization uses this tool to avoid strategic surprise and to ensure its long-term health. Research has found a positive relationship between environmental scanning and profits.[1] After studying the techniques presented in this chapter, you should be able to identify the aspects of a firm's environment that are most strategically important. In other words, external environmental scanning will reveal the dependencies a firm has on aspects of its environment, identify the nature of change in the environment and how it will affect firm performance, and point to the opportunities and threats an organization will experience. What will result is an understanding of the most significant environmental forces to which an organization must respond and an appraisal of the long-term prospects of profitability and survival.

IDENTIFYING EXTERNAL ENVIRONMENTAL VARIABLES

> **societal environment** the forces outside the industry that do not directly influence short-run business activities but often influence its long-run decisions

In undertaking environmental scanning, strategic managers must first be aware of the many variables within an organization's societal and task environments. The **societal environment** includes general forces that do not directly touch on the short-run activities of the organization but that can, and often do, influence its long-run decisions. These forces, shown in **Figure 3–1** on page 52 are as follows:

- **Economic** forces that regulate the exchange of materials, money, energy, and information
- **Technological** forces that generate problem-solving inventions
- **Political-legal** forces that allocate power and provide constraining and protecting laws and regulations
- **Socio-cultural** forces that influence the values, mores, and customs of society

Figure 3–1 Scanning the External Environment

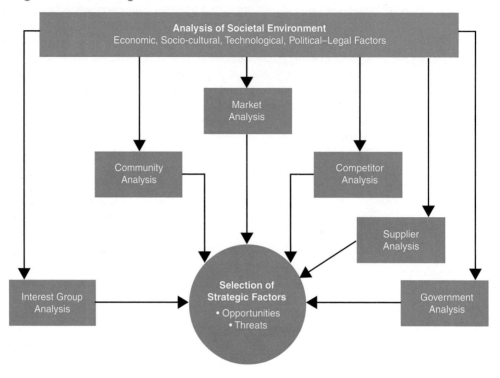

task environment indi-
viduals or groups that
directly affect the
organization and are
affected by its actions

industry analysis the
examination of the key
competitive factors
within the task
environment

The **task environment** includes those individuals or groups that directly affect the organization and, in turn, are affected by it. These are governments, local communities, suppliers, competitors, customers, creditors, employees and labour unions, special-interest groups, and trade associations. A large part of an organization's task environment is the industry within which it operates, that is, the collection of organizations that produce similar or competitive products. **Industry analysis** refers to an examination of key factors within the task environment that will affect strategic decision making and firm performance. Both the societal and task environments must be monitored to detect the strategic factors that are likely to have a strong impact on organizational success or failure.

Scanning the Societal Environment

The number of possible strategic factors in the societal environment is very high. The number becomes enormous when we realize that, generally speaking, each country in the world can be represented by its own unique set of societal forces—some of which are very similar to those of neighbouring countries and some of which are very different.

For example, even though Korea and China share Asia's Pacific Rim area with Thailand, Taiwan, and Hong Kong (sharing many similar cultural values), they have very different views about the role of business in society. It is generally believed in Korea and China (and to a lesser extent in Japan) that the role of business is primarily to contribute to national development; whereas in Hong Kong, Taiwan, and Thailand (and to a lesser extent in the Philippines, Indonesia, Singapore, and Malaysia), the role of business is primarily to make profits for the shareholders.[2] Such differences may translate into different trade regulations and varying difficulty in repatriating profits (transferring profits from a foreign subsidiary to an organization's headquarters).

Monitoring Societal Trends   As noted in **Table 3–1**, organizations can categorize their societal environment into four areas and focus their scanning in each area to determine the relevance of those variables to the organization. Obviously trends in any one area may be very important to the firms in one industry but of lesser importance to firms in other industries. In other words, environmental analysis must be undertaken with an eye on a *particular* organization's activities, determining which aspects of the societal environment are most important to the organization's strategic decision making.

Table 3–1 Elements of the Societal Environment

Economic	Technological	Political-Legal	Socio-cultural
GDP trends	Total government spending for R & D	Antitrust regulations	Lifestyle changes
Interest rates	Total industry spending for R & D	Environmental protection laws	Career expectations
Money supply			Consumer activism
Inflation rates	Focus of technological efforts	Tax laws	Rate of family formation
Unemployment levels		Special incentives	Growth rate of population
Wage/price controls	Patent protection	Foreign trade regulations	Age distribution of population
Devaluation/revaluation	New products	Attitudes toward foreign companies	Regional shifts in population
Energy availability and cost	New developments in technology transfer from lab to marketplace	Laws on hiring and promotion	Life expectancies
Disposable and discretionary income	Productivity improvements through automation	Stability of government	Birth rates
	Internet availability		
	Telecommunication infrastructure		

Trends in the *economic* part of the societal environment can have an obvious impact on business activity. For example, an increase in interest rates means fewer sales of major home appliances. Why? A rising interest rate tends to be reflected in higher mortgage rates. Because higher mortgage rates increase the cost of buying a house, the demand for new and used houses tends to fall. Because most major home appliances are sold when people change houses, a reduction in house sales soon translates into a decline in sales of refrigerators, stoves, and dishwashers and reduced profits for everyone in that industry.

Changes in the *technological* part of the societal environment can also have a great impact on multiple industries. For example, improvements in computer microprocessors have led not only to the widespread use of home computers, but also to better automobile engine performance in terms of power and fuel economy through the use of microprocessors to monitor fuel injection. A number of developments in technology are forecast to have a significant impact during the decade ending in 2010:

- **Portable Information Devices and Electronic Networking:** Combining the computing power of the personal computer, the networking of the internet, the images of the television, and the convenience of the telephone, these appliances will soon be used by more than 30% of the population of industrialized nations to make phone calls, send email, and transmit data and documents. Even now, homes, autos, and offices are being connected (via wires and wireless technology) into intelligent networks that interact with one another.

Personal digital assistants (PDAs) are increasingly powerful, communicate freely with personal computers, and have internet access capabilities. The traditional stand-alone desktop computer may soon join the manual typewriter as a historical curiosity.

■ **Fuel Cells and Alternative Energy Sources:** The use of wind, geothermal, hydroelectric, solar, and biomass power—among other alternative energy sources—should increase from their present level of 10% to about 30% by the end of the decade. Once used exclusively to power spacecraft, fuel cells offer the prospect of pollution-free electrical power. Fuel cells chemically combine hydrogen and oxygen to produce electricity with water as a by-product. Although it will take a number of years before fuel cells replace gas-powered engines or vast power-generation plants, this technology is already providing an alternative source of power for large buildings.

■ **Virtual Personal Assistants:** Very smart computer programs that monitor email, faxes, and phone calls will be able to take over routine tasks, such as writing a letter, retrieving a file, making a phone call, or screening requests. Acting like a secretary, a person's virtual assistant (VA) could substitute for that person at meetings or in dealing with routine actions.

■ **Genetically Altered Organisms:** A convergence of biotechnology and agriculture is creating a new field of life sciences. Plant seeds can be genetically modified to produce more needed vitamins or to make them less attractive to pests and more able to survive. Animals could be similarly modified for desirable characteristics and to eliminate genetic disabilities and diseases.

■ **Smart, Mobile Robots:** Robot development has been limited by a lack of sensory devices and sophisticated artificial intelligence systems. Improvements in these areas mean that robots will perform more sophisticated factory work, run errands, do household chores, and assist people with disabilities.[3]

Trends in the *political-legal* part of the societal environment have a significant impact not only on the level of competition within an industry, but also on which strategies might be successful.[4] For example, periods of strict enforcement of the Canadian Competition Act directly influence corporate growth strategy. (For a summary of this act's major elements, see **Table 3–2**.) When Canadian Airlines International and Air Canada were both experiencing financial difficulties, federal regulators blocked several mergers in the interest of preserving competition. A foreign content clause was used to block American Airlines' investment in Canadian Airlines, and the high social costs of restricted competition were used to justify blocking Onex Corporation's proposal to acquire Air Canada. As large companies find it more difficult to acquire another firm in the same industry or a related one (horizontal merging), they often consider diversifying into unrelated industries or different countries.[5] In Europe, the formation of the European Union has led to an increase in merger activity across national boundaries.

Demographic trends are part of the *socio-cultural* aspect of the societal environment. **Demography** is the study of human populations, and it can help us predict trends in demand for products, how populated schools and universities will become, and the state of the health-care system. The combination of lower birth rates and increased life expectancy create an aging population that naturally has different characteristics from a younger one. The increasing size of the over-55 segment of the population has made it the fastest-growing age group in all developed countries. Companies with an eye on the future can find many opportunities in the sale of products and services to the growing number of "woofies" (well-off old folks)—defined as people over 55 with money to spend.[6] These people are more likely to purchase recreational vehicles, take ocean cruises, and enjoy leisure sports such as boating, fishing, and bowling. They are also in need of financial services and health care.

This trend can mean increasing sales for firms like Winnebago (RVs), Carnival Cruise Lines, and Brunswick (sports equipment), among others. To attract older customers, retailers will need

demography the study of human populations

Table 3–2 Major Elements of the Competition Act

Illegal trade practices Article 50 (1)	• Discriminating against competitors by witholding discounts, rebates, allowances • Lessening competition by selling products in one area of Canada at lower prices than in others • Selling products at unreasonably low prices to lessen competition or eliminate a competitor
Deceptive telemarketing Article 52 (3)	• Making false or misleading representations • Conducting lotteries where fees are charged or the number or value of prizes is not disclosed • Offering a product free or at a very low price in consideration of purchasing another product • Selling a product at a price grossly in excess of its fair market value
Conspiracy Article 45 (1)	• Limiting facilities for transporting, producing, manufacturing, supplying, storing, or dealing in any product • Prevening or unduly limiting production or competition through collusion
Bid-rigging Article 47 (1)	• Making an agreement not to submit a bid in response to a call for tender • Making bid submissions that are prepared by agreement or arrangement between multiple bidders
Price maintenance Article 61 (1)	• Attempting to upwardly influence (or discourage reduction of) the price at which a product is sold • Refusing to supply a product because of the low-pricing policy of the reseller

Source: Competition Act, Chapter C-34, **http://laws.justice.gc.ca/en/c-34/text.html** (accessed February 5, 2003).

to place seats in their larger stores so aging shoppers can rest. Washrooms need to be more accessible. Signs need to be larger. Restaurants need to raise the level of lighting so diners can read their menus. Home appliances need simpler and larger controls. Already, the market for road bikes is declining and sales of treadmills and massagers for aching muscles have increased.

Here are seven socio-cultural trends in Canada that are helping to define what North America and the world will soon look like:

1. **Increasing environmental awareness:** Recycling and conservation are becoming more than slogans. McDonalds's, for example, eliminated the use of Styrofoam packaging for its sandwiches in favour of paper wrappers. Most municipalities have curbside recycling programs for newsprint, cardboard, and most containers (tin, glass, plastic, and Tetra Pak). Provinces like Nova Scotia have deposits on all beverage containers, half of which are refunded when containers are returned to a designated environmental centre.

2. **Growth of the seniors market:** As their numbers increase, people over age 55 will become an even more important market. Already some companies are segmenting the senior population into Young Matures, Older Matures, and the Elderly—each having a different set of attributes, attitudes, and interests. Differences in disposable income, physical ability, and need for convenience provide segmenting opportunities in this growing portion of the Canadian population.

3. **Impact of Generation Y:** Born after 1980 to the boomer and X generations, this cohort may end up being as large as the boomer generation. Called the echo generation by David K. Foot, author of *Boom, Bust & Echo*,[7] this generation is largest in Ontario and western Canada because so many boomers left Quebec and the Atlantic provinces to seek employment. In 1996 there were 6.9 million members of the echo generation in Canada. Expect this cohort to have a strong impact on future products and services.

4. **Decline of the mass market:** Niche markets are beginning to define the marketers' environment. People want products and services that are adapted more to their personal needs. For example, Estée Lauder's "All Skin" and Maybelline's "Shades of You" lines of cosmetic products are specifically made for African-origin women. "Mass customization"—the making and marketing of products tailored to a person's requirements (as demonstrated by Dell and Gateway Computers)—is replacing the mass production and marketing of the same product in some markets.

5. **Changing pace and location of life:** Instant communication via fax machines, cell phones, email and overnight mail enhances efficiency, but it also puts more pressure on people. Merging the personal computer with the communication and entertainment industry through telephone lines, satellite dishes, and cable television increases consumer choice. Workers can leave overcrowded urban areas for small towns, telecommuting via personal computers and modems.

6. **Changing household composition:** Single-person households are becoming increasingly common in Canada. Both the marriage and divorce rates dropped slightly between 1992 and 2000. Over this time period there was a trend of fewer families of two or more people related by marriage or common law and fewer families with children. The number of lone-parent families rose, with an increasing number of these families being headed by women (83.4% in 2000).[8] In other words, a household clearly is no longer the same as it was once portrayed in *The Brady Bunch* in the 1970s or even *The Cosby Show* in the 1980s.

7. **Increasing diversity of the workforce and markets:** Canada has almost four million people who identify themselves as "visible minorities."[9] The proportion rose from 4.7% of the total population in 1981 to 13.4% in 2001. In other words, the visible minority population is growing faster than the total population. Of the immigrants who came to Canada in the 1990s, 73% were members of visible minority groups. In the past, most immigrants to Canada came from Europe, including the United Kingdom. But today, because of changing immigration policies and international events that encouraged the movement of refugees, most come from Asian countries. Fifty-eight percent of immigrants who arrived in Canada between 1991 and 2001 came from Asia and the Middle East. Some minority groups such as Japanese Canadians and African Canadians have longer histories in Canada and are more likely to be Canadian-born. The province with the highest proportion of visible minorities is British Columbia, accounting for 22% of its total population. Because of the religious and cultural traditions associated with different ethnic groups that affect consumer preferences, new market segments are appearing that previously may have been too small to be profitable.

International Societal Considerations   Each country or group of countries in which a company operates presents a whole new societal environment with a different set of economic, technological, political-legal, and socio-cultural variables for the company to face. International societal environments vary so widely that an organization's internal environment and strategic management process must be very flexible. Cultural trends in Germany, for example, have resulted in the inclusion of worker representatives in corporate strategic planning. Differences in societal environments strongly affect the ways in which a **multinational corporation** (MNC), a company with significant assets and activities in multiple countries, conducts its marketing, financial, manufacturing, and other functional activities. For example, the existence of regional associations like the European Union, the North American Free Trade Zone, and Mercosur in South America has a significant impact on the competitive "rules of the game" both for those MNCs operating within these areas and for those MNCs wanting to enter them.

multinational corporation a company with significant assets and activities in multiple countries

currency convertibility
the ease with which one currency can be converted into a foreign currency

To account for the many differences among societal environments from one country to another, consider **Table 3–3**. It includes a list of economic, technological, political-legal, and socio-cultural variables for any particular country or region. For example, an important economic variable for any firm investing in a foreign country is **currency convertibility**. Without convertibility, a company operating in Russia cannot convert its profits from rubles to dollars. In terms of socio-cultural variables, many Asian cultures (especially China) are less concerned with the value of human rights than are European and North American cultures. Some Asian companies actually contend that American companies are trying to impose Western human rights requirements on them in an attempt to make Asian products less competitive by raising their costs.[10]

Before planning its strategy for a particular international location, a company must scan the particular country environment(s) in question for opportunities and threats, and compare these with its own organizational strengths and weaknesses. For example, to operate successfully in a global industry such as automobiles, tires, electronics, or watches, a company must be prepared to establish a significant presence in the three developed areas of the world known collectively as the **Triad**. This term was coined by the Japanese management expert Kenichi Ohmae, and it refers to the three developed markets of Japan, North America, and Western Europe, which now form a single market with common needs.[11] Focusing on the Triad is essential for an MNC pursuing success in a global industry, according to Ohmae, because close to 90% of all high–value-added, high-technology manufactured goods are produced and consumed in North America, Western Europe, and Japan. Ideally a company should have a significant presence in each of these regions so that it can develop, produce, and market its products simultaneously in all three areas. Otherwise, it will lose competitive advantage to Triad-oriented MNCs. No longer can an MNC develop and market a new product in one part of the world before it exports it to other developed countries.

Triad the three major economic zones in the world: Japan, North America, and Western Europe

Focusing only on the developed nations, however, causes an organization to miss important market opportunities in the developing nations of the world. Although these nations may

Table 3–3 Some Important Variables in *International* Societal Environments

Economic	Technological	Political-Legal	Socio-cultural
Economic development	Regulations on technology transfer	Form of government	Customs, norms, values
Per capita income	Energy availability/cost	Political ideology	Language
Climate	Natural resource availability	Tax laws	Demographics
GDP trends	Transportation network	Stability of government	Life expectancies
Monetary and fiscal policies	Skill level of workforce	Government attitude toward foreign companies	Social institutions
Unemployment level	Patent-trademark protection	Regulations on foreign ownership of assets	Status symbols
Currency convertibility	Internet availability	Strength of opposition groups	Lifestyle
Wage levels	Telecommunication infrastructure	Trade regulations	Religious beliefs
Nature of competition		Protectionist sentiment	Attitudes toward foreigners
Membership in regional economic associations		Foreign policies	Literacy level
		Terrorist activity	Human rights
		Legal system	Environmentalism

not have developed to the point that they have significant demand for a broad spectrum of products, they may very likely be on the threshold of rapid growth in the demand for specific products. This would be the ideal time for a company to enter this market—before competition is established. The key is to be able to identify the "trigger point" when demand for a particular product or service is ready to boom. See the **Global Issue** feature for an in-depth explanation of a technique to identify the optimum time to enter a particular market in a developing nation.

Global Issue

Identifying Potential Markets in Developing Nations

Research by the Deloitte & Touche Consulting Group reveals that the demand for a specific product increases exponentially at certain points in a country's development. Identifying this trigger point of demand is thus critical to entering emerging markets at the best time. A **trigger point** is the time when enough people have enough money to buy what a company has to sell but before competition is established. This creates significant first-mover advantages for the firm that enters these developing markets when the time is right. Determining when the time is right can be done using the concept of **purchasing power parity (PPP)**. PPP has its basis in the "law of one price," which states that when exchange rates, taxes, and transportation costs are set aside, the price of a given product traded on world markets will not vary by country of origin. *The*

Economist created its famous Big Mac Index in 1986 to gauge the extent to which currencies were at their correct exchange rate. They did so by comparing the prices of McDonald's Big Mac sandwiches in different countries, which in theory should be essentially the same. Not surprisingly, they were not.

PPP can be used to estimate the material wealth a nation can purchase, rather than the financial wealth it creates, as typically measured by Gross Domestic Product (GDP). As a result, restating a nation's GDP in PPP terms reveals much greater spending power than factoring in exchange rates would suggest. For example, a Big Mac costing $2.99 in Canada can be purchased for the equivalent of $1.63 in China. Consequently the people of China can enjoy the same standard of living (with respect to Big Macs) as people in Canada with only 55% of the money. Correcting a nation's wealth for PPP restates all Chinese Big Macs at their equivalent Canadian price value of $2.99. Using PPP, China becomes the world's second-largest economy after the United States, with Brazil, Mexico, and India moving ahead of Canada into the top 10 world markets. Understanding the purchasing power inherent in a country's economy is an important step in assessing its profit potential.

Source: Summarized from D. Fraser and M. Raynor, "The Power of Parity," *Forecast* (May/June, 1996), pp. 8–12. Numbers used in this example are based on average prices and exchange rates in 2002.

trigger point the point in time when sufficient demand exists for a product to warrant market entry

purchasing power parity the economic theory that predicts that a product's cost will be independent of its country of origin after controlling for exchange rates, taxes, and transportation costs

Scanning the Task Environment

As shown in **Figure 3–1**, an organization's scanning of the environment will include analyses of all the relevant elements in the task environment. These analyses take the form of individual reports written by various people in different parts of the firm. At Procter & Gamble (P&G), for example, people from each of the brand management teams work with key people from the sales and market research departments to research and write a "competitive activity report" each quarter on each of the product categories in which P&G competes. People in purchasing also write similar reports concerning new developments in the industries that supply P&G. These and other reports are then summarized and transmitted up the corporate hierarchy for top management to use in strategic decision making. If a new development is reported regarding a particular product category, top management may then send memos asking people throughout the organization to watch for and report on developments in related product areas. The many reports resulting from these scanning efforts, when boiled down to their essentials, act as a detailed list of external strategic factors.

IDENTIFYING EXTERNAL STRATEGIC FACTORS

Why do companies often respond differently to the same environmental changes? One reason is that managers differ in their ability to recognize and understand external strategic issues and factors. No firm can successfully monitor all external factors. Choices must be made regarding which factors are important (most significantly influencing organizational performance) and which are not. Even though managers may agree that strategic importance determines what variables are consistently tracked, they sometimes miss or choose to ignore crucial new developments.[12] Personal values and functional experiences of an organization's managers as well as the success of current strategies are likely to bias both their perception of what is important to monitor in the external environment and their interpretations of what they perceive.[13]

strategic myopia a cognitive bias that prevents unfamiliar or unexpected information from being accurately incorporated into strategic decision making

This rejection of unfamiliar as well as negative information is called **strategic myopia**.[14] This is a rather common phenomenon in organizations, especially successful ones. Because firms have a proven track record of results, they are often very reluctant to change their strategy or their practices, even if the environment around them has changed significantly or organizational performance declines. The first step in an organization changing its strategy (or at least questioning its efficacy) is the systematic gathering of external information.

One way to identify and analyze developments in the external environment is to use the issues priority matrix, shown in **Figure 3–2**, as follows:

1. Identify a number of likely trends emerging in the societal and task environments. These are strategic environmental issues, the important factors that, if the trends continue, will significantly affect what the industry will look like in the near future and how profitable existing organizations in it will be.

Figure 3–2 Issues Priority Matrix

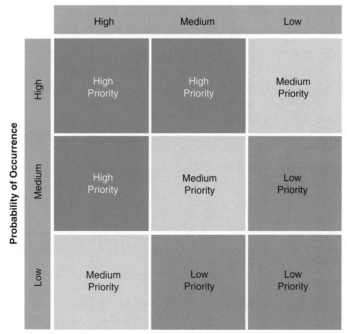

Source: Reprinted from L.L. Lederman, "Foresight Activities in the U.S.A.: Time for a Re-Assessment?" *Long-Range Planning* (June 1984), p. 46. Copyright © 1984. Reprinted with permission from Elsevier Science.

2. Assess the likelihood that these trends will actually continue. High probability events clearly call for immediate managerial attention in formulating strategies. Low probability events are usually just monitored rather than acted upon, because they are not likely to adversely affect firm performance.

3. Estimate the likely impact of each of these trends on the organization being examined. Those with the most significant potential effect on an organization take the highest priority. Anything that threatens firm survival or profitability would fall into this category. Among the events that are likely to occur, the ones that are unlikely to have any material effect on the organization, its key stakeholders, or its reputation will often not attract top management's attention until the time arrives that their impact is potentially greater.

external strategic factors the dominant environmental trends that have a relatively high probability of both occurrence and impact on the organization

An organization's **external strategic factors** are those key environmental trends that are judged to have both a medium to high probability of occurrence and a medium to high probability of impact on the organization. The issues priority matrix helps managers determine which environmental trends should be merely scanned (low priority) and which should be monitored as strategic factors (high priority) and acted upon. Those environmental trends judged to be an organization's strategic factors are then categorized favourably as opportunities or unfavourably as threats and included in the strategy formulation process.

THE COMPETITIVE ADVANTAGE OF NATIONS

Michael Porter, an authority on competitive strategy, encourages us to first examine the external environment at the national level. Classical theories of international trade predicted that factor endowments such as land, labour, and infrastructure would give a nation a comparative advantage. In other words, by virtue of having particular factor endowments, some nations would be more efficient in producing some products than others. Porter's diamond of national advantage (see **Figure 3–3**), however, shows that factor conditions represent only one source of advantage. Nations can create strong industries by developing skilled labour, advanced technology, government support, and a culture of innovation and investment. The corners of the diamond represent four distinct bases of national advantage:[15]

1. **Factor Conditions.** Countries, or geographic regions within countries, can create strategically important factors like skilled resources and technology. Local disadvantages in factors of production will force innovation and change, so that new advantages are created. For example, high-cost labour has led to increased use of technology as well as new human resource management practices that increase organizational commitment and reduce voluntary turnover.

2. **Demand Conditions.** Countries with large domestic markets for particular products are usually at an advantage when they begin exporting products into foreign markets. The combination of economies of scale and experience often leads to efficiencies in organizations that give them certain advantages. Although Canada is a relatively small economy, especially in comparison with the United States, it is home to many large, successful organizations in the telecommunications, financial services, and automobile manufacturing industries. A demanding local market and the experience that firms gain from serving it lead to national advantage and allow Canadian organizations to gain from the increased globalization of many markets (globalization is discussed in more detail later in this chapter).

3. **Related and Supporting Industries.** Competitive industries in a local economy allow other organizations to acquire less costly and higher quality inputs. For example, Canada's strength in natural resource extraction and electrical generation gives a variety of manufacturers a cost advantage over their foreign rivals. The stronger a nation's

upstream industries are, the greater the potential for competitive advantage in its downstream industries.

4. **Firm Strategy, Structure, and Rivalry.** As will be discussed in the following section, five competitive forces determine the extent of rivalry within industries. Although low rivalry makes an industry more attractive for the firms in it, over the long term this lack of rivalry removes any pressure from organizations to innovate and improve. In Canada this is evident in the telecommunications and airline industries, where government regulations had restricted competition in the past. With new competitors all trying to outperform each other, consumers have better selection at lower prices than ever before. As a result, organizations are forced to strengthen their competitive advantages, which will, in turn, allow them to be more successful in global markets.

In conclusion, Porter's diamond of national advantage is a framework for understanding why nations have strength in certain industry sectors but not others. This is important to understand prior to undergoing a detailed analysis of industry competitive forces, because a nation's bases of advantage will influence all organizations operating in it. Central to this framework is an assumption that organizations will innovate and change only when forced to, in other words when there is a healthy amount of competition or rivalry. Experience has shown this to be at least partly true. Understanding the bases of a nation's advantage should provide the starting point of an analysis of a firm's external environment. Before delving in detail into the competitive forces within a particular industry, use the diamond of national advantage to understand the structural conditions within a nation's economy that affect the profit potential of its organizations.

Figure 3–3 Determinants of National Advantage

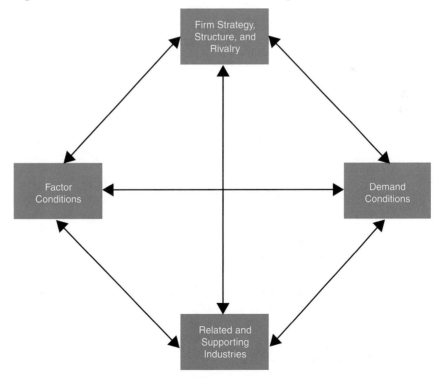

3.2 Industry Analysis: Analyzing the Task Environment

industry the collection of firms producing a similar product or service

An **industry** is defined as a group of firms producing a similar product or service. An examination of the important stakeholder groups, such as suppliers and customers, in a particular organization's task environment is a part of industry analysis.

PORTER'S APPROACH TO INDUSTRY ANALYSIS

Michael Porter contends that an organization should be most concerned with the intensity of rivalry within its own industry. Porter's view of strategic management is that certain industries are more attractive than others based on the competitive forces contained in them. He also contends that *within* any given industry, the intensity of competition varies and is therefore not experienced equally by all organizations. Because Porter sees the industry as being the major determinant of an organization's profitability, he suggests that organizations create strategies to position themselves favourably vis-à-vis these competitive forces. By defending against them, actively shaping them, or anticipating shifts in factors underlying these competitive forces, organizations can secure above-average levels of profits and increase their chances of survival.

The intensity of rivalry within an industry is determined by basic competitive forces, which are depicted in **Figure 3–4**. "The collective strength of these forces determines the ultimate profit potential in the industry, where profit potential is measured in terms of long-run return on invested capital."[16] In carefully scanning its industry, the organization must assess the importance to its success of each of the six forces: threat of new entrants, rivalry among existing firms, threat of substitute products or services, bargaining power of buyers, bargaining power of suppliers, and relative power of other stakeholders.[17] The stronger each of these forces is, the more limited companies are in their ability to raise prices and earn greater profits. Although Porter mentions only five forces, a sixth—other stakeholders—is discussed here to reflect the power that governments, local communities, and other groups from the task environment wield over industry activities.

Using the model in **Figure 3–4**, a high or strong force is viewed as unfavourable (or a threat) because it is likely to reduce profits. A weak or low force, in contrast, is viewed as favourable (or an opportunity) because it may allow the company to earn greater sales, profits, or market share in the future. In the short run, these forces act as constraints on a company's activities. In the long run, however, it may be possible for a company, through its choice of strategy, to change the strength of one or more of the forces to the company's advantage. For example, to pressure its customers (PC makers) to purchase more of Intel's latest microprocessors for use in their PCs, Intel supported the development of sophisticated software that required increasingly larger amounts of processing power. In the mid-1990s Intel began selling 3-D graphics chips—not because it wanted to be in that business, but because 3-D chips necessitated significant new processing power (provided of course by Intel). Intel also introduced software that made it easier for network administrators to manage PCs on their networks, which Intel believed would help sell more PCs and neutralize a threat from network computers.[18] A strategist can analyze any industry by understanding the foundations of each competitive force and assessing its impact on rivalry within the industry.

Threat of New Entrants

New entrants to an industry typically bring to it new capacity, a desire to gain market share, and substantial resources. They are, therefore, threats to an established organization. The threat of entry depends on the profit potential of an industry, the presence of obstacles that

Figure 3–4 Forces Driving Industry Competition

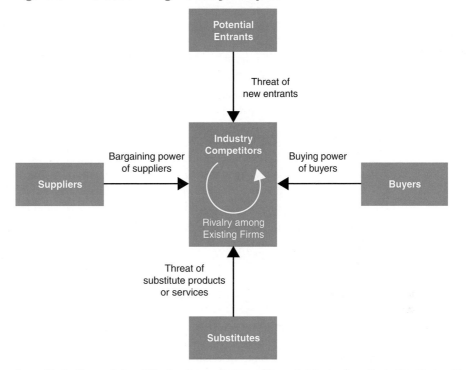

Source: Used with permission of The Free Press, a Division of Simon & Schuster, from *Competitive Strategy: Techniques for Analyzing Industries and Competitors* by Michael E. Porter. Copyright © 1980, 1988 by The Free Press.

entry barrier an obstacle that makes it difficult, time-consuming, or costly for a new company to enter an otherwise profitable industry

discourage or prevent new firms from entering the industry, and the reaction or retaliation that can be expected from existing competitors. An **entry barrier** is an obstruction that makes it difficult, time-consuming, or costly for a company to enter an industry. For example, no new domestic automobile companies have been successfully established in North America since the 1930s because of the high capital requirements to build production facilities and to develop a dealer distribution network. Another example is the Toronto Transit Commission, which has provided all public transit in the metropolitan Toronto region for many years. What explains these relatively static industries? If industry profits exist and no firms are entering the industry, some obstacles to entry must exist. Here are some common barriers to entry:

- **Economies of Scale:** Scale economies are usually derived from large capital investments that allow for high-volume production at low unit costs. These economies favour larger firms that produce at higher output levels. Unless a new rival can make the capital investment and produce at a high enough output level, the presence of economies of scale can deter entry by making profitability difficult to achieve. For example, Intel's large market share and high production levels gave it a significant cost advantage over any new (smaller) rival in the production and sale of microprocessors. Intel was thus able to remain one of America's most profitable companies for many years without encountering any increased competition.

- **Product Differentiation:** When products have a commodity-like status, buyers are usually willing to purchase from whatever source of supply is cheapest. Product differentiation, however, means that established products have some sort of uniqueness that customers desire. New entrants would therefore have to overcome existing loyalties and either provide better value or differentiate their products in such a way as to capture sales from existing firms. Differentiation makes market entry a costlier and riskier option. Corporations like Procter & Gamble and General Mills, who manufacture products like Tide laundry detergent and Cheerios breakfast cereal, create high entry barriers through their high levels of advertising and promotion, forcing new entrants to engage in similar marketing campaigns to educate customers about their products' features and benefits.

- **Capital Requirements:** The need to invest significant financial resources (in manufacturing facilities, research and development, or marketing) creates a huge risk in terms of an up-front cost that must be incurred prior to any sales or profits being achieved. Because the risk of entry increases with significant start-up costs, industry profits must be sufficiently high to justify market entry. The manufacture of large commercial airplanes by any would-be competitor to Boeing and Airbus entails significant barriers to entry: the production facilities and technical expertise necessary to develop and build the product. Similarly, the acquisition of a fleet of aircraft and the hiring of necessary crew on the ground and in the air create significant barriers to entry for national airlines such as Air Canada and British Airways.

- **Switching Costs:** For many consumer products, buyers can very easily purchase from different sellers on each purchase occasion. If buyers incur some sort of cost each time they switch sellers, then a barrier to entry is created by making a new product relatively expensive for the buyer. For example, once a software program like Excel or Word becomes established in an office, office managers are very reluctant to switch to a new program because of the high costs of training and of reconfiguring data.

- **Access to Distribution Channels:** Sometimes established firms have already secured superior distribution arrangements that place them at an advantage over new entrants. This is usually most noticeable in retailing. Small organizations often have difficulty obtaining shelf space for their goods or finding a wholesaler to carry them because large retailers give priority to the established firms who can pay for the advertising needed to generate high customer demand.

- **Proprietary Product Technology:** Innovative products that are sufficiently different from existing products can be patented and thereby protected from competition. Similarly, technical knowledge or managerial expertise can be retained within a firm through secrecy and confidentiality agreements. Both of these arrangements provide benefits to existing firms that discourage the entry of new firms into the industry. In the pharmaceutical industry a combination of huge R & D costs, a complex regulatory process of drug approvals, and lengthy patent protection discourage the entry of new firms into the industry. Pfizer, one of the world's largest pharmaceutical firms, is earning tremendous profits from Lipitor (to lower cholesterol levels), Viagra (for erectile dysfunction), and Zoloft (for depression and obsessive-compulsive disorder). The profits Pfizer earns while these drugs remain under patent protection are used to finance R & D into new products that can sustain its market-leading position and continue to discourage the entry of new firms into the industry.

- **Government Policy:** Governments can limit entry into an industry through licensing requirements, either by restricting access to raw materials, such as oil in environmentally protected areas, or by granting monopoly rights to certain firms. The Canadian government also has foreign ownership limits in most public utilities and transportation services as a safeguard against the erosion of service and the increase of prices in more remote areas of the country.

Rivalry among Existing Firms

In most industries, organizations are mutually dependent. A competitive move by one firm can be expected to have a noticeable effect on its competitors and thus may cause retaliation.

For example, the entry by mail order companies such as Dell and Gateway into a PC industry previously dominated by IBM, Apple, and Compaq increased the level of competitive activity to such an extent that any price reduction or new product introduction is now quickly followed by similar moves from other PC makers. The same is true of prices in the Canadian airline industry, with the entry of discount airlines like WestJet and CanJet encouraging Air Canada to create discount divisions of its own business like Jazz and Tango. According to Porter, intense rivalry is related to the presence of several factors, including these:

- **Number and Power of Competitors:** When competitors are few and roughly equal in size, such as in the automobile and major home appliance industries, they watch each other carefully to make sure that any move by another firm is matched by an equal countermove. Oligopolistic market structures are characterized by firms' competitive interdependence, and their strategic commitment to an industry leads them to engage in continued competition rather than exiting the industry as competition increases. In contrast, when industries contain many firms, one firm may feel that its aggressive strategic moves will go unnoticed. Often a small firm can gradually strengthen its competitive position without negatively affecting larger, established rivals.

- **Slow Industry Growth:** When demand is growing, new entrants can enter the market while existing firms can still increase their sales. In other words when demand is growing, one firm's gain is not necessarily another firm's loss. But as industry growth slows, firms can grow only by taking market share away from a rival firm. This has been noticeable in the beer industry, where firm strategies cannot realistically be directed at growing the market (increasing the demand for beer). Instead they are directed at differentiating and positioning through R & D and advertising, creating rather intense market-share competition.

- **Commodification:** If a product possesses a commodity-like status (that is, an absence of unique features), buyers make their purchases based primarily on availability and price. Many people buy gas for their car based on location and price because they view gas as a commodity. If it doesn't matter who sells the gas, then consumers will go to a station that is easy to access and sells its product at the going price. This is exactly what we expect in highly competitive industries, where no one firm is able to charge a higher price than any other because of the ease of substitution. Gas stations are, however, attempting to differentiate by adding services at their locations (for instance, Tim Hortons outlets at some Esso stations), creating loyalty through reward programs (Petro Canada's Petro Points, Esso's Esso Extra, Shell's association with Air Miles), and strategic co-operative relationships (Sunoco and the Canadian Automobile Association).

- **High Fixed Costs:** When firms incur significant fixed costs to create production capacity, they experience pressure to fill capacity, which floods the market and puts downward pressure on prices. Because airlines must fly their planes on a schedule regardless of the number of paying passengers for any one flight, they offer cheap standby fares whenever a plane has empty seats.

- **Height of Exit Barriers:** Exit barriers keep a company from leaving an industry, either as a result of financial investments or strategic commitments to an industry. The brewing industry, for example, has a low percentage of companies that voluntarily leave the industry because breweries have large investments in specialized assets with few uses except for making beer. Closing manufacturing facilities often results in tremendous costs from the breaking of labour agreements and losses on the sale of production equipment, as well as the need to arrange for servicing of existing client bases. Sometimes organizations will not leave an industry whose attractiveness is declining because the costs of exit are too high; they instead stay around and engage in highly competitive tactics that often have a negative effect on the industry as a whole, as the example of Canadian Airlines International shows. The inability of Canadian Airlines to achieve economies of scale put it in a situation where it tried to increase sales by cutting prices. What resulted was a series of price wars that brought poor profits for virtually all Canadian airlines. The government's unwillingness first to allow significant American investment in Canadian Airlines and then to permit it to merge with Air Canada also acted as exit barriers.

Threat of Substitute Products or Services

Substitute products are those products that appear to be different but can satisfy the same need as another product. For example, fax machines are a substitute for the mail or a courier, aspartame is a substitute for sugar, and bottled water is a substitute for soft drinks. According to Porter, "substitutes limit the potential returns of an industry by placing a ceiling on the prices firms in the industry can profitably charge."[19] To the extent that switching costs are low, substitutes may have a strong effect on an industry. Tea can be considered a substitute for coffee. If the price of coffee goes up high enough, coffee drinkers will slowly begin switching to tea. The price of tea thus puts a price ceiling on the price of coffee. Identifying possible substitute products or services is sometimes a difficult task. It means searching for products or services that can perform the same function or provide the same benefits, even though they have a different appearance and may not appear to be easily substitutable. Substitute products create the strongest unfavourable competitive force when they improve value for consumers, that is, they improve the price-performance relationship.

Bargaining Power of Buyers

Buyers inherently possess a certain amount of power—to purchase a product from one firm or another. By virtue of these choices, buyers are always powerful. Some buyers can be more powerful than others, however, having the ability to put downward pressure on prices and upward pressure on quality or quantity of the product provided. Buyers are powerful when some of the following factors hold true:

- A buyer purchases a large proportion of the seller's product or service (for example, oil filters purchased by a major auto maker). When a large portion of an organization's sales go to one buyer, that buyer becomes very important because the seller comes to rely on its business.

- A buyer has the potential or the willingness to integrate backward by producing the product itself (for example, a newspaper chain could make its own paper). If an organization has the ability to make some of its components rather than having to buy them, it is in a better position to demand more favourable purchasing arrangements.

- Products are standard or undifferentiated, giving buyers many choices of supply (for example, motorists can choose among many gas stations). A perfectly competitive industry such as dry cleaning or gas retailing illustrates the power that buyers have by virtue of the choices available to them.

- If switching costs are low, a buyer can change suppliers with little difficulty. In absence of anything that ties a buyer to a particular seller, the threat of switching gives power to a buyer because sellers are motivated to provide better value in order to retain customers (for example, office supplies are easily purchased from Staples, Grand & Toy, and Corporate Express).

- The purchased product represents a high percentage of a buyer's costs, thus providing the buyer with an incentive to shop around for a lower price (for example, gasoline purchased for resale by convenience stores accounts for half their total costs). This makes buyers particularly price-sensitive, which gives them a certain amount of power over suppliers in terms of their unwillingness to accept certain price increases.

- A buyer is not particularly profitable. This makes it very sensitive to costs and service differences, and encourages it to pressure sellers for better prices and payment terms (for example, Nortel is becoming increasingly price-sensitive as it reports significant losses and seeks ways to return to profitability).

- The purchased product is unimportant to the final quality or price of a buyer's product. When this is the case, it can be easily substituted without adversely affecting the final product (for example, electric wire bought for use in lamps). On the other hand, when the quality is very important (for example, jet engines in commercial aircraft) and equipment failure would have catastrophic consequences, the buyer has little bargaining power with the supplier.

Bargaining Power of Suppliers

Suppliers can affect an industry through their ability to raise prices or reduce the quality of purchased goods and services. A supplier or supplier group is powerful if some of the following factors apply:

- The supplier industry is dominated by a few companies, but it sells to many (for example, the petroleum industry). Because buyers have fewer choices, selling firms can be more demanding in terms of delivery schedules, credit terms, and prices.

- Its product or service is unique or it has built up switching costs (for example, word processing software). When few direct substitutes exist, supplying firms experience little direct competition and can therefore use their power over buyers who are dependent on them.

- Suppliers are able to integrate forward and compete directly with their present customers (for example, a microprocessor producer like Intel can make PCs). The ability of firms to engage in more in-house activities acts as a control over potentially powerful suppliers.

- A purchasing industry buys only a small portion of the supplier group's goods and services and is thus unimportant to the supplier (for example, sales of lawn mower tires are less important to the tire industry than are sales of auto tires). In contrast, if an industry is very important, then the success of the buyer will be closely tied to the success of the supplier, so suppliers will be encouraged to be reasonable in their terms and conditions.

RELATIVE POWER OF OTHER STAKEHOLDERS

stakeholder a constituent who can affect an organization's activities and/or be affected by them

complementor a firm whose product works well, or complements, that of another firm

Another force should be added to Porter's list to include a variety of stakeholder groups from the task environment. A **stakeholder** is defined as a constituent (group or individual) who can affect an organization's activities and/or be affected by them. Insofar as they are not included in any of Porter's five competitive forces, attention must be given to governments, local communities, creditors, trade associations, special-interest groups, unions, shareholders, and **complementors** (companies whose products work well with those of a firm). Because of the interdependence of organizations today, it is increasingly important for them to develop expertise in forming and managing strategic alliances, engaging in strategic outsourcing and balancing the demands of various stakeholders. Recognizing the fact that organizations are often embedded in networks of organizations and constituents that affect each other, it is important to systematically examine how a firm's strategy influences all members of its network, not just its owners or shareholders. The benefit of including the influence of stakeholders in an analysis of the task environment is that it forces strategic decision makers to consider the impact their actions will have on important constituencies in their environment. Incorporating the interests and needs of various stakeholders into the strategy formulation process avoids the possibility of neglecting the interests of many constituencies that are not explicitly considered by Porter's industry competitive analysis. This minimizes the opportunity for inadvertently creating dissatisfaction in a particular stakeholder group or neglecting its interests in the strategic development process.

The importance of these stakeholders varies by industry. For example, environmental groups in Prince Edward Island have kept plastic and metal soft drink containers off the island in favour of glass bottles that are reusable and recyclable through a provincial program. This has effectively raised costs across the board, with the greatest impact being felt by marginal producers who could not absorb all of the new costs. In Vancouver, smoking in restaurants and bars has been prohibited for many years. Public concern with the effects of second-hand smoke has brought about the gradual elimination of smoking in public places across Canada. The traditionally strong power of national unions in automobile manufacturing and integrated steel production has effectively raised costs throughout these industries. In contrast, unions are of little importance in computer software development and telecommunications hardware manufacturing. (Expectations of stakeholders are discussed in further detail in **Chapter 7**.)

INDUSTRY EVOLUTION

Over time, most industries evolve through a series of stages from growth through maturity to eventual decline. The strength of each of the forces mentioned earlier varies according to the stage of industry evolution. The industry life cycle is useful for explaining and predicting trends among the forces driving industry competition. For example, when an industry is new, people often buy the product regardless of price because it fulfills a unique need. This is probably a **fragmented industry**—no firm has a large market share and each firm serves only a small piece of the total market in competition with others (for example, Chinese restaurants and dry cleaning services). As new competitors enter the industry, prices drop as a result of competition. Companies use the experience curve (to be discussed in **Chapter 4**) and economies of scale to reduce costs faster than the competition. Companies integrate to reduce costs even further by acquiring their suppliers and distributors. Competitors try to differentiate their products from one another's to avoid the fierce price competition common to a maturing industry.

fragmented industry
an industry with a relative large number of firms with equal power and market share

By the time an industry enters maturity, products tend to become more like commodities. This is now a **consolidated industry**—dominated by a few large firms, each of which struggles to differentiate its products from those of the competition. As buyers become more sophisticated over time, purchasing decisions are based on better information. Price becomes a dominant concern, given a minimum level of quality and features. One example of this trend is the video cassette recorder industry. By the 1990s, VCRs had reached the point where there were few major differences among them. Consumers realized that because slight improvements cost significantly more money, it made little sense to pay more than the minimum for a VCR.

consolidated industry
an industry dominated by a small number of large and powerful firms

As an industry moves through maturity toward possible decline, its products' growth rate of sales slows, and sales may even begin to decrease. To the extent that exit barriers are low, firms will begin converting their facilities to alternative uses or will sell them to another firm. The industry will tend to consolidate around fewer but larger competitors. In the case of the North American major home appliance industry, it changed from being a fragmented industry (pure competition) comprising hundreds of appliance manufacturers in its early years to a consolidated industry (mature oligopoly) comprising five companies controlling almost all appliance sales. A similar consolidation is occurring now in European major home appliances.

CATEGORIZING INTERNATIONAL INDUSTRIES

multidomestic industry an industry that comprises local firms, usually reflective of strong pressures for localization

global industry an industry that operates worldwide, where firms will invest and produce in numerous geographic locations

According to Porter, world industries vary on a continuum from multidomestic to global (see **Figure 3–5**).[20] **Multidomestic industries** are specific to each country or group of countries. This type of international industry is a collection of essentially domestic industries, like retailing and insurance. The activities in a subsidiary of a multinational corporation (MNC) in this type of industry are essentially independent of the activities of the MNC's subsidiaries in other countries. Within each country, it has a manufacturing facility to produce goods for sale in that country. The MNC is thus able to tailor its products or services to the specific needs of consumers in a particular country or group of countries having similar societal environments.

Global industries, in contrast, operate worldwide, with MNCs making only small adjustments for country-specific circumstances. A global industry is one in which an MNC's activities in one country are significantly affected by its activities in other countries. MNCs produce products or services in various locations throughout the world and also sell them throughout the world. Examples of global industries are commercial aircraft, television sets, semiconductors, copiers, automobiles, watches, and tires. The largest industrial organizations in the world in terms of dollar sales are, for the most part, multinational corporations operating in global industries.

Two factors tend to determine whether an industry will be primarily multidomestic or primarily global:

- *Pressure for coordination* within the multinational corporations operating in that industry
- *Pressure for local responsiveness* on the part of individual country markets

To the extent that the pressure for coordination is strong and the pressure for local responsiveness is weak for multinational corporations within a particular industry, that industry will tend to become global. In contrast, when the pressure for local responsiveness is strong and the pressure for coordination is weak for multinational corporations in an industry, that industry will tend to be multidomestic. Between these two extremes lie a number of industries with varying characteristics of both multidomestic and global industries. These are illustrated in **Figure 3–6** on page 70. For example, the "hybrid" industry is characterized by relatively high pressures for responsiveness, but only a moderate amount of coordination between the subsidiary and parent company. This can occur, for example, when there are large economies of scale that encourage large-scale, integrated operations, yet sufficient local differences to prevent standard products from being developed. In situations such as these, customized products can be created for local markets using the R & D and core products of the parent. In industries such as telecommunications, local differences in infrastructure and regulations prevent standard products from being developed, yet there are benefits of leveraging investments in R & D for the larger, more global firm. In the "regional" industry, there are minimal local differences, but there are limits to the industry's globalization. In industries involving bulky or

Figure 3–5 Continuum of International Industries

Multidomestic ◄──────────────────────────────► **Global**

Industry in which companies tailor their products to the specific needs of consumers in a particular country.
- Retailing
- Insurance
- Banking

Industry in which companies manufacture and sell the same products, with only minor adjustments made for individual countries around the world.
- Automobile
- Tires
- Television sets

Figure 3–6 Categorization of International Industries

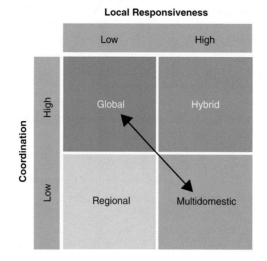

perishable products (for example gravel, cement, produce), there are significant costs to ship products great distances. So despite there being a relatively homogeneous market for a product, there may be economic or regulatory obstacles to globalization.

From the previous discussion we can see that international industries can take many different forms. Moving along the continuum from multidomestic to global, there are different benefits to the organization—the former provides greater customer responsiveness, the latter greater efficiencies. The strategies most successful in each type of industry try to maximize the benefits associated with coordination and local responsiveness. The dynamic tension between these two factors is contained in the phrase "Think globally, but act locally."

INTERNATIONAL RISK ASSESSMENT

Many organizations develop elaborate information networks and computerized systems to evaluate and rank investment risks. Smaller companies often outsource these activities, hiring outside consultants to provide political-risk assessments. Among the many systems that exist to assess political and economic risks are the Political System Stability Index, the Business Environment Risk Index, Business International's Country Assessment Service, and Frost and Sullivan's World Political Risk Forecasts.[21] Business International provides subscribers with continuously updated information on conditions in 63 countries. A Boston company called International Strategies offers an Export Hotline that faxes information to callers for only the cost of the call. Regardless of the source of data, a firm must develop its own method of assessing risk. It must decide on its most important risk factors and then assign weights to each.

STRATEGIC GROUPS

strategic group a set of firms that pursue essentially similar strategies with similar resources

A **strategic group** is a set of business units or firms that "pursue similar strategies with similar resources."[22] Categorizing firms in any one industry into strategic groups is very useful as a way of better understanding the competitive environment.[23] Because an organization's structure and culture tend to reflect the kinds of strategies it follows, companies or business units belonging to a particular strategic group within the same industry tend to be strong rivals and tend to be more similar to one another than to competitors in other strategic groups within the same industry.

For example, although McDonald's and Outback Steakhouse are a part of the same restaurant industry, they have different missions, objectives, and strategies, and thus belong to different strategic groups. They generally have very little in common and pay little attention to each other when planning competitive actions. Burger King and Wendy's, however, have a great deal in common with McDonald's in terms of their similar strategy of producing a high volume of low-priced meals targeted for sale to the average family. Consequently they are strong rivals and are organized to operate similarly.

Strategic groups in a particular industry can be mapped by plotting the market positions of industry competitors on a two-dimensional graph using two strategic variables as the vertical and horizontal axes (for an example see **Figure 3–7**).

1. Select two broad strategic characteristics that differentiate companies in an industry from one another and are not highly correlated. The choice of variables will vary by industry but can include things such as distribution channel, product line, integration, cost position, customer service, price level, and branding.

2. Plot the firms using these two characteristics as the dimensions.

3. Draw a circle around those companies that are closest to one another as one strategic group, varying the size of the circle in proportion to the group's share of total industry sales. You could also name each strategic group with an identifying title for ease of interpretation.

Figure 3–7 Strategic Group Map of Canadian Hardware Retail Industry

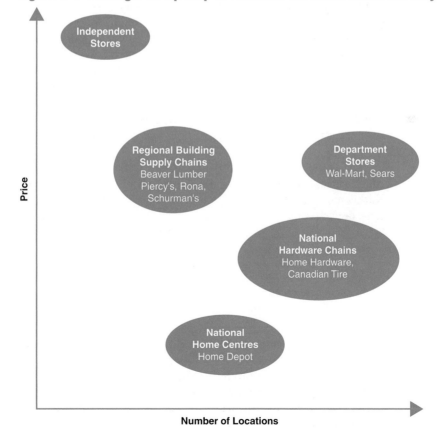

Preparing a strategic group map allows strategic decision makers to see the competitive positions of rival firms. By systematically assessing all firms along particular strategic dimensions, analysts can identify which firms are pursuing essentially similar strategies and therefore pose the most direct competition with one another. It is possible that an industry has only one strategic group if all firms follow essentially the same strategy. More likely, however, is the presence of multiple strategic groups. Why do we observe this phenomenon? Sometimes it is due to the differences in capabilities of industry players, their past practices that contributed to their current success, or the vision of their leaders. Once strategic group mapping has revealed industry clusters, decision makers are in a much better position to determine which firms pose the greatest competitive threat. As a general rule, organizations belonging to the same strategic group experience the most intense rivalry because they follow essentially the same strategy and target essentially the same customers.

mobility barrier an obstacle to an organization's movement between strategic groups that makes movement difficult, time-consuming, or costly

Examining the strategic group map for empty spaces points toward relatively noncompetitive segments of the industry that may reflect opportunities. The freedom to move between strategic groups will be a function of **mobility barriers**, factors that prevent or discourage the movement of an organization from one strategic group to another. The presence of mobility barriers explains how some firms in an industry can remain more profitable than their rivals—they occupy a competitive position toward which movement is hindered by mobility barriers. This can also explain why an organization is unable to abandon a strategic group with intense rivalry and move toward an unoccupied competitive space identified in a strategic group map.

HYPERCOMPETITION

Most industries today are facing an ever-increasing level of environmental uncertainty. They are becoming more complex and more dynamic. Industries that used to be multidomestic are becoming global. Flexible, aggressive, innovative new competitors are moving into established markets to rapidly erode the advantages of large, previously dominant firms. Distribution channels vary from country to country and are being altered daily through the use of sophisticated information systems. Closer relationships with suppliers are being forged to reduce costs, increase quality, and gain access to new technology. Companies learn to quickly imitate the successful strategies of market leaders, and it becomes harder to sustain any competitive advantage for very long. Consequently, the level of competitive intensity is increasing in most industries.

hypercompetition a competitive environment characterized by high levels of uncertainty and dynamism

Richard D'Aveni's popular book *Hypercompetition* describes a new competitive reality in which change, rather than stability, is the norm. As increased environmental turbulence reaches more industries, a state of **hypercompetition** results in which new strategic tools need to be used. According to D'Aveni:

> In hypercompetition the frequency, boldness, and aggressiveness of dynamic movement by the players accelerates to create a condition of constant disequilibrium and change. Market stability is threatened by short product life cycles, short product design cycles, new technologies, frequent entry by unexpected outsiders, repositioning by incumbents, and tactical redefinitions of market boundaries as diverse industries merge. In other words, environments escalate toward higher and higher levels of uncertainty, dynamism, heterogeneity of the players, and hostility.[24]

cannibalization when a company loses sales of one product to another of its own products

In hypercompetitive industries such as computers, competitive advantage comes from an up-to-date knowledge of environmental trends and competitive activity coupled with a willingness to risk a current advantage for a possible new advantage. Companies must be willing to **cannibalize** their own products (replacing popular products before competitors do so) to prolong their competitive advantage. As a result, industry or competitive intelligence has never been more important. See the boxed example to learn how Microsoft is operating in the hypercompetitive industry of computer software.

Microsoft Operates in a Hypercompetitive Industry

Microsoft is a hypercompetitive firm operating in a hypercompetitive industry. It has used its dominance in operating systems (DOS and Windows) to move into a very strong position in application programs like word processing and spreadsheets (Word and Excel). Even though Microsoft held 90% of the market for personal computer operating systems in 1992, it still invested millions in developing the next generation: Windows 95 and Windows NT. Instead of trying to protect its advantage in the profitable DOS operating system, Microsoft actively sought to replace DOS with various versions of Windows. Before hypercompetition, most experts argued against cannibalization of a company's own product line because it destroys a very profitable product instead of harvesting it like a "cash cow." According to this line of thought, a company would be better off defending its older products. New products would be introduced only if it could be proven that they would not take sales away from current products. Microsoft was one of the first companies to disprove this argument against cannibalization.

Bill Gates, Microsoft's co-founder, chairman, and CEO, realized that if his company didn't replace its own DOS product line with a better product, someone else would (such as IBM with OS/2 Warp). He knew that success in the software industry depends not so much on company size but on moving aggressively to the next competitive advantage before a competitor does. "This is a hypercompetitive market," explained Gates. "Scale is not all positive in this business. Cleverness is the position in this business." By 2000, Microsoft still controlled over 90% of operating systems software and had achieved a dominant position in applications software as well.

Source: R.A. D'Aveni, *Hypercompetition* (New York: Free Press, 1994), p. 2.

The idea that many industries will evolve to a hypercompetitive state poses a challenge to the relatively static industry analysis described in the previous section. D'Aveni's fundamental assumptions are quite different from Porter's, which results in a shifting emphasis on the importance of competitive forces. Recall that Porter's competitive analysis was geared toward finding attractive (that is, not overly competitive) industries and operating in these areas of relatively low competitive rivalry. D'Aveni, on the other hand, studies industries in which competition is extremely high and environmental change is extremely rapid. In other words, there are no places of low competitive rivalry in hypercompetitive markets. And if there are no particularly favourable industries (or profitable niches within them), what should strategic decision makers do?

Here we see D'Aveni's contribution to strategic thinking in terms of his willingness to reject the notion that a sustainable competitive advantage is "difficult, if not impossible." Rather than looking to the industry for competitive forces to neutralize or protect themselves against, organizations should create advantage by "actively disrupting advantages of others to adapt the world to themselves." So rather than trying to analyze competitive forces and create a strategy that positions the firm favourably against them, under hypercompetition firms should undertake a series of initiatives that build a set of temporary advantages and create market disruptions. (Hypercompetition is discussed in more detail in **Chapter 5**.)

IDENTIFYING KEY SUCCESS FACTORS

Within any industry or in a particular strategic group there are usually certain variables, key success factors, that a company's management must understand in order to be successful.

key success factors
characteristics of an industry that significantly affect the competitive positions of all firms in it

Key success factors are defined as those variables that can affect significantly the competitive positions of all companies within the industry or strategic group. These are the variables that most directly affect the success of an organization. Typically varying from industry to industry, they are usually determined by the economic and technological characteristics of the industry and by the competitive weapons on which the firms in the industry have built their strategies.[25] For example, in the major home appliance industry, a firm must achieve low costs, typically by building large manufacturing facilities dedicated to making multiple versions of one type of appliance, such as washing machines. Since most major home appliances in Canada are sold through large retailers such as Sears, The Bay, Home Depot, and Future Shop, a firm must have a strong presence in the mass merchandiser distribution channel. It must offer a full line of appliances and provide a just-in-time delivery system to keep store inventory and ordering costs to a minimum. Because the consumer expects reliability and durability in an appliance, a firm must have excellent process R & D. Any appliance manufacturer that is unable to deal successfully with these key success factors will likely not survive.

Key success factors usually relate to strategic variables, product qualities, and organizational capabilities that combine to create value for consumers. How does a strategist determine key success factors for an industry or a particular market niche? The first step in this analysis is to examine successful firms and compare them with unsuccessful firms. What explains the relative performance of different firms in the industry? In what ways are their strategies, production systems, management practices, and product offerings similar? Understanding these key differences can be enhanced through competitive intelligence (discussed in detail below). A second step in this analysis is to engage in consumer research that determines the elements of a product (from its physical attributes, brand, distribution, price, warranty, etc.) that are salient in the purchase decision. What makes one product provide more value to a buyer than another? What differences seem to matter the most and which the least?

The process of identifying key success factors is a critical activity in the environmental scanning process. It is extremely important that organizations know the factors that influence buying decisions and the different ways in which they can organize and provide their products to the market. Identifying key success factors therefore acts as a focusing tool, directing strategic attention toward certain decisions that must be made extremely carefully. In the home appliance industry discussed earlier, logistics management and retail channel management stand out as areas in which organizations must develop or strengthen capabilities. If they can do this, then they can expect to secure a strong competitive position in the industry. If they cannot, they can expect to be outperformed by rivals who have been able to develop internal competencies that match the key success factors present in the industry.

3.3 Competitive Intelligence

Much external environmental scanning is done on an informal and individual basis. Information is obtained from a variety of sources: suppliers, customers, industry publications, employees, industry experts, industry conferences, and the internet.[26] For example, scientists and engineers working in a firm's R & D lab can learn about new products and competitors' ideas at professional meetings. Someone from the purchasing department, speaking with supplier-representatives, may also uncover valuable bits of information about a competitor. A study of product innovation found that 77% of all product innovations in scientific instruments and 67% in semiconductors and printed circuit boards were initiated by the customer in the form of inquiries and complaints.[27] In these industries, the sales force and service departments must be especially vigilant.

competitive intelligence a formal program of gathering information on a company's competitors and customers

Competitive intelligence is a formal program of gathering information about a company's competitors and customers. It is designed to aid organizations in anticipating changes in the environment and developing appropriate strategies in response to those changes. To gain the full benefit of a competitive intelligence program, information on industry trends, legal precedents, government regulation, technological developments, local country politics, and the economy all need to be assessed. The relative strength of a rival can only be determined in the context of these types of environmental factors.

Until recently, few North American organizations had fully developed competitive intelligence programs. In contrast, all Japanese organizations involved in international business and most large European companies have active intelligence programs.[28] This situation is changing, however. Competitive intelligence is now one of the fastest growing fields within strategic management.[29] At General Mills, for example, all employees have been trained to recognize and tap sources of competitive information. A recent survey of large corporations revealed that 78% of them reported competitive intelligence activities within their firm.[30]

Most organizations rely on outside organizations to provide them with environmental data. Firms such as A.C. Nielsen provide subscribers with bimonthly data on brand share, retail prices, percentages of stores stocking an item, and percentages of stock-out stores. Analysts can use this data to spot regional and national trends as well as to assess market share. Information on market conditions, government regulations, competitors, and new products can be bought from "information brokers" such as MarketResearch.com and Finsbury Data Services. Company and industry profiles are generally available from the Hoover's Online website. Many business organizations have established their own in-house libraries and computerized information systems to deal with the growing mass of available information. In addition to formal, published sources, a number of informal sources of information can be used, including a company's sales brochures and corporate communications, employees who know a lot about customers and competitors, customers themselves, customer service employees who hear about first-hand experience with rival products, and trade shows where new products are introduced.

Some companies, however, choose to use industrial espionage or other intelligence-gathering techniques to get their information straight from their competitors. Approaching current or former employees of their competitors and using private contractors, some firms attempt to steal trade secrets, technology, business plans, and pricing strategies. For example, Avon Products hired private investigators to retrieve from a public dumpster documents (some of them shredded) that Mary Kay Corporation had thrown away. Even Procter & Gamble, which defends itself like a fortress from information leaks, is vulnerable. A competitor was able to learn the precise launch date of a concentrated laundry detergent in Europe when one of its people visited the factory where machinery was being made. Simply asking a few questions about what a certain machine did, whom it was for, and when it would be delivered was all that was necessary.

To combat the increasing theft of company secrets, the US government passed the Economic Espionage Act in 1996. The law makes it illegal (with fines up to $5 million and 10 years in jail) to steal any material whose value derives from its secrecy and that a business has taken "reasonable efforts" to keep secret.[31] Canada has no similar law, but professionals usually adhere to a code of ethics as defined by the Society of Competitive Intelligence Professionals (**www.scip.org**), which urges strategists to stay within existing laws and to act ethically when searching for information. The society states that illegal activities are foolish because the vast majority of worthwhile competitive intelligence is available publicly via annual reports, websites, and public libraries.

3.4 Forecasting

Environmental scanning provides reasonably hard data on the present situation and current trends, but intuition and luck are needed to predict accurately whether these trends will continue. The resulting forecasts are, however, usually based on a set of assumptions that may or may not be valid.

DANGER OF ASSUMPTIONS

Faulty underlying assumptions are the most frequent cause of forecasting errors. Nevertheless, many managers who formulate and implement strategic plans rarely consider that their success is based on a series of assumptions. Many long-range plans are simply based on projections of the current situation.

One example of what can happen when a corporate strategy rests on the very questionable assumption that the future will simply be an extension of the present is that of Tupperware, the company that originated air-tight, easy-to-use plastic food storage containers. Much of the company's success had been based on Tupperware parties in the 1950s, when housewives gathered in one another's homes to socialize and play games while the local Tupperware lady demonstrated and sold new products. Management assumed during the following decades that Tupperware parties would continue to be an excellent distribution channel. Its faith in this assumption blinded it to information about changing lifestyles (two-career families) and the likely impact on sales. Even in the 1990s, when Tupperware executives realized that their sales forecasts were no longer justified, they were unable to improve their forecasting techniques until they changed their assumption that the best way to sell Tupperware was at a Tupperware party. Consequently, Rubbermaid and other competitors, who chose to market their containers in grocery and discount stores, continued to grow at the expense of Tupperware.[32]

USEFUL FORECASTING TECHNIQUES

extrapolation extending past trends to predict future performance

Various techniques are used to forecast future situations. Each has its proponents and critics. A study of nearly 500 of the world's largest corporations revealed trend **extrapolation** to be the most widely practised form of forecasting—more than 70% use this technique either occasionally or frequently.[33] Simply stated, extrapolation is the extension of present trends into the future. It rests on the assumption that the world is reasonably consistent and changes slowly in the short run. Time-series methods are approaches of this type; they attempt to carry a series of historical events forward into the future. The basic problem with extrapolation is that a historical trend is based on a series of patterns or relationships among so many different variables that a change in any one of these can drastically alter the future direction of the trend. As a general rule, the further back into the past you can find relevant data supporting the trend, the more confidence you can have in the prediction.

brainstorming a process of idea generation that encourages all ideas and discourages evaluating them at an early stage

Delphi technique a decision-making process that relies on experts to assess the probability of particular events occurring

Brainstorming, seeking expert opinion, and statistical modelling are also very popular forecasting techniques. **Brainstorming** is a non-quantitative approach requiring simply the presence of people with some knowledge of the situation to be predicted. The basic ground rule is to propose ideas without first mentally screening them. No criticism is allowed. Ideas tend to build on previous ideas until a consensus is reached. This is a good technique to use with operating managers who have more faith in "gut feeling" than in more quantitative "number crunching" techniques. The **Delphi technique** is based on expert opinion. Separate experts independently assess the likelihood of specified events. These assessments are combined and sent back to each expert for fine tuning until an agreement is reached.

statistical modelling a mathematical technique that identifies and measures causal factors in time series data

Statistical modelling is a quantitative technique that attempts to discover causal or at least explanatory factors that link two or more time series together. Examples of statistical modelling are regression analysis and other econometric methods. Although very useful for grasping past trends, statistical modelling, like trend extrapolation, is based on historical data. As the pattern of relationships changes, the accuracy of the forecast deteriorates. Other forecasting techniques, such as cross-impact analysis (CIA) and trend-impact analysis (TIA), have not established themselves successfully as regularly employed tools.

scenario planning the identification of several possible future scenarios, used as the basis for plans should each scenario occur

Scenario planning, originated by Royal Dutch Shell, appears to be the most widely used forecasting technique after trend extrapolation. Scenarios are focused descriptions of different likely futures presented in a narrative fashion. The scenario thus may be merely a written description of some future state, in terms of key variables and issues, or it may be generated in combination with other forecasting techniques. An industry scenario is a forecast description of a particular industry's likely future. Such a scenario is developed by analyzing the probable impact of future societal forces on key groups in a particular industry. The process may operate as follows:[34]

1. Examine possible shifts in the societal variables globally.
2. Identify uncertainties in each of the forces of the task environment (for example, potential entrants, competitors, likely substitutes, buyers, suppliers, and other key stakeholders).
3. Make a range of plausible assumptions about future trends.
4. Combine assumptions about individual trends into internally consistent scenarios.
5. Analyze the industry situation that would prevail under each scenario.
6. Determine the sources of competitive advantage under each scenario.
7. Predict competitors' behaviour under each scenario.
8. Select the scenarios that are either most likely to occur or most likely to have a strong impact on the future of the company. Use these scenarios in strategy formulation.

3.5 Summary of Environmental Analysis

After strategic managers have scanned the societal and task environments and identified a number of likely external factors for their particular organization, they may want to summarize their analysis of these factors in a way that identifies high-priority factors in the strategy formulation process. This can be accomplished in the following steps:

1. Extract the most critical external strategic factors from the issues priority matrix and assess their likely impact on firm performance. From this matrix you should be able to identify the variables that will most likely have a negative impact on firm performance if current strategies continue to be used. Assessing the likelihood of these environmental changes occurring and estimating their impact on firm performance can provide the rationale for a strategic change that will defend the firm against these unfavourable environmental forces. Similarly, you can identify opportunities that the firm is currently well-equipped to exploit, estimating the improved performance that will result from continuing with current strategies.
2. Identify the six forces in the task environment and assess how favourably or unfavourably they affect the organization. Although organizations can prosper in what most would consider unattractive industries, as a general rule, the more intense the rivalry within an industry, the more difficult it will be to remain profitable in it. Porter's five competitive

forces plus the interests of relevant stakeholders can suggest future strategies that can position the firm more favourably against these forces, thereby increasing profitability and the ability to withstand competition.

3.   Determine key success factors for the industry or strategic group and ensure these activities are a fundamental part of the organization's strategic priorities. Key success factors, by definition, are really must-have properties. Sometimes they will be industry-wide; at other times they may vary across strategic groups. Once identified, key success factors need to be incorporated into an organization's products and activities to strengthen its competitive advantage and present a product to the market that provides superior value.

4.   Use strategic group maps to determine which competitors deserve the most attention and examine the nature of their competitive positions. The identification of the strategic groups with the most intense rivalry and the lowest profits will suggest strategic changes in the direction of more favourable competitive positions. Once differences in competitive positions are identified, an assessment of mobility barriers will indicate the ease with which firms can move from one strategic group to another in pursuit of less intense rivalry and higher profits.

The results of these four tasks will provide strategic managers with insight into the industry in which the firm competes and the environment within which it operates. What a good environmental analysis should present is a systematic assessment of how the organization interacts with other individuals, groups, and organizations, what trends may result in deteriorating firm performance, and what future directions strategists should carefully examine to make strategic decisions that enhance profitability and survival.

3.6 Impact of the Internet on Environmental Scanning and Industry Analysis

The internet has changed the way in which the strategist engages in environmental scanning. It provides the quickest means to obtain data on almost any subject. A recent joint study of 77 companies by the American Productivity & Quality Center and the Society of Competitive Intelligence Professionals reveals that 73% of the firms ranked the internet as being used to a "great" or "very great" extent. Other mentioned sources of information were competitor offerings and products (66%), industry experts (62%), personal industry contacts (60%), online databases (56%), market research (55%), and the sales force (54%).[35] Although the scope and quality of internet information is increasing geometrically, it is also littered with "noise," misinformation, and utter nonsense. For example, a number of corporate websites are sending unwanted guests to specially constructed bogus sites.[36]

Unlike the library, the internet lacks the tight bibliographic control standards that exist in the print world. There is no ISBN or Dewey Decimal System to identify, search, and retrieve a document. Many web documents lack the name of the author and the date of publication. A web page providing useful information may be accessible on the web one day and gone the next. Unhappy ex-employees, radical environmentalists, and prank-prone hackers create websites to attack and discredit an otherwise reputable organization. Rumours with no basis in fact are spread via chat rooms and personal websites. This creates a serious problem for the researcher. How can one evaluate the information found on the internet?

A basic rule in intelligence gathering is that before a piece of information can be used in any report or briefing, it must first be evaluated in two ways. *First, the source of the information should be judged in terms of its truthfulness and reliability.* How trustworthy is the source? How well can a researcher rely upon it for truthful and correct information? One approach is to rank the reliability of the source as A (extremely reliable), B (reliable), C (of unknown reliability), D (probably unreliable), or E (of very questionable reliability). The reliability of a source can be judged on the basis of the author's credentials, the organization sponsoring the information, and past performance, among other factors. *Second, the information or data should be judged in terms of the likelihood of its being correct.* The correctness of the data may be ranked as 1 (correct), 2 (probably correct), 3 (of unknown correctness), 4 (doubtful), or 5 (extremely doubtful). The correctness of a piece of data or information can be judged on the basis of its agreement with other bits of separately obtained information or with a general trend supported by previous data.

For every piece of information found on the internet, the intelligence gatherer must list not only the address of the webpage, but also the evaluation of the information. Information found through library research in sources such as *Moody's Industrials*, *Standard & Poor's*, or *Value Line* can generally be evaluated as having a reliability of A. The correctness of the data can still range anywhere from 1 to 5, but in most instances it is likely to be either 1 or 2, and probably it is no worse than 3 or 4. Other sources may be less reliable.

Sites such as those sponsored by Industry Canada (**http://strategis.ic.gc.ca**), Statistics Canada (**www.statcan.ca**), and Hoover's Online (**www.hoovers.com**) are extremely reliable. Company sponsored websites are generally reliable but are not the place to go for trade secrets, strategic plans, or proprietary information. For one thing, many firms think of their websites primarily in terms of marketing, and they provide little data aside from product descriptions and distribution channels. Other companies provide their latest financial statements and links to other useful websites. Nevertheless, some companies in very competitive industries install software on their websites to ascertain a visitor's web address. Visitors with a competitor's domain name are thus screened before they are given access to certain web pages. They may not be allowed beyond the product information page, or they may be sent to a bogus website containing misinformation.

Much time spent searching the internet can be saved through the effective use of search engines, websites that search the internet for names and key words typed in by the user. The search engines most used by competitive intelligence professionals are AltaVista (50%), Yahoo! (25%), and Lycos (15%).[37] The most popular search engines in North America, according to a large Nielsen//NetRating study of home and business internet surfers, are Google (29.5%), Yahoo! (28.9%), and MSN (27.6%).[38]

Although information about publicly held corporations is widely available, it is much harder to obtain information about privately held companies. For a comparison of the type of information generally available on publicly and privately held companies, see the **Internet Issue** feature on page 80.

Internet Issue

Competitor Information Available on the Internet

Type of Information	Likelihood of Finding Data on the Net for Publicly Held Company	Likelihood of Finding Data on the Net for Privately Held Company
Total Annual Sales	Very high	Very low
Sales and Profitability by Product Line or Distribution Channel	Very low	Very low
Market Sizes in Segments of Interest	Depends on the market: High for large companies, low for small "niche" firms	Same as for publicly held
Trends in Marketing, Technology, Distribution	Same as above	Same as for publicly held
Prices, Including the Lowest Prices to Best Customers	Very low	Very low
Marketing Strategy	Some information available from trade articles and analyst reports, but incomplete and dated	Even less than for publicly held
Sales and Technical Literature on Products	Strong likelihood, but often incomplete; less chance for detailed technical information	Even less than for publicly held
Number of Employees Working on Certain Products or in Particular Departments	Highly unlikely	Highly unlikely
Compensation Levels	Top management generally available; others unlikely	Will not be found
Customer Opinions Regarding Strengths and Weaknesses	Available from trade articles and industry reports; at best, may be incomplete and dated	Less likely than for publicly held
Feedback on Firm's Own Products and Services	Will not be found; look for independent user chat rooms	Same as for publicly held

Source: Adapted from C. Klein, "Overcoming 'Net Disease,'" *Competitive Intelligence Magazine* (July–September 1999), p. 31.

Discussion Questions

1. Discuss how a development in an organization's societal environment can affect the organization through its task environment.

2. According to Porter, what determines the level of competitive intensity in an industry?

3. According to Porter's discussion of industry analysis, is Pepsi a substitute for Coca-Cola?

4. How can a decision maker identify strategic factors in the organization's external international environment?

5. What are stakeholders and how do they figure in an analysis of the environment?

6. What are the fundamental differences between Michael Porter's and Richard D'Aveni's approaches to understanding the competitive environment?

Strategic Practice Exercise

What are the forces driving competition in the airline industry? Using the approach to industry analysis discussed in this chapter, evaluate each of the six forces in the task environment to ascertain what drives the level of competitive intensity in this industry.

The deregulation of the Canadian airline industry in the mid-1980s created an intense rivalry between Air Canada and Canadian Airlines. Canadian Airlines was strong in western Canada as a result of its acquisitions in Canadian Pacific and Wardair. Air Canada had its strength in central and eastern Canada but was in transition from being a crown corporation to becoming a publicly traded one. The presence of two national airlines created a situation of excess capacity and duplicated routes, which in turn led to regular price discounting. It was not long before both airlines were in financial difficulty. During the 1990s a number of small carriers such as Royal Airlines, Air Transat, Canada 3000, and WestJet were established, offering low-price alternatives to the two national carriers. These low-price, restricted-route airlines were able to make healthy profits in markets where price-sensitive consumers were willing to trade frequency and flight connections for reduced fares and no-frills service.

The government has always regulated the airline industry, not only as concerns the maintenance and operation of airplanes, but also with regard to foreign ownership and route availability. For a long time the government was unwilling to facilitate the consolidation of the airline industry, preventing American Airlines' bid for controlling interest in Canadian Airlines and then Onex Corporation's takeover of Air Canada. The government appeared torn between, on the one hand, a reluctance to interfere with market forces in the airline industry through subsidies of either national carrier, and on the other hand, a desire to protect the Canadian public from a monopoly airline that they were fearful would cut service to more remote areas of the country and raise fares.

Most countries have a national airline, and Canada is no exception. These airlines are usually at least partially government owned, often receiving subsidies and favourable treatment vis-à-vis transit regulations. For example, no foreign carrier can transport passengers between two Canadian cities, even if their plane travels between them. So a flight that runs from London, England, to Montreal, and then to Toronto is unable to pick up any new passengers in Montreal, although it can continue to fly its original passengers to Toronto.

Costs are still relatively high for most of the world's major airlines because of the high cost of new airplanes. One new commercial jet costs anywhere between $40 million and $150 million. By 2003, Airbus Industries and Boeing provided virtually all large commercial planes. Bombardier is a market leader in the regional and private jet segments. Major airlines were forced to buy new planes to become more fuel-efficient, increase safety, and reduce maintenance. Airlines that chose to stay with an old fleet had to deal with numerous higher costs. Fuel surcharges reflecting the steadily increasing price of petroleum, airport security fees introduced after the September 11 terrorist attacks in the United States, and the airport improvement fees charged by most airports in the country all pass along a variety of costs to consumers.

1. Evaluate each of the forces currently driving competition in the Canadian airline industry. Score each competitive force and provide a brief rationale for your assessment.

   Threat of New Entrants: High, Medium, or Low?

   Rivalry among Existing Firms: High, Medium, or Low?

   Threat of Substitutes: High, Medium, or Low?

   Bargaining Power of Buyers/Distributors: High, Medium, or Low?

   Bargaining Power of Suppliers: High, Medium, or Low?

   Relative Power of Other Stakeholders (such as _____): High, Medium, or Low?

2. Which of these forces are changing? How will this affect the overall level of competitive intensity in the airline industry in the future? Would you invest or look for a job in this industry? What do recent financial results of Canadian airlines indicate about the attractiveness of this industry?

Notes

1. J.B. Thomas, S.M. Clark, and D.A. Gioia, "Strategic Sensemaking and Organizational Performance: Linkages among Scanning, Interpretation, Action, Outcomes," *Academy of Management Journal* (April 1993), pp. 239–270; J.A. Smith, "Strategies for Start-Ups," *Long Range Planning* (December 1998), pp. 857–872.

2. P. Lasserre and J. Probert, "Competing on the Pacific Rim: High Risks and High Returns," *Long Range Planning* (April 1994), pp. 12–35.

3. W.E. Halal, "The Top 10 Emerging Technologies," *Special Report* (World Future Society, 2000).

4. F. Dobbin and T.J. Dowd, "How Policy Shapes Competition: Early Railroad Foundings in Massachusetts," *Administrative Science Quarterly* (September 1997), pp. 501–529.

5. A. Shleifer and R.W. Viskny, "Takeovers in the 1960s and the 1980s: Evidence and Implications," in *Fundamental Issues in Strategy: A Research Agenda*, edited by R.P. Rumelt, D.E. Schendel, and D.J. Teece (Boston: Harvard Business School Press, 1994), pp. 403–418.

6. J. Wyatt, "Playing the Woofie Card," *Fortune* (February 6, 1995), pp. 130–132.

7. D.K. Foot (with Daniel Stoffman), *Boom, Bust & Echo: How to Profit from the Coming Demographic Shift* (Toronto: MacFarlane Walter & Ross, 1996).

8. Statistics Canada, Catalogue No. 11-008 (Spring 2002).

9. Statistics Canada, "Canada's Ethnocultural Portrait: The Changing Mosaic," Catalogue No. 96F0030XIE2001008 (2001). As defined in the Employment Equity Act, visible minorities are persons, other than Aboriginal people, who are non-Caucasian in race or non-white in colour.

10. J. Naisbitt, *Megatrends Asia* (New York: Simon & Schuster, 1996), p. 79.

11. K. Ohmae, "The Triad World View," *Journal of Business Strategy* (Spring 1987), pp. 8–19.

12. B.K. Boyd and J. Fulk, "Executive Scanning and Perceived Uncertainty: A Multidimensional Model," *Journal of Management*, Vol. 22, No. 1 (1996), pp. 1–21.

13. R.A. Bettis and C.K. Prahalad, "The Dominant Logic: Retrospective and Extension," *Strategic Management Journal* (January 1995), pp. 5–14; J.M. Stofford and C.W.F. Baden-Fuller, "Creating Corporate Entrepreneurship," *Strategic Management Journal* (September 1994), pp. 521–536; J.M. Beyer, P. Chattopadhyay, E. George, W.H. Glick, and D. Pugliese, "The Selective Perception of Managers Revisited," *Academy of Management Journal* (June 1997), pp. 716–737.

14. H.I. Ansoff, "Strategic Management in a Historical Perspective," in *International Review of Strategic Management*, Vol. 2, No. 1 (1991), edited by D.E. Hussey (Chichester, England: Wiley, 1991), p. 61.

15. M.E. Porter, *The Competitive Advantage of Nations* (New York: Free Press, 1990).

16. M.E. Porter, *Competitive Strategy* (New York: Free Press, 1980), p. 3.

17. This summary of the forces driving competitive intensity is taken from Porter, *Competitive Strategy*, pp. 7–29.

18. P.N. Avakian, "Political Realities in Strategy," *Strategy & Leadership* (October, November, December 1999), pp. 42–48.

19. M.E. Porter, *Competitive Strategy*, p. 23.

20. M.E. Porter, "Changing Patterns of International Competition," *California Management Review* (Winter 1986), pp. 9–40.

21. T.N. Gladwin, "Assessing the Multinational Environment for Corporate Opportunity," in *Handbook of Business Strategy*, edited by W.D. Guth (Boston: Warren, Gorham and Lamont, 1985), pp. 7.28–7.41.

22. K.J. Hatten and M.L. Hatten, "Strategic Groups, Asymmetrical Mobility Barriers, and Contestability," *Strategic Management Journal* (July–August 1987), p. 329.

23. A. Fiegenbaum and H. Thomas, "Strategic Groups as Reference Groups: Theory, Modeling and Empirical Examination of Industry and Competitive Strategy," *Strategic Management Journal* (September 1995), pp. 461–476; H.R. Greve, "Managerial Cognition and the Mimetic Adoption of Market Positions: What You See Is What You Do," *Strategic Management Journal* (October 1998), pp. 967–988.

24. R.A. D'Aveni, *Hypercompetition* (New York: The Free Press, 1994), pp. xiii–xiv.

25. C.W. Hofer and D. Schendel, *Strategy Formulation: Analytical Concepts* (St. Paul, Minnesota: West Publishing Co., 1978), p. 77.

26. "Information Overload," *Journal of Business Strategy* (January–February 1998), p. 4.

27. E. Von Hipple, *Sources of Innovation* (New York: Oxford University Press, 1988), p. 4.

28. L. Kahaner, *Competitive Intelligence* (New York: Simon & Schuster, 1996).

29. S.M. Shaker and M.P. Gembicki, *WarRoom Guide to Competitive Intelligence* (New York: McGraw-Hill, 1999), p. 10.

30. R.G. Vedder, "CEO and CIO Attitudes about Competitive Intelligence," *Competitive Intelligence Magazine* (October–December 1999), pp. 39–41.

31. B. Flora, "Ethical Business Intelligence Is NOT Mission Impossible," *Strategy & Leadership* (January/February 1998), pp. 40–41.

32. L.M. Grossman, "Families Have Changed but Tupperware Keeps Holding Its Parties," *The Wall Street Journal* (July 21, 1992), pp. A1, A13.

33. H.E. Klein and R.E. Linneman, "Environmental Assessment: An International Study of Corporate Practices," *Journal of Business Strategy* (Summer 1984), p. 72.

34. This process of scenario development is adapted from M.E. Porter, *Competitive Advantage* (New York: Free Press, 1985), pp. 448–470.

35. S.H. Miller, "Developing a Successful CI Program: Preliminary Study Results," *Competitive Intelligence Magazine* (October–December 1999), p. 9.

36. S.H. Miller, "Beware Rival's Web Site Subterfuge," *Competitive Intelligence Magazine* (January–March 2000), p. 8.

37. S.M. Shaker and M.P. Gembicki, *WarRoom Guide to Competitive Intelligence* (New York: McGraw-Hill, 1999), pp. 113–115.

38. Statistics reported are based on audience reach: the percentage of home and work internet users estimated to have used a particular search engine at least once during a given month. *Source*: "Nielsen//NetRatings Search Engine Ratings," www.nielsen-netratings.com (accessed March 3, 2003).

CHAPTER 4

Internal Scanning:
Organizational Analysis

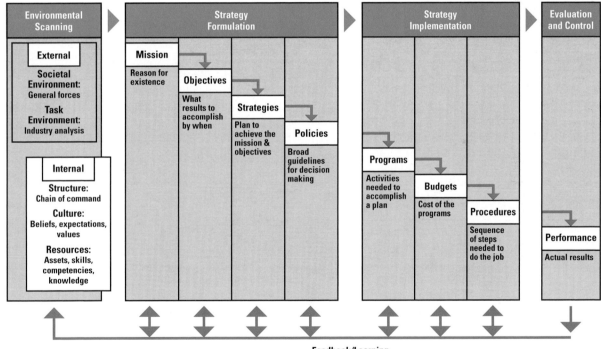

Environmental Scanning	Strategy Formulation	Strategy Implementation	Evaluation and Control

External
Societal Environment: General forces
Task Environment: Industry analysis

Internal
Structure: Chain of command
Culture: Beliefs, expectations, values
Resources: Assets, skills, competencies, knowledge

Mission
Reason for existence

Objectives
What results to accomplish by when

Strategies
Plan to achieve the mission & objectives

Policies
Broad guidelines for decision making

Programs
Activities needed to accomplish a plan

Budgets
Cost of the programs

Procedures
Sequence of steps needed to do the job

Performance
Actual results

Feedback/Learning

Learning Objectives

After reading this chapter you should be able to

> Understand the resource-based view of a firm
>
> Use the value chain and VRIO framework to assess an organization's competitive advantage
>
> Scan functional resources to determine their fit with a firm's strategy
>
> Assess the importance of internal factors to building competitive advantage and inhibiting imitation

IMAX Corporation was founded in 1967 by four Canadians who learned of an innovative film transport system that had been developed in Australia. At that time there was still nothing more advanced than century-old claw and sprocket mechanisms to transport film through a projector. These mechanisms worked well enough for film sizes up to 70 mm, but they could not handle the wider films that were becoming more common as theatres used increasingly large screens. An Australian engineer had developed a process that moved film through a projector in caterpillar-like waves using compressed air jets to cushion the film movement. He took out a patent on this "rolling loop" process and began to find buyers for his patent rights. Fortunately for the people at IMAX, there weren't all that many.

The first IMAX film was shown at Osaka's 1970 Exposition, only two years after the company purchased the world rights to the rolling loop technology prototype. To project images on such a large screen, a special wide-angle production lens was required. No such lens was available commercially. But Canadian firm Ernest Leitz designed and built an 88 mm lens specially for the job. Normal projector lamps were not going to do the job either. IMAX first tried a 12 kW water-cooled xenon lamp developed by the US military for its searchlights. The lamp was certainly bright enough, but it was so hot that it would set anything close to it on fire. The solution was a series of water-cooled metal and quartz mirrors that provided sufficient brightness without generating tremendous amounts of heat. Once the projection equipment was sorted out, IMAX needed to develop a new type of film that would run smoothly through the projector. They chose a Mylar material because it could be joined using ultrasonic welding, resulting in a very smooth and strong join that would not break, even with repeated use.

The initial success of IMAX was due to technological innovativeness that had created a movie experience like no other. Screen sizes of 60 by 80 feet (18 by 25 metres) or larger accompanied by multi-channel sound create a unique film experience. There are now more than 225 IMAX cinemas in 30 countries, most recently China and Russia. Alongside this push to expand the number of countries that have IMAX theatres, IMAX has had tremendous success with its latest innovation, digital remastering (DRM). This has allowed IMAX to take Disney classics like *The Lion King* and *Fantasia 2000* to the big screen. These large-format releases have used the original films with very few changes, but the large screen and the elaborate sound system enhance the viewing experience. The DRM process transfers original 35 mm images to IMAX's 70 mm frame format, which is 10 times the size of the original image. This process opens up the possibility of reformatting a number of films with action-packed content that appeal to large family audiences. IMAX's technological innovativeness is thus creating a second life for many Hollywood films. Sales from the 2002 release of *Beauty and the Beast* have helped to reverse a trend in poor earnings at IMAX, a result of a high debt load, high corporate costs, and slow growth in developing new digital markets.

As the history of IMAX indicates, the success of many organizations can be attributed to a competitive advantage that is rooted in organizational resources. This example shows how a combination of organizational resources can exploit environmental opportunities, resulting in a worldwide market presence.[1]

4.1 A Resource-Based Approach to Organizational Analysis

internal strategic factors strengths and weaknesses of the organization that allow it to capture opportunities or avoid threats in the environment

organizational analysis the process of identifying an organization's resources in order to determine their fit with the environment and strategy

Scanning and analyzing the external environment for opportunities and threats is not enough to give an organization a competitive advantage. Analysts must also look within the organization itself to identify **internal strategic factors**—those critical strengths and weaknesses that are likely to determine whether the firm will be able to take advantage of opportunities while avoiding threats. This internal scanning is often referred to as **organizational analysis** and is concerned with identifying and developing an organization's resources.

The tools for external environmental scanning presented in **Chapter 3** allowed organizational decision makers to identify the key strategic issues to which they had to respond. By identifying environmental opportunities and threats, decision makers could develop strategies to fit with the environment. Looking outside the organization is, however, only part of the challenge for strategists. What is an opportunity for one firm might not be for another because not all firms have the same resource endowments. In other words, a clear understanding of the types of resources an organization has and how it uses them is necessary to ensure that the optimal strategy is chosen, key success factors are strengthened, and competitive advantage is protected.

Analyzing the resources of an organization as part of the strategic management process allows for the findings of environmental analysis to be customized for a particular organization. Relying on environmental analysis alone, we might be tempted to think that there are "good" industries to be in, or "good" strategic groups to occupy. This logic is faulty when the organization is viewed as a collection of resources that can be used for a variety of purposes. From this resource-based view of the firm, performance is attributable primarily to the resources an organization has and how they are deployed. This view implies that organizational analysis, the process of identifying how best to use organizational resources in pursuit of a given strategy, is a critical managerial activity. A related activity is also critical to managers: planning for the development of strategy-critical resources that can lead to competitive advantage. Strategic decision makers must therefore know what key external environment factors to address, in addition to acquiring and managing the resources necessary for successful strategy implementation.

resource an organizational attribute used to achieve organizational goals

competitive advantage the superior competitive position of an organization that results from using its resources to successfully implement strategy and subsequently withstand competition

A **resource** is an asset, a competency, a process, a skill, or knowledge controlled by the organization. In this book, the term "resources" is used in its broadest sense to refer to what others might consider either resources or capabilities. Elsewhere, the term "resources" is sometimes used to refer to tangible assets of a firm (for example money, equipment, and people), while "capabilities" is the word used to signify the ability of an organization to coordinate or exploit its resources. For the sake of simplicity, the term "resource" is used here to refer to any organizational attribute that can give rise to **competitive advantage**, a superior competitive position that will allow the organization to earn above-average levels of profit. This use of the term "resource" is based on the belief that making distinctions between resources and capabilities is not particularly valuable to strategic decision makers and may simply reflect a theoretical distinction.[2]

A resource is a strength if it provides a company with a competitive advantage. It is something the firm does, or has the potential to do, particularly well relative to the abilities of existing or potential competitors. A resource is a weakness if it is something the organization does poorly or doesn't have the capacity to do, although its competitors have that capacity. Jay Barney, in his VRIO (Value, Rareness, Imitability, and Organization) framework of analysis, proposes four questions to evaluate each of a firm's key resources and the extent to which it contributes to competitive advantage.

1. **Value:** Does the resource provide value to consumers? Can it be used to capture opportunity or minimize threats? Can it contribute to profitable growth?

2. **Rareness:** Do other competitors possess the resource? Is it easy to acquire or transfer? The more firms there are that possess a particular resource, the less likely an organization will be to put itself at any relative advantage by using it.

3. **Imitability:** Is the resource costly or time-consuming for others to imitate? Is it proprietary or generic? Does it exist in a single source or in a number of interrelated processes? Anything that puts a rival organization at a cost disadvantage will create a competitive advantage for the firm possessing that resource.

4. **Organization:** Is the firm organized to exploit the resource? Does it have the employees, the management, and the capital necessary to use the resource optimally? Organizations must be aware of the potential of the resources they do possess, and develop a structure and culture that uses them in a way that supports its strategy.

If the answer to these questions is yes for a particular resource, that resource is considered a strength and a distinctive competency.[3] It in turn will lead to a competitive advantage of a certain degree.

USING RESOURCES TO GAIN COMPETITIVE ADVANTAGE

An organization experiences a competitive advantage when its behaviours create above-average returns and allow it to withstand competition. At the root of this concept, therefore, are *value* and *difference*. The VRIO framework provides a systematic way of looking at organizational resources to determine how strong a competitive advantage will be. But how does an organization know that its resources are being used optimally to create the strongest competitive advantage possible? What different forms can value and difference take in creating advantage? A competitive advantage therefore requires three things:

1. Customers perceive an important difference between the producer's products and those of rival firms.

2. A resource gap exists between the producer and rival firms that allows for these product differences.

3. Differences in product attributes and the resource gap underlying them can be expected to endure over time.[4]

Competitive advantage is therefore firmly rooted in differences between rival firms—differences in the products they offer for sale and differences in organizational resources. But being different is not necessarily sufficient for competitive advantages to arise. These differences must be valued in the market for the organization to gain from them. This can usually reflected in three ways:

- Tangible differences in product attributes such as price, quality, function, availability, and post-sales service

- Consumer preference for these differences as they reflect key buying criteria

- The ability of product differences to command the attention and loyalty of a significant customer base, called a "footprint in the market"

Underlying the ability to create these differences are resource differences that competitors cannot readily imitate. Understanding resource gaps between competitive firms is therefore crucial to determining the extent to which an organization will experience a competitive advantage. Proposing that a company's sustained competitive advantage is primarily determined by its resource endowments in relation to rival firms, Robert Grant proposes a five-step resource-based approach to strategy analysis.

1. Identify and classify the firm's resources in terms of strengths and weaknesses.

2. Combine the firm's strengths into specific capabilities. Organizational capabilities—often called **core competencies**—are the things that an organization can do exceedingly well. When these capabilities, or competencies, are superior to those of competitors, they are often called **distinctive competencies**.

3. Appraise the profit potential of these resources and capabilities in terms of two things: their potential for sustainable competitive advantage and the firm's ability to harvest the profits resulting from the use of these resources and capabilities.

4. Select the strategy that best exploits the firm's resources and capabilities relative to external opportunities.

5. Identify resource gaps and invest in upgrading weaknesses.[5]

As indicated in the second step above, when an organization's resources are combined, they form a number of capabilities. In the example of IMAX Corporation, IMAX has world-class capabilities in engineering and technological innovation. It has used these capabilities to create high-quality sounds and images in large-screen formats, in addition to enhancing previously produced films for re-release in new formats. At the heart of its products is proprietary technology, some of which it licensed and successfully commercialized, while others were developed internally.

DETERMINING THE SUSTAINABILITY OF AN ADVANTAGE

Just because a firm is able to use its resources and capabilities to develop a competitive advantage does not mean it will be able to sustain the advantage. Two characteristics determine the sustainability of a firm's distinctive competency (or competencies): durability and imitability.

Durability is the rate at which a firm's underlying resources (including its core competencies) depreciate or become obsolete. New technology can make a company's core competency obsolete or irrelevant. For example, Intel's skills in using basic technology developed by others to manufacture and market quality microprocessors was a crucial capability until management realized that the firm had taken current technology as far as possible with the Pentium chip. Without basic R & D of its own, the company would have slowly lost its competitive advantage to others.

Imitability is the rate at which a firm's underlying resources (including its core competencies) can be duplicated by others. To the extent that a firm's distinctive competency gives it competitive advantage in the marketplace, competitors will do what they can to learn and imitate that set of skills and capabilities. Competitors' efforts may range from **reverse engineering** (taking apart a competitor's product to find out how it works) to hiring employees from the competitor, to outright patent infringement. A core competency can be easily imitated to the extent that it is transparent, transferable, and replicable.

■ **Transparency** is the speed with which other firms can understand the relationship of resources and capabilities supporting a successful firm's strategy. For example, Gillette has always supported its dominance in the marketing of razors with excellent R & D. A competitor could never understand how the Sensor or Mach 3 razor was produced simply by taking one apart. Gillette's Sensor razor design, in particular, was very difficult to copy, partially because the manufacturing equipment needed to produce it was so expensive and complicated.

---

core competencies capabilities an organization excels at

distinctive competencies capabilities that are superior to those of rival firms

durability of competitive advantage the rate at which the organizational resources creating competitive advantage depreciate, become obsolete, or become inefficient

imitability of competitive advantage the rate at which the organizational resources creating competitive advantage can be copied by rivals

reverse engineering the process of taking apart a product to determine how it functions and/or how it was made

transparency how quickly other firms understand the relationship of resources and capabilities supporting a successful firm's strategy

Transferability the ability of a firm to gather resources and capabilities to support a competitive challenge

replicability the ability of a firm to duplicate resources and capabilities to imitate another firm's success

- **Transferability** is the ability of competitors to gather the resources and capabilities necessary to support a competitive challenge. For example, it may be very difficult for a winemaker in the United States to duplicate a Canadian winery's key resources of land and climate that result in the world's best icewine. If the know-how required in the winemaking process is added to the list of a vineyard's valuable resources, transferring resources becomes extremely difficult.

- **Replicability** is the ability of competitors to use duplicated resources and capabilities to imitate another firm's success. For example, Wal-Mart's sophisticated cross-docking system, which provides the company a substantial cost advantage by improving its ability to reduce shipping and handling costs, has proved difficult to replicate. Although Wal-Mart has the same resources in terms of retail space, employee skills, and equipment as many other discount chains, it has the unique capability to manage its resources for maximum productivity.[6]

explicit knowledge knowledge that can be easily learned, articulated, and communicated

tacit knowledge knowledge that resides in an organization's culture or people's attitudes, behaviour, and memory that is difficult to observe, learn, or understand

It is relatively easy to learn and imitate another company's core competency or capability if it derives from **explicit knowledge**, that is, knowledge that can be easily articulated and communicated. This is the type of knowledge that competitive intelligence activities can quickly identify and communicate. **Tacit knowledge**, in contrast, is knowledge that is *not* easily communicated because it is deeply rooted in employee experience or in an organization's culture.[7] Tacit knowledge is more valuable and more likely to lead to a sustainable competitive advantage than is explicit knowledge because it is much harder for competitors to imitate. The knowledge may be complex and combined with other types of knowledge in an unclear fashion in such a way that even management cannot clearly explain the competency.[8] Because Procter & Gamble's successful approach to brand management is primarily composed of tacit knowledge, the firm's top management is very reluctant to make any significant modifications to it, fearing that they might destroy the very thing they are trying to improve.

slow-cycle resources resources protected from imitation through their basis in tacit knowledge or proprietary knowledge

fast-cycle resources tangible resources relatively easily imitated because of their basis in explicit knowledge

An organization's resources and capabilities can be placed on a continuum indicating the extent to which they are durable and can't be imitated (that is, aren't transparent, transferable, or replicable) by another firm. This continuum of sustainability is depicted in **Figure 4–1**. At one extreme are **slow-cycle resources**, which are sustainable because they are shielded by patents, geography, strong brand names, or tacit knowledge. These resources and capabilities are distinctive competencies because they provide a sustainable competitive advantage. Gillette's Sensor razor is a good example of a product built around slow-cycle resources. The other extreme includes **fast-cycle resources**, which face the highest imitation pressures because they are based on a concept or technology that can be easily duplicated, such as Sony's Walkman. To the extent that a company has fast-cycle resources, the primary way it can compete successfully is through increased speed from lab to marketplace. Otherwise, it has no real sustainable competitive advantage. For example, with its low-cost position, reputation for safe, on-time flights, and its dedicated workforce, WestJet has successfully built a sustainable competitive advantage based on relatively slow-cycle resources. Its resources are durable and can't be easily imitated because they lack transparency, transferability, and replicability.

4.2 Value Chain Analysis

value chain analysis a systematic way of examining organizational activities that identifies sources of competitive advantage

A good way to begin an organizational analysis is to ascertain where a firm's products are located in the overall value chain. A value chain is a linked set of value-creating activities beginning with the acquisition from suppliers of basic raw materials, moving on to a series of value-added activities involved in producing and marketing a product or service, continuing with the distributor's efforts to get the finished goods into the hands of the consumer, and concluding with after-sales service and support. The focus of **value chain analysis** is to

Figure 4–1 Continuum of Resource Sustainability

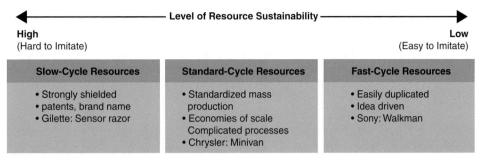

Source: Suggested by J.R. Williams, "How Sustainable Is Your Competitive Advantage?" *California Management Review* (Spring 1992), p. 33. Copyright © 1992 by the Regents of the University of California. Reprinted by permission of the Regents.

examine the organization in the context of the overall chain of value-creating activities, of which the firm may be only a small part.

Very few organizations encompass a product's entire value chain. Ford Motor Company did when it was managed by its founder, Henry Ford I. During the 1920s and 1930s, the company owned its own iron mines, ore-carrying ships, and a small rail line to bring ore to its mile-long River Rouge plant in Detroit. A similar case is that of J.D. Irving, Limited, a diversified, family-owned company based in Saint John, New Brunswick. Irving is highly integrated in both its paper products and oil businesses, choosing to conduct as many value chain activities as possible in-house rather than to rely on outside suppliers or distributors. In its oil business, Irving controls just about all activities except for exploration. It has large refining operations in eastern Canada, an aviation division that supplies many North American airlines, a home heating division that sells and maintains high-efficiency home heating systems, a natural gas division using gas from the Sable Island project, a lubricants division that tests and distributes a wide range of industrial products, a large fleet to transport its products to various production facilities, and a large network of retail service stations. Irving Forest Products manufactures a full and wide range of forest products including kraft pulp, newsprint, tissue, and corrugated medium. Irving owns and operates 16 sawmills in eastern Canada, producing softwood and hardwood lumber as well as many value-added products. An integrated sea, rail, and truck transportation network supports the movement of Irving's forest products to markets in the Caribbean, Europe, and the northeastern United States.

INDUSTRY VALUE CHAIN ANALYSIS

The value chains of most industries can be split into two segments: *upstream* and *downstream*. In the petroleum industry, for example, upstream refers to oil exploration, drilling, and moving the crude oil to the refinery, and downstream refers to refining the oil plus the transporting and marketing of gasoline and refined oil to distributors and gas station retailers. Even though most large oil companies are completely integrated, they often vary in the amount of expertise they have at each part of the value chain. Irving Oil, for example, has its greatest expertise downstream in marketing and retailing. Others, such as PanCanadian Petroleum, are more dominant in upstream activities such as exploration.

An industry can be analyzed in terms of the profit margin available at any one point along the value chain. For example, the auto manufacturers' revenues and profits are divided among many value chain activities, including manufacturing, new and used car sales, gasoline retailing, insurance, after-sales service and parts, and lease financing. From a revenue standpoint, auto manufacturers dominate the industry, accounting for almost 60% of total industry revenues. Profits are, however, a different matter. Auto leasing is the most profitable activity in the value chain, followed by insurance and auto loans. The core activities of manufacturing and distribution, however, earn significantly smaller shares of the total industry profits than they do of total revenues. For example, since auto sales have become marginally profitable, dealerships are now emphasizing service and repair. As a result of various differences along the industry value chain, manufacturers have moved aggressively into auto financing. Ford, for example, generates nearly half its profits from financing, even though financing accounts for less than 20% of the company's revenues.[9]

In analyzing the complete value chain of a product, note that even if a firm operates up and down the entire industry chain, it usually has an area of primary expertise where its primary activities lie. A company's **centre of gravity** is the part of the chain that is most important to the company and the point where its greatest expertise and capabilities lie—its core competencies. According to J.R. Galbraith, a company's centre of gravity is usually the point at which the company started. After a firm successfully establishes itself at this point by obtaining a competitive advantage, one of its first strategic moves is to move forward or backward along the value chain to reduce costs, guarantee access to key raw materials, or guarantee distribution.[10] This process is called *vertical integration* and is discussed in more detail in **Chapter 6**.

The idea of a centre of gravity can also be understood by thinking of an organization's core competencies. By definition a core competency is the activity that the organization performs best. As a result, it is usually central to the success of the organization. Bombardier, for example, became successful by inventing the snowmobile. Next it developed expertise in the research and development of motors, which it subsequently used in a variety of transportation products. Ricoh Corporation was one of the world's largest camera manufacturers before it adapted its lens technologies for use in photocopiers and optical disk storage systems. Nortel built on its telephone and packet switching devices to take advantage of the networking demands created by increased internet usage. As all of these examples illustrate, a strength in one value chain activity can be used to build strength in adjacent activities, or it can be leveraged into other related products or markets. According to the resource-based view of the firm, organizations will be successful when they acquire the resources that allow their business units to adapt quickly to changing opportunities. Without strength in at least one value chain activity, the organization has little chance of withstanding competition and has a very weak foundation for future growth.

centre of gravity the value chain activity that is most central to the success of a firm

VALUE CHAIN ANALYSIS

Each organization has its own internal value chain of activities. See **Figure 4–2** for an example of a value chain. Michael Porter proposes that a manufacturing firm's **primary activities** usually begin with inbound logistics (raw materials handling and warehousing), go through an operations process in which a product is manufactured, and continue on to outbound logistics (warehousing and distribution), marketing and sales, and finally service (installation, repair, and sale of parts). Several **support activities**, such as procurement (purchasing), technology development (R & D), human resource management, and firm infrastructure (accounting, finance, strategic planning), ensure that the primary value chain activities operate effectively and efficiently. Each of a company's product lines has its own distinctive value chain. Because most organizations make several different products or services, an internal analysis of the firm involves analyzing a series of different value chains.

primary activities activities involved in the physical creation of a product, its sale to buyers, and post-sale service

support activities activities that support primary activities by providing various organization-wide functions

The systematic examination of individual value activities can lead to a better understanding of a firm's strengths and weaknesses. According to Porter, "Differences among competitor value chains are a key source of competitive advantage."[11] Value chain analysis involves the following three steps:

1. *Identify Value Activities.* The first step is to identify and isolate the technologically distinct

Figure 4–2 An Organization's Value Chain

Source: Adapted and reprinted with the permission of The Free Press, an imprint of Simon & Schuster, from *Competitive Advantage: Creating and Sustaining Superior Performance* by Michael E. Porter, p. 37. Copyright © 1985, 1988 by Michael E. Porter.

activities necessary for producing the product. For example, broad categories like manufacturing should be broken down into specific activities based on product flow, so that each can be analyzed for its relative value contribution. Everything an organization does needs to be captured in a primary or support activity so that areas of strength and weakness can be identified. Where is the most value created? The answer to this question points to activities that can be considered strengths (core competencies). Do any of the strengths provide competitive advantage such that they can be labelled distinctive competencies? Where is the least value created? The answer to this points to areas of weakness. These can be the target of development programs or may be considered for outsourcing.

2. *Examine the "linkages" within the value chain.* The value chain is not simply a collection of independent activities but rather a network of interdependent activities. Linkages are the connections between the way one activity (for example, marketing) is performed and the cost of performance of another (for example, quality control). In seeking ways for an organization to gain competitive advantage in the marketplace, look for ways to optimize or coordinate the linkages between activities in order to gain competitive advantage. There are three generic ways to do this:

    ■ The same function can be performed in different ways with different results. For example, quality inspection of 100% of output by the workers themselves instead of the usual 10% by quality control inspectors might increase production costs, but that increase could be more than offset by the savings obtained from reducing the number of repair people needed to fix defective products and increasing the amount of salespeople's time devoted to selling instead of exchanging defective products.

    ■ The efficiency of direct activities can be improved by superior indirect activities. For example, better information systems allow large retailers like Canadian Tire to manage its inventory more efficiently, gather real-time data from its stores, and interface with its larger suppliers. This can reduce costs in logistics management, minimize transportation costs by reducing the number of deliveries to stores, and eliminate many inventory stockouts.

- Activities performed internally will reduce the need to service products in the field. For example, the Six Sigma quality program used at Bombardier can substantially reduce service costs of the transportation equipment it sells around the world. This reflects a trade-off in activities, a decision to spend more in one area not only to spend much less in another, but also to enhance the organization's reputation for quality.[12]

3. *Identify possible areas for achieving economies of scope.* Each value element, such as advertising or manufacturing, has an inherent economy of scale in which activities are conducted at their lowest possible cost per unit of output. If a particular product is not being produced at a high enough level to reach economies of scale in distribution, another product could be used to share the same distribution channel. This is an example of economies of scope, which result when the value chains of two separate products or services share activities, such as the same marketing channels or manufacturing facilities. For example, the cost of joint production of multiple products can be less than the cost of separate production.

4.3 Scanning Functional Resources

The simplest way to begin an analysis of a firm's value chain is by carefully examining its traditional functional areas for potential strengths and weaknesses. Functional resources include not only the financial, physical, and human assets in each area, but also the ability of the people in each area to formulate and implement the necessary functional objectives, strategies, and policies. The resources include the knowledge of analytical concepts and procedural techniques common to each area as well as the ability of the people in each area to use them effectively. If used properly, these resources serve as strengths to carry out value-added activities and support strategic decisions. In addition to the usual business functions of marketing, finance, R & D, operations, human resources, and information systems, we also discuss structure and culture as key parts of a business organization's value chain.

BASIC ORGANIZATIONAL STRUCTURES

organizational structure how work is divided between people, grouped into departments, and coordinated to achieve organizational goals

simple structure an organizational structure with little departmentalization and hierarchy, controlled directly by the CEO

functional structure an organizational structure built around groupings of people doing similar jobs

Although there is an almost infinite variety of structural forms, certain basic types predominate in modern complex organizations. **Figure 4–3** illustrates three basic types of **organizational structures.** Generally speaking, each structure tends to support some strategies over others.

- **Simple structures** have no functional or product categories and are appropriate for a small, entrepreneur-dominated company with one or two product lines that operates in a reasonably small, easily identifiable market niche. Employees tend to be generalists and supervision tends to occur directly, through the chain of command. The strength of this structure lies in having a small number of people working in close proximity, each knowing a great deal about most activities. This type of structure is usually quite flat, calling for a minimum of supervisors and managers between line workers and the CEO.

- **Functional structures** are appropriate for a medium-sized firm with several related product lines in one industry, or to organize the smaller divisions of larger organizations. Employees tend to be specialists in the business functions important to that industry, such as manufacturing, marketing, finance, and human resources. This structure permits efficiency gains from the fact that people performing similar functions are working closely

Figure 4–3 Basic Organizational Structures

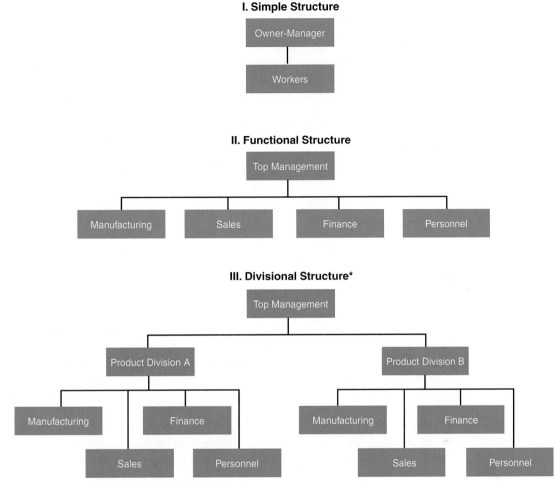

*Conglomerate structure is a variant of the divisional structure.

together. Not only are there benefits from learning associated with this, but there is also the possibility of eliminating the duplication of support activities in multiple departments. Within a functional department, communication should be enhanced because of employees' similar backgrounds and training.

divisional structure an organizational structure built around groupings of products, customers, or geographic markets to allow for customization and fast response within each division

conglomerate structure a form of divisional structure characterized by largely independent businesses in distinct markets, operating under one corporate umbrella

- **Divisional structures** are appropriate for a large organization with many product lines in several related industries, or in different geographic locations. Employees tend to be functional specialists organized according to product or market distinctions. The Royal Bank of Canada, for example, groups its various services primarily into personal and commercial sectors. It also has separate divisions for insurance, investments, capital markets, and global services. Beyond this, there are geographic divisions to reflect the physical separation of markets like Asia and the Caribbean, as well as the local regulations of these markets. The **conglomerate structure** is a variant of the divisional structure. It is appropriate for a large organization with many distinct or autonomous businesses in unrelated industries. Each division represents an autonomous product division that receives leadership from the CEO.

If the current organizational structure does not easily support a strategy under consideration, management must decide whether the proposed strategy is feasible or whether the structure should be changed to a more advanced structure such as the matrix or network. (Structural design is discussed further in **Chapter 7**.)

ORGANIZATIONAL CULTURE: THE COMPANY WAY

There is an oft-told story of a person new to a company asking an experienced co-worker what an employee should do when a customer calls. The old-timer responds: "There are three ways to do any job: the right way, the wrong way, and the company way. Around here, we always do things the company way." In most organizations, the "company way" is derived from the organization's culture. **Organizational culture** is the collection of beliefs, expectations, and values learned and shared by an organization's members and transmitted from one generation of employees to another. The organizational culture generally reflects the values of the founder(s) and the mission of the firm.[13] It gives a company a sense of identity: *This is who we are. This is what we do. This is what we stand for.* The culture includes the dominant orientation of the company, such as research and development at Hewlett-Packard, customer service

organizational culture
the shared understandings of appropriate behaviour within an organization

---

TELUS Implements All-Employee Stock Option Plan

TELUS Mobility of Burnaby, BC, implemented an innovative plan designed as a competitive advantage in retaining and attracting talent and rewarding employees. By extending employee stock options to every employee in the company, TELUS has set itself apart in the Canadian telecommunications industry. In March 2001 it launched a three-year plan to provide 300 stock options to each and every employee (beyond management, who were already participating in an existing plan). According to the Conference Board of Canada, only 6.5% of mid- to large-sized businesses in Canada currently provide universal employee stock options.

"The TELUS employee stock options plan is fundamental in building a truly high-performance culture," said Darren Entwistle, TELUS president and CEO. "It is the TELUS team that will set our company apart and give us a competitive advantage, so it is very important we motivate and reward employees by linking employee wealth creation to company performance. The federal human resources minister spoke of a critical skilled-worker shortage in Canada and I can tell you TELUS is not being caught off-guard," Entwistle added. "I'm proud to say our company is leading the way with this significant demonstration of TELUS' commitment to employees and, by extension, shareholders.

"Beyond employees, our shareholders benefit from TELUS' enhanced ability to attract and retain skilled people and through TELUS' new, performance-based culture of which the stock options plan is an important element," said Entwistle. "The stock options plan is part of a major program underway at TELUS aimed at cultivating a performance culture based on teamwork, growth and innovation. The program makes culture a key competitive advantage and includes education and training incentives and support."

Source: www.telusmobility.com/about/press_room/releases/march_2001_TELUS_all-employee_stock_options.html (accessed July 24, 2003).

at Nordstrom, or product quality at Maytag. It often includes a number of informal work rules (forming the "company way") that employees follow without question. These work practices over time become part of a company's unquestioned tradition. The example of TELUS Mobility shows how a high-performance organizational culture can be used to create a strong competitive advantage.

cultural intensity the degree of acceptance of an organization's culture

Organizational culture has two distinct attributes, intensity and integration.[14] **Cultural intensity** is the degree to which members of a unit accept the norms, values, or other cultural content associated with the unit. This shows the culture's depth. Organizations with strong norms promoting a particular value, such as quality at Maytag, have intensive cultures, whereas new firms (or those in transition) have weaker, less intensive cultures. Employees in an intensive culture tend to exhibit consistent behaviour; that is, they tend to act similarly over time. **Cultural integration** is the extent to which units throughout an organization share a common culture. This is the culture's breadth. Organizations with a pervasive dominant culture may be hierarchically controlled and power-oriented, such as a military unit, and have highly integrated cultures. All employees tend to hold the same cultural values and norms. In contrast, a company that is structured into diverse units by functions or divisions usually exhibits some strong subcultures (for example, R & D versus manufacturing) and a less integrated organizational culture.

cultural integration the extent to which a culture is shared by all the members of an organization

Organizational culture fulfills several important functions in an organization:

1. It conveys a sense of identity to employees.

2. It helps generate employee commitment to something greater than themselves.

3. It adds to the stability of the organization as a social system.

4. It serves as a frame of reference for employees to use to make sense out of organizational activities and to use as a guide for appropriate behaviour.[15]

Organizational culture shapes the behaviour of people in the organization. Because these cultures have a powerful influence on the behaviour of people at all levels, they can strongly affect a firm's ability to shift its strategic direction. A strong culture should not only promote survival, but it should also create the basis for a superior competitive position. For example, a culture emphasizing constant renewal may help a company adapt to a changing, hypercompetitive environment.[16] To the extent that a firm's distinctive competency is embedded in an organization's culture, it will be a form of tacit knowledge and very difficult for a competitor to imitate.[17] Organizations with strong cultures, however, experience a trade-off with respect to their ability to adapt and respond in the context of environmental change. Strong cultures promote reliable performance in relatively stable environments, but as volatility increases, the reliability benefits of strong cultures disappear. This suggests that strong-culture firms are better at exploiting established competencies than discovering new ones that might better suit changing environmental conditions.[18] See the **Global Issue** feature to see how the Swiss company ABB Asea Brown Boveri AG uses its organizational culture to develop and maintain a competitive advantage in a global industry.

A change in mission, objectives, strategies, or policies is not likely to be successful if it is in opposition to the accepted culture of the firm. Foot-dragging and even sabotage may result as employees fight to resist a radical change in philosophy. As with organizational structure, if an organization's culture is compatible with a new strategy, it is an internal strength. But if the organizational culture is not compatible with the proposed strategy, it is a serious weakness.

Global Issue

ABB Uses Organizational Culture as a Competitive Advantage

Zurich-based ABB Asea Brown Boveri AG is a worldwide builder of power plants, electrical equipment, and industrial factories in 140 countries. By establishing one set of values throughout its global operations, ABB's management believes that the company will gain an advantage over its rivals Siemens AG of Germany, France's Alcatel-Alsthom NV, and the US's General Electric Company.

Percy Barnevik, Swedish chairman of ABB, managed the merger that created ABB from Sweden's Asea AB and Switzerland's BBC Brown Boveri Ltd. At that time both companies were far behind the world leaders in electrical equipment and engineering. Barnevik introduced his concept of a company with no geographic base—one that had many

"home" markets that could draw on expertise from around the globe. To do this, he created a set of 500 global managers who could adapt to local cultures while executing ABB's global strategies. These people are multilingual and move around each of ABB's 5000 profit centres in 140 countries. Their assignment is to cut costs, improve efficiency, and integrate local businesses with the ABB world view.

ABB requires local business units, such as Mexico's motor factory, to report both to one of ABB's travelling global managers and to a business area manager who sets global motor strategy for ABB. When the goals of the local factory conflict with worldwide priorities, it is up to the global manager to resolve the conflict.

Few multinational corporations are as successful as ABB in getting global strategies to work with local operations. In agreement with the resource-based view of the firm, Barnevik states, "Our strength comes from pulling together.... If you can make this work real well, then you get a competitive edge out of the organization which is very, very difficult to copy."

Source: J. Guyon, "ABB Fuses Units with One Set of Values," *The Wall Street Journal* (October 2, 1996), p. A15. Copyright © 1996 by *The Wall Street Journal*. Reprinted by permission of *The Wall Street Journal* via the Copyright Clearance Center.

STRATEGIC MARKETING ISSUES

The marketing manager is the company's primary link to the customer and the competition. The manager, therefore, must be especially concerned with the market position and marketing mix of the firm.

Market Position and Segmentation

Market position deals with the question, Who are our customers? It refers to the selection of specific areas for marketing concentration and can be expressed in terms of market, product, and geographical locations. Through market research, organizations are able to practise market segmentation with various products or services so that managers can discover what niches to seek, which new types of products to develop, and how to ensure that a company's many products do not directly compete with one another.

Marketing Mix

The marketing mix refers to the particular combination of key variables under the organization's control that can be used to affect demand and to gain competitive advantage. These variables are product, place, promotion, and price. Within each of these four variables are several subvariables, listed in **Table 4–1**, which should be analyzed in terms of their effects on divisional and firm performance.

Product Life Cycle

One of the most useful concepts in marketing, insofar as strategic management is concerned, is that of the product life cycle. As depicted in **Figure 4–4**, the product life cycle is a graph

Table 4–1 Marketing Mix Variables

Product	Place	Promotion	Price
Quality	Channels	Advertising	List price
Features	Coverage	Personal selling	Discounts
Options	Locations	Sales promotion	Allowances
Style	Inventory	Publicity	Payment pereiods
Brand name	Transport	Credit items	
Packing			
Sizes			
Services			
Warranties			
Returns			

Source: Philip Kotler, *Marketing Management: Analysis, Planning, and Control*, 4th edition (Upper Saddle River, NJ: Prentice Hall, 1980), p. 89. Copyright © 1980. Reprinted by permission of Pearson Education, Inc., Upper Saddle River, NJ.

showing time plotted against the dollar sales of a product as it moves from introduction through growth and maturity to decline. This concept enables a marketing manager to examine the marketing mix of a particular product or group of products in terms of its position in its life cycle.

STRATEGIC FINANCIAL ISSUES

The financial manager must ascertain the best sources of funds, uses of funds, and control of funds. Cash must be raised from internal or external (local and global) sources and allocated for different uses. The flow of funds in the operations of the organization must be monitored.

Figure 4–4 Product Life Cycle

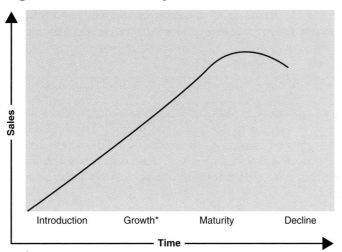

*The right end of the Growth stage is often called Competitive Turbulence because of price and distribution competition that shakes out the weaker competitors. For further information, see C.R. Wasson, *Dynamic Competitive Strategy and Product Life Cycles*, 3rd edition (Austin, TX: Austin Press, 1978).

To the extent that an organization is involved in international activities, currency fluctuations must be dealt with to ensure that profits aren't wiped out by the rise or fall of the dollar versus the yen, euro, or other currencies. Benefits in the form of returns, repayments, or products and services must be given to the sources of outside financing. All these tasks must be handled in a way that complements and supports overall strategy. A firm's capital structure (amounts of debt and equity) can influence its strategic choices. For example, increased debt tends to increase risk aversion and decrease the willingness of management to invest in R & D.[19]

Financial Leverage

The mix of externally generated short-term and long-term funds in relation to the amount and timing of internally generated funds should be appropriate to the organizational objectives, strategies, and policies. The concept of **financial leverage** (the ratio of total debt to total assets) is helpful in describing how debt is used to increase the earnings available to common shareholders. When the company finances its activities by sales of bonds or notes instead of through stock, the earnings per share are boosted; the interest paid on the debt reduces taxable income, but fewer shareholders share the profits than if the company had sold more stock to finance its activities. The debt, however, does raise the firm's break-even point above what it would have been if the firm had financed from internally generated funds only. High leverage may therefore be perceived as a strength in times of prosperity and ever-increasing sales, or as a weakness in times of a recession and falling sales. This is because leverage acts to magnify the effect on earnings per share of an increase or decrease in dollar sales. Research indicates that greater leverage has a positive impact on performance for firms in stable environments, but a negative impact for firms in dynamic environments.[20]

financial leverage the ability of an organization to use debt to maximize shareholder wealth

Capital Budgeting

capital budgeting the process of comparing the returns of alternative capital investments

Capital budgeting is the analyzing and ranking of possible investments in fixed assets such as land, buildings, and equipment in terms of the additional outlays and additional receipts that will result from each investment. A good finance department will be able to prepare such capital budgets and to rank them on the basis of some accepted criteria or hurdle rate (for example, years to pay back investment, rate of return, or time to break-even point) for the purpose of strategic decision making. Most firms have more than one hurdle rate and vary it as a function of the type of project being considered. Projects with high strategic significance, such as entering new markets or defending market share, will often have low hurdle rates.[21]

STRATEGIC RESEARCH AND DEVELOPMENT (R & D) ISSUES

The R & D manager is responsible for suggesting and implementing a company's technological strategy in light of its objectives and policies. The manager's job, therefore, involves (1) choosing among alternative new technologies to use within the organization, (2) developing methods of embodying the new technology in new products and processes, and (3) deploying resources so that the new technology can be successfully implemented.

R & D Intensity, Technological Competence, and Technology Transfer

R & D intensity the proportion of an organization's sales spent on research and development

The company must make available the resources necessary for effective research and development. A company's **R & D intensity** (its spending on R & D as a percentage of sales revenue) is a principal means of gaining market share in global competition. The amount spent on

R & D often varies by industry. For example, the US computer software industry spends an average of 13.5% of its sales dollar for R & D, whereas the paper and forest products industry spends only 1.0%.[22] A good guideline for R & D spending is that a firm should spend at a rate that is considered normal for that particular industry unless its strategic plan calls for unusual expenditures.

Simply spending money on R & D or new projects does not mean, however, that the money will produce useful results. For example, a few years ago Pharmacia Upjohn spent more of its revenues on research than any other company in any industry (18%) but was still ranked low in innovation.[23] A company's R & D unit should be evaluated for technological competence in both the development and the use of innovative technology. Not only should the organization make a consistent research effort (as measured by reasonably constant expenditures that result in usable innovations), it should also be proficient in managing research personnel and integrating their innovations into its day-to-day operations. If a company is not proficient in technology transfer, the process of taking a new technology from the laboratory to the marketplace, it will not gain much advantage from its technological advances. For example, Xerox Corporation has been criticized for failing to take advantage of various innovations (such as the mouse and the graphical user interface for personal computers) developed originally in its sophisticated Palo Alto Research Center.

R & D Mix

Basic R & D is conducted by scientists in well-equipped laboratories where the focus is on theoretical problem areas. The best indicators of a company's capability in this area are its patents and research publications. Product R & D concentrates on marketing and is concerned with product or product-packaging improvements. The best measurements of ability in this area are the number of successful new products introduced and the percentage of total sales and profits coming from products introduced within the past five years. Engineering (or process) R & D is concerned with engineering, concentrating on quality control and the development of design specifications and improved production equipment. A company's capability in this area can be measured by consistent reductions in unit manufacturing costs and by the number of product defects.

Most organizations will have a mix of basic, product, and process R & D, a mix that will vary by industry, company, and product line. The balance of these types of research is known as the R & D mix and should be appropriate to the strategy being considered and to each product's life cycle. For example, it is generally accepted that product R & D normally dominates the early stages of a product's life cycle (when the product's optimal form and features are still being debated), whereas process R & D becomes especially important in the later stages (when the product's design is solidified and the emphasis is on reducing costs and improving quality).

Impact of Technological Discontinuity on Strategy

technological discontinuity the replacement of old technologies by new ones as a result of innovation

The R & D manager must determine when to abandon present technology and when to develop or adopt new technology. Richard Foster of McKinsey and Company states that the displacement of one technology by another—**technological discontinuity**—is a frequent and strategically important phenomenon. Such a discontinuity occurs when a new technology cannot simply be used to enhance the current technology but actually substitutes for that technology to yield better performance. For each technology within a given field or industry, according to Foster, the plotting of product performance against research effort and expenditures on a graph results in an S-shaped curve. He describes the process depicted in **Figure 4–5**:

> *Early in the development of the technology a knowledge base is being built and progress requires a relatively large amount of effort. Later, progress comes more easily. And then, as the limits of that technology are approached, progress becomes slow and expensive. That is when R & D dollars should be allocated to technology with more potential. That is also—not so incidentally—when a competitor who has bet on a new technology can sweep away your business or topple an entire industry.*[24]

Computerized information technology is currently on the steep upward slope of its S-curve, where relatively small increments in R & D effort result in significant improvement in performance. This is an example of Moore's law, which states that silicon chips (microprocessors) double in complexity every 18 months. Proposed by Gordon Moore, co-founder of Intel, in 1965, the law originally stated that processor complexity would double in one year, but Moore soon changed it to two years. Others changed it to 18 months—the number now generally accepted. In 1965, 16 components could be placed on a silicon chip. By 2000, that number had grown exponentially to 10 million. According to Moore, "Moore's Law has been the name given to everything that changes exponentially in the industry."[25]

C.M. Christensen explains in *The Innovator's Dilemma* why this transition occurs when a "disruptive technology" enters an industry. In a study of computer disk drive manufacturers, he explains that established market leaders are typically reluctant to move in a timely manner to a new technology. This reluctance to switch technologies—even when the firm is aware of the new technology and may have even invented it—is because the resource allocation process in most companies gives priority to those projects, typically based on the old technology, with the greatest likelihood of generating a good return on investment. Those projects are the ones that appeal to the firm's current customers, whose products are also based on the characteristics of the old technology. For example, in the 1980s a disk drive manufacturer's customers, PC manufacturers, wanted a faster $5\frac{1}{4}$-inch drive with greater capacity. These PC makers were not interested in the new $3\frac{1}{2}$-inch drives based on the new technology because at that time the smaller drives were slower and had less capacity. The advantages of smaller size were irrelevant to them since these companies primarily made desktop personal computers that were designed to hold large drives.

Figure 4–5 Technological Discontinuity

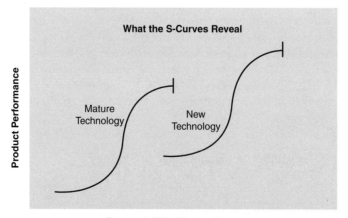

In the corporate planning process, it is generally assumed that incremental progress in technology will occur. But past developments in a given technology cannot be extrapolated into the future because every technology has its limits. The key to competitiveness is to determine when to shift resources to a technology with more potential.

Source: P. Pascarella, "Are You Investing in the Wrong Technology?" *Industry Week* (July 25, 1983), p. 38. Copyright © 1983 Penton Media, Inc., Cleveland, Ohio. All rights reserved. Reprinted with permission from *Industry Week.*

A new technology is generally riskier and of little appeal to the current customers of established firms. Products derived from a new technology are more expensive and do not meet the customers' requirements, which are based on the old technology. New entrepreneurial firms are typically more interested in the new technology because it is one way to appeal to a developing market niche in a market currently dominated by established companies. Even though the new technology may be more expensive to develop, it offers performance improvements in areas that are attractive to this small niche, though they may be of no consequence to the customers of the established competitors.

This was the case with the entrepreneurial manufacturers of $3\frac{1}{2}$-inch disk drives. These smaller drives appealed to the PC makers who were trying to increase their small PC market share by offering laptop computers. Size and weight were more important to these customers than were capacity and speed. By the time the new technology was developed to the point that the $3\frac{1}{2}$-inch drive matched and even surpassed the $5\frac{1}{4}$-inch drive in terms of speed and capacity (in addition to size and weight), it was too late for the established $5\frac{1}{4}$-inch disk drive firms to switch to the new technology. Once their customers began demanding smaller products using the new technology, the established firms were unable to respond quickly and lost their leadership position in the industry. They were able to remain in the industry (with a much reduced market share) only insofar as they were able to utilize the new technology to be competitive in the new product line.[26]

STRATEGIC OPERATIONS ISSUES

The primary task of the operations (manufacturing or service) manager is to develop and operate a system that will produce the required number of products or services, with a certain quality, at a given cost, within an allotted time. Many of the key concepts and techniques popularly used in manufacturing can be applied to service businesses.

intermittent systems a production process that produces items sequentially, either individually or in batches

In very general terms, manufacturing can be intermittent or continuous. In **intermittent systems** (job shops), the item is normally processed sequentially, but the work and sequence of the process vary. An example is an auto body repair shop. At each location, the tasks determine the details of processing and the time required for them. These job shops can be very labour-intensive. For example, a job shop usually has little automated machinery and thus a low level of fixed costs. It has a fairly low break-even point, but its variable cost line (comprising wages and costs of special parts) has a relatively steep slope. Because most of the costs associated with the product are variable (many employees earn piece-rate wages), a job shop's variable costs are higher than those of automated firms. Its advantage over other firms is that it can operate at low levels and still be profitable. After a job shop's sales reach break-even, however, the huge variable costs as a percentage of total costs keep the profit per unit at a relatively low level. In terms of strategy, this firm should look for a niche in the marketplace for which it can produce and sell a reasonably small quantity of goods.

continuous system a production process that produces items in a continuous process

In contrast, **continuous systems** are those laid out as lines on which products can be continuously assembled or processed. An example is an automobile assembly line. A firm using continuous systems invests heavily in fixed investments such as automated processes and highly sophisticated machinery. Its labour force, relatively small but highly skilled, earns salaries rather than piece-rate wages. Consequently this firm has a high amount of fixed costs. It also has a relatively high break-even point, but its variable cost line rises slowly. This is an example of **operating leverage**, the impact of a specific change in sales volume on net operating income. The advantage of high operating leverage is that once the firm reaches break-even, its profits rise faster than do those of less automated firms having lower operating leverage. Continuous systems reap benefits from economies of scale. In terms of strategy, this firm needs to find a high-demand niche in the marketplace for which it can produce and sell a large quantity of goods. However, a firm with high operating leverage is likely to suffer huge losses during a recession. During an economic downturn, the firm with less automa-

operating leverage a cost/profit relationship where relatively small changes in sales volume translate into relatively large increases in net income

tion and thus less leverage is more likely to survive comfortably because a drop in sales primarily affects variable costs. It is often easier to lay off labour than to sell off specialized plants and machines.

Experience Curve

experience curve the decline in costs associated with accumulated experience

A conceptual framework that many large organizations have used successfully is the **experience curve** (originally called the learning curve). The experience curve suggests that unit production costs decline by some fixed percentage (commonly 20% to 30%) each time the total accumulated volume of production in units doubles. The actual percentage varies by industry and is based on many variables: the amount of time it takes a person to learn a new task, scale economies, product and process improvements, and lower raw materials costs, among others. For example, in an industry with an 85% experience curve, an organization might expect a 15% reduction in unit costs for every doubling of volume. The total costs per unit can be expected to drop from $100, when the total production is 10 units, to $85 ($100 × 85%) when production doubles to 20 units, and to $72.25 ($85 × 85%) when it doubles again to 40 units. Achieving these results often means investing in R & D and fixed assets; higher fixed costs and less flexibility thus result. Nevertheless the manufacturing strategy is one of building capacity ahead of demand to achieve the lower unit costs that develop from the experience curve. When it has reached some future point on the experience curve, the organization should price the product or service very low to pre-empt competition and increase market demand. The resulting high number of units sold and high market share should result in high profits, based on the low unit costs.

Management commonly uses the experience curve in estimating the production costs of (1) a new product made with the current techniques and processes or (2) a current product if it were produced by newly introduced techniques or processes. The concept was first applied in the airframe industry and can be applied in the service industry as well. For example, an office-cleaning company can reduce its costs per employee by having its workers use the same equipment and techniques to clean many adjacent offices in one office building rather than cleaning just a few offices in each of several buildings. Although many firms have used experience curves extensively, an unquestioning acceptance of the industry norm (such as 80% for the airframe industry or 70% for integrated circuits) is very risky. The experience curve of the industry as a whole might not hold true for a particular company for a variety of reasons.

Flexible Manufacturing for Mass Customization

mass customization production systems that can profitably produce small batches of individually customized products

flexible manufacturing production systems that can profitably generate low-volume output of many different products

Recently the use of large, continuous, mass-production facilities to take advantage of experience-curve economies has been criticized. The use of **C**omputer-**A**ssisted **D**esign and **C**omputer-**A**ssisted **M**anufacturing (CAD/CAM) and robot technology means that learning times are shorter and products can be economically manufactured in small, customized batches in a process called **mass customization**—the low-cost production of individually customized goods and services.[27] Economies of scope (in which common parts of the manufacturing activities of various products are combined to gain economies even though small numbers of each product are made) replace economies of scale (in which unit costs are reduced by making large numbers of the same product) in flexible manufacturing. **Flexible manufacturing** permits the low-volume output of custom-tailored products at relatively low unit costs through economies of scope. It is thus possible to have the cost advantages of continuous systems with the customer-oriented advantages of intermittent systems.

STRATEGIC HUMAN RESOURCE MANAGEMENT (HRM) ISSUES

The primary task of the manager of human resources is to improve the match between individuals and jobs. A good HRM department should know how to use attitude surveys and other feedback devices to assess employees' satisfaction with their jobs and with the organization as a whole. HRM managers should also use job analysis to obtain job description information about what each job needs to accomplish in terms of quality and quantity. Up-to-date job descriptions are essential not only for proper employee selection, appraisal, training, and development for wage and salary administration, and for labour negotiations, but also for summarizing the organization-wide human resources in terms of employee-skill categories. Just as a company must know the number, type, and quality of its manufacturing facilities, it must also know the kinds of people it employs and the skills they possess. The best strategies are meaningless if employees do not have the skills to carry them out or if jobs cannot be designed to accommodate the available workers. Hewlett-Packard, for example, uses employee profiles to ensure that it has the right mix of talents to implement its planned strategies.

Use of Teams

Management is beginning to realize that it must be more flexible in its utilization of employees in order for human resources to be a strength. Human resource managers, therefore, need to be knowledgeable about work options such as part-time work, job sharing, flex-time, extended leaves, contract work, and especially the proper use of teams. Many large companies are successfully using **autonomous (self-managing) work teams**, in which a group of people work together without a supervisor to plan, coordinate, and evaluate their own work.[28] Nortel found that productivity and quality increased with work teams to such an extent that it was able to reduce the number of quality inspectors by 40%.[29]

> **autonomous work teams** work groups that function in the absence of a formal supervisor
>
> **cross-functional work teams** teams that consist of employees from many functional areas, each contributing to the production of a finished product

One way to move a product more quickly through its development stage is to use **cross-functional work teams**. Instead of developing products in a series of steps—beginning with a request from sales, which leads to design, then to engineering, purchasing, and finally manufacturing (often resulting in a costly product rejected by the customer)—companies are tearing down the traditional walls separating the departments so that people from each discipline can get involved in projects early on. In a process called concurrent engineering, the once-isolated specialists now work side by side and compare notes constantly in an effort to design cost-effective products with features customers want. Taking this approach enabled car manufacturers like Volvo and Chrysler to reduce the product development cycle by almost 50%.[30] For such cross-functional work teams to be successful, the groups must receive training and coaching. Otherwise, poorly implemented teams may worsen morale, create divisiveness, and raise the level of cynicism among workers.[31]

Union Relations and Temporary Workers

If the organization is unionized, a good human resource manager should be able to work closely with the union. Union membership in Canada has grown steadily during the last century, periods of war notwithstanding. In 2001 there were just over four million union members in Canada. The greatest change in union membership has been the increase in female members, who now account for half of the country's union members. In the past, unions represented blue-collar manufacturing labourers, most of whom were white males who worked full-time. Today we see increasing representation of part-time workers and white-collar workers in a wider range of industries. These changes can be attributed to the increasing participation of women in the labour force in general, in addition to unionization of the public sector where large numbers of women work. The growth in Canadian union membership since 1967 can be attributed almost exclusively to increasing numbers of female members. At the same time, de-industrialization has resulted in significant job losses in the manufacturing sector, a traditional union stronghold.[32]

Outside Canada, the average proportion of unionized workers among major industrialized nations is around 50%. European unions tend to be militant, politically oriented, and much less interested in working with management to increase efficiency. Nationwide strikes can occur quickly. Japanese unions are typically tied to individual companies and are usually supportive of management. In America, union membership has steadily dropped to approximately 15%. These differences among countries have significant implications for the management of multinational organizations.

To increase flexibility, avoid layoffs, and reduce labour costs, organizations are using more temporary workers. Since 1975, the proportion of these workers has increased to almost 20% of the workforce. Most of this increase is due to more **involuntary part-time work**, the work done by people who desire full-time work but cannot find it. Sometimes part-time working arrangements are mutually beneficial to workers and their employers. People with family responsibilities or students, for instance, may prefer to work part-time. The involuntary part-time workers, however, are forced into working fewer hours than they would like, perhaps even working for multiple employers to work the equivalent of full-time hours. Often part-time workers are paid significantly less than their full-time counterparts. This combination of lower wages and shorter hours creates working conditions that put a certain amount of strain on workers and their families. Many employers, however, still prefer to use part-time workers because of the cost savings that result. Lower wages, fewer benefits, and virtually no job security all provide incentives for organizations to use more part-time workers. On the other hand, part-time workers are usually less attached to their jobs and more likely to quit when dissatisfied. These workers are often employed by small private-sector organizations, where opposition to unions tends to be the strongest and unions have the toughest job of organizing workers.[33]

involuntary part-time work the work done by people employed part-time who are unable to find full-time work

Quality of Work Life and Human Diversity

Human resource departments have found that to reduce employee dissatisfaction and unionization efforts (or, conversely, to improve employee satisfaction and existing union relations), they must consider the **quality of work life** in the design of jobs. Partially a reaction to the traditionally heavy emphasis on technical and economic factors in job design, quality of work life emphasizes improving the human dimension of work. The knowledgeable human resource manager, therefore, should be able to improve the organization's quality of work life by (1) introducing participative problem solving, (2) restructuring work, (3) introducing innovative reward systems, and (4) improving the work environment. The idea is that these improvements will lead to a more participative organizational culture and thus higher productivity and quality products. Ford Motor Company, for example, is rebuilding and modernizing its famous River Rouge plant using flexible equipment and new processes. Employees will work in teams and use internet-connected PCs on the shop floor to share their concerns instantly with suppliers or product engineers. Workstations are being redesigned to make them more ergonomic and to reduce repetitive strain injuries. "If you feel good while you're working," said a Ford representative, "I think quality and productivity will increase, and Ford thinks that too, otherwise, they wouldn't do this."[34]

quality of work life workers' attitudes toward their jobs

"Human diversity" refers to the mix in the workplace of people from different races, cultures, and backgrounds. Realizing that North American demographics are shifting toward an increasing percentage of minorities and women in the workforce, companies are now concerned with hiring and promoting people without regard to ethnic background or sex.

According to a study reported by *Fortune* magazine, companies that pursue diversity outperform the S&P 500.[35] Good human resource managers should be working to ensure that people are treated fairly on the job and not harassed by prejudiced co-workers or managers. Otherwise, they may find themselves subject to lawsuits. The Coca-Cola Company, for example, agreed to pay $192.5 million because of discrimination against African-American salaried employees in pay, promotions, and evaluations from 1995 and 2000. According to chairman and CEO Douglas Daft, "Sometimes things happen in an unintentional manner. And I've made it clear that can't happen anymore."[36]

An organization's human resources are especially important in today's world of global communication and transportation systems. For example, on a visit to China during the spring of 2000, one of the Coca-Cola Company's executives was challenged by Chinese reporters regarding the company's racial problems. Advances in technology are copied almost immediately by competitors around the world, but people are not as willing to move to other companies in other countries. This means that the only long-term resource advantage remaining to organizations operating in the industrialized nations may lie in the area of skilled human resources. Research does reveal that competitive strategies are more successfully executed in those companies with a high level of commitment to their employees than in those firms with less commitment.[37]

STRATEGIC INFORMATION SYSTEMS/TECHNOLOGY ISSUES

The primary task of the manager of information systems/technology is to design and manage the flow of information in an organization in ways that improve productivity and decision making. Information must be collected, stored, and synthesized in such a manner that it will answer important operating and strategic questions. The growth of the global internet economy is forcing organizations to make significant investments in this functional area. (See the **Internet Issue** feature.) Investments in information systems/technology are growing 11% annually even though 70% of all investments are either not completed or exceed cost projections by nearly 200%.[38]

Internet Issue

The Growing Global Internet Economy

Electronic commerce (ecommerce) is poised to grow rapidly throughout the world to a total of $6.9 trillion in internet sales by 2004. According to a report by Forrester Research titled *Global Ecommerce Approaches Hypergrowth*, internet sales in the United States should increase to $3.2 trillion by 2004 and account for 46.4% of the global internet economy. The Asia-Pacific region should grow to $1.6 trillion in sales and account for 23.2% of total internet sales. Western Europe should reach $1.5 trillion in sales (21.7% of the total). After a slow start, Latin America's internet sales should total $82.9 billion and account for 1.2% of total world internet sales. Technologically, Latin America lags behind North America and Western Europe but is being pushed by trading partners who are sophisticated internet users to invest in crucial technology infrastructure such as phone lines, computers, internet hosts, and cell phones. With Brazil and Argentina leading the way in liberalizing trade, the economic climate is rapidly improving. By 2004, Brazil should generate $64 billion on its own in online sales. Eastern Europe, Africa, and the Middle East are still facing the same problems that Latin America is now overcoming and will account for only $68.6 billion in sales, a mere 0.9% of the total world sales. The rest of the world's internet sales will total $450 billion for the remaining 6.6% of total world sales.

Source: "Hypergrowth for E-Commerce?" *The Futurist* (September–October 2000), p. 15.

A firm's information system can be a strength or a weakness in all elements of strategic management. It can not only aid in environmental scanning and in controlling a company's many activities, it can also be used as a strategic weapon in gaining competitive advantage. For example, American Hospital Supply (AHS), a leading manufacturer and distributor of a broad line of products for doctors, laboratories, and hospitals, developed an order entry distribution system that directly linked the majority of its customers to AHS computers. The system was successful because it simplified ordering processes for customers, reduced costs for both AHS and the customer, and allowed AHS to provide pricing incentives to the customer. As a result, customer loyalty was high and AHS's share of the market became large.

Information systems/technology offers four main contributions to firm performance. First (beginning in the 1970s with mainframe computers), it is used to automate existing back-office processes, such as payroll, human resource records, and accounts payable and receivable, and to establish huge databases. Second (since the 1980s), it is used to automate individual tasks, such as keeping track of clients and expenses, through the use of personal computers with word processing and spreadsheet software. Corporate databases are accessed to provide sufficient data for analysis and to create what-if scenarios. These first two contributions tend to focus on reducing costs.

Third (since the 1990s), information systems/technology is used to enhance key business functions, such as marketing and operations. This third contribution focuses on productivity improvements. The system provides customer support and help in distribution and logistics. For example, FedEx found that by allowing customers to directly access its package-tracking database via its website instead of their having to ask a human operator, the company saved up to $2 million annually.[39] Business processes are analyzed to increase efficiency and productivity via re-engineering. Enterprise resource planning application software, by firms such as SAP and Oracle, is used to integrate worldwide business activities so that employees need to enter information only once and that information is available to all corporate systems (including accounting) around the world. Fourth (since 2000), it is used to develop competitive advantage. The focus is now on taking advantage of opportunities via supply chain management, ecommerce, and knowledge management. Currently, most companies devote 85% of their IS/IT budget to the first two utility functions, 12% to productivity enhancement, and only 3% to efforts to gain competitive advantage.[40]

Current trends in information systems include the increasing use of the internet for marketing, intranets for internal communication, and extranets for logistics and distribution. An intranet is an information network within an organization that also has access to the external worldwide internet. Intranets typically begin as ways to provide employees with company information such as lists of product prices, fringe benefits, and company policies. They are then converted into extranets for supply chain management. An extranet is an information network within an organization that is available to key suppliers and customers. The key issue in building an extranet is the creation of firewalls to block extranet users from accessing the firm's or other users' confidential data. Once this is accomplished, companies can allow employees, customers, and suppliers to access information and conduct business on the internet in a completely automated manner. By connecting these groups, companies hope to obtain a competitive advantage by reducing the time needed to design and bring new products to market, slashing inventories, customizing manufacturing, and entering new markets.[41]

4.4 Summary of Internal Factors

After strategists have scanned the internal organizational environment and identified key strategic factors for their particular organization, their analysis needs to summarize their findings in a way that is useful to strategic decision makers. Strategists should use the VRIO framework (**V**alue, **R**areness, **I**mitability, and **O**rganization) to assess the importance of each of the factors that might be considered strengths.

1. Identify the most important strengths and weaknesses within the organization. Focus on the ones that are key to creating value and directly affect firm performance. The organization should focus on developing the resources that influence performance most significantly.

2. Assess the probable impact of those resources on the company's current strategic position.

3. Match the organization's strengths to key success factors identified in external environmental scanning. Determine how well management is addressing any resource gaps that may exist.

4. Evaluate the extent to which the organization is strengthening and/or protecting the resources that give it competitive advantage.

The assessment of organizational strengths and weaknesses can be conducted by using the instructions for a strategic audit found in the **Appendix**. The audit provides a checklist of questions by area of concern. For example, Part IV of the audit examines structure, culture, and resources. It looks at resources in terms of the functional areas of marketing, finance, R & D, operations, human resources, and information systems, among others.

After accomplishing the four tasks outlined above, you will be in a better position to identify the resource strengths a firm has and the steps it must take to nurture these core competencies into a strong basis of competitive advantage. The resource-based view of the firm encourages us to think of the organization as a bundle of resources that is used to produce and deliver a product to market. Organizations with superior resources should therefore achieve above-average performance. It is not only important to have superior resources, but also to use them in a way that creates some sort of sustainable difference in the organization's strategy. Determining how an organization performs activities in the pursuit of a unique competitive position, and how it protects them from imitation, are critical managerial activities.[42]

The ability of an organization to secure a competitive advantage comes from its ability to perform a collection of activities in a way that provides better value to consumers than that of rivals. Activities are therefore the source of competitive advantage, but they can be performed because of the resources an organization has.[43] What makes an organization successful is its ability to (1) perform different activities from its rivals or (2) perform similar activities in different ways. Either of these uses of resources should create a competitive advantage for the firm, the strength of which will be a function of durability and imitability as discussed earlier. We can look to the activities of WestJet—see **Figure 4–6** on page 108 for a set of related activities reflecting its choices about what to do (be a discount airline) and what not to do (compete head to head with Air Canada). Any strategy requires that choices be made, and the more an organization's activities become part of a web of activities, the stronger its competitive advantage should be.

The WestJet business model, patterned on that of the highly successful Southwest Airlines, is characterized by three activities:

■ Targeting price-sensitive passengers

■ Offering a limited number of short- to medium-range direct flights

■ Running a low-cost, no-frills passenger airline

This strategy, based on five strategic variables, has been tremendously successful, even post–September 11, when many airlines experienced severe performance declines. By offering limited customer service, select routes between major cities in western Canada, low ticket prices, reliability in arrivals and departures, and an efficient workforce, WestJet has created a

Figure 4–6 WestJet Value-Creating Activities

network of activities that rivals have difficulty matching. This network of activities indicates the various types of fit that make this business model successful for WestJet. First, there is *consistency among activities.* For WestJet, the most important aspect of its strategy is the low price of its tickets. All activities the organization performs must therefore link to this low-cost strategy. For example, WestJet minimizes the size of its fleet and uses only one type of aircraft to save training and maintenance costs. It also chooses to offer more limited customer service so it can provide consumers with cheaper tickets. It also uses its company website to provide schedule and fare information, as well as ticket sales that avoid travel agent commissions. Second, *activities reinforce each other.* Beyond having consistent activities that strengthen its low-cost position and appeal to the price-sensitive traveller, WestJet uses activities that reinforce each other. It uses simple advertisements that inform consumers of its newest routes and its everyday low fares. It makes decisions on its routes and customer service in a way that emphasizes a common need for safe, reliable, low-cost air travel in Canada. Its highly motivated and personable workforce create a pleasant flying experience that offsets some of the services WestJet does not offer in order to offer cheaper flights.[44]

What makes this strategy successful for WestJet, and why have other airlines had difficulty imitating it? The answer lies in the fact that competitive advantages based on systems of activities are more sustainable than those built on individual resources.[45] This difference results from the difficulty of imitating a network of activities (many activities would need to be performed differently to copy this strategy) and the unwillingness of many organizations to stop performing the activities that do not reinforce a low-cost strategy (such as offering hot meals, connecting flights, and worldwide travel alliances). The process of scanning the internal environment provides the organization with an opportunity to assess the strengths and weaknesses of its organizational resources. It also encourages managers to think about how the activities it performs fit together in a way that will allow it to do something better than rival firms, creating a more sustainable advantage in the process.

4.5 Impact of the Internet on Internal Scanning and Organizational Analysis

supply chain management the managing of supplier networks to create efficiencies in the organization and its partners

The expansion of the marketing-oriented internet into intranets and extranets is making significant contributions to organizational performance through supply chain management and virtual teams. **Supply chain management** is the forming of networks for sourcing raw materials, manufacturing products or creating services, storing and distributing the goods, and delivering them to customers and consumers.[46] Industry leaders are integrating modern information systems into their value chains to harmonize company-wide efforts and to achieve competitive advantage. For example, Heineken beer distributors input actual depletion figures and replenishment orders to the Dutch brewer through their linked webpages. This interactive planning system generates time-phased orders based on actual usage rather than on projected demand. Distributors are then able to modify plans based on local conditions or changes in marketing. Heineken uses these modifications to adjust brewing and supply schedules. As a result of this system, lead times have been reduced from the traditional 10 to 12 weeks to 4 to 6 weeks. This time saving is especially useful in an industry competing on product freshness. In another example, Procter & Gamble participates in an information network to move the company's line of consumer products through Wal-Mart's many stores. As part of the network with Wal-Mart, P&G knows by cash register and by store what products have passed through the system each day. The network is linked by satellite communications on a real-time basis. With actual point-of-sale information, products are replenished to meet current demand and minimize stockouts while maintaining exceptionally low inventories.[47]

virtual teams teams whose members communicate via telecommunication and information technologies, often across great distances

Virtual teams are groups of geographically and/or organizationally dispersed co-workers who assemble using a combination of telecommunications and information technologies to accomplish an organizational task.[48] Internet, intranet, and extranet systems are combining with other new technologies such as desktop videoconferencing and collaborative software to create a new workplace in which teams of workers are no longer restrained by geography, time, or organizational boundaries. As more companies outsource some of the activities previously conducted internally, the traditional organizational structure is being replaced by a series of virtual teams whose members rarely, if ever, meet face to face. Such teams may be established as temporary groups to accomplish a specific task or may be more permanent to address continuing issues such as strategic planning. Membership on these teams is often fluid, depending on the task to be accomplished. They may include not only employees from different functions within a company, but also members of various stakeholder groups, such as suppliers, customers, and law or consulting firms. The use of virtual teams to replace traditional face-to-face work groups is being driven by five trends:

1. Flatter organizational structures with increasing cross-functional coordination needs
2. Turbulent environments requiring more inter-organizational co-operation
3. Increasing employee autonomy and participation in decision making
4. Higher knowledge requirements derived from a greater emphasis on service
5. Increasing globalization of trade and corporate activity[49]

Discussion Questions

1. What is the relevance of the resource-based view of the firm to strategic management in a global environment?

2. How can value chain analysis help identify a company's strengths and weaknesses?

3. In what ways can an organization's structure and culture be internal strengths or weaknesses?

4. What are the advantages and disadvantages of management's using the experience curve to determine strategy?

5. How might a firm's management decide whether it should continue to invest in current known technology or in new but untested technology? What factors might encourage or discourage such a shift?

Strategic Practice Exercise

Can you analyze an organization using the internet? Try the following exercise.

1. Form teams of around five people. Find the Internet 100 Index from the latest copy of *USA Today*. The index is divided into the e-Commerce 50 and the e-Business 50. The e-Commerce 50 is comprises four subindustries: e-Retail, e-Finance, e-New Media, and e-Service Providers. The e-Business 50 comprises three subindustries: e-Infrastructure, e-Services/Solutions, and e-Advertising.

2. Each team selects four companies plus one assigned by the instructor. (The list of companies from which assignments will be made is Amazon.com, E-loan, Cisco Systems, AOL, Yahoo!, and DoubleClick.) Provide the instructor with your list.

3. Conduct research on each of your five companies *using the internet only*.

4. Write a three-to-six-page double-spaced typed report for each of the five companies. The report should answer the following questions:

a. Does the firm have any core competencies? Are any of these distinctive (better than the competition) competencies? Does the firm have any competitive advantage? Provide a SWOT analysis.

b. What is the likely future of this firm? Will the company survive industry consolidation?

c. Would you buy stock in this company? Assume that your team has $25 000 to invest. Allocate the money among your five companies. Be specific. List the five companies, the number of shares purchased of each, the cost of each share as of a given date, and the total cost for each purchase assuming a typical commission used by an internet broker, such as E*TRADE. (This part of your report will be common to all members of your team.)

Questions for Discussion

1. Discuss patents in terms of a basis of competitive advantage. Use the properties of competitive advantages to discuss the ability of proprietary and generic manufacturers to earn profits and withstand competition.

2. What is the purpose of patent legislation? Explain how it is justified despite being contrary to the Competition Act. Evaluate the costs and benefits of patent legislation to organizations, consumers, and society as a whole.

3. Differences in the regulation of drug prices in Canada and the United States have created a large trade in cross-border shipments of drugs into the United States. Discuss the basis of this controversy and consider a socially responsible solution to it.

4. Discuss the activities of pharmaceutical firms in terms of Carroll's types of responsibilities. How can the recent agreements to cut the prices of AIDS drugs in African countries be explained in terms of social responsibility?

Video Resource: "Drug Manufacturing," *Venture* #853, November 10, 2002.

CHAPTER 5

Strategy Formulation: Situation Analysis and Business Strategy

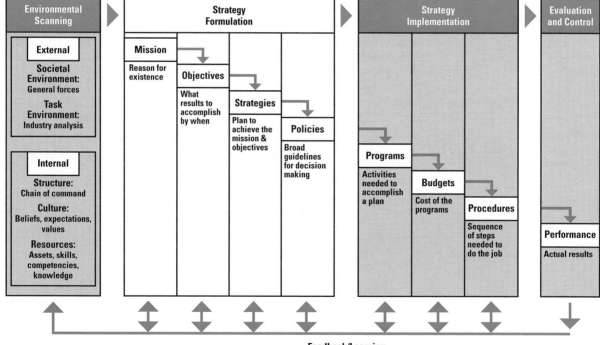

Learning Objectives

After reading this chapter you should be able to

Organize the findings of environmental analysis using a SWOT analysis

Generate strategic options using the TOWS matrix

Understand the basic competitive and co-operative strategies available to organizations

Customize strategy recommendations according to industry competitive structure and intensity of competition

Understand the range of competitive tactics that can be used to implement strategy

Le Château was founded in 1959 by Herschel Segal, a Montreal native whose family owned a small, local fashion business. His first business was a clothing store that dealt in surplus inventory from his father's business, Peerless Clothing. Quickly he realized that there was no place for fashion-conscious young Canadians to buy affordable clothing. His focus on a younger market segment and European-inspired fashion gave Le Château its original success, providing the basis for expansion throughout Canada. He went public in 1983 and remains a dominant market presence in Canadian retailing.

The growth of Le Château from a small clearance house to one of the strongest retailers in Canada is evidence of a successful competitive strategy. The cornerstone of its strategy is to provide inexpensive trendy fashions to young shoppers, a market segment that has typically been unpredictable and disloyal to any particular retailer. Although Le Château ran into financial difficulties by its ill-fated expansion into the United States in the late 1980s, Segal has successfully turned around the company's operations by improving the quality of his designs and thereby creating more value for customers. For years he was content to provide "disposable fashion," trendy styling but low-quality. This reputation eventually caught up with Le Château, and customers took their business to other stores where they received better value. By introducing a quality control system and hiring experts in textile engineering, the company was able to add a new quality dimension to its product. To make consumers aware of this, and to reposition Le Château away from a low-quality position, it has increased its advertising to convince consumers that its "cheap chic" products provide superior value for cost-conscious consumers. The company's primary target is 13- to 25-year-old women who crave new fashions but have limited purchasing power. One way it has found to signal the trendiness of its product is to avoid discounting, a strategy that risks sending the message that a product isn't fashionable. Segal has used his key organizational design, production, and marketing resources to keep Le Château profitable. At a time when many of its rivals are in difficulty, Le Château seems to be improving its position in the tremendously competitive Canadian retailing industry. A strategy that strikes the balance between fashion and low price has been key to its success. By continuing to restructure management and maintain a tight focus, Segal seems poised to continue this trend of success well into the future.

Le Château is successful because its strategy makes a trade-off that many organizations have been unable or unwilling to make successfully. By incorporating elements of a differentiation strategy, focusing on a narrow market segment, and offering products that are both fashionable and inexpensive, Le Château has created a strategy designed to give it an advantage in a very competitive industry. This success shows how aspects of the business competitive strategies discussed in this chapter can be assembled in ways to create a sustainable market position in an industry known for its vulnerability to the economy and high levels of competition.[1]

5.1 Situation Analysis: SWOT Analysis

SWOT analysis an organizing framework that categorizes organizational resources as strengths or weaknesses, and environmental factors as opportunities or threats

distinctive competencies an organization's unique resources and the value-creating activities that use them

Strategy formulation is often referred to as strategic planning or long-range planning and is concerned with developing an organization's mission, objectives, strategies, and policies. It begins with situation analysis: the process of finding a strategic fit between external opportunities and internal strengths while working around external threats and internal weaknesses. As shown in **Figure 1–6**: Strategic Decision-Making Process (in **Chapter 1**), this is step 5: analyzing strategic factors in light of the current situation using **SWOT analysis**. "SWOT" is an acronym used to describe the particular Strengths, Weaknesses, Opportunities, and Threats that are strategic factors for a specific company. SWOT analysis should not only result in the identification of an organization's **distinctive competencies**—the particular capabilities and resources that a firm possesses and the superior way in which they are used—but also in the identification of opportunities that the firm is not currently able to take advantage of because of a lack of appropriate resources. Over the years, SWOT analysis has proven to be the most enduring analytical technique used in strategic management. For example, a survey of manufacturing and service companies reported the five most-used tools and techniques in strategic analysis to be (1) spreadsheet "what-if" analysis, (2) analysis of key or critical success factors, (3) financial analysis of competitors, (4) SWOT analysis, and (5) core capabilities analysis.[2]

It can be said that the essence of strategy is opportunity divided by capacity.[3] An opportunity by itself has no real value unless a company has the capacity (that is, the resources) to take advantage of that opportunity. This approach, however, considers only opportunities and strengths when considering alternative strategies. By itself, a distinctive competency in a key resource or capability is no guarantee of competitive advantage. Weaknesses in other resource areas can prevent a strategy from being successful. This points to an important issue facing strategic managers: Should we invest more in our strengths to make them even stronger (a distinctive competency), or should we invest in our weaknesses to at least make them competitive? A SWOT analysis can help with this type of decision.

SWOT analysis, by itself, is not a panacea. This approach has been criticized because of the difficulty it imposes of forcing a factor into one of two categories, its omission of a basis to reflect the importance or priorities associated with each factor, and its idea that positive factors (strengths and opportunities) offset negatives ones (weaknesses and threats).[4] These criticisms notwithstanding, the SWOT framework is a widely recognized system for presenting the findings of a strategic analysis. The techniques of environmental analysis (**Chapter 3**) and organizational analysis (**Chapter 4**) need to come together in a systematic way in order for strategists to make decisions that have the highest probability of improving long-run firm performance. Forcing analysis to assess the favourability of key environmental variables and organizational attributes puts strategists in a position to search for strategies that optimally use organizational resources, identify and address resource gaps, capture favourable trends in the external environment, and adapt to the changing context in which the organization operates. A SWOT analysis allows decision makers to make these critical decisions with a clear understanding of the favourable and unfavourable aspects of the environment and the organization. Neglecting any one of these creates the possibility of faulty strategic decision making and therefore the possibility of a strategy less likely to improve long-run firm performance.

FINDING A PROPITIOUS NICHE

propitious niche a favourable market segment that is well-suited to the organization but not to its rivals

One desired outcome of analyzing strategic factors is identifying a niche where an organization can use its core competencies to take advantage of a particular market opportunity. A niche is a need in the marketplace that is currently unsatisfied. The goal is to find a **propitious niche**—an extremely favourable niche—that is so well-suited to the firm's internal and external environment that other organizations are not likely to challenge or dislodge it.[5] A niche is propitious to the extent that it currently is just large enough for one firm to satisfy its demand. After a firm has found and filled that niche, it is not worth a potential competitor's time or money to also go after the same niche.

strategic window a temporary market opportunity that an organization is capable of capturing

Finding such a niche is not always easy. A firm's management must be always looking for a **strategic window**, that is, a unique market opportunity that is available only for a particular time. The first firm through a strategic window can occupy a propitious niche and discourage competition (if the firm has the required internal strengths). One company that has successfully found a propitious niche is Frank J. Zamboni & Company, the manufacturer of the machines that smooth the ice at ice-skating rinks. Frank Zamboni invented the unique tractor-like machine in 1949, and no one since then has found a substitute. Before the machine was invented, people had to clean and scrape the ice by hand to prepare the surface for skating. Now hockey fans look forward to intermissions just to watch the Zamboni slowly drive up and down the ice rink, turning rough, scraped ice into a smooth mirror surface—almost like magic. So long as Zamboni's company is able to produce the machines in the quantity and quality desired at a reasonable price, it's not worth another company's effort to go after Frank Zamboni & Company's propitious niche.

As the niche grows, so can the company within that niche—by increasing its operations' capacity or through alliances with larger firms. The key is to identify a market opportunity in which the first firm to reach that market segment can obtain and keep dominant market share. For example, Church & Dwight was the first company to successfully market sodium bicarbonate for use in cooking. Its Arm & Hammer brand baking soda has approximately a 95% market share in North America. The propitious niche concept is crucial to the software industry. Small initial demand in emerging markets allows new entrepreneurial ventures to go after niches too small to be noticed by established companies. When Microsoft developed its first disk operating system (DOS) in 1980 for IBM's personal computers, for example, the demand for such open systems software was very small—a small niche for a then very small Microsoft. The company was able to fill that niche and to successfully grow with it.

Niches can also change—sometimes faster than a firm can adapt to that change. A company's managers may discover in their situation analysis that they need to invest heavily in the firm's capabilities to keep them competitively strong in a changing niche. South African Breweries (SAB), for example, took this approach when management realized that the only way to keep competitors out of its market was to continuously invest in increased productivity and infrastructure in order to keep its prices very low. See the **Global Issue** feature to see how SAB was able to successfully defend its market niche during significant changes in its environment.

Global Issue

SAB Defends Its Propitious Niche

Out of 50 beers drunk by South Africans, 49 are brewed by South African Breweries (SAB). Founded more than a century ago, SAB controlled most of the local beer market by 1950 with brands like Castle and Lion. When the government repealed the ban on the sale of alcohol to blacks in the 1960s, SAB and other brewers competed for the rapidly growing market. SAB fought successfully to retain its dominance of the market. With the end of apartheid, foreign brewers have been tempted to break SAB's near-monopoly but have been deterred by the entry barriers SAB has created.

Entry Barrier #1

Every year for the past two decades SAB has reduced its prices. The "real" (adjusted for inflation) price of its beer is now half what it was during the 1970s. SAB has been able to achieve this through a continuous emphasis on productivity improvements—boosting production while cutting the workforce almost in half. Keeping prices low has been the key to SAB's avoiding charges of abusing its monopoly.

Entry Barrier #2

In South Africa's poor and rural areas, roads are rough and electricity is undependable. SAB has a great deal of experience in transporting crates to remote villages along bad roads and making sure that distributors have refrigerators (and electricity generators if needed). Many of its distributors are former employees who have been helped by the company to start their own trucking businesses.

Entry Barrier #3

Most of the beer sold in South Africa is sold through unlicensed pubs called shebeens, most of which date back to apartheid when blacks were not allowed licences. Although the current government of South Africa would be pleased to grant pub licences to blacks, the shebeen owners don't want them. They enjoy not paying any taxes. SAB cannot sell directly to the shebeens, but it does sell to them indirectly through wholesalers. The government, in turn, ignores the situation, preferring that people drink SAB beer rather than potentially deadly moonshine.

To break into South Africa, a new entrant would have to build large breweries and a substantial distribution network. SAB would, in turn, probably reduce its prices still further to defend its market. The difficulties of operating in South Africa are too great, the market is growing too slowly, and (given SAB's low-cost position) the likely profit margin is too low to justify entering the market. Some foreign brewers, such as Heineken, would rather use SAB to distribute their products throughout South Africa. As a result, SAB is now the world's fifth largest brewer by volume. With its home market secure, SAB's management considered acquiring a global brewer such as Bass in June 2000 but decided against it because of the high price.

Source: "Big Lion, Small Cage," *The Economist* (August 12, 2000), p. 56. Reprinted with permission.

5.2 Review of Mission and Objectives

A re-examination of an organization's current mission and objectives must be made before alternative strategies can be generated and evaluated. Even when formulating strategy, decision makers tend to concentrate on the alternatives—the action possibilities—rather than on a mission to be fulfilled and objectives to be achieved. This tendency is so attractive because it is much easier to deal with alternative courses of action that exist right here and now than to really think about what you want to accomplish in the future. The end result is that we often choose strategies that set our objectives for us, rather than having our choices incorporate clear objectives and a mission statement.

Problems in performance can derive from an inappropriate statement of mission, which may be too narrow or too broad. If the mission does not provide a *common thread* (a unifying theme) for an organization's businesses, managers may be unclear about where the company is heading. Objectives and strategies might be in conflict with each other. Divisions might be competing against one another, rather than against outside competition, to the detriment of the organization as a whole.

A company's objectives can also be inappropriately stated. They can either focus too much on short-term operational goals or be so general that they provide little real guidance. There may be a gap between planned and achieved objectives. When such a gap occurs, either the strategies have to be changed to improve performance or the objectives need to be adjusted downward to be more realistic. Consequently, objectives should be constantly reviewed to ensure their usefulness. For example, many new Canadian digital TV channels have failed to capture a critical mass of viewers to ensure their survival. A recent survey showed that approximately a third of all new digital channels have fewer than 1000 viewers in any given minute. Together, these 57 new channels have less than a 2% share of prime time viewing.[6] Channels like The Green Channel and Pride TV are now forced into making some tough choices as a result of these performance gaps. These difficulties stem from the inability of digital cable and direct-to-home satellite systems to take significant market share away from basic cable subscribers. As unique and innovative as many of these new channels may be, many cable subscribers do not know they exist. Many tough choices are ahead for these speciality channels, whose strategies have stemmed from the idea that new programming will encourage basic cable subscribers to upgrade their systems.

5.3 Generating Alternative Strategies Using a TOWS Matrix

Thus far we have discussed how a firm uses SWOT analysis to assess its situation. SWOT can also be used to generate a number of possible alternative strategies. The TOWS Matrix (TOWS is just another way of saying SWOT) illustrates how the external opportunities and threats facing a particular organization can be matched with that company's internal strengths and weaknesses to result in four sets of possible strategic alternatives (See **Figure 5–1**). This is a good way to use brainstorming to create alternative strategies that might not otherwise be considered. It forces strategic managers to create various kinds of aggressive and defensive strategies. It can be used to generate corporate as well as business strategies.

To generate a TOWS matrix, take the following steps:

1. Use the SWOT analysis framework to identify the most significant strategic factors in the organization's internal and external environment.

2. Generate a series of possible strategies for the company or business unit under consideration based on particular combinations of the four sets of factors:

    ■ *SO Strategies* are generated by thinking of ways in which a company or business unit could use its strengths to take advantage of opportunities.
    ■ *ST Strategies* consider a company's or unit's strengths as a way to avoid threats.
    ■ *WO Strategies* attempt to take advantage of opportunities by overcoming weaknesses.

    ■ *WT Strategies* are basically defensive and primarily act to minimize weaknesses and avoid threats.

The TOWS Matrix is very useful for generating a series of alternatives that the decision makers of a company or business unit might not otherwise have scrutinized. It can be used for the organization as a whole or it can be used for a specific business unit within an organization. It provides generic directions for organizational strategies: *aggressive* ones that capture environmental opportunities or *defensive* ones that protect or defend against environmental threats. Each of these generic directions would be further subdivided into two types, one based on *using* existing organizational strengths and the other on *developing* organizational

Figure 5–1 TOWS Matrix

INTERNAL FACTORS (IFAS) EXTERNAL FACTORS (EFAS)	Strengths (S) List 5–10 *internal* strengths here	Weaknesses (W) List 5–10 *internal* weaknesses here
Opportunities (O) List 5–10 *external* opportunities here	**SO Strategies** Generate strategies here that use **strengths** to take **advantage** of **opportunities**	**WO Strategies** Generate strategies here that take **advantage** of **opportunities** by **overcoming weaknesses**
Threats (T) List 5–10 *external* threats here	**ST Strategies** Generate strategies here that use **strengths** to **avoid threats**	**WT Strategies** Generate strategies here that **minimize weaknesses** and **avoid threats**

Source: Reprinted from *Long-Range Planning*, April 1982. H. Weihrich, "The TOWS Matrix—A Tool for Situational Analysis," p. 60. Copyright 1982, with permission from Elsevier Science.

strengths. We say these strategies are generic because they can apply to any type of organization, in any type of industry—even not-for-profit organizations. Using this comparison of environmental and organizational strategic factors, decision makers are encouraged to think "outside the box" toward a wider range of solutions that improve firm performance in distinct ways. How to choose among possible strategies is discussed in more detail in **Chapter 7**.

5.4 Business Strategies

business strategy an organization's plan to improve performance of a single business unit, or of the entire organization if operating in only one market

Whereas the TOWS matrix identifies different directions a strategy can take (aggressive or defensive), another approach is to evaluate each business unit within an organization in terms of possible competitive and co-operative strategies. **Business strategy** focuses on improving the competitive position of a company's or business unit's products or services within the specific industry or market segment that the company or business unit serves. Business strategy can be competitive (battling against all competitors for advantage) or co-operative (working with one or more competitors to gain advantage against other competitors). Questions about business strategy involve asking how the organization or its divisions should compete or co-operate in each industry.

PORTER'S GENERIC COMPETITIVE STRATEGIES

competitive strategy an organizational strategy based on independent decisions designed to improve the organization's performance relative to that of rivals

Competitive strategy raises the following questions:

- Should we compete on the basis of low cost (and thus price), or should we differentiate our products or services on some other basis, such as quality or service? This question is based on how different an organization wants to be from its rivals.
- Should we compete head to head with our major competitors for the biggest but most sought-after share of the market, or should we focus on a niche in which we can satisfy a less sought-after but also profitable segment of the market? This question is based on how large a competitive scope an organization desires.

Michael Porter proposes two generic competitive strategies for outperforming other organizations in a particular industry: cost leadership and differentiation.[7] From an extensive analysis of successful American firms, of many sizes and in many different industries, Porter observed differences in organizational strategy that were highly correlated with performance. In other words, the strategies of successful firms were different from those of unsuccessful firms. A process of looking at the differences between the strategies of successful and unsuccessful firms led to these two broad categories of generic competitive strategies. These strategies represent a set of choices made by the organization to improve its long-run performance in two different ways.

- *Cost leadership strategy* is the ability of a company or a business unit to design, produce, and market a comparable product more efficiently than its competitors. Performance improves from earning higher margins than rival firms.
- *Differentiation strategy* is the ability to provide unique and superior value to the buyer in terms of product quality, special features, or after-sale service. Performance improves from avoiding direct competition with rivals and making competitive products less substitutable.

competitive scope the size of an organization's target market

Porter further proposes that a firm's competitive advantage in an industry is determined by its **competitive scope**, that is, the breadth of the company's or business unit's target market. Before using either of the generic competitive strategies (cost leadership or differentiation), the organization or unit must choose the range of product varieties it will produce, the distribution channels it will employ, the types of buyers it will serve, the geographic areas in which it will sell, and the array of related industries in which it will also compete. This should reflect an understanding of the firm's unique resources. Simply put, a company or business unit can choose a broad target (that is, aim at the middle of the mass market) or a narrow target (that is, aim at a market niche). Combining these two types of target markets with the two competitive strategies results in the four variations of generic strategies depicted in **Figure 5–2**. When these two generic strategies have a broad mass-market target, they are simply called *cost leadership* and *differentiation*. When they are focused on a market niche (narrow target), however, they are called *focused cost leadership* and *focused differentiation*. Although research does indicate that established firms pursuing broad-scope strategies outperform firms following narrow-scope strategies in terms of return on assets (ROA), new entrepreneurial firms have a better chance of surviving if they follow a narrow-scope over a broad-scope strategy.[8]

cost leadership strategy a broad scope competitive strategy based on organizational efficiency and price-based competition

Cost leadership is an efficiency-based competitive strategy that aims at the broad mass market and requires "aggressive construction of efficient-scale facilities, vigorous pursuit of cost reductions from experience, tight cost and overhead control, avoidance of marginal customer accounts, and cost minimization in areas like R & D, service, sales force, advertising, and so on."[9] Because of its lower costs, the cost leader is able to charge a lower price for its products than its competitors and still make a satisfactory profit. Some companies successfully following this strategy are Wal-Mart, WestJet, Timex, and Gateway 2000. Having a low-cost position also gives a company or business unit a defence against rivals. Its lower costs allow it to continue to earn profits during times of heavy competition. Its high market share means that it will have high bargaining power relative to its suppliers (because it buys in large quantities). Its low price will also serve as a barrier to entry because few new entrants will be able to match the leader's cost advantage. As a result, cost leaders are likely to earn above-average returns on investment.

differentiation strategy a broad scope competitive strategy based on creating products perceived as different from rival offerings, which in turn will not compete solely on price

Differentiation is also aimed at the broad mass market but involves the creation of a product or service that is perceived throughout its industry as unique. The company or business unit may then charge a premium for its product. This specialty can be associated with design or brand image, technology, features, dealer network, or customer service. Differentiation is a viable strategy for earning above-average returns in a specific business because the resulting brand loyalty lowers customers' sensitivity to price. Increased costs can

Figure 5–2 Porter's Generic Competitive Strategies

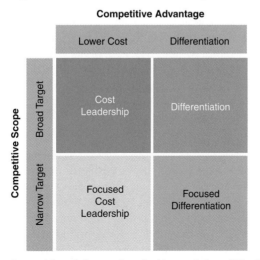

Source: Adapted from and used with permission of The Free Press, an imprint of Simon & Schuster, from *The Competitive Advantage of Nations* by Michael E. Porter, p. 39. Copyright © 1990 by Michael E. Porter.

usually be passed on to the buyers. Buyer loyalty also serves as an entry barrier—new firms must develop their own distinctive competencies to differentiate their products in some way in order to compete successfully. Examples of companies that have successfully used a differentiation strategy are Walt Disney Productions, KitchenAid, Nike, Apple Computer, and Mercedes-Benz. Research suggests that a differentiation strategy is more likely to generate higher profit margins than is a low-cost strategy because differentiation creates a better entry barrier. A low-cost strategy is more likely, however, to generate increases in market share.[10]

focused cost leadership strategy a narrow scope competitive strategy based on based on organizational efficiency and price-based competition

Focused cost leadership is a low-cost competitive strategy that focuses on a particular buyer group or geographic market. The organization attempts to serve only this niche, to the exclusion of others. In using this strategy, the company or business unit seeks a cost advantage in its target segment. A good example of this strategy is Fadal Engineering. Fadal focuses its efforts on building and selling no-frills machine tools to small manufacturers. Fadal achieved cost focus by keeping overhead and R & D to a minimum and by focusing its marketing efforts strictly on its market niche. The cost focus strategy is valued by those who believe that a company or business unit that focuses its efforts is better able to serve its narrow strategic target more efficiently than can its competition. It does, however, require a trade-off between profitability and overall market share.

focused differentiation strategy a narrow scope competitive strategy based on creating products perceived as different from rival offerings, which in turn will not compete solely on price

Focused differentiation strategies, like focused cost leadership, concentrate on a particular buyer group, product line segment, or geographic market. This is the strategy successfully followed by independent clothing boutiques, local arts and crafts producers, Porsche, and local health food stores. In using a differentiation focus, the company or business unit seeks differentiation in a targeted market segment. This strategy is valued by those who believe that a company or a unit that focuses its efforts is better able to serve the special needs of a narrow strategic target more effectively than can its competition. This is the strategy being used so successfully by Nova Scotian Crystal, a Halifax-based producer of hand-crafted crystal giftware. Their strategy is to produce unique, high-quality handmade products and distribute them very selectively. Because they do not use machines in the process of blowing and carving crystal, they are unable to offer low-cost products. Instead they position their product as an exclusive high-end gift or souvenir product. The company remains small in size to minimize many of its organizational costs, keeping inventory levels low and using its own sales staff to educate consumers about its high-value products.

Risks in Competitive Strategies

No one competitive strategy is guaranteed to achieve success, and some companies that have successfully implemented one of Porter's competitive strategies have found that they could not sustain the strategy. As shown in **Table 5–1**, each of the generic strategies has its risks. For example, a company following a differentiation strategy must ensure that the higher price it charges for its higher quality is not priced too far above the competition; otherwise customers will not see the extra quality as worth the extra cost.

Issues in Competitive Strategies

Porter argues that to be successful, a company or business unit must achieve one of the preceding generic competitive strategies. An organization failing to do this will do nothing particularly well—Porter refers to this as being "stuck in the middle." Being caught between generic strategies, the organization will have no competitive advantage and will earn below-average profits. His logic here is that pursuing any of the generic competitive strategies requires making trade-offs: choosing to do one thing will prevent the organization from doing another. For example, an organization that invests large amounts of money in production equipment to mass-produce its products will not be able to easily customize products for

Table 5–1 Risks of Generic Competitive Strategies

Risks of Cost Leadership	Risks of Differentiation	Risks of Focus
Cost leadership is not sustained: • Competitors intimate. • Technology changes. • Other bases for cost leadership erode. Proximity in differentiation is lost.	Differentiation is not sustained: • Competitors imitate. • Bases for differentiation become less important to buyers. Cost proximity is lost.	The focus strategy is imitated. The target segment becomes structurally unattractive: • Structure erodes. • Demand disappears. Broadly targeted competitors overwhelm the segment: • The segment's differences from other segments narrow. • The advantages of a broad line increase.
Cost focusers achieve even lower cost in segments.	Differentiation focusers achieve even greater differentiation in segments.	New focusers subsegment the industry.

Source: Adapted/reprinted with permission of The Free Press, an imprint of Simon & Schuster, from *Competitive Advantage: Creating and Sustaining Superior Performance* by Michael E. Porter, p. 21. Copyright © 1985 by Michael E. Porter.

particular customers' needs. An example of a business that may be facing a problem of this kind is the personal computer division at Hewlett-Packard (HP). For years, HP was a niche player following a differentiation focus strategy in personal computers. Their products were high-quality and expensive. In the mid-1990s HP left the niche and competed instead in the broad-target market. To compete with its lower cost rivals such as Dell and Gateway, HP reduced prices. HP's switch from a narrow-target to a broad-target competitive strategy had its downside. In moving to the mass market, HP had not kept up its quality image (thus losing its differentiation) and had thus far failed to achieve the lower cost position. This example shows two things. First, it is difficult to change from one type of generic strategy to another. As will be discussed later in this chapter, different strategies require different organizational resources. It might be relatively easy to quickly decide to change strategies, but acquiring or developing the resources necessary to implement the new strategy is a much slower process. Second, there are often fundamental trade-offs that must be made pursuing any competitive strategy. Often the pursuit of efficiencies prevents firms from incorporating many product attributes, which makes it difficult to simultaneously compete on both product attributes and price.

Despite Porter's assertion that organizations should not pursue more than one generic strategy simultaneously, research does not support the argument that a firm or unit must choose between differentiation and lower cost to be successful.[11] What of companies that attempt to achieve *both* a low-cost and a high-differentiation position? When Home Depot entered the Canadian market, it provided high levels of service, broad and deep product lines, and guaranteed lowest prices. Its combination of information technology to minimize inventory costs and skilled sales associates allow it to provide very high levels of service and a low price. The Japanese auto companies of Toyota, Nissan, and Honda are often presented as examples of successful firms able to successfully follow both of these generic strategies. Thanks to advances in technology, a company may be able to design quality into a product or service in such a way that it can achieve both high quality and high market share, thus lowering costs.[12] Porter recognizes that many different kinds of potentially profitable competitive strategies exist. Although there is generally room for only a few companies to successfully pursue the mass-market cost leadership strategy (because it is so dependent on achieving dominant market share), there is room for an almost unlimited number of differentiation and focus strategies (depending on the range of possible desirable features and the number of identifiable market niches). Quality, alone, has eight different dimensions—each with the potential of providing a product with a competitive advantage (see **Table 5–2).**

Most entrepreneurial ventures follow focus strategies. The successful ones differentiate their product from those of their competitors in the areas of quality and service, and they focus the product on customer needs in a segment of the market, thereby achieving a dominant share of that part of the market. These companies go after opportunities in market niches too small to justify retaliation from the market leaders. Veteran entrepreneur Norm Brodsky argues that it's often much easier for a small company to compete against a big company than against a well-run small company. "We beat the giants on service. We beat them on flexibility. We beat them on location and price."[13]

Industry Structure and Competitive Strategy

fragmented industry
an industry with a relatively large number of small- to medium-sized firms, all having similar amounts of market power

Although each of Porter's generic competitive strategies may be used in any industry, certain strategies are more likely to succeed than others in some instances. In a **fragmented industry**, for example, where many small- and medium-sized local companies compete for relatively small shares of the total market, focus strategies will likely predominate. Fragmented industries are typical for products in the early stages of their life cycle. If few economies are to be gained through size, no large firms will emerge and entry barriers will be low, allowing a stream of new entrants into the industry. Convenience stores, veterinary care, used-car sales, and funeral homes are examples.

If a company is able to overcome the limitations of a fragmented market, however, it can reap the benefits of a broadly targeted cost leadership or differentiation strategy. Until Pizza Hut and Pizza Pizza were able to use advertising to differentiate themselves from local competitors, the Canadian fast-food pizza business was a fragmented industry comprising primarily locally owned pizza parlours, each with its own distinctive product and service offering.

consolidated industry
an industry with a small number of large and relatively powerful firms

As an industry matures, fragmentation is overcome and the industry tends to become a **consolidated industry** dominated by a few large companies. Although many industries begin as fragmented, battles for market share and creative attempts to overcome local or niche

Table 5–2 The Eight Dimensions of Quality

1. **Performance**	Primary operating characteristics, such as a washing machine's cleaning ability
2. **Features**	"Bells and whistles," like cruise control in a car, that supplement the basic functions
3. **Reliability**	Probability that the product will continue functioning without any significant maintenance
4. **Conformance**	Degree to which a product meets standards. When a customer buys a product out of the warehouse, it will perform identically to that viewed on the showroom floor.
5. **Durability**	Number of years of service a consumer can expect from a product before it significantly deteriorates. Differs from reliability in that a product can be durable, but still need a lot of maintenance.
6. **Serviceability**	Product's ease of repair
7. **Aesthetics**	How a product looks, feels, sounds, tastes, or smells
8. **Perceived Quality**	Product's overall reputation. Especially important if there are no objective, easily used measures of quality.

Source: Adapted from D.A. Garvin, *Managing Quality: The Strategic and Competitive Edge* (New York: Free Press, 1988).

market boundaries often increase the market share of a few companies. After product standards become established for minimum quality and features, competition shifts to a greater emphasis on cost and service. Slower growth, over-capacity, and knowledgeable buyers combine to put a premium on a firm's ability to achieve cost leadership or differentiation along the dimensions most desired by the market. Research and development shifts from product to process improvements. Overall product quality improves, and costs are reduced significantly.

strategic rollup rapid acquisition of independent businesses for the purpose of consolidating an industry and securing a dominant position in it

The **strategic rollup** was developed in the mid-1990s as an efficient way to quickly consolidate a fragmented industry. With the aid of money from venture capitalists, an entrepreneur acquires hundreds of owner-operated small businesses. The resulting large firm creates economies of scale by building regional or national brands, applies best practices across all aspects of marketing and operations, and hires more sophisticated managers than the small businesses could previously afford. Rollups differ from conventional mergers and acquisitions in three ways: (1) They involve large numbers of firms, (2) the acquired firms are typically owner-operated, and (3) the objective is not to gain incremental advantage, but to reinvent an entire industry.[14] Rollups are currently under way in the funeral industry, led by the American firm Services Corporation International (SCI) and the Canadian firm the Loewen Group (recently acquired by the American firm the Alderwoods Group). Many independent funeral homes were family-owned and ill-prepared for the issue of succession. Consolidators would buy independent funeral homes in areas where they had developed clusters of homes, centralizing many of the support activities of the funeral home to increase efficiency. The result of this activity is a consolidated industry where small independent funeral homes are gradually being driven out of business because they lack the economies of scale and the managerial expertise possessed by larger consolidators like SCI and Loewen.[15]

Once consolidated, the industry becomes one in which cost leadership and differentiation tend to be combined to various degrees. A firm can no longer gain high market share simply through low price. The buyers are more sophisticated and demand a certain minimum level of quality for price paid. The same is true for firms emphasizing high quality. Either the quality must be high enough and valued by the customer sufficiently to justify the higher price or the price must be dropped (through lowering costs) to compete effectively with the lower-priced products. This consolidation is taking place worldwide in the automobile, airline, and home appliance industries.

Hypercompetition and Competitive Strategy

In his book *Hypercompetition*, D'Aveni proposes that it is becoming increasingly difficult to sustain a competitive advantage for very long. "Market stability is threatened by short product life cycles, short product design cycles, new technologies, frequent entry by unexpected outsiders, repositioning by incumbents, and tactical redefinitions of market boundaries as diverse industries merge."[16] Consequently, a company or business unit must constantly work to improve its competitive advantage. It is not enough to be just the lowest cost competitor. Through continuous improvement programs, competitors are usually working to lower their costs as well. Firms must find new ways not only to reduce costs further, but also to add value to the product or service being provided.

The same is true of a firm or unit that is following a differentiation strategy. Maytag Company, for example, was successful for many years by offering the most durable brand in major home appliances. Their ad campaigns about the lonely Maytag repairman endured for decades. The company was able to charge the highest prices for Maytag brand washing machines. When other competitors improved the quality of their products, however, it became increasingly hard for customers to justify Maytag's significantly higher price. Consequently Maytag was forced not only to add new features to its products, but also to reduce costs through improved manufacturing processes so that its prices were no longer out of line with those of the competition. This illustrates D'Aveni's contention that as industries become hypercompetitive, it becomes harder to sustain a competitive advantage. Firms initially compete on cost and quality until an abundance of high-quality, low-priced goods result. This occurred in the North American major home appliance industry by 1980. In a second stage of competition, the competitors move into untapped markets. Others usually imitate these moves until the moves become too risky or expensive. This epitomized the major home appliance industry during the 1980s and 1990s, as firms moved first to Europe and then into Asia and South America.

According to D'Aveni, firms then raise entry barriers to limit competitors. Economies of scale, distribution agreements, and strategic alliances made it all but impossible for a new firm to enter the major home appliance industry by the end of the twentieth century. After the established players have entered and consolidated all new markets, the next stage is for the remaining firms to attack and destroy the strongholds of other firms. Maytag's 1995 decision to divest its European division and concentrate on improving its position in North America could be a prelude to building a North American stronghold while Whirlpool, GE, and Electrolux are distracted by European and worldwide investments. Eventually, according to D'Aveni, the remaining large global competitors work their way to a situation of perfect competition in which no one has any advantage and profits are minimal.

Before hypercompetition, strategic initiatives provided competitive advantage for many years, perhaps for decades. This is no longer the case. According to D'Aveni, as industries become hypercompetitive, there is no such thing as a sustainable competitive advantage. Successful strategic initiatives in this type of industry typically last only months to a few years. The only way a firm in this kind of dynamic industry can sustain any competitive advantage is through a continuous series of multiple short-term initiatives aimed at replacing a firm's current successful products with the next generation of products before the competitors can do so. Intel and Microsoft are taking this approach in the hypercompetitive computer industry.

Hypercompetition views competition, in effect, as a distinct series of ocean waves on what used to be a fairly calm stretch of water. As industry competition becomes more intense, the waves grow higher and require more dexterity to handle. Although a strategy is still needed to sail from point A to point B, more water turbulence means that a craft must continually adjust course to suit each new large wave. One danger of D'Aveni's concept of hypercompetition, however, is that it may lead to an overemphasis on short-term tactics (to be discussed in the next section) over long-term strategy. Too much of an orientation toward each individual wave of hypercompetition could cause a company to focus too much on short-term temporary advantage and not enough on achieving its long-term objectives through building sustainable competitive advantage. (Hypercompetition is also discussed as part of external environmental scanning in **Chapter 3.**)

Which Competitive Strategy Is Best?

Before selecting one of Porter's generic competitive strategies for a company or business unit, management should assess its feasibility in terms of company or business unit resources and capabilities. Porter lists some of the commonly required skills and resources, as well as organizational requirements, in **Table 5–3.** It is also important to consider the stage of industry evolution (discussed in detail in **Chapter 3**) and choose a generic strategy that addresses the greatest challenges associated with each stage. The choice of strategy is therefore based on an assessment of the greatest opportunity associated with each stage of industry evolution, and an understanding of the industry competitive forces present in each. Although there are no hard-and-fast rules, some characteristics of each stage of industry evolution and guidelines for strategic development are outlined next.

Table 5–3 Requirements for Generic Competitive Strategies

Generic Strategy	Commonly Required Skills and Resources	Common Organizational Requirements

Cost Leadership	• Sustained capital investment and access to capital
	  • Process engineering skills
	  • Intense supervision of labour
	  • Products designed for ease of manufacture
	  • Low-cost distribution system
		• Tight cost control
		• Frequent, detailed control reports
		• Structured organization and responsibilities
		• Incentives based on meeting strict quantitative targets

Differentiation	• Strong marketing abilities • Product engineering • Creative flair • Strong capability in basic research • Corporate reputation for quality or technological leadership • Long tradition in the industry or unique combination of skills drawn from other businesses • Strong co-operation from channels	• Strong coordination among functions in R&D, product development, and marketing • Subjective measurement and incentives instead of quantitative measures • Amenities to attract highly skilled labour, scientists, or creative people
Focus	• Combination of the above policies directed at the particular strategic target	• Combination of the above policies directed at the particular strategic target

Source: Adapted/reprinted with permission of The Free Press, an imprint of Simon & Schuster, from *Competitive Strategy: Techniques for Analyzing Industries and Competitors* by Michael E. Porter, pp. 40–41. Copyright © 1980, 1988 by The Free Press.

- *Emerging Industries.* New industries that have been recently formed are usually a result of technological or regulatory changes. In this stage, sales growth is slow because of buyers' unfamiliarity with products, high prices, and poor distribution channels. Organizations are therefore faced with considerable *uncertainty*—over what product features to provide, optimal pricing levels, speed of consumer acceptance, and competitive response. Strategies for dealing with these uncertainties include developing internal strengths along the value chain and enhancing learning capabilities, and co-operating with other new firms to create product standards and achieve economies of scale, so that first-mover advantages are maximized.

- *Mature Industries.* As industries mature, market growth slows down and eventually stops. Because sales growth is minimal (demand might only come from replacement demand at this stage), firms become increasingly competitive. This *competition for market share* gives buyers more power and puts downward pressure on prices. Organizations are therefore faced with intense rivalry, which they can combat by focusing on improving internal efficiency, improving customer service, or expanding into less-developed international markets where rivalry is less intense.

- *Declining Industries.* When the size of a market actually decreases, industries are said to be in decline. This occurs most frequently because of technological substitution, changes in consumer tastes, regulatory changes, or increased international competition. Competition in this stage can be particularly intense, especially if exit barriers exist that discourage or prevent firms from leaving an otherwise unattractive industry. Especially when firms have large-scale production facilities, *intense rivalry* occurs as firms try to use existing capacity and keep average unit costs low. Strategies for dealing with this rivalry include striving for market leadership through pursuing a cost leadership strategy or focusing on an underserved market niche that the firm is able to serve. If these strategies fail, organizations may be left no choice but to divest or liquidate the business.

Competitive Tactics

tactic a detailed plan of how a strategy will be implemented

Studies of decision making report that half the decisions made in organizations fail because of poor tactics.[17] A **tactic** is a specific operating plan detailing how a strategy is to be implemented in terms of when and where it is to be put into action. By their nature, tactics are narrower in their scope and shorter in their time horizon than are strategies. Tactics, therefore, may be viewed (like policies) as a link between the formulation and implementation of strategy. Some of the tactics available to implement competitive strategies are *timing* tactics (when) and market *location* tactics (where).

Timing Tactics: When to Compete

first mover the first organization to reach the market with a new product

first mover advantages the profits earned by the first mover, before new entrants increase competition and gain market share

The first company to manufacture and sell a new product or service is called the **first mover** (or pioneer). Some **first mover advantages** are that the company is able to establish a reputation as an industry leader, move down the learning curve to assume the cost leader position, and earn temporarily high profits from buyers who value the product or service very highly. A successful first mover can also set the standard for all subsequent products in the industry. A company that sets the standard "locks in" customers and is then able to offer further products based on that standard.[18] Microsoft was able to do this in software with its Windows operating system, and Netscape garnered more than 80% share of the internet browser market by being first to commercialize the product successfully. Research does indicate that moving first or second into a new industry or foreign country results in greater market share and shareholder wealth than does moving later.[19] This is only true, however, if the first mover has sufficient resources to both exploit the new market and to defend its position against later arrivals with greater resources.[20]

late mover organizations that enter a market after the first mover has taken the initial risks of market development

late mover advantages the reduced costs and risks associated with allowing the first mover to establish the demand for the product

Being a first mover does, however, have its disadvantages. These disadvantages can be, conversely, advantages enjoyed by **late mover** firms. **Late mover advantages** may include being able to imitate the technological advances of others (and thus keep R & D costs low), keeping risks down by waiting until a new market is established, and taking advantage of the first mover's natural inclination to ignore market segments.[21] Once Netscape had established itself as the standard for internet browsers, Microsoft used its huge resources to directly attack Netscape's position. It did not want Netscape to also set the standard in the developing and highly lucrative intranet market inside organizations. Research suggests that the advantages and disadvantages of first and late movers may not always generalize across industries because of differences in entry barriers and the resources of the specific competitors.[22]

Location Tactics: Where to Compete

A company or business unit can implement a competitive strategy either offensively or defensively. Either set of tactics can result in improved firm performance, but the choice should be made based on the resources currently possessed by the organization. It is always wise to engage in offensive tactics from a position of strength because they are usually met with strong competitive response. In absence of a strong competitive position, defensive tactics are wise because they allow the organization to develop its resources for future use, either aggressively or defensively.[23]

offensive tactic a decision or action taking effect outside an organization's current market location

Offensive Tactics An **offensive tactic** usually takes place in an established competitor's market location. Following are some of the methods used to attack a competitor's position:

- **Frontal Assault:** The attacking firm goes head to head with its competitor. It matches the competitor in every category from price to promotion to distribution channel. To be successful, the attacker must not only have superior resources but also the willingness to persevere. This is generally a very expensive tactic and may serve to awaken a sleeping giant (a number of small telecom firms in Canada did this to Bell in long-distance telephone service), depressing profits for the whole industry.

- **Flanking Manoeuvre**: Rather than going straight for a competitor's position of strength with a frontal assault, a firm may attack a part of the market where the competitor is weak. The Canadian chartered banks have made moves into insurance, mutual funds, financial planning, and brokerage, gradually developing strength in a range of financial services. They can offer these services to clients in one location, increasing sales to those consumers who desire convenience or display loyalty to their banking institution. To be successful, the flanker must be patient and willing to carefully expand out of the relatively undefended market niche or else face retaliation by an established competitor.

- **Bypass Attack**: Rather than attacking the established competitor frontally or on its flanks, a company or business unit may choose to change the rules of the game. This is the type of logic that D'Aveni says is necessary in a hypercompetitive industry. This tactic attempts to cut the market out from under the established defender by offering a new type of product that makes the competitor's product unnecessary. For example, instead of competing directly against Microsoft's Windows 95 operating system, Netscape chose to use Java "applets" in its internet browser so that an operating system and specialized programs were no longer necessary to run applications on a personal computer.

- **Encirclement**: Usually evolving out of a frontal assault or flanking manoeuvre, encirclement occurs as an attacking company or unit encircles the competitor's position in terms of products or markets or both. The encircler has greater product variety (a complete product line ranging from low to high price) and/or serves more markets (it dominates every secondary market). Home Depot and Wal-Mart used these tactics when they entered Canada. By offering broader and deeper product lines than established retailers, these large companies were able to beat the competition on both price and selection. Many small retailers were unable to withstand this competition. Even large retailers like Kmart could not break out of the encirclement tactics Wal-Mart used so effectively.

- **Guerrilla Warfare**: Instead of a continual and extensive, resource-expensive attack on a competitor, a firm or business unit may choose to "hit and run." Guerrilla warfare is characterized by the use of small, intermittent assaults on different market segments held by the competitor. In this way, a new entrant or small firm can make some gains without seriously threatening a large, established competitor and evoking some form of retaliation. To be successful, the firm or unit conducting guerrilla warfare must be patient enough to accept small gains and to avoid pushing the established competitor to the point that it must respond or else lose face. Microbreweries, which make beer for sale to local customers, use this tactic against national brewers like Labatt.

defensive tactic a decision or action taking effect in an organization's current market location

Defensive Tactics   A **defensive tactic** usually takes place in the firm's own current market position as a defence against possible attack by a rival. According to Porter, defensive tactics aim to lower the probability of attack, divert attacks to less threatening avenues, or lessen the intensity of an attack. Instead of directly increasing competitive advantage, they make a company's or business unit's competitive advantage more sustainable by causing a challenger to conclude that an attack is unattractive. These tactics deliberately reduce short-term profitability to ensure long-term profitability.[24] Here are some methods used to protect an organization's competitive position:

- **Raise Structural Barriers**: Entry barriers act to block a challenger's logical avenues of attack. Some of the most important entry-barrier strategies according to Porter are the following:
  1.   Offer a full line of products in every profitable market segment to close off any entry

points (for example, Coca-Cola offers unprofitable non-carbonated beverages to keep competitors off store shelves).

2. Block channel access by signing exclusive agreements with distributors.
3. Raise buyer switching costs by offering low-cost training to users.
4. Raise the cost of gaining trial users by keeping prices low on items new users are most likely to purchase.
5. Increase scale economies to reduce unit costs.
6. Foreclose alternative technologies through patenting or licensing.
7. Limit outside access to facilities and personnel.
8. Tie up suppliers by obtaining exclusive contracts or purchasing key locations.
9. Avoid suppliers that also serve competitors.
10. Encourage the government to raise barriers such as safety and pollution standards or favourable trade policies.

- **Increase Expected Retaliation**: This tactic is any action that increases the perceived threat of retaliation for an attack. For example, management may strongly defend any erosion of market share by drastically cutting prices or matching a challenger's promotion through a policy of accepting any price-reduction coupons for a competitor's product. This counter-attack is especially important in markets that are very important to the defending company or business unit. For example, when the Clorox Company challenged Procter & Gamble in the detergent market with Clorox Super Detergent, P&G retaliated by test marketing its liquid bleach, Lemon Fresh Comet, in an attempt to scare Clorox into retreating from the detergent market. When new discount airlines like CanJet and WestJet started flying between cities in the east and west of Canada, respectively, Air Canada reacted by dropping its prices to keep price-conscious customers from switching airlines. In fact at one point it dropped its prices so much, it was ordered to raise them to avoid predatory pricing.

- **Lower the Inducement for Attack**: A third type of defensive tactic is to reduce a challenger's expectation of future profits in the industry. As WestJet has done, a company can deliberately keep prices low and constantly invest in cost-reducing measures. With prices kept very low, there is little profit incentive for a new entrant.

Co-operative Strategies

co-operative strategy partnering with other firms to gain competitive advantage

Competitive strategies and tactics are used to gain competitive advantage within an industry by battling against other firms. These are not, however, the only business strategy options available to a company or business unit for competing successfully within an industry. **Co-operative strategies** can also be used to gain competitive advantage within an industry by working with other firms. The reason an organization chooses a co-operative strategy over a competitive one is usually that certain resource gaps prevent it from acting independently. There is usually some connection between the value chains of organizations entering into co-operative relationships that provides a benefit to each organization that it could not achieve independently. This usually happens in one of two ways. The first is through the sharing of resources between organizations, which creates strength in more activities. Logical partnerships would offset weaknesses in each other's value chain, where, for example, one organization's strength in R & D and manufacturing could be combined with another organization's strength in sales and marketing. The second way is through one organization's provision of either a source of raw materials or components for the other organization's product, or a seller or distributor for it. These partnerships extend each organization's value chain by linking to a partner's value chain on either the upstream or downstream end of its own. This is what we often see when Canadian firms partner with distributors in China and Japan to gain market access.

Collusion

collusion co-operative firm behaviour intended to influence the forces of supply and demand in a market

The two general types of co-operative strategies are collusion and strategic alliances. **Collusion** is the active co-operation of firms within an industry to reduce output and raise prices in order to get around the normal economic law of supply and demand. Collusion may be explicit, where firms co-operate through direct communication and negotiation, or tacit, where firms co-operate indirectly through an informal system of signals. Explicit collusion is illegal in most countries. For example, in February 2001, Tokai Carbon Co., Ltd. of Japan pleaded guilty to aiding its competitors to implement a foreign-directed conspiracy in Canada. Members of this group agreed to fix prices and to divide world markets for graphite electrodes between themselves. They colluded to have Tokai refrain from selling directly into Canada, a market dominated by UCAR Inc. and SGL Canada Inc. By colluding in this way, Tokai helped a price-fixing scheme to succeed in Canada. Through Tokai's agreement to stay out of the Canadian market, competition was reduced and the sole Canadian producers had a near monopoly position. The prices of graphite electrode prices in Canada increased by more than 90% between 1992 and 1997.[25]

Collusion can also be tacit, in which case there is no direct communication among competing firms. Tacit collusion is actually a normal practice in oligopolies, where competitive interdependence is high. It is most likely to be successful if (1) there are a small number of identifiable competitors, (2) costs are similar among firms, (3) one firm tends to act as the "price leader," (4) there is a common industry culture that accepts co-operation, (5) sales are characterized by a high frequency of small orders, (6) large inventories and order backlogs are normal ways of dealing with fluctuations in demand, and (7) there are high entry barriers to keep out new competitors.[26] Even tacit collusion can, however, be illegal. Regulatory bodies such as the Competition Bureau want to ensure that collusion does not unfairly lessen competition or permit organizations to exert undue influence on consumers.

Strategic Alliances

strategic alliance a mutually beneficial partnership between organizations

A **strategic alliance** is a partnership of two or more organizations or business units to achieve strategically significant objectives that are mutually beneficial.[27] Alliances between companies or business units have become a fact of life in modern business. More than 20 000 alliances occurred between 1992 and 1997, quadruple the total five years earlier.[28] Some alliances are very short-lived, only lasting long enough for one partner to establish a beachhead in a new market. Over time, conflicts over objectives and control often develop between the partners. For these and other reasons, between 30% and 50% of all alliances perform unsatisfactorily.[29] Others are more long-lasting and may even be the prelude to a full merger between two companies. A recent study found that firms involved in strategic alliances had 11% higher revenues and a 20% higher growth rate than companies not involved in alliances.[30]

Companies or business units may form a strategic alliance for a number of reasons, including these:

1. **To obtain technological or manufacturing capabilities**: For example, Intel formed a partnership with Hewlett-Packard to use HP's capabilities in RISC technology in order to develop the successor to Intel's Pentium microprocessor.

2. **To obtain access to specific markets**: Rather than buy a foreign company or build breweries of its own in other countries, Anheuser-Busch chose to license the right to brew and market Budweiser to other brewers, such as Labatt in Canada, Modelo in Mexico, and Kirin in Japan.

3. **To reduce financial risk**: For example, because the costs of developing a new large jet airplane were becoming too high for any one manufacturer, Boeing, Aerospatiale of France,

British Aerospace, Construcciones Aeronáuticas of Spain, and Deutsche Aerospace of Germany planned a joint venture to design such a plane.

4. **To reduce political risk**: To gain access to China, ensuring a positive relationship with the often restrictive Chinese government, and to develop products well-suited to local tastes, the Vancouver-based coffee company Blenz formed a joint venture with China Coffee Holdings Inc. to develop Blenz Coffee retail outlets in China.

5. **To achieve or ensure competitive advantage**: General Motors and Toyota formed Nummi Corporation as a joint venture to give Toyota a manufacturing facility in the United States and to give GM access to Toyota's low-cost, high-quality manufacturing expertise.[31]

Co-operative arrangements between companies and business units fall along a continuum from weak and distant to strong and close. (See **Figure 5–3**.) The types of alliances range from mutual service consortia to joint ventures and licensing arrangements to value chain partnerships.[32]

Mutual Service Consortia

mutual service consortium a partnership based on the sharing of resources

A **mutual service consortium** is a partnership of similar companies in similar industries that pool their resources to gain a benefit that is too expensive to develop alone, such as access to advanced technology. For example, IBM of the United States, Toshiba of Japan, and Siemens of Germany formed a consortium to develop new generations of computer chips. As part of this alliance, IBM offered Toshiba its expertise in chemical mechanical polishing to help develop a new manufacturing process using ultraviolet lithography to etch tiny circuits in silicon chips.[33] The mutual service consortia is a fairly weak and distant alliance—appropriate for partners who want to work together but not to share their core competencies. There is usually very little interaction or communication between the partners.

Joint Venture

joint venture a strategic partnership that creates a separate organization to develop a business opportunity

A **joint venture** is a "co-operative business activity, formed by two or more separate organizations for strategic purposes, that creates an independent business entity and allocates ownership, operational responsibilities, and financial risks and rewards to each member, while preserving their separate identity/autonomy."[34] Along with licensing arrangements, joint ventures lie at the midpoint of the continuum and are formed to pursue an opportunity that needs a capability from two companies or business units, such as the technology of one and the distribution channels of another.

Joint ventures are the most popular form of strategic alliance. They often occur because the companies involved do not want to or cannot legally merge permanently. Joint ventures provide a way to temporarily combine the different strengths of partners to achieve an outcome of value to both. For example, Toys "R" Us and Amazon.com formed a joint venture in

Figure 5–3 Continuum of Strategic Alliances

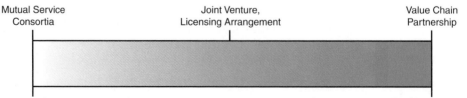

| Mutual Service Consortia | Joint Venture, Licensing Arrangement | Value Chain Partnership |

Weak and Distant — **Strong and Close**

Source: Suggested by R.M. Kanter, "Collaborative Advantage: The Art of Alliances," *Harvard Business Review* (July–August 1994), pp. 96–108. Copyright © 2001 by the President and Fellows of Harvard College, all rights reserved.

August 2000 called Toysrus.com to act as an online toy store. Amazon was to include the joint venture on its website, ship the products, and handle customer service. In turn, Toys "R" Us was to choose and buy the toys, using its purchasing power to get the most desired toys at the best price.[35]

Extremely popular in international undertakings because of financial and political-legal constraints, joint ventures are a convenient way for organizations to work together without losing their independence. Disadvantages of joint ventures are the same as with any type of partnership, including loss of control, lower profits, probability of conflicts with partners, and the likely transfer of technological advantage to the partner. Joint ventures are often meant to be temporary, especially by companies that view them as a way to rectify a competitive weakness until they can achieve long-term dominance in the partnership. Partially for this reason, joint ventures have a high failure rate. Research does indicate, however, that joint ventures tend to be more successful when the partners have equal ownership in the venture and are mutually dependent on each other for results.[36]

licensing arrangement an agreement to grant production or distribution rights to another organization in a different country

Licensing Arrangement
A **licensing arrangement** is an agreement in which the licensing firm grants rights to another firm in another country or market to produce and/or sell a product. The licensee pays compensation to the licensing firm in return for technical expertise. Licensing is an especially useful strategy if the trademark or brand name is well known but the multinational corporation does not have sufficient funds to finance a direct entry into the country. Canadian breweries Labatt and Molson use this strategy to produce and market their beer brands in the United States, South America, and Europe. This strategy also becomes important if the country makes entry via investment either difficult or impossible. The danger always exists, however, that the licensee might develop its competency to the point that it becomes a competitor to the licensing firm. Therefore, a company should never license its distinctive competency, even for some short-run advantage.

value chain partnership a long-term alliance between a producer and a supplier or distributor to obtain mutual advantage

Value Chain Partnership
A **value chain partnership** is a strong and close alliance in which one company or unit forms a long-term arrangement with a key supplier or distributor for mutual advantage. For example, to improve the quality of parts they purchase, North American car companies have decided to work more closely with fewer suppliers and to involve them more in product design decisions. Mopar has a partnership for original equipment parts and accessories for Dodge, Jeep, and Chrysler vehicles. With car manufacturers increasingly using just-in-time production systems, good working relationships with major suppliers are particularly important. Activities that had been previously done internally by an auto maker are being outsourced to suppliers specializing in those activities. A value chain partnership helps solidify these relationships and encourages both parties to work together to improve efficiency and coordination. Research suggests that suppliers who engage in long-term relationships are more profitable than suppliers with multiple short-term contracts.[37] For an example, see the **Internet Issue** feature on the internet value chain partnership between Cisco Systems and its suppliers, on page 134.

All forms of strategic alliances are filled with uncertainty. There are many issues that need to be dealt with when the alliance is initially formed and others that emerge later. Many problems revolve around the fact that a firm's alliance partners may also be its competitors, either now or in the future. One thorny issue in any strategic alliance is how to co-operate without giving away the company or business unit's core competency. "Particularly when advanced technology is involved, it can be difficult for partners in an alliance to co-operate and openly share strategic know-how, but it is mandatory if the joint venture is to succeed."[38] It is therefore important that a company or business unit that is interested in joining or forming a strategic alliance consider the pointers for strategic alliance success listed in **Table 5–4** on page 134.

Internet Issue

Business to Business at Cisco Systems

Every day Cisco Systems, successful manufacturer of internet servers, posts its requirements for components on an extranet, a dedicated internet-based networck connecting the company to 32 manufacturing plants. Although Cisco does not own these plants, each plant has completed a lengthy process of certification ensuring that each meets Cisco's quality and other standards. Within hours of the posting, these suppliers respond with a price, a delivery time, and a record of their recent performance in terms of reliability and product quality.

Cisco then chooses which bid to select and the deal is finalized.

This process has replaced 50 purchasing agents who used to assemble the same information using telephones and faxes. The operation, which used to take three to four days, now takes only hours. The purchasing agents are instead managing the quality of the components.

Three aspects of Cisco's supply system are especially significant. One is the use of the electronic market to set prices. This is characteristic of online auctions and of business-to-business value chain relationships. A second is the exchange of information between buyer and seller. The internet allows the inexpensive flow of information in a way never before realized. Third is the extent to which Cisco outsources activities that many other companies do internally. The ability of the internet to connect multiple departments together with suppliers and distributors in other companies makes outsourcing both effective and efficient.

Source: "Trying to Connect You," *The Economist E-Management Survey* (November 11, 2000), p. 28. Reprinted with permission.

Table 5–4 Recommendations for Strategic Alliance Success

- Have a clear strategic purpose. Integrate the alliance with each partner's strategy. Ensure that mutual value is created for all partners.
- Find a fitting partner with compatible goals and complementary capabilities.
- Identify likely partnering risks and deal with them when the alliance is formed.
- Allocate tasks and responsibilities so that each partner can specialize in what it does best.
- Create incentives for cooperation to minimize differences in corporate culture or organization fit.
- Minimize conflicts among the partners by clarifying objectives and avoiding direct competition in the marketplace.
- If an international alliance, ensure that those managing it have comprehensive cross-cultural knowledge.
- Exchange human resources to maintain communication and trust. Don't allow individual egos to dominate.
- Operate with long-term time horizons. The expectation of future gains can minimize short-term conflicts.
- Develop multiple joint projects so that any failures are counterbalanced by successes.
- Agree upon a monitoring process. Share information to build trust and keep projects on target. Monitor customer responses and service complaints.
- Be flexible in terms of willingness to renegotiate the relationship in terms of environmental changes and new opportunities.
- Agree upon an exit strategy for when the partners' objectives are achieved or the alliance is judged a failure.

Sources: Compiled from B. Gomes-Casseres, "Do You Really Have an Alliance Strategy?" *Strategy & Leadership* (September/October 1998), pp. 6–11; L. Segil, "Strategic Alliances for the 21st Century," *Strategy & Leadership* (September/October 1998), pp. 12–16; A.C. Inkpen and K.-Q. Li, "Joint Venture Formation: Planning and Knowledge Gathering for Success," *Organizational Dynamics* (Spring 1999), pp. 33–47. Inkpen and Li provide a checklist of 17 questions on p. 46.

5.5 Impact of the Internet on Business Strategy

The initial impact of the internet was on marketing. "Business-to-consumer" (B2C) described the activities of many dot-com start-ups selling items directly to consumers via their websites. The best-known of these first entrants or pioneers was Amazon.com, the successful marketer of books and related merchandise. Not wanting to be disadvantaged late entrants, established manufacturers became active participants on the internet. They supplemented their current distribution networks with direct selling through their own internet sites or formed marketing alliances with technologically competent web-based businesses. One such alliance is the Toysrus.com joint venture.

"Business to business" (B2B) describes the launching of web portals aimed at electronically connecting buyers with suppliers, strengthening collective purchasing activities, and auctioning inventory. Dick Hunter, head of Dell Computer's supply chain management, states that one purpose of B2B is for information to replace inventory. For example, the companies supplying Dell with metal and plastic boxes for Dell's computers are located within 145 kilometres of Dell's assembly plant. They have access to Dell's real-time information on its use of their products. On the basis of Dell's usage of their parts, they make more and ship them as needed to Dell's plant. In turn, the suppliers keep only a day's worth of finished stock on hand. "If our information was 100% right," asserts Hunter, "the only inventory that would exist would be in transit."[39]

The B2B consortium is a recent example of the use of co-operative strategies to obtain competitive advantage. Traditional competitors are forming internet consortia to centralize many activities, such as purchasing, that had previously been done internally. General Motors, Ford, and Chrysler have established an auto parts exchange called Covisint. Boeing, Lockheed Martin, Raytheon, and BAE Systems have formed the Global Aerospace & Defence Trading Exchange. Hewlett-Packard, Compaq, and 10 other computer makers have created Ehitex.com. Goodyear, Michelin, Bridgestone, and four other tire makers have formed RubberNetwork.com. Although these consortia are being formed with great expectations, there have been problems. For example, Covisint has three project leaders (one for each auto maker) who are battling over what to charge and how much trading data to allow users to access. The US Federal Trade Commission is reviewing these consortia among erstwhile competitors for antitrust issues. Since Covisint's owners collectively dominate the North American automobile market, there could easily be collusion. According to Dana Corporation, an auto components supplier, "We're concerned about how big this gorilla is going to be. There's only so much room to squeeze prices."[40]

Although B2B is still in its initial stages, Hau Lee, director of the Global Supply Chain Management Forum at Stanford University, proposes that business-to-business commerce will move through four stages of development:

Stage 1: *Information, such as demand forecasts and sales data, is exchanged.* Companies work to define common standards for inventory and point-of-sale to allow better planning.

Stage 2: *Companies move beyond data transfer to exchanging information.* For example, when Wal-Mart's Florida stores ran out of mosquito repellent during a heat wave, the company discovered that Warner Lambert, its supplier, was able to track weather forecasts to predict future peaks in demand. The sharing of this information enabled both companies to do better.

Stage 3: *Companies exchange the right to make decisions.* For example, since Wal-Mart sells disposable diapers made by P&G, which are made with sticky tape from 3M, the three companies are experimenting with a system allowing one person instead of three to make the ordering decision for all three companies.

Stage 4: *Companies exchange work and roles.* The manufacturer becomes a retailer and the retailer moves to a support role. For example, companies such as VooDooCycles and Cannondale, makers of sport bicycles, are increasingly taking customers' orders directly and only then building the bicycles. Since a high-quality bike needs last-minute adjustments before it is ready for the customer, bicycle retailers are needed to perform this crucial service as well as to facilitate purchases of helmets and other paraphernalia.[41]

Discussion Questions

1. What industry forces might cause a propitious niche to disappear?
2. Is it possible for a company or business unit to follow a cost leadership strategy and a differentiation strategy simultaneously? Why or why not?
3. Is it possible for a company to have a sustainable com- petitive advantage when its industry becomes hyper- competitive?
4. What are the advantages and disadvantages of being a first mover in an industry? Give some examples of first mover and late mover firms. Were they successful?
5. Why are many strategic alliances temporary?

Strategic Practice Exercise

This exercise can be conducted individually or in groups, inside or outside class. Its goal is to draw linkages between firm strategy and resources. First, pick an *industry* with which you are familiar (for example automobile manufac- turing, fast food, retail clothing, passenger airlines). Second, identify different *organizations* within this industry that are pursuing different competitive or co-operative strategies. Draw upon whatever library or internet sources you have at your disposal, as well as whatever knowledge you have as a consumer. Third, identify the key aspects of the organiza- tion's *strategy* and classify it according to the different com- petitive and co-operative types discussed in this chapter. Fourth, determine what *resources* are most critical for suc- cessfully pursuing this strategy. Fifth, discuss the reasons why different organizations are pursuing different strategies and how effectively they are doing so. In other words, what *strategic groups* exist in this industry, and how attractive is each? Sixth, determine what *resources* are necessary in order for these firms to engage in the activities and/or behaviours necessary for success? Finally, what *actions* should these organizations take to reduce the vulnerabilities of these strategies (see **Table 5–1** for a summary).

Notes

1. "The Clothes That Made the Man," *Canadian Business* (February 17, 2003), pp. 36–39.
2. K.W. Glaister and J.R. Falshaw, "Strategic Planning: Still Going Strong?," *Long Range Planning* (February 1999), pp. 107–116.
3. T. Brown, "The Essence of Strategy," *Management Review* (April 1997), pp. 8–13.
4. T. Hill and R. Westbrook, "SWOT Analysis: It's Time for a Product Recall," *Long Range Planning* (February 1997), pp. 46–52.
5. W.H. Newman, "Shaping the Master Strategy of Your Firm," *California Management Review*, Vol. 9, No. 3 (1967), pp. 77–88.
6. "Nobody's Watching," *National Post Business* (December 2002) pp. 53–54.
7. M.E. Porter, *Competitive Strategy* (New York: The Free Press, 1980), pp. 34–41, as revised in M.E. Porter, *The Competitive Advantage of Nations* (New York: The Free Press, 1990), pp. 37–40.
8. J.O. DeCastro and J.J. Chrisman, "Narrow-Scope Strategies and Firm Performance: An Empirical Investigation," *Journal of Business Strategies* (Spring 1998), pp. 1–16; T.M. Stearns, N.M. Carter, P.D. Reynolds, and M.L. Williams, "New Firm Survival: Industry, Strategy, and Location," *Journal of Business Venturing* (January 1995), pp. 23–42.
9. Porter, *Competitive Strategy*, p. 35.
10. R.E. Caves and P. Ghemawat, "Identifying Mobility Barriers," *Strategic Management Journal* (January 1992), pp. 1–12.
11. C. Campbell-Hunt, "What Have We Learned about Generic Competitive Strategy? A Meta Analysis," *Strategic Management Journal* (February 2000), pp. 127–154.
12. M. Kroll, P. Wright, and R.A. Heiens, "The Contribution of Product Quality to Competitive Advantage: Impacts on Systematic Variance and Unexplained Variance in Returns," *Strategic Management Journal* (April 1999), pp. 375–384.
13. N. Brodsky, "Size Matters," *INC.* (September 1998), pp. 31–32.
14. P.F. Kocourek, S.Y. Chung, and M.G. McKenna, "Strategic Rollups: Overhauling the Multi-Merger Machine," *Strategy + Business* (2nd Quarter 2000), pp. 45–53.
15. J.A. Tannenbaum, "Acquisitive Companies Set Out to 'Roll Up' Fragmented Industries," *The Wall Street Journal* (March 3, 1997), pp. A1, A6.

16. R.A. D'Aveni, *Hypercompetition* (New York: The Free Press, 1994), pp. xiii–xiv.

17. P.C. Nutt, "Surprising but True: Half the Decisions in Organizations Fail," *Academy of Management Executive* (November 1999), pp. 75–90.

18. Some refer to this as the economic concept of "increasing returns." Instead of reaching a point of diminishing returns when a product saturates a market and the curve levels off, the curve continues to go up as the company takes advantage of setting the standard to spin off new products that use the new standard to achieve higher performance than competitors. See J. Alley, "The Theory That Made Microsoft," *Fortune* (April 29, 1996), pp. 65–66.

19. H. Lee, K.G. Smith, C.M. Grimm, and A. Schomburg, "Timing, Order and Durability of New Product Advantages with Imitation," *Strategic Management Journal* (January 2000), pp. 23–30; Y. Pan and P.C.K. Chi, "Financial Performance and Survival of Multinational Corporations in China," *Strategic Management Journal* (April 1999), pp. 359–374; R. Makadok, "Can First-Mover and Early-Mover Advantages Be Sustained in an Industry with Low Barriers to Entry/Imitation?" *Strategic Management Journal* (July 1998), pp. 683–696; B. Mascarenhas, "The Order and Size of Entry into International Markets," *Journal of Business Venturing* (July 1997), pp. 287–299.

20. G.J. Tellis and P.N. Golder, "First to Market, First to Fail? Real Causes of Enduring Market Leadership," *Sloan Management Review* (Winter 1996), pp. 65–75.

21. For an in-depth discussion of first and late mover advantages and disadvantages, see D.-S. Cho, D.-J. Kim, and D.K. Rhee, "Latecomer Strategies: Evidence from the Semiconductor Industry in Japan and Korea," *Organization Science* (July–August 1998), pp. 489–505.

22. T.S. Schoenecker and A.C. Cooper, "The Role of Firm Resources and Organizational Attributes in Determining Entry Timing: A Cross-Industry Study," *Strategic Management Journal* (December 1998), pp. 1127–1143.

23. Summarized from various articles by L. Fahey in *The Strategic Management Reader*, edited by L. Fahey (Englewood Cliffs, NJ: Prentice-Hall, 1989), pp. 178–205.

24. This information on defensive tactics is summarized from M.E. Porter, *Competitive Advantage* (New York: Free Press, 1985), pp. 482–512.

25. http://strategis.ic.gc.ca/SSG/ct02114e.html (accessed March 28, 2003).

26. Much of the content on co-operative strategies was summarized from J.B. Barney, *Gaining and Sustaining Competitive Advantage* (Reading, Mass.: Addison-Wesley, 1997), pp. 255–278.

27. E.A. Murray, Jr., and J.F. Mahon, "Strategic Alliances: Gateway to the New Europe?" *Long Range Planning* (August 1993), p. 103.

28. H. Meyer, "My Enemy, My Friend," *Journal of Business Strategy* (September–October 1998), pp. 42–46.

29. T.K. Das and B.-S. Teng, "Instabilities of Strategic Alliances: An Internal Tensions Perspective," *Organization Science* (January–February 2000), pp. 77–101.

30. L. Segil, "Strategic Alliances for the 21st Century," *Strategy & Leadership* (September/October 1998), pp. 12–16.

31. E.A. Murray Jr., and J.F. Mahon, "Strategic Alliances: Gateway to the New Europe?" *Long Range Planning* (August 1993), pp. 105–106.

32. R.M. Kanter, "Collaborative Advantage: The Art of Alliances," *Harvard Business Review* (July–August 1994), pp. 96–108.

33. B. Bremner, Z. Schiller, T. Smart, and W.J. Holstein, "Keiretsu Connections," *Business Week* (July 22, 1996), pp. 52–54.

34. R.P. Lynch, *The Practical Guide to Joint Ventures and Corporate Alliances* (New York: John Wiley and Sons, 1989), p. 7.

35. H. Green, "Double Play," *Business Week E-Biz* (October 23, 2000), pp. EB42–EB46.

36. L.L. Blodgett, "Factors in the Instability of International Joint Ventures: An Event History Analysis," *Strategic Management Journal* (September 1992), pp. 475–481; J. Bleeke and D. Ernst, "The Way to Win in Cross-Border Alliances," *Harvard Business Review* (November–December 1991), pp. 127–135; J.M. Geringer, "Partner Selection Criteria for Developed Country Joint Ventures," in *International Management Behavior*, 2nd edition, edited by H.W. Lane and J.J. DiStephano (Boston: PWS-Kent, 1992), pp. 206–216.

37. K.Z. Andrews, "Manufacturer/Supplier Relationships: The Supplier Payoff," *Harvard Business Review* (September–October 1995), pp. 14–15.

38. P. Lorange, "Black-Box Protection of Your Core Competencies in Strategic Alliances," in *Co-operative Strategies: European Perspectives*, edited by P.W. Beamish and J.P. Killing (San Francisco: The New Lexington Press, 1997), pp. 59–99.

39. "Enter the Eco-System," *The Economist E-Management Survey* (November 11, 2000), p. 30.

40. N. Weinberg, "Herding Cats," *Forbes* (July 24, 2000), pp. 108–110.

41. "Enter the Eco-System," *The Economist E-Management Survey* (November 11, 2000), p. 34.

CHAPTER 6

Strategy Formulation: Corporate Strategy

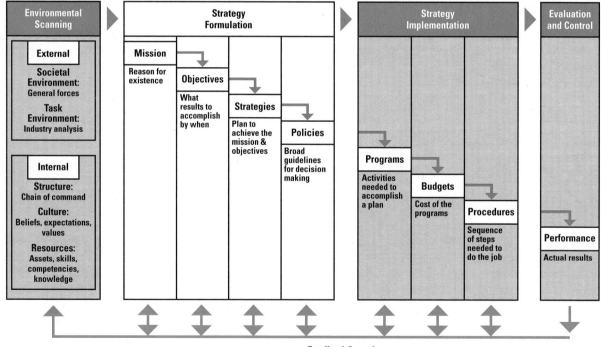

Environmental Scanning

External

Societal Environment: General forces

Task Environment: Industry analysis

Internal

Structure: Chain of command

Culture: Beliefs, expectations, values

Resources: Assets, skills, competencies, knowledge

Strategy Formulation

Mission — Reason for existence

Objectives — What results to accomplish by when

Strategies — Plan to achieve the mission & objectives

Policies — Broad guidelines for decision making

Strategy Implementation

Programs — Activities needed to accomplish a plan

Budgets — Cost of the programs

Procedures — Sequence of steps needed to do the job

Evaluation and Control

Performance — Actual results

Feedback/Learning

Learning Objectives

After reading this chapter you should be able to identify and formulate strategies for a multibusiness firm based on

Corporate directional strategies of growth, stability, or retrenchment

Portfolio analysis techniques to guide decisions to enter and exit businesses

Parenting subsidiaries and business units to generate competitive advantage

conglomerate discount the amount by which the share price of a conglomerate understates its assets

Canadian Pacific (CP) was one of Canada's oldest businesses, with roots in building the cross-country railway more than 120 years ago. Since that time Canadian Pacific had grown into a diversified conglomerate with revenues in excess of $18 billion. But in October 2001, Canadian Pacific announced that it would break the organization apart to create five separate, publicly traded businesses. Its interests in petroleum, railways, coal, shipping, and hotels would therefore not be managed and financed by one organization but rather by five separate boards, each representing different stakeholder groups. Part of the reason for this separation is to minimize the **conglomerate discount**, a situation that arises when the value of a conglomerate is less than the estimated value of the total of its business units.

Analysts observed that the CP conglomerate was overdue for a breakup. At its peak, CP had 10 divisions in disparate industries. At one point management desired this much diversification because while one division's performance might be struggling, others wouldn't be. As the organization grew, its management and control became increasingly complex. And over time as trade became increasingly liberalized and competition more global, CP's divisions desired to become more of an international force rather than simply a national one. This change was accompanied by shareholder pressure for CP to separate operations in different sectors so their performance could be more accurately assessed by the markets, and each division could act with more strategic autonomy. If each division were an autonomous, publicly traded company, it could use its own equity to acquire competitors as well as protect itself from the effects of other divisions' performance. CP's five businesses are now (1) PanCanadian Energy, (2) CP Ships, (3) Fairmont Hotels & Resorts, (4) CP Railway and (5) Fording Inc. (coal production).

The corporate strategy of breaking up a conglomerate into independent corporations allows the performance of each to be independently judged. It also opens up the possibility for new merger and acquisition activity. For example, Fording is the world's second-largest producer of metallurgical coal. It is now a possible acquisition target because of the downturn in the global economy and reduced crude steel production (which uses coal). On the other hand, PanCanadian engaged in a merger of equals with Alberta Energy to avoid being acquired by larger American competitors. Despite the falling energy prices at the time of CP's privatization, many of Canada's resource companies are vulnerable to foreign takeovers. The merger of PanCanadian and Alberta Energy to form EnCana Corp. was intended to provide the new firm a large enough capital base to facilitate international expansion and to make it competitive with its larger foreign rivals.[1]

6.1 Corporate Strategy

corporate strategy the way a multibusiness organization enters and exits industries to improve its long-run performance

The story of Canadian Pacific's breakup illustrates the importance of corporate strategy to a firm's survival and success. **Corporate strategy** deals with three key issues facing the corporation as a whole:

1. The firm's overall orientation toward growth, stability, or retrenchment (*directional strategy*)

2. The industries or markets in which the firm competes through its products and business units (*portfolio strategy*)

3. The manner in which management coordinates activities, transfers resources, and cultivates capabilities among product lines and business units (*parenting strategy*)

Corporate strategy is primarily about the choice of direction for the firm as a whole.[2] This is true whether the firm is a small, one-product company or a large multinational corporation. In a large multibusiness company, however, corporate strategy is also about managing various product lines and business units for maximum value. In this instance, corporate headquarters must play the role of the organizational "parent," in that it must deal with various product and business unit "children." Even though each product line or business unit has its own competitive or co-operative strategy that it uses to obtain its own competitive advantage in the marketplace, the corporation must coordinate these different business strategies so that the corporation as a whole succeeds as a "family."[3]

Corporate strategy, therefore, includes decisions regarding the flow of financial and other resources to and from a company's product lines and business units. Through a series of coordinating devices, a company transfers skills and capabilities developed in one unit to other units that need such resources. In this way, it attempts to obtain synergies among numerous product lines and business units so that the corporate whole is greater than the sum of its individual business unit parts.[4] All corporations, from the smallest company offering one product in only one industry to the largest conglomerate operating in many industries with many products, must at one time or another consider one or more of these issues.

To deal with each of the key issues, this chapter is organized into three parts that examine corporate strategy in terms of *directional strategy* (orientation toward growth), *portfolio analysis* (coordination of cash flow among units), and *corporate parenting* (building corporate synergies through resource sharing and development).

6.2 Directional Strategy

directional strategy an organization's orientation toward expansion or contraction of its portfolio of businesses

Just as every product or business unit must follow a business strategy to improve its competitive position, every organization must decide its orientation toward growth—its **directional strategy**—by asking the following three questions:

1. Should we expand, cut back, or continue our operations unchanged?

2. Should we concentrate our activities within our current industry or should we diversify into other industries?

3. If we want to grow and expand nationally and/or globally, should we do so through internal development or through external acquisitions, mergers, or strategic alliances?

An organization's directional strategy comprises three general orientations (sometimes called grand strategies):

- *Growth* strategies, which expand the company's activities
- *Stability* strategies, which make no change to the company's current activities
- *Retrenchment* strategies, which reduce the company's level of activities

Having chosen their company's general orientation (such as growth), managers can select from several more specific corporate strategies such as concentration within one product line or industry or diversification into other products or industries. (See **Figure 6–1.**) These

Figure 6–1 Corporate Directional Strategies

• GROWTH	• STABILITY	• RETRENCHMENT

Concentration
  Vertical Growth
  Horizontal Growth
Diversification
  Concentric
  Conglomerate
	Pause/Proceed with Caution
	No Change
	Profit
		Turnaround
		Captive Company
		Sell-out/Divestment
		Bankruptcy/Liquidation

strategies are useful both to corporations operating in only one industry with one product line and to those operating in many industries with many product lines.

GROWTH STRATEGIES

By far the most widely pursued corporate directional strategies are those designed to achieve growth in sales, assets, profits, or some combination. Companies that do business in expanding industries must grow to survive. Continuing growth means increasing sales and a chance to take advantage of the experience curve to reduce the per-unit cost of products sold, thereby increasing profits. This cost reduction becomes extremely important if an organization's industry is growing quickly and competitors are engaging in price wars in attempts to increase their shares of the market. Firms that have not reached "critical mass" (that is, gained the necessary economy of large-scale production) will face large losses unless they can find and fill a small but profitable niche where higher prices can be offset by special product or service features. That is why Bombardier chose to concentrate its activities in a small number of industry sectors; it could thereby attain economies of scale and technological leadership in each. Its critical mass in railway transportation equipment, regional jets, and recreational products allow it to be a strong competitive presence in these industries, deterring entry of new firms and allowing it to reinvest in the innovations that will strengthen its market dominance.

An organization can grow internally by expanding its operations both globally and domestically, or it can grow externally through mergers, acquisitions, and strategic alliances. A **merger** is a transaction involving two or more corporations in which stock is exchanged, but from which only one corporation survives. Mergers usually occur between firms of somewhat similar size and are usually "friendly." One example is the merging of PanCanadian and Alberta Energy discussed in this chapter's opening section. An **acquisition** is the purchase of a company that is completely absorbed as an operating subsidiary or division of the acquiring corporation. One example is Bombardier's acquisition of Lear Jet, the American producer of executive jets. Acquisitions usually occur between firms of different sizes and can be either friendly or hostile. Hostile acquisitions are often called takeovers.

A strategic alliance is a partnership of two or more organizations or business units to achieve strategically significant objectives that are mutually beneficial. Essentially these types of partnerships accomplish the same objectives as mergers and acquisitions, but do so by contractual arrangements rather than outright ownership. See **Chapter 5** for a detailed discussion of strategic alliances.

Growth is a very attractive strategy for two key reasons:

- Growth based on increasing market demand may mask flaws in a company—flaws that would be immediately evident in a stable or declining market. A growing flow of revenue into a highly leveraged organization can create a large amount of *organization slack* (unused resources) that can be used to quickly resolve problems and conflicts between

merger a friendly purchase of one organization by another

acquisition a complete absorption of one organization by another

departments and divisions. Growth also provides a big cushion for a turnaround in case a strategic error is made. Large firms also have more bargaining power than small firms and are more likely to obtain support from key stakeholders in case of difficulty.

■ A growing firm offers more opportunities for advancement, promotion, and interesting jobs. Growth itself is exciting and ego-enhancing for CEOs. The marketplace and potential investors tend to view a growing corporation as a "winner" or "on the move." Executive compensation tends to get bigger as an organization increases in size. Large firms are also more difficult to acquire than are smaller ones; thus an executive's job is more secure.

The two basic growth strategies are concentration on the current product line(s) in one industry and diversification into other product lines in other industries.

Concentration Strategies

If a company's current product lines have real growth potential, concentration of resources on those product lines makes sense as a strategy for growth. The two basic concentration strategies are vertical growth and horizontal growth. Growing firms in a growing industry tend to choose these strategies before they try diversification.

Vertical Growth   Vertical growth can be achieved by taking over a function previously provided by a supplier or by a distributor. The company, in effect, grows by making its own supplies or by distributing its own products. This may be done to reduce costs, gain control over a scarce resource, guarantee quality of a key input, or obtain access to potential customers. This growth can be achieved either internally by expanding current operations or externally through acquisitions. Henry Ford, for example, used internal company resources to build his River Rouge Plant outside Detroit. The manufacturing process was integrated to the point that iron ore entered one end of the long plant and finished automobiles rolled out the other end into a huge parking lot. In contrast, Cisco Systems, the maker of internet hardware, chose the external route to vertical growth by purchasing Radiata, Inc., a maker of chip sets for wireless networks. This acquisition gave Cisco access to technology permitting wireless communications at speeds previously possible only with wired connections.[5]

vertical integration
the extent to which an organization's value chain includes all activities from extracting raw materials to selling products to end-users

Vertical growth results in **vertical integration**—the degree to which a firm operates vertically in multiple locations on an industry's value chain, from extracting raw materials to manufacturing to retailing. More specifically, assuming a function previously provided by a supplier is called **backward integration**, that is, going backward on an industry's value chain. This is sometimes called upstream integration. For example, Thai Rayon Public Co. Ltd. pursued a backward integration strategy when it acquired a 50% equity stake in AV Cell Inc., a New Brunswick wood pulp producer. By owning a producer of rayon grade wood pulp, the main raw material in rayon fabric, Thai Rayon was able to establish an assured supply of raw material, obtain better purchasing power in buying, and achieve stability in purchase prices.[6]

backward integration
extending the organization's value chain toward the source of raw materials and component parts

Assuming a function previously provided by a distributor is labelled **forward integration**, that is, going forward on an industry's value chain. This is sometimes called downstream integration. For example, Air Canada created its own travel agency, Destina.ca, to provide full-service travel arrangements to holiday travellers. In addition, by increasing the services available through its website, it includes many activities traditionally performed by travel agents in its value chain. Both strategic moves are examples of forward integration: performing more services in the forward end of the organization's value chain.

forward integration
extending the organization's value chain toward the end-users of its products

Vertical growth is a logical strategy for an organization or business unit with a strong competitive position in a highly attractive industry—especially when technology is predictable and markets are growing.[7] To keep and even improve its competitive position, the company may use backward integration to minimize resource acquisition costs and inefficient operations as well as forward integration to gain more control over product distribution. The firm, in effect, builds on its distinctive competency by expanding along the industry's value chain to gain greater competitive advantage.

Although backward integration is usually more profitable than forward integration, any type of integration can be disadvantageous for an organization. In fact the relative scarcity of highly integrated firms suggests that their benefits may be overshadowed by costs. What might discourage an organization from becoming increasingly integrated? First, it can reduce its strategic flexibility. The resulting encumbrance of expensive specialized assets that might be hard to sell could create an exit barrier, preventing the organization from leaving that particular industry if it became unprofitable. Second, there may be cost disadvantages associated with having the supply of raw materials come from only one place. If other suppliers are able to provide lower-cost materials, the integrated firm will be placed at a cost disadvantage by its inability to easily change suppliers.

Transaction cost economics proposes that vertical integration is more efficient than contracting for goods and services in the marketplace when the transaction costs of buying goods on the open market become too great. When highly integrated firms become excessively large and bureaucratic, however, the costs of managing the internal transactions may become greater than simply purchasing the needed goods externally, thus justifying outsourcing over vertical integration. See the **Theory As It Applies** feature on how transaction cost economics helps explain why firms vertically integrate.

Theory As It Applies

Transaction Cost Economics Analyzes Vertical Growth Strategy

Why do organizations use vertical growth to permanently own suppliers or distributors when they could simply purchase individual items when needed on the open market? Transaction cost economics is a branch of institutional economics that attempts to answer this question. Beginning with work by Coase and extended by Williamson, transaction cost economics proposes that ownership of resources through vertical growth is more efficient than contracting for goods and services in the marketplace when the transaction costs of buying goods on the open market become too great. Transaction costs include the basic costs of drafting, negotiating, and safeguarding a market agreement (a contract) as well as the later managerial costs when the agreement is creating problems (goods aren't being delivered on time or quality is lower than needed), renegotiation costs (costs of meetings and phone calls), and the costs of settling disputes (lawyers' fees and court costs).

According to Williamson, three conditions must be met before an organization will prefer internalizing a vertical transaction through ownership over contracting for the transaction in the marketplace: (1) a high level of uncertainty must surround the transaction, (2) assets involved in the transaction must be highly specialized to the transaction, and (3) the

transaction must occur frequently. If there is a high level of uncertainty, it will be impossible to write a contract covering all contingencies and it is likely that the contractor will act opportunistically to exploit any gaps in the written agreement, thus creating problems and increasing costs. If the assets being contracted for are highly specialized (goods or services with few alternative uses), there are likely to be few alternative suppliers, thus allowing the contractor to take advantage of the situation and increase costs. The more frequent the transactions, the more opportunity for the contractor to demand special treatment and thus increase costs further.

Vertical integration is not always more efficient than the marketplace, however. When highly vertically integrated firms become excessively large and bureaucratic, the costs of managing the internal transactions may become greater than simply purchasing the needed goods externally, thus justifying outsourcing over ownership. The usually hidden management costs (excessive layers of management, endless committee meetings needed for interdepartmental coordination, and delayed decision making due to excessively detailed rules and policies) add to the internal transaction costs, thus reducing the effectiveness and efficiency of vertical integration. The decision to own or to contract is, therefore, based on the particular situation surrounding the transaction and the ability of the organization to manage the transaction internally both effectively and efficiently.

Sources: O.E. Williamson and S.G. Winter, editors, *The Nature of the Firm: Origins, Evolution, and Development* (New York: Oxford University Press, 1991); E. Mosakowski, "Organizational Boundaries and Economic Performance: An Empirical Study of Entrepreneurial Computer Firms," *Strategic Management Journal* (February 1991), pp. 115–133; P.S. Ring and A.H. Van De Ven, "Structuring Cooperative Relationships Between Organizations," *Strategic Management Journal* (October 1992), pp. 483–498.

full integration ownership and control of 100% of an organization's value chain activities

A company's degree of vertical integration can range from total ownership of the value chain needed to make and sell a product to no ownership at all.[8] (See **Figure 6–2.**) Under **full integration**, a firm internally makes 100% of its key supplies and completely controls its distributors. Large oil companies, such as Royal Dutch Shell, are fully integrated. They own the oil rigs that pump the oil out of the ground, the ships and pipelines that transport the oil, the refineries that convert the oil to gasoline, and the trucks that deliver the gasoline to company-owned and franchised gas stations.

taper integration ownership and control of a portion of an organization's value chain activities, the rest of which is purchased from outside suppliers

If an organization is uncomfortable with the disadvantages of full vertical integration as discussed previously, it may choose either taper or quasi-integration strategies. With **taper integration**, a firm internally produces only a portion of its own requirements and buys the rest from outside suppliers. For instance, Irving Oil extracts and refines its own oil and gas for resale in eastern Canada and the United States, but it also purchases crude oil in the open market to meet consumer demand. In terms of distributors, a taper-integrated firm may sell part of its goods through company-owned stores and the rest through intermediaries. Sony illustrates this type of integration, where its products are sold through its own retailer, The Sony Store, in addition to electronics retailers like Future Shop and department stores like The Bay and Sears.

quasi-integration partial control of suppliers through partnerships or minority equity positions

With **quasi-integration**, a company does not make any of its key supplies but purchases most of its requirements from outside suppliers that are under its partial control. For example, by purchasing 20% of the common stock of a key supplier, In Focus Systems, Motorola guaranteed its access to In Focus's technology and enabled itself to establish a joint venture with In Focus to manufacture flat-panel video displays.[9] An example of forward quasi-integration would be a large pharmaceutical firm that acquires part interest in a drugstore chain to guarantee that its drugs have access to the distribution channel. Purchasing part interest in a key supplier or distributor usually provides a company with a seat on the other firm's board of directors, thus guaranteeing the acquiring firm both information and control.

long-term contracts contractual agreements for two organizations to provide goods and services to each other

A company may not want to invest in suppliers or distributors but may still desire to guarantee access to needed supplies or distribution channels. In this case, it may use contractual agreements. **Long-term contracts** are agreements between two separate firms to provide agreed-upon goods and services to each other for a specified period of time. This cannot really be considered to be vertical integration unless the contract specifies that the supplier or distributor cannot have a similar relationship with a competitive firm. In this case, the supplier or distributor is really a captive company that, although officially independent, does most of its business with the contracted firm and is formally tied to the other company through a long-term contract.

outsourcing the purchase of goods and services from third parties

Recently there has been a movement away from vertical growth strategies (and thus vertical integration) toward co-operative contractual relationships with suppliers and even with competitors. These relationships range from **outsourcing**, in which resources are purchased from outsiders through long-term contracts instead of being made in-house (for example, Hewlett-Packard buys all its laser engines from Canon for HP's laser jet printers), to strategic alliances, in which partnerships, technology licensing agreements, and joint ventures supplement a firm's capabilities (for example, Toshiba has used strategic alliances with GE, Siemens, Motorola, and Ericsson to become one of the world's leading electronics companies).[10] Often

Figure 6–2 Vertical Integration Continuum

Full Integration	Taper Integration	Quasi-integration	Long-Term Contract

Source: Suggested by K.R. Harrigan, *Strategies for Vertical Integration* (Lexington, Mass.: Lexington Books, D.C. Heath, 1983), pp. 16–21.

outsourcing is used when an organization has little expertise in particular value chain activities that are not part of its core business. For example, Cara is a food-service giant that owns Harvey's and Swiss Chalet. It also provides much of the food that is consumed on Canadian airlines and in Canadian airports.

Horizontal Growth Horizontal growth can be achieved by expanding the firm's products into other geographic locations or by increasing the range of products and services offered to current markets. In this case, the company expands sideways at the same location on the industry's value chain. For example, Dell Computers followed a horizontal growth strategy when it extended its mail order business to Europe and to China. A company can grow horizontally through internal development or externally through acquisitions or strategic alliances with another firm in the same industry.

Horizontal growth results in increasing **horizontal integration**—the degree to which a firm operates in multiple geographic locations at the same point in an industry's value chain. Horizontal integration for a firm may range from full to partial ownership to long-term contracts. For example, KLM, the Dutch airline, purchased a controlling stake (partial ownership) in Northwest Airlines to obtain access to American and Asian markets. KLM was unable to acquire all of Northwest's stock because of US government regulations forbidding foreign ownership of a domestic airline. Air Canada chose to enter into a partnership with other major airlines to accomplish the same objectives without having to make any direct investment itself. The Star Alliance is a network of passenger airlines that collaborate to offer a complete arrangement for travellers, far beyond what any one airline could provide.

Diversification Strategies

When an industry consolidates and becomes mature, most of the surviving firms have reached the limits of growth using vertical and horizontal growth strategies. Unless the competitors are able to expand internationally into less mature markets, they may have no choice but to diversify into different industries if they want to continue growing. The two basic diversification strategies are concentric and conglomerate.

Concentric (Related) Diversification Growth through **concentric diversification** into a related industry may be a very appropriate corporate strategy when a firm has a strong competitive position but industry attractiveness is low. By focusing on the characteristics that have given the company its distinctive competency, the company uses those very strengths as its means of diversification. The firm attempts to secure strategic fit in a new industry where the firm's product knowledge, its manufacturing capabilities, and the marketing skills it used so effectively in the original industry can be put to good use.[11] The organization's original products or processes must be related in some way to the new ones, possessing some common thread that allows certain value-chain activities to be transferred between business units or shared between them. Sometimes this can create **synergy**, the concept that two businesses (or business units) will generate more profits together than they could separately. The point of commonality may be similar technology, customer usage, distribution, managerial skills, or product similarity.

Power Corporation of Canada is a diversified management and holding company. It has holdings in leading financial services and the communications sector. Through its European-based affiliate Pargesa group, Power Corporation holds significant positions in major media, energy, water, waste services, and specialty mineral companies. It also has diversified interests in Asia. Diversified organizations such as this typically grow by external means: mergers or acquisitions. This occurs because it is often very time-consuming to build a new business from the ground up, and it is rare for the parent organization to have the necessary expertise to do

horizontal integration the extent to which an organization operates in multiple geographic locations

concentric diversification the addition of related businesses to an organization's portfolio of businesses

synergy the increase in firm value when a diversified organization earns greater returns than if each business unit were independently owned

so. Instead, organizations seeking to enter related industries tend to acquire established firms and integrate them into existing operations.

Conglomerate (Unrelated) Diversification When management realizes that the current industry is unattractive and that the firm lacks outstanding abilities or skills that it could easily transfer to related products or services in other industries, the most likely strategy is **conglomerate diversification**—diversifying into an industry unrelated to its current one. Rather than maintaining a common thread throughout their organization, strategic managers who adopt this strategy are primarily concerned with financial considerations of cash flow or risk reduction. For example, the Irving Group of Companies, one of the largest family-controlled businesses in Canada, has operations in food processing (Cavendish Farms), bus transportation and cargo (Acadia Lines), paper products (Irving Tissue), shipping services (Midland Transport), oil refining and retailing (Irving Oil), and J.D. Irving (construction and shipbuilding). Similarly, Onex Corporation is a diversified Canadian company that creates value for its shareholders by building global, industry-leading companies. It attempts to manage risk by diversifying by industry and geography. It has operations in electronics manufacturing (Celestica), customer management services (ClientLogic), automotive products and logistics (Dura Automotive, J.L. French Automotive, Performance Logistics Group), commercial vehicles (Bostrom Holdings, Magnatrax), communications (Radian Communication), sugar refining (Rogers/Lantic), insurance (InsLogic), and entertainment (Loews Cineplex, Galaxy Entertainment, Phoenix Pictures).

The emphasis in conglomerate diversification is on financial considerations rather than on the product–market commonalities at the basis of concentric diversification. A cash-rich company with few opportunities for growth in its industry might, for example, move into another industry where opportunities are great but cash is hard to find. Another instance of conglomerate diversification might be when a company with a seasonal and, therefore, uneven cash flow purchases a firm in an unrelated industry with complementing seasonal sales that will level out the cash flow.

conglomerate diversification the addition of unrelated businesses to an organization's portfolio of businesses

International Entry Options

In today's world, growth usually has international implications. Research indicates that going international is positively associated with firm profitability.[12] An organization can select from several strategic options the most appropriate method for it to use in entering a foreign market or establishing manufacturing facilities in another country. The options vary from simple exporting to acquisitions to management contracts. See the **Global Issue** feature to see how Wal-Mart is using international entry options in a horizontal growth strategy to expand in Europe.

Global Issue

Wal-Mart Enters International Markets

How can Wal-Mart continue to grow? From its humble beginnings in Bentonville, Arkansas, the company has successfully grown such that its discount stores can now be found in most every corner of the United States. Wal-Mart long ago surpassed Sears as the largest retailer in the United States.

Over the next few years most of the company's growth will likely continue to come from expansion within the United States, but an increasing percentage will be coming from international markets. The company's first attempts to expand outside the country in the early 1990s flopped miserably. It offered the wrong products, such as tennis balls that wouldn't bounce in high-altitude Mexico City and 110-volt appliances in Argentina, where 220 volts is the norm. Learning from those early attempts, Wal-Mart opened profitable stores in Canada, Mexico, China, Brazil, and Britain. Of the company's total 1998 sales, 9% came from international operations. Management wanted to raise that amount to 20% by 2001.

After closing a losing operation in Indonesia, management altered its strategy to focus on becoming a major retailer in Europe. In December 1997, Wal-Mart purchased the 21-store German Tertkauf chain. A year later, it strengthened its hold in Germany by acquiring 74 Interspar stores. It took months of remodelling the stores with wider aisles, better lighting, and more checkout counters before the stores were rechristened as Wal-Marts. In 1999, Wal-Mart bought Britain's 229-store Asda Group, the country's third largest grocery chain. Nevertheless, according to Hubertus Pellengahr of the Association of German Retailers, "They will have to grow a lot to gain critical mass."

Not content to grow by acquisition, Wal-Mart announced in July 2000 a three-year plan to open 50 new locations in Germany and to double its share of the European discount market to 20%. Given difficulties in obtaining building permits from the German bureaucracy, management negotiated with Germany's largest retailer, Metro AG, to swap subsidiaries. This would give Wal-Mart two additional German chains. Given that non-unionized Wal-Mart was now dealing with German unions, analysts wondered whether management could turn the money-losing German operation into a profitable one.

Sources: L. Kim, "Crossing the Rhine," *U.S. News & World Report* (August 14, 2000); "Wal-Mart to Buy British Food Chain," *Des Moines Register* (June 15, 1999), p. 9S; P. Geitner, "Wal-Mart Rises in Germany," *Des Moines Register* (December 11, 1999), p. 12S; *Money* (December, 1999), p. 162.

Some of the more popular options for international entry are as follows:

exporting shipping domestically produced products to other countries for distribution and sale

- *Exporting:* A good way to minimize risk and experiment with a specific product is **exporting**, shipping goods produced in the company's home country to other countries for marketing. The company could choose to handle all critical functions itself, or it could contract these functions to an export management company. Exporting is becoming increasingly popular for small businesses because of the internet, fax machines, toll-free telephone numbers, and overnight air express services, which reduce the once-formidable costs of going international.

licensing granting production or distribution rights to organizations in another country

- *Licensing:* Under a **licensing** agreement, the licensing firm grants rights to another firm in the host country to produce and/or sell a product. The licensee pays compensation to the licensing firm in return for technical expertise. This is an especially useful strategy if the trademark or brand name is well-known, but the company does not have sufficient funds to finance its entering the country directly. Labatt uses this strategy to produce and market Guinness beer in North America. Currently it produces this brand in Toronto, under the supervision and quality standards of Guinness Limited, and both sells it domestically and exports it to the United States. This strategy can become important if the country makes entry via investment either difficult or impossible (as is the case with passenger airlines, public utilities, and defence-related products). As discussed in **Chapter 5**, however, the danger that the licensee might become a competitor to the licensing firm should prevent a company from ever licensing its distinctive competency.

franchising granting rights to an organization's name, products, and business model in another country

- *Franchising:* Under a **franchising** agreement, the franchiser grants rights to another company to open a retail store using the franchiser's name and operating system. In exchange, the franchisee pays the franchiser a percentage of its sales as a royalty. Franchising provides an opportunity for firms to establish a presence in countries where the population or per capita spending is not sufficient to support a major expansion effort.[13]

- *Joint Ventures:* The rate of joint venture formation between North American companies and international partners has been growing steadily since 1985.[14] It is the most popular strategy used to enter a new country.[15] Companies often form joint ventures to combine the resources and expertise needed to develop new products or technologies. A joint venture also enables a firm to enter a country that restricts foreign ownership. The corporation can enter another country with fewer assets at stake and thus lower risk. For example, when Mexico privatized its railroads in 1996 (two years after the North American Trade Agreement was ratified), the Kansas City Southern (KCS) saw an opportunity to form one complete railroad from Mexico's industrialized northeast to Canada. KCS jointly bid with the Mexican shipping line Transportacion Maritima Mexicana (with whom it would jointly operate the Mexican rail system) to purchase 80% of Grupo Transportacion Ferroviaria Mexicana (TFM). KCS then formed an alliance with Canadian National Railway to complete the route.[16] A joint venture may be an association between a company and a firm in the host country or a government agency in that country. A quick method of obtaining local management, it also reduces the risks of expropriation and harassment by host country officials. Sometimes international joint ventures are formed because of economies of scale or the cost differences between operations in different nations. For example, Mountain Province Diamonds Inc. and joint-venture partner De Beers Canada Exploration Inc. (De Beers Canada) have agreed to conduct a bulk sample program in the Northwest Territories. The approximate cost of this program is $10 million.

acquisition the purchasing of a foreign firm operating in the same industry

■ *Acquisitions:* A relatively quick way to move into an international area is through **acquisition**—purchasing another company already operating in that area. Synergistic benefits can result if the company acquires a firm with strong complementary product lines and a good distribution network. Research does suggest that wholly owned subsidiaries are more successful in international undertakings than are strategic alliances, such as joint ventures.[17] This is one reason why firms more experienced in international markets take a higher ownership position when making a foreign investment.[18] In some countries, however, acquisitions can be difficult to arrange because of a lack of available information about potential candidates. Government restrictions on ownership, such as the Canadian requirement that limits foreign ownership of airlines, public utilities, and banks, can also discourage acquisitions. Foreign acquisitions are also appealing where local tastes and brands differ, and larger organizations seek to gain economies of scale by creating a worldwide presence. Interbrew, a large Belgian brewer that refers to itself as "The World's Local Brewer," uses a strategy to build strong local platforms in the world's major beer markets. Through acquisitions they have created a strong brand portfolio that gives them leading positions in almost every market in which they operate. Their acquisition of Labatt has helped them to achieve a market-leading position in Canada. They use this brand as a cornerstone of their strategy in the Canadian market: promoting a domestic lager brand in each local market. They support this primary brand with at least one other brand from Interbrew's large portfolio (including Alexander Keith's, Kokanee, Rolling Rock, and Becks).

production sharing performing different value chain activities in different regions based on favourable local economies

■ *Production Sharing:* Coined by Peter Drucker, the term **production sharing** means the process of combining the higher labour skills and technology available in the developed countries with the lower cost labour available in developing countries. The current trend is to move data processing and programming activities offshore to places such as Ireland, India, Barbados, Jamaica, the Philippines, and Singapore, where wages are lower, English is spoken, and telecommunications are in place.

turnkey operation a ready-to-use production facility sold to a foreign country

■ *Turnkey Operations:* A **turnkey operation** is typically the result of a contract for the construction of operating facilities in exchange for a fee. The facilities are transferred to the host country or firm when they are complete. The customer is usually a government agency of, for example, a Middle Eastern country that has decreed that a particular product must be produced locally and under its control. For example, Fiat built an auto plant in Russia to produce an older model of Fiat under a Russian brand name. Multinational corporations that perform turnkey operations are frequently industrial equipment manufacturers that supply some of their own equipment for the project and that commonly sell replacement parts and maintenance services to the host country. They thereby create customers as well as future competitors.

management contract providing management and consulting services in foreign countries where management expertise is lacking

■ *Management Contracts:* A large corporation operating throughout the world is likely to have a large amount of management talent at its disposal. A **management contract** offers a means through which an organization may use some of its personnel to assist a firm in a host country for a specified fee and period of time. Management contracts are common when a host government expropriates part or all of a foreign-owned company's holdings in its country. The contracts allow the firm to continue to earn some income from its investment and keep the operations going until local management is trained.

Controversies in Directional Growth Strategies

Is vertical growth better than horizontal growth? Is concentric diversification better than conglomerate diversification? Although the research is not in complete agreement, growth into areas related to a company's current product lines is generally more successful than is growth into completely unrelated areas.[19] For example, one study of various growth projects examined how many were considered successful, that is, still in existence after 22 years. These were the results: vertical growth, 80%; horizontal growth, 50%; concentric diversification, 35%; and conglomerate diversification, 28%.[20]

In terms of diversification strategies, research suggests that the relationship between relatedness and performance is curvilinear, in an inverted U-shaped curve. If a new business is very similar to that of the acquiring firm, it adds little new to the corporation and only marginally improves performance. If the new business is completely different from the acquiring company's businesses, there may be very little potential for any synergy. If, however, the new business provides new resources and capabilities in a different, but similar, business, the likelihood of a significant performance improvement is high.[21]

Is internal growth better than external growth? Organizations can follow the growth strategies of either concentration or diversification through the internal development of new products and services or through external acquisitions, mergers, and strategic alliances. The value of global acquisitions and mergers increased enormously in the 1990s.[22] Although not yet conclusive, the research indicates that firms that grow through acquisitions do not perform financially as well as firms that grow through internal means.[23] Studies do reveal that more than two-thirds of acquisitions are failures primarily because the premiums paid were too high for them to earn their cost of capital.[24] That has been frequently discussed as the root of the financial problems at Indigo. The high price paid for Chapters, in addition to the overcapacity Indigo now has a result of its competitive days when the two firms built rival superstores, contributed to a $47 million loss reported in 2002. Analysts suggest that in Heather Reisman's efforts to take over Chapters at all costs, she paid up to triple the fair share price for Chapters.[25] Other research indicates, however, that acquisitions have a higher survival rate than do new internally generated business ventures.[26] It is likely that neither strategy is best by itself and that some combination of internal and external growth strategies is better than using one or the other exclusively.[27]

STABILITY STRATEGIES

An organization may choose stability over growth by continuing its current activities without any significant change in direction. Although sometimes viewed as a lack of strategy, the stability family of corporate strategies can be appropriate for a successful organization operating in a reasonably predictable environment.[28] They are very popular with small business owners who have found a niche and are happy with their success and the manageable size of their firms. Stability strategies can be very useful in the short run, but they can be dangerous if followed for too long (as many small-town retailers discovered when Wal-Mart came to town, or small Atlantic pharmacies when Lawtons did much the same thing). Some of the more popular of these strategies are the pause/proceed with caution, no change, and profit strategies.

Pause/Proceed with Caution Strategy

pause/proceed with caution strategy a temporary strategy of maintaining the status quo until environmental uncertainty is reduced

A **pause/proceed with caution strategy** is, in effect, a time out—an opportunity to rest before continuing a growth or retrenchment strategy. It is a very deliberate attempt to make only incremental improvements until a particular environmental situation changes. It is typically conceived as a temporary strategy to be used until the environment becomes more hospitable or to enable a company to consolidate its resources after prolonged rapid growth. This was the strategy Dell Computer Corporation followed in 1993 after its growth strategy had resulted in more growth than it could handle. Explained CEO Michael Dell, "We grew 285% in two years, and we're having some growing pains." Selling personal computers by mail enabled Dell to underprice Compaq Computer and IBM, but it could not keep up with the needs of the $2 billion, 5600-employee company selling PCs in 95 countries. Dell did not give up on its growth strategy; it merely put it temporarily in limbo until the company was able to hire new managers, improve the structure, and build new facilities.

No Change Strategy

no change strategy an overt choice to make no changes to strategy, based on perceived stability in the environment and satisfaction with firm performance

Rarely articulated as a definite strategy, a **no change strategy** is a decision to do nothing new—a choice to continue current operations and policies for the foreseeable future. A no change strategy's success depends on a lack of significant change in an organization's situation. The relative stability created by the firm's modest competitive position in an industry facing little or no growth encourages the company to continue on its current course, making only small adjustments for inflation in its sales and profit objectives. There are no obvious opportunities or threats; nor are there any significant strengths or weaknesses. Few aggressive new competitors are likely to enter such an industry. The corporation has probably found a reasonably profitable and stable niche for its products. Unless the industry is undergoing consolidation, the relative comfort that a company in this situation experiences is likely to encourage the company to follow a no change strategy in which the future is expected to continue as an extension of the present. Most small-town businesses probably follow this strategy, such as independent restaurants, clothiers, and barbershops. Funeral homes would have typically followed the same strategy until consolidators like Canada's Loewen Group dramatically changed the industry.

Profit Strategy

profit strategy a deceptive strategy that creates the appearance of profits at times of declining sales or other difficulties

A **profit strategy** is a decision to do nothing new in a worsening situation but instead to act as though the company's problems are only temporary. The profit strategy is an attempt to artificially support profits when a company's sales are declining by reducing investment and short-term discretionary expenditures. Rather than announcing the company's poor position to shareholders and the investment community at large, top management may be tempted to follow this very seductive strategy. Blaming the company's problems on a hostile environment (such as anti-business government policies, unethical competitors, finicky customers, or greedy lenders), management defers investments and/or cuts expenses (such as R & D, maintenance, and advertising) to stabilize profits during this period. It may even sell one of its product lines for the cash flow benefits. Obviously the profit strategy is useful only to help a company get through a temporary difficulty. Unfortunately the strategy is seductive and if continued long enough will lead to a serious deterioration in an organization's competitive position. The profit strategy is therefore usually top management's passive, short-term, and often self-serving response to the situation.

RETRENCHMENT STRATEGIES

A company may pursue retrenchment strategies when it has a weak competitive position in some or all of its product lines, resulting in poor performance—sales are down and profits are becoming losses. These strategies impose a great deal of pressure to improve performance. In an attempt to eliminate the weaknesses that are dragging the company down, management may follow one of several retrenchment strategies ranging from turnaround or becoming a captive company to selling out, bankruptcy, or liquidation.

Turnaround Strategy

turnaround strategy a strategy of improving efficiencies, often performed after a merger with, or acquisition of, a poorly run firm

The **turnaround strategy** emphasizes the improvement of operational efficiency and is probably most appropriate when an organization's problems are pervasive but not yet critical. Analogous to a weight-reduction diet, the two basic phases of a turnaround strategy are contraction and consolidation.[29]

Contraction is the initial effort to quickly "stop the bleeding" with a general across-the-board cutback in size and costs. The second phase, *consolidation*, implements a program to stabilize the now-leaner corporation. To streamline the company, plans are developed to reduce unnecessary overhead and to make functional activities cost-justified. This is a crucial time for the organization. If the consolidation phase is not conducted in a positive manner, many of the best people leave the organization. An over-emphasis on downsizing and cutting costs coupled with a heavy hand by top management is usually counterproductive and can actually hurt performance.[30] If, however, all employees are encouraged to get involved in productivity improvements, the firm is likely to emerge from this retrenchment period a much stronger and better organized company. It has improved its competitive position and is able once again to expand the business. See the boxed feature for a description of IBM's effective use of the turnaround strategy.

Turnaround Strategy: IBM Becomes "Internet Business Machines"

During the 1970s and 1980s, IBM dominated the computer industry worldwide. It was the market leader in both large mainframe and small personal computers. Along with Apple Computer, IBM set the standard for all personal computers. Even up to now—when IBM no longer dominates the field—personal computers are still identified as being either Apple or IBM-style PCs.

IBM's problems came to a head in the early 1990s. The company's computer sales were falling. More companies were choosing to replace their large, expensive mainframe computers with personal computers, but they weren't buying the PCs from IBM. An increasing number of firms like Hewlett-Packard, Dell, Gateway, and Compaq had entered the industry. They offered IBM-style PC "clones" that were considerably cheaper and often more advanced than IBM's PCs. IBM's falling revenues meant corporate losses—$15 billion in cumulative losses from 1991 through 1993. Industry experts perceived the company as a bureaucratic dinosaur that could no longer adapt to changing conditions. Its stock price fell to $40 with no end in sight.

IBM's board of directors in 1993 hired a new CEO, Louis Gerstner, to lead a corporate turnaround strategy at "Big Blue" (the nickname IBM earned from its rigid dress code policies). To stop the flow of red ink, the company violated its long-held "no lay-offs" policy by reducing its workforce 40%. Under Gerstner, IBM reorganized its sales force around specific industries such as retailing and banking. Decision making was made easier. Previously, according to Joseph Formichelli, a top executive with the PC division, he "had to go through seven layers to get things done." Firing incompetent employees could take a year, "so you pawned them off on another group." Strategy presentations were hashed over so many times "they got watered down to nothing." Under Gerstner, however, formal presentations were no longer desired. The emphasis switched to quicker decision making and a stronger customer orientation.

At the same time that Gerstner was beginning his turnaround strategy in 1994, David Grossman, a recently hired IBM programmer, was arguing that the future of the computer lay in the developing internet. According to Grossman, "I came from a progressive computing environment and was telling people at IBM that there was this thing called UNIX—there was an Internet. No one knew what I was talking about." Teamed with John Patrick, a career person with IBM who also served on a strategy task force, and David Singer, a researcher who had written one of the first Gopher programs, Grossman began building a corporate intranet and eventually created a formal internet group with Patrick as chief technical officer. Recalled Patrick, "A lot of people were saying, 'How do you make money at this?' I said, 'I have no idea. All I know is that this is the most powerful, important form of communication both inside and outside the company that has ever existed....' From the beginning, our goal was to help IBM become the Internet Business Machines company."

From 1994 to 2000, the company transformed itself from being a besieged computer maker to a dominant service provider. Its Global Services unit has grown from almost nothing to a $30 billion business with more than 135 000 employees. By the end of 1998, IBM had completed 18 000 ebusiness consulting engagements—a third of which were internet-related. In a 1999 report to financial analysts, CEO Gerstner stated, "... IBM is already generating more [ebusiness] revenue and certainly more profits than all of the top Internet companies combined."

Sources: G. Hamel, "Waking Up IBM," *Harvard Business Review* (July–August 2000), pp. 137–146; I. Sager, "Inside IBM: Internet Business Machines," *Business Week E.Biz* (December 13, 1999), pp. EB20–EB40; B. Ziegler, "Gerstner's IBM Revival: Impressive, Incomplete," *Wall Street Journal* (March 25, 1997), pp. B1, B4.

Captive Company Strategy

captive company strategy giving up an organization's independence in exchange for resources and security provided by another

A **captive company strategy** is the giving up of independence in exchange for security. A company with a weak competitive position may not be able to engage in a full-blown turnaround strategy. The industry may not be sufficiently attractive to justify such an effort from either the current management or from investors. Nevertheless a company in this situation faces poor sales and increasing losses unless it takes some action. Management desperately searches for an "angel" by offering to be a captive company to one of its larger customers in order to guarantee the company's continued existence with a long-term contract. In this way, the organization may be able to reduce the scope of some of its functional activities, such as marketing, thus reducing costs significantly. The weaker company gains certainty of sales and production in return for becoming heavily dependent on one firm for at least 75% of its sales. For example, to become the sole supplier of an auto part to General Motors, Simpson Industries of Birmingham, Michigan, agreed to let a special team from GM inspect its engine parts facilities and books, and interview its employees. In return, nearly 80% of the company's production was sold to GM through long-term contracts.[31]

Sell-Out/Divestment Strategy

sell-out strategy selling the business unit due to a weak competitive position and poor firm performance

If an organization with a weak competitive position in its industry is unable either to pull itself up by its bootstraps or to find a customer to which it can become a captive company, it may have no choice but to sell out. The **sell-out strategy** makes sense if management can still obtain a good price for its shareholders and the employees can keep their jobs by selling the entire company to another firm. The hope is that another company will have the necessary resources and determination to return the company to profitability. This is what Bombardier is doing in response to its $1 billion fourth quarter loss in 2003. The firm's stock value is at an eight-year low based on concerns over poor jet sales resulting from the decline of many North American airlines post–September 11. It has decided to sell off its recreational products division that makes Ski-Doo and Sea-Doo vehicles, in addition to all-terrain vehicles. Markets for most of these products are mature, which is making profit margins very thin. By spinning off this division Bombardier can focus on customer relations in two core areas: airplanes and trains.

divestment shutting down unprofitable operations and selling assets

If the corporation has multiple business lines and it chooses to sell off a division with low growth potential, this is called **divestment**. This is what CIBC did when it shut down its US electronic banking operations (Amicus FSB and CIBC National Bank) in 2002. Because these operations were not profitable, it was unlikely that a buyer would be found. CIBC therefore decided to just shut down the operation and transfer customer deposits to another institution.[32]

Bankruptcy/Liquidation Strategy

bankruptcy or liquidation strategy a last-resort strategy where assets are sold or management is turned over to the courts

When a company finds itself in the worst possible situation with a poor competitive position in an industry with few prospects, management has only a few alternatives—all of them distasteful. Because no one is interested in buying a weak company in an unattractive industry, the firm must pursue a **bankruptcy or liquidation strategy**. Bankruptcy involves giving up management of the firm to the courts in return for some settlement of the organization's obligations. Top management hopes that once the court decides the claims on the company, the company will be stronger and better able to compete in a more attractive industry. Air Canada filed for bankruptcy protection in April 2003. It did this in order to protect itself from creditors while it restructures into a more competitive and profitable airline. While under bankruptcy protection, Air Canada will continue to fly as it holds talks with creditors, unions, and suppliers. Its recent advertisements are aimed at reassuring passengers that flights will keep operating and that Air Canada isn't going out of business.

In contrast to bankruptcy, which seeks to perpetuate the corporation, liquidation is the termination of the firm. Because the industry is unattractive and the company too weak to be sold as a going concern, management may choose to convert as many saleable assets as possible to cash, which is then distributed to the shareholders after all obligations are paid. The benefit of liquidation over bankruptcy is that the board of directors, as representatives of the shareholders, together with top management make the decisions instead of turning them over to the court, which may choose to ignore shareholders completely. An example is NeoStar, a retail computer software chain that operated in Canada and the United States under the names Babbage's and Software Etc. It liquidated its assets because its lenders, director, and shareholders failed to reach an agreement on the terms of a financing transaction. NeoStar auctioned off its assets and ceased operations entirely in 1996.

At times, top management must be willing to select one of these less desirable retrenchment strategies. Unfortunately, many top managers are unwilling to admit that their company has serious weaknesses for fear that they may be personally blamed. Even worse, top management may not even perceive that crises are developing. When these top managers do eventually notice trouble, they are prone to attribute the problems to temporary environmental disturbances and tend to follow profit strategies. Even when things are going terribly wrong, top management is greatly tempted to avoid liquidation in the hope of a miracle. Thus, an organization needs a strong board of directors who, to safeguard shareholders' interests, can tell top management when to quit.

6.3 Portfolio Analysis

Chapter 5 dealt with how individual product lines and business units can gain competitive advantage in the marketplace by using competitive and co-operative strategies. Companies with multiple product lines or business units must also ask themselves how these various products and business units should be managed to boost overall corporate performance, keeping these questions in mind:

- How much of our time and money should we spend on our best products and business units to ensure that they continue to be successful?

- How much of our time and money should we spend developing new costly products, most of which will never be successful?

portfolio analysis a technique to analyze the returns of the business units of a firm

One of the most popular aids to developing corporate strategy in a multibusiness corporation is **portfolio analysis**. Although its popularity has dropped since the 1970s and 1980s, when more than half of the largest business corporations used portfolio analysis, it is still used by around 27% of Fortune 500 firms in corporate strategy formulation.[33] Portfolio analysis puts corporate headquarters into the role of an internal banker. In portfolio analysis, top management views its product lines and business units as a series of investments from which it expects a profitable return. The product lines and business units form a portfolio of investments that top management must constantly juggle to ensure the best return on the organization's invested money. Two of the most popular approaches are the BCG (Boston Consulting Group) Growth-Share Matrix and the GE Business Screen. This concept can also be used to develop strategies for international markets.

BCG GROWTH-SHARE MATRIX

BCG Growth Share Matrix a portfolio analysis technique that categorizes businesses into stars, dogs, cash cows, and question marks

The **BCG Growth-Share Matrix**, depicted in **Figure 6–3,** is the simplest way to portray an organization's portfolio of investments. Each of the corporation's product lines or business units is plotted on the matrix according to both the growth rate of the industry in which it competes and its relative market share. A unit's relative competitive position is defined as its market share in the industry divided by that of the largest other competitor. By this calculation, a relative market share above 1.0 belongs to the market leader. The business growth rate is the percentage of market growth, that is, the percentage by which sales of a particular business unit classification of products have increased. The matrix assumes that, other things being equal, a growing market is attractive.

The line separating areas of high and low relative competitive position is set at 1.5 times. A product line or business unit must have relative strengths of this magnitude to ensure that it will have the dominant position needed to be a "star" or "cash cow." On the other hand, a product line or unit having a relative competitive position less than 1.0 has "dog" status.[34] Each product or unit is represented in **Figure 6–3** by a circle. The area of the circle represents the relative significance of each business unit or product line to the corporation in terms of assets used or sales generated.

The BCG Growth-Share Matrix has a lot in common with the product life cycle. As a product moves through its life cycle, it is categorized into one of four types for the purpose of funding decisions:

- *Question marks* (sometimes called "problem children" or "wildcats") are new products that have the potential for success but need a lot of cash for development. If such a product is to gain enough market share to become a market leader and thus a star, money must be taken from more mature products and spent on a question mark.

- *Stars* are market leaders typically at the peak of their product life cycle and are usually able to generate enough cash to maintain their high share of the market. When their market growth rate slows, stars become cash cows.

- *Cash cows* typically bring in far more money than is needed to maintain their market share. In this declining stage of their life cycle, these products are "milked" for cash that will be invested in new question marks.

- *Dogs* have low market share and do not have the potential (because they are in an unattractive industry) to bring in much cash. Question marks unable to obtain a dominant market share (and thus become stars) by the time the industry growth rate inevitably slows become dogs. According to the BCG Growth-Share Matrix, dogs should be either sold off or managed carefully for the small amount of cash they can generate.

Underlying the BCG Growth-Share Matrix is the concept of the experience curve (discussed in **Chapter 4**). The key to success is assumed to be market share. Firms with the highest market share tend to have a cost leadership position based on economies of scale, among other things. If a company is able to use the experience curve to its advantage, it should be able to manufacture and sell new products at a price low enough to garner early market share leadership (assuming no successful imitation by competitors). Once the product becomes a star, it is destined to be very profitable, considering its inevitable future as a cash cow.

Having plotted the current positions of its product lines or business units on a matrix, a company can project their future positions, assuming no change in strategy. Present and

Figure 6–3 BCG Growth-Share Matrix

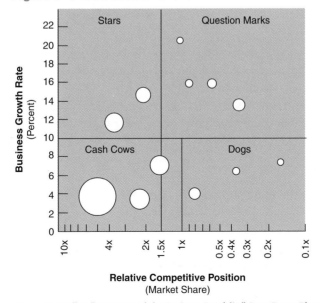

Source: B. Hedley, "Strategy and the Business Portfolio," *Long Range Planning* (February 1977), p. 12. Reprinted with permission from Elsevier Science.

projected matrixes can thus be used to help identify major strategic issues facing the organization. The goal of any company is to maintain a balanced portfolio so it can be self-sufficient in cash and always working to harvest mature products in declining industries to support new ones in growing industries.

The BCG Growth-Share Matrix is a very well-known portfolio concept with some clear advantages. It is quantifiable and easy to use. Cash cows, dogs, and stars are an easy-to-remember way to refer to an organization's business units or products. It can highlight the business units that need attention in terms of improving market share or identifying changes in market growth. The assumption at the base of this model is that industry growth and market share are highly correlated to profitability, but contradictory examples abound. For example, Olivetti is still profitably selling manual typewriters through mail order catalogues, and Labatt is profitable in a mature industry that has not grown for decades. But as with any categorization, the use of "high" and "low" to form four categories is very simplistic. Sometimes business units are near the boundaries of these categories, which makes it difficult to label them.

GE BUSINESS SCREEN

GE Business Screen a portfolio analysis technique that categorizes businesses based on industry attractiveness and competitive position

General Electric, with the assistance of the McKinsey and Company consulting firm, developed a more complicated matrix. As depicted in **Figure 6–4**, the **GE Business Screen** includes nine cells based on long-term industry attractiveness and business strength or competitive position. The GE Business Screen, in contrast to the BCG Growth-Share Matrix, includes much more data in its two key factors than just business growth rate and comparable market share. For example, at GE, industry attractiveness includes market growth rate, industry profitability, size, and pricing practices, among other possible opportunities and threats. Business strength or competitive position includes market share as well as technological position, profitability, and size, among other possible strengths and weaknesses.[35]

The individual product lines or business units are identified by a letter and plotted as circles on the GE Business Screen. The area of each circle is in proportion to the size of the industry in terms of sales. The pie slices within the circles depict the market share of each product line or business unit. To plot product lines or business units on the GE Business Screen, follow these four steps:

1. Select criteria to rate the industry for each product line or business unit. Assess overall industry attractiveness for each product line or business unit on a scale from 1 (very unattractive) to 5 (very attractive).

2. Select the key factors needed for success in each product line or business unit. Assess business strength or competitive position for each product line or business unit on a scale of 1 (very weak) to 5 (very strong).

3. Plot each product line's or business unit's current position on a matrix like that depicted in **Figure 6–4**.

4. Plot the firm's future portfolio assuming that present corporate and business strategies remain unchanged. Is there a performance gap between projected and desired portfolios? If so, this gap should serve as a stimulus to seriously review the corporation's current mission, objectives, strategies, and policies.

Overall the nine-cell GE Business Screen is an improvement over the BCG Growth-Share Matrix. The GE Business Screen considers many more variables and does not lead to such simplistic conclusions. It recognizes, for example, that the attractiveness of an industry can be assessed in many different ways (other than simply using growth rate), and it thus allows users to select whatever criteria they feel are most appropriate to their situation. This portfolio

Figure 6–4 General Electric's Business Screen

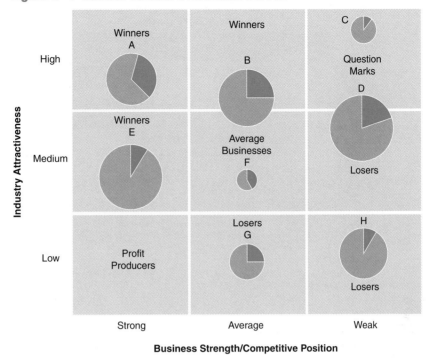

Source: Adapted from *Strategic Management in GE*, Corporate Planning and Development, General Electric Corporation. Used by permission of General Electric Company.

matrix, however, does have some shortcomings. As with the BCG matrix, having to give numerical estimates of industry attractiveness and business strength or competitive position gives the appearance of objectivity, but the resulting numbers are in reality subjective judgments that may vary from one person to another. And again, any business units near the boundaries of each category are problematic to assess. Because this model is based on industry attractiveness as an important determinant of business unit profitability, it becomes difficult to assess the potential of new products or business units in developing industries.

INTERNATIONAL PORTFOLIO ANALYSIS

To aid international strategic planning, portfolio analysis can be applied to international markets.[36] Two factors form the axes of the matrix in **Figure 6–5** on page 160. A country's attractiveness comprises its market size, the market rate of growth, the extent and type of government regulation, and economic and political factors. A product's competitive strength comprises its market share, product fit, contribution margin, and market support. Depending on where a product fits on the matrix, it should either receive more funding or be harvested for cash.

Portfolio analysis might not be useful, however, to corporations operating in a global industry rather than a multidomestic one. In discussing the importance of global industries, Porter argues against the use of portfolio analysis on a country-by-country basis:

> *In a global industry, however, managing international activities like a portfolio will undermine the possibility of achieving competitive advantage. In a global industry, a firm must in some way integrate its activities on a world-wide basis to capture the linkage among countries.*[37]

Figure 6–5 Portfolio Matrix for Plotting Products by Country

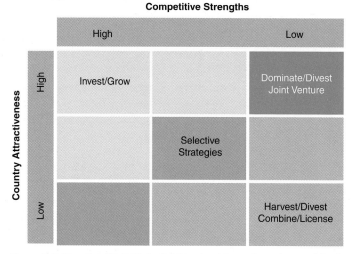

Source: G.D. Harrell and R.O. Kiefer, "Multinational Strategic Market Portfolios," *MSU Business Topics* (Winter 1981), p. 7. Reprinted by permission.

ADVANTAGES AND LIMITATIONS OF PORTFOLIO ANALYSIS

Portfolio analysis is commonly used in strategy formulation because it offers certain advantages:

- It encourages top management to evaluate each of the corporation's businesses individually and to set objectives and allocate resources for each.
- It stimulates the use of externally oriented data to supplement management's judgment.
- It raises the issue of cash flow availability for use in expansion and growth.
- Its graphic depiction facilitates communication.

Portfolio analysis does, however, have some very real limitations that have caused some companies to reduce their use of this approach:

- It is not easy to define product/market segments.
- It suggests the use of standard strategies that can miss opportunities or be impractical.
- It provides an illusion of scientific rigour when in reality positions are based on subjective judgments.
- Its value-laden terms like "cash cow" and "dog" can lead to self-fulfilling prophecies.
- It is not always clear what makes an industry attractive or where a product is in its life cycle.
- Counterintuitive findings exist. For example, General Mills' Bisquick brand of flour is a product that would have been written off years ago, based on portfolio analysis alone. And businesses like WestJet should be doomed by virtue of the industry to which they belong.

6.4 Corporate Parenting

Campbell, Goold, and Alexander, authors of *Corporate-Level Strategy: Creating Value in the Multibusiness Company,* contend that corporate strategists must address two crucial questions:

- Which businesses should this company own, and why?
- What organizational structure, management processes, and philosophy will foster superior performance from the company's business units?[38]

Portfolio analysis attempts to answer these questions by examining the attractiveness of various industries and by managing business units for cash flow, that is, by using cash generated from mature units to build new product lines. Unfortunately portfolio analysis fails to deal with the questions of which industries an organization should enter or how an organization can attain synergy among its product lines and business units. As suggested by its name, portfolio analysis tends to primarily view matters financially, regarding business units and product lines as separate and independent investments.

Corporate parenting, in contrast, views the corporation in terms of resources and capabilities that can be used to build business unit value as well as generate synergies across business units. According to Campbell, Goold, and Alexander:

> *Multibusiness companies create value by influencing—or parenting—the businesses they own. The best parent companies create more value than any of their rivals would if they owned the same businesses. Those companies have what we call parenting advantage.*[39]

Corporate parenting generates corporate strategy by focusing on the core competencies of the parent corporation and on the value created from the relationship between the parent and its businesses. In the form of corporate headquarters, the parent has a great deal of power in this relationship. If there is a good fit between the parent's skills and resources and the needs and opportunities of the business units, the corporation is likely to create value. If, however, there is not a good fit, the corporation is likely to destroy value.[40] This approach to corporate strategy is useful not only in deciding which new businesses to acquire, but also in choosing how each existing business unit should be managed. This appears to be the secret to the success of General Electric under CEO Jack Welch. According to one analyst:

> *... he and his managers really add value by imposing tough standards of profitability and by disseminating knowledge and best practice quickly around the GE empire. If some manufacturing trick cuts costs in GE's aero-engine repair shops in Wales, he insists it be applied across the group.*[41]

The primary job of corporate headquarters is, therefore, to obtain synergy among the business units by providing needed resources to units, transferring skills and capabilities among the units, and coordinating the activities of shared unit functions to attain economies of scope (as in centralized purchasing).[42] This is in agreement with the concept of the learning organization discussed in **Chapter 1,** in which the role of the large firm is to facilitate and transfer the knowledge assets and services throughout the organization.[43] This is especially important given that three-quarters of a modern company's market value stems from its intangible assets—the organization's knowledge.[44]

DEVELOPING A CORPORATE PARENTING STRATEGY

Campbell, Goold, and Alexander recommend that the search for appropriate corporate strategy involve three analytical steps:

1. *Examine each business unit (or target firm in the case of acquisition) in terms of its strategic factors.* People in the business units probably identified the strategic factors when they were generating business strategies for their units.

2. *Examine each business unit (or target firm) in terms of areas in which performance can be improved.* These are considered to be parenting opportunities. For example, two business units might be able to gain economies of scope by combining their sales forces. In another instance, a unit may have good, but not great, manufacturing and logistics skills. A parent company having world-class expertise in these areas can improve that unit's performance.

---

corporate parenting
the relationship between a parent and its subsidiaries in terms of flows of resources and how these are used to create value

The corporate parent could also transfer some people from one business unit having the desired skills to another unit in need of those skills. People at corporate headquarters may, because of their experience in many industries, spot areas where improvements are possible that even people in the business unit may not have noticed. Unless specific areas are significantly weaker than the competition, people in the business units may not even be aware that these areas could be improved, especially if each business unit only monitors its own particular industry.

3. *Analyze how well the parent corporation fits with the business unit (or target firm).* Corporate headquarters must be aware of its own strengths and weaknesses in terms of resources, skills, and capabilities. To do this, the corporate parent must ask whether it has the characteristics that fit the parenting opportunities in each business unit. It must also ask whether there is a misfit between the parent's characteristics and the critical success factors of each business unit.

PARENTING-FIT MATRIX

parenting fit matrix a classification of the relationship between a parent company and its subsidiaries

Campbell, Goold, and Alexander further recommend the use of a **parenting-fit matrix** that summarizes the various judgments regarding corporate/business unit fit for the corporation as a whole. Instead of describing business units in terms of their growth potential, competitive position, or industry structure, such a matrix emphasizes their fit with the corporate parent. As shown in **Figure 6–6**, the parenting-fit matrix comprises two dimensions: the positive contributions that the parent can make and the negative effects the parent can make. The combination of these two dimensions creates five different positions—each with its own implications for corporate strategy.

Figure 6–6 Parenting-Fit Matrix

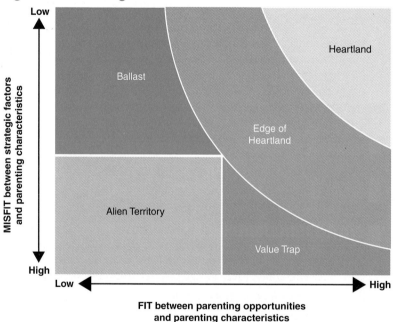

Source: Adapted from M. Alexander, A. Campbell, and M. Goold, "A New Model for Reforming the Planning Review Process," *Planning Review* (January/February 1995), p. 17. Copyright © MCB University Press Ltd. Reprinted with permission.

Heartland Businesses

heartland business a business unit whose needs fit with the resources and skills of the parent

According to Campbell, Goold, and Alexander, business units that lie in the top right corner of the matrix should be at the heart of the organization's future. These **heartland businesses** have opportunities for improvement by the parent, and the parent understands their strategic factors well. These businesses should have priority for all corporate activities.

Edge-of-Heartland Businesses

edge-of-heartland business a business unit whose needs fit with only some of the resources and skills of the parent

For **edge-of-heartland businesses**, some parenting characteristics fit the business, but others do not. The parent may not have all the characteristics needed by a unit, or the parent may not really understand all of the unit's strategic factors. For example, a unit in this area may be very strong in creating its own image through advertising—a critical success factor in its industry (such as in perfumes). The corporate parent may, however, not have this strength and tends to leave this to its advertising agency. If the parent were to force the unit to abandon its own creative efforts in favour of using the corporation's favourite ad agency, the unit may flounder. Such business units are likely to consume much of the parent's attention, as the parent tries to understand them better and transform them into heartland businesses. In this instance, the parent needs to know when to interfere in business unit activities and strategies and when to keep at arm's length.

Ballast Businesses

ballast business a business unit whose needs fit the resources and skills of the parent, but contain few parenting opportunities

Ballast businesses fit very comfortably with the parent corporation but contain very few opportunities to be improved by the parent. This is likely to be the case in units that have been with the corporation for many years and have been very successful. The parent may have added value in the past, but it can no longer find further parenting opportunities. Like cash cows, ballast businesses may be important sources of stability and earnings. They can, however, also be a drag on the corporation as a whole by slowing growth and distracting the parent from more productive activities. Some analysts might put IBM's mainframe business units in this category. Because there is always a danger that environmental changes could move a ballast business unit into alien territory, corporate decision makers should consider divesting this unit as soon as they can get a price that exceeds the expected value of future cash flows.

Alien Territory Businesses

alien territory business a business unit where there is little opportunity for parenting and a significant misfit with the parent

Alien territory businesses have little opportunity to be improved by the corporate parent, and a misfit exists between the parenting characteristics and these units' strategic factors. There is little potential for value creation but high potential for value destruction on the part of the parent. Usually small, these units are often remnants of past experiments with diversification, businesses acquired as part of a larger purchase, or pet projects of senior managers. Even though corporate headquarters may admit that there is little fit, there may be reasons for keeping a unit: it is currently profitable, there are few buyers, the parent has made commitments to the unit's managers, or it is a favourite of the chairman. Because the corporate parent is probably destroying value in its attempts to improve fit, Campbell, Goold, and Alexander recommend that the corporation divest this unit while it still has value.

Value Trap Businesses

value trap business a business unit that fits well with the parent's skills and resources, but is not strategically understood by the parent

Value trap businesses fit well with parenting opportunities, but they are a misfit with the parent's understanding of the units' strategic factors. This is where corporate headquarters can make a big error by mistaking what it sees as opportunities for ways to improve the business unit's profitability or competitive position. For example, in its zeal to make the unit a world-class manufacturer (because the parent has world-class manufacturing skills), it may not notice that the unit is primarily successful because of its unique product development and niche marketing expertise. The potential for possible gain blinds the parent to the downside risks of doing the wrong thing and destroying the unit's core competencies.

HORIZONTAL STRATEGY AND MULTIPOINT COMPETITION

A horizontal strategy is a corporate strategy that cuts across business unit boundaries to build synergy across business units and to improve the competitive position of one or more business units. When used to build synergy, it acts like a parenting strategy. When used to improve the competitive position of one or more business units, it can be thought of as a corporate competitive strategy. In **multipoint competition**, large multibusiness corporations compete against other large multibusiness firms in a number of markets. These multipoint competitors are firms that compete with each other in not just one business unit but a number of them. At one time or another, a cash-rich competitor may choose to build its own market share in a particular market to the disadvantage of another corporation's business unit. Although each business unit has primary responsibility for its own business strategy, it may sometimes need some help from its corporate parent, especially if the competitor business unit is getting heavy financial support from its corporate parent. In this instance, corporate headquarters develops a horizontal strategy to coordinate the various goals and strategies of related business units.[45]

> **multipoint competition**
> when large companies compete directly against similar firms in a number of markets simultaneously

For example, Procter & Gamble, Kimberly-Clark, Scott Paper, and Johnson & Johnson compete with one another in varying combinations of consumer paper products, from disposable diapers to facial tissues. If (purely hypothetically) Johnson & Johnson had just developed a toilet tissue with which it chose to challenge Procter & Gamble's high-share Charmin brand in a particular district, it might charge a low price for its new brand to build sales quickly. Procter & Gamble might choose not to respond to this attack on its share by cutting prices on Charmin. Because of Charmin's high market share, Procter & Gamble would lose significantly more sales dollars in a price war than Johnson & Johnson would with its initially low-share brand. To retaliate, Procter & Gamble might thus challenge Johnson & Johnson's high-share baby shampoo with Procter & Gamble's own low-share brand of baby shampoo in a different district. Once Johnson & Johnson had perceived Procter & Gamble's response, it might choose to stop challenging Charmin so that Procter & Gamble would stop challenging Johnson & Johnson's baby shampoo.

Multipoint competition and the resulting use of horizontal strategy may actually slow the development of hypercompetition in an industry. The realization that an attack on a market leader's position could result in a response in another market leads to mutual forbearance in which managers behave more conservatively toward multimarket rivals and competitive rivalry is reduced.[46] In one industry, for example, multipoint competition resulted in firms being less likely to exit a market. "Live and let live" replaced strong competitive rivalry.[47] Multipoint competition is likely to become even more prevalent in the future as corporations become global competitors and expand into more markets through strategic alliances.[48]

6.5 Impact of the Internet on Corporate Strategy

One impact of the growth of the internet is that corporations are rethinking what businesses they should be in. For example, Emerson Electric, the 110-year-old St. Louis manufacturer of electrical motors, refrigeration components, and industrial tools, is now positioning itself in power backup systems for computers. In January 2000, Emerson purchased Jordan Industries Inc.'s telecommunications-products business. Three months later, Emerson bought the power supply division of Swedish phone maker Ericsson. With the power grid reaching its capacity, electrical outages are becoming more commonplace in the United States. For example, the state of California suffered under "rolling blackouts" in 2001 because of insufficient power generation capacity.

Emerson's acquisitions mean that the company could now provide reliable power backup capability for its customers. When the power goes out, Emerson's components act to switch the power from one source to another and regulate the voltage. Emerson provides the generators and fuel cells to generate the temporary electricity. These products have become crucial for any company that relies on the internet for conducting business. Intira Corp., a St. Louis web-hosting company, suffered a seven-hour outage due to a malfunctioning transformer but was able to stay online thanks to Emerson equipment. According to John Steensen, Intira's chief technology officer, "All of our affected customers would have gotten a month of free service if we had gone down, costing us hundreds of thousands of dollars." The acquisitions significantly increased Emerson's sales and made the power unit the largest and fastest growing of Emerson's five strategic business units (SBUs). Cisco Systems, WorldCom, and Intel are Emerson customers. Emerson's management is estimating that its high-tech power-systems business will grow at 15% to 20% annually for the foreseeable future.[49]

Any company considering entering international markets must consider the impact of the internet. Simply creating a website is likely to result in inquiries from people in foreign countries where the company may have no experience. (See the **Internet Issue** feature for internet usage by country and by language.) A few years ago, The Doll Collection was a barely profitable neighbourhood retail shop in Louisville, Kentucky, with a staff of three people. Looking for an inexpensive way to boost its sales, one of the employees, Jason Walters, suggested putting a web-page—**www.dollpage.com**—on the internet. After spending two weeks learning the internet computer language, HTML, Walters designed a simple site showcasing well-known dolls like Barbie and Madam Alexander to attract buyers. Employees of The Doll Collection were amazed by the response—much of which came from outside North America. Sales jumped 375%. In one year the shop had become a global retailer, marketing Barbie and Madam Alexander dolls to people in almost every country, including Japan, China, and Australia.[50]

Internet Issue
Global Online Population

In the year 2000 it was predicted that by 2002, 490 million people throughout the world would have achieved internet access. For every 1000 people, 80 would be using the web. By the end of 2005, the number is expected to rise to 118 per 1000 people. Fifteen countries will account for nearly 82% of these worldwide internet users. The United States in 2000 accounted for 43% of the total 259 million worldwide. This percentage was predicted to drop to 33% in 2002 and only 27% in 2005. The top 10 nations with the most internet users in 2000 were these:

Country	Internet Users (in thousands)
1. United States	110 825
2. Japan	18 156
3. United Kingdom	13 156
4. Canada	12 277
5. Germany	12 285
6. Australia	6 837
7. Brazil	6 790
8. China	6 308
9. France	5 696
10. South Korea	5 688

Given that four of the top 10 countries using the internet speak English, it is no surprise that English has become the dominant language of the internet. In 1996, it was the first language of 80% of internet users. As other countries become active in the internet, that figure is changing. By 2000, only 49.9% of internet users had English as their first language.

Chinese was second with 7.6%, followed by Japanese at 7.2%, German at 5.9%, and Spanish at 5%.

Source: J. Kirchner, "Global Online Population," *PC Magazine* (June 6, 2000), p. 23; R.O. Crockett, "Surfing in Tongues," *Business Week E.Biz* (December 11, 2000), p. EB 18.

Discussion Questions

1. How does horizontal growth differ from vertical growth as a corporate strategy? From concentric diversification?

2. What are the trade-offs between an internal and an external growth strategy? Which approach is best as an international entry strategy?

3. Is stability really a strategy or just a term for no strategy?

4. Compare and contrast SWOT analysis with portfolio analysis.

5. How is corporate parenting different from portfolio analysis? How is it alike? Is it a useful concept in a global industry?

Strategic Practice Exercise

On March 14, 2000, Stephen King, the horror writer, published his new book, *Riding the Bullet*, on the internet before it appeared in print. Within 24 hours, around 400 000 people had downloaded the book—even though most of them also needed to download the software to read the book. The unexpected demand crashed servers. According to Jack Romanos, president of Simon & Schuster, "I don't think anybody could have anticipated how many people were out there who are willing to accept the written word in a paperless format." To many, this announced the coming of the electronic novel. Environmentalists welcomed the possibility that ebooks would soon replace paper books and newspapers, thus reducing pollution coming from paper mills and landfills. The King book was easy to download and took less time than a trip to the bookstore. Critics argued that the King book used the internet because at 66 pages, it was too short to be a standard printed novel. It was also free, so there was nothing to discourage natural curiosity. Some people in the industry remarked that 75% of those who downloaded the

book did not read it.[51] To explore issues related to this event, perform the following exercise:

1. Form into small groups in the class to discuss the future of internet publishing.

2. Consider the following questions as discussion guides:
   - What are the advantages and disadvantages of electronic publishing?
   - Should newspaper and book publishers convert to electronic publishing over paper?
   - *The Wall Street Journal* and others publish in both paper and electronic formats. Has this been a success?
   - Would you prefer this textbook and others in an electronic format?
   - How would publishers distribute books and textbooks?

3. Present your group's conclusions to the class.

Notes

1. "CP's Long Goodbye," *Canadian Business* (September 2, 2001) p. 21; "Breaking Up Is Good To Do," *Canadian Business* (October 15, 2001) p. 15.
2. R.P. Rumelt, D.E. Schendel, and D.J. Teece, "Fundamental Issues in Strategy," in *Fundamental Issues in Strategy: A Research Agenda,* edited by R.P. Rumelt, D.E. Schendel, and D.J. Teece (Boston: HBS Press, 1994), p. 42.
3. This analogy of corporate parent and business unit children was initially proposed by A. Campbell, M. Goold, and M. Alexander. See "Corporate Strategy: The Quest for Parenting Advantage," *Harvard Business Review* (March–April, 1995), pp. 120–132.
4. M.E. Porter, "From Competitive Strategy to Corporate Strategy," in *International Review of Strategic Management*, Vol. 1, edited by D.E. Husey (Chichester, England: John Wiley & Sons, 1990), p. 29.
5. "Cisco Buys Wireless Chip-Set Maker," *The [Ames] Tribune* (November 11, 2000), p. B7.

6. www.thairayon.com/pr01.htm

7. J.W. Slocum, Jr., M. McGill, and D.T. Lei, "The New Learning Strategy: Anytime, Anything, Anywhere," *Organizational Dynamics* (Autumn 1994), p. 36.

8. K.R. Harrigan, *Strategies for Vertical Integration* (Lexington, Mass.: Lexington Books, D.C. Heath, 1983), pp. 16–21.

9. L. Grant, "Partners in Profit," *U.S. News and World Report* (September 20, 1993), pp. 65–66.

10. For a discussion of the pros and cons of contracting versus vertical integration, see J.T. Mahoney, "The Choice of Organizational Form: Vertical Financial Ownership versus Other Methods of Vertical Integration," *Strategic Management Journal* (November 1992), pp. 559–584.

11. A.Y. Ilinich and C.P. Zeithaml, "Operationalizing and Testing Galbraith's Center of Gravity Theory," *Strategic Management Journal* (June 1995), pp. 401–410.

12. A. Delios and P.W. Beamish, "Geographic Scope, Product Diversification, and the Corporate Performance of Japanese Firms," *Strategic Management Journal* (August 1999), pp. 711–727.

13. E. Elango and V.H. Fried, "Franchising Research: A Literature Review and Synthesis," *Journal of Small Business Management* (July 1997), pp. 68–81.

14. S. Sherman, "Are Strategic Alliances Working?" *Fortune* (September 21, 1992), p. 77.

15. J.E. McCann, III, "The Growth of Acquisitions in Services," *Long Range Planning* (December 1996), pp. 835–841.

16. P. Gogoi and G. Smith, "The Way to Run a Railroad," *Business Week* (October 23, 2000), pp. 106–110.

17. B. Voss, "Strategic Federations Frequently Falter in Far East," *Journal of Business Strategy* (July/August 1993), p. 6; S. Douma, "Success and Failure in New Ventures," *Long Range Planning* (April 1991), pp. 54–60.

18. A. Delios and P.W. Beamish, "Ownership Strategy of Japanese Firms: Transactional, Institutional, and Experience Approaches," *Strategic Management Journal* (October 1999), pp. 915–933.

19. K. Ramaswamy, "The Performance Impact of Strategic Similarity in Horizontal Mergers: Evidence from the U.S. Banking Industry," *Academy of Management Journal* (July 1997), pp. 697–715; D.J. Flanagan, "Announcements of Purely Related and Purely Unrelated Mergers and Shareholder Returns: Reconciling the Relatedness Paradox," *Journal of Management*, Vol. 22, No. 6 (1996), pp. 823–835; D.D. Bergh, "Predicting Diversification of Unrelated Acquisitions: An Integrated Model of Ex Ante Conditions," *Strategic Management Journal* (October 1997), pp. 715–731.

20. J.M. Pennings, H. Barkema, and S. Douma, "Organizational Learning and Diversification," *Academy of Management Journal* (June 1994), pp. 608–640.

21. L.E. Palich, L.B. Cardinal, and C.C. Miller, "Curvilinearity in the Diversification-Performance Linkage: An Examination of Over Three Decades of Research," *Strategic Management Journal* (February 2000), pp. 155–174.

22. "The Great Merger Wave Breaks," *The Economist* (January 27, 2001), pp. 59–60.

23. W.B. Carper, "Corporate Acquisitions and Shareholder Wealth: A Review and Exploratory Analysis, "*Journal of Management* (December 1990), pp. 807–823; P.G. Simmonds, "Using Diversification As a Tool for Effective Performance," *Handbook of Business Strategy, 1992/93 Yearbook*, edited by H.E. Glass and M.A. Hovde (Boston: Warren, Gorham & Lamont, 1992), pp. 3.1–3.7; B.T. Lamont and C.A. Anderson, "Mode of Corporate Diversification and Economic Performance," *Academy of Management Journal* (December 1985), pp. 926–936.

24. M.L. Sirower, *The Synergy Trap* (NY: Free Press, 1997); B. Jensen, "Make It Simple! How Simplicity Could Become Your Ultimate Strategy," *Strategy & Leadership* (March/April 1997), p. 35.

25. "Case Study: Indigo Books & Music Inc.," *National Post Business* (December 2002), pp. 45–48.

26. J.M. Pennings, H. Barkema, and S. Douma, "Organizational Learning and Diversification," *Academy of Management Journal* (June 1994), pp. 608–640.

27. E.C. Busija, H.M. O'Neill, and C.P. Zeithaml, "Diversification Strategy, Entry Mode, and Performance: Evidence of Choice and Constraints," *Strategic Management Journal* (April 1997), pp. 321–327; A. Sharma, "Mode of Entry and Ex-Post Performance," *Strategic Management Journal* (September 1998), pp. 879–900.

28. A. Inkpen and N. Choudhury, "The Seeking of Strategy Where It Is Not: Towards a Theory of Strategy Absence," *Strategic Management Journal* (May 1995), pp. 313–323.

29. J.A. Pearce II and D.K. Robbins, "Retrenchment Remains the Foundation of Business Turnaround," *Strategic Management Journal* (June 1994), pp. 407–417.

30. J.R. Morris, W.F. Cascio, and C.E. Young, "Downsizing after All These Years," *Organizational Dynamics* (Winter 1999), pp. 78–87; P.H. Mirvis, "Human Resource Management: Leaders, Laggards, and Followers," *Academy of Management Executive* (May 1997), pp. 43–56; J.K. DeDee and D.W. Vorhies, "Retrenchment Activities of Small Firms During Economic Downturn: An Empirical Investigation," *Journal of Small Business Management* (July 1998), pp. 46–61.

31. J.B. Treece, "U.S. Parts Makers Just Won't Say 'Uncle,'" *Business Week* (August 10, 1987), pp. 76–77.

32. "Quaker Oats Gives Up on Snapple, Sells It at a $1.4 Billion Loss," *Des Moines Register* (March 28, 1997), p. 8S.

33. B.C. Reimann and A. Reichert, "Portfolio Planning Methods for Strategic Capital Allocation: A Survey of Fortune 500 Firms," *International Journal of Management* (March 1996), pp. 84–93; D.K. Sinha, "Strategic Planning in the Fortune 500," *Handbook of Business Strategy, 1991/92 Yearbook*, edited by H.E. Glass and M.A. Hovde (Boston: Warren Gorham & Lamont, 1991), p. 9.6.

34. B. Hedley, "Strategy and the Business Portfolio," *Long Range Planning* (February 1977), p. 9.

35. R.G. Hamermesh, *Making Strategy Work* (New York: John Wiley & Sons, 1986), p. 14.

36. G.D. Harrell and R.O. Kiefer, "Multinational Strategic Market Portfolios," *MSU Business Topics* (Winter 1981), p. 5.

37. M.E. Porter, "Changing Patterns of International Competition," *California Management Review* (Winter 1986), p. 12.

38. A. Campbell, M. Goold, and M. Alexander, *Corporate-Level Strategy: Creating Value in the Multibusiness Company* (New York: John Wiley & Sons, 1994). See also M. Goold, A. Campbell, and M. Alexander, "Corporate Strategy and Parenting Theory," *Long Range Planning* (April 1998), pp. 308–318.

39. A. Campbell, M. Goold, and M. Alexander, "Corporate Strategy: The Quest for Parenting Advantage," *Harvard Business Review* (March–April 1995), p. 121.

40. Campbell, Goold, and Alexander, p. 122.

41. "Jack's Gamble," *The Economist* (October 28, 2000), pp. 13–14.

42. D.J. Collis, "Corporate Strategy in Multibusiness Firms," *Long Range Planning* (June 1996), pp. 416–418; D. Lei, M.A. Hitt, and R. Bettis, "Dynamic Core Competencies Through Meta-Learning and Strategic Context," *Journal of Management*, Vol. 22, No. 4 (1996), pp. 549–569.

43. D.J. Teece, "Strategies for Managing Knowledge Assets: The Role of Firm Structure and Industrial Context," *Long Range Planning* (February 2000), pp. 35–54.

44. C. Havens and E. Knapp, "Easing into Knowledge Management," *Strategy & Leadership* (March/April 1999), pp. 4–9.

45. M.E. Porter, *Competitive Advantage* (New York: Free Press, 1985), pp. 317–382.

46. J. Gimeno and C.Y. Woo, "Hypercompetition in a Multimarket Environment: The Role of Strategic Similarity and Multimarket Contact in Competitive De-Escalation," *Organization Science* (May/June 1996), pp. 322–341.

47. W. Boeker, J. Goodstein, J. Stephan, and J.P. Murmann,

"Competition in a Multimarket Environment: The Case of Market Exit," *Organization Science* (March/April 1997), pp. 126–142.

48. J. Gimeno and C.Y. Woo, "Multimarket Contact, Economies of Scope, and Firm Performance," *Academy of Management Journal* (June 1999), pp. 239–259.

49. D. Little, "Emerson Electric Jump-Starts Itself," *Business Week* (July 24, 2000), pp. 78–80.

50. L. Beresford, "Global Smarts, Toy Story," *Entrepreneur* (February 1997), p. 38.

51. "Learning to E-Read," *The Economist Survey E-Entertainment* (October 7, 2000), p. 22.

CHAPTER 7

Strategy Formulation: Functional Strategy and Strategic Choice

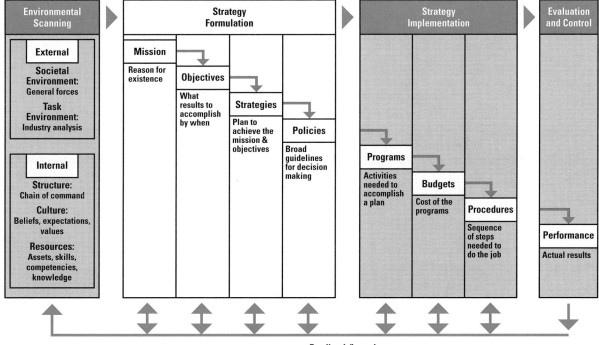

Feedback/Learning

Learning Objectives

After reading this chapter you should be able to

Identify a variety of functional strategies that can be used to achieve organizational goals and objectives

Understand how to strategically outsource to strengthen competitive advantage

Recognize pitfalls in the process of identifying strategic options

Use organizational scenarios to evaluate strategic proposals

Use multiple criteria and decision-making processes to improve the quality of strategic choices

The increasingly competitive nature of business and the rapid pace of environmental change mean that organizations have to be flexible and continuously looking for ways to strengthen competitive advantage. One way many organizations are doing this is through strategically outsourcing some of their value chain activities. This trend toward outsourcing has created opportunities for organizations like Aramark, a large food services, cleaning, and maintenance organization. Significant growth is currently expected in the outsourcing of a variety of services. Today, 10% of medium and large organizations outsource at least some activities. Five years from now, that number is expected to reach 50%.[1]

More and more we see organizations outsourcing value-creating activities to specialist organizations like Aramark so they can focus their energies and resources on their core competencies. Aramark's roots are in vending machines, but it quickly grew into a vending and food service business. In the mid-1960s it took advantage of the growth in commercial air travel and attendance at sporting events to enter the leisure services industry. In the 1970s it diversified into uniforms, health care, and child care services. Its strategy was one of partnering with organizations to provide superior services that were not in the core business areas of their clients. For example, at Procter & Gamble's Yonge Street offices in Toronto, Aramark's food services developed an "Eat Smart" cafeteria program. Eat Smart has been certified by Ontario's Healthy Restaurant Program, which, based on nominations by health inspectors and reviews by the province, identifies establishments that provide healthy eating. Aramark's program met standards relating to healthy menu choices, food safety, and smoke-free premises, which bolstered Procter & Gamble's image in the community as a health-conscious employer and drew endorsements from the Canadian Cancer Society and the Heart and Stroke Foundation of Ontario.[2] Eat Smart contributed to Procter & Gamble's ability to create a healthy and productive workforce, but without requiring the company to develop its own expertise in food services. Partnerships such as these not only allow Aramark to continue making gains into the institutional food services market, but also develop the business and improve working conditions at clients like Procter & Gamble.

7.1 Functional Strategy

functional strategy the approach or plan used by functional areas of an organization to achieve the organization's overall goals and objectives

Functional strategy is the approach a functional area takes to achieve organizational and business unit objectives and strategies by maximizing resource productivity. It is concerned with developing and nurturing competencies to provide a company or business unit with a competitive advantage. Just as a multidivisional corporation has several business units, each with its own business strategy, each business unit has its own set of departments, each with its own functional strategy.

The orientation of the functional strategy is dictated by the organization's strategy. For example, a business unit following a competitive strategy of differentiation through high quality needs a manufacturing functional strategy that emphasizes relatively expensive quality-assurance processes over cheaper high-volume production; a human resource functional strategy that emphasizes the hiring and training of a highly skilled, and therefore costly, workforce; and a marketing functional strategy that emphasizes distribution channel "pull," using advertising to increase consumer demand, over "push," using promotional allowances to retailers. If a business unit were to follow a low-cost competitive strategy, however, a different set of functional strategies would be needed.

Just as a competitive strategy may need to vary from one region of the world to another, functional strategies may need to vary from region to region. When Mr. Donut expanded into Japan, for example, it had to market its products not as breakfast food, but as snack food. Because the Japanese had no breakfast coffee-and-doughnut custom, they preferred to eat the doughnuts in the afternoon or evening. Mr. Donut restaurants were thus located near railroad stations and supermarkets. All signs were in English to appeal to the Japanese interest in Western culture.

CORE COMPETENCIES

As defined earlier in **Chapter 4**, a core competency is something that an organization can do exceedingly well. It is a key strength. It may also be called a core capability because it includes a number of constituent skills. For example, a core competency of Avon Products is its expertise in door-to-door selling. FedEx has a core competency in information technology. An organization must continually reinvest in its core competencies or risk losing them.[3] When these competencies or capabilities are superior to those of the competition, they are called distinctive competencies. Although it is typically not an asset in the accounting sense, a core competency is a very valuable resource—it does not "wear out." In general, the more core competencies are used, the more refined they get and the more valuable they become. To be considered a distinctive competency, the competency must meet three tests:[4]

1. *Customer value:* It must make a disproportionate contribution to customer-perceived value. In other words, resources need to be used in a way that satisfies customer demand and meets unmet wants or needs in the market.

2. *Uniqueness:* It must be unique and superior to competitor capabilities. Unique competencies allow the organization to outperform its rivals and therefore put it at an advantage for as long as it can maintain its uniqueness.

3. *Extendability:* It must be something that can be used to develop new products or services, or to enter new markets. Ideally these competencies become part of a reinforcing cycle, where strengths get stronger as they are put to use and regularly improved upon. These competencies can be a springboard to future growth, acting as the core of new innovations in products or processes.

Even though a distinctive competency is certainly considered an organization's key strength, a key strength may not always be a distinctive competency. As competitors attempt to imitate another company's competency in a particular functional area, what was once a distinctive competency becomes a minimum requirement to compete in the industry.[5] Even though the competency may still be a core competency and thus a strength, it is no longer unique. For example, when Maytag was alone in offering high-quality washing machines in North America, its ability to make exceedingly reliable and durable products was a distinctive competency. As other appliance makers imitated its quality control and design processes, this ability continued to be a key strength (that is, a core competency) of Maytag, but it was less and less a distinctive competency.

Where do these competencies come from? An organization can gain access to a distinctive competency in four ways:[6]

- It may be an asset endowment, such as a key patent, coming from the founding of the company. Xerox, for instance, grew on the basis of its original copying patent.

- It may be acquired from someone else. Whirlpool bought a worldwide distribution system when it purchased Philips's appliance division, and Bombardier became a world leader in aerospace by acquiring Canadair, De Haviland, and Shorts Brothers.

- It may be shared with another business unit or alliance partner. Apple Computer worked with a design firm to create the special appeal of its Apple II and iMac computers.

- It may be carefully built and accumulated over time within the company. Honda carefully extended its expertise in small motor manufacturing from motorcycles to automobiles and lawn mowers. Cirque du Soleil grew from a one-show touring circus into a diversified global multimedia giant valued at more than $800 million, through the creativity and innovativeness of its founders.

For core competencies to be distinctive competencies, they must be superior to those of the competition. As more industries become hypercompetitive (discussed in **Chapter 3**), it will be increasingly difficult to keep a core competency distinctive. These resources are likely either to be imitated or made obsolete by new technologies. As previously discussed, some competencies are more easily imitated than others. If an organization is unable to prevent or slow down the pace of imitation, it needs to continue to develop new competencies in order to stay a step ahead of the competition.

For a functional strategy to have the best chance of success, it should be built on a distinctive competency residing within that functional area. If an organization does not have a distinctive competency in a particular functional area, that functional area could be a candidate for outsourcing.

THE SOURCING DECISION: WHERE SHOULD FUNCTIONS BE HOUSED?

outsourcing acquiring products or services from an independent organization

Where should a function be housed? Should it be integrated within the organization or purchased from an outside contractor? **Outsourcing** is acquiring from someone else a product or service that had been previously provided internally. For example, DuPont contracted out project engineering and design to Morrison Knudsen; AT&T outsourced its credit card processing to Total System Services; and Northern Telecom outsourced its electronic component manufacturing to Comptronix. Outsourcing is becoming an increasingly important part of strategic decision making and an important way to increase efficiency and often quality. Firms competing in global industries in particular must search worldwide for the most appropriate suppliers. Such searches have created a significant amount of new business activity in Canada for businesses like Convergys, which provides billing and customer service support for a variety of organizations. The combination of a weak Canadian dollar, advanced telecommunications infrastructure, an educated workforce, and government incentives has contributed to the location of a large number of call centres in New Brunswick and Nova Scotia, servicing mainly American clients in the wireless telephone market.

Studies show that outsourcing results on average in a 9% reduction in costs and a 15% increase in capacity and quality.[7] For example, Motorola sold its factories in Iowa and Ireland to Celestica Inc. for $70 million. Motorola then agreed to pay Celestica more than $1 billion over three years to make handsets, pagers, two-way radios, and other accessories for Motorola. Celestica, which was once a factory of IBM in Toronto, offered jobs to many of Motorola's employees in Iowa and Ireland. Motorola then shifted manufacturing from its plant in Florida to the Ireland plant it had just sold to Celestica, so that its Florida facility could concentrate on software design and administration. According to Motorola's management, this was part of a broad effort to make the organization's supply chain more efficient, consolidate its manufacturing operations, and improve financial performance.[8]

Most manufacturing firms outsource at least one activity. The most frequently outsourced activities are general and administrative (78%), human resources (77%), transportation and distribution (66%), information systems (63%), manufacturing (56%), marketing (51%), and finance and accounting (18%). Studies show that approximately 25% of the respondents have been disappointed in their outsourcing results. About half of the firms reported bringing an outsourced activity back in-house. Nevertheless, experts predict not only that the number of companies engaging in outsourcing will increase, but also that these companies will outsource an increasing number of functions, especially in customer service, bookkeeping, financial and clerical, sales and telemarketing, and mailroom.[9] The market for outsourced services in Canada alone was approximately $54 billion in 2000 (see **Figure 7–1.**)

Sophisticated strategists, according to Quinn, no longer think just of market share or vertical integration as the keys to strategic planning:

> *Instead they concentrate on identifying those few core service activities where the company has or can develop: (1) a continuing strategic edge and (2) long-term streams of new products to satisfy future customer demands. They develop these competencies in greater depth than anyone else in the world. Then they seek to eliminate, minimize, or outsource activities where the company cannot be pre-eminent, unless those activities are essential to support or protect the chosen areas of strategic focus.*[10]

The key to outsourcing is to purchase from outside only those activities that are not key to the company's distinctive competencies. Otherwise, the company may give up the very capabilities that made it successful in the first place—thus putting itself on the road to eventual decline. Therefore, in determining functional strategy, the strategist must do three things:

- Identify the company's or business unit's core competencies

- Ensure that the competencies are continually being strengthened

- Manage the competencies in the way that best preserves the competitive advantage they create

An outsourcing decision depends on the fraction of total value-added that the activity under consideration represents and the amount of potential competitive advantage in that

Figure 7–1 Canadian Outsourcing Market

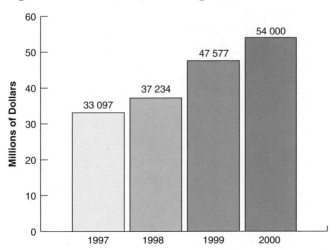

Source: Dun & Bradstreet Canada, advertising supplement in *Canadian Business*, September 24, 1999.

activity for the company or business unit (see the outsourcing matrix in **Figure 7–2**). A firm should consider outsourcing any activity or function that has low potential for competitive advantage. In other words, any low value-creating activity that does not reflect a distinctive competency is a candidate for outsourcing. If that activity constitutes only a small part of the total value of the firm's products or services, it should be purchased on the open market (assuming that quality providers of the activity are available). If, however, the activity contributes highly to the company's products or services, the firm should purchase it through long-term contracts with trusted suppliers or distributors. A firm should always produce at least some of the activity or function (taper vertical integration) if that activity has the potential for providing the company some competitive advantage. Full vertical integration should only be considered, however, when that activity or function adds significant value to the company's products or services in addition to providing competitive advantage. (Vertical integration was discussed in greater detail in **Chapter 6**.)

Outsourcing does, however, have some disadvantages. For example, GE's introduction of a new washing machine was delayed three weeks by production problems at a supplier company to which it had contracted out key work. Some companies have found themselves locked into long-term contracts with outside suppliers that are no longer competitive.[11] Some authorities propose that the cumulative effect of continued outsourcing steadily reduces a firm's ability to learn new skills and to develop new core competencies.[12] Are there lessons to be learned from the difficulties organizations have had with outsourcing? Unsuccessful outsourcing efforts typically have three common characteristics:[13]

- The firm's finance and legal departments and its vendors dominated the decision process.
- Vendors were not pre-qualified based on total capabilities.
- Short-term benefits dominated decision making.

Outsourcing has become an important issue in all industries, especially in global industries such as automobiles, where cost competition is fierce. General Motors, for example, was faced with a strike by its Canadian unions when it wanted to outsource some operations. The

Figure 7–2 Proposed Outsourcing Matrix

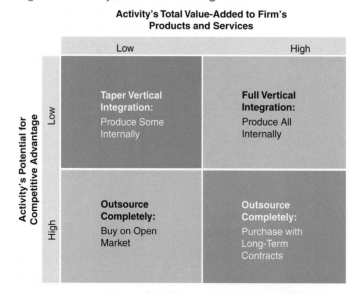

Source: J.D. Hunger and T.L. Wheelen, "Proposed Outsourcing Matrix." Copyright © 1996 by Wheelen and Hunger Associates. Reprinted by permission.

unions were very concerned that such outsourcing would reduce union employment and increase the number of low-paying jobs. Expect this issue to continue in importance throughout the world as more industries become global.

MARKETING STRATEGY

marketing strategy an organization's choices on product, pricing, promotion, and distribution intended to achieve organizational objectives

market development a marketing strategy that either develops new markets for existing products or attempts to increase the sales of existing products in current markets

product development a marketing strategy that achieves growth by developing new products, either for existing or new markets

brand extension a marketing strategy that uses a successful brand to market a new product

Marketing strategy deals with pricing, selling, and distributing a product. Using a **market development** strategy, a company or business unit can (1) capture a larger share of an existing market for current products through market saturation and market penetration or (2) develop new markets for current products. Consumer product giants such as Procter & Gamble, Colgate-Palmolive, and Unilever are experts at using advertising and promotion to implement a market saturation or penetration strategy to gain the dominant market share in a product category. As seeming masters of the product life cycle, these companies are able to extend product life almost indefinitely through "new and improved" variations of product and packaging that appeal to most market niches. These companies also follow the second market development strategy by taking a successful product they market in one part of the world and marketing it elsewhere. Noting the success of their pre-soak detergents in Europe, for example, both P&G and Colgate successfully introduced this type of laundry product to North America under the trade names of Biz and Axion.

Using the **product development** strategy, a company or unit can either (1) develop new products for existing markets, or (2) develop new products for new markets. Church & Dwight has had great success following the first product development strategy by developing new products to sell to its current customers. Acknowledging the widespread appeal of its Arm & Hammer brand baking soda, the company generated new uses for its sodium bicarbonate by reformulating it as toothpaste, deodorant, and detergent. Using a successful brand name to market other products is called **brand extension** and is a good way to appeal to a company's current customers. Roots has extended its brand from shoes and sweatshirts to accessories like bags and watches, perfumes, and for a short while, even a commercial airline. It used its reputation for quality and style along with being Canadian to launch these new products. Arm & Hammer successfully followed the second product development strategy by developing new pollution reduction products (using sodium bicarbonate compounds) for sale to coal-fired electric utility plants—a very different market from grocery stores.

There are other elements to a marketing strategy that an organization can pursue alongside these types of growth strategies. For example, a company or business unit can choose between a push or a pull promotional strategy. Many big food and consumer product companies in the United States and Canada have followed a **push strategy** by spending a large amount of money on trade promotion to gain or hold shelf space in retail outlets. Trade promotion includes discounts, in-store special offers, and advertising allowances designed to "push" products through the distribution system. The Kellogg Company recently decided to change its emphasis from a push to a **pull strategy**, in which advertising "pulls" the products through the distribution channels. The company now spends more money on consumer advertising designed to build brand awareness so that shoppers will ask for the products. Research has indicated that a high level of advertising (a key part of a pull strategy) is most beneficial to leading brands in a market.[14] The difference between these types of promotional strategies is illustrated in **Figure 7–3**.

push strategy using effective selling and trade promotions to push a product through distribution channels to customers

pull strategy investing in advertising and promotion to stimulate consumer demand

channel conflict a situation where intermediaries act in competition with each other for customers

All marketing strategies must somehow deal with distribution, how an organization's products are made available to the consumer. Should a company use distributors and dealers to sell its products or should it sell directly to mass merchandisers? Using both channels simultaneously can lead to **channel conflict** problems. To increase the sales of its lawn tractors and mowers, for example, John Deere decided to sell the products not only through its current dealer network, but also through mass merchandisers like Home Depot. Deere's dealers,

Figure 7–3 Push and Pull Promotional Strategies

Source: P. Kotler, G. Armstrong, and P.H. Cunningham, *Principles of Marketing*, 4th Canadian edition (Scarborough: Prentice-Hall, 1999), p. 482. Reprinted with permission from Pearson Education Canada Inc.

however, were furious. They considered Home Depot a key competitor. The dealers were concerned that Home Depot's ability to underprice them would eventually lead to their becoming little more than repair facilities for their competition, leaving them with insufficient sales to stay in business.[15]

When pricing a new product, a company or business unit can follow one of two strategies. For new-product pioneers, **price skimming** offers the opportunity to "skim the cream" from the top of the demand curve with a high price while the product is novel and competitors are few. Once sales to these segments decline, prices are lowered to reach the next highest point of the demand curve. This process continues until no more customers remain who are willing to pay a premium price for the product. **Penetration pricing**, in contrast, attempts to hasten market development and offers the pioneer the opportunity to use the experience curve to gain market share with a low price and dominate the industry. Depending on organizational and business unit objectives and strategies, either of these choices may be desirable to a particular company or unit. Penetration pricing is, however, more likely than price skimming to raise a unit's operating profit in the long term.[16]

FINANCIAL STRATEGY

Financial strategy examines the financial implications of corporate and business-level strategic options and identifies the best financial course of action. It can also provide competitive advantage through a lower cost of funds and a flexible ability to raise capital to support a business strategy. Financial strategy usually attempts to maximize the financial value of the firm.

The trade-off between achieving the desired debt-to-equity ratio and relying on internal long-term financing via cash flow is a key issue in financial strategy. Many small companies and family businesses try to avoid all external sources of funds in order to avoid outside entanglements and to keep control of the company within the family. Many financial analysts believe, however, that only by financing through long-term debt can an organization use financial leverage to boost earnings per share, thus raising stock price and the overall value of the company. Research indicates that higher debt levels not only deter takeover by other firms (by making the company less attractive), but also lead to improved productivity and improved cash flows by forcing management to focus on core businesses.[17] On the other hand, higher

---

price skimming a pricing strategy that initially sets a high price for a new product to earn maximum profits, then gradually lowers prices

penetration pricing a low-price strategy aimed at quickly attracting large numbers of buyers

financial strategy an organization's plan of how to generate the necessary funds to achieve its goals and objectives

levels of debt commit organizations to higher financing costs that must be made on a fixed schedule. This introduces a level of risk into the organization's financial position, making it more vulnerable to a decline in sales or an increase in costs.

Research reveals that a firm's financial strategy is influenced by its corporate diversification strategy. Equity financing, for example, is preferred for related diversification while debt financing is preferred for unrelated diversification.[18] The recent trend away from unrelated to related acquisitions explains why the number of acquisitions being paid for entirely with stock increased from only 2% in 1988 to 50% in 1998.[19]

One type of financial strategy is the **leveraged buyout** (LBO). In a leveraged buyout, a company is acquired in a transaction financed largely by debt—usually obtained from a third party, such as an insurance company or an investment banker. Ultimately the debt is paid with money generated from the acquired company's operations or by the sale of its assets. The acquired company, in effect, pays for its own acquisition. Management of the LBO is then under tremendous pressure to keep the highly leveraged company profitable. Unfortunately the huge amount of debt on the acquired company's books may actually cause its eventual decline by focusing management's attention on short-term matters. One study of LBOs revealed that the financial performance of the typical LBO usually falls below the industry average in the fourth year after the buyout. The firm declines because of inflated expectations, utilization of all slack, management burnout, and a lack of strategic management.[20] Often the only solution is to go public once again by selling stock to finance growth.

The management of dividends to shareholders is an important part of a corporation's financial strategy. Corporations in fast-growing industries such as computers and computer software often do not declare dividends. They use the money they might have spent on dividends to finance rapid growth. If the company is successful, its growth in sales and profits is reflected in a higher stock price—eventually resulting in a hefty capital gain when shareholders sell their common stock. Other corporations that do not face rapid growth must support the value of their stock by offering generous and consistent dividends.

A recent financial strategy being used by large, established corporations to highlight a high-growth business unit in a popular sector of the stock market is to develop a tracking stock. A **tracking stock** is a type of common stock tied to one portion of an organization's business. This strategy allows established companies to highlight a high-growth business unit without selling the business. By keeping the unit as a subsidiary with its common stock separately identified, the corporation is able to keep control of the subsidiary and yet allow the subsidiary the ability to fund its own growth with outside money. It goes public as an initial public offering (IPO) and pays dividends based on the unit's performance. Because the tracking stock is actually an equity interest in the parent company (not the subsidiary), another company cannot acquire the subsidiary by buying its shares. Examples of corporations using tracking stocks as part of their financial strategy are AT&T (AT&T Wireless), Sprint (Sprint PCS), J.C. Penney (Eckerd Drugs), and Staples (Staples.com).[21]

RESEARCH AND DEVELOPMENT (R & D) STRATEGY

R & D strategy deals with product and process innovation and improvement. It also deals with the appropriate mix of different types of R & D (basic, product, or process) and with the question of how new technology should be accessed—internal development, external acquisition, or through strategic alliances.

One of the R & D choices is to be either a technological leader in which one pioneers an innovation or a technological follower in which one imitates the products of competitors. Porter suggests that deciding to become a technological leader or follower can be a way of achieving either overall low cost or differentiation (see **Table 7–1** on page 176).

One example of an effective use of the *leader* R & D functional strategy to achieve a

---

leveraged buyout using almost exclusively borrowed funds to acquire an organization

tracking stock a class of common stock linked to one business unit of a diversified firm

R & D strategy the types of R & D used and how it will be accessed to achieve organizational goals and objectives

Table 7–1 Research and Development Strategy and Competitive Advantage

	Technological Leadership	Technological Followership
Cost Advantage	Pioneer the lowest cost product design. Be the first firm down the learning curve. Create low-cost ways of performing value activities.	Lower the cost of the product or value activities by learning from the leader's experience. Avoid R & D costs through imitation.
Differentiation	Pioneer a unique product that increases buyer value. Innovate in other activities to increase buyer value.	Adapt the product or delivery system more closely to buyer needs by learning from the leader's experience.

Source: Adapted/reprinted with the permission of The Free Press, an imprint of Simon & Schuster, from *Competitive Advantage: Creating and Sustaining Superior Performance* by Michael E. Porter, p. 181. Copyright © 1985 by Michael E. Porter.

differentiation competitive advantage is Nike, Inc. Nike spends more than most in the industry on R & D to differentiate the performance of its athletic shoes from that of its competitors. As a result, its products have become the favourite of the serious athlete. An example of the use of the *follower* R & D functional strategy to achieve a low-cost competitive advantage is Cott Beverages, the world's leading supplier of retail branded soft drinks. Cott is able to produce a new beverage, upon customer request, at a lower price than its rivals.

An increasing number of companies are working with their suppliers to help them keep up with changing technology. They are beginning to realize that a firm cannot be competitive technologically only through internal development. For example, Chrysler Corporation's skilful use of parts suppliers to design everything from car seats to drive shafts has enabled it to spend consistently less money than its competitors to develop new car models. Strategic technology alliances are one way to combine the R & D capabilities of two companies. Maytag Company worked with one of its suppliers to apply fuzzy logic technology to its new IntelliSense dishwasher. The partnership enabled Maytag to complete the project in a shorter amount of time than if it had tried to do it alone.[22]

OPERATIONS STRATEGY

operations strategy a plan of how and where a product or service will be produced

Operations strategy determines how and where a product or service is to be manufactured, the level of vertical integration in the production process, and the deployment of physical resources. It should also deal with the optimum level of technology the firm should use in its operations processes. See the **Global Issue** feature to see how differences in national conditions can lead to differences in product design and manufacturing facilities from one country to another.

Advanced Manufacturing Technology (AMT) is revolutionizing operations worldwide and should continue to have a major impact as organizations strive to integrate diverse business activities using computer-aided design and manufacturing (CAD/CAM) principles. The use of CAD/CAM, flexible manufacturing systems, computer numerically controlled systems, automatically guided vehicles, robotics, manufacturing resource planning, optimized production technology, and just-in-time contribute to increased flexibility, quick response time, and higher productivity. Such investments also act to increase the company's fixed costs and could cause significant problems if the company is unable to achieve economies of scale or scope.

Global Issue

International Differences Alter Whirlpool's Operations Strategy

To better penetrate the growing markets in developing nations, Whirlpool decided to build a "world washer." This new type of washing machine was to be produced in Brazil, Mexico, and India. Lightweight, with substantially fewer parts than its North American counterpart, its performance was to be equal to or better than anything on the world market while being competitive in price with the most popular models in these markets. The goal was to develop a complete product, process, and facility design package that could be used in different countries with low initial investment. Originally the plan had been to make the same low-cost washer in identical plants in each of the three countries.

Significant differences in each of the three countries forced Whirlpool to change its product design to suit each nation's situation. According to Lawrence Kremer, senior vice-

president of global technology and operations, "Our Mexican affiliate, Vitromatic, has porcelain and glassmaking capabilities. Porcelain baskets made sense for them. Stainless steel became the preferred material for the others." Costs also affected decisions. "In India, for example, material costs may run as much as 200% to 800% higher than elsewhere, while labor and overhead costs are comparatively minimal," added Kremer. Another consideration was the garments to be washed in each country. For example, saris—the 5.5-metre lengths of cotton or silk with which Indian women drape themselves—needed special treatment in an Indian washing machine, forcing additional modifications.

Manufacturing facilities also varied from country to country. Brastemp, Whirlpool's Brazilian partner, built its plant of precast concrete to address the problems of high humidity. In India, however, the construction crew cast the concrete and allowed it to cure; then five or six people, using chain, block, and tackle, raised each three-ton slab into place. Instead of using one building, Mexican operations used two, one housing the flexible assembly lines and stamping operations and an adjacent facility housing the injection moulding and extrusion processes.

Source: A.A. Ullmann, "Whirlpool Corporation, 1993: A Metamorphosis," in Wheelen and Hunger, *Strategic Management and Business Policy*, 5th edition (Reading, Mass.: Addison-Wesley, 1995), pp. 713–715.

A firm's manufacturing strategy is often affected by a product's life cycle. As the sales of a product increase, there will be an increase in production volume ranging from lot sizes as low as one in a job shop (one-of-a-kind production using skilled labour) through connected line batch flow (components are standardized; each machine functions like a job shop but is positioned in the same order as the parts are processed) to lot sizes as high as 100 000 or more per year for flexible manufacturing systems (parts are grouped into manufacturing families to produce a wide variety of mass-produced items) and dedicated transfer lines (highly automated assembly lines making one mass-produced product using little human labour). According to this concept, the product becomes standardized into a commodity over time in conjunction with increasing demand. Flexibility thus gives way to efficiency.[23]

Increasing competitive intensity in many industries has forced companies to switch from traditional mass production using dedicated transfer lines to a continuous improvement production strategy. A **mass production** system was an excellent method to produce a large amount of low-cost, standard goods and services. Employees worked on narrowly defined, repetitive tasks under close supervision in a bureaucratic and hierarchical structure. Quality, however, often tended to be fairly low. Learning how to do something better was the prerogative of management; workers were expected only to learn what was assigned to them. This system tended to dominate manufacturing until the 1970s. Under the continuous improvement system developed by Japanese firms, empowered cross-functional teams strive constantly to improve production processes. Managers become more like coaches. The result is a large quantity of low-cost, standard goods and services, but with high quality. The key to continuous improvement is the acknowledgement that workers' experience and knowledge can help managers solve production problems and contribute toward tightening variances and reducing errors. Because continuous improvement enables firms to use the same low-cost competitive strategy as do mass production firms but at a significantly higher level of quality, it is rapidly replacing mass production as an operations strategy.

mass production a production system of large quantities of standard products

modular manufacturing a production system based on just-in-time delivery of components and subassemblies

The automobile industry is currently experimenting with the strategy of **modular manufacturing** in which pre-assembled subassemblies are delivered as they are needed (just-in-time) to a company's assembly line workers, who quickly piece the modules together into a finished product. For example, General Motors built a new automotive complex in Brazil to make its new subcompact, the Celta. Sixteen of the seventeen buildings are occupied by suppliers, including Delphi, Lear, and Goodyear. These suppliers deliver pre-assembled modules (which together constitute 85% of the final value of each car) to GM's building for assembly. In a process new to the industry, the suppliers act as a team to build a single module comprising the motor, transmission, fuel lines, rear axle, brake-fluid lines, and exhaust system, which is then installed as one piece. GM is hoping that this manufacturing strategy will enable it to produce 100 vehicles annually per worker, compared with the standard rate of 30 to 50 autos.[24] Ford and Chrysler have also opened similar modular facilities in Brazil.

The concept of a product's life cycle eventually leading to one-size-fits-all mass production is being increasingly challenged by the new concept of mass customization. Appropriate for an ever-changing environment, **mass customization** requires that people, processes, units, and technology reconfigure themselves to give customers exactly what they want, when they want it. In contrast to mass production, mass customization requires flexibility and quick responsiveness. Managers coordinate independent, capable individuals. An efficient linkage system is crucial. The result is low-cost, high-quality, customized goods and services. Mass customization is having a significant impact on product development. Under a true mass customization system, no one knows exactly what the next customer will want. Therefore, no one can know exactly what product the company will be creating or producing next. Because it is becoming increasingly difficult to predict what product–market opportunity will open up next, it is harder to create a long-term vision of the company's products.

mass customization a large-scale yet flexible production system generating customized products

One example of mass customization is the "Personal Pair" system Levi Strauss introduced to combat the growing competition from private label jeans. The customer is measured at one of the company's Personal Pair outlets, the measurements are sent to Levi's by computer, and the made-to-order jeans arrive a few days later. The jeans cost more than an off-the-shelf pair. Levi Strauss then launched Original Spin, offering more options plus men's jeans. More choices are now available to the customer without any increase in store inventory. For example, a fully stocked Levi's store carries approximately 130 pairs of jeans for any given waist and inseam. That number virtually increases to 430 with Personal Pair and to 750 with Original Spin. Lands' End is currently working to develop special body scanning booths that will create an electronic 3-D model of a person's body that will sit in memory at a website. Mattel is hoping to soon allow individuals to customize the manufacturing of their own Barbie doll. According to Mattel's marketing vice-president, Anne Parducci, "We are going to build a database of children's names to develop a one-to-one relationship with these girls."[25]

lean manufacturing a strategy of identifying and eliminating waste in the production process

A relatively new manufacturing concept is **lean manufacturing**, a production strategy that identifies and eliminates waste (non-value-added activities) through continuous improvement.[26] Developed in Japan by Toyota, this strategy involves not only manufacturing processes, but also organizational culture. In a lean environment, products are made just-in-time, and quality management is embedded into all processes. Production teams are often empowered to make decisions that will improve productivity and quality. In other words, lean manufacturing strives for perfection by eliminating waste and pursuing the highest quality standards. This focus on waste is something unique about lean manufacturing. Waste is anything the customer is not willing to pay for. This can take several forms, such as overproduction (producing more of the product than is needed, or before it is needed), waiting (bottlenecks in production flow), inventory (raw materials and work-in-progress arising from large production runs with long cycle times), transportation (the time and expense of moving people or products to the next stage of production), and defective products (resulting from poor process control, faulty design, improperly maintained equipment, or inadequate training).[27] Companies like Active Burgess in Windsor, a complete tooling solutions provider specializing in plastic injection moulds for the automotive industry, have had tremendous success with this system. For example, they have reduced their lead time (the time between the receipt of an order and its shipment) almost by half, from 28 weeks to 16 weeks.[28]

PURCHASING STRATEGY

purchasing strategy the way in which inputs into the production process are obtained

Purchasing strategy deals with obtaining the raw materials, parts, and supplies needed to perform the operations function. The basic purchasing choices are multiple, sole, and parallel sourcing. Under multiple sourcing, the purchasing company orders a particular part from several vendors. Multiple sourcing has traditionally been considered superior to other purchasing approaches because (1) it forces suppliers to compete for the business of an important buyer, thus reducing purchasing costs, and (2) if one supplier could not deliver, another usually could, thus guaranteeing that parts and supplies would always be on hand when needed. Multiple sourcing was one way a purchasing firm could control the relationship with its suppliers. So long as suppliers could provide evidence that they could meet the product specifications, they were kept on the purchaser's list of acceptable vendors for specific parts and supplies. Unfortunately the common practice of accepting the lowest bid often compromised quality.

just-in-time a production system that minimizes inventory by having raw materials and components arrive only very shortly before they are required

W. Edward Deming, a well-known management consultant, strongly recommended sole sourcing as the only manageable way to obtain high supplier quality. Sole sourcing relies on only one supplier for a particular part. Given his concern with designing quality into a product in its early stages of development, Deming argued that the buyer should work closely with the supplier at all stages. This reduces both cost and time spent on product design as well as improves quality. It can also simplify the purchasing company's production process by using the **just-in-time** (JIT) concept of arranging for purchased parts to arrive at the plant just when they are needed rather than keeping inventories. The concept of sole sourcing is being taken one step further in JIT II, in which vendor sales representatives actually have desks next to the purchasing company's factory floor, attend production status meetings, visit the R & D lab, and analyze the purchasing company's sales forecasts. These in-house suppliers write sales orders for which the purchasing company is billed. Developed by Lance Dixon at Bose Corporation, JIT II is also being used at IBM, Honeywell, and Ingersoll-Rand. Karen Dale, purchasing manager for Honeywell's office supplies, said she was very concerned about confidentiality when JIT II was first suggested to her. Now she has five suppliers working with her 20 buyers and reports few problems.[29]

parallel sourcing using multiple suppliers to reduce dependencies

Sole sourcing reduces transaction costs and builds quality by having purchaser and supplier work together as partners rather than as adversaries. Sole sourcing means that more companies are going to have longer relationships with fewer suppliers. Sole sourcing does, however, have its limitations. If a supplier is unable to deliver a part, the purchaser has no alternative but to delay production. Multiple suppliers can provide the purchaser with better information about new technology and performance capabilities. The limitations of sole sourcing have led to the development of parallel sourcing. In **parallel sourcing**, two suppliers are the sole suppliers of two different parts, but they are also backup suppliers for each other's parts. In case one vendor cannot supply all of its parts on time, the other vendor would be asked to make up the difference.[30]

The internet is increasingly being used both to find new sources of supply and to keep inventories replenished. For example, Hewlett-Packard introduced a web-based procurement system to enable its 84 000 employees to buy office supplies from a standard set of suppliers. The new system enabled the company to save $60 million to $100 million annually in purchasing costs.[31] See the **Internet Issue** feature on page 180 to learn how David Crosier, vice-president for supply-chain management at Staples, uses the internet to keep the retailer stocked with Post-it Notes and Scotch Tape from 3M.

LOGISTICS STRATEGY

logistics strategy the way inputs enter, and products leave, the manufacturing process

Logistics strategy deals with the flow of products into and out of the manufacturing process. Three trends are evident: centralization, outsourcing, and the use of the internet. To gain logistical synergies across business units, organizations began centralizing logistics in the headquarters group. This centralized logistics group usually contains specialists with expertise in different transportation modes such as rail or trucking. They work to aggregate shipping volumes across the entire organization to gain better contracts with shippers. Companies like Amoco Chemical, Georgia-Pacific, Marriott, and Union Carbide view the logistics function as an important way to differentiate themselves from the competition, to add value, and to reduce costs.

Many companies have found that outsourcing logistics reduces costs and improves delivery time. For example, Hewlett-Packard (HP) contracted with Roadway Logistics to manage its inbound raw materials warehousing in Vancouver. Nearly 140 Roadway employees replaced 250 HP workers, who were transferred to other HP activities.[32]

Many companies are using the internet to simplify their logistical systems. For example, Ace Hardware created an online system for its retailers and suppliers. An individual hardware store can now see on the website that ordering 210 cases of wrenches is cheaper than ordering 200 cases. Since a full pallet comprises 210 cases of wrenches, an order for a full pallet means that the supplier doesn't have to pull 10 cases off a pallet and repackage them for storage. There is less chance for loose cases to be lost in delivery and the paperwork doesn't have to be redone. As a result, Ace's transportation costs are down 18% and warehouse costs have been cut 28%. As shown in the **Internet Issue** feature,[33] 3M's new system enabled it to save $10 million annually in maintenance and customer-service costs.

Internet Issue

Staples Uses Internet to Replenish Inventory from 3M

David Crosier was mad. As the vice-president for supply-chain management for Staples, the office supplies retailer, Crosier couldn't even find a Post-it Note to write down the complaint that his stores were consistently low on 3M products. Crosier would send an order to the Minnesota Mining & Manufacturing Company (3M) for 10 000 rolls of Scotch Tape and receive only 8000. Even worse, the supplies from 3M often arrived late, causing stockouts of popular products. Crosier then discovered 3M's new online ordering system for office supplies. The website enabled 3M to reduce customer frustration caused by paper forms and last-minute phone calls by eliminating error-prone steps in purchasing. Since Staples started to use 3M's website, Crosier reports that 3M's fill rate has improved by 20% and that its on-time performance has almost doubled. "The technology takes a lot of inefficiencies out of the supply-chain process," says Crosier.

This improvement at 3M was initiated by Allen Messerli, information manager at 3M, over a five-year period. Since 1997, 3M has invested $30 million in the project. Ongoing maintenance costs of keeping the system current are $2.6 million. Before implementing this online system, 3M had serious problems with its finished goods inventory, distribution, and customer service. For example, nearly 40% of its North American customer records had invalid addresses. Bloated finished goods inventory in 1998 caused a 45% drop in earnings. With more than 70 000 employees around the world, 3M had difficulty linking employees, managers, and customers because of incompatible networks. With its new Global Enterprise Data Warehouse, 3M is now delivering customer, product, sales, inventory, and financial data directly to its employees and partners, who can access the information via the internet (at www.3m.com). The company reports saving $10 million annually in maintenance and customer-service costs. More accurate and current sales reporting is saving an additional $2.5 million per year. The new technology improved productivity, boosting global sales. Supply-chain managers like David Crosier at Staples are pleased to make the internet an important part of their purchasing strategy.

Source: D. Little, "3M: Glued to the Web," *Business Week E.Biz* (November 2000), pp. EB65–EB70. Reprinted by special permission, copyright © 2000 by The McGraw-Hill Companies, Inc.

HUMAN RESOURCE MANAGEMENT (HRM) STRATEGY

human resource management strategy the way an organization determines and meets its labour needs

HRM strategy, among other things, addresses the issue of whether a company or business unit should hire a large number of low-skilled employees who receive low pay, perform repetitive jobs, and most likely quit after a short time (the McDonald's restaurant strategy) or hire skilled employees who receive relatively high pay and are cross-trained to participate in *self-managing work teams*. As work increases in complexity, the more suited it becomes for teams, especially in the case of innovative product development efforts. Multinational corporations are increasingly using self-managing work teams in their foreign affiliates as well as in home country operations.[34] Research indicates that the use of work teams leads to increased quality and productivity as well as to higher employee satisfaction and commitment.[35]

Many North American and European companies are not only using increasing numbers of part-time and temporary employees, they are also experimenting with using temporary (or contingent) employees from agencies. As previously discussed in **Chapter 4**, many employers are using more part-time and contingent workers because of the cost savings and strategic flexibility that result. The combination of lower wages, fewer benefits, and virtually no job security all provide incentives for organizations to use more of them. The ease with which specialist workers can be obtained from agencies makes it easier for organizations to be responsive to environmental changes. It is far easier for an organization to hire a contract worker with a particular skill set than it is to train one itself or engage in the recruiting and selection to hire one.

Companies are finding that having a diverse workforce can be a competitive advantage. Research reveals that firms with a high degree of racial diversity following a growth strategy have higher productivity than firms with less racial diversity.[36] Avon Company, for example, was able to turn around its unprofitable inner-city markets by putting African-American and Hispanic managers in charge of marketing to these markets.[37] Diversity in terms of age and national origin also offers benefits. DuPont's use of multinational teams has helped the company develop and market products internationally. McDonald's has discovered that older workers perform as well as, if not better than, younger employees.

INFORMATION SYSTEMS STRATEGY

information systems strategy the way computer technology is used to achieve organizational goals and objectives

Organizations are increasingly adopting **information systems strategies** in that they are turning to information systems technology to provide business units with competitive advantage. When FedEx first provided its customers with PowerShip computer software to store addresses, print shipping labels, and track package location, its sales jumped significantly. UPS soon followed with its own MaxiShip software. Viewing its information system as a distinctive competency, FedEx continued to push for further advantage against UPS by using its website to enable customers to track their packages. FedEx exploits this competency in its advertisements by showing how customers can track the progress of their shipments.

Multinational organizations are finding that the use of a sophisticated intranet allows them to practise *follow-the-sun management*, in which project team members living in one country can pass their work to team members in another country in which the workday is just beginning. Thus, night shifts are no longer needed.[38] The development of instant translation software is also enabling workers to have online communication with co-workers in other countries who use a different language. Lotus Translation Services for Sametime is a Java-based application that can deliver translated text during a chat session or an instant message in 17 languages. Another software, e-lingo, offers a multilingual search function and web surfing as well as text and email translation.[39]

7.2 Strategies to Avoid

Several strategies, which could be considered corporate, business, or functional, are very dangerous. Managers who have made a poor analysis or lack creativity may be trapped into considering some of the following strategies. The strategic logic underlying each strategy and the risks associated with it are presented in **Table 7–2**.

- **Follow the Leader:** Imitating a leading competitor's strategy might seem to be a good idea, but it ignores a firm's particular strengths and weaknesses and the possibility that the leader may be wrong. Fujitsu Ltd., the world's second-largest computer maker, was driven since the 1960s by the sole ambition of catching up to IBM. Like IBM, Fujitsu competed primarily as a mainframe computer maker. So devoted was it to catching IBM, however, that it failed to notice that the mainframe business had reached maturity by 1990 and was no longer growing.

- **Bet the Firm:** Sometimes a strategy can have such a strong impact on an organization's performance that if it is not successful, the organization will not survive. This can occur when strategies are chosen that are only able to succeed under a very specific set of circumstances. The best illustrations of this are the dot-com companies that sprung up out of nowhere in the late 1990s as internet technology diffused rapidly throughout the world, especially in North America. These companies "bet the firm" on their ability to use new technology to create ebusiness opportunities for traditional organizations. Unfortunately, may of these dot-com companies simply made huge losses because there was no solid business model for the use of the innovative technologies they possessed.

- **Hit Another Home Run:** If a company is successful because it pioneered an extremely successful product, it tends to search for another super product that will ensure growth and prosperity. As with betting on long shots at the horse races, the probability of finding another winner of the same magnitude is slight. Polaroid spent a lot of money developing an "instant" movie camera, but the public ignored it in favour of the camcorder.

- **Arms Race:** Entering into a spirited battle with another firm for increased market share might increase sales revenue, but that increase will probably be more than offset by increases in advertising, promotion, R & D, and manufacturing costs. Since the deregulation of airlines, price wars and rate "specials" have contributed to the low profit margins or bankruptcy of many commercial airlines such as Canada 3000, Royal Airlines, and Greyhound Air.

- **Do Everything:** When faced with several interesting opportunities, management might tend to leap at all of them. At first, an organization might have enough resources to develop each idea into a project, but money, time, and energy are soon exhausted as the many projects demand large infusions of resources. The Walt Disney Company's expertise in the entertainment industry led it to acquire the ABC television network. As the company churned out new motion pictures and television programs like *Who Wants To Be a Millionaire*, it also spent $750 million to build new theme parks and buy a cruise line (as well as a hockey team). By 2000, even though sales continued to increase, net income was falling.[40]

- **Losing Hand:** An organization might have invested so much in a particular strategy that top management is unwilling to accept its failure. Believing that it has too much invested to quit, the organization continues to "throw good money after bad." Pan American Airlines, for example, chose to sell its Pan Am Building and Intercontinental Hotels, the most profitable parts of the organization, to keep its money-losing airline flying. Continuing to suffer losses, the company followed this strategy of shedding assets for cash until it had sold off everything and gone bankrupt.

Table 7–2 Strategies to Avoid

Strategy	Underlying Logic	Risks
Follow the Leader	Leading firms have the winning formula	Misfit with organizational resources
Bet the Firm	Large financial gains if successful	High cost of failure
Hit Another Home Run	What worked in the past will work in the future	Strategic inflexibility
Arms Race	Larger market share will result in higher profits	Intense rivalry and/or price wars
Do Everything	All opportunities should be pursued	Resources spread too thinly and trade-offs not made
Losing Hand	More resources will result in improved performance	Escalation of commitment

7.3 Strategic Choice: Selection of the Best Strategy

After the advantages and disadvantages of the potential alternatives have been identified and evaluated, one strategy must be selected for implementation. By now, it is likely that many feasible alternatives will have emerged. How is the best strategy determined?

Perhaps the most important criterion is the ability of the proposed strategy to deal with the specific strategic factors developed earlier in the SWOT analysis. If the alternative doesn't take advantage of environmental opportunities and organizational strengths/competencies, and lead away from environmental threats and organizational weaknesses, it will probably fail.

Another important consideration in the selection of a strategy is the ability of each alternative to satisfy agreed-on objectives with the least resources and the fewest negative side effects. It is, therefore, important to develop a tentative implementation plan so that the difficulties that management is likely to face are addressed. This should be done in light of societal trends, the industry, and the company's situation based on the construction of scenarios.

CONSTRUCTING ORGANIZATIONAL SCENARIOS

organizational scenarios forecasts of financial performance associated with different strategic alternatives

Organizational scenarios are pro forma balance sheets and income statements that forecast the effect each alternative strategy and its various programs will likely have on divisional and organizational return on investment. In a survey of *Fortune* 500 firms, 84% reported using computer simulation models in strategic planning. Most of these were simply spreadsheet-based simulation models dealing with "what-if" questions.[41]

The recommended scenarios are simply extensions of the industry scenarios discussed in **Chapter 3**. If, for example, industry scenarios suggest the probable emergence of a strong market demand in a specific country for certain products, a series of alternative strategy scenarios can be developed. The alternative of acquiring another firm having these products in that country can be compared with the alternative of a green-field development (building new operations in that country). Using three sets of estimated sales figures (optimistic, pessimistic, and most likely) for the new products over the next five years, the two alternatives can be evaluated in terms of their effect on future company performance as reflected in its probable future financial statements. Pro forma (estimated future) balance sheets and income statements can be generated with spreadsheet software like Excel on a personal computer.

To construct a scenario, follow these steps:

1. *Use industry scenarios* (discussed in **Chapter 3**) to develop a set of assumptions about the task environment (in the specific country under consideration). For example, 3M requires the general manager of each business unit to describe annually what his or her industry will look like in 15 years. List *optimistic, pessimistic,* and *most likely* assumptions for key economic factors such as the GDP (gross domestic product), CPI (consumer price index), and prime interest rate, and for other key external strategic factors such as governmental regulation and industry trends. This should be done for every country or region in which the organization has significant operations that will be affected by each strategic alternative. These same underlying assumptions should be listed for each of the alternative scenarios to be developed.

2. *Develop common-size financial statements* (to be discussed in **Appendix**) for the company's or business unit's previous years, to serve as the basis for the trend analysis projections of pro forma financial statements. Use the Scenario Box form in **Table 7–3**.

   a. Use the historical common-size percentages to estimate the level of revenues, expenses, and other categories in pro forma statements for future years.

   b. Develop for each strategic alternative a set of *optimistic, pessimistic,* and *most likely* assumptions about the impact of key variables on the company's future financial statements.

   c. Forecast three sets of figures for both sales and cost of goods sold for at least five years into the future.

   d. Analyze historical data and make adjustments based on the environmental assumptions listed earlier. Do the same for other figures that can vary significantly.

   e. Assume for other figures that they will continue in their historical relationship to sales or some other key determining factor. Plug in expected inventory levels, accounts receivable, accounts payable, R & D expenses, advertising and promotion expenses, capital expenditures, and debt payments (assuming that debt is used to finance the strategy), among others.

   f. Consider not only historical trends, but also programs that might be needed to implement each alternative strategy (such as building a new manufacturing facility or expanding the sales force).

3. *Construct detailed pro forma financial statements* for each strategic alternative.

   a. List the actual figures from this year's financial statements in the left column of the spreadsheet.

   b. List to the right of this column the optimistic figures for years 1 through 5.

   c. Go through this same process with the same strategic alternative, but now list the pessimistic figures for the next five years.

   d. Do the same with the most likely figures.

   e. Develop a similar set of *optimistic* (O), *pessimistic* (P), and *most likely* (ML) pro forma statements for the second strategic alternative. This process generates six different pro forma scenarios reflecting three different situations (O, P, and ML) for two strategic alternatives.

   f. Calculate financial ratios and common-size income statements and balance sheets to accompany the pro forma statements.

g. Compare the assumptions underlying the scenarios with these financial statements and ratios to determine the feasibility of the scenarios. For example, if cost of goods sold drops from 70% to 50% of total sales revenue in the pro forma income statements, this drop should result from a change in the production process or a shift to cheaper raw materials or labour costs, rather than from a failure to keep the cost of goods sold in its usual percentage relationship to sales revenue when the predicted statement was developed.

The result of this detailed scenario construction should be anticipated net profits, cash flow, and net working capital for each of three versions of the two alternatives for five years into the future. A strategist might want to go further into the future if the strategy is expected to have a major impact on the company's financial statements beyond five years. The result of this work should provide sufficient information on which forecasts of the likely feasibility and probable profitability of each of the strategic alternatives could be based.

Obviously these scenarios can quickly become very complicated, especially if three sets of acquisition prices and development costs are calculated. Nevertheless this sort of detailed "what-if" analysis is needed to realistically compare the projected outcome of each reasonable alternative strategy and its attendant programs, budgets, and procedures. Regardless of the quantifiable pros and cons of each alternative, the actual decision will probably be influenced by several subjective factors like those described in the following sections.

Table 7–3 Scenario Box for Use in Generating Financial Pro Forma Statements

Factor	Last Year	Historical Average	Trend Analysis	Projections[1] 200- O	P	ML	200- O	P	ML	200- O	P	ML	Comments
GDP													
CPI													
Other													
Sales units													
Dollars													
COGS													
Advertising and marketing													
Interest expense													
Plant expansion													
Dividends													
Net profits													
EPS													
ROI													
ROE													
Other													

Note:
1. **O** = Optimistic; **P** = Pessimistic; **ML** = Most Likely.

Source: T.L. Wheelen and J.D. Hunger. Copyright ©1993 by Wheelen and Hunger Associates. Reprinted by permission.

Management's Attitude toward Risk

The attractiveness of a particular strategic alternative is partially a function of the amount of risk it entails. **Risk** comprises not only the *probability* that the strategy will be effective, but also of the *amount of assets* the organization must allocate to that strategy and the *length of time* the assets will be unavailable for other uses. Because of variation among countries in terms of customs, regulations, and resources, companies operating in global industries must deal with a greater amount of risk than firms operating only in one country. The greater the assets involved and the longer they are committed, the more likely top management is to demand a high probability of success. Do not expect managers with no ownership position in a company to have much interest in putting their jobs in danger with a risky decision. Research does indicate that managers who own a significant amount of stock in their firms are more likely to engage in risk-taking actions than are managers with no stock.[42]

A high level of risk was why Intel's board of directors found it difficult to vote for a proposal in the early 1990s to commit $5 billion to making the Pentium microprocessor chip—five times the amount needed for its previous chip. In looking back on that board meeting, then-CEO Andy Grove remarked, "I remember people's eyes looking at that chart and getting big. I wasn't even sure I believed those numbers at the time." The proposal committed the company to building new factories, something Intel had been reluctant to do. A wrong decision would mean that the company would end up with a killing amount of overcapacity. Based on Grove's presentation, the board decided to take the gamble. Intel's resulting manufacturing expansion eventually cost $10 billion, but it resulted in Intel's obtaining 75% of the microprocessor business and huge cash profits.[43]

Risk might be one reason that significant innovations occur more often in small firms than in large, established organizations. The small firm managed by an entrepreneur is willing to accept greater risk than would a large firm of diversified ownership run by professional managers.[44] It is one thing to take a chance if you are the primary shareholder and are not concerned with periodic changes in the value of the company's common stock. It is something else if the corporation's stock is widely held and acquisition-hungry competitors or takeover artists surround the company like sharks every time the company's stock price falls below some external assessment of the firm's value.

A new approach to evaluating alternatives under conditions of high environmental uncertainty is to use real options theory. According to the **real options approach**, when the future is highly uncertain, it pays to have a broad range of options open. This is in contrast to using **net present value** (NPV) to calculate the value of a project by predicting its payouts, adjusting them for risk, and subtracting the amount invested. By boiling everything down to one scenario, NPV doesn't provide any flexibility in case circumstances change. NPV is also difficult to apply to projects in which the potential payoffs are currently unknown. The real options approach, however, deals with these issues by breaking the investment into stages. Management allocates a small amount of funding to initiate multiple projects, monitors their development, and then cancels the projects that aren't successful and funds those that are doing well. This approach is very similar to the way venture capitalists fund an entrepreneurial venture in stages of funding based on the venture's performance. Organizations using the real options approach are Chevron for bidding on petroleum reserves, Airbus for calculating the costs of airlines changing their orders at the last minute, and the Tennessee Valley Authority for outsourcing electricity generation instead of building its own plant. Because of its complexity, the real options approach is not worthwhile for minor decisions or for projects requiring a full commitment at the beginning.[45] What this approach does offer, however, is a way to minimize potential losses while not affecting upside gains. This occurs by viewing a capital expenditure (for example a plant expansion, increased R & D, or an acquisition) as a call option—the organization has the right but not the obligation to commence and continue with the expenditure. By breaking a larger investment into stages, losses can be contained if results in any given stage are subpar. This is particularly important when payoffs are uncertain or unpredictable. If earlier states of the investment are successful, further investments can then be made.

Pressures from Stakeholders

The attractiveness of a strategic alternative is affected by its perceived compatibility with the key stakeholders in an organization's task environment. Creditors want to be paid on time. Unions exert pressure for comparable wage and employment security. Governments and interest groups demand social responsibility. Shareholders want dividends. All of these pressures must be given some consideration in the selection of the best alternative.

Stakeholders can be categorized in terms of their (1) interest in the organization's activities and (2) relative power to influence the organization's activities.[46] Using the Stakeholder Priority Matrix depicted in **Figure 7–4**, each stakeholder group may be placed in one of the nine cells.

Strategic managers should ask four questions to assess the importance of stakeholder concerns in a particular decision:

1. How will this decision affect each stakeholder, especially those given high and medium priority?
2. How much of what each stakeholder wants are they likely to get under this alternative?
3. What are they likely to do if they don't get what they want?
4. What is the probability that they will do it?

Figure 7–4 Stakeholder Priority Matrix

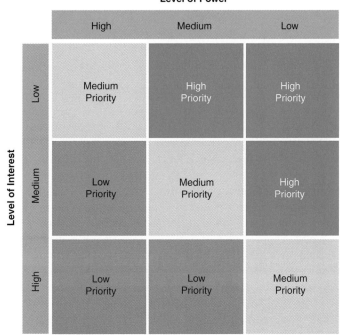

Source: Suggested by C. Anderson, "Values-Based Management," *Academy of Management Executive* (November 1997), p, 31. Reprinted by permission of *Academy of Management Executive* via the Copyright Clearance Center.

Strategy makers should be better able to choose strategic alternatives that minimize external pressures and maximize the probability of gaining stakeholder support. In addition, top management can propose a political strategy to influence its key stakeholders. Some of the most commonly used political strategies include constituency building, political action committee contributions, advocacy advertising, lobbying, and coalition building.

Pressures from the Organizational Culture

If a strategy is incompatible with the organizational culture, the likelihood of its success is very low. Foot-dragging and even sabotage will result as employees fight to resist a radical change in organizational philosophy. Precedents from the past tend to restrict the kinds of objectives and strategies that can be seriously considered.[47] The "aura" of the founders of an organization can linger long past their lifetimes because their values have been imprinted on an organization's members.

In evaluating a strategic alternative, the strategy makers must consider organizational culture pressures and assess the strategy's compatibility with the organizational culture. If there is little fit, management must decide whether it should take one of these options:

- Take a chance on ignoring the culture
- Manage around the culture and change the implementation plan
- Try to change the culture to fit the strategy
- Change the strategy to fit the culture

Further, a decision to proceed with a particular strategy without a commitment to change the culture or manage around the culture (both very tricky and time-consuming) is dangerous. Nevertheless restricting an organization to only those strategies that are completely compatible with its culture might eliminate from consideration the most profitable alternatives. (See **Chapter 9** for more information on managing organizational culture.)

Needs and Desires of Key Managers

Even the most attractive alternative might not be selected if it is contrary to the needs and desires of important top managers. Personal characteristics and experience do affect a person's assessment of an alternative's attractiveness.[48] A person's ego may be tied to a particular proposal to the extent that all other alternatives are strongly lobbied against. As a result, he or she may have unfavourable forecasts altered so that they are more in agreement with the desired alternative.[49] A key executive might influence other people in top management to favour a particular alternative so that objections to it are ignored. For example, Nextel's CEO, Daniel Akerson, decided that the best place to locate the corporation's 500-person national headquarters would be the Washington, DC, area, close to his own home.[50]

Industry and cultural backgrounds affect strategic choice. For example, executives with strong ties within an industry tend to choose strategies commonly used in that industry. Executives who have come to the firm from another industry and have strong ties outside the industry tend to choose different strategies from what is being currently used in their industry.[51] Research reveals that executives from Korea, the United States, Japan, and Germany tend to make different strategic choices in similar situations because they use different decision criteria and weights. For example, Korean executives emphasize industry attractiveness, sales, and market share in their decisions, whereas US executives emphasize projected demand, discounted cash flow, and ROI.[52]

There is a tendency to maintain the status quo, which means that decision makers continue with existing goals and plans beyond the point when an objective observer would recommend a change in course. Some executives show a self-serving tendency to attribute the firm's problems not to their own poor decisions, but to environmental events out of their control such as government policies or a poor economic climate.[53] Negative information about a particular course of action to which a person is committed may be ignored because of a desire to appear competent or because of strongly held values regarding consistency. It may take a crisis or an unlikely event to cause strategic decision makers to seriously consider an alternative they had previously ignored or discounted.[54] For example, it wasn't until the CEO of ConAgra, a multinational food products company, had a heart attack that ConAgra started producing the Healthy Choice line of low-fat, low-cholesterol, low-sodium frozen-food entrees.

Process of Strategic Choice

There is an old story at General Motors:

> At a meeting with his key executives, CEO Alfred Sloan proposed a controversial strategic decision. When asked for comments, each executive responded with supportive comments and praise. After announcing that they were all in apparent agreement, Sloan stated that they were not going to proceed with the decision. Either his executives didn't know enough to point out potential downsides of the decision, or they were agreeing to avoid upsetting the boss and disrupting the cohesion of the group. The decision was delayed until a debate could occur over the pros and cons.[55]

strategic choice the way strategic options are evaluated and selected

Strategic choice is the evaluation of alternative strategies and selection of the best alternative. There is mounting evidence that when an organization is facing a dynamic environment, the best strategic decisions are not arrived at through consensus when everyone agrees on one alternative. They actually involve a certain amount of heated disagreement and even conflict. This is certainly the case for firms operating in a global industry. Because unmanaged conflict often carries a high emotional cost, authorities in decision making propose that strategic managers use "programmed conflict" to raise different opinions regardless of the personal feelings of the people involved.[56] Two techniques help strategic managers avoid the consensus trap that Alfred Sloan found:

devil's advocate a role in which a person identifies problems or difficulties with any strategic option

1. **Devil's Advocate:** The concept of the devil's advocate originated in the medieval Roman Catholic Church as a way of ensuring that impostors were not canonized as saints. One trusted person was selected to find and present all reasons why the person should not be canonized. When applied to strategic decision making, the devil's advocate (who may be an individual or a group) is assigned to identify potential pitfalls and problems with a proposed alternative strategy in a formal presentation.

dialectical inquiry a process whereby the relative merits of strategic options are compared and subsequently used for selecting among them

2. **Dialectical Inquiry:** The dialectic philosophy, which can be traced back to Plato and Aristotle and more recently to Hegel, involves combining two conflicting views—the thesis and the antithesis—into a synthesis. When applied to strategic decision making, dialectical inquiry requires that two proposals using different assumptions be generated for each alternative strategy under consideration. After advocates of each position present and debate the merits of their arguments before key decision makers, either one of the alternatives or a new compromise alternative is selected as the strategy to be implemented.

Research generally supports the conclusion that the two techniques of devil's advocate and dialectical inquiry are equally superior to the practice of consensus in decision making, especially when the firm's environment is dynamic. The debate itself, rather than its particular format, appears to improve the quality of decisions by formalizing and legitimizing constructive conflict and by encouraging critical evaluation. Both lead to better assumptions and recommendations and to a higher level of critical thinking among the people involved.[57]

strategy shadow committee a group of people who observe the strategy development process as a basis for making improvements to it

Another approach to generating a series of diverse and creative strategic alternatives is to use a **strategy shadow committee**. At Anheuser-Busch, top management established such a committee comprising employees at least two to three echelons below the executive-level strategy committee. Members of the shadow committee serve for two years. During that time they see all materials and attend all meetings of the executive strategy committee. One year the shadow committee was taken off-site and asked what was wrong with management and what the company should be doing differently. The group's report was then given to the board of directors.[58]

Regardless of the process used to generate strategic alternatives, each resulting alternative must be rigorously evaluated in terms of its ability to meet four criteria:[59]

1. **Success.** It must have a good probability of success. Does it provide an acceptable level of return at an acceptable level of risk? Is there some way to strengthen competitive position or competitive advantage using this strategy?

2. **Ability to Implement.** It must be doable in a practical sense. Does the organization have the resources, structure, and culture necessary to implement the changes necessary with the new strategy?

3. **Completeness.** It must take into account all the key strategic issues. Is the strategic direction consistent with consumer behaviour trends, product life cycles, industry evolution, value chain analysis, and industry competitive structure?

4. **Internal Consistency.** It must make sense on its own as a strategic decision for the entire firm and not contradict key goals, policies, and strategies currently being pursued by the firm or its units. Is it consistent with the history and traditions of the organization and the values of top management? Is it consistent with the interests and needs of organizational stakeholders?

7.4 Development of Policies

The selection of the best strategic alternative is not the end of strategy formulation. The organization must now engage in developing policies. Policies define the broad guidelines for implementation. Flowing from the selected strategy, policies provide guidance for decision making and actions throughout the organization. At Bombardier, for example, it is a policy to be a market leader in whatever industry the company competes in. This policy gives clear guidance to managers throughout the organization. Another example of such a policy is that of Casey's General Stores that a new service or product line may be added to its stores only when the product or service can be justified in terms of increasing store traffic.

Policies tend to be rather long-lived and can even outlast the particular strategy that created them. Interestingly, these general policies—such as "The customer is always right" or "Research and development should get first priority on all budget requests"—can become, in time, part of an organization's culture. Such policies can make the implementation of specific strategies easier. They can also restrict top management's strategic options in the future. Thus, a change in strategy should be followed quickly by a change in policies. Managing policy is one way to manage the organizational culture.

7.5 Impact of the Internet on Functional Strategy

Every time a person clicks on a banner or views a product on the internet, website operators add this information to that person's digital trail. The user doesn't have to purchase anything because a decision not to buy is almost as important as a decision to buy. The data is used to answer questions such as these: Why did the customer visit our site but not buy our products? Is our checkout process too long? Did the customer come from an affiliate site? Should we have offered this person a discount or special offer? The answers to these questions can strongly influence a company's marketing functional strategy.

Tracking potential online customers is the rationale for *electronic customer relationship management (eCRM) software*. Divided into the three areas of marketing, services, and sales, eCRM is the fastest-growing area of the software industry. The marketing part of eCRM is growing at a rate of 50% annually and is divided into the fields of analytics, emarketing, and personalization. According to Phil Fernandez, executive vice-president of E.piphany, an eCRM developer, "*Analytics* helps you to understand the customer. *E-marketing* helps structure how you reach out to that customer, and *personalization* is about using all that knowledge to create a personalized experience."

Analytics software creates information from data gathered from a number of customer *touch points*, both online and offline. Combining demographic data with sales information from customer records can indicate how purchases vary by demographic group. Online activity records can tell what particular groups of customers buy, what webpages they tend to visit, and their tastes. Companies such as Accrue, digiMine, Coremetrics, NetGenesis, Personify, and MicroStrategy offer software that can analyze customer data and turn it into usable reports. Hoover's Online used analytics software to analyze website traffic, create customer profiles, and classify users by market segment. According to Craig Lakey, vice-president of marketing for Hoover's Online, "Using Personify's technology, we were able to analyze where people were going and promote areas that they were ignoring. We were able to cross-promote other aspects of the site. Just by virtue of analyzing what we found, we tripled the traffic on the business travel channel."

Emarketing software is used to keep track of which marketing campaigns succeed and which fail, as well as to plan future marketing programs. The analytics stage answers questions such as, Of the people who bought Gucci bags, how many also bought Calvin Klein shirts? In the emarketing stage, companies use the answers to allow a firm to offer discounts on Gucci bags via email to customers who bought Calvin Klein shirts. Companies offering emarketing software are Annuncio, Broadbase Software, E.piphany, and Responsys.com.

Personalization software allows businesses to offer products uniquely relevant to the individual visitor to a website by creating a web experience tailored to that individual's taste. Amazon.com uses this software to inform people who purchase a book or CD that people who previously bought that item also bought items by another author or artist. As at Amazon.com, statistical correlation techniques are used to find other website visitors with similar patterns of behaviour and analyze the behaviour of these like-minded people to make recommendations for further purchases. Personalization software also uses neural network-based artificial intelligence to model website visitors on the basis of their "clickstream" (a sequence of webpages selected by a visitor) and purchase behaviour. Personalization is superior to blindly emailing coupons to potential customers because it is more closely connected to that person's interests. Personalization software is still in the development stage but has a lot of appeal to companies with an internet presence. Some of the companies offering personalization software are Net Perceptions, Angara, the Art Technology Group, Blaze Software, and BroadVision. According to Lynne Harvey, senior consultant with the Patricia Seybold Group, "The number of touch points is expanding, so there will be an increased demand by the customers for companies to be more responsive, as opposed to the old way, where you had a pre-defined offer and you hoped that someone would be attracted enough to buy it."[60]

Thanks to eCRM software, firms are now able to practise *dynamic pricing*, a controversial pricing practice in which different customers pay different prices for the same product or service. Tried by Amazom.com, this practice uses a customer's address, record of previous purchases, sites visited, and other information to decide whether the customer is price-sensitive. If the software puts the customer in a price-sensitive category, the customer is offered a low price. Otherwise, the customer pays a premium. Other firms practise *dynamic service*, in which they offer varying levels of service for the same price. Customers are coded based on the profitability of their business. Using a customer's code, phone centres or websites route customers to different queues. The most profitable customers have fees waived and receive special offers the typical customer doesn't know exist.[61] Gambling casinos have used this marketing strategy for years to encourage "high rollers" who are prone to spending (and losing) a large amount of money in gambling establishments.

Discussion Questions

1. How can an organization identify its core competencies? Its distinctive competencies?

2. When should an organization or business unit outsource a function or activity?

3. Why is penetration pricing more likely than skim pricing to raise a company's or a business unit's operating profit in the long run?

4. How does mass customization support a business unit's competitive strategy?

5. What is the relationship of policies to strategies?

Strategic Practice Exercise

Wal-Mart is a very successful mass marketing retailer with stores throughout North America and an increasing presence in Europe, South America, and Asia. The company is known for its distinctive competency in information systems and distribution logistics. According to Michael Campbell, CEO of Campbell Software, "Wal-Mart is so far ahead of the [technology] curve because they were the first ones to embrace the fact that they are in the information business."[62]

In 1996, management decided to establish a position for the company on the internet. During this period of time, when its brick and mortar stores were registering double-digit sales and earnings growth, Wal-Mart's virtual store on the internet had continual problems. For example, in 1999 the company was forced to warn web customers that it couldn't guarantee Christmas delivery of goods ordered after December 14. A redesigned and expanded website debuted in February 2000 but was criticized for its cumbersome design, slow downloading time, and poor search engine. In September 2000, it was ranked 47th out of 50 retail sites by Media Metrix.[63]

Timothy Mullaney, a columnist for *Business Week's* e-biz section, compared Wal-Mart's website during September 2000 with that of Amazon.com. He found that Wal-Mart's website didn't measure up to its own brick and mortar stores, much less to Amazon. He rated Walmart.com a failure on content, convenience, and fun. Among its faults were the following: Walmart.com settled for taking orders rather than enticing visitors (as Amazon did) to consider things they hadn't thought of buying. Compared with Amazon.com, he found the site boring. Its homepage comprised a long list of categories. The site provided basic data on each product offered but failed to provide any reviews of the products or show them in use. In contrast, Amazon.com's website provided reviews by both Amazon and 33 users supplemented by a table that let the user compare the features of one CD player with those of other players. Simple one-click boxes referred the user to accessories and batteries. Amazon.com tailored its recommendations to the visitor's tastes and interests, whereas Walmart.com made generic suggestions that fit few visitors. Walmart.com's navigation features were poor. The site contained a number of broken or poorly designed links. For example, a request for romantic comedies starring Tom Hanks led to *Nightmare at 43 Hillcrest*, a drama about drug-dealing. Prices and shipping costs were, however, about the same at both sites. The columnist summed up his experience with the statement, "Right now, Amazon.com is a very good store, and Walmart.com is still learning the online fundamentals."[64]

Reacting to the poor performance of its website, Wal-Mart's management hired Jeanne Jackson as the new CEO of Walmart.com. Hired during the spring of 2000 from Banana Republic, where she had been CEO as well as head of the company's catalogue and web operations, Jackson vowed to make the largest brick and mortar retailer into a successful virtual retailer. She closed the website in late September for remodelling and opened it a few weeks later as a much leaner site without personalized promotions or 3-D graphics. Although the site had a more streamlined and intuitive layout in 2001, critics found it dull. CEO Jackson continued to be optimistic. The online efforts of Sears, Kmart, and Target were still in their infancy. Jackson commented, "This is a marathon. It's not a sprint."

1. Given that Wal-Mart has a distinctive competency in information technology, why has it done so poorly on the internet?

2. Considering that as of early 2001, almost no dot-com retailer (including Amazon.com) had yet to show a profit, why all the fuss about internet retailing?

3. Is the marriage of "bricks" and "clicks" the right formula for marketing success on the internet?

4. Should Wal-Mart be investing in the internet at a time when it has so many alternative growth opportunities throughout the world?

5. What advice would you give Jeanne Jackson regarding Walmart.com?

Notes

1. *Canadian Business*, September 24, 1999.

2. www.aramark.ca (accessed May 2, 2003).

3. M.A. Hitt, B.W. Keats, and S.M. DeMarie, "Navigating in the New Competitive Landscape: Building Strategic Flexibility and Competitive Advantage in the 21st Century," *Academy of Management Executive* (November 1998), pp. 22–42. According to the authors, failure to reinvest in a core competency will result in its becoming a "core rigidity."

4. G. Hamel and S.K. Prahalad, *Competing for the Future* (Boston: Harvard Business School Press, 1994), pp. 202–207.

5. Ibid, p. 211.

6. P.J. Verdin and P.J. Williamson, "Core Competencies, Competitive Advantage and Market Analysis: Forging the Links," in *Competence-Based Competition*, edited by G. Hamel and A. Heene (New York: John Wiley and Sons, 1994), pp. 83–84.

7. B. Kelley, "Outsourcing Marches On," *Journal of Business Strategy* (July/August 1995), p. 40.

8. BridgeNews, "Motorola Will Cut 2,870 Jobs in Outsourcing Deal," *The [Ames] Tribune* (December 11, 2000), p. D4.

9. J. Greco, "Outsourcing: The New Partnership," *Journal of Business Strategy* (July/August 1997), pp. 48–54.

10. J.B. Quinn, "The Intelligent Enterprise: A New Paradigm," *Academy of Management Executive* (November 1992), pp. 48–63.

11. J.A. Byrne, "Has Outsourcing Gone Too Far?" *Business Week* (April 1, 1996), pp. 26–28.

12. D. Lei and M.A. Hitt, "Strategic Restructuring and Outsourcing: The Effect of Mergers and Acquisitions and LBOs on Building Firm Skills and Capabilities," *Journal of Management*, Vol. 21, No. 5 (1995), pp. 835–859.

13. Kelley, "Outsourcing Marches On," p. 40.

14. S.M. Oster, *Modern Competitive Analysis*, 2nd edition (New York: Oxford University Press, 1994), p. 93.

15. M. Springer, "Plowed Under," *Forbes* (February 21, 2000), p. 56.

16. W. Redmond, "The Strategic Pricing of Innovative Products," *Handbook of Business Strategy, 1992/1993 Yearbook*, edited by H.E. Glass and M.A. Hovde (Boston: Warren, Gorham and Lamont, 1992), pp. 16.1–16.13.

17. A. Safieddine and S. Titman in April 1999, *Journal of Finance* As summarized by D. Champion, "The Joy of Leverage," *Harvard Business Review* (July–August 1999), pp. 19–22.

18. R. Kochhar and M.A. Hitt, "Linking Corporate Strategy to Capital Structure: Diversification Strategy, Type and Source of Financing," *Strategic Management Journal* (June 1998), pp. 601–610.

19. A. Rappaport and M.L. Sirower, "Stock or Cash?" *Harvard Business Review* (November–December 1999), pp. 147–158.

20. D. Angwin and I. Contardo, "Unleashing Cerberus: Don't Let Your MBOs Turn on Themselves," *Long Range Strategy* (October 1999), pp. 494–504.

21. S. Scherreik, "Tread Carefully When You Buy Tracking Stocks," *Business Week* (March 6, 2000), pp. 182–184.

22. S. Stevens, "Speeding the Signals of Change," *Appliance* (February 1995), p. 7.

23. J.R. Williams and R.S. Novak, "Aligning CIM Strategies to Different Markets," *Long Range Planning* (February 1990), pp. 126–135.

24. J. Wheatley, "Super Factory—or Super Headache," *Business Week* (July 31, 2000), p. 66.

25. G. Hamel, "Strategy As Revolution," *Harvard Business Review* (July–August, 1996), p. 73; and E. Schonfeld, "The Customized, Digitized, Have-It-Your-Way Economy," *Fortune* (September 28, 1998), pp. 115–124.

26. J.P. Womak and D.T. Jones, *Lean Thinking: Banish Waste and Create Wealth in Your Corporation* (New York: Simon & Schuster, 1996).

27. H.H. Millar, *An Introduction to Lean Enterprise* (Halifax: Saint Mary's University Business Development Centre, 2003).

28. www.leanadvisors.com (accessed May 4, 2003).

29. F.R. Bleakley, "Some Companies Let Supplier Work on Site and Even Place Orders," *Wall Street Journal* (January 13, 1995), pp. A1, A6.

30. J. Richardson, "Parallel Sourcing and Supplier Performance in the Japanese Automobile Industry," *Strategic Management Journal* (July 1993), pp. 339–350.

31. S. Roberts-Witt, "Procurement: The HP Way," *PC Magazine* (November 21, 2000), pp. iBiz 21–22.

32. J. Bigness, "In Today's Economy, There Is Big Money To Be Made in Logistics," *The Wall Street Journal* (September 6, 1995), pp. A1, A9.

33. F. Keenan, "Logistics Gets a Little Respect," *Business Week* (November 20, 2000), pp. E.Biz 112–116.

34. B.L. Kirkman and D.L. Shapiro, "The Impact of Cultural Values on Employee Resistance to Teams: Toward a Model of Globalized Self-Managing Work Team Effectiveness," *Academy of Management Review* (July 1997), pp. 730–757.

35. R.D. Banker, J.M. Field, R.G. Schroeder, and K.K. Sinha, "Impact of Work Teams on Manufacturing Performance: A Longitudinal Field Study," *Academy of Management Journal* (August 1996), pp. 867–890; B.L. Kirkman and B. Rosen, "Beyond Self-Management: Antecedents and Consequences of Team Empowerment," *Academy of Management Journal* (February 1999), pp. 58–74.

36. O.C. Richard, "Racial Diversity, Business Strategy, and Firm Performance: A Resource-Based View," *Academy of Management Journal* (April 2000), pp. 164–177.

37. G. Robinson and K. Dechant, "Building a Business Case for Diversity," *Academy of Management Executive* (August 1997), pp. 21–31.

38. J. Greco, "Good Day Sunshine," *Journal of Business Strategy* (July/August 1998), pp. 4–5.

39. W. Howard, "Translate Now," *PC Magazine* (September 19, 2000), p. 81.

40. R. Grover and D. Polek, "Millionaire Buys Disney Time," *Business Week* (June 26, 2000), pp. 141–144.

41. D.K. Sinha, "Strategic Planning in the Fortune 500," *Handbook of Business Strategy, 1991/1992 Yearbook*, edited by H.E. Glass and M.A. Hovde (Boston: Warren, Gorham and Lamont, 1991), pp. 9.6–9.8.

42. T.B. Palmer and R.M. Wiseman, "Decoupling Risk Taking from Income Stream Uncertainty: A Holistic Model of Risk," *Strategic Management Journal* (November 1999), pp. 1037–1062.

43. D. Clark, "All the Chips: A Big Bet Made Intel What It Is Today; Now It Wagers Again," *The Wall Street Journal* (June 6, 1995), pp. A1, A5.

44. L.W. Busenitz and J.B. Barney, "Differences between Entrepreneurs and Managers in Large Organizations: Biases and Heuristics in Strategic Decision-Making," *Journal of Business Venturing* (January 1997), pp. 9–30.

45. P. Coy, "Exploiting Uncertainty," *Business Week* (June 7, 1999), pp. 118–124. For further information on real options, see M. Amram and N. Kulatilaka, "Uncertainty: The New Rules for Strategy," *Journal of Business Strategy* (May/June 1999), pp. 25–29; M. Amram and N. Kulatilaka, "Disciplined Decisions: Aligning Strategy with the Financial Markets," *Harvard Business Review* (January–February 1999), pp. 95–104; T.A. Luehrman, "Strategy As a Portfolio of Real Options," *Harvard Business Review* (September–October 1998), pp. 89–99; T.A. Luehrman, "Investment Opportunities As Real Options: Getting Started with the Numbers," *Harvard Business Review* (July–August 1998), pp. 51–67; R.G. McGrath, "Falling Forward: Real Options Reasoning and Entrepreneurial Failure," *Academy of Management Review* (January 1999), pp. 13–30.

46. C. Anderson, "Values-Based Management," *Academy of Management Executive* (November 1997), pp. 25–46.

47. H.M. O'Neill, R.W. Pouder, and A.K. Buchholtz, "Patterns in the Diffusion of Strategies across Organizations: Insights from the Innovation Diffusion Literature," *Academy of Management Executive* (January 1998), pp. 98–114.

48. B.B. Tyler and H.K. Steensma, "Evaluating Technological Collaborative Opportunities: A Cognitive Modeling Perspective," *Strategic Management Journal* (Summer 1995), pp. 43–70; D. Duchan, D.P. Ashman, and M. Nathan, "Mavericks, Visionaries, Protestors, and Sages: Toward a Typology of Cognitive Structures for Decision Making in Organizations," *Journal of Business Strategies* (Fall 1997), pp. 106–125; P. Chattopadhyay, W.H. Glick, C.C. Miller, and G.P. Huber, "Determinants of Executive Beliefs: Comparing Functional Conditioning and Social Influence," *Strategic Management Journal* (August 1999), pp. 763–789; B. Katey and G.G. Meredith, "Relationship among Owner/Manager Personal Values, Business Strategies, and Enterprise Performance," *Journal of Small Business Management* (April 1997), pp. 37–64.

49. C.S. Galbraith and G.B. Merrill, "The Politics of Forecasting: Managing the Truth," *California Management Review* (Winter 1996), pp. 29–43.

50. M. Leuchter, "The Rules of the Game," *Forecast* (May/June 1996), pp. 16–23.

51. M.A. Geletkanycz and D.C. Hambrick, "The External Ties of Top Executives: Implications for Strategic Choice and Performance," *Administrative Science Quarterly* (December 1997), pp. 654–681.

52. M.A. Hitt, M.T. Dacin, B.B. Tyler, and D. Park, "Understanding the Differences in Korean and U.S. Executives' Strategic Orientation," *Strategic Management Journal* (February 1997), pp. 159–167; L.G. Thomas III and G. Waring, "Competing Capitalisms: Capital Investment in American, German, and Japanese Firms," *Strategic Management Journal* (August 1999), pp. 729–748.

53. J.A. Wagner III and R.Z. Gooding, "Equivocal Information and Attribution: An Investigation of Patterns of Managerial Sensemaking," *Strategic Management Journal* (April 1997), pp. 275–286.

54. J. Ross and B.M. Staw, "Organizational Escalation and Exit: Lessons from the Shoreham Nuclear Power Plant," *Academy of Management Journal* (August 1993), pp. 701–732; P.W. Mulvey, J.F. Veiga, and P.M. Elsass, "When Teammates Raise a White Flag," *Academy of Management Executive* (February 1996), pp. 40–49.

55. R.A. Cosier and C.R. Schwenk, "Agreement and Thinking Alike: Ingredients for Poor Decisions," *Academy of Management Executive* (February 1990), p. 69.

56. A.C. Amason, "Distinguishing the Effects of Functional and Dysfunctional Conflict on Strategic Decision Making: Resolving a Paradox for Top Management Teams," *Academy of Management Journal* (February 1996), pp. 123–148; A.C. Amason and H.J. Sapienza, "The Effects of Top Management Team Size and Interaction Norms on Cognitive and Affective Conflict," *Journal of Management*, Vol. 23, No. 4 (1997), pp. 495–516.

57. D.M. Schweiger, W.R. Sandberg, and P.L. Rechner, "Experiential Effects of Dialectical Inquiry, Devil's Advocacy, and Consensus Approaches to Strategic Decision Making," *Academy of Management Journal* (December 1989), pp. 745–772; G. Whyte, "Decision Failures: Why They Occur and How To Prevent Them," *Academy of Management Executive* (August 1991), pp. 23–31; R.L. Priem, D.A. Harrison, and N.K. Muir, "Structured Conflict and Consensus Outcomes in Group Decision Making," *Journal of Management*, Vol. 21, No. 4 (1995), pp. 691–710.

58. G. Hamel, "Turning Your Business Upside Down," *Fortune* (June 23, 1997), p. 87.

59. S.C. Abraham, "Using Bundles To Find the Best Strategy," *Strategy & Leadership* (July/August/September 1999), pp. 53–55.

60. C. Medford, "Know Who I Am," *PC Magazine* (January 16, 2001), pp. 136–148, S.L. Roberts-Witt, "Personalization: Is It Worth It?" *PC Magazine* (December 19, 2000), pp. iBiz 8–12.

61. P. Krugman, "The Cost of Convenience," *The [Ames] Tribune* (October 5, 2000), p. A6; D. Brady, "Customer Service?" *Business Week* (October 23, 2000), pp. 119–128.

62. J. Jordan and D. Svetcov, "Data-Crunching Santa," *U.S. News & World Report* (December 21, 1998), pp. 44–48.

63. W. Zellner, "Will Walmart.com Get It Right This Time?" *Business Week* (November 6, 2000), pp. 104–112.

64. T.J. Mullaney, "This Race Isn't Even Close," *Business Week* (December 18, 2000), pp. 208–210.

Nova Scotian Crystal

The production of crystal glass started in Venice in the Middle Ages, gradually developing throughout Europe as Italian glass-workers migrated to other countries. Ireland has emerged as an important producing country, with Waterford Crystal being a leading brand synonymous with luxury and quality. Crystal was originally made by hand, with the skills of blowing, cutting, engraving, molding, and enamel work being key to the unique and beautiful designs of the world's leading crystal manufacturers.

But even companies like Waterford Crystal struggled with profitability. Cheaper products of rival firms used lower lead content, but consumers cannot easily see the difference. Product designs were easily copied, making it difficult for higher quality producers to make the investment in designs, skilled labour, and equipment necessary to grow. As economic conditions worsened throughout the 1980s, many crystal manufacturers decided to go high-tech, using automated equipment for cutting and blowing. Crystal, as a luxury product, was vulnerable to economic downturns, and the low dollar values in Canada and the United States contributed to the decline in crystal imports.

As profiled in this video, Nova Scotian Crystal uses traditional mouth-blowing and hard-cutting techniques. The opportunity that Denis Ryan saw was a group of Irish crystal workers that had lost their jobs due to the increased mechanization of most of the world's largest crystal producers. Rather than following the trend of going high-tech, Nova Scotian Crystal did exactly the opposite. The only modern machines they use are computers. Everything else is done or guided by hand, using traditional tools and equipment. Ryan and his partner, Rod McCulloch, now run the only crystal manufacturer in Canada, employing thirty people and attracting approximately 50 000 tourists a year at their Halifax waterfront location. Its annual sales are in excess of $1 million, catering to approximately 15 000 customers looking for a personalized touch.

Despite the uniqueness and quality of Nova Scotian Crystal's products, sales and profitability goals have not been achieved. Part of the problem is the relatively small market size for high-end crystal and the single Halifax location that distributes it. The product has attracted a number of high-end retailers, but the company has declined all offers. Their choice was to stay small and keep the handmade character of the product and only sell the product where knowledgeable staff is on hand. There are plans to open more outlets, but not to use retailers or online distributors who might not be able to provide consumers with the information they need to justify the expense of these premium products.

Concepts Illustrated in the Video

Strategy formulation	Competitive tactics (timing)
SWOT analysis	Marketing strategy
Propitious niche	Human resources management strategy
Competitive strategy	Management's attitude toward risk

Discussion Questions

1. What generic competitive strategy is being used by Nova Scotian Crystal? Discuss the risks inherent in this type of strategy. Have they found a propitious niche?

2. Conduct a SWOT analysis. What are its key findings?

3. What strategic variables would be most useful in conducting a strategic group map of the crystal industry? What are the key success factors for each type of producer?

4. Discuss the competitive dynamics in the crystal industry. How favourably does Nova Scotian Crystal appear to be positioned against these forces? What actions can they take to protect themselves against competitive forces?

5. What is the competitive advantage of Nova Scotian Crystal? Discuss this in terms of durability and imitability.

6. In what ways do the functional strategies of marketing and production fit into the overall competitive strategy of Nova Scotian Crystal? What tradeoffs are being made as a result? Comment on the suitability of these choices and how they will likely affect firm performance.

Video Resource: "Crystal Update," *Venture* #846, September 22, 2002.

Tyler Brûlé and *Wallpaper* Magazine

There may be no better testimonials to the power of design improving life quality than Winnipeg's Tyler Brûlé. In less than a decade, he has become a Canadian global brand himself. *Wallpaper*, launched in 1996, transformed him into an overnight style expert. Wink, his "multi-disciplinary creative agency" founded in 1998, has just finished rebranding the former Swissair into "swiss," an endeavour he is extremely proud of. Brûlé describes this effort as nothing less than reinventing the culture of air travel. Wink is currently at work on projects as diverse as a new Swiss Visa card and a glass department store in the Kuwaiti desert. Even Brûlé's choice of kitchen appliance is newsworthy—the *New York Times Magazine* recently ran a feature on the Zyliss hand-held food chopper simply because he had praised it as "an amazing piece of democratic design." Similar to the "Oprah effect" on novels, Brûlé quickly came to be an authority on anything and everything stylish. He capitalized on this success tremendously.

Wallpaper's timing was excellent, catching the mid-'90s style trend that was not reflected in magazines. High-end advertisers lined up, wanting to cash in on the unity of the magazine's editorial and advertising. It wasn't unheard of for the magazine to send unattractive ads back for restyling. The media took notice, making *Wallpaper*'s influence disproportionate with its circulation. It quickly went from a circulation of less than 50 000 to now around 135 000. *Wallpaper* created so much attention that in 1997 Time Inc. bought the title for US$1.6 million after just four issues. Brûlé, who was about to declare bankruptcy, kept a 15% stake and editorial control, plus a contract to develop new projects. But they wanted it to be the next Martha Stewart Living, something Brûlé never envisioned for the magazine. The trouble was, *Wallpaper* was never destined to be the mass-market money-maker that Martha Stewart Living was (her current legal situation notwithstanding). Nor was Brûlé willing to play front person. He was never interested in becoming a celebrity editor or having his photo in the magazine.

In 2002, Brûlé was given the go ahead to buy back *Wallpaper* and *Spruce*, a fashion magazine he launched in 2001, as well as Wink, all of which were operating under the AOL Time Warner umbrella. Then Time Inc. bought IPC Media and put *Wallpaper* and Wink under that company's management. It was not an arrangement Brûlé liked—his authority was reduced, and his extravagant editorial spending questioned. By May 2002, Brûlé found himself out of a job. Now he directs his attention toward Wink, whose clients include Selfridges and Puma, and which won the contest to redesign Swissair in 2001. The concept, says Brûlé, was to celebrate aviation: "Let's make the aircraft look like aircraft, let's make it recognizable. And it has to be built on a foundation of Swiss typography and graphic design." His detailed recommendations included cleaning the exteriors of the planes, installing flattering lighting, and removing the greasy-hair marks on the windows. Predictably, swiss's new modernist look resembles a *Wallpaper* layout.

Concepts Illustrated in the Video

Strategy formulation	Organizational culture
Propitious niche	Leadership
Identifying market trends	Mergers and acquisitions
Core and distinctive competencies	Diversification strategies

Discussion Questions

1. Discuss the conditions that led to the rapid success of *Wallpaper*. In what ways did Brûlé's growth plans adhere to one of the generic strategy options in the TOWS matrix?

2. What resources and capabilities did Brûlé attempt to use in order to diversify into related industries (i.e., advertising and fashion)? Discuss the value chain activities most likely to be shared between these businesses and what role Brûlé himself should play in each business.

3. Discuss Brûlé's role in *Wallpaper* once it was acquired by Time Inc. In what ways would the organizations structure, cultures, policies/procedures, and leadership change after this type of acquisition. Comment on Brûlé's decision to sell *Wallpaper*, and what changes he should have anticipated as a consequence of this decision. In what ways has Brûlé's leadership influenced the businesses in which he has been involved?

Video Resource: "Wallpaper Tyler Brûlé Update," *Venture* #829, May 26, 2002.

CHAPTER 8

Strategy Implementation: Organizing for Action

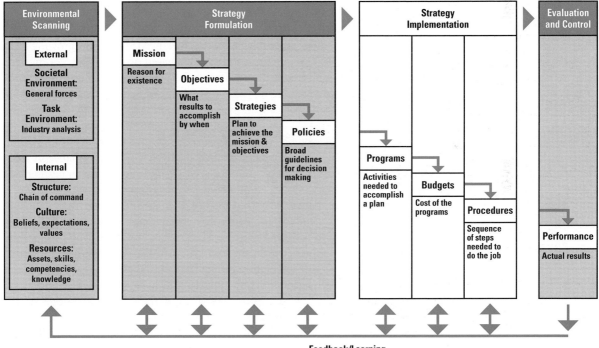

Learning Objectives

After reading this chapter you should be able to

Develop programs, budgets, and procedures to implement organizational strategy

Understand the stages of organizational development and the structures that characterize them

Identify obstacles to organizational change

Construct matrix and network structures to support flexible and nimble organizational strategies

Design jobs to implement strategy

Montreal-based BCE Inc. (Bell Canada Enterprises) had an impressive record of profitability and growth throughout the 1990s, due in large part to the success of Nortel. In 2000, BCE spun off a majority of its equity in Nortel to its shareholders and began a series of acquisitions designed to reduce its dependence on the telephone industry. In attempting to transform itself into an internet-oriented multimedia firm, BCE created business units in telecom infrastructure (Bell Canada, Teleglobe, and Bell Canada International), media (CTV television, *The Globe and Mail* newspaper, the Sympatico-Lycos internet portal) and ecommerce (BCE Emergis). The restructuring of BCE was a way of implementing a new corporate strategy in response to the decline of Nortel, which had previously made up 95% of BCE's market cap. No longer able to count on earnings growth from Nortel, BCE needed a rapidly growing business unit to fuel future growth. The new BCE strategy was based on convergence, providing customers more value by delivering connectivity and content simultaneously. Bell Globalmedia (the combination of CTV, *The Globe and Mail*, and Sympatico) was to provide this content, as a complement to the core businesses areas of phone service, long-distance, and DSL.[1]

It is too early to tell whether BCE's strategy of convergence, and the diversification upon which it is built, will be effective. Bell Globalmedia had relatively poor performance in 2001, largely a result of weak advertising revenue. The worldwide economic slowdown hasn't made it easy for these new businesses to show a contribution to BCE's bottom line. On a strategic level it makes sense to pursue connectivity convergence, that is, combining voice, data, and multimedia into one network. Content and connectivity may prove to be more difficult to implement. This is partly due to the differences between media executives who produce the content and engineers who run the networks themselves. The different backgrounds, culture, and language of these groups make integration difficult. As well, there is a real possibility of attracting the attention of federal regulators by appearing to have a network provider give preferential treatment to its own content providers. Both of these factors suggest that the implementation of a convergence strategy that on the surface makes complete strategic sense might face tremendous difficulties in the implementation phase. Cases such as this illustrate the point that making strategic decisions is relatively easy compared with undertaking the actions necessary to turn those decisions into improved performance.

8.1 Strategy Implementation

strategy implementation the activities an organization must perform in acting on its strategic plans

Strategy implementation is the sum total of the activities and choices required for the execution of a strategic plan. It is the process by which strategies and policies are put into action through the development of programs, budgets, and procedures. Although implementation is usually considered after strategy has been formulated, implementation is a key part of strategic management. Strategy formulation and strategy implementation should thus be considered as two sides of the same coin. Poor implementation has been blamed for a number of strategic failures. Studies show that half of all acquisitions fail to achieve what was expected of them, and one out of four international ventures does not succeed.[2] A study of the 700 largest mergers from 1996 to 1998 found that 83% of the mergers failed to increase the acquirer's shareholder value within a year of completing the merger.[3]

To begin the implementation process, strategy makers must consider these questions:

- *Who* are the people who will carry out the strategic plan?
- *What* must be done to align the company's operations in the new intended direction?
- *How* is everyone going to work together to do what is needed?

These questions and similar ones should have been addressed initially when the advantages and disadvantages of strategic alternatives were analyzed. They must also be addressed again before appropriate implementation plans can be made. Unless top management can answer these basic questions satisfactorily, even the best planned strategy is unlikely to provide the desired outcome.

A survey of *Fortune* 500 firms revealed that more than half of the organizations experienced the following problems when they attempted to implement a strategic change.[4] These problems are listed in order of frequency:

1. Implementation took more time than originally planned.
2. Unanticipated major problems arose.
3. Activities were ineffectively coordinated.
4. Competing activities and crises took attention away from implementation.
5. The involved employees had insufficient capabilities to perform their jobs.
6. Lower-level employees were inadequately trained.
7. Uncontrollable external environmental factors created problems.
8. Departmental managers provided inadequate leadership and direction.
9. Key implementation tasks and activities were poorly defined.
10. The information system inadequately monitored activities.

8.2 Who Implements Strategy?

Depending on how the firm is organized, those who implement strategy will probably be a much more diverse set of people than those who formulate it. In most large, multi-industry organizations, the implementers are everyone in the organization. Vice-presidents of functional areas and directors of divisions or SBUs work with their subordinates to put together large-scale implementation plans. Plant managers, project managers, and unit heads put together plans for their specific plants, departments, and units. Therefore, every operational manager down to the first-line supervisor and every employee is involved in some way in implementing corporate, business, and functional strategies.

Many of the people in the organization who are crucial to successful strategy implementation probably have little to do with the development of the corporate strategy and even the business strategy. Therefore, they might be unaware of the vast amount of data and work that went into the formulation process. Unless changes in mission, objectives, strategies, and policies and their importance to the company are communicated clearly to all operational managers, there can be a lot of resistance and foot-dragging. Managers might hope to influence top management into abandoning its new plans and returning to its old ways. This is one reason why involving people from all organizational levels in the formulation and the implementation of strategy tends to result in better organizational performance.

8.3 What Must Be Done?

The managers of divisions and functional areas work with their fellow managers to develop programs, budgets, and procedures for the implementation of strategy. They also work to achieve synergy among the divisions and functional areas in order to establish and maintain a company's distinctive competency.

DEVELOPING PROGRAMS, BUDGETS, AND PROCEDURES

Strategy implementation consists of establishing programs to create a series of new organizational activities, budgets to allocate funds to the new activities, and procedures to handle the day-to-day details.

Programs

program the activities necessary for a strategic plan to be successfully implemented

The purpose of a **program** is to make the strategy action-oriented. As discussed in **Chapter 1**, a program is a statement of the activities or steps needed to implement strategy. These steps often begin with broadly defined actions based on priority components of strategy. For example, Canada Post and its affiliate Purolator Courier installed sophisticated information systems to enable courier customers to order supplies, schedule pickups, and track shipments. They also incorporated lean manufacturing concepts to deal with increasing competition in postal services. New competitors and alternative technologies required internal changes to keep costs down and remain competitive. Scouts Canada has also adopted new programs to achieve its mission of contributing to the education of young people. It is the country's leading youth organization, offering programs for young people of ages 5 to 26 across Canada. To move toward a more accessible organization serving boys and girls, it had to develop new programs that appealed to today's youth, like ScoutsAbout and Extreme Adventure. It also needed to recruit new leaders to deliver these new programs and facilitate the transition from a boys-only organization to one involving a cross-section of Canadian youth throughout their formative years in an informal educational process.[5]

One way to examine the likely impact new programs will have on an existing organization is to compare proposed programs and activities with current programs and activities. A matrix of change can help managers decide how quickly change should proceed, in what order changes should take place, whether to start at a new site, and whether the proposed systems are stable and coherent. As shown in **Figure 8–1**, target practices (new programs) for a manufacturing plant are drawn on the vertical axis, and existing practices (current activities) are drawn on the horizontal axis. As shown, any new strategy will likely involve a sequence of new programs and activities. Any one of these may conflict with existing practices or activities, creating implementation problems. Use the following steps to create the matrix:

1. Compare each of the new programs/target practices with each other to see whether they are complementary (+), interfering (–), or have no effect on each other (leave blank).

2. Examine existing practices/activities for their interactions with each other using the same symbols.

3. Compare each new program/target practice with each existing practice/activity for any interaction effects. Place the appropriate symbols in the cells in the lower right part of the matrix.

4. Evaluate each program/activity in terms of its relative importance to achieving the strategy or getting the job accomplished.

5. Examine the overall matrix to identify problem areas where proposed programs are likely to either interfere with each other or with existing practices/activities. Note in **Figure 8–1** that the proposed program of installing flexible equipment interferes with the proposed program of assembly line rationalization. The two new programs need to be changed so that they no longer conflict with each other. Note also that the amount of change necessary to carry out the proposed implementation programs (target practices) is a function of the number of times each program interferes with existing practices/activities. In other words, the more minus signs and the fewer plus signs there are in the matrix, the more implementation problems can be expected.

The matrix offers useful guidelines on where, when, and how fast to implement change.[6]

Figure 8–1 The Matrix of Change

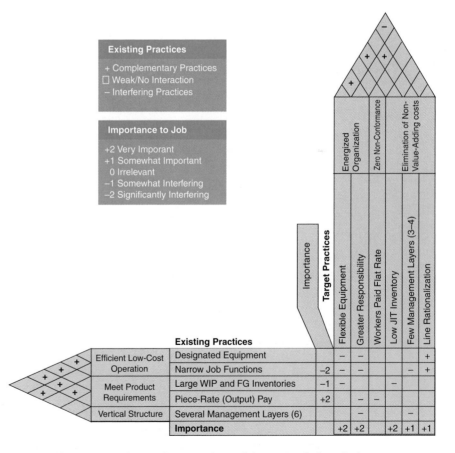

Source: E. Brynjolfsson, A.A. Renshaw, and M. Van Alstyne, "The Matrix of Change," *Sloan Management Review* (Winter 1997), p. 43. Reprinted by permission of publisher. Copyright © 1997 by Massachusetts Institute of Technology. All rights reserved.

It can be used to address the following types of questions:

- **Feasibility:** Do the proposed programs and activities constitute a coherent, stable system? Are the current activities coherent and stable? Is the transition likely to be difficult?
- **Sequence of Execution:** Where should the change begin? How does the sequence affect success? Are there reasonable stopping points?
- **Location:** Are we better off instituting the new programs at a new site or can we reorganize the existing facilities at a reasonable cost?
- **Pace and Nature of Change:** Should the change be slow or fast, incremental or radical? Which blocks of current activities must be changed at the same time?
- **Stakeholder Evaluations:** Have we overlooked any important activities or interactions? Should we get further input from interested stakeholders? Which new programs and current activities offer the greatest sources of value?

Budgets

budget a financial projection of the financial needs of a department or division

After programs have been developed, the **budget** process begins. Planning a budget is the last real check an organization has on the feasibility of its selected strategy. An ideal strategy might be found to be completely impractical only after specific implementation programs are costed in detail. The importance of budgeting rests on the fact that doing things differently takes time and costs money. If a new strategic plan is put in place that requires departments and divisions to do things differently, then they need to be provided with the financial resources to do so. And because new strategies almost always involve organizational change, budget increases or reallocations will almost always be necessary. What managers must ensure is that the activities that are critical to the success of an organization's strategy and that provide it with a competitive advantage are not starved of resources. Budgets that are too large waste organizational resources and make them unavailable for performing activities critical to the success of the organization. Proper budgeting can therefore have a significant effect on the strategy implementation process and must be closely matched.

Procedures

procedures the standardized ways of implementing organizational programs

After the program, divisional, and corporate budgets are approved, **procedures** must be developed. Often called standard operating procedures (SOPs), they typically detail the various activities that must be carried out to complete an organization's programs. Once in place, they must be updated to reflect any changes in technology as well as in strategy. These procedures ensure that the day-to-day operations will be consistent over time (that is, next week's work activities will be the same as this week's) and consistent among locations (that is, each retail store will operate in the same manner as the others). For example, to ensure that its policies are carried out to the letter in every one of its fast-food retail outlets, McDonald's has done an excellent job of developing very detailed procedures (and policing them).

Procedures are therefore a type of coordinating mechanism that is essential to organizing the firm. Procedures prescribe how work is to be done and what behaviours are expected without the need for direct supervision. Through socialization and training, workers are shown the company way and taught organizational policies that will make behaviour consistent throughout the organization. This is particularly important in terms of trying to encourage the behaviours that will support the implementation of an organization's strategy, especially when workers are located in many different locations or perform highly interdependent work. The more central an activity is to an organization's competitive advantage, the more important it becomes to create some sort of policy surrounding it.

Procedures don't have to resemble the McDonald's style of very detailed policies. Consider Scouts Canada's activities in developing youth programs. In addition to achieving this mission, Scouts Canada must provide for the safety and well-being of children while taking part in their programs. Although they have always done this, recent societal changes have now made it critical for Scouts Canada to earn and maintain trust in its operations. This has become a new critical success factor for the organization, and as a result new policies are being developed to ensure consistency and display to parents that children are safe when they take part in scouting events. Two policy changes have recently been introduced. The first involves no longer transporting children to scouting events, in order to remove responsibility and liability from the organization. Many scouting groups now help to organize car pools and ride-sharing to help members access programs and attend events that they would previously have been bused to. The second involves always having at least two leaders present at any scouting event. This will prevent any one-on-one situation between leaders and children that might be construed as inappropriate, while also improving the leader-to-member ratio. This policy is intended to protect the safety of all involved, which combined with police record checks of leaders, contributes to the image of Scouts Canada as a responsible organization that provides a safe environment in which children can socialize and learn.[7]

ACHIEVING SYNERGY

One of the goals to be achieved in strategy implementation is synergy between and among functions and business units. This is the reason why organizations commonly reorganize after an acquisition. **Synergy** is said to exist for a divisional corporation if the return on investment (ROI) of each division is greater than what the return would be if each division were an independent business. Synergy can take place in one of six forms:[8]

synergy when two or more divisions of an organization work together in a way that produces a higher return than the divisions could earn independently

1. **Shared Know-How:** Combined units often benefit from sharing knowledge or skills. This is a leveraging of core competencies.

2. **Coordinated Strategies:** Aligning the business strategies of two or more business units may provide an organization significant advantage by reducing inter-unit competition and developing a coordinated response to common competitors (horizontal strategy).

3. **Shared Tangible Resources:** Combined units can sometimes save money by sharing resources, such as a common manufacturing facility or R & D lab.

4. **Economies of Scale or Scope:** Coordinating the flow of products or services of one unit with that of another unit can reduce inventory, increase capacity utilization, and improve market access.

5. **Pooled Negotiating Power:** Combined units can combine their purchasing to gain bargaining power over common suppliers to reduce costs and improve quality. The same can be done with common distributors.

6. **New Business Creation:** Exchanging knowledge and skills can facilitate new products or services by extracting discrete activities from various units and combining them in a new unit or by establishing joint ventures among internal business units.

8.4 How Is Strategy to Be Implemented? Organizing for Action

Before plans can lead to actual performance, an organization should be appropriately structured, programs should be adequately staffed, and activities should be directed toward achieving desired objectives. (Organizational structure is reviewed briefly in this chapter; staffing, directing, and control activities are covered in **Chapters 9 and 10**.)

Any change in strategy is very likely to require some sort of change in the way an organization is structured and in the kind of skills needed in particular positions. Managers must, therefore, closely examine the way their company is structured to decide what, if any, changes should be made in the way work is accomplished. Should activities be grouped differently? Should the authority to make key decisions be centralized at headquarters or decentralized to managers in distant locations? Should the company be managed like a "tight ship" with many rules and controls, or "loosely" with few rules and controls? Should the organization be organized into a "tall" structure with many layers of managers, each having a narrow span of control (that is, few employees per supervisor) to allow for better control of subordinates; or should it be organized into a "flat" structure with fewer layers of managers, each having a wide span of control (that is, more employees per supervisor), giving more freedom to subordinates?

STRUCTURE FOLLOWS STRATEGY

In a classic study of large corporations such as DuPont, General Motors, Sears, and Standard Oil, Alfred Chandler concluded that structure follows strategy—that is, changes in corporate strategy lead to changes in organizational structure.[9] He also concluded that organizations follow a pattern of development from one kind of structural arrangement to another as they expand. According to Chandler, these structural changes occur because the old structure, having been pushed too far, has caused inefficiencies that have become too obviously detrimental to bear. Chandler, therefore, proposed the following sequence of events:

1. New strategy is created.
2. New administrative problems emerge.
3. Economic performance declines.
4. New appropriate structure is invented.
5. Profit returns to its previous level.

Chandler found that in their early years, organizations tend to have a centralized functional organizational structure that is well-suited to producing and selling a limited range of products. As they add new product lines, purchase their own sources of supply, and create their own distribution networks, they become too complex for highly centralized structures. To remain successful, they need to shift to a decentralized structure with several semi-autonomous divisions (referred to in **Chapter 4** as divisional structures).

Alfred P. Sloan, past CEO of General Motors, detailed how GM conducted such structural changes in the 1920s.[10] He saw decentralization of structure as "centralized policy determination coupled with decentralized operating management." After top management had developed a strategy for the total corporation, the individual divisions (Chevrolet, Buick, and so on) were free to choose how to implement that strategy. GM found the decentralized multidivisional structure, patterned after the organizational structure at DuPont, to be extremely effective in allowing the maximum amount of freedom for product development. Return on investment (ROI) was used as a financial control. (ROI is discussed in more detail in **Chapter 10**.)

There is somewhat mixed empirical support for Chandler's proposition that structure follows strategy. There is also evidence that structure influences strategy.[11] How should we make sense of this apparently contradictory finding? As mentioned earlier, changes in the environment tend to be reflected in changes in an organization's strategy, thus leading to changes to its structure. Strategy, structure, and the environment need to be closely aligned; otherwise, organizational performance will likely suffer.[12] For example, a business unit following a differentiation strategy needs more freedom from headquarters to be successful than does another unit following a low-cost strategy.[13] These examples illustrate that organizations change their structure to support a particular strategy. There are cases, however, where organizations are too large, complex, and steeped in tradition to quickly or easily change their structures, even if there might be a demonstrated need to. Organizations in this situation would therefore select strategies that fit with their current organizational structures and practices. In other words, the fit between strategy and structure is achieved by selecting from strategies that can be implemented via current organizational structures. This is only the reverse of Chandler's proposition. At the end of the day it is probably less important what comes first (the strategy or the structure). What is critical, however, is that there is an alignment between the two.

Although organizational structure must vary with different environmental conditions, which, in turn, affect an organization's strategy, there is no agreement about an optimal organizational design. What was appropriate for organizations in the 1920s might not be appropriate today. Firms in the same industry do, however, tend to organize themselves similarly. For example, automobile manufacturers tend to emulate General Motors' divisional concept, whereas consumer-goods producers tend to emulate the brand-management concept (a type of matrix structure) pioneered by Procter & Gamble. The general conclusion seems to be that firms following similar strategies in similar industries tend to adopt similar structures. This is once again evidence of the tight link between strategy and structure discussed in the previous paragraph. What is clear from this observation is that different structures seem to be able to support particular strategies better than others. The presence of a relatively limited number of organizational designs in any given industry is testament to the fact that these designs are more favourable than others. In the sections that follow you will see how the stage of an organization's development and its life cycle influence the type of organizational structure most likely to be successful in helping organizations achieve their goals and objectives.

STAGES OF ORGANIZATIONAL DEVELOPMENT

Successful organizations tend to follow a pattern of structural development as they grow and expand. Beginning with the simple structure of the entrepreneurial firm (in which everybody does everything), they usually (if they are successful) get larger and organize along functional lines with marketing, production, and finance departments. With continuing success, the company adds new product lines in different industries and organizes itself into interconnected divisions. The differences among these three structural stages of organizational development in terms of typical problems, objectives, strategies, reward systems, and other characteristics are specified in detail in **Table 8–1** on page 206.

Stage I: Simple Structure

Stage I is typified by the entrepreneur, who founds the company to promote an idea (product or service). The entrepreneur tends to make all the important decisions personally and is involved in every detail and phase of the organization. The Stage I company has little formal structure, which allows the entrepreneur to directly supervise the activities of every employee (see **Figure 4–3** in **Chapter 4** for an illustration of the simple, functional, and divisional structures). Planning is usually short range or reactive. The typical managerial functions of planning, organizing, directing, staffing, and controlling are usually performed to a very limited degree, if at all. The greatest strengths of a Stage I corporation are its flexibility and dynamism. The drive of the entrepreneur energizes the organization in its struggle for growth. Its greatest weakness is its extreme reliance on the entrepreneur to decide general strategies as well as detailed procedures. If the entrepreneur falters, the company usually flounders. This is referred to as a **crisis of leadership**.[14]

crisis of leadership the failure of an entrepreneur's leadership to deal with growth and increasing complexity

Stage I describes Newbridge Networks Corporation at the time it was founded, in 1986. Now a worldwide leader in the design, manufacture, marketing, and service of a comprehensive family of networking solutions, it started much more modestly in Kanata, Ontario, serving the networking needs of mostly Canadian businesses. At that time, the communications needs of organizations were just starting to take off, and the relatively limited number of products available and the small market size allowed for the organization to prosper in an entrepreneurial mode. By the early 1990s, growth had been so significant, with consumers demanding more sophisticated products, that a transition took place to a new structure

Table 8–1 Factors Differentiating Stage I, II, and III Companies

Function	Stage I	Stage II	Stage III
1. Sizing up: Major problems	Survival and growth dealing with short-term operating problems.	Growth, rationalization, and expansion of resources, providing for adequate attention to product problems.	Trusteeship in management and investment and control of large, increasing, and diversified resources. Also, important to diagnose and take action on problems at division level.
2. Objectives	Personal and subjective.	Profits and meeting functionally oriented budgets and performance targets.	ROI, profits, earnings per share.
3. Strategy	Implicit and personal; exploitation of immediate opportunities seen by owner-manager.	Functionally oriented moves restricted to "one product" scope; exploitation of one basic product or service field.	Growth and product diversification; exploitation of general business opportunities.
4. Organization: Major characteristic of structure	One unit, "one-man show."	One unit, functionally specialized group.	Multi-unit general staff office and decentralized operating divisions.
5. (a) Measurement and control	Personal, subjective control based on simple accounting system and daily communication and observation.	Control grows beyond one person; assessment of functional operations necessary; structured control systems evolve.	Complex formal system geared to comparative assessment of performance measures, indicating problems and opportunities and assessing management ability of division managers.
5. (b) Key performance indicators	Personal criteria, relationships with owner, operating efficiency, ability to solve operating problems.	Functional and internal criteria such as sales, performance compared with budget, size of empire, status in group, personal relationships, etc.	More impersonal application of comparisons such as profits, ROI, P/E ratio, sales, market share, productivity, product leadership, personnel development, employee attitudes, public responsibility.
6. Reward-punishment system	Informal, personal, subjective; used to maintain control and divide small pool of resources to provide personal incentives for key performers.	More structured; usually based to a greater extent on agreed policies as opposed to personal opinion and relationships.	Allotment by "due process" of a wide variety of different rewards and punishments on a formal and systematic basis. Company-wide policies usually apply to many different classes of managers and workers with few major exceptions for individual cases.

Source: D.H. Thain, "Stages of Corporate Development," *Ivey Business Journal* (formerly *Ivey Business Quarterly*), (Winter 1969), p. 37. Copyright © 1969 by Ivey Management Services.

characterized by increased formalization and departmentalization. This marks the transition to a Stage II organization.

Stage II: Functional Structure

Stage II is the point when the entrepreneur is replaced by a team of managers who have functional specialization. The transition to this stage requires a substantial managerial style change for the chief officer of the company, especially if he or she was the Stage I entrepreneur. He or she must learn to delegate; otherwise, having additional staff members yields no benefits to the organization. The previous example of growth at Newbridge Networks illustrates the functional specialization that is so often necessary to successful organization growth. To transform itself into the global R & D and manufacturing organization it now is, functional specialities needed to be developed that would allow Newbridge to quickly and profitably offer new products to the market. For example, in 1993 it developed the ATM access switch that delivered fully integrated access, switching and control of data, image, video, and voice communications. Creating the development tools that would allow Newbridge to produce high-quality products in a short amount of time was facilitated by the move toward a functional structure, along with the professional management of each functional area by specialists. Once into Stage II, the strategies tend to be directed at dominance of the industry, often through vertical and horizontal growth. The great strength of a Stage II organization lies in its concentration and specialization in one industry. Strategies at this stage should continue to develop core competencies and solidify the organization's market-leading position.

By concentrating on one industry while that industry remains attractive, a Stage II company can be very successful. Once a functionally structured firm diversifies into other products in different industries, however, the advantages of the functional structure break down. A **crisis of autonomy** can now develop in which people managing diversified product lines need more decision-making freedom than top management is willing to delegate to them. The company needs to move to a different structure.

Stage III: Divisional Structure

Stage III is typified by the organization's managing diverse product lines in numerous industries; it decentralizes the decision-making authority. These organizations grow by diversifying their product lines and expanding to cover wider geographical areas. They move to a divisional structure with a central headquarters and decentralized operating divisions—each division or business unit is a functionally organized Stage II company. They may also use a conglomerate structure if top management chooses to keep its collection of Stage II subsidiaries operating autonomously. A **crisis of control** can now develop in which the various units act to optimize their own sales and profits without regard to the overall organization, whose headquarters seems so far away and almost irrelevant.

Recently divisions have been evolving into strategic business units (SBUs) to better reflect product–market considerations. Headquarters attempts to coordinate the activities of its operating divisions or SBUs through performance- and results-oriented control and reporting systems, and by stressing corporate planning techniques. The units are not tightly controlled but are held responsible for their own performance results. Therefore, to be effective, the company has to have a decentralized decision-making process. The greatest challenge experienced by Stage III firms is that, because they are usually so large and complex, strategy tends to become relatively inflexible. Larger, more established organizations often experience stronger tendencies toward inertia than smaller, newer ones. Part of this can be because of the belief that what has worked in the past will continue to work well in the future. The longer the organization's history, the harder it is to change structure and strategy.[15] In other words,

crisis of autonomy a situation when increasing numbers of products and markets create conflict between functional areas, which no longer have the necessary autonomy to achieve their goals

crisis of control conflicting goals and priorities of semi-autonomous business units, creating the need for an organizational structure that encourages coordination, co-operation, and integration

strategic persistence and a difficulty in making changes to a large organization (like moving a large ship in the water) represent the managerial challenges associated with Stage III firms.

Stage IV: Beyond SBUs

red tape crisis a situation when an organization's increasing size and complexity make rules and procedures ineffective in dealing with growth and change, prohibiting more responsible and collaborative structures

Even with its evolution into strategic business units during the 1970s and 1980s, the divisional form is not the last word in organizational structure. The use of SBUs may result in a **red tape crisis** in which the corporation has grown too large and complex to be managed through formal programs, and rigid systems and procedures take precedence over problem solving. Under conditions of (1) increasing environmental uncertainty, (2) greater use of sophisticated technological production methods and information systems, (3) the increasing size and scope of worldwide business organizations, (4) a greater emphasis on multi-industry competitive strategy, and (5) a more educated cadre of managers and employees, new advanced forms of organizational structure have emerged and are continuing to emerge. These structures attempt to emphasize collaboration over competition in the managing of an organization's multiple overlapping projects and developing businesses.

The *matrix* and the *network* are two possible candidates for a fourth stage in corporate development—a stage that not only emphasizes horizontal over vertical connections between people and groups, but also organizes work around temporary projects in which sophisticated information systems support collaborative activities. It is likely that this stage of development will have its own crisis as well—a sort of **pressure-cooker crisis**. Employees in these collaborative organizations will eventually grow emotionally and physically exhausted from the intensity of teamwork and the heavy pressure for innovative solutions.[16]

pressure-cooker crisis difficulties associated with working in organizations that require increased teamwork and collaboration with larger numbers of people

Obstacles to Changing Stages

Organizations often find themselves in difficulty because there are obstacles to moving into the next logical stage of development. Obstacles to development may be internal (such as lack of resources, lack of ability, or a refusal of top management to delegate decision making to others) or they may be external (such as economic conditions, labour shortages, and lack of market growth). For example, Chandler noted in his study that the successful founder or CEO in one stage was rarely the person who created the new structure to fit the new strategy, and that, as a result, the transition from one stage to another was often painful. This was true of General Motors Corporation under the management of William Durant, Ford Motor Company under Henry Ford I, Polaroid Corporation under Edwin Land, Apple Computer under Steven Jobs, and Hayes Microcomputer Products under Dennis Hayes. (See the **Internet Issue** feature on page 210 for what happened to the company founded by the inventor of the modern modem.)

This difficulty in moving to a new stage is compounded by the founder's tendency to manoeuvre around the need to delegate by carefully hiring, training, and grooming his or her own team of managers. The team tends to maintain the founder's influence throughout the organization long after the founder is gone. This is what happened at Walt Disney Productions when the family continued to emphasize Walt Disney's policies and plans long after he was dead. Although this may often be an organization's strength, it may also be a weakness—to the extent that the culture supports the status quo and blocks needed change.

The likelihood of encountering these types of obstacles to change will be a function of how critical or urgent the change is perceived to be. This is largely determined by the current level of firm performance and the extent to which organizations and their stakeholders are content with it. As summarized in **Table 8–2**, there are distinct types of changes that are characterized by different perceptions of the need for change. As the discussion in this section indicated, there is usually some sort of crisis or performance problem that indicates a need for

Table 8–2 Identifying Obstacles to Organizational Change

	Anticipatory	**Reactive**	**Crisis**
Firm performance	High	Declining	Low
Need for change	Not demonstrated	Somewhat evident	Obvious
Management's role	Show need for change	Determine where to start	Acquire resources to make changes quickly
Major obstacles	Lack of commitment to change	Disagreement over what changes to make	Recruiting people to assist turnaround

Source: Adapted from M.M. Crossan, J.N. Fry, and J.P. Killing's *Strategic Analysis and Action*, 5th edition (Toronto: Prentice Hall, 2002), p. 178. Reprinted with permission by Pearson Education Canada Inc.

change. This explains why anticipatory change is likely the most difficult to implement. On the other hand, the organization facing a serious crisis might be painfully aware of the need for change but lack the resources to be able to do so. Any way you look at strategic change, you see potential obstacles. Good strategists should therefore use different techniques to minimize the effects of the obstacles they are most likely to encounter.

ORGANIZATIONAL LIFE CYCLE

organizational life cycle a model of organizational evolution that passes through five stages over time

Instead of considering stages of development in terms of structure, the organizational life cycle approach places the primary emphasis on the dominant issue facing the firm. Organizational structure is therefore a secondary concern. The **organizational life cycle** describes how organizations grow, develop, and eventually decline. It is the organizational equivalent of the product life cycle in marketing. These stages are Birth (Stage I), Growth (Stage II), Maturity (Stage III), Decline (Stage IV), and Death (Stage V). The impact of these stages on corporate strategy and structure is summarized in **Table 8–3**. Note that the first three stages of the organizational life cycle are similar to the three commonly accepted stages of corporate development mentioned previously. The only significant difference is the addition of Decline and Death stages to complete the cycle. Even though a company's strategy may still be sound, its aging structure, culture, and processes may be such that they prevent the strategy from being executed properly. Its core competencies become core rigidities no longer able to adapt to changing conditions—thus the company moves into the Decline stage.[17]

Movement from Growth to Maturity to Decline and finally to Death is not, however, inevitable. A Revival phase may occur sometime during the Maturity or Decline stages. The

Table 8–3 Organizational Life Cycle

	Stage I	**Stage II**	**Stage III***	**Stage IV**	**Stage V**
Dominant Issue	Birth	Growth	Maturity	Decline	Death
Popular Stategies	Concentration in a niche	Horizontal and vertical growth	Concentric and conglomerate diversification	Profit strategy followed by retrenchment	Liquidation or bankruptcy
Likely Structure	Entrepreneur-dominated	Functional management emphasized	Decentralization into profit or investment centres	Structural surgery	Dismemberment of structure

*An organization may enter a *Revival Phase* either during the Maturity or Decline stages and thus extend the organization's life.

organization's life cycle can be extended by managerial and product innovations.[18] Revival often occurs during the implementation of a turnaround strategy. This is what happened at Lionel, the maker of toy electric trains. Founded by Joshua Lionel Cowen in 1900 to make electrical devices, Lionel came to define the toy "electric train." In 1953, Lionel sold three million engines and freight cars, making it the biggest toy manufacturer in the world. By the mid-1960s, the company was in decline. Electric trains were becoming a historical curiosity. Slot cars and space toys were in demand. Train hobbyists preferred the smaller HO gauge electric train over Lionel's larger train because HO gauge trains were more realistic and used less space. The company barely managed to remain in business over the next three decades. In 1999, Lionel's new owners hired Richard Maddox, a lifelong train enthusiast and an executive close to retirement at toy company Bachmann Industries. Maddox and his executive team worked to update Lionel's trains with new models and the latest technology. He improved the catalogue and established dozens of licensing agreements. "We're trying to excel in things whimsical, clever," said Maddox. The unofficial Lionel historian, Todd Wagner, discovered long-forgotten blueprints of trains from the 1920s and 1930s that were gathering dust in old Lionel storerooms. The company is now using those plans to build more authentic historical models. The reinvigorated company's sales increased 15% in 2000 and were expected to increase by the same amount in 2001.[19]

Internet Issue

The Founder of the Modem Blocks Transition to Stage II

Would there be an internet without the modem? Although most large organizations now rent digital T1 lines for fast internet access, most individuals and small business owners still access the World Wide Web using the same type of modem and command set invented by Dennis Hayes.

Dennis Hayes is legendary not only for inventing the personal computer modem, but also for driving his company into bankruptcy—not once, but twice. Hayes and retired partner Dale Heatherington founded Hayes Microcomputer Products two decades ago when they invented a device called the Hayes Smartmodem, which allowed personal computers to communicate with each other through telephone lines via the Hayes Standard AT Command Set. The modem was needed to convert voice analogue data into the digital data needed by computers. Modem sales boomed from $4.8 million in 1981 to $150 million in 1985. When competitors developed low-cost modems, Hayes delayed until the early 1990s to respond with its own low-priced version. Sales and profits plummeted. Hayes lost its dominant position to US Robotics. Management problems mounted. Creditors and potential investors looking into the company's books and operations found them a shambles. According to one investment banker, "The factory was in complete disarray." The company reported its first loss in 1994,

by which time the company was nearly $70 million in debt. In November 1994, Hayes applied for protection from creditors under Chapter 11 of the US Bankruptcy Code.

Under the leadership of its founder, the company underwent a turnaround during 1995. Still in second place with a 9.3% market share of modem sales in North America, the company up was put up for sale by Hayes. He turned down a bid of $140 million from rival Diamond Multimedia Systems and instead accepted only $30 million for 49% of the company from Asian investors. Although the offer required Hayes to relinquish the title of CEO, he would still be chairman of the board. He explained his decision as deriving from his unwillingness to completely let go of his baby. "I'll be able to have input, through the board and as chairman, that will best use my abilities. What I was concerned about was that someone would come in and... slash a part of the company without understanding how it fit in."

The company, renamed Hayes Corporation, continued to suffer losses. On October 9, 1998, the company declared Chapter 11 bankruptcy for the last time. Unable to find further financing to turn things around, the company was forced to sell its brands, manufacturing facilities, and distribution offices to the Canadian firm Zoom Telephonics (www.zoomtel.com), for $5.3 million. It sold its website domain name, Hayes.com, its service centre, and its spare parts inventories to Modem Express (www.modemexpress.com), a seller of refurbished "orphan" products. The company founded by Dennis Hayes now exists only as a division of another company.

Sources: D. McDermott, "Asians Rejuvenate Hayes Microcomputer," *The Wall Street Journal* (May 6, 1996), p. A10; plus information gathered from company websites and Hayes Company documents within the SEC's Edgar database.

Unless a company is able to resolve the critical issues facing it in the Decline stage, it is likely to move into Stage V, corporate death—also known as bankruptcy. This is what happened to Montgomery Ward, Pan American Airlines, Macy's Department Stores, Baldwin-United, Eastern Airlines, Colt's Manufacturing, Orion Pictures, and Wheeling-Pittsburgh Steel, as well as many other firms. So many internet ventures went bankrupt during 2000 that *Fortune* magazine listed 135 internet companies on its "Dot-Com Deathwatch."[20] As in the cases of Johns-Manville, International Harvester, and Macy's—all of which went bankrupt—a corporation might nevertheless rise like a phoenix from its own ashes and live again under the same or a different name. CanJet, a division of Nova Scotia's IMP group, ceased operations during the time Air Canada was aggressively competing with rival regional airlines. After not operating for two years, it resumed service at a time when government regulations shielded CanJet form the predatory pricing of Air Canada and fewer discount airlines were in the sky.

Few organizations will move through these five stages in order. Some may, for example, never move past Stage II. Others, like General Motors, might go directly from Stage I to Stage III. A large number of entrepreneurial ventures jump from Stage I or II directly into Stage IV or V. Hayes Microcomputer Products, for example, went from the Growth to Decline stage under Dennis Hayes. The key is to be able to identify indications that a firm is in the process of changing stages and to make the appropriate strategic and structural adjustments to ensure that corporate performance is maintained or even improved. This is what the successful internet auction firm eBay did when it hired Meg Whitman from Hasbro as CEO to professionalize its management and to improve its marketing.

ADVANCED TYPES OF ORGANIZATIONAL STRUCTURES

The basic structures (simple, functional, divisional, and conglomerate) were discussed earlier in **Chapter 4** and summarized under the first three stages of corporate development. A new strategy may require more flexible characteristics than the traditional functional or divisional structure can offer. Today's business organizations are becoming less centralized with a greater use of cross-functional work teams. **Table 8–4** depicts some of the changing structural characteristics of modern corporations. Although many variations and hybrid structures contain these characteristics, two forms stand out: the matrix structure and the network structure.

Table 8–4   Changing Structural Characteristics of Modern Corporations

Old Organizational Design	New Organizational Design
One large organization	Mini-business units and co-operative relationships
Vertical communication	Horizontal communication
Centralized top-down decision making	Decentralized participative decision making
Vertical integration	Outsourcing and virtual organizations
Work/quality teams	Autonomous work teams
Functional work teams	Cross-functional work teams
Minimal training	Extensive training
Specialized job design focused on individual	Value-chain team-focused job design

Source: Adapted from B. Macy and H. Izumi, "Organizational Change, Design, and Work Innovation: A Meta-Analysis of 131 North American Field Studies—1961–1991," in Woodman: *Research in Organizational Change and Development*, Vol. 7, JAI Press (1993), p. 298. Copyright © 1993 with permission from Elsevier Science.

Matrix Structure

matrix structure an
organizational structure
characterized by dual
accountability, where
departments maintain
two types of specialization simultaneously

Most organizations find that organizing around either functions (in the functional structure) or products and geography (in the divisional structure) provides an appropriate organizational structure. The **matrix structure**, in contrast, may be very appropriate when organizations conclude that neither functional nor divisional forms, even when combined with horizontal linking mechanisms like strategic business units, are right for their situations. In matrix structures, two different specializations are combined simultaneously at the same level of the organization (see **Figure 8–2**). Employees have two superiors, for example a product or project manager and a functional manager. The "home" department—that is, engineering, manufacturing, or sales—is usually functional and is reasonably permanent. People from these functional units are often assigned temporarily to one or more product units or proj-

Figure 8–2 Matrix and Network Structures

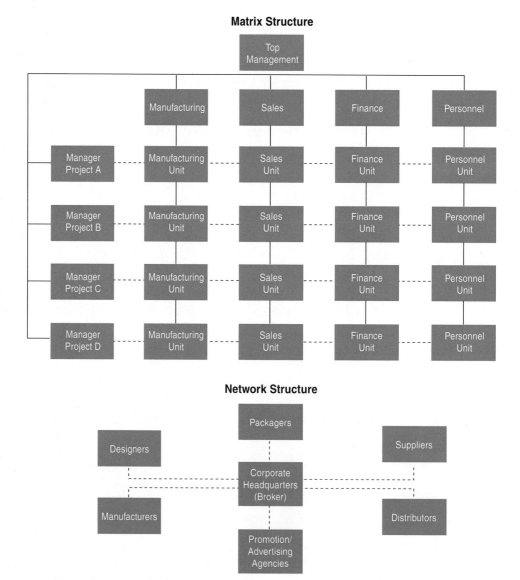

ects. The product units or projects are usually temporary and act like divisions in that they are differentiated on a product–market basis.

Pioneered in the aerospace industry, the matrix structure was developed to combine the stability of the functional structure with the flexibility of the product form. The matrix structure is very useful when the external environment (especially its technological and market aspects) is very complex and changeable. It does, however, produce conflicts revolving around duties, authority, and resource allocation. To the extent that the goals to be achieved are vague and the technology used is poorly understood, a continuous battle for power between product and functional managers is likely. The matrix structure is often found in an organization or within an SBU when the following three conditions exist:[21]

- Ideas need to be cross-fertilized across projects or products.
- Resources are scarce.
- Abilities to process information and to make decisions need to be improved.

Three distinct phases exist in the development of the matrix structure:[22]

1. **Temporary Cross-Functional Task Forces:** These are initially used when a new product line is being introduced. A project manager is in charge as the key horizontal link. Chrysler has extensively used this approach in product development.

2. **Product/Brand Management:** If the cross-functional task forces become more permanent, the project manager becomes a product or brand manager and a second phase begins. In this arrangement, function is still the primary organizational structure, but product or brand managers act as the integrators of semi-permanent products or brands. Considered by many a key to the success of Procter & Gamble, brand management has been widely imitated by other consumer product firms around the world.

3. **Mature Matrix:** The third and final phase of matrix development involves a true dual-authority structure. Both the functional and product structures are permanent. All employees are connected to both a vertical functional superior and a horizontal product manager. Functional and product managers have equal authority and must work well together to resolve disagreements over resources and priorities. The dual accountability associated with the matrix structure makes it unique. Although individuals will have dual responsibilities (usually functional and product) and therefore report to two people, there exists tremendous potential for customer responsiveness and innovation by preventing some of the problems with functional silos present in many organizations.

Network Structure—The Virtual Organization

network structure an organizational structure characterized by partnerships and alliances of organizations to produce and distribute products

virtual organization an organization consisting of partnerships and alliances that provide value-creating activities

A newer and somewhat more radical organizational design, the **network structure** (see **Figure 8–2**) is an example of what could be termed "non-structural" by its virtual elimination of in-house business functions. Many activities are outsourced. A corporation organized in this manner is often called a **virtual organization** because it comprises a series of project groups or collaborations linked by constantly changing non-hierarchical, cobweb-like networks.[23]

The network structure becomes most useful when the environment of a firm is unstable and is expected to remain so. Under such conditions, there is usually a strong need for innovation and quick response. Instead of having salaried employees, an organization may contract with people for a specific project or length of time. Long-term contracts with suppliers and distributors replace services that the company could provide for itself through vertical integration. Electronic markets and sophisticated information systems reduce the transaction costs of the marketplace, thus justifying a "buy" over a "make" decision. Rather than being located in a single building or area, an organization's business functions are scattered worldwide. The organization is, in effect, only a shell, with a small headquarters acting as a "broker," electronically connected to some completely owned divisions, partially owned subsidiaries, and other independent companies. In its ultimate form, the network organization is a series of independent firms or business units linked together by computers in an information system that designs, produces, and markets a product or service.[24]

An example of a complete network organization is Just Toys. The New York City company licenses characters like Disney's Little Mermaid, Hanna-Barbera's Flintstones, and Marvel Entertainment's Spider-Man to make bendable polyvinyl chloride figures called Bend-Ems. The manufacturing and administrative work for Bend-Ems is contracted out. The company has only 30 employees. If a toy isn't selling well, production can be reduced and shipments stopped almost immediately. It would take Mattel or Hasbro months to react in a similar situation.

Other companies such as Nike, Reebok, and Benetton use the network structure in their operations function by subcontracting manufacturing to other companies in low-cost locations around the world. For control purposes, the Italian-based Benetton maintains what it calls an "umbilical cord" by assuring production planning for all its subcontractors, planning materials requirements for them, and providing them with bills of labour and standard prices and costs, as well as technical assistance to make sure their quality is up to Benetton's standards.

The network organization structure provides an organization with increased flexibility and adaptability to cope with rapid technological change and shifting patterns of international trade and competition. It allows a company to concentrate on its distinctive competencies, while gathering efficiencies from other firms that are concentrating their efforts in their areas of expertise. The network does, however, have disadvantages. Some believe that the network is really only a transitional structure because it is inherently unstable and subject to tensions.[25] The availability of numerous potential partners can be a source of trouble. Contracting out functions to separate suppliers or distributors may keep the firm from discovering any synergies by combining activities. If a particular firm overspecializes in only a few functions, it runs the risk of choosing the wrong functions and thus becoming non-competitive.

Cellular Organization: A New Type of Structure?

cellular organization a hybrid organizational structure consisting of a collection of production cells that flexibly form and function to achieve organizational goals

Miles, Snow, Mathews, Miles, and Coleman propose that the evolution of organizational forms is leading from the matrix and the network to the cellular. According to them, "a **cellular organization** is composed of cells (self-managing teams, autonomous business units, etc.) that can operate alone but that can interact with other cells to produce a more potent and competent business mechanism." It is this combination of independence and interdependence that allows the cellular organizational form to generate and share the knowledge and expertise to produce continuous innovation. The cellular form includes the dispersed entrepreneurship of the divisional structure, customer responsiveness of the matrix, and self-organizing knowledge and asset sharing of the network.[26] As proposed, the cellular structure is similar to a current trend in industry of using internal joint ventures to temporarily combine specialized expertise and skills within a corporation to accomplish a task that individual units alone could not accomplish.[27]

The impetus for such a new structure is the pressure for a continuous process of innovation in all industries. Each cell has an entrepreneurial responsibility to the larger organization. Beyond knowledge creation and sharing, the cellular form adds value by keeping the firm's total knowledge assets more fully in use than any other type of structure. Cellular organization is beginning to appear in those firms focused on rapid product and service innovation—providing unique or state-of-the-art offerings.

RE-ENGINEERING AND STRATEGY IMPLEMENTATION

Re-engineering is the radical redesign of business processes to achieve major gains in cost, service, or time. It is not in itself a type of structure, but it is an effective way to implement a turnaround strategy.

Re-engineering strives to break away from the old rules and procedures that develop and become ingrained in every organization over the years. These may be a combination of policies, rules, and procedures that have never been seriously questioned because they were established years earlier. These may range from "Credit decisions are made by the credit department" to "Local inventory is needed for good customer service." These rules of organization and work design were based on assumptions about technology, people, and organizational goals that may no longer be relevant. Rather than attempting to fix existing problems through minor adjustments and fine-tuning existing processes, the key to re-engineering is to ask, If this were a new company, how would we run this place? In other words, would we do this a different way if we could start from scratch? In this way business process re-engineering encourages us to fundamentally rethink the way work is accomplished in the organization, without dwelling on what steps might be necessary to make these changes. The focus on "processes" gets managers thinking about what exactly happens as the product is produced, or the service provided. Does every task that gets performed actually increase its value? Are there ways to do this faster, or with fewer resources? Does the current organizational structure help or hinder the efficiency of processes? All of these types of questions can be addressed by re-engineering, even if the organization is unable or unwilling to engage in the large-scale changes that define re-engineering. Even small steps toward this ideal can provide tremendous benefits for organizations. In fact small steps might be more successful in the long run because the magnitude of the changes might make them appear more acceptable to organizational members. Without the fear of failure associated with radical organizational change, fewer obstacles to change may exist, which should increase the likelihood of success.

Michael Hammer, who popularized the concept, suggests the following principles for re-engineering:[28]

- Organize around outcomes, not tasks. Design a person's or a department's job around an objective or outcome instead of a single task or series of tasks.

- Have those who use the output of the process perform the process. With computer-based information systems, processes can now be re-engineered so that the people who need the result of the process can do it themselves.

- Subsume information-processing work into the real work that produces the information. People or departments that produce information can also process it for use instead of just sending out raw data for others in the organization to interpret.

- Treat geographically dispersed resources as though they were centralized. With modern information systems, companies can provide flexible service locally while keeping the actual resources in a centralized location for co-ordination purposes.

- Link parallel activities instead of integrating their results. Instead of having separate units perform different activities that must eventually come together, have them communicate while they work so that they can do the integrating.

- Put the decision point where the work is performed, and build control into the process. The people who do the work should make the decisions and be self-controlling.

- Capture information once and at the source. Instead of having each unit develop its own database and information processing activities, the information can be put on a network so that all can access it.

Studies of the performance of re-engineering programs show mixed results. Several companies have had success with re-engineering. One study of North American financial firms found, "The average reengineering project took 15 months, consumed 66 person-months of effort, and delivered cost savings of 24%."[29] In a survey of 782 organizations using re-engineering, 75% of the executives said their companies had succeeded in reducing operating expenses and increasing productivity. Although only 47% stated that their companies had succeeded in generating revenue growth and 37% at raising market share, 70% of the respondents stated that their companies planned to use re-engineering in the future.[30] Nevertheless, other studies report that anywhere from 50% to 70% of re-engineering programs fail to achieve their objectives.[31]

DESIGNING JOBS TO IMPLEMENT STRATEGY

job design studying the content of jobs to make them more efficient and motivating

Organizing a company's activities and people to implement strategy involves more than simply redesigning an organization's overall structure; it also involves redesigning the way jobs are done. With the increasing emphasis on re-engineering, many companies are beginning to rethink their work processes with an eye toward phasing unnecessary people and activities out of the process. Process steps that had traditionally been performed sequentially can be improved by performing them concurrently using cross-functional work teams. Harley-Davidson, for example, has managed to reduce total plant employment by 25% while reducing by 50% the time needed to build a motorcycle. Restructuring through fewer people requires broadening the scope of jobs and encouraging teamwork. The design of jobs and subsequent job performance are, therefore, increasingly being considered as sources of competitive advantage.

job characteristics model a tool for diagnosing the motivating potential in jobs based on five core job characteristics and the psychological states they create

Job design refers to the study of individual tasks in an attempt to make them more relevant to the company and to the employee(s). To minimize some of the adverse consequences of task specialization, organizations have turned to job design techniques: job enlargement (combining tasks to give a worker more of the same type of duties to perform), job rotation (moving workers through several jobs to increase variety), and job enrichment (altering the jobs by giving the worker more autonomy and control over activities). The **job characteristics model** is a good example of how paying attention to the content of jobs can affect employee motivation and satisfaction (see the **Theory As It Applies** feature and **Figure 8–3**).

Theory As It Applies

Designing Jobs with the Job Characteristics Model

The job characteristics model is an approach to job design based on the belief that tasks can be described in terms of certain objective characteristics and that these characteristics affect employee motivation. In other words, jobs can be designed so that workers are more motivated and satisfied to do them, and the quality of their work is increased. Any job can be described by these five core job dimensions:

- **Skill variety:** the number and type of activities employees perform
- **Task identity:** completing whole and identifiable pieces of work
- **Task significance:** the degree of impact the job has on the lives of others
- **Autonomy:** the amount of freedom, independence, and discretion individuals have in doing their job
- **Feedback:** the availability of direct and clear information about on-the-job performance

The job characteristics model suggests that improved personal and work outcomes will be obtained by designing jobs that will create certain psychological states in workers:

- **Experienced meaningfulness:** viewing the job as important, valuable, and worthwhile as a result of skill variety, task identity, and task significance

- **Experienced responsibility:** experiencing a personal responsibility for results of their jobs as a result of autonomy
- **Knowledge of results:** absorption of regular feedback on how workers are performing in relation to targets

These psychological states lead to improved personal outcomes, such as intrinsic motivation, performance, and satisfaction, as well as improved outcomes for employers, such as reduced absenteeism and turnover. Techniques that managers could use to design better jobs include the following:

1. Combine tasks to increase task variety and to enable workers to identify with what they are doing.
2. Form natural work units to make workers more responsible and accountable for the performance of their jobs.
3. Establish client relationships so each worker will know what performance is required and why.

4. Vertically load the job by giving workers increased authority and responsibility over their activities.
5. Open feedback channels by providing workers with information on how they are performing.

Research supports the job characteristics model as a way to improve job performance through job enrichment. Although there are several other approaches to job design, practising managers seem increasingly to follow the prescriptions of this model as a way of improving productivity and product quality.

Sources: J.R. Hackman and G.R. Oldham, *Work Redesign* (Reading, Mass.: Addison-Wesley, 1980), pp. 135–141; G. Johns, J.L. Xie, and Y. Fang, "Mediating and Moderating Effects in Job Design," *Journal of Management* (December 1992), pp. 657–676; R.W. Griffin, "Effects of Work Redesign on Employee Perceptions, Attitudes, and Behaviors: A Long-Term Investigation," *Academy of Management Journal* (June 1991), pp. 425–435.

Figure 8–3 The Job Characteristics Model

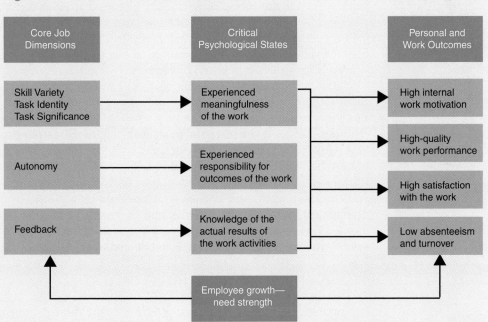

Source: J.R. Hackman and G.R. Oldham, *Work Redesign* (p. 90) Copyright © 1980. Reprinted by permission of Pearson Education, Inc., Upper Saddle River, NJ.

A good example of how job design can be effectively used is the introduction of work teams and job progression at MacMillan Bloedel. As a large integrated forest products company, MacMillan Bloedel made numerous attempts in the 1980s to introduce changes to jobs at British Columbia's Chemainus Sawmill in an effort make the plant cost-competitive. The 1927 sawmill had at one point employed 600 unionized workers but was unable to be profitable in the face of its old equipment and high labour costs. It had even been shut down while the company and union discussed how changes could be made. Together, union and management put together a plan to save the mill that involved innovative work practices and equipment. Along with downsizing the workforce to approximately 125 people, the new Chemaimus Sawmill was organized very differently. Key to the success of the mill was the use of teams, ranging in size from three to nine workers. Individual workers were trained as they moved from the low-paying jobs up to higher-paying ones they were qualified to do. After a certain number of hours at the low-paying job, the worker was ready to move up to the next job, where he or she was trained by the experienced worker. Although this meant that a large portion of workers were paid at the top pay category, this system was an important source of motivation. It also permitted job rotation within teams so that knowledge that was formerly specific to a job or a person was now more widely shared.[32]

8.5 International Issues in Strategy Implementation

multinational corporation an organization with investment and facilities in several geographic locations around the world and a worldwide perspective in its operations

An international company is one that engages in any combination of activities, from exporting or importing to full-scale manufacturing, in foreign countries. The **multinational corporation (MNC)**, in contrast, is a highly developed international company with a deep involvement throughout the world, plus a worldwide perspective in its management and decision making. For a multinational corporation to be considered global, it must manage its worldwide operations as if they were totally interconnected. This approach works best when the industry has moved from being multidomestic (each country's industry is essentially separate from the same industry in other countries; an example is retailing) to global (each country is a part of one worldwide industry; an example is consumer electronics).

Strategic alliances, such as joint ventures and licensing agreements, between a multinational company and a local partner in a host country are becoming increasingly popular as a means by which a corporation can gain entry into other countries, especially less developed countries. The key to the successful implementation of these strategies is the selection of the local partner. Each party needs to assess not only the strategic fit of each company's project strategy, but also the fit of each company's respective resources. A successful joint venture may require as much as two years of prior contact between the two parties.

The design of an organization's structure is strongly affected by the company's stage of development in international activities and the types of industries in which the company is involved. The issue of centralization versus decentralization becomes especially important for a multinational corporation operating in both multidomestic and global industries.

STAGES OF INTERNATIONAL DEVELOPMENT

Organizations operating internationally tend to evolve through five common stages, both in their relationships with widely dispersed geographic markets and in the manner in which they structure their operations and programs:

- **Stage 1 (Domestic Company):** The primarily domestic company exports some of its products through local dealers and distributors to foreign countries. The impact on the organization's structure is minimal because an export department at corporate headquarters handles everything.

- **Stage 2 (Domestic Company with Export Division):** Success in Stage 1 leads the company to establish its own sales company with offices in other countries to eliminate the intermediaries and to better control marketing. Because exports have now become more important, the company establishes an export division to oversee foreign sales offices.

- **Stage 3 (Primarily Domestic Company with International Division):** Success in earlier stages leads the company to establish manufacturing facilities in addition to sales and service offices in key countries. The company now adds an international division with responsibilities for most of the business functions conducted in other countries.

- **Stage 4 (MNC with Multidomestic Emphasis):** Now a full-fledged multinational corporation, the company increases its investments in other countries. The company establishes a local operating division or company in the host country, such as Ford of Britain, to better serve the market. The product line is expanded, and local manufacturing capacity is established. Managerial functions (product development, finance, marketing, and so on) are organized locally. Over time, the parent company acquires other related businesses, broadening the base of the local operating division. As the subsidiary in the host country successfully develops a strong regional presence, it achieves greater autonomy and self-sufficiency. The operations in each country are, nevertheless, managed separately, as if each were a domestic company.

- **Stage 5 (MNC with Global Emphasis):** The most successful multinational corporations move into a fifth stage in which they have worldwide personnel, R & D, and financing strategies. Typically operating in a global industry, the MNC denationalizes its operations and plans product design, manufacturing, and marketing around worldwide considerations. Global considerations now dominate organizational design. The global MNC structures itself in a matrix form around some combination of geographic areas, product lines, and functions. All managers are now responsible for dealing with international as well as domestic issues.

Research provides some support for some concept of the stages of international development, but it does not necessarily support the preceding sequence of stages. For example, a company may initiate production and sales in multiple countries without having gone through the steps of exporting or having local sales subsidiaries. In addition, any one corporation can be at different stages simultaneously, with different products in different markets at different levels. Firms may also leapfrog across stages to a global emphasis. Developments in information technology are changing the way business is being done internationally. See the **Global Issue** feature to see how FedEx is using its expertise in information technology to help customers sidestep the building of a costly logistical infrastructure to take advantage of global markets. Nevertheless, the stages concept provides a useful way to illustrate some of the structural changes corporations undergo when they increase their involvement in international activities.

Global Issue

FedEx Provides the Infrastructure for Companies to Become Global

Globalization is becoming a permanent and irreversible part of economic life. A key reason is the use of information system technology to connect operations around the world. The internet—via email, chat rooms, and websites in multiple languages—provides instantaneous communication 24 hours a day. *Enterprise resource planning (ERP) systems*, such as SAP's R/3 software, can manage all of a corporation's internal operations (including international) in a single powerful network. ERP is able to unite customers and suppliers so that they can transact business with each other online. Retailers like Wal-Mart are going global and are pressuring suppliers to have global sourcing and pricing.

FedEx is a key force behind globalization, but not just because it delivers 2.8 million packages in 210 countries each day. It is using information technology to remake its clients' worldwide supply and distribution systems. FedEx is becoming the global logistical backbone for many of its customers. Using its technology, FedEx manages its customers' worldwide inventory, warehousing, distribution, and customs clearance. It can help a customer assemble and make products by securing supplies globally in a reliable and cost-effective manner. It is able to do this because it is able to electronically track any of its shipments at any point in time. This provides FedEx with a distinctive competency, which it is able to use to provide valuable service to others. With a guarantee of on-time delivery, customers are able to reduce costly inventories and institute just-in-time systems. According to CEO and chairman Frederick Smith, "We decided years ago that the most important element in this business is information technology, and we have geared everything to that philosophy—recruitment, training, and

compensation. Fail-safe precision is the key to it all."

Dell Computer Corporation eliminated its costly distribution infrastructure in favour of using FedEx to coordinate the assembly of computers and their customs clearance and shipping from a manufacturing centre in Malaysia to customers in Japan and Taiwan. By managing National Semiconductor Corporation's global warehousing and distribution systems, FedEx was able to reduce its customer's total costs of logistics from 3% to 1.9% of revenues.

Source: J.E. Garten, "Why the Global Economy Is Here to Stay," *Business Week* (March 23, 1998), p. 21. By special permission, copyright © 1998 by The McGraw-Hill Companies, Inc.

CENTRALIZATION VERSUS DECENTRALIZATION

A basic dilemma that a multinational corporation faces is how to organize authority centrally so that it operates as a vast interlocking system that achieves synergy, and at the same time decentralize authority so that local managers can make the decisions necessary to meet the demands of the local market or host government.[33] To deal with this problem, MNCs tend to structure themselves either along product groups or geographic areas. They may even combine both in a matrix structure—the design chosen by 3M Corporation and Asea Brown Boveri (ABB), among others.[34] One side of 3M's matrix represents the company's product divisions; the other side includes the company's international country and regional subsidiaries.

Two examples of usual international structures are Nestlé and American Cyanamid. Nestlé's structure is one in which significant power and authority have been decentralized to geographic entities. This structure is similar to that depicted in **Figure 8–4**, in which each geographic set of operating companies has a different group of products. In contrast, American Cyanamid has a series of centralized product groups with worldwide responsibilities. To depict Cyanamid's structure, the geographical entities in **Figure 8–4** would have to be replaced by product groups or strategic business units.

The *product-group structure* of American Cyanamid enables the company to introduce and manage a similar line of products around the world. This allows the corporation to centralize decision making along product lines and to reduce costs. The *geographic-area structure* of Nestlé, in contrast, allows the company to tailor products to regional differences and to achieve regional coordination. This decentralizes decision making to the local subsidiaries. As industries move from being multidomestic to more globally integrated, multinational corporations are increasingly switching from the geographic-area to the product-group structure. Texaco, Inc., for example, changed to a product-group structure by consolidating its international, US, and new business opportunities under each line of business at its White Plains, New York, headquarters. The logic behind this type of structure is that "by placing groups which will perform similar work in the same location, they will be able to share information, ideas, and resources more readily—and move critical information throughout the organization."[35]

Simultaneous pressures for decentralization to be locally responsive and centralization to be maximally efficient are causing interesting structural adjustments in most large corporations. Companies are attempting to decentralize those operations that are culturally oriented and closest to the customers: manufacturing, marketing, and human resources. At the same time, the companies are consolidating less visible internal functions, such as research and development, finance, and information systems, where there can be significant economies of scale.

Figure 8–4 Geographic Area Structure for a Multinational Corporation

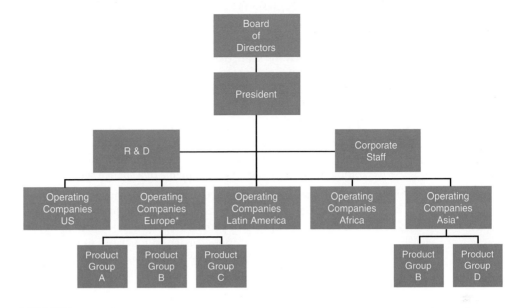

*Note: Because of space limitations, product groups for only Europe and Asia are shown here.

8.6 Managing Organizational Change

One thing that should be clear from the material presented in this book is that organizations can rarely withstand competition or grow without undergoing some type of organizational change. As markets become increasingly competitive, globalization increases, consumer tastes change, and technologies develop, it is becoming increasingly important for organizations to be able to make strategic and operational changes quickly and efficiently. It is not uncommon for organizations to undertake moderate organizational changes at least once a year, and major ones every four or five.[36] When organizations think strategically, they continuously strive to match organizational resources with the external environment in a way that will improve long-run performance. Doing so requires a strong vision of *where* the organization wants to be, and a clear idea of *how* it wants to get there. As part of implementing strategy, managers need to create an organization that is supportive of the activities that create value for consumers and build competitive advantage for the firm. These goals and strategies need to be reviewed regularly and revised as needed in light of changing circumstances. In this way, strategic management is characterized as an ongoing process based on a willingness to change. Despite the importance of change to the success of an organization, change agendas are usually met with mixed success. Most change efforts encounter problems, such as taking longer than expected, costing more money than planned, causing problems in morale and motivation, or not delivering the intended performance improvements.

A large part of the problem with many change efforts is the human resistance they often run into. One way to minimize the problems associated with organizational change is to assess who might resist the changes and for what reasons. The four most common reasons people resist change are these:[37]

1. *Self-interest.* If people think they will lose something of value by changing, then they will likely resist it. Often people focus on their own best interests rather than those of the

organization as a whole. Unfortunately many organizational changes do create "winners" and "losers," which spurs the desire for individuals to protect themselves and their departments by resisting organizational changes.

2. *Misunderstanding and lack of trust.* People will resist change when they do not understand either the need for change or how it will affect them. These situations occur most frequently when trust is lacking between the decision makers who initiate the changes and the employees who will have to do things differently.

3. *Different assessments.* Organizational members often disagree on how much sense a change makes, or how great its benefits will actually be. Often the people making strategic decisions will have more relevant information that has been analyzed prior to announcing a change agenda. Differences in information available throughout the organization can lead to different assessments of a change agenda, which can lead to resistance.

4. *Low tolerance for change.* When organizations change, people need to change along with them. Yet not all people are as willing or able to change as others. When new skills or behaviours are required of people, they often learn them at a pace that is too slow for the organization. People can only change so much, or so quickly. Yet many organizational change efforts fail because these limitations to employees' tolerance for change are ignored or underestimated.

An important first step in implementing any organizational change is, therefore, assessing the possible sources of resistance that will be encountered. Doing so will not only alert managers to potential obstacles in the change process, but also indicate a range of tactics they can use to positively influence the people involved. **Table 8–5** identifies six methods for dealing with resistance to change, and the situations in which they are most commonly used.

8.7 Impact of the Internet on Organizational Design and Structure

The Cluetrain Manifesto, a book written by Levine, Locke, Searls, and Weinberger, proposes 95 theses about how the internet is changing the world and the way it does business. Many of today's companies are still stuck in traditional, conservative mindsets, creating virtual barriers between themselves and the people they hope to reach. The book argues that the internet has "something special" about it, the "voice," that sets it apart from any other medium. The internet connects people to each other, allowing them to have conversations and comment on things in a forum that joins a wealth of knowledge from different resources. The **hyperlinked organization** is a new type of developing organization, which provides all employees easy access to one another and to people outside the organization in a rich variety of ways, ranging from email to personal websites. Workers and markets speak the same language.

> **hyperlinked organization** an organization that connects its members and customers with internet technology

According to Levine et al., bringing the internet into an organization changes things in unpredictable ways. The new hyperlinked organization contains several major themes:[38]

- **Hyperlinked and Decentralized:** There is no central authority on the web; it consists of hundreds of millions of pages linked together by the author of each individual page. Organizations become hyperlinked when they decentralize their teams, committees, task forces, and individuals. Official structure is set aside in favour of networks of trusted colleagues.

- **Hypertime:** With the internet, people can look for information and connections at their own pace and under their own control any time of the day or week without having to search for a parking place or obtain a library card. In a hyperlinked organization, schedules

Table 8–5 Methods for Dealing with Resistance to Change

Approach	Commonly used in situations	Advantages	Drawbacks
Education + communication	Where there is a lack of information or inaccurate information and analysis.	Once persuaded, people will often help with the implementation of the change.	Can be very time-consuming if lots of people are involved.
Participation + involvement	Where the initiators do no have all the information they need to design the change, and where others have considerable power to resist.	People who participate will be committed to implementing change, and any relevant information they have will be inegrated into the change plan.	Can be very time-consuming if participators design an inappropriate change.
Facilitation + support	Where people are resisting because of adjustment problems.	No other approach works as well with adjustment problems.	Can be time-consuming and expensive, and still fail.
Negotiation + agreement	Where someone or some group will clearly lose out in a change, and where that group has considerable power to resist.	Sometimes it is a relatively easy way to avoid major resistance.	Can be too expensive in many cases if it alerts others to negotiate for compliance.
Manipulation + co-optation	Where other tactics will not work, or are too expensive.	It can be a relatively quick and inexpensive solution to resistance problems.	Can lead to future problems if people feel manipulated.
Explicit + Implicit coercion	Where speed is essential, and the change initiators possess considerable power.	It is speedy, and can overcome any kind of resistance.	Can be risky if it leaves people mad at the initiators.

Source: John P. Kotter & Leonard A. Schlesinger, "Choosing Strategies for Change," *Harvard Business Review*, March/April 1979, p. 111.

are driven locally, not centrally, created by local groups and individuals. Traditional deadlines are replaced by a team's motivation to help a customer or co-worker.

- **Directly Accessible:** The internet provides direct access for everyone on the planet to every piece of information made available. Hyperlinked organizations replace the old mindset of hoarding information with new, wide-open policies that encourage collaboration over intranets, moving individual tasks to group tasks, and bringing in people because they have the necessary skills and shared interests, not because of their position in the hierarchy.

- **Full of Rich Data:** The currency of the internet is pages of information. The various types of internet communication (especially email) allow the hyperlinked organization to link staff, management, and customers who can tell stories, create valuable narratives, and explore the many ways to translate ideas using each participant's distinctive voice.

- **Broken:** Because the internet is a large, complex network controlled by no one, it will always be somewhat "broken." Any search of the internet is bound to find many dead links and dead ends (those "sticky" sites that refuse to allow the visitor to use the browser to go back to a previous web page). Although the traditional hierarchy demanded predictability and consistency, the hyperlinked organization looks for innovation and expects mistakes and slightly broken systems and structures, which are always in a state of repair and rebuilding.

- **Borderless:** Traditional organizations and networks were concerned as much with security as with access. They were usually very clear where one department ended and another began—even within the same company. People had access to important information only if they "had a need to know." In contrast, the internet was designed so that one page could be linked to another without obtaining the author's permission. Because of the way links work, it is often hard to tell whether one is still on the same webpage or on another page located in another part of the world. Hyperlinked organizations accept that borders between units are permeable and changing. Intranets and extranets allow companies to share previously unknown processes with customers and to solicit ideas and suggestions from them. They also allow internal communications to flow more easily, replacing closed meeting rooms with email discussion groups and group intranet sites. As the hurdles to membership lower, the boundaries begin to blur.

According to *The Cluetrain Manifesto*, the structures of organizations must change if they are to be effective in a changing, global, internet-linked environment. This suggests that traditional organization structures must adopt more of the characteristics of the matrix, the network, and the cellular forms of organization.

Discussion Questions

1. How should a corporation attempt to achieve synergy among functions and business units?

2. How should an owner-manager prepare a company for its movement from Stage I to Stage II?

3. How can a corporation keep from sliding into the Decline stage of the organizational life cycle?

4. Is re-engineering just another management fad or does it offer something of lasting value?

5. How is the cellular organization different from the network structure?

Strategic Practice Exercise

The Synergy Game

SETUP

Put three to five chairs on either side of a room facing each other in the front of the class. Put a table in the middle with a bell in the middle of the table.

PROCEDURE

The instructor/moderator divides the class into teams of three to five people. Each team selects a name for itself. The instructor/moderator lists the team names on the board. The first two teams come to the front and sit in the chairs facing each other. The instructor/moderator reads a list of products or services being provided by an actual company. The winning team must identify (1) possible sources of synergy and (2) the actual company being described. For example, if the products or services listed are family restaurants, airline catering, hotels, and retirement centres, the synergy is standardized food service and hospitality settings and the company is The Marriott Corporation. The first team to successfully name the company and the synergy wins the round.

After one practice session, the game begins. Each of the teams is free to discuss the question with other team members. Once one of the two teams thinks that it has the

answer to both parts of the question, it must be the first to ring the bell to announce its answer. If it gives the correct answer, it is deemed the winner of round one. Both parts of the answer must be given for a team to have the correct answer. If a team correctly provides only one part, that answer is still wrong—no partial credit. The instructor/moderator does not say which part of the answer, if either, was correct. The second team then has the opportunity to state the answer. If the second team is wrong, both teams may try once more. If neither chooses to try again, the instructor/moderator may (1) declare no round winner and both teams sit down, (2) allow the next two teams to provide the answer to round one, or (3) go on to the next round with the same two teams. Two new teams then come to the front for the next round. Once all groups have played once, the winning teams play each other. Rounds continue until there is a grand champion. The instructor should provide a suitable prize, such as candy bars, for the winning team.

This exercise was developed by Professors Yolanda Sarason of Colorado State University and Catherine Banbury of St. Mary's College and Purdue University, and presented at the Organizational Behavior Teaching Conference, June 1999. Copyright © 1999 by Yolanda Sarason and Catherine Banbury. Adapted with permission.

Notes

1. "Case Study Scenario: BEC Inc.," *National Post Business* (May 2002, pp. 29–34).

2. J.W. Gadella, "Avoiding Expensive Mistakes in Capital Investment," *Long Range Planning* (April 1994), pp. 103–110; B. Voss, "World Market Is Not for Everyone," *Journal of Business Strategy* (July/August 1993), p.4.

3. J.I. Rigdon, "The Integration Game," *Red Herring* (July 2000), pp. 356–366.

4. L.D. Alexander, "Strategy Implementation: Nature of the Problem," *International Review of Strategic Management*, Vol. 2, No. 1, edited by D.E. Hussey (New York: John Wiley & Sons, 1991), pp. 73–113.

5. www.scouts.ca (accessed May 7, 2003).

6. E. Brynjolfsson, A.A. Renshaw, and M. Van Alstyne, "The Matrix of Change," *Sloan Management Review* (Winter 1997), pp. 37–54.

7. www.scouts.ca (accessed May 9, 2003).

8. M. Goold and A. Campbell, "Desperately Seeking Synergy," *Harvard Business Review* (September–October 1998), pp. 131–143.

9. A.D. Chandler, *Strategy and Structure* (Cambridge, Mass.: MIT Press, 1962).

10. A.P. Sloan, Jr., *My Years with General Motors* (Garden City, NY: Doubleday, 1964).

11. T.L. Amburgey and T. Dacin, "As the Left Foot Follows the Right? The Dynamics of Strategic and Structural Change," *Academy of Management Journal* (December 1994), pp. 1427–1452; M. Ollinger, "The Limits of Growth of the Multidivisional Firm: A Case Study of the U.S. Oil Industry from 1930–90," *Strategic Management Journal* (September 1994), pp. 503–520.

12. D.F. Jennings and S.L. Seaman, "High and Low Levels of Organizational Adaptation: An Empirical Analysis of Strategy, Structure, and Performance," *Strategic Management Journal* (July 1994), pp. 459–475; L. Donaldson, "The Normal Science of Structured Contingency Theory," in *Handbook of Organization Studies*, edited by S.R. Clegg, C. Hardy, and W.R. Nord (London: Sage Publications, 1996), pp. 57–76.

13. A.K. Gupta, "SBU Strategies, Corporate-SBU Relations, and SBU Effectiveness in Strategy Implementation," *Academy of Management Journal* (September 1987), pp. 477–500.

14. L.E. Greiner, "Evolution and Revolution as Organizations Grow," *Harvard Business Review* (May–June 1998), pp. 55–67. This is an updated version of Greiner's classic 1972 article.

15. D. Miller and M.-J. Chen, "Sources and Consequences of Competitive Inertia," *Administrative Science Quarterly* (Volume 39, 1994), pp. 1–23.

16. Greiner, p. 64. Although Greiner simply labelled this as the *"?" crisis*, the term "pressure-cooker" seems apt.

17. W.P. Barnett, "The Dynamics of Competitive Intensity," *Administrative Science Quarterly* (March 1997), pp. 128–160; D. Miller, *The Icarus Paradox: How Exceptional Companies Bring About Their Own Downfall* (New York: Harper Business, 1990).

18. D. Miller and P.H. Friesen, "A Longitudinal Study of the Corporate Life Cycle," *Management Science* (October 1984), pp. 1161–1183.

19. J. Green, "The Toy-Train Company that Thinks It Can," *Business Week* (December 4, 2000), pp. 64–69.

20. G. David, F. Garcia, and I. Gashurov, "Welcome to the Valley of the Damned.Com," *Fortune* (January 22, 2001), p. 52.

21. L.G. Hrebiniak and W.F. Joyce, *Implementing Strategy* (New York: Macmillan, 1984), pp. 85–86.

22. S.M. Davis and P.R. Lawrence, *Matrix* (Reading, Mass.: Addison-Wesley, 1977), pp. 11–24.

23. J.G. March, "The Future Disposable Organizations and the Rigidities of Imagination," *Organization* (August/November 1995), p. 434.

24. M.P. Koza and A.Y. Lewin, "The Coevolution of Network Alliances: A Longitudinal Analysis of an International Professional Service Network," *Organization Science* (September/October 1999), pp. 638–653.

25. For more information on managing a network organization, see G. Lorenzoni and C. Baden-Fuller, "Creating a Strategic Center to Manage a Web of Partners," *California Management Review* (Spring 1995), pp. 146–163.

26. R.E. Miles, C.C. Snow, J.A. Mathews, G. Miles, and H.J. Coleman, Jr., "Organizing in the Knowledge Age: Anticipating the Cellular Form," *Academy of Management Executive* (November 1997), pp. 7–24.

27. J. Naylor and M. Lewis, "Internal Alliances: Using Joint Ventures in a Diversified Company," *Long Range Planning* (October 1997), pp. 678–688.

28. Summarized from M. Hammer, "Reengineering Work: Don't Automate, Obliterate," *Harvard Business Review* (July–August 1990), pp. 104–112.

29. S. Drew, "BPR in Financial Services: Factors for Success," *Long Range Planning* (October 1994), pp. 25–41.

30. "Do As I Say, Not As I Do," *Journal of Business Strategy* (May/June 1997), pp. 3–4.

31. K. Grint, Reengineering History: Social Resonances and Business Process Reengineering," *Organization* (July 1994), pp. 179–201; A. Kleiner, "Revisiting Reengineering," *Strategy + Business* (3rd Quarter 2000), pp. 27–31.

32. http://labour-travail.hrdc-drhc.gc.ca/pdf/pdf_e/bloedel-en.pdf (accessed May 11, 2003).

33. J.H. Taggart, "Strategy Shifts in MNC Subsidiaries," *Strategic Management Journal* (July 1998), pp. 663–681.

34. C.A. Bartlett and S. Ghoshal, "Beyond the M-Form: Toward a Managerial Theory of the Firm," *Strategic Management Journal* (Winter 1993), pp. 23–46.

35. A. Sullivan, "Texaco Revamps Executive Structure to Focus on Business, Not Geography," *The Wall Street Journal* (October 3, 1996), p. B15.

36. Stephen A. Allen, "Organizational Choice and General Influence Networks for Diversified Companies," *Academy of Management Journal* (September 1978), p. 341.

37. John P. Kotter & Leonard A. Schlesinger, "Choosing Strategies for Change," *Harvard Business Review* (March–April 1979), pp. 106–114.

38. R. Levine, C. Locke, D. Searls, and D. Weinberger, *The Cluetrain Manifesto* (Cambridge, Mass.: Perseus Books, 2000). Originally posted on a website at www.cluetrain.com, *The Cluetrain Manifesto* has now reached the status of a cult book within the internet community.

CHAPTER 9

Strategy Implementation: Staffing and Directing

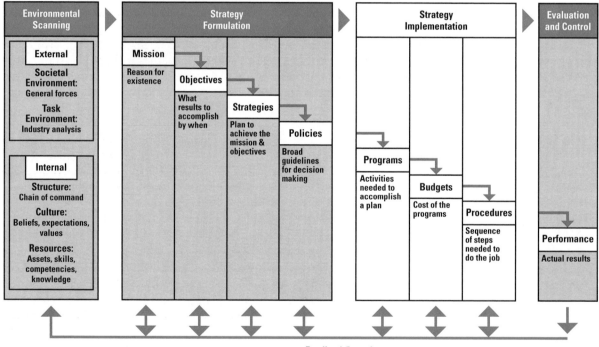

Environmental Scanning

External

Societal Environment: General forces

Task Environment: Industry analysis

Internal

Structure: Chain of command

Culture: Beliefs, expectations, values

Resources: Assets, skills, competencies, knowledge

Strategy Formulation

Mission

Reason for existence

Objectives

What results to accomplish by when

Strategies

Plan to achieve the mission & objectives

Policies

Broad guidelines for decision making

Strategy Implementation

Programs

Activities needed to accomplish a plan

Budgets

Cost of the programs

Procedures

Sequence of steps needed to do the job

Evaluation and Control

Performance

Actual results

Feedback/Learning

Learning Objectives

After reading this chapter you should be able to

Understand the link between strategy and staffing decisions

Choose from several selection processes to better match people and jobs

Scan functional resources to determine their fit with firm strategy

Understand how to implement an effective downsizing program

Manage organizational culture to effectively support organizational strategies

Formulate action plans

Relate cultural differences to successful leadership

Canada's third-largest integrated steelmaker, Algoma Steel Inc. of Sault Ste. Marie, has a history of bringing itself out of bankruptcy and finding a way to keep its mills running. But in 2001, Algoma lost approximately $400 million and sought bankruptcy protection for the third time. Once again a deal was reached between creditors, employees, directors, and governments that gave Algoma one more chance to turn its money-losing operations around.

Algoma's financial difficulties over the years make it hard to attract and retain a good top management team. In August 2002 CEO Sandy Adam retired, which once again left Algoma in the difficult position of being a poor performing organization in search of a leader. Rumours circulated that Adam had been pushed out by the new controlling shareholder group, formerly New York bondholders who replaced their US$397 million debt with shorter-term notes and common shares (representing 75% ownership). Others wondered whether Adam "didn't want to be at the helm when the ship goes down for a third and final time." Perhaps we will never know. The leadership challenge at Algoma is, however, daunting. One problem is Algoma's reliance on low-margin commodity steel products, which are difficult to profit from under its relatively inefficient plants and high debt load. Compounding this problem is an American tariff on imported steel, a response to lobbying from American producers who claimed that foreign dumping was responsible for the low steel prices in America and the closure of numerous mills. And there is the ever-present threat of mini-mills, which now account for approximately half the steel produced in North America. The combination of using scrap metal as an input and labour from non-unionized facilities allows them to undercut integrated producers like Algoma.

The management challenges at Algoma are significant. Not only does the organization need to find a CEO at a time when Algoma has very little to offer an experienced executive, but there is an urgency to turn around operations quickly in order to keep the company alive. After a new leader is found, tough strategic decisions will need to be made about the company's product mix and how to defend against the competitive threat of mini-mills. In the long term, efficiency gains will need to be made. These will likely come from investments in new capital equipment as well as adjustments to the workforce and the organization's structure.[1]

This example illustrates how, in order to succeed, a strategy must be implemented with carefully considered programs overseen by skilled management. This chapter discusses strategy implementation in terms of staffing and leading. *Staffing* focuses on the selection and use of employees. *Leading* emphasizes the use of programs to better align employee interests and attitudes with a new strategy.

9.1 Staffing

staffing the set of
human resource man-
agement practices used
to implement organiza-
tional strategy

The implementation of new strategies and policies often calls for new human resource management priorities and a different use of personnel. Such **staffing** issues can involve hiring
new people with new skills, firing people with inappropriate or substandard skills, and/or
training existing employees to learn new skills.

If growth strategies are to be implemented, new people may need to be hired and trained.
Experienced people with the necessary skills need to be found for promotion to newly created
managerial positions. When a corporation follows a strategy of growth through acquisition, it
may find that it needs to replace several managers in the acquired company. Recent studies
have shown that the percentage of an acquired company's top management team who either
quit or were asked to leave was around 25% after the first year, 35% after the second year, 48%
after the third year, 55% after the fourth year, and 61% after five years.[2] It is one thing to lose
excess employees after a merger, but it is something else to lose highly skilled people who are
difficult to replace. To deal with problems such as this, some companies are appointing special integration managers to shepherd companies through the implementation process of an
acquisition. To be a successful integration manager, a person should have (1) a deep knowledge of the acquiring company, (2) a flexible management style, (3) an ability to work in cross-
functional project teams, (4) a willingness to work independently, and (5) sufficient emotional
and cultural intelligence to work well with people from all backgrounds.[3]

If an organization adopts a retrenchment strategy, however, a large number of people may
need to be laid off or fired, and top management, as well as the divisional managers, will need
to specify the criteria to be used in making these personnel decisions. Should employees be
fired on the basis of low seniority or on the basis of poor performance? Sometimes corporations find it easier to close or sell off an entire division than to choose which individuals to fire.

STAFFING FOLLOWS STRATEGY

As in the case of structure, staffing requirements are likely to follow a change in strategy. For
example, promotions should be based not only on current job performance, but also on whether
a person has the skills and abilities to do what is needed to implement the new strategy.

Hiring and Training Requirements Change

Having formulated a new strategy, an organization may find that it needs to either hire different people or retrain current employees to implement it. Consider the introduction of
team-based production at MacMillan Bloedel mentioned in **Chapter 8**. Employee selection
and training were crucial to the success of the new manufacturing strategy because workers
would now have to learn multiple jobs and work in a team setting. It was this new combination of skills and abilities that allowed for the tremendous productivity improvements that
prevented the closure of the Chemainus Sawmill.

One way to implement a company's business strategy, such as overall low cost, is through
training and development. A recent study found that 71% of "leading" companies rated staff
learning and training as important or very important compared with 62% of the other companies.[4] Another study of manufacturing firms revealed that those with training programs had
19% higher productivity than those without such a program. Another study found that a doubling of formal training per employee resulted in a 7% reduction in scrap.[5] Training is especially important for a differentiation strategy emphasizing quality or customer service. Firms
pursuing this type of strategy need to make investments in training because of the inherent
inseparability of experienced customer service and the organization's employees. In other

words, customer service is experienced as an interaction between people, and the organizations that excel at providing customer service usually make significant investments in training. Skilled labour is also one of the most important contributors to the growth of organizations. This translates into approximately 30 hours of training per employee per year.[6] Evidence of the importance of skilled labour can be seen in the findings of a large survey of Canadian organizations that found 52% had training programs to improve skills of employees at all levels of the organization, and 36% had formal training programs.[7] In 2000, the average per capita expenditures on training and development across all industries was $859 per year. Companies in primary industries spent the most, $1560, followed by technology and communication at $1437, financial services at $1171 and provincial and federal governments at $1057. The average expenditure on training and development was 1.8% of payroll.[8]

Matching the Manager to the Strategy

The most appropriate type of general manager needed to effectively implement a new corporate or business strategy depends on the desired strategic direction of the firm or business unit. Executives with a particular mix of skills and experiences may be classified as an executive type and paired with a specific corporate strategy. For example, an organization following a concentration strategy emphasizing vertical or horizontal growth would probably want an aggressive new chief executive with a great deal of experience in that particular industry—a *dynamic industry expert*. A diversification strategy, in contrast, might call for someone with an analytical mind who is highly knowledgeable in other industries and can manage diverse product lines—an *analytical portfolio manager*. A firm choosing to follow a stability strategy would probably want as its CEO a *cautious profit planner*, a person with a conservative style, a production or engineering background, and experience with controlling budgets, capital expenditures, inventories, and standardization procedures. Weak companies in a relatively attractive industry tend to turn to a type of challenge-oriented executive known as the *turnaround specialist* to save the company. Albert J. Dunlap, known as "Chainsaw Al" or "Rambo in Pinstripes," was a premier example of a turnaround "artist" who saved troubled corporations by trimming expenses and downsizing the workforce. After restoring Scott Paper to profitability, Dunlap successfully did the same to Sunbeam Corporation. Unfortunately, Dunlap was unable to build a company once he had turned it around, so he chose to acquire three companies—each showing losses and needing to be "turned around." Dunlap was soon fired by the board in favour of an executive with a less mercurial management style who could regain the confidence of both investors and the employees.[9] If a company cannot be saved, a *professional liquidator* might be called on by a bankruptcy court to close the firm and liquidate its assets. Research tends to support the conclusion that as a firm's environment changes, it tends to change the type of top executive to implement a new strategy.[10] For example, during the 1990s when the emphasis was on growth in a company's core products or services, the most desired background for a CEO was either in marketing or international, in contrast to the emphasis on finance during the 1980s when conglomerate diversification was popular.[11]

This approach is in agreement with Chandler's ideas presented in **Chapter 8**. Chandler suggested that the most appropriate CEO of a company would change as a firm moved from one stage of development to another. Because priorities certainly change over an organization's life, successful organizations need to select managers who have skills and characteristics appropriate to the organization's particular stage of development and position in its life cycle. For example, founders of firms tend to have functional backgrounds in technological specialties, whereas successors tend to have backgrounds in marketing and administration.[12] A change in the environment leading to a change in a company's strategy also leads to a change in the top management team. For example, a trend in the 1990s of using internally focused, efficiency-oriented strategies led to the domination of top management teams by older managers with longer company and industry tenure, and with efficiency-oriented backgrounds in operations, engineering, and accounting.[13]

A large study of organizations over a 25-year period revealed that CEOs in these companies tended to have the same functional specialization as the former CEO, especially when the past CEO's strategy continued to be successful. This may be a pattern for successful organizations.[14] In particular, it explains why so many prosperous companies tend to recruit their top executives from one particular area. At Procter & Gamble, the route to the CEO's position has traditionally been through brand management with a strong emphasis on marketing—and more recently international experience. In other firms, the route may be through manufacturing, marketing, accounting, or finance, depending on what the corporation has always considered its key area (and its overall strategic orientation).

SELECTION AND MANAGEMENT DEVELOPMENT

Selection and development are important not only to ensure that people with the right mix of skills and experiences are initially hired, but also to help them grow on the job so that they might be prepared for future promotions.

Executive Succession: Insiders versus Outsiders

executive succession
the process of planning for and replacing key top managers

Executive succession is the process of replacing a key top manager. Given that two-thirds of all major organizations worldwide replaced their CEO at least once between 1995 and 2000, for instance, it is important that the firm plan for this eventuality.[15] It is especially important for a company that usually promotes from within to prepare its current managers for promotion. Companies known for being excellent training grounds for executive talent are Xerox, Royal Bank of Canada, Bristol-Myers Squibb, General Electric, Hewlett-Packard, McDonalds, McKinsey & Company, Microsoft, Nike, PepsiCo, Pfizer, and Procter & Gamble. Some of the best practices for top management succession are encouraging boards to help the CEO create a succession plan, identifying succession candidates below the top layer, measuring internal candidates against outside candidates to ensure the development of a comprehensive set of skills, and providing appropriate financial incentives.[16] See the boxed feature to see how Hewlett-Packard identifies those with potential for executive leadership positions.

Prosperous firms tend to look outside for CEO candidates only if they have no obvious internal candidates. Firms in trouble, however, tend to choose outsiders to lead them.[17] For example, one study of 22 firms undertaking a turnaround strategy found that the CEO was replaced in all but two companies. Of all the changes of CEO (several firms had more than one CEO during this period), only 25% were insiders—75% were outsiders.[18] The probability of an outsider being chosen to lead a firm that is in difficulty increases if there is no internal heir apparent, the last CEO was fired, and if the board of directors comprises a large percentage of outsiders.[19] Boards realize that the best way to force a change in strategy is to hire a new CEO with no connections to the current strategy.[20]

Identifying Abilities and Potential

**performance appraisal
system** A system that
standardizes performance appraisals and
makes them objective
by providing uniform
processes and criteria

A company can identify and prepare its people for important positions in several ways. One approach is to establish a sound **performance appraisal system** to identify good performers with promotion potential. A survey of corporate planners and human resource executives revealed that approximately 80% made some attempt to identify managers' talents and behavioural tendencies so that they could place a manager with a likely fit to a given competitive

---

How Hewlett-Packard Identifies Potential Executives

Hewlett-Packard identifies those with high potential for executive leadership by looking for six broad competencies that the company believes are necessary:

1. *Practice the HP way* by building trust and respect, focusing on achievement, demonstrating integrity, being innovative with customers, contributing to the community, and developing organizational decision making.

2. *Lead change and learning* by recognizing and acting on signals for change, leading organizational change, learning from organizational experience, removing barriers to change, developing self, and challenging and developing others.

3. *Know the internal and external environments* by anticipating global trends, acting on trends, and learning from others.

4. *Lead strategy setting* by inspiring breakthrough business strategy, leading the strategy-making process, committing to business vision, creating long-range strategies, building financial strategies, and defining a business-planning system.

5. *Align the organization* by working across boundaries, implementing competitive cost structures, developing alliances and partnerships, planning and managing core business, and designing the organization.

6. *Achieve results* by building a track record, establishing accountability, supporting calculated risks, making tough individual decisions, and resolving performance problems.

Source: R.M. Fulmer, P.A. Gibbs, and M. Goldsmith, "The New HP Way: Leveraging Strategy with Diversity, Leadership Development and Decentralization," *Strategy & Leadership* (October/November/December, 1999), pp. 21–29.

---

strategy.[21] A company should examine its human resource system to ensure not only that people are being hired without regard to their racial, ethnic, or religious background, but also that they are being identified for training and promotion in the same manner. Diversity in management could be a competitive advantage in a multi-ethnic world. With more women in the workplace, an increasing number are moving into top management. Recent studies are suggesting that female executives score higher than men on motivating others, fostering communication, producing high-quality work, and listening to others, while there is no difference in strategic planning or in analyzing issues.[22] Another study showed that cultural and racial diversity in organizations interacted with business strategy in determining firm performance. This was important in showing that diversity does in fact add value and, within the proper context, contributes to an organization's competitive advantage.[23] More specifically, a more diverse workforce is more costly to coordinate, so when sales growth is low or negative, there may be no bottom-line improvement associated with a diverse workforce.

assessment centres a selection technique that uses simulations of organizational work to gauge performance potential

Many large organizations are using **assessment centres** to evaluate a person's suitability for an advanced position. Organizations such as the Canadian government, IBM, Sears, and GE have successfully used assessment centres. Because each is specifically tailored to its organization, these assessment centres are unique. They use special interviews, management games, in-basket exercises, leaderless group discussions, case analyses, decision-making exercises, and oral presentations to assess the potential of employees for specific positions. Promotions into these positions are based on performance levels in the assessment centre. Many assessment centres have been able to accurately predict subsequent job performance.

job rotation moving employees between jobs to increase their experience in different types of work

Job rotation, moving people from one job to another, is also used in many large organizations to ensure that employees are gaining the appropriate mix of experiences to prepare them for future responsibilities. Rotating people among divisions is one way that the corporation can improve the level of organizational learning. For example, companies that pursue related diversification strategies through internal development make greater use of interdivisional transfers of people than do companies that grow through unrelated acquisitions. Apparently the companies that grow internally attempt to transfer important knowledge and skills throughout the corporation in order to achieve some sort of synergy.[24] In addition to conferring these benefits, job rotation makes work more satisfying and meaningful for employees, according to the Job Characteristics Model (as discussed in **Chapter 8**). So not only does the broad range of skills help the organization develop important learning qualities that will make it more efficient and responsive, but job rotation also makes jobs better for the people occupying them and leads to improved workplace attitudes.

PROBLEMS IN RETRENCHMENT

downsizing the planned elimination of jobs

Downsizing (sometimes called "rightsizing") refers to the planned elimination of positions or jobs. This program is often used to implement retrenchment strategies. Because the financial community is likely to react favourably to announcements of downsizing from a company in difficulty, such a program may provide some short-term benefits such as raising the company's stock price. If not done properly, however, downsizing may result in less, rather than more, productivity. One study found that a 10% reduction in people resulted in only a 1.5% reduction in costs, profits increased in only half the firms downsizing, and that the stock price of downsized firms increased over three years, but not as much as did that of firms that did not downsize.[25] Why were the results so marginal? Another study of downsizing revealed that about two-thirds of the time, either the wrong jobs were eliminated or blanket offers of early retirement prompted managers, even those considered invaluable, to leave. After the layoffs, the remaining employees had to do not only their work but also the work of the people who had gone. Because the survivors often didn't know how to do the tasks that were new to them, morale and productivity plummeted.[26] Another result of downsizing is that creativity drops significantly (affecting new product development) and it becomes very difficult to keep high performers from leaving the company.[27] In addition, cost-conscious executives tend to defer maintenance, skimp on training, delay new product introductions, and avoid risky new businesses—all of which leads to lower sales and eventually to lower profits.

Downsizing occurs in virtually all sectors of the Canadian economy, in both unionized and non-unionized facilities. Despite the mixed success with downsizing, there is little to suggest that this management practice will continue to reduce costs and increase the strategic flexibility of organizations. A recent study showed that a majority of Canadian businesses underwent some sort of downsizing between 1995 and 1997.[28] The job losses that took place at this time were mostly low-skilled jobs, requiring only skills that were relatively commonplace in the workforce. In other words, some people and some jobs are more likely to be targets of downsizing than others.

A good retrenchment strategy can thus be implemented well in terms of organizing but poorly in terms of staffing. A situation can develop in which retrenchment feeds on itself and acts to further weaken rather than strengthen the company. Research indicates that companies undertaking cost-cutting programs are four times more likely than others to cut costs again, typically by reducing staff.[29] This happened at Eastman Kodak and Xerox during the 1990s, but the companies were still having difficulty in 2001. In contrast, firms that downsize successfully undertake a strategic reorientation, not just a bloodletting of employees. Research shows that when companies use downsizing as part of a larger restructuring program to narrow company focus, they enjoy better performance.[30]

There are no standard recipes for how to downsize successfully. Consider the following guidelines that have been proposed:[31]

- **Eliminate unnecessary work instead of making across-the-board cuts.** Spend the time to research where money is going and eliminate the task, not the workers, if it doesn't add value to what the firm is producing. Reduce the number of administrative levels rather than the number of individual positions. Look for interdependent relationships before eliminating activities. Identify and protect core competencies.

- **Contract out work that others can do more cheaply.** For example, many organizations contract out their mailroom and printing services to Xerox, payroll and benefits administration to Ceredian, and food services to Aramark. Outsourcing may be cheaper than vertical integration and poses no strategic threat to the organization because these activities do not significantly contribute to competitive advantage.

- **Plan for long-run efficiencies.** Don't simply eliminate all postponable expenses, such as maintenance, R & D, and advertising, in the unjustifiable hope that the environment will become more supportive. Continue to hire, grow, and develop—particularly in critical areas.

- **Communicate the reasons for actions.** Tell employees not only why the company is downsizing, but also what the company is trying to achieve. Promote educational programs.

- **Invest in the remaining employees.** Because most survivors in a corporate downsizing will probably be doing different tasks from what they were doing before the change, firms need to draft new job specifications, performance standards, appraisal techniques, and compensation packages. Additional training is needed to ensure that everyone has the proper skills to deal with expanded jobs and responsibilities. Empower key individuals or groups, and emphasize team building. Identify, protect, and mentor people with leadership talent.

- **Develop value-added jobs to balance out job elimination.** When no other jobs are currently available within the organization to transfer employees to, management must consider other staffing alternatives. Harley-Davidson, for example, worked with the company's unions to find other work for surplus employees by moving work previously done by suppliers into Harley plants.

Adhering to as many of these guidelines as possible will increase the likelihood of achieving the goals of downsizing while minimizing some of the potentially dysfunctional consequences. Whatever approach to downsizing is used, it must start with an assessment of the organization's current workforce and a determination of future requirements. When downsizing must occur, it is because there is a mismatch between these two. Sometimes an organization can effectively make the workforce adjustments it needs by a combination of attrition and a hiring freeze, stopping the flow of employees into the organization. Often this method does not create results quickly enough, so more active strategies to retrain and transfer existing employees or terminate work arrangements are necessary. **Figure 9–1** on page 234 shows a range of downsizing techniques used by Canadian organizations.

INTERNATIONAL ISSUES IN STAFFING

Implementing a strategy of international expansion takes a lot of planning and can be very expensive. Nearly 80% of mid-size and larger companies send their employees abroad, and 45% plan to increase the number they have on foreign assignment. A complete package for

Figure 9–1 Canadian Downsizing Practices

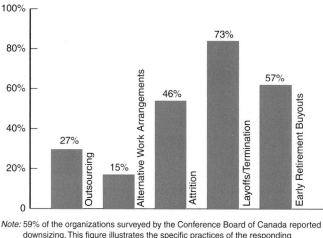

Note: 59% of the organizations surveyed by the Conference Board of Canada reported downsizing. This figure illustrates the specific practices of the responding organizations. Reporting of multiple downsizing practices was possible.

Source: Compensation Planning Outlook 1997, The Conference Board of Canada.

one executive working in another country costs from $300 000 to $1 million annually. Nevertheless, between 10% and 20% of all managers sent abroad returned early because of job dissatisfaction or difficulties in adjusting to a foreign country. Of those who stayed for the duration of their assignment, nearly one-third did not perform as well as expected. One-fourth of those completing an assignment left their company within one year of returning home—often leaving to join a competitor.[32] One common mistake is failing to educate the person about the customs in other countries.

Because of cultural differences, managerial style and human resource practices must be tailored to fit the particular situations in other countries. Since only 11% of human resource managers have ever worked abroad, most have little understanding of a global assignment's unique personal and professional challenges and thus fail to develop the training necessary for such an assignment.[33] Ninety percent of companies select employees for an international assignment based on their technical expertise, while ignoring other areas.[34] This situation is, however, improving. Multinational corporations are now putting more emphasis on inter-cultural training for those managers being sent on an assignment to a foreign country. This training is one of the commonly cited reasons for the lower expatriate failure rates—6% or less—for European and Japanese MNCs, which have emphasized cross-cultural experiences, compared with a 35% failure rate for US-based MNCs.[35]

To improve organizational learning, many multinational corporations are providing their managers with international assignments lasting as long as five years. Upon their return to headquarters, these expatriates have an in-depth understanding of the company's operations in another part of the world. This has value to the extent that these employees communicate this understanding to others in decision-making positions. Unfortunately, not all corporations appropriately manage international assignments. While out of the country, a person may be overlooked for an important promotion (out of sight, out of mind). Upon the employee's return to the home country, co-workers may deprecate the out-of-country experience as a waste of time.

A study of 750 US, Japanese, and European companies found that the companies that do a good job of managing foreign assignments follow three general practices:[36]

- When making international assignments, they focus on transferring knowledge and developing global leadership.

- They give foreign assignments to people whose technical skills are matched or exceeded by their cross-cultural abilities.
- They end foreign assignments with a deliberate repatriation process with career guidance and jobs in which the employees can apply what they learned in their assignments.

Once an organization has established itself in another country, it hires and promotes people from the host country into higher-level positions. For example, most large multinational corporations (MNCs) attempt to fill managerial positions in their subsidiaries with well-qualified citizens of the host countries. Unilever and IBM take this approach to international staffing. This policy serves to placate nationalistic governments and to better attune management practices to the host country's culture. The danger in using primarily foreign nationals to staff managerial positions in subsidiaries is the increased likelihood of suboptimization (the local subsidiary ignores the needs of the larger parent corporation). This makes it difficult for a multinational corporation to meet its long-term, worldwide objectives. To a local national in an MNC subsidiary, the corporation as a whole is an abstraction. Communication and coordination across subsidiaries become more difficult. As it becomes harder to coordinate the activities of several international subsidiaries, an MNC will have serious problems operating in a global industry.

Another approach to staffing the managerial positions of multinational corporations is to use people with an international orientation, regardless of their country of origin or host country assignment. This is a widespread practice among European firms. For example, Electrolux, a Swedish firm, had a French director in its Singapore factory. Using third-country "nationals" can allow for more opportunities for promotion than does Unilever's policy of hiring local people, but it can also result in more misunderstandings and conflicts with the local employees and with the host country's government.

Some organizations draw on the skills of immigrants and their children to staff key positions when negotiating entry into another country and when selecting an executive to manage the company's new foreign operations. For example, when General Motors wanted to learn more about business opportunities in China, it turned to Shirley Young, a vice-president of marketing at GM. Born in Shanghai and fluent in the Chinese language and customs, Young was instrumental in helping GM negotiate a $1 billion joint venture with Shanghai Automotive to build a Buick plant in China. With other Chinese Americans, Young formed a committee to advise GM on relations with China. Although just a part of a larger team of GM employees working on the joint venture, Young coached GM employees on Chinese customs and traditions.[37]

Multinational corporations with a high level of international interdependence among activities need to provide their managers with significant international assignments and experiences as part of their training and development. Such assignments provide future corporate leaders with a series of valuable international contacts in addition to a better personal understanding of international issues and global linkages among corporate activities. Executive recruiters report that more major corporations are now requiring candidates to have international experience.[38]

9.2 Leading

leading a managerial activity that motivates and coordinates an organization's human resources

Implementation also involves **leading** people to use their abilities and skills most effectively and efficiently to achieve organizational objectives. Without direction, people tend to do their work according to their personal view of what tasks should be done, how, and in what order. They may approach their work as they have in the past or emphasize those tasks that they most enjoy—regardless of the organization's priorities. This can create real problems, particularly if the company is operating internationally and must adjust to customs and traditions in other countries. This direction may take the form of management leadership, communicated norms of behaviour from the organizational culture, or agreements among workers in autonomous work groups. It may also be accomplished more formally through action planning or through programs such as management by objectives and total quality management.[39]

MANAGING ORGANIZATIONAL CULTURE

organizational culture
the shared understandings of appropriate behaviour within an organization

Because an organization's culture can exert a powerful influence on the behaviour of all employees, it can strongly affect a company's ability to shift its strategic direction. A problem for a strong culture is that a change in mission, objectives, strategies, or policies is not likely to be successful if it is in opposition to the accepted culture of the company. **Organizational culture** has a strong tendency to resist change because its very reason for existence often rests on preserving stable relationships and patterns of behaviour. For example, the male-dominated, Japanese-centred organizational culture of the giant Mitsubishi Corporation created problems for the company when it implemented its growth strategy in North America. The alleged sexual harassment of its female employees by male supervisors resulted in a lawsuit and a boycott of the company's automobiles by the National Organization for Women.[40]

There is no one best organizational culture. An optimal culture is one that best supports the mission and strategy of the company of which it is a part. This means that, like structure and staffing, organizational culture should support the strategy. Unless new strategy is in complete agreement with the culture, any significant change in strategy should be followed by a modification of the organization's culture. Although organizational culture can be changed, it may often take a long time and it requires much effort. A key job of management involves managing organizational culture. In doing so, management must evaluate what a particular change in strategy means to the organizational culture, assess whether a change in culture is needed, and decide whether an attempt to change the culture is worth the likely costs.

Assessing Strategy–Culture Compatibility

When implementing a new strategy, a company should take the time to assess strategy–culture compatibility (see **Figure 9–2**). Consider the following questions regarding the corporation's culture:

1. Is the planned strategy compatible with the company's current culture? If yes, full steam ahead. Tie organizational changes into the company's culture by identifying how the new strategy will achieve the mission better than the current strategy does. *If not...*

2. Can the culture be easily modified to make it more compatible with the new strategy? If yes, move forward carefully by introducing a set of culture-changing activities such as minor structural modifications, training and development activities, and/or hiring new managers who are more compatible with the new strategy. For example, implementing a strategy aimed at reducing costs requires making changes in how some things are done but often leaves the organization's structure intact. Here the culture would have to adapt to these modifications in order for productivity to increase. *If not...*

3. Is management willing and able to make major organizational changes and accept probable delays and a likely increase in costs? If yes, manage around the culture by establishing a new structural unit to implement the new strategy. Sometimes radical changes are needed to be more competitive. In situations were current structures, cultures, and procedures are very inflexible, management might decide to establish a completely new division that operates in a fundamentally different way. This is what General Motors did by creating its Saturn division. *If not...*

Figure 9–2 Assessing Strategy–Culture Compatibility

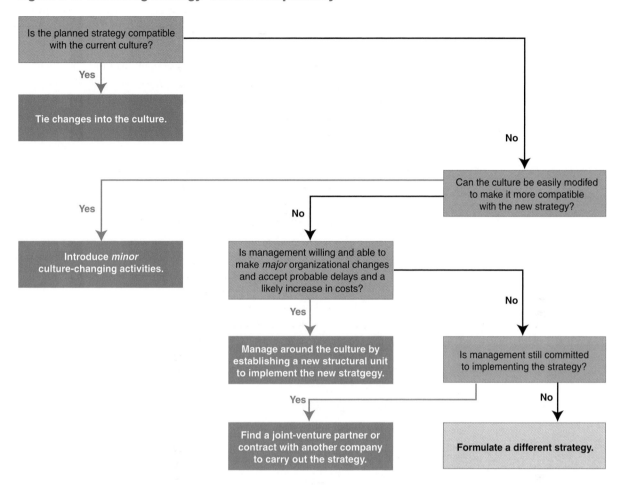

4. Is management still committed to implementing the strategy? *If it is,* find a joint-venture partner or contract with another company to carry out the strategy. *If not,* formulate a different strategy.

Managing Cultural Change through Communication

Communication is a key to the effective management of any type of change. It is necessary for positively effecting change, but not sufficient. Rationale for strategic changes should be communicated to workers not only in newsletters and speeches, but also in training and development programs. Companies in which major cultural changes have taken place successfully had the following characteristics in common:[41]

- The CEO and other top managers had a strategic vision of what the company could become and communicated this vision to employees at all levels. The current performance of the company was compared with that of its competition and constantly updated.

- The vision was translated into the key elements necessary to accomplish that vision. For example, if the vision called for the company to become a leader in quality or service, aspects of quality and service were pinpointed for improvement and appropriate measurement systems were developed to monitor them. These measures were communicated widely through contests, formal and informal recognition, and monetary rewards, among other devices.

As indicated in **Chapter 8**, organizational change is always difficult. Not only do organizational members need to be convinced of the need for change, but it is very rare that organizational changes do not create winners and losers. In other words, it is very difficult to change any part of an organization without affecting people, jobs, and practices *throughout* the organization. Organizational culture is particularly difficult to change because it is intangible; it does not exist in any particular place so it cannot be studied, transformed, or moved around. Because of this, changing organizational culture is *always* difficult. Organizational culture is based on the beliefs and assumptions that organizational members have. To change cultures, people must learn to think in different ways and come to hold different ideas about how things should be done. An interesting study of cultural change at Nova Scotia Power showed that management's cultural change program was viewed as just a passing management fad, and as a result it was resisted just about every step of the way.[42] The process of changing cultures is a slow one and needs to be consistently reinforced by communication and action. Top leadership support is critical in this process, as is the willingness to adjust the workforce through selection and socialization so that person–organization fit is increased.[43] See the boxed insert for a discussion of how a cultural change was introduced at Suncor.

Cultural Change at Suncor

Suncor Energy Inc. of Calgary experienced significant performance problems in the early 1990s. Contributing to its poor profits were a major downsizing, a serious fire at one of its refineries, and inter-group communication problems. Part of Suncor's return to profitability came from a cultural change that started with a new vision. It defined a core purpose to "consistently deliver outstanding achievements in Canadian petroleum and related businesses." To do this, it moved to a "more flexible, more innovative environment that is open to ideas and focuses on individual initiative." In other words, a new way of doing things was going to be required to achieve its core purpose. By keeping employees informed of changes, Suncor was able to earn "a level of trust and commitment that made the turnaround happen quickly and professionally." Changing an organization's culture requires changing practices, procedures, and routines. Because many aspects of the organization must change at once, cultural change tends to be a major event in many organizations. To increase the likelihood of a successful cultural change, organizations must do two things:

- Create an awareness of the need for change and the risks of not doing so
- Build a belief that all employees are part of the change and key to its success

Only after taking steps to insure awareness and involvement will employees be committed to the process of change. And without this commitment, any change agenda will be likely to fail.

Source: "Changing the Corporate Culture from Downsizing to Growth," *Canadian Speeches* (June 1996), pp. 45–50, quoted in S.R. Robbins and N. Langton, *Organizational Behaviour: Concepts, Controversies, Applications,* 2nd Canadian edition (Toronto: Pearson Education, 2001), p. 593. Reprinted with permission by Pearson Education Canada Inc.

Managing Diverse Cultures Following an Acquisition

When a company is merging with or acquiring another company, top management must give some consideration to a potential clash of organizational cultures. Research shows that integrating culture is a top challenge for many companies.[44] It is dangerous to assume that the firms can simply be integrated into the same reporting structure. The greater the gap between the cultures of the acquired firm and the acquiring firm, the faster executives in the acquired firm quit their jobs and valuable talent is lost.

There are four general methods of managing two different cultures (See **Figure 9–3**). The choice of which method to use should be based on (1) how much members of the acquired firm value preserving their own culture and (2) how attractive they perceive the culture of the acquirer to be.[45]

1. **Integration** involves a relatively balanced give-and-take of cultural and managerial practices between the merger partners, and no strong imposition of cultural change on either company. It merges cultures in such a way that the separate cultures of both firms are preserved in the resulting culture. This is what occurred in the creation of Aliant Telecom (formed by the merger of Island Tel, New Tel, MT&T, NB Tel). Top management in various divisions were drawn from all the formerly independent companies, in an attempt to keep the best parts of all organizations and to treat all cultures with equal respect.

2. **Assimilation** involves the domination of one organization over the other. The domination is not forced, but it is welcomed by members of the acquired firm, who may feel for many reasons that their culture and managerial practices have not produced success. The acquired firm surrenders its culture and adopts the culture of the acquiring company. See the boxed feature describing this method of acculturation when Admiral was acquired by Maytag Corporation.

Figure 9–3 Methods of Managing the Culture of an Acquired Firm

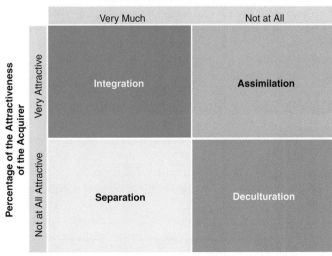

How Much Members of the Acquired Firm Value Preservation of Their Own Culture

Source: A. Nahavardi and A.R. Malekzadeh, "Acculturation in Mergers and Acquisitions," *Academy of Management Review* (January 1988), p. 83. Copyright © 1988 by the Academy of Management. Reprinted by permission of Academy of Management via the Copyright Clearance Center.

3. **Separation** is characterized by a separation of the two companies' cultures. They are structurally separated, without cultural exchange. This is what happened in some instances when the Canadian chartered banks acquired larger brokerages after industry deregulation in the late 1980s. For example, CIBC acquired Wood Gundy to be able to provide a full range of financial and brokerage services for personal and commercial clients. The two organizations were kept somewhat separate, with little effort made to integrate people, structures, and cultures. But after years of mediocre performance, the operations of the two organizations were more extensively merged.

4. **Deculturation** involves the disintegration of one company's culture resulting from unwanted and extreme pressure from the other to impose its culture and practices. This is the most common and most destructive method of dealing with two different cultures. It is often accompanied by much confusion, conflict, resentment, and stress. This is a primary reason why so many executives tend to leave after their firm is acquired.[46] Such a merger typically results in poor performance by the acquired company and its eventual divestment. In the CIBC–Wood Gundy example previously discussed, the organization

---

Admiral Assimilates Maytag's Culture

Maytag's organizational culture had been dominated[47] almost from the beginning of the company by the concept of quality. Maytag employees took great pride in being known as the "dependability people." Over the years, Maytag Company consistently advertised that their repairmen were "lonely" because Maytag products rarely, if ever, needed repair.

Admiral's history had, however, been quite different. Prior to Maytag's purchase of Magic Chef (and thus Admiral) in 1986, Admiral had been owned by three different corporations. Its manufacturing plant in Galesburg, Illinois, had deteriorated to a dismal level by the time Maytag acquired it. Refrigerators sometimes rolled off the assembly line with screws driven in crooked and temperature balances askew.

Maytag's management had always wanted to have its own Maytag brand refrigerator. That was one reason why it purchased Admiral. But it was worried that Admiral might not be able to produce a quality product to Maytag's specifications. To improve Admiral's quality, Maytag's top management decided to integrate Admiral directly into Maytag Company operations. As a result, all Admiral functional departments, except marketing, reported directly to the Maytag Company president.

Under the direction of Leonard Hadley, while he was serving as Maytag Company president, a project was initiated to design and manufacture a refrigerator for the Maytag brand at the Admiral plant. When Hadley first visited Admiral's facilities to discuss the design of a Maytag line of refrigerators, Admiral personnel asked Hadley when the name on their plant's water tower would be changed from Admiral to Maytag. Hadley (acknowledging Maytag's cultural concerns regarding quality) responded: "When you earn it."

The refrigerator resulting from the Maytag–Admiral collaboration was a huge success. The project crystallized corporate management's philosophy for forging synergies among the Maytag companies while simultaneously allowing the individual expertise of those units to flourish. Admiral's employees were willing to accept the dominance of Maytag's strong quality-oriented culture because they respected it. In turn, they expected to be treated with some respect for their tradition of skill in refrigeration technology.

first tried a separation approach, and then followed it up with a deculturation approach based on CIBC's hierarchical structure and more conservative strategies. At that time, many brokers left the organization to pursue opportunities in less formalized and bureaucratic brokerages. The markedly different types of cultures in banks (conservative and cautious) and brokerages (entrepreneurial and risk-taking) made the task of merging difficult.

ACTION PLANNING

action plan detailed steps to be performed in the strategy implementation process

Activities can be directed toward accomplishing strategic goals through action planning. At a minimum, an **action plan** states what actions are going to be taken, by whom, during what time frame, and with what expected results. After a program has been selected to implement a particular strategy, an action plan should be developed to put the program in place.

Take the example of a company choosing forward vertical integration through the acquisition of a retailing chain as its growth strategy. Now that it owns its own retail outlets, it must integrate the stores into the company. One of the many programs it would have to develop is a new advertising program for the stores. See **Table 9–1** for an example of an action plan for a new advertising and promotion program. The resulting action plan to develop a new advertising program should include much of the following information:

1. **Specific actions to be taken to make the program operational:** One action might be to contact three reputable advertising agencies and ask them to prepare a proposal for a new radio and newspaper ad campaign based on the theme "Jones Surplus is now a part of Ajax Continental. Prices are lower. Selection is better."

2. **Dates to begin and end each action:** Time would have to be allotted not only to select and contact three agencies, but also to allow them sufficient time to prepare a detailed proposal. For example, allow one week to select and contact the agencies plus three months for them to prepare detailed proposals to present to the company's marketing director. Also allow some time to decide which proposal to accept.

3. **Person (identified by name and title) responsible for carrying out each action:** List someone—such as Jan Lewis, advertising manager, or Rick Carter, advertising assistant—who can be put in charge of each action.

4. **Person responsible for monitoring the timeliness and effectiveness of each action:** Indicate that Jan Lewis is responsible for ensuring that the proposals are of good quality and are priced within the planned program budget. She will be the primary company contact for the ad agencies and will report on the progress of the program once a week to the company's marketing director.

5. **Expected financial and physical consequences of each action:** Estimate when a completed ad campaign will be ready to show top management and how long it will take after approval to begin to air the ads. Estimate also the expected increase in store sales over the six-month period after the ads are first aired. Indicate whether "recall" measures will be used to help assess the ad campaign's effectiveness plus how, when, and by whom the recall data will be collected and analyzed.

6. **Contingency plans:** Indicate how long it will take to get an acceptable ad campaign to show top management if none of the initial proposals is acceptable.

Action plans are important for several reasons. First, action plans serve as a link between strategy formulation and evaluation and control. Second, the action plan specifies what needs to be done differently from the way operations are currently carried out. Third, during the evaluation and control process that comes later, an action plan helps in both the appraisal of

Table 9–1 Example of an Action Plan

Action Plan for Jan Lewis, Advertising Manager, and Rick Carter, Advertising Assistant, Ajax Continental

Program Objective: To Run a New Advertising and Promotion Campaign for the Combined Jones Surplus/Ajax Continental Retail Stores for the Coming Holiday Season Within a Budget of $XX.

Program Activities:
1. Identify 3 Best Ad Agencies for New Campaign.
2. Ask 3 Ad Agencies to Submit a Proposal for a New Advertising and Promotion Campaign for Combined Stores.
3. Agencies Present Proposals to Marketing Manager.
4. Select Best Proposal and Inform Agencies of Decision.
5. Agency Presents Winning Proposal to Top Management.
6. Ads Air on TV and Promotions Appear in Stores.
7. Measure Results of Campaign in Terms of Viewer Recall and Increase in Store Sales.

Action Steps	Responsibility	Start–End
1. A. Review previous programs	Lewis & Carter	1/1–2/1
B. Discuss with boss	Lewis & Smith	2/1–2/3
C. Decide on 3 agencies	Lewis	2/4
2. A. Write specifications for ad	Lewis	1/15–1/20
B. Assistant writes ad request	Carter	1/20–1/30
C. Contact ad agencies	Lewis	2/5–2/8
D. Send request to 3 agencies	Carter	2/10
E. Meet with agency acct. execs	Lewis & Carter	2/16–2/20
3. A. Agencies work on proposals	Acct. Execs	2/23–5/1
B. Agencies present proposals	Carter	5/1–5/15
4. A. Select best proposal	Lewis	5/15–5/20
B. Meet with winning agency	Lewis	5/22–5/30
C. Inform losers	Carter	6/1
5. A. Fine-tune proposal	Acct. Exec	6/1–7/1
B. Presentation to management	Lewis	7/1–7/3
6. A. Ads air on TV	Lewis	9/1–12/24
B. Floor displays in stores	Carter	8/20–12/24
7. A. Gather recall measures of ads	Carter	9/1–12/24
B. Evaluate sales data	Carter	1/1–1/10
C. Prepare analysis of campaign	Carter	1/10–2/15

performance and in the identification of any remedial actions, as needed. In addition, the explicit assignment of responsibilities for implementing and monitoring the programs may contribute to better motivation.

MANAGEMENT BY OBJECTIVES

management by objectives a program of goals and feedback mechanisms, set by organization-wide participation, that is designed to improve organizational performance

Management by objectives (MBO) is an organization-wide approach to help ensure purposeful action toward desired objectives. MBO links organizational objectives to the behaviour of individuals. Because it is a system that links plans with performance, it is a powerful implementation technique. The MBO process involves four steps:

1. Establishing and communicating organizational objectives

2. Setting individual objectives (through superior–subordinate interaction) that help implement organizational ones

3. Developing an action plan of activities needed to achieve the objectives

4. Periodically (at least quarterly) reviewing performance as it relates to the objectives and including the results in the annual performance appraisal

MBO provides an opportunity for the organization to connect the objectives of people at each level to those at the next higher level. MBO, therefore, acts to tie together corporate, business, and functional objectives, as well as the strategies developed to achieve them. One of the real benefits of MBO is that it can reduce the amount of internal politics operating within a large organization. Political actions within a firm can cause conflict and create divisions between the very people and groups who should be working together to implement strategy. People are less likely to jockey for position if the company's mission and objectives are clear and they know that the reward system is based not on game playing, but on achieving clearly communicated, measurable objectives.

An interesting example of implementing MBO can be seen in the Research Branch of Agriculture Canada. Prior to using MBO, this branch had experienced many organizational changes, some a result of changes in government policy, others from changes in the department's own management. These changes were made to increase the "response of research to the needs of all segments of the Canadian food production industry. Central agencies of government have sought ways of predicting the benefits of research before it was started and of measuring its effectiveness before it was finished." Despite good intentions, may of the changes they made resulted in higher administrative costs and a decentralization of research programs that created some duplication of effort.[48] Dissatisfied with some of the results of previous organizational changes, the branch started to use MBO. First it identified scientists, their objectives, and the amount of time they devoted to each research project. With this information, rather than just relying on estimates, the branch was able to track the amount of research being done in each agricultural discipline. A meeting of directors formalized the final step in the MBO process. "Each station director was to receive commitments from scientists to meet specific goals and objectives, to establish a precise system of accountability, and to integrate management by objectives with estimates of monetary requirements and personnel assessments."[49] To further solidify the changes made under MBO and spread knowledge about branch research in various areas, a branch newspaper, *Tableau*, was launched.

TOTAL QUALITY MANAGEMENT

total quality management an operational philosophy based on commitment to customer satisfaction and continuous improvement

Total quality management (TQM) is an operational philosophy committed to customer satisfaction and continuous improvement. TQM is committed to excellence and to being the best in all functions. Because TQM aims to reduce costs and improve quality, it can be used as a program to implement either an overall low-cost or differentiation business strategy. About 92% of manufacturing companies and 69% of service firms have implemented some form of quality management practices.[50] Nevertheless, a report by McKinsey & Company reported that two-thirds of the TQM programs it examined had failed to produce expected improvements. An analysis of the successes and failures of TQM concluded that the key is top management. Successful TQM programs occur in those companies in which "top managers move beyond defensive and tactical orientations to embrace a developmental orientation."[51] TQM has four objectives:

1. Better, less variable quality of the product and service

2. Quicker, less variable response in processes to customer needs

3. Greater flexibility in adjusting to customers' shifting requirements

4. Lower cost through quality improvement and elimination of non-value-adding work[52]

According to TQM, faulty processes, not poorly motivated employees, are the cause of defects in quality. The program involves a significant change in organizational culture, requiring strong leadership from top management, employee training, empowerment of lower level employees (giving people more control over their work), and teamwork for it to succeed in a company. TQM emphasizes prevention, not correction. Inspection for quality still takes place, but the emphasis is on improving the process to prevent errors and deficiencies. Thus, quality circles or quality improvement teams are formed to identify problems and to suggest how to improve the processes that may be causing the problems. These are TQM's essential ingredients:[53]

- **An intense focus on customer satisfaction:** Everyone (not just people in the sales and marketing departments) understands that their jobs exist only because of customer needs. Thus, all jobs must be approached in terms of how it will affect customer satisfaction.

- **Internal as well as external customers:** An employee in the shipping department may be the internal customer of another employee who completes the assembly of a product, just as a person who buys the product is a customer of the entire company. An employee must be just as concerned with pleasing the internal customer as in satisfying the external customer.

- **Accurate measurement of every critical variable in a company's operations:** This means that employees have to be trained in what to measure, how to measure, and how to interpret the data. A rule of TQM is "you only improve what you measure."

- **Continuous improvement of products and services:** Everyone realizes that operations need to be continuously monitored to find ways to improve products and services.

- **New work relationships based on trust and teamwork:** The idea of empowerment—giving employees wide latitude in how they go about achieving the company's goals—is an important part of TQM. Research indicates that the key to TQM success lies in executive commitment, an open organizational culture, and employee empowerment.

Bombardier Inc. has incorporated TQM principles into its Six Sigma quality program that puts customer needs first, providing a systematic analysis to help in the continuous improvement of processes throughout the organization. This program is consistent with Bombardier's goals of meeting or exceeding customer, employee, and growth objectives. "Selecting the most promising resources to support this program on a full-time basis and involving everyone in the organization through learning and participation shows the commitment of the organization to making Six Sigma happen."[54] Trade liberalization and privatization in transportation industries have significantly increased competition for companies like Bombardier. As a result, successful firms must make measurable improvements in productivity and quality. Bombardier's mission to be an industry leader meets the challenge of these tougher requirements through TQM programs that refine procedures and enhance product quality. The result has been greater customer satisfaction.

INTERNATIONAL CONSIDERATIONS IN LEADING

In a study of 53 different national cultures, Hofstede found that each nation's unique culture could be identified using five dimensions. He found that national culture is so influential that it tends to overwhelm even a strong organizational culture. In measuring the differences among these dimensions of national culture from country to country, he was able to explain why a certain management practice might be successful in one nation but fail in another.[55]

1. **Power distance** is the extent to which a society accepts an unequal distribution of power in organizations. Malaysia and Mexico scored highest, whereas Germany and Austria

scored lowest. People in those countries scoring high on this dimension tend to prefer autocratic to more participative managers. In organizational contexts, the smaller the power distance, the more workers would be included and consulted in decision-making processes, and the more democratic their leaders' style would be. Hofstede speculated that understanding superiors, colleagues, and subordinates in work contexts would be facilitated by understanding previous experiences in the family and schools, where ideas about power distance are formed.

2. **Uncertainty avoidance** is the extent to which a society feels threatened by uncertain and ambiguous situations. This dimension reflects the level of discomfort in unstructured situations. Greece and Japan scored highest on disliking ambiguity, whereas the United States and Singapore scored lowest. People in those nations scoring high in this dimension tend to want career stability, formal rules, and clear-cut measures of performance. Standardization and formalization are sought out by organizational members as uncertainty-reducing mechanisms. In contrast, in cultures that are low-scoring in uncertainty avoidance, organizational members dislike rules, whether they are written or unwritten. Their acceptance of uncertainty makes them more tolerant of opinions different from their own.

3. **Individualism–collectivism** is the extent to which a society values individual freedom and independence of action compared with a tight social framework and loyalty to the group. The United States and Canada scored highest on individualism, whereas Mexico and Guatemala scored lowest. People in those nations scoring high on individualism tend to value individual success through competition. In organizational contexts, the importance of the task dominates concern over interpersonal relationships. Relationships are only valued to the extent they help accomplish tasks and contribute to individual successes. In contrast, cultures low on individualism (or high on collectivism) tend to value group success through co-operation. At work, relationships prevail over the tasks themselves, and workers have a strong sense of belonging to their organization.

4. **Masculinity–femininity** refers to the distribution of roles between the sexes. Hofstede's study showed that women's values differ less among societies than men's values, but that men's values varied tremendously. In some societies men's values were very assertive and competitive in comparison with women's, but in others they were modest and caring and quite similar to women's values. Femininity is the label for the modest and caring end of this continuum, while masculinity is the label for the assertive end. Japan and Mexico scored highest on masculinity, whereas France and Sweden scored lowest (or highest on femininity). People in those nations scoring high on masculinity tend to value clearly defined sex roles where men dominate and to emphasize performance and independence. Assertiveness is appreciated, and decisiveness is valued. In contrast, cultures scoring low on masculinity (and thus high on femininity) tend to value equality of the sexes where power is shared and to emphasize the quality of life and interdependence. Here assertiveness is ridiculed, self-monitoring behaviour is eschewed, and the quality of working life is valued over individual careers.

5. **Long- versus short-term orientation** is the extent to which society is oriented toward the past or the future. A long-term time orientation emphasizes the importance of hard work, education, and persistence as well as the importance of thrift. Organizations in these cultures should value strategic planning and other management techniques with a long-term payback. A short-term orientation, in contrast, emphasizes "a respect for tradition, fulfilling social obligations and protecting one's face."[56] Organizations in these cultures reward deference to superiors and clear status differentials between workers. Hong Kong and Japan scored highest on short-term orientation, whereas Pakistan scored the lowest.

These dimensions of national culture may help to explain why some management practices work well in some countries but not in others. For example, management by objectives (MBO), which originated in the United States, has succeeded in Germany, according to Hofstede, because the idea of replacing the arbitrary authority of the boss with the impersonal authority of mutually agreed-upon objectives fits the low power distance that is a dimension of the German culture. It has failed in France, however, because the French are used to high power distances—to accepting orders from a highly personalized authority. In addition, some of the difficulties experienced by US companies in using Japanese-style quality circles in TQM may stem from the extremely high value that American culture places on individualism. The differences between the US and Mexico in the dimensions of power distance (Mexico 104 versus US 46) and individualism–collectivism (US 91 versus Mexico 30) may help explain why some companies operating in both countries have difficulty adapting to the differences in customs.[57]

When one successful company in a country merges with another successful company in another country, the clash of organizational cultures is compounded by the clash of national cultures. With the value of cross-border mergers and acquisitions totalling $720 billion in 1999, the management of cultures is becoming a key issue in strategy implementation.[58] See the **Global Issue** feature to learn how differences in national and organizational cultures created conflict when Upjohn Company of the United States and Pharmacia AB of Sweden merged.

Global Issue

Cultural Differences Create Implementation Problems in Merger

When Upjohn Pharmaceuticals of Kalamazoo, Michigan, and Pharmacia AB of Stockholm, Sweden, merged in 1995, employees of both sides were optimistic for the newly formed Pharmacia & Upjohn, Inc. Both companies were second-tier competitors fighting for survival in a global industry. Together, the firms would create a global company that could compete scientifically with its bigger rivals.

Because Pharmacia had acquired an Italian firm in 1993, it also had a large operation in Milan. American executives scheduled meetings throughout the summer of 1996, only to cancel them when their European counterparts could not attend. Although it was common knowledge in Europe that most Swedes take the entire month of July for vacation and that Italians take off all of August, this was not common knowledge in Michigan. Differences in management styles became a special irritant. Swedes were used to an open system with autonomous work teams. Executives sought the whole group's approval before making an important decision. Upjohn executives followed the more traditional American top-down approach. Upon taking command of the newly merged firm, Dr. Zabriskie (who had been Upjohn's CEO), divided the company into departments reporting to the new London headquarters. He required frequent reports, budgets, and staffing updates. The Swedes reacted negatively to this top-down management hierarchical style. "It was degrading," said Stener Kvinnsland, head of Pharmacia's cancer research in Italy before he quit the new company.

The Italian operations baffled the Americans, even though the Italians felt comfortable with a hierarchical management style. Italy's laws and unions made layoffs difficult. Italian data and accounting were often inaccurate. Because the Americans didn't trust the data, they were constantly asking for verification. In turn, the Italians were concerned that the Americans were trying to take over Italian operations. At Upjohn, all workers were subject to testing for drug and alcohol abuse. Upjohn also banned smoking. At Pharmacia's Italian business centre, however, waiters poured wine freely every afternoon in the company dining room. Pharmacia's boardrooms were stocked with humidors for executives who smoked cigars during long meetings. After a brief attempt to enforce Upjohn's policies, the company dropped both the no-drinking and no-smoking policies for European workers.

Although the combined company had cut annual costs by $200 million, overall costs of the merger reached $800 million, some $200 million more than projected. Nevertheless, Jan Eckberg, CEO of Pharmacia before the merger, remained confident of the new company's ability to succeed. He admitted, however, that "we have to make some smaller changes to release the full power of the two companies."

Multinational corporations must pay attention to the many differences in cultural dimensions around the world and adjust their management practices accordingly. Cultural differences can easily go unrecognized by a headquarters staff that may interpret these differences as personality defects, whether the people in the subsidiaries are locals or expatriates. When conducting strategic planning in a multinational corporation, top management must be aware that the process will vary in accord with the national culture where a subsidiary is located. For example, in one MNC, the French expect concepts and key questions and answers. North American managers provide heavy financial analysis. Germans give precise dates and financial analysis. Information is usually late from Spanish and Moroccan operations and quotas are typically inflated. It is up to management to adapt to the differences.[59] Hofstede and Bond conclude: "Whether they like it or not, the headquarters of multinationals are in the business of multicultural management."[60]

9.3 Impact of the Internet on Staffing and Leading in Organizations

intranet a computer network to share information among an organization's employees

The widespread acceptance of the internet has created demand for the development of intranets in most large organizations. An **intranet** is an internal internet created for the use of an organization's employees. The availability of the World Wide Web, servers, chat rooms, bulletin boards, and electronic mail allows companies to use their existing technologies to build intranets without needing additional investment in hardware or software. Intranets support the development of virtual teams, disseminate information about the company's products and services, provide information about internal job openings and health benefits, and offer email and file transfer services so that people can transfer project information from one personal computer to another. Unlike the internet, an intranet is owned entirely by the corporation. Information posted on an intranet cannot be accessed by the general public without their being provided explicit access privileges. Intranets are protected from unauthorized entry by firewalls, software programs that check and verify the credentials of potential users. Unlike other technologies, intranets don't need standard hardware platforms, such as IBM or Macintosh, on which an application resides. The vast majority of companies report a positive return from their intranet investment.[61]

Intranets can be either static (updated periodically) or dynamic (updated continuously). Examples of static information are phone directories, internal job openings, employee benefits information, company news releases, corporate events, technical documents, and company policies and procedures. Examples of dynamic information are sales, inventory, and expense account transactions.

STATIC INTRANET APPLICATIONS

The primary goal of static intranet applications is to provide information when and if people need it. For example, a number of large corporations are installing internal directories where an employee can type key skills or experiences into the computer and get back the names and résumés of other employees within the firm who have those skills or experiences. Deere & Company uses a "People Who Know" database to help people with questions find people with answers. Bruce Boardman, head of metals research at Deere, states that the cost of the system is "less than the salary of one engineer—it pays for itself at least half a dozen times a year," especially when the production line stops and someone needs help immediately.

When Bechtel Corporation created a new division called Bechtel Systems & Infrastructure, Inc. (BSII), it developed a skills directory for the unit. The division was a combination of all Bechtel's work for governments around the world and included 6000 people.

According to Mary O'Donnell of BSII's human resource department, "We didn't know all the skills we had." The directory, based on Lotus Notes, contains employee résumés listing a person's skills; current project and when it will be completed; past projects; military, international, and supervisory experience; and other information. Together with online Notes forums called "twigs" (technical working groups), the system provides a way to find answers to technical questions. It also enables the division to staff jobs more quickly.

NatWest Markets, the investment banking division of Britain's NatWest Group, developed a Green Book containing the names of 800 people arranged by area of expertise within the five categories of financial products, industry sectors, geography, support, and business intelligence. About 100 of the people are "knowledge coordinators" who have volunteered to direct other employees not only to other people, but to legal documents or files. Interestingly, the people are not listed by titles. According to Victoria Ward, NatWest Markets' chief knowledge officer: "I'm not interested in titles. It might turn out that one of our best experts in securitization works in the equities unit, not in the debt unit. This is about function, not form."[62]

DYNAMIC INTRANET APPLICATIONS

Intranets can also be used effectively to process and exchange dynamic information by linking employees with company databases and proprietary transaction systems such as inventory and purchasing systems. Software like HotOffice allows project co-workers to access folders and read posted documents. The HotOffice system includes a bulletin board, group calendar, personal calendars, virtual meeting rooms for real-time discussions, and private email. For real-time collaboration over a LAN (local area network), Lotus Sametime is a software package that includes text chat and whiteboard applications as well as application sharing.[63] (See the **Internet Issue** feature for an example of how business people use the net to interact over long distances.)

Ford Motor Company's intranet connects 120 000 workstations at offices and factories worldwide to thousands of Ford websites containing proprietary information like market research, analyses of competitors' components, and rankings of the most efficient suppliers of parts. Its product development system allows engineers, designers, and suppliers to work from the same data. Every vehicle team has a website where team members can post questions and progress reports, note bottlenecks, and resolve issues. According to Paul Blumberg, director of product development, sharing such information widely has helped Ford reduce the time to get new models into production from 36 to 24 months. The company links its dealers into the intranet so they can order vehicles from the assembly plant, check on production status, and change orders up to seven days before a car is finished. The dealers are then able to offer custom ordering and delivery on every car or truck.[64]

ADVANTAGES AND DISADVANTAGES OF INTRANETS[65]

Intranets have many *advantages*, among them the following:

- **Speed, effectiveness, and relatively low cost:** Less time and money is spent on printing reams of paper and disseminating it to employees who often just dump it in the trash.
- **Elimination of time and space barriers:** People can find answers to their questions regardless of the time or the location.

■ **Basis in existing infrastructure:** Once a firm has the hardware in place to use the internet, it is very easy to create an intranet.

■ **Ease of use:** Accessing information on an intranet is much simpler and faster than digging into filing cabinets to find policy folders or calling friends to find an expert on a particular problem.

■ **Enhancement of productivity:** The time spent in searching for information is significantly reduced.

Intranets also have some *disadvantages*, including these:

■ **Need for information and hyperlinks to be continually updated:** Nothing is more frustrating than being sent to a site that is no longer operating or one that contains out-of-date information. Employees need to be periodically reminded to update their résumés.

■ **Frequent need for technology to be updated:** The increasing use of virtual work teams is pushing the development of video and voice systems on computers, requiring investments in newer, more powerful, and faster personal computers and workstations.

■ **Need for technical support to maintain the system:** People must be trained on how to use the intranet. Someone must monitor what people put on the intranet, such as résumés, to ensure that the information is correct.

■ **The critical issue of security:** Even well-constructed firewalls cannot keep out serious hackers who like to meddle with confidential documents. Industrial espionage is always a concern for companies in highly competitive or defence-related industries.

■ **The issue of access:** Unless all employees have access to the intranet, many of the advantages may be lost.

Internet Issue

Virtual Teams Use the Net to Operate at Long Distance

Christine Martin, president and CEO of the consulting firm TLCi, tells how her company uses the net for both the internal and external transaction of business.

My company is a virtual company in three ways:

First, our CFO and Ops Director works from eastern Canada, while the company is headquartered in Southern California. We meet every morning over the Internet, employing a videocam along with audio. If the Internet connection is not satisfactory, we work over the telephone. We regularly address our strategic plan and work on our various client projects together. This is a highly productive and beneficial arrangement.

Second, TLCi has various strategic partners with whom we are connected virtually. We use e-mail on a regular basis. We send important links and information, and exchange drafts and final documents (such as business plans) over the Internet. We find e-mail to be the best vehicle for exchanging working documents, saving time and ensuring accuracy.

Third, to ensure ourselves against catastrophe, we regularly update our virus-protection software and back up files religiously. We also manage our own Web site, to make sure that company information is always current. Future projects include videoconferencing with clients worldwide.

Source: C. Martin, "Virtual Companies: A Reality," *EntreWorld Discussion ListServe* (December 18, 2000). Reprinted by permission.

Discussion Questions

1. What skills should a person have for managing a business unit following a differentiation strategy? Why? What should a company do if no one is available internally and the company has a policy of promotion from within?

2. When should someone from outside the company be hired to manage the company or one of its business units?

3. What are some ways to implement a retrenchment strategy without creating a lot of resentment and conflict with labour unions?

4. How can organizational culture be changed?

5. Why is an understanding of national cultures important in strategic management?

Strategic Practice Exercise

Staffing involves finding the person with the right blend of characteristics, such as personality, training, and experience, to implement a particular strategy. The Keirsey Temperament Sorter is designed to identify different kinds of personality. It is similar to other instruments derived from Carl Jung's theory of psychological types, such as the Myers-Briggs, the Singer-Loomis, and the Grey-Wheelright. The questionnaire identifies four temperament types: Guardian (SJ), Artisan (SP), Idealist (NF), and Rational (NT). *Guardians* have natural talent in managing goods and services. They are dependable and trustworthy. *Artisans* have keen senses and are at home with tools, instruments, and vehicles. They are risk-takers and like action. *Idealists* are concerned with growth and development and like to work with people. They prefer friendly co-operation over confrontation and conflict. *Rationalists* are problem solvers who like to know how things work. They work tirelessly to accomplish their goals. Each of these four types has four variants.[66] To learn more about these temperament types, do the following exercise:

1. Access the Keirsey Temperament Sorter using your internet browser (**www.keirsey.com/cgi-bin/keirsey/ newkts.cgi**).

2. Once you complete and score the questionnaire, print the description of your personality type.

3. Read the information on the website about each personality type. Become familiar with each.

4. Bring to class a sheet of paper containing your name and your personality type: Guardian, Artisan, Idealist, or Rational. Your instructor will either put you into a group containing people with the same predominant style or into a group with representatives from each type. She or he may then give each group a number. The instructor will then give the teams a project to accomplish. Each group will have approximately 30 minutes to do the project. It may be to solve a problem, analyze a short case, or propose a new entrepreneurial venture. The instructor will provide you with very little guidance beyond forming and numbering the groups, giving them the project, and keeping track of time. He or she may move from group to group to sit in on each team's progress. When the time is up, the instructor will ask a spokesperson from each group to (1) describe the process the group went through and (2) present orally each group's ideas. After each group makes its presentation, the instructor may choose one or more of the following activities:

- On a sheet of paper, each person in the class identifies his or her personality type and votes which team did the best on the project.
- The class as a whole tries to identify each group's dominant decision-making style in terms of how they did their assignment. See how many people vote for one of the four types for each team.
- Each member of a group guesses if she or he was put into a team comprising the same personality types or in one comprising all four personality types.

Keirsey challenges the assumption that people are basically the same in the ways that we think, feel, and approach problems. Keirsey argues that it is far less desirable to attempt to change others (because doing so has little likelihood of success) than to attempt to understand, work with, and take advantage of normal differences. Companies can use this type of questionnaire to help team members understand how each person can contribute to team performance.

Notes

1. "Case Study: Algoma Steel Inc.," *National Post Business* (August 2002), pp. 23–26.
2. The numbers are approximate averages from three separate studies of top management turnover after mergers. See M. Lubatkin, D. Schweiger, and Y. Weber, "Top Management Turnover in Related M&A's: An Additional Test of the Theory of Relative Standing," *Journal of Management* 25, 1 (1999), pp. 55–73.
3. R.N. Ashkenas and S.C. Francis, "Integration Managers: Special Leaders for Special Times," *Harvard Business Review* (November–December 2000), pp. 108–116.
4. "Training and Human Resources," *Business Strategy News Review* (July 2000), p. 6.
5. *High Performance Work Practices and Firm Performance* (Washington, DC: U.S. Department of Labor, Office of the American Workplace, 1993), pp. i, 4.
6. J. Baldwin, *Innovation, Training and Success* (Ottawa: Industry Canada, 1999).
7. J. Baldwin, W. Chandler, C. Le, and T. Papailiadis, *Strategies for Success: A Profile of Growing Small and Medium-Sized Enterprises in Canada* (Ottawa: Statistics Canada, Catalogue 88-513-XPB, 1994).
8. *Training and Development Outlook 2001* (Ottawa: The Conference Board of Canada).
9. For further details, see J.A. Byrne, *Chainsaw: The Notorious Career of Al Dunlap in the Era of Profit-at-Any-Price* (New York: Harper Business, 1999).
10. D.K. Datta and N. Rajagopalan, "Industry Structure and CEO Characteristics: An Empirical Study of Succession Events," *Strategic Management Journal* (September 1998), pp. 833–852; A.S. Thomas and K. Ramaswamy, "Environmental Change and Management Staffing: A Comment," *Journal of Management* (Winter 1993), pp. 877–887; J.P. Guthrie, C.M. Grimm, and K.G. Smith, "Environmental Change and Management Staffing: An Empirical Study," *Journal of Management* (December 1991), pp. 735–748.
11. J. Greco, "The Search Goes On," *Journal of Business Strategy* (September/October 1997), pp. 22–25; W. Ocasio and H. Kim, "The Circulation of Corporate Control: Selection of Functional Backgrounds on New CEOs in Large U.S. Manufacturing Firms, 1981–1992," *Administrative Science Quarterly* (September 1999), pp. 532–562.
12. R. Drazin and R.K. Kazanjian, "Applying the Del Technique to the Analysis of Cross-Classification Data: A Test of CEO Succession and Top Management Team Development," *Academy of Management Journal* (December 1993), pp. 1374–1399; W.E. Rothschild, "A Portfolio of Strategic Leaders," *Planning Review* (January/February 1996), pp. 16–19.
13. R. Subramanian and C.M. Sanchez, "Environmental Change and Management Staffing: An Empirical Examination of the Electric Utilities Industry," *Journal of Business Strategies* (Spring 1998), pp. 17–34.
14. M. Smith and M.C. White, "Strategy, CEO Specialization, and Succession," *Administrative Science Quarterly* (June 1987), pp. 263–280.
15. A. Bianco, L. Lavelle, J. Merrit, and A. Barrett, "The CEO Trap," *Business Week* (December 11, 2000), pp. 86–92.
16. D.C. Carey and D. Ogden, *CEO Succession: A Window on How Boards Do It Right When Choosing a New Chief Executive* (New York: Oxford University Press, 2000).
17. A.A. Buchko and D. DiVerde, "Antecedents, Moderators, and Consequences of CEO Turnover: A Review and Reconceptualization," Paper presented to Midwest Academy of Management, Lincoln, Nebraska, 1997, p. 10; W. Ocasio, "Institutionalized Action and Corporate Governance: The Reliance on Rules of CEO Succession," *Administrative Science Quarterly* (June 1999), pp. 384–416.
18. C. Gopinath, "Turnaround: Recognizing Decline and Initiating Intervention," *Long Range Planning* (December 1991), pp. 96–101.
19. K.B. Schwartz and K. Menon, "Executive Succession in Failing Firms," *Academy of Management Journal* (September 1985), pp. 680–686; A.A. Cannella, Jr., and M. Lubatkin, "Succession as a Sociopolitical Process: Internal Impediments to Outsider Selection," *Academy of Management Journal* (August 1993), pp. 763–793; W. Boeker and J. Goodstein, "Performance and Succession Choice: The Moderating Effects of Governance and Ownership," *Academy of Management Journal* (February 1993), pp. 172–186.
20. W. Boeker, "Executive Migration and Strategic Change: The Effect of Top Manager Movement on Product–Market Entry," *Administrative Science Quarterly* (June 1997), pp. 213–236.
21. P. Lorange and D. Murphy, "Bringing Human Resources into Strategic Planning: System Design Characteristics," in *Strategic Human Resource Management*, edited by C.J. Fombrun, N.M. Tichy, and M.A. Devanna (New York: John Wiley & Sons, 1984), pp. 281–283.
22. R. Sharpe, "As Leaders, Women Rule," *Business Week* (November 20, 2000), pp. 75–84.
23. O.C. Richard, "Racial Diversity, Business Strategy, and Firm Performance: A Resource-Based View," *Academy of Management Journal* (Vol. 43, 2000), pp. 164–177.
24. R.A. Pitts, "Strategies and Structures for Diversification," *Academy of Management Journal* (June 1997), pp. 197–208.
25. K.E. Mishra, G.M. Spreitzer, and A.K. Mishra, "Preserving Employee Morale During Downsizing," *Sloan Management Review* (Winter 1998), pp. 83–95.
26. B. O'Reilly, "Is Your Company Asking Too Much?" *Fortune* (March 12, 1990), p. 41. For more information on the emotional reactions of survivors of downsizing, see C.R. Stoner and R.I. Hartman, "Organizational Therapy: Building Survivor Health & Competitiveness," *SAM Advanced Management Journal* (Summer 1997), pp. 15–31, 41.
27. T.M. Amabile and R. Conti, "Changes in the Work Environment for Creativity during Downsizing," *Academy of Management Journal* (December 1999), pp. 630–640; A.G. Bedeian and A.A. Armenakis, "The Cesspool Syndrome: How Dreck Floats to the Top of Declining Organizations," *Academy of Management Executive* (February 1998), pp. 58–67.
28. *Compensation Planning Outlook 1997* (Ottawa: The Conference Board of Canada, 1997).
29. *The Wall Street Journal* (December 22, 1992), p. B1.
30. G.D. Bruton, J.K. Keels, and C.L. Shook, "Downsizing the Firm: Answering the Strategic Questions," *Academy of Management Executive* (May 1996), pp. 38–45.
31. M.A. Hitt, B.W. Keats, H.F. Harback, and R.D. Nixon, "Rightsizing: Building and Maintaining Strategic Leadership and Long-Term Competitiveness," *Organizational Dynamics* (Autumn 1994), pp. 18–32. For additional suggestions, see T. Mroczkowski and M. Hanaoka, "Effective Rightsizing Strategies in Japan and America: Is There a Convergence of Employment Practices?" *Academy of Management Executive* (May 1997), pp. 57–67.
32. J.S. Black and H.B. Gregersen, "The Right Way to Manage Expats," *Harvard Business Review* (March–April 1999), pp. 52–61.
33. Black and Gregersen, p. 54.
34. J.I. Sanchez, P.E. Spector, and C.L. Cooper, "Adapting to a Boundaryless World: A Developmental Expatriate Model," *Academy of Management Executive* (May 2000), pp. 96–106.
35. R.L. Tung, *The New Expatriates* (Cambridge, Mass.: Ballinger, 1988); J.S. Black, M. Mendenhall, and G. Oddou, "Toward a Comprehensive Model of International Adjustment: An Integration of Multiple Theoretical Perspectives," *Academy of Management Review* (April 1991), pp. 291–317.

36. Black and Gregersen, p. 54.
37. G. Stern, "GM Executive's Ties to Native Country Help Auto Maker Clinch Deal in China," *The Wall Street Journal* (November 2, 1995), p. B7.
38. K. Roth, "Managing International Interdependence: CEO Characteristics in a Resource-Based Framework," *Academy of Management Journal* (February 1995), pp. 200–231.
39. J.S. Lublin, "An Overseas Stint Can Be a Ticket to the Top," *The Wall Street Journal* (January 29, 1996), pp. B1, B2.
40. P. Elstrom and S.V. Brull, "Mitsubishi's Morass," *Business Week* (June 3, 1996), p. 35.
41. G.G. Gordon, "The Relationship of Corporate Culture to Industry Sector and Corporate Performance," in *Gaining Control of the Corporate Culture,* edited by R.H. Kilmann, M.J. Saxton, R. Serpa, and Associates (San Francisco: Jossey-Bass, 1985), p. 123; T. Kono, "Corporate Culture and Long-Range Planning," *Long Range Planning* (August 1990), pp. 9–19.
42. J.H. Mills, *Making Sense of Organizational Change* (London: Routledge, 2003).
43. J.A. Chatman, "Matching People and Organizations: Selection and Socialization in Public Accounting Firms," *Administrative Science Quarterly* (Vol. 36, 1991), pp. 459–484.
44. T.J. Tetenbaum, "Seven Key Practices that Improve the Chance for Expected Integration and Synergies," *Organizational Dynamics* (Autumn 1999), pp. 22–35.
45. A.R. Malekzadeh and A. Nahavandi, "Making Mergers Work by Managing Cultures," *Journal of Business Strategy* (May/June 1990), pp. 53–57; A. Nahavandi and A.R. Malekzadeh, "Acculturation in Mergers and Acquisitions," *Academy of Management Review* (January 1988), pp. 79–90.
46. Lubatkin, Schweiger, and Weber, pp. 55–73.
47. J.J. Keller, "Why AT&T Takeover of NCR Hasn't Been a Real Bell Ringer," *The Wall Street Journal* (September 19, 1995), pp. A1, A5.
48. http://collections.ic.gc.ca/agrican/pubweb/hs270044.asp (accessed May 24, 2003).
49. Ibid.
50. S.S. Masterson and M.S. Taylor, "Total Quality Management and Performance Appraisal: An Integrative Perspective," *Journal of Quality Management 1,* No. 1 (1996), pp. 67–89.
51. T.Y. Choi and O.C. Behling, "Top Managers and TQM Success: One More Look after All These Years," *Academy of Management Executive* (February 1997), pp. 37–47.
52. R.J. Schonberger, "Total Quality Management Cuts a Broad Swath—Through Manufacturing and Beyond," *Organizational Dynamics* (Spring 1992), pp. 16–28.
53. T.C. Powell, "Total Quality Management as Competitive Advantage: A Review and Empirical Study," *Strategic Management Journal* (January 1995), pp. 15–37.
54. www.bombardier.com/index.jsp?id=1_0&lang=en&file=/en/1_0/1_11/vol03_02/1_11_03.jsp (accessed May 24, 2003).
55. G. Hofstede, *Cultures and Organizations: Software of the Mind* (London: McGraw-Hill, 1991); G. Hofstede and M.H. Bond, "The Confucius Connection: From Cultural Roots to Economic Growth," *Organizational Dynamics* (Spring 1988), pp. 5–21; R. Hodgetts, "A Conversation with Geert Hofstede," *Organizational Dynamics* (Spring 1993), pp. 53–61.
56. G. Hofstede, "The Business of International Business Is Culture," in T. Jackson, editor, *Cross-Cultural Management* (Oxford: Butterworth-Heinemann, 1995), pp. 150–165.
57. Hofstede and Bond, "The Confucius Connection," pp. 12–13.
58. "Emerging-Market Indicators," *The Economist* (October 7, 2000), p. 124.
59. T.T. Herbert, "Multinational Strategic Planning: Matching Central Expectations to Local Realities," *Long Range Planning* (February 1999), pp. 81–87.
60. Hofstede and Bond, "The Confucius Connection," p. 20.
61. U.G. Gupta and F.J. Hebert, "Is Your Company Ready for an Intranet?" *SAM Advanced Management Journal* (Autumn 1998), pp. 11–17, 26.
62. T.A. Stewart, "Does Anyone Around Here Know...?" *Fortune* (September 29, 1997), pp. 279–280.
63. C. Metz, "Work Together," *PC Magazine* (July 2000), pp. 171–172.
64. M.J. Cronin, "Ford's Intranet Success," *Fortune* (March 30, 1998), p. 158.
65. Gupta and Hebert, p. 16.
66. D. Keirsey, *Please Understand Me II* (Del Mar, Calif.: Prometheus Nemesis Book Co., 1998).

CHAPTER 10

Evaluation and Control

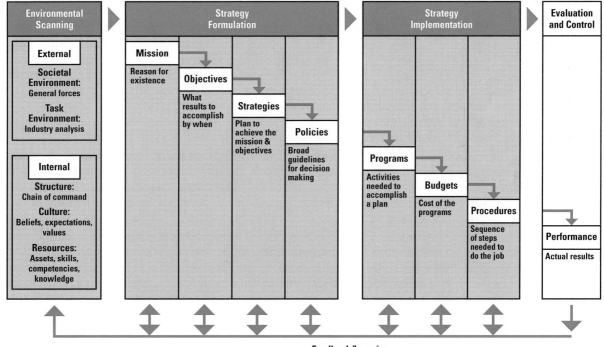

Learning Objectives

After reading this chapter you should be able to

Choose among different measures to assess performance

Use the balanced scorecard approach to develop key performance measures

Understand the problems in measuring performance in organizational contexts

Develop control systems to support organizational strategies

Many Canadian organizations have experienced considerable changes as a result of increasing globalization. The high degree of foreign ownership in many industries creates an awkward situation for many Canadian divisions—parent companies may shift operations to countries where costs are lower, taxes or regulations are more favourable, or specialized labour is more readily available. These threats have made Canadian divisions consider their role in a global organization, where each subsidiary has a larger mandate. As a result, the subsidiary assumes increased responsibility in terms of geographic markets served, which requires increased strategic control over many value-creating activities. For example, Westinghouse Canada has the responsibility for gas turbines in all geographic markets, and 3M Canada has a North American mandate for Scotch-Brite scouring pads and transparent duct tape.[1]

What is especially important for subsidiaries is to prepare themselves for the ongoing globalization of so many industries. This means that organizations must gather and analyze a large amount of information, about major world markets as well as their own internal operations. Often there is competition among subsidiaries for global product mandates, so managers must be proactive in obtaining the types of information that will allow them to put together a winning proposal. One key element of this is a measurement system that assesses the performance of core activities. By tracking how well existing resources are used, and demonstrating evaluation and control processes to enhance performance, subsidiaries can demonstrate what they do particularly well, and how they can be used to make different products or provide different services. The physical separation of the subsidiary makes it difficult for head office managers to have the knowledge of what a division does particularly well, and what role it can play in capturing new global opportunities. Especially as product divisions with large mandates replace international divisions of MNCs, head office decision makers need to be kept abreast of the current performance and future potential of their organizations' subsidiaries.[2] A good system of evaluation and control is one important aspect of this.

evaluation and control process a system of monitoring and feedback that tracks an organization's progress toward achieving its goals and objectives

The **evaluation and control process** ensures that the company is achieving what it set out to accomplish. It compares performance with desired results and provides the feedback necessary for management to evaluate results and take corrective action, as needed. This process can be viewed as a five-step feedback model, as depicted in **Figure 10–1**.

1. **Determine what to measure.** Top managers and operational managers need to specify what implementation processes and results will be monitored and evaluated. The processes and results must be capable of being measured in a reasonably objective and consistent manner. The focus should be on the most significant elements in a process— the ones that account for the highest proportion of expense or the greatest number of problems. Measurements must be found for all important areas, regardless of difficulty.

2. **Establish standards of performance.** Standards used to measure performance are detailed expressions of strategic objectives. They are measures of acceptable performance results. Each standard usually includes a tolerance range, which defines acceptable deviations. Standards can be set not only for final output, but also for intermediate stages of production output.

3. **Measure actual performance.** Measurements must be made at predetermined times.

4. **Compare actual performance with the standard.** If actual performance results are within the desired tolerance range, the measurement process stops here.

5. **Take corrective action.** If actual results fall outside the desired tolerance range, action must be taken to correct the deviation. The following questions must be answered:

   a. Is the deviation only a chance fluctuation?
   b. Are the processes being carried out incorrectly?
   c. Are the processes appropriate to the achievement of the desired standard? Action must be taken that will not only correct the deviation, but will also prevent its happening again.
   d. Who is the best person to take corrective action?

The purpose of having a good strategic control system is to be able to identify performance gaps early enough that corrective action can be taken. In other words, regular measurement of key operating and financial results can indicate problem areas in an organization's value chain long before these problems become too difficult to fix and the problems become too large. If organizations had to wait until their fiscal year-end to find out that performance is lacking, or until small cost overruns accumulated into large ones, steering them back on course would be a much more difficult task. For these reasons, it is important for organizations to regularly monitor their activities and assess their movement toward achieving their goals and objectives.

10.1 Evaluation and Control in Strategic Management

Evaluation and control information consists of performance data and activity reports (gathered in Step 3 of **Figure 10–1**). If undesired performance results from inappropriate use of strategic management processes, operational managers must know about it so that they can correct the employee activity. Top management need not be involved. If, however, undesired performance results from the processes themselves, top managers, as well as operational managers, must know about it so that they can develop new implementation programs or procedures. Evaluation and control information must be relevant to what is being monitored. One of the obstacles to effective control is the difficulty in developing appropriate measures of important activities and outputs.

Figure 10–1 Evaluation and Control Process

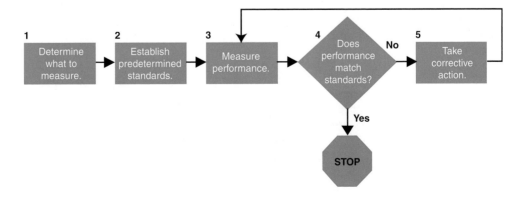

An application of the control process to strategic management is depicted in **Figure 10–2**. It provides strategic managers with a series of questions to use in evaluating an implemented strategy. Such a strategy review is usually initiated when a gap appears between a company's financial objectives and the expected results of current activities. After answering the proposed

Figure 10–2 Evaluating an Implemented Strategy

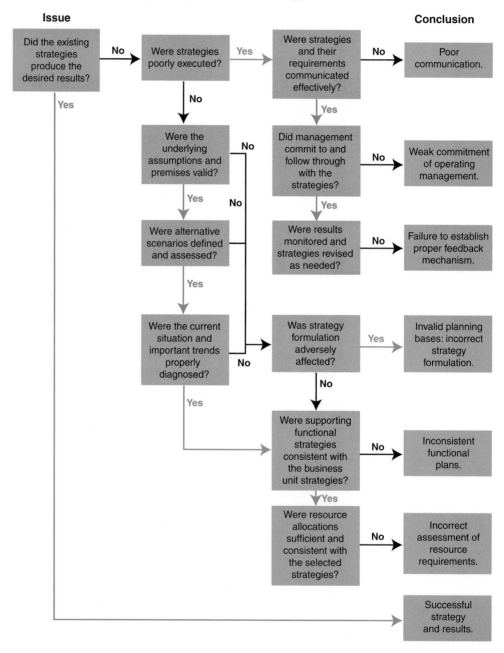

Source: Jeffery A. Schmidt, "The Strategic Review," *Planning Review* (July/August 1988), p. 15. Copyright © 1988 by MCB University Press Ltd. Reprinted with permission.

set of questions, a manager should have a good idea of where the problem originated and what must be done to correct the situation.

10.2 Measuring Performance

performance the organization's output resulting from strategy implementation

Performance is the end result of activity. Which measure one should select to assess performance depends on the organizational unit to be appraised and the objectives to be achieved. The objectives that were established earlier in the strategy formulation part of the strategic management process (dealing with profitability, market share, and cost reduction, among others) should certainly be used to measure organizational performance once the strategies have been implemented.

APPROPRIATE MEASURES

Some measures, such as return on investment (ROI), are appropriate for evaluating the corporation's or division's ability to achieve a profitability objective. This type of measure, however, is inadequate for evaluating additional corporate objectives such as social responsibility or employee development. Even though profitability is a corporation's major objective, ROI can be computed only after profits are totalled for a period. It tells what happened after the fact—not what is happening or what will happen. A firm, therefore, needs to develop measures that predict likely profitability. These are referred to as **steering controls** because they measure variables that influence future profitability. One example of this type of control is the use of control charts in Statistical Process Control (SPC). In SPC, workers and managers maintain charts and graphs detailing quality and productivity on a daily basis. They are thus able to make adjustments to the system before it gets out of control.[3]

steering control measures of variables that affect future profitability

TYPES OF CONTROLS

Controls can be established to focus on actual performance results (output), on the activities that generate the performance (behaviour), or on resources that are used in performance (input). Each is briefly discussed below:[4]

1. **Behaviour controls** specify how something is to be done through policies, rules, standard operating procedures, and orders from a superior. This type of control is most often used when measurable standards are impractical to develop, as is often the case when organizations try to develop a culture of customer satisfaction or innovativeness. Sometimes called bureaucratic controls, behaviour controls develop predictability and consistency by specifying *how* work is done. By standardizing behaviours, outcomes become predictable. For example, McDonald's specifies how food is prepared and customers are served so that the customer experience is the same at all of its restaurants. Because it specifies how work is done, predictability and accuracy are enhanced.

2. **Output controls** specify what is to be accomplished by focusing on the end result of the behaviours through the use of objectives and performance targets or milestones. This type of control is most often used when the final specifications of a product are particularly important. The means to this end may be difficult to standardize, so instead the control is over the finished product (for example its dimensions, quality, customer returns, and costs). This is usually measured by sampling of finished products to determine the extent to which they meet standards. Corrective action is taken only when these standards are not being met. For example, hotel operations like Four Seasons and

Fairmont strive for high levels of guest satisfaction so that clients will continue to use their hotels in the future. Standardizing outputs is one way many organizations try to satisfy and retain customers.

3. **Input controls** focus on resources, such as knowledge, skills, abilities, values, and motives of employees. This type of control is most often used when standardizing behaviours and outputs is difficult to accomplish. The focus then becomes standardizing the inputs into an organization, so that the quality of the finished product is more predictable. We see this type of control used in many professional service organizations like BearingPoint (formerly KPMG Consulting). By being a selective recruiter and devoting considerable resources to training and development, BearingPoint ensures that its consultants have the knowledge and skills necessary to provide high-quality services for its clients. Through careful selection, socialization, and training, organizations are able to assemble a workforce that has both the knowledge required and the desire to strive toward organizational goals.

Behaviour, output, and input controls are not interchangeable. Behaviour controls (such as following company procedures, making sales calls to potential customers, and getting to work on time) are most appropriate when performance results are hard to measure but the cause–effect connection between activities and results is clear. Output controls (such as sales quotas, specific cost-reduction or profit objectives, and surveys of customer satisfaction) are most appropriate when specific output measures have been agreed on but the cause–effect connection between activities and results is not clear. Input controls (such as number of years of education and experience) are most appropriate when output is difficult to measure and there is no clear cause–effect relationship between behaviour and performance (such as in college teaching). Organizations following the strategy of conglomerate diversification tend to emphasize output controls with their divisions and subsidiaries (presumably because they are managed independently of each other); whereas, corporations following concentric diversification use all three types of controls (presumably because synergy is desired).[5] Even if all three types of control are used, one or two of them may be emphasized more than another depending on the circumstances. For example, as a multinational corporation moves through its stages of development, its emphasis on control will likely shift from being primarily output at first, to behavioural, and finally to input control.[6]

ISO 9000 Standards Series a quality assurance program based on measuring and assessing the quality of all organizational processes

One example of an increasingly popular behaviour control is the **ISO 9000 Standards Series** on quality management and assurance developed by the International Standards Association of Geneva, Switzerland. The ISO 9000 series (comprising five sections from 9000 to 9004) is a way of objectively documenting a company's high level of quality operations. ISO 9000 and 9004 contain guidelines for use with the other sections; 9001 is the most comprehensive standard; 9002 is less stringent; 9003 is used only for inspecting and testing procedures. A company wanting certification would probably document its process for product introductions, among other things. ISO 9001 would require this firm to separately document design input, design process, design output, and design verification—a large amount of work. Although the average total cost for a company to be certified is close to $250 000, the annual savings are around $175 000 per company.[7]

Many organizations view ISO 9000 certification as assurance that a supplier sells quality products. Firms such as Bombardier, Nortel Networks, Hewlett-Packard, and 3M have facilities registered to ISO standards. Companies in many countries, including Canada, Mexico, Japan, the United States, and the European Union (EU), are requiring ISO 9000 certification of their suppliers. By 1996, close to 100 000 firms were registered worldwide.[8] A recent survey of manufacturing executives showed that 51% of the executives found that certification increased their international competitiveness. Other executives noted that it signalled their commitment to quality and gave them a strategic advantage over non-certified competitors.[9]

ACTIVITY-BASED COSTING

activity-based costing
an accounting system
that allocates costs to
the value-creating activ-
ities used to produce a
product

Activity-based costing (ABC) is a new accounting method for allocating indirect and fixed costs to individual products or product lines based on the value-added activities going into that product.[10] This accounting method is thus very useful in doing a value chain analysis of a firm's activities for making outsourcing decisions. Traditional cost accounting, in contrast, focuses on valuing a company's inventory for financial reporting purposes. To obtain a unit's cost, cost accountants typically add direct labour to the cost of materials. Then they compute overhead from rent to R & D expenses, based on the number of direct labour hours it takes to make a product. To obtain unit cost, they divide the total by the number of items made during the period under consideration.

Traditional cost accounting is useful when direct labour accounts for most of total costs and a company produces just a few products requiring the same processes. This may have been true of companies during the early part of the twentieth century, but it is no longer relevant today when overhead may account for as much as 70% of manufacturing costs. Because overhead is such a significant component of many organizations' costs, allocation errors lead to pricing errors, which could easily bankrupt the company. The appropriate allocation of indirect costs and overhead has thus become crucial for decision making. The traditional volume-based cost-driven system systematically understates the cost per unit of products with low sales volumes and products with a high degree of complexity. Similarly, it overstates the cost per unit of products with high sales volumes and with a low degree of complexity.[11]

ABC accounting allows accountants to charge costs more accurately than the traditional method because it allocates overhead far more precisely. For example, imagine a production line in a pen factory where black pens are made in high volume and blue pens in low volume. Assume it takes eight hours to retool (reprogram the machinery) to shift production from one kind of pen to the other. The total costs include supplies (the same for both pens), the direct labour of the line workers, and factory overhead. In this instance, a very significant part of the overhead cost is the cost of reprogramming the machinery to switch from one pen to another. If the company produces 10 times as many black pens as blue pens, then 10 times more reprogramming costs will be allocated to the black pens than to the blue pens under traditional cost accounting methods. This approach underestimates, however, the true cost of making the blue pens.

ABC accounting, in contrast, first breaks down pen manufacturing into its activities. It is then very easy to see that it is the activity of changing pens that triggers the cost of retooling. The ABC accountant calculates an average cost of setting up the machinery and charges it against each batch of pens that requires retooling regardless of the size of the run. Thus, a product carries only those costs for the overhead it actually consumes. Management is now able to discover that its blue pens cost almost twice as much as do the black pens. Unless the company is able to charge a higher price for its blue pens, it cannot make a profit on these pens. Unless there is a strategic reason why it must offer blue pens (such as a key customer who must have a small number of blue pens with every large order of black pens, or a marketing trend away from black to blue pens), the company will earn significantly greater profits if it completely stops making blue pens.[12]

PRIMARY MEASURES OF CORPORATE PERFORMANCE

The days when simple financial measures such as ROI or EPS were used alone to assess overall corporate performance are coming to an end. Analysts now recommend a broad range of methods to evaluate the success or failure of a strategy. Some of these methods are stakeholder measures, measures of shareholder value, and the balanced scorecard approach. Even though each of these methods has its supporters as well as detractors, the current trend is clearly toward more complicated financial measures and an increasing use of non-financial measures of corporate performance.[13] For example, research indicates that companies pursuing strategies founded on innovation and new product development now tend to favour non-financial over financial measures.[14]

Traditional Financial Measures

return on investment a profitability index: the ratio of after-tax earnings to total assets

earnings per share a profitability index: the ratio of after-tax earnings less dividends to the average number of common shares outstanding

return on equity a profitability index: the ratio of after-tax earnings to shareholders' equity

The most commonly used measure of corporate performance (in terms of profits) is **return on investment (ROI)**. ROI is simply the result of dividing net income after taxes by total assets. Although using ROI has several advantages, it also has several distinct limitations. (See **Table 10–1**.) Although ROI gives the impression of objectivity and precision, it can be easily manipulated.

Earnings per share (EPS), dividing net earnings by the number of shares of common stock issued, also has several deficiencies as an evaluation of past and future performance. First, because alternative accounting principles are available, EPS can have several different but equally acceptable values, depending on the principle selected for its computation. Second, because EPS is based on accrual income, the conversion of income to cash can be near term or delayed. Therefore, EPS does not consider the time value of money. **Return on equity (ROE)**, dividing net income by total equity, also has its share of limitations because it is also

Table 10–1 Advantages and Limitations of Using ROI As a Measure of Corporate Performance

Advantages

1. ROI is a single comprehensive figure influenced by everything that happens.
2. It measures how well the division manager uses the property of the company to generate profits. It is also a good way to check on the accuracy of capital investment proposals.
3. It is a common denominator that can be compared with many entities.
4. It provides an incentive to use existing assets efficiently.
5. It provides an incentive to acquire new assets only when doing so would increase the return.

Limitations

1. ROI is very sensitive to depreciation policy. Depreciation write-off variances between divisions affect ROI performance. Accelerated depreciation techniques increase ROI, conflicting with capital budgeting discounted cash-flow analysis.
2. ROI is sensitive to book value. Older plants with more depreciated assets have relatively lower investment bases than newer plants (note also the effect of inflation), thus increasing ROI. Note that asset investment may be held down or assets disposed of in order to increase ROI performance.
3. In many firms that use ROI, one division sells to another. As a result, transfer pricing must occur. Expenses incurred affect profit. Since, in theory, the transfer price should be based on the total impact on firm profit, some investment centre managers are bound to suffer. Equitable transfer prices are difficult to determine.
4. If one division operates in an industry that has favourable conditions and another division operates in an industry that has unfavourable conditions, the former division will automatically "look" better than the other.
5. The time span of concern here is short range. The performance of division managers should be measured in the long run. This is top management's time span capacity.
6. The business cycle strongly affects ROI performance, often despite managerial performance.

Source: "Advantages and Limitations of ROI As a Measure of Corporate Performance," from *Organizational Policy and Strategic Management: Text and Cases,* 2nd edition, by James M. Higgins, copyright © 1983. Reproduced by permission of South-Western College Publishing, a division of Thomson Learning.

derived from accounting-based data. In addition, EPS and ROE are often unrelated to a company's stock price. Because of these and other limitations, ROI, EPS, and ROE by themselves are not adequate measures of corporate performance. Nevertheless, they are still better than the measures proposed by internet start-ups during the 1990s. (See the **Internet Issue** feature on page 262 for an example of how Amazon.com used "eyeballs" as its primary measure of performance.)

Stakeholder Measures

Each stakeholder has its own set of criteria to determine how well the corporation is performing. These criteria typically deal with the direct and indirect impact of corporate activities on stakeholder interests. Top management should establish one or more simple stakeholder measures for each stakeholder category so that it can keep track of stakeholder concerns (see **Table 10–2**).

Table 10–2 A Sample Scorecard for "Keeping Score" with Stakeholders

Stakeholder Category	Possible Near-Term Measures	Possible Long-Term Measures
Customers	Sales ($ and volume) New customers Number of new customer needs met ("tries")	Growth in sales Turnover of customer base Ability to control price

Suppliers	Cost of raw material
	Delivery time
	Inventory
	Availability of raw material
		Growth rates of:
		    Raw material costs
		    Delivery time
		    Inventory
		New ideas from suppliers

Financial community	EPS Stock price Number of "buy" lists ROE	Ability to convince Wall Street of strategy Growth in ROE
Employees	Number of suggestions Productivity Number of grievances	Number of internal promotions Turnover
Congress	Number of new pieces of legislation that affect the firm Access to key members and staff	Number of new regulations that affect industry Ratio of "cooperative" vs. "competitive" encounters
Consumer advocate (CA)	Number of meetings Number of "hostile" encounters Number of times coalitions formed Number of legal actions	Number of changes in policy due to CA Number of CA-initiated "calls for help"
Environmentalists	Number of meetings Number of hostile encounters Number of times coalitions formed Number of EPA complaints Number of legal actions	Number of changes in policy due to environmentalists Number of environmentalist "calls for help"

Source: R.E. Freeman, *Strategic Management: A Stakeholder Approach* (Boston: Ballinger Publishing Company, 1984), p. 179. Copyright © 1984 by R.E. Freeman. Reprinted by permission.

Internet Issue

"Eyeballs" and "MUUs": Questionable Performance Measures

When Amazon.com's investor relations team went to Denver in September 2000 to seek funding from Marsico Capital Management, a mutual fund company, it presented its usual performance story. Even though the company had never shown a profit, the team asserted that Amazon.com had a "first to market" advantage and that its website received an extremely high number of "monthly unique visitors" and "eyeballs." Although such presentations had in the past raised millions of dollars for the company in stock purchases, it failed this time. Marsico was more concerned with when the company would become profitable. The Amazon.com team left empty-handed.

Until 2000, investors had been so enamoured with new internet firms that they made decisions based on novel measures of performance and firm valuation. They looked at measures such as "stickiness" (length of website visit), "eyeballs" (number of people who visit a website), and "mindshare" (brand awareness). Mergers and acquisitions were priced on multiples of "MUUs" (monthly unique users) or even on registered users. Since practically all the dot-com (internet) firms

failed to earn a profit, investors and analysts used these measures to estimate what the firms might be worth sometime in the future. By 2000, however, "the market concluded the [net stock] valuations were insane," commented Charles Wolf, analyst with UBS Warburg.

With a debt of $2.1 billion, Amazon.com had an accumulated net loss from 1994 through 2000 of $1.75 billion. Its management had proposed that as the company grew in scale, its operations would become more efficient, and its gross margin per customer would improve. The question from investors was—when? For example, Amazon.com in 2000 averaged $160.01 annually in revenue from each of its 17 million customers for books and CDs. The annual cost of these books and CDs was $139.22, leaving a gross profit of $20.79 per customer. Annual marketing expenses amounted to $42.47 per customer. Using the traditional profit measure, Amazon.com was losing $21.68 per person. This didn't include an additional $19.83 per person for warehousing, shipping, customer service, and other operating expenses. The company did sell prominent positions on its website to firms such as Drugstore.com for $105 million and car-dealer Greenlight.com for $145 million. With sufficient sales of space on its website, it could become profitable soon. Since Amazon.com realized an 80% margin from this sort of advertising, it was not so much an internet retailer as a newspaper or television station existing off advertising.

Sources: E. Schonfeld, "How Much Are Your Eyeballs Worth?" *Fortune* (February 21, 2000), pp. 197–204; N. Byrnes, "Eyeballs, Bah! Figuring Dot-Coms' Real Worth," *Business Week* (October 30, 2000), p. 62; R. Barker, "Amazon: Cheaper—But Cheap Enough?" *Business Week* (December 4, 2000), p. 172.

Shareholder Value

Because of the belief that accounting-based numbers such as return on investment, return on equity, and earnings per share are not reliable indicators of a corporation's economic value, many corporations are using shareholder value as a better measure of corporate performance and strategic management effectiveness. **Shareholder value** can be defined as the present value of the anticipated future stream of cash flows from the business plus the value of the company if liquidated. Arguing that the purpose of a company is to increase shareholder wealth, shareholder value analysis concentrates on cash flow as the key measure of performance. The value of an organization is thus the value of its cash flows discounted back to their present value, using the business's cost of capital as the discount rate. As long as the returns from a business exceed its cost of capital, the business will create value and be worth more than the capital invested in it.

shareholder value the present value of anticipated future cash flows of an organization

Two other shareholder value measures are economic value added (EVA) and market value added (MVA). Well-known companies such as Coca-Cola, General Electric, AT&T, Whirlpool, Quaker Oats, Eli Lilly, Georgia-Pacific, Polaroid, Sprint, Teledyne, and Tenneco have adopted MVA and/or EVA as the best yardstick for corporate performance. The benefit of these types of measures over EPS (which measures accounting results) is that they attempt to gauge true economic performance.

economic value added a financial indicator of an organization's profitability in excess of its cost of capital

Economic value added (EVA) has become an extremely popular shareholder value method of measuring corporate and divisional performance and may be on its way to replacing ROI as the standard performance measure. EVA measures the difference between the pre-strategy and post-strategy value for the business. Simply put, EVA is after-tax operating income minus the total annual cost of capital. This is the formula to measure EVA:

$$\text{EVA} = \left(\begin{array}{c}\text{After tax}\\\text{operating income}\end{array}\right) - \left(\begin{array}{c}\text{investment in assets} \times\\\text{weighted average cost of capital}\end{array}\right)^{15}$$

The cost of capital combines the cost of debt and equity. The annual cost of borrowed capital is the interest charged by the firm's banks and bondholders. To calculate the cost of equity, assume that shareholders generally earn about 6% more on stocks than on government bonds. If long-term treasury bills are selling at 7.5%, the firm's cost of equity should be 13.5%—more if the firm is in a risky industry. A corporation's overall cost of capital is the weighted-average cost of the firm's debt and equity capital. The investment in assets is the total amount of capital invested in the business, including buildings, machines, computers, and investments in R & D and training (allocating costs annually over their useful life). Since the typical balance sheet understates the investment made in a company, Stern Stewart has identified 150 possible adjustments before EVA is calculated.[16] Multiply the firm's total investment in assets by the weighted-average cost of capital. Subtract that figure from after-tax operating income. If the difference is positive, the strategy (and the management employing it) is generating value for the shareholders. If it is negative, the strategy is destroying shareholder value.[17] Using EVA as an indicator of performance, decision makers will be able to identify the profitability of the organization (or any of its divisions) in excess of the cost of the investments necessary to generate that profit. This reflects wealth it has created for its shareholders above what they should minimally expect based on a firm's cost of capital.

Roberto Goizueta, CEO of Coca-Cola, explains, "We raise capital to make concentrate, and sell it at an operating profit. Then we pay the cost of that capital. Shareholders pocket the difference."[18] Managers can improve their company's or business unit's EVA by (1) earning more profit without using more capital, (2) using less capital, and (3) investing capital in high-return projects. Studies have found that companies using EVA outperform their median competitor by an average of 8.43% of total return annually.[19] EVA does, however, have some limitations. For one thing, it does not control for size differences across plants or divisions. As with ROI, managers can manipulate the numbers. As with ROI, EVA is an after-the-fact measure and cannot be used as a steering control.[20] Although proponents of EVA argue that EVA (unlike ROI, ROE, and/or ROS [return on sales]) has a strong relationship to stock price, other studies do not support this contention.[21]

market value added
financial indicator of the appreciation of an organization's value in excess of its shareholders' investments in it

Market value added (MVA) is the difference between the market value of an organization and the capital contributed by shareholders and lenders. Like net present value, it measures the stock market's estimate of the net present value of a firm's past and expected capital investment projects. As such, MVA is the present value of future EVA.[22] This is how MVA is calculated:

1. First, add all the capital that has been put into a company—from shareholders, bondholders, and retained earnings.

2. Reclassify certain accounting expenses, such as R & D, to reflect that they are actually investments in future earnings. This provides the firm's total capital. So far, this is the same approach taken in calculating EVA.

3. Using the current stock price, total the value of all outstanding stock, adding it to the company's debt. This is the company's market value. If the company's market value is greater than all the capital invested in it, the firm has a positive MVA—meaning that management (and the strategy it is following) has created wealth. In some cases, however, the market value of the company is actually less than the capital put into it—shareholder wealth is being destroyed.

Microsoft, General Electric, Intel, and Coca-Cola tend to have high MVAs, whereas General Motors and RJR Nabisco have low ones.[23] Studies have shown that EVA is a predictor of MVA. Consecutive years of positive EVA generally lead to a soaring MVA.[24] Research also reveals that CEO turnover is significantly correlated with MVA and EVA, whereas ROI and ROE are not. This suggests that EVA and MVA may be more appropriate measures of the market's evaluation of a firm's strategy and its management than are the traditional measures of corporate perform-ance.[25] Nevertheless, these measures consider only the financial interests of the shareholder and ignore other stakeholders, such as environmentalists and employees.

Balanced Scorecard Approach: Using Key Performance Measures

Rather than evaluate a corporation using a few financial measures, Kaplan and Norton argue for a "balanced scorecard," including non-financial as well as financial measures.[26] This approach is especially useful given that research indicates that non-financial assets explain 50% to 80% of a firm's value.[27] The **balanced scorecard** combines financial measures that tell the results of actions already taken with operational measures on customer satisfaction, inter-nal processes, and the corporation's innovation and improvement activities—the drivers of future financial performance. The benefit of this approach to assessing organizational per-formance is that it forces managers to look at performance from different perspectives. From each of these four perspectives, specific goals and measures need to be developed as part of an integrated strategic control system. To get a balanced view of financial and operational meas-ures, the balanced scorecard approach has all organizations examine the following:

balanced scorecard a set of measures giving a comprehensive view of organizational performance

1. *Financial Perspective:* **How do we appear to shareholders?** The financial measures dis-cussed earlier in this chapter fit into this perspective. Are an organization's activities con-tributing to bottom-line performance, and in what different ways can these assessments be made? Although financial results are important, relying on them can create a short-term focus on results that does not assess the development of a range of organizational competencies that will affect long-run performance.

2. *Customer Perspective:* **How do customers view us?** Because most organizations have a mission or vision that focuses on the customer, measures of how customers view the organization and its activities can supplement financial measures. Doing this involves translating broad statements of customer-orientation into specific measures that matter to customers—in other words the factors that will influence the benefits obtained from using the organization's products. Generic customer concerns include time, quality, per-formance, service, and price. By conducting market research and customer satisfaction surveys, organizations are able to understand the basis of customer satisfaction. They are then able to make changes to their products and processes to improve customer views of the organization.

3. *Internal Business Perspective:* **What must we excel at?** Knowledge of what is important to customers needs to be positioned alongside what the organization must do internally. There is a tight link between customer satisfaction and the activities of the organization—processes, decisions, and actions that develop and market a product. Internal measures should therefore identify the activities and processes that have the largest impact on customer satisfaction. Often this is supported by information systems that gather and summarize information for organizational decision makers. As with any type of control system, monitoring performance data can indicate problem areas early on, while there is still time to address them.

4. *Innovation and Learning Perspective:* **Can we continue to improve and create value?** The previously discussed perspectives reveal the basis of competitive success—what is important to customers and what organizational activities are necessary to deliver them.

But in increasingly competitive industries, and with globalization changing the nature of competition, these bases of success are changing more rapidly than ever. An organization therefore needs the ability to innovate and learn in ways that create more value for customers, which in turn creates value for shareholders. By developing superior, innovative products, improving operating efficiencies, and constantly re-evaluating its strategies, an organization can look ahead to what is likely to make it most successful in the future and determine what changes need to be made today to remain competitive.

To put the balanced scorecard into practice, goals in each area (for example, avoiding bankruptcy in the financial area) are assigned one or more measures, as well as a target and an initiative. These measures can be thought of as **key performance measures**—measures that are essential for achieving a desired strategic option.[28] For example, a company could include cash flow, quarterly sales growth, and ROE as measures for success in the financial area. It could include market share (competitive position goal) and percentage of new sales coming from new products (customer acceptance goal) as measures under the customer perspective. It could include cycle time and unit cost (manufacturing excellence goal) as measures under the internal business perspective. It could include time to develop next generation products (technology leadership objective) under the innovation and learning perspective.

Several companies are starting to use one or more variations of the scorecard and view it as complementary to its knowledge management activities. A study of the *Fortune* 500 firms in the United States and the *Post* 300 firms in Canada revealed the most popular non-financial measures to be customer satisfaction, customer service, product quality, market share, productivity, service quality, and core competencies. New product development, corporate culture, and market growth were not far behind.[29]

> **key performance measures** measurable signals of achieving goals in each area of the balanced scorecard

Evaluating Top Management

Through its strategy, audit, and compensation committees, a board of directors closely evaluates the job performance of the CEO and the top management team. Of course, it is concerned primarily with overall corporate profitability as measured quantitatively by return on investment, return on equity, earnings per share, and shareholder value. The absence of short-run profitability certainly contributes to the firing of any CEO. The board, however, is also concerned with other factors.

Members of the compensation committees of today's boards of directors generally agree that a CEO's ability to establish strategic direction, build a management team, and provide leadership are more critical in the long run than are a few quantitative measures. The board should evaluate top management not only on the typical output-oriented quantitative measures, but also on behavioural measures—factors relating to its strategic management practices. The specific items that a board uses to evaluate its top management should be derived from the objectives that both the board and top management agreed on earlier. If better relations with the local community and improved safety practices in work areas were selected as objectives for the year (or for five years), these items should be included in the evaluation. In addition, other factors that tend to lead to profitability might be included, such as market share, product quality, or investment intensity. Although the number of boards that conduct systematic evaluations of their CEOs is increasing, it is estimated that no more than half of boards do so.

> **management audits** systematic examinations of the performance of management

Management audits are very useful to boards of directors in evaluating management's handling of various corporate activities. Management audits have been developed to evaluate activities such as corporate social responsibility, functional areas such as the marketing department, and divisions such as the international division, as well as to evaluate the corporation itself in a strategic audit. The strategic audit is explained in detail later in the **Appendix** of this book.

PRIMARY MEASURES OF DIVISIONAL AND FUNCTIONAL PERFORMANCE

Companies use a variety of techniques to evaluate and control performance in divisions, SBUs, and functional areas. If an organization comprises SBUs or divisions, it will use many of the same performance measures (ROI or EVA, for instance) that it uses to assess overall corporate performance. To the extent that it can isolate specific functional units such as R & D, the corporation may develop responsibility centres. It will also use typical functional measures such as market share and sales per employee (marketing), unit costs and percentage of defects (operations), percentage of sales from new products and number of patents (R & D), and turnover and job satisfaction (HRM). For example, FedEx uses Enhanced Tracker software with its COSMOS database to track the progress of its 2.5 million to 3.5 million shipments daily. As a courier is completing her or his day's activities, the Enhanced Tracker asks whether the person's package count equals the Enhanced Tracker's count. If the count is off, the software helps reconcile the differences.[30]

During strategy formulation and implementation, top management approves a series of programs and supporting operating budgets from its business units. During evaluation and control, actual expenses are contrasted with planned expenditures and the degree of variance is assessed. This is typically done on a monthly basis. In addition, top management will probably require periodic statistical reports summarizing data on such key factors as the number of new customer contracts, volume of received orders, and productivity figures.

Responsibility Centres

responsibility centre a part of an organization that is assessed separately from the rest of the organization as a way to enhance control

Control systems can be established to monitor specific functions, projects, or divisions. Budgets are one type of control system that is typically used to control the financial indicators of performance. **Responsibility centres** are used to isolate units so that they can be evaluated separately from the rest of the corporation. Each responsibility centre, therefore, has its own budget and is evaluated on its use of budgeted resources. It is headed by the manager responsible for the centre's performance. The centre uses resources (measured in terms of costs or expenses) to produce a service or a product (measured in terms of volume or revenues). There are five major types of responsibility centres. The type is determined by the way the corporation's control system measures these resources and services or products.

1. **Standard Cost Centres:** This type is primarily used in manufacturing facilities. Standard (or expected) costs are computed for each operation on the basis of historical data. In the evaluation of the centre's performance, its total standard costs are multiplied by the units produced. The result is the expected cost of production, which is then compared with the actual cost of production.

2. **Revenue Centres:** Production, usually in terms of unit or dollar sales, is measured without consideration of resource costs (for example, salaries). The centre is thus judged in terms of effectiveness rather than efficiency. The effectiveness of a sales region, for example, is determined by comparing its actual sales with its projected or previous year's sales. Profits are not considered because sales departments have very limited influence over the cost of the products they sell.

3. **Expense Centres:** Resources are measured in dollars without consideration for service or product costs. Thus, budgets will have been prepared for engineered expenses (those costs that can be calculated) and for discretionary expenses (those costs that can be only estimated). Typical expense centres are administrative, service, and research departments. They cost an organization money, but they only indirectly contribute to revenues.

4. **Profit Centres:** Performance is measured in terms of the difference between revenues (which measure production) and expenditures (which measure resources). A profit

centre is typically established whenever an organizational unit has control over both its resources and its products or services. By having such centres, a company can be organized into divisions of separate product lines. The manager of each division is given autonomy to the extent that she or he is able to keep profits at a satisfactory (or better) level.

Some organizational units that are not usually considered potentially autonomous can, for the purpose of profit centre evaluations, be made so. A manufacturing department, for example, can be converted from a standard cost centre (or expense centre) into a profit centre; it is allowed to charge a transfer price for each product it "sells" to the sales department. The difference between the manufacturing cost per unit and the agreed-upon transfer price is the unit's "profit."

Transfer pricing is commonly used in vertically integrated corporations and can work well when a price can be easily determined for a designated amount of product. Even though most experts agree that market-based transfer prices are the best choice, only 30% to 40% of companies use market price to set the transfer price. (Of the rest, 50% use cost; 10% to 20% use negotiation.)[31] When a price cannot be set easily, however, the relative bargaining power of the centres, rather than strategic considerations, tends to influence the agreed-upon price. Top management has an obligation to make sure that these political considerations do not overwhelm the strategic ones. Otherwise, profit figures for each centre will be biased and provide poor information for strategic decisions at both corporate and divisional levels.

5. **Investment Centres:** Because many divisions in large manufacturing corporations use significant assets to make their products, their asset base should be factored into their performance evaluation. Thus, it is insufficient to focus only on profits, as in the case of profit centres. An investment centre's performance is measured in terms of the difference between its resources and its services or products. For example, two divisions in a corporation made identical profits, but one division owns a $3 million plant, whereas the other owns a $1 million plant. Both make the same profits, but one is obviously more efficient; the smaller plant provides the shareholders with a better return on their investment. The most widely used measure of investment centre performance is return on investment (ROI).

Most single-business organizations, such as Air Canada, tend to use a combination of cost, expense, and revenue centres. In these organizations, most managers are functional specialists and manage against a budget. Total profitability is integrated at the corporate level. Multidivisional corporations with one dominating product line, such as Labatt's, which have diversified into a few businesses, but which still depend on a single product line (such as beer) for most of their revenue and income, generally use a combination of cost, expense, revenue, plus profit centres. Other multidivisional corporations, such as BCE Inc., tend to emphasize investment centres—although in various units throughout the corporation other types of responsibility centres are also used. One problem with using responsibility centres, however, is that the separation needed to measure and evaluate a division's performance can diminish the level of co-operation among divisions that is needed to attain synergy for the corporation as a whole. (This problem is discussed later in this chapter under "Suboptimization.")

Using Benchmarking to Evaluate Performance

benchmarking A comparison of products, services, and practices with those of leading companies

According to Xerox Corporation, the company that pioneered this concept, **benchmarking** is "the continual process of measuring products, services, and practices against the toughest competitors or those companies recognized as industry leaders."[32] Benchmarking, an increasingly popular program, is based on the concept that it makes no sense to reinvent something that someone else is already using. It involves openly learning how others do something better than one's own company, so that one can not only imitate but perhaps even improve on the other company's current techniques. The benchmarking process usually involves the following steps:

- Identify the area or process to be examined. It should be an activity that has the potential to determine a business unit's competitive advantage.
- Find behavioural and output measures of the area or process and obtain measurements.
- Select an accessible set of competitors and best-in-class companies against which to benchmark. These may very often be companies that are in completely different industries but perform similar activities. For example, when Xerox wanted to improve its order fulfillment, it went to L.L. Bean, the successful mail-order firm, to learn how it achieved excellence in this area.
- Calculate the differences between the company's performance measurements and those of the best-in-class and determine why the differences exist.
- Develop tactical programs for closing performance gaps.
- Implement the programs and then compare the resulting new measurements with those of the best-in-class companies.

Benchmarking has been found to produce best results in companies that are already well managed. Apparently poorer performing firms tend to be overwhelmed by the discrepancy between their performance and the benchmark, and they tend to view the benchmark as too difficult to reach.[33] Nevertheless, a survey of a broad cross-section of companies in different industries indicated that more than 70% were using benchmarking in either a major or limited manner.[34] Cost reductions range from 15% to 45%.[35] Benchmarking can also increase sales, improve goal setting, and boost employee motivation.[36] The average benchmarking study costs around $100 000 and involves 30 weeks of effort.[37]

INTERNATIONAL MEASUREMENT ISSUES

The three most widely used techniques for international performance evaluation are return on investment, budget analysis, and historical comparisons. In one study, 95% of the corporate officers interviewed stated that they use the same evaluation techniques for foreign and domestic operations. Rate of return was mentioned as the single most important measure.[38] However, ROI can cause problems when it is applied to international operations. Because of foreign currencies, different rates of inflation, different tax laws, and the use of transfer pricing, both the net income figure and the investment base may be seriously distorted.[39]

A study of 79 MNCs revealed that international transfer pricing from one country unit to another is primarily used not to evaluate performance but to minimize taxes.[40] Taxes are an important issue for MNCs given that corporate tax rates vary from more than 40% in Canada, Japan, Italy, and the United States to 25% in Bolivia, 15% in Chile, and 10% to 15% in Zambia.[41] In countries where corporate tax rates are relatively high, as in Canada, foreign firms can be tempted to artificially inflate the value of Canadian deliveries in order to reduce the profits and thus the taxes of their subsidiaries.[42] Parts made in a subsidiary of an MNC in a low-tax country such as Singapore or China can be shipped to its subsidiary in a high-tax country such as Canada or the United States at such a high price that the subsidiary reports very little profit (and thus pays few taxes), while the Singapore subsidiary reports a very high profit (but also pays few taxes because of the lower tax rate). An MNC can, therefore, earn more profit worldwide by reporting less profit in high-tax countries and more profit in low-tax countries. Transfer pricing is an important factor, given that 56% of all trade in the triad and one-third of all international trade comprises inter-company transactions.[43] Transfer pricing can thus be one way the parent company can reduce taxes and "capture profits" from a subsidiary. Other common ways of transferring profits to the parent company (often referred to as the repatriation of profits) are through dividends, royalties, and management fees.[44]

and (3) insufficient implementation support.[47] Over the two-year period of installing R/3, Owens-Corning had to completely overhaul its operations. Because R/3 was incompatible with Apple Computer's very organic corporate culture, the company was able to apply it only to its order management and financial operations, but not to manufacturing.

DIVISIONAL AND FUNCTIONAL IS SUPPORT

At the divisional or SBU level of a corporation, the information system should be used to support, reinforce, or enlarge its business-level strategy through its decision support system. An SBU pursuing a strategy of overall cost leadership could use its information system to reduce costs either by improving labour productivity or improving the use of other resources such as inventory or machinery. Merrill Lynch took this approach when it developed Prism software to provide its 500 US retail offices with quick access to financial information in order to boost brokers' efficiency. Another SBU, in contrast, might want to pursue a differentiation strategy. It could use its information system to add uniqueness to the product or service and contribute to quality, service, or image through the functional areas. Canada Post wanted to use superior service and internal efficiency to develop a competitive advantage that would allow it to withstand the many forms of competition it was facing (new technology shrinking the demand for mail/courier and gains from large American couriers like FedEx). It invested significantly in several types of information systems to measure and track the performance of its delivery service. It combined this with a redesign of its operations using lean manufacturing concepts. Together, these gave Canada Post and its affiliate Purolator Courier improved efficiency and effectiveness in a wide range of delivery services in Canada.

10.4 Problems in Measuring Performance

The measurement of performance is a crucial part of evaluation and control. The lack of quantifiable objectives or performance standards and the inability of the information system to provide timely and valid information are two obvious control problems. Without objective and timely measurements, it would be extremely difficult to make operational, let alone strategic, decisions. Nevertheless, the use of timely, quantifiable standards does not guarantee good performance. The very act of monitoring and measuring performance can cause side effects that interfere with overall corporate performance. Among the most frequent negative side effects are a short-term orientation and goal displacement.

SHORT-TERM ORIENTATION

Top executives report that in many situations they analyze neither the long-term implications of present operations on the strategy they have adopted nor the operational impact of a strategy on the corporate mission. Long-run evaluations are often not conducted because executives (1) don't realize their importance, (2) believe that short-run considerations are more important than long-run considerations, (3) aren't personally evaluated on a long-term basis, or (4) don't have the time to make a long-run analysis.[48] There is no real justification for the first and last "reasons." If executives realize the importance of long-run evaluations, they make the time needed to conduct them. Even though many chief executives point to immediate pressures from the investment community and to short-term incentive and promotion plans to support the second and third reasons, evidence does not always support their claims.[49]

Many accounting-based measures do, however, encourage a short-term orientation. **Table 10–1** indicates that one of the limitations of ROI as a performance measure is its short-term nature. In theory, ROI is not limited to the short run, but in practice it is often difficult to use this measure to realize long-term benefits for the company. Because managers can often manipulate both the numerator (earnings) and the denominator (investment), the resulting ROI figure can be meaningless. Advertising, maintenance, and research efforts can be reduced. Mergers can be undertaken that will do more for this year's earnings (and next year's pay-cheque) than for the division's or corporation's future profits. Research of firms that engaged in major acquisitions revealed that even though they performed poorly after the acquisition, the acquiring firms' top management still received significant increases in compensation.[50] Expensive retooling and plant modernization can be delayed as long as a manager can manipulate figures on production defects and absenteeism.

Research supports the conclusion that many CEOs and their friends on the board of directors' compensation committee manipulate information to provide themselves a pay raise. For example, CEOs tend to announce bad news—thus reducing the company's stock price—just before the issuance of stock options. Once the options are issued, the CEOs tend to announce good news—thus raising the stock price and making their options more valuable.[51] Board compensation committees tend to expand the peer group comparison outside their industry to include lower performing firms to justify a high raise to the CEO. They tend to do this when the company performs poorly, the industry performs well, the CEO is already highly paid, and shareholders are powerful and active.[52]

GOAL DISPLACEMENT

goal displacement
an unintended consequence of strategic control where the relationship between means and ends no longer supports organizational goal accomplishment

Monitoring and measuring performance (if not carefully done) can actually result in a decline in overall corporate performance. **Goal displacement** is the confusion of means with ends and occurs when activities originally intended to help managers attain corporate objectives become ends in themselves—or are adapted to meet ends other than those for which they were intended. Two types of goal displacement are behaviour substitution and suboptimization.

Behaviour Substitution

behaviour substitution
an unintended consequence of reward systems, where the behaviours that are measured and rewarded replace those that best accomplish organizational goals

Behaviour substitution refers to the phenomenon of substitution of activities that do not lead to goal accomplishment for activities that do, because the wrong activities are being rewarded. Managers, like most people, tend to focus more of their attention on those behaviours that are clearly measurable than on those that are not. Employees often receive little to no reward for engaging in hard-to-measure activities such as co-operation and initiative. However, easy-to-measure activities might have little to no relation to the desired good performance. Rational people, nevertheless, tend to work for the rewards that the system has to offer. Therefore, people tend to substitute behaviours that are recognized and rewarded for those behaviours that are ignored, without regard to their contribution to goal accomplishment. An old navy quip sums up this situation: "What you inspect (or reward) is what you get." Sears thought that it would improve employee productivity by tying performance to rewards. It therefore paid commissions to its auto shop employees as a percentage of each repair bill. Behaviour substitution resulted as employees altered their behaviour to fit the reward system. The result was over-billed customers, charges for work never done, and a scandal that tarnished the company's reputation for many years.[53] The effect of measurement on behaviour seems to be that quantifiable measures drive out non-quantifiable measures. In other words, what gets measured gets done; what does not get measured will eventually disappear.

Suboptimization

suboptimization the situation where an organizational unit optimizes its goal accomplishment to the detriment of the organization as a whole

Suboptimization refers to when a unit optimizes its goal accomplishment to the detriment of the organization as a whole. The emphasis in large corporations on developing separate responsibility centres can create some problems for the corporation. To the extent that a division or functional unit views itself as a separate entity, it might refuse to co-operate with other units or divisions in the same corporation if co-operation could in some way negatively affect its performance evaluation. The competition between divisions to achieve a high ROI can result in one division's refusal to share its new technology or work process improvements. One division's attempt to optimize the accomplishment of its goals can cause other divisions to fall behind and thus negatively affect overall corporate performance. One common example of suboptimization occurs when a marketing department approves an early shipment date to a customer as a means of getting an order and forces the manufacturing department into overtime production for this one order. Production costs are raised, which reduces the manufacturing department's overall efficiency. The end result might be that, although marketing achieves its sales goal, the corporation as a whole fails to achieve its expected profitability. This was the cause of many problems at Provincial Papers Inc. in Thunder Bay. Once a coated paper manufacturing division of Abitibi-Price, Provincial Papers struggled as an independent organization in the context of the increasing globalization of the industry, overcapacity worldwide, and restrictive trade barriers in Europe. As the company experienced increasingly poor financial returns, it felt pressure to make sales any way it could. This contributed to a large number of changes to production processes and scheduling to create samples for custom paper products, which increased costs to the point where the firm was not improving its bottom line despite increasing its sales. By having a sales force that was under so much pressure to make sales, the organization as a whole suffered as products were not able to be profitably delivered. Gradually the company ended up with large inventories and high development costs as new custom paper products were promised to customers. To add to its problems, Provincial Papers was convicted of several environmental offences in 2000 and fined $200 000 for depositing "acutely lethal effluent... into fish-bearing waters."[54]

10.5 Guidelines for Proper Control

In designing a control system, top management should remember that controls should follow strategy. Unless controls ensure the use of the proper strategy to achieve objectives, there is a strong likelihood that dysfunctional side effects will completely undermine the implementation of the objectives. The following guidelines are recommended:

1. **Control should involve only the minimum amount of information** needed to give a reliable picture of events. Too many controls create confusion. Focus on the strategic factors by following the 80/20 rule: monitor those 20% of the factors that determine 80% of the results.

2. **Controls should monitor only meaningful activities and results**, regardless of measurement difficulty. If co-operation among divisions is important to corporate performance, some form of qualitative or quantitative measure should be established to monitor co-operation.

3. **Controls should be timely** so that corrective action can be taken before it is too late. Steering controls, controls that monitor or measure the factors influencing performance, should be stressed so that advance notice of problems is given.

4. **Long-term and short-term controls should be used**. If only short-term measures are emphasized, a short-term managerial orientation is likely.

5. **Controls should aim at pinpointing exceptions**. Only those activities or results that fall outside a predetermined tolerance range should call for action.

6. **Emphasize the reward of meeting or exceeding standards** rather than punishment for failing to meet standards. Heavy punishment of failure typically results in goal displacement. Managers will fudge reports and lobby for lower standards.

To the extent that the culture complements and reinforces the strategic orientation of the firm, there is less need for an extensive formal control system. In their book *In Search of Excellence*, Peters and Waterman state that "the stronger the culture and the more it was directed toward the marketplace, the less need was there for policy manuals, organization charts, or detailed procedures and rules. In these companies, people way down the line know what they are supposed to do in most situations because the handful of guiding values is crystal clear."[55]

10.6 Corporate Governance

Strategic control systems are designed to ensure that an organization's strategy is successfully implemented, and that ample warning is given to managers if it is not. The organization must be structured in a way that facilitates organizational goal accomplishment, but organizational members must also be motivated to do what is best for the organization as a whole. Agency theory is useful as a backdrop for strategic control because it recognizes that as individuals (and the departments they work in) act in their own interests, they might not necessarily act in the interests of the organization and its owners. Simply put, agency theory states that individuals will act in self-interested ways. In organizations, an agency situation arises because owners or shareholders (the principal) delegate the day-to-day management of the organization to managers (the agent). An agency problem arises when the principal and agent have different goals. To overcome these types of agency problems, strategic control systems are developed to align the interests of principals and agents. How is this accomplished? In large part it is done by corporate governance mechanisms that provide shareholders, through a board of directors, with the information necessary to review performance and provide input into the management of the firm so that goal conflict is reduced.

A corporation is a mechanism established to allow different parties to contribute capital, expertise, and labour for their mutual benefit. The investor or shareholder participates in the profits of the enterprise without taking responsibility for the operations. Management runs the company without being responsible for personally providing the funds. To make this possible, laws have been passed so that shareholders have limited liability and, correspondingly, limited involvement in a corporation's activities. That involvement does include, however, the right to elect directors who have a legal duty to represent the shareholders and protect their interests. As representatives of the shareholders, directors have both the authority and the responsibility to establish basic corporate policies and to ensure that they are followed.[56]

The board of directors has, therefore, an obligation to approve all decisions that might affect the long-run performance of the corporation. This means that the corporation is fundamentally governed by the board of directors overseeing top management, with the concurrence of the shareholders. The term **corporate governance** refers to the relationship among these three groups in determining the direction and performance of the corporation.[57]

Over the past decade, shareholders and various interest groups have seriously questioned the role of the board of directors in corporations. They are concerned that outside board members often lack sufficient knowledge, involvement, and enthusiasm to do an adequate job of providing guidance to top management. The general public has not only become more

corporate governance
the mechanism by which shareholders, through a board of directors, oversee and influence an organization's management

aware and more critical of many boards' apparent lack of responsibility for corporate activities, it has also begun to push government to demand accountability. As a result, the board as a rubber stamp of the CEO or as a bastion of the "old boy" selection system is being replaced by more active, more professional boards.

ownership concentration the situation when a small number of large investors own a large proportion of a corporation's shares

In Canada, **ownership concentration** is relatively high, which results in large institutional investors having a tremendous amount of influence in organizational strategy through their ownership stake. Pension funds and mutual funds represent some of the largest institutional investors in Canada, and they are becoming increasingly interested in ensuring their interests are heard and acted upon, and that governance mechanisms are in place to safeguard their investments and control the decisions of management. Ownership concentration makes it easier to influence managerial decision making because institutional investors can be represented at shareholder meetings by people who command a large amount of respect by virtue of their equity investments in the organization. The greater the degree of ownership concentration, the greater the chance that management's decisions will be made in ways that maximize shareholder value and consider their claims.

Because they are able to exert influence on an organization's management, institutional investors act as a governance mechanism in the way a stock market does. But in contrast to diffuse ownership situations where coordination among shareholders is difficult, concentrated ownership allows for more powerful governance. In Canada, approximately 70% of publicly traded stocks are owned by institutions, but in the United States this figure is only about 50%. These investors are becoming increasingly interested in organizations' strategic decisions, especially in the post-Enron era when so many Canadian institutional investors and banks lost a tremendous amount of money. The fraudulent management and accounting practices of Enron, Adelphia, and Tyco sent a signal to all equity investors of the uncontrolled ambition and greed of some executives and the virtual disregard for shareholders and employees that went along with it. Canada has its own examples, albeit on a smaller scale:

- **YBM Magnex:** YBM's key disclosure documents did not disclose all material facts and changes in its affairs forthwith, essentially disclosing good news with little hesitation but restricting the disclosure of bad news. YBM's disclosures led investors and creditors to believe that the risks it faced were no greater than the inherent risks faced by any company operating in Eastern Europe. The Ontario Securities Commission found this to be untrue.

- **Cartaway Resources:** In 1995 Cartaway announced it had acquired claims in Voisey Bay and issued press releases indicating promising test results showing nickel and copper deposits. These reports were misleading, but they caused stock prices to rise dramatically in the short run.

- **Bre-X Minerals:** In what is perhaps Canada's most famous case of corporate wrongdoing, stock prices plunged from the equivalent of $281 per share to less than $0.02 after questions about the company's gold values and the reported suicide of one of the geologists who found the property. Share prices originally skyrocketed after reports of huge gold deposits in an Indonesian rain forest. After its owners made millions, Bre-X eventually admitted that the size of gold deposits had been overstated. This announcement left thousand of shareholders with virtually worthless stocks.

executive compensation the use of financial incentives to align the interests of the owners and managers of a corporation

The popular press has written a great deal lately about **executive compensation**, most specifically about the extremely high levels of compensation and its apparent disconnect from firm performance. As a governance mechanism, executive compensation is intended to create goal alignment as any incentive-based pay system would. By using compensation (salaries, bonuses, and stock options) as an incentive, these plans are intended to tie an executive's performance to that of the organization. Because executives are also shareholders, the potential for agency problems caused by the separation of ownership and management is minimized. The logic here is that the interests of shareholders and the organization are aligned when there is no longer a clear distinction between owners and managers. This logic notwithstanding, it is difficult to reward decisions that are in the long-run interest of the organization when there is an inability to accurately measure something in the short-run, or even to be certain how today's decisions will affect tomorrow's performance. Adding to the complexity of creating effective incentive-based pay systems are the circumstances beyond the control of executives (for example competitive response and social changes) that affect the outcomes of their decisions. Despite the imperfect nature of executive compensation as a governance mechanism, there surely is a benefit to having as tight a link as possible between the performance of an organization and that of its executives. In the popular press there is constant questioning of what are viewed as excessive compensation packages—Magna International's chairman Frank Stronach has taken home on average approximately $45 million a year since 2000, and the Bank of Montreal's Tony Comper grossed close to $25 million in 1999. These large figures might be justified if these incentives are in fact aligning the interests of managers with those of shareholders and other stakeholders. The risk is that they are not and that a great deal of money gets channelled to a very small number of people.

RESPONSIBILITIES OF THE BOARD

Laws and standards defining the responsibilities of boards of directors vary from country to country. For example, board members in Ontario face more than a hundred provincial and federal laws governing director liability. The United States, however, has no clear national standards or federal laws. Specific requirements of directors vary, depending on the state in which the corporate charter is issued. There is, nevertheless, a developing worldwide consensus concerning the major responsibilities of a board. Interviews with directors from eight countries (Canada, France, Germany, Finland, Switzerland, the Netherlands, the United Kingdom, and Venezuela) revealed strong agreement on the following five board responsibilities, listed in order of importance:[58]

1. Setting corporate strategy, overall direction, mission, or vision
2. Hiring and firing the CEO and top management
3. Controlling, monitoring, or supervising top management
4. Reviewing and approving the use of resources
5. Caring for shareholder interests

Directors must make certain, in addition to the duties just listed, that the corporation is managed in accordance with the laws of the province in which it is incorporated. They must also ensure management's adherence to laws and regulations, such as those dealing with the issuance of securities, insider trading, and other conflict-of-interest situations. They must also be aware of the needs and demands of constituent groups so that they can achieve a judicious balance among the interests of these diverse groups while ensuring the continued functioning of the corporation.

In a legal sense, the board is required to direct the affairs of the corporation but not to manage them. It is charged by law to act with due care, or **due diligence**. If a director or the board as a whole fails to act with due care and, as a result, the corporation is in some way harmed, the careless director or directors can be held personally liable for the harm done. This is no small concern given that one survey of outside directors revealed that more than 40% had been named as part of a lawsuit against the corporation.[59]

due diligence the legal obligation of the board of directors to direct the affairs of the corporation to safeguard owners' interests

Role of the Board in Strategic Management

How does a board of directors fulfill these many responsibilities? The role of the board of directors in strategic management is to carry out three basic tasks:

- **Monitor**: By acting through its committees, a board can keep abreast of developments inside and outside the corporation, bringing to management's attention developments it might have overlooked. A board should at least carry out this task.

- **Evaluate and influence:** A board can examine management's proposals, decisions, and actions; agree or disagree with them; give advice and offer suggestions; outline alternatives. More active boards perform this task in addition to the monitoring one.

- **Initiate and determine:** A board can delineate a corporation's mission and specify strategic options to its management. Only the most active boards take on this task in addition to the two previous ones.

Board of Directors Continuum

A board of directors is involved in strategic management to the extent that it carries out the three tasks of monitoring, evaluating and influencing, and initiating and determining. The board of directors continuum shown in **Figure 10–3** shows the possible degree of involvement (from low to high) in the strategic management process. As types, boards can range from phantom boards with no real involvement to catalyst boards with a very high degree of involvement. Research does suggest that active board involvement in strategic management is positively related to corporate financial performance.[60]

Highly involved boards tend to be very active. They take their tasks of monitoring, evaluating, and influencing, plus initiating and determining, very seriously; they provide advice when necessary and keep management alert. As depicted in **Figure 10–3,** their heavy involvement in the strategic management process places them in the active participation or even catalyst positions. For example, in a survey of directors of large US corporations, more than 60% indicated that they were deeply involved in the strategy-setting process. In the same survey, 54% of the respondents indicated that their boards participated in an annual retreat or special planning session to discuss company strategy. Nevertheless, only slightly more than 32% of the boards helped develop the strategy. More than two-thirds of the boards reviewed

Figure 10–3 Board of Directors Continuum

DEGREE OF INVOLVEMENT IN STRATEGIC MANAGEMENT ➡

Low (Passive) ⟵ ⟶ High (Active)

Phantom	Rubber Stamp	Minimal Review	Nominal Participation	Active Participation	Catalyst
Never knows what to do, if anything; no degree of involvement.	Permits officers to make all decisions. It votes as the officers recommend on action issues.	Formally reviews selected issues that officers bring to its attention.	Involved to a limited degree in the performance or review of selected key decisions, indicators, or programs of management.	Approves, questions, and makes final decisions on missions, strategy, policies, and objectives. Has active board committees. Performs fiscal and management audits.	Takes the leading role in establishing and modifying the mission, objectives, strategy, and policies. It has a very active strategy committee.

Source: T.L. Wheelen and J.D. Hunger, "Board of Directors Continuum." Copyright © 1994 by Wheelen and Hunger Associates. Reprinted by permission.

strategy only after it had been first developed by management. Another 1% admitted playing no role at all in strategy.[61]

As a board becomes less involved in the affairs of the corporation, it moves farther to the left on the continuum. On the far left are passive phantom or rubber stamp boards that typically never initiate or determine strategy unless a crisis occurs. In these situations, the CEO also serves as chairman of the board, personally nominates all directors, and works to keep board members under his or her control by giving them the "mushroom treatment": throw manure on them and keep them in the dark.

Generally, the smaller the corporation, the less active is its board of directors. In an entrepreneurial venture, for example, the privately held corporation may be 100% owned by the founders, who also manage the company. In this case, there is no need for an active board to protect the interests of the owner-manager shareholders; the interests of the owners and the managers are identical. In this instance, a board is really unnecessary and only meets to satisfy legal requirements. If stock is sold to outsiders to finance growth, however, the board becomes more active. Key investors want seats on the board so they can oversee their investment. To the extent that they still control most of the stock, however, the founders dominate the board. Friends, family members, and key shareholders usually become members, but the board acts primarily as a rubber stamp for any proposals put forward by the owner-managers. This cozy relationship between the board and management should change, however, when the corporation goes public and stock is more widely dispersed. The founders, who are still acting as management, may sometimes make decisions that conflict with the needs of the other shareholders (especially if the founders own less than 50% of the common stock). In this instance, problems could occur if the board fails to become more active in terms of its roles and responsibilities.

Most large, publicly owned corporations have boards that operate at some point between nominal and active participation. A recent study of boards of directors found the following:[62]

- Thirty percent of the boards actively worked with management to develop strategic direction (**active/catalyst**).
- Thirty percent worked to revise as well as ratify management's proposals (**minimal/nominal participation**).
- Forty percent merely ratified management's strategic proposals (**phantom/rubber stamp**).

The boards of most publicly owned corporations comprise both inside and outside directors. Inside directors (sometimes called management directors) are typically officers or executives employed by the corporation. Outside directors (sometimes called non-management directors) may be executives of other firms but are not employees of the board's corporation. Although there is no clear evidence indicating that a high proportion of outsiders on a board results in improved corporate performance, there is a trend in the United States toward increasing the number of outsiders on boards. The typical large corporation had an average of 11 directors in 1999 (down from 12 directors in 1994), of whom two were insiders (down from three in 1994 and five in 1973).[63] Even though outsiders account for slightly more than 80% of the board members in these large American corporations (approximately the same as in Canada), they only account for about 42% of board membership in small US companies.[64] People who favour a high proportion of outsiders state that outside directors are less biased and more likely to evaluate management's performance objectively than are inside directors. This is the main reason why the New York Stock Exchange requires that all companies listed on the exchange have an audit committee comprising only independent, outside members. This view is in agreement with agency theory, which states that problems arise in corporations because the agents (top management) are not willing to bear responsibility for their decisions unless they own a substantial amount of stock in the corporation. The theory suggests that a majority of a board needs to be from outside the firm so that top management is prevented from acting selfishly to the detriment of the shareholders. See the **Theory As It Applies** feature for a discussion of Agency Theory contrasted with Stewardship Theory.

Theory As It Applies

Agency Theory versus Stewardship Theory in Corporate Governance

Managers of large, modern, publicly held corporations are typically not the owners. In fact, most of today's top managers own only nominal amounts of stock in the corporation they manage. The real owners (shareholders) elect boards of directors who hire managers as their agents to run the firm's day-to-day activities. Once hired, how trustworthy are these executives? Do they put themselves or the firm first?

Agency Theory

As suggested in the classic study by Berle and Means, top managers are, in effect, "hired hands" who may very likely be more interested in their personal welfare than that of the shareholders. For example, management might emphasize strategies, such as acquisitions, that increase the size of the firm (to become more powerful and to demand increased pay and benefits) or that diversify the firm into unrelated businesses (to reduce short-term risk and to allow them to put less effort into a core product line that may be facing difficulty) but that result in a reduction in dividends and/or stock price.

Agency theory is concerned with analyzing and resolving two problems that occur in relationships between principals (owners or shareholders) and their agents (top management):

1. The agency problem that arises when (a) the desires or objectives of the owners and the agents conflict or (b) it is difficult or expensive for the owners to verify what the agent is actually doing. One example occurs when top management is more interested in raising its own salary than in increasing stock dividends.

2. The risk-sharing problem that arises when the owners and agents have different attitudes toward risk. Executives may not select risky strategies because they fear losing their jobs if the strategy fails.

According to agency theory, the likelihood that these problems will occur increases when stock is widely held (no one shareholder owns more than a small percentage of the total common stock), when the board of directors comprises people who know little of the company or who are personal friends of top management, and when a high percentage of board members are inside (management) directors.

To better align the interests of the agents with those of the owners and to increase the corporation's overall performance, agency theory suggests that top management have a significant degree of ownership in the firm and/or a strong financial stake in its long-term performance. In support of this argument, research does indicate a positive relationship between corporate performance and the amount of stock owned by directors.

Stewardship Theory

In contrast, stewardship theory suggests that executives tend to be more motivated to act in the best interests of the corporation than in their own self-interest. Whereas agency theory focuses on extrinsic rewards that serve the lower level needs, such as pay and security, stewardship theory focuses on the higher order needs, such as achievement and self-actualization. Stewardship theory argues that senior executives over time tend to view the corporation as an extension of themselves. Rather than using the firm for their own ends, these executives are most interested in guaranteeing the continued life and success of the corporation. The relationship between the board and top management is thus one of principal and steward, not principal and agent ("hired hand"). Stewardship theory notes that in a widely held corporation, the shareholder is free to sell her or his stock at any time. A diversified investor may care little about risk at the company level—preferring that management assume extraordinary risk as long as the return is adequate. Because executives in a firm cannot so easily leave their jobs when in difficulty, they are more interested in a merely satisfactory return and put heavy emphasis on the firm's continued survival. Thus, stewardship theory would argue that in many instances top management may care more about a company's long-term success than do more short-term-oriented shareholders.

For more information about agency and stewardship theory, see J.H. Davis, F.D. Schoorman, and L. Donaldson, "Toward a Stewardship Theory of Management," *Academy of Management Review* (January 1997), pp. 20–47. See also P.J. Lane, A.A. Cannella Jr., and M.H. Lubatkin, "Agency Problems As Antecedents to Unrelated Mergers and Diversification: Amihud and Lev Reconsidered," *Strategic Management Journal* (June 1998), pp. 555–578, and M.L. Hayward and D.C. Hambrick, "Explaining the Premiums Paid for Large Acquisitions: Evidence of CEO Hubris," *Administrative Science Quarterly* (March 1997), pp. 103–127.

In contrast, those who prefer inside over outside directors contend that outside directors are less effective than are insiders because the outsiders are less likely to have the necessary interest, availability, or competency. Directors may sometimes serve on so many boards that they spread their time and interest too thinly to actively fulfill their responsibilities. They could also point out that the term "outsider" is too simplistic—some outsiders are not truly objective and should be considered more as insiders than as outsiders. For example, there are these types of directors:

1. **Affiliated directors** who, though not really employed by the corporation, handle the legal or insurance work for the company or are important suppliers (thus dependent on the current management for a key part of their business). These outsiders face a conflict of interest and are not likely to be objective.

2. **Retired directors** who used to work for the company, such as the past CEO (who is partly responsible for much of the corporation's current strategy and probably groomed the current CEO as his or her replacement). Many boards of large firms keep the firm's recently retired CEO on the board for a year or two after retirement as a courtesy, especially if he or she performed well as the CEO. It is almost certain, however, that this person will not be able to objectively evaluate the corporation's performance. Nevertheless, a recent survey found that only 29% of directors surveyed indicated that their boards required the former CEO to leave the board upon retirement.[65]

3. **Family directors** who are descendants of the founder and own significant blocks of stock (with personal agendas based on a family relationship with the current CEO). The Schlitz Brewing Company, for example, was unable to complete its turnaround strategy with a non-family CEO because family members serving on the board wanted their money out of the company, forcing it to be sold.[66]

The majority of outside directors are active or retired CEOs and COOs of other corporations. Others are major investors or shareholders, academicians, attorneys, consultants, former government officials, and bankers. Given that approximately 60% of the outstanding stock in the largest US and UK corporations is now owned by institutional investors, such as mutual funds and pension plans, these investors are taking an increasingly active role in board membership and activities.[67] In Germany, bankers are represented on almost every board—primarily because they own large blocks of stock in German corporations. In Denmark, Sweden, Belgium, and Italy, however, investment companies assume this role. For example, the investment company Investor AB casts 42.5% of the Electrolux AB shareholder votes, thus guaranteeing itself positions on the Electrolux board. Surveys of large US corporations found that 75% of the boards in 1999 had at least one female director—up from 60% in 1992 and only 11% in 1972—with 25% now having two female directors. Boards having at least one minority member increased from 9% in 1973 to 60% in 1999 (African-American: 39%; Latino: 12%; Asian: 9%).

The globalization of business is having an impact on board membership. By 1998, 10% of all directors of companies surveyed internationally by the Conference Board's Global Corporate Governance Research Center were non-nationals, up from 6% three years earlier. Europe is the most "globalized" region of the world, with 71% of companies reporting one or more non-national directors, followed by North America, where the figure was 60% in 1998. Asian and Latin American boards are still predominantly staffed by nationals.[68] See the **Global Issue** feature showing how a Korean manufacturing firm added a non-Korean director to its board of directors.

Outside directors serving on the boards of large corporations in 1999 annually earned on average (median) $33 000. Almost 90% of these corporations also provided some form of payment through stock options or grants—raising the median annual total compensation to $43 700.[69] Directors serving on the boards of small companies usually received much less (around $10 000). One study found directors to hold on average 3% of their corporations' outstanding stock.[70]

The vast majority of inside directors include the chief executive officer, chief operating officer, and presidents or vice-presidents of key operating divisions or functional units. Few, if any, inside directors receive any extra compensation for assuming this extra duty. Very rarely does a North American board include any lower level operating employees.

Global Issue

POSCO Adds a Non-Korean Director

In an attempt to make Korean businesses more attractive to foreign investors, the South Korean government recommended that companies listed on the stock exchange introduce a two-tiered structure. One structure was to consist entirely of non-executive (outside) directors. One of the few companies to immediately adopt this new system of governance was Pohang Iron & Steel Company, Ltd. (POSCO), the world's

largest steelmaker. POSCO was listed on the New York Stock Exchange and had significant operations in the United States plus a joint venture with U.S. Steel. According to Youn-Gil Ro, corporate information team manager, "We needed professional advice on international business practices as well as American practices."

Among the eight outside directors added to the board in early 1997 was Samuel Chevalier, an international financier from the United States. Chevalier had previously sat on boards in Hong Kong and Brazil and had no problem travelling long distances to attend board meetings. To overcome language problems, Youn-Gil Ro explained, "There are simultaneous interpretations during the meetings, and agendas and other materials are written in English as well as Korean."

Source: Globalizing the Board of Directors: Trends and Strategies (New York: The Conference Board, 1999), p. 16.

MEMBERS OF A BOARD OF DIRECTORS

Co-determination: Should Employees Serve on Boards?

co-determination
including company workers in the board of directors to have a greater role in corporate governance

Co-determination, the inclusion of a corporation's workers on its board, began only recently in the United States. Corporations such as Chrysler, Northwest Airlines, United Airlines (UAL), and Wheeling-Pittsburgh Steel have added representatives from employee associations to their boards as part of union agreements or employee stock ownership plans (ESOPs). For example, United Airlines workers traded 15% in pay cuts for 55% of the company (through an ESOP) and 3 of the firm's 12 board seats. In this instance, workers represent themselves on the board not so much as employees, but primarily as owners. At Chrysler, however, the United Auto Workers union obtained a seat on the board as part of a union contract agreement in exchange for changes in work rules and reductions in benefits. Nevertheless, this position on the board did not last long at Chrysler. In situations like this, when a director represents an internal stakeholder, critics raise the issue of conflict of interest. Can a member of the board, who is privy to confidential managerial information, function, for example, as a union leader whose primary duty is to fight for the best benefits for union members?

Although the movement to place employees on the boards of directors of US companies shows little likelihood of increasing (except through employee stock ownership), the European experience reveals an increasing acceptance of worker participation (without ownership) on corporate boards. Germany pioneered co-determination during the 1950s with a two-tiered system: a supervisory board elected by shareholders and employees to approve or decide corporate strategy and policy, and a management board (comprising primarily top management) appointed by the supervisory board to manage the company's activities. Worker representatives in specific industries such as coal, iron, and steel were given equal status with management on policy-making supervisory boards. In other industries, however, workers only elect one-third of supervisory board membership. At Siemens AG, for example, shareholders elect only 10 people to the supervisory board. Employees of Siemens and "dependent" firms elect seven members, with employee labour unions electing three more members for a total of another 10. This 20-member supervisory board elects a 17-member management board to actually run the company.[71]

Most other Western European countries have either passed similar co-determination legislation (as in Sweden, Denmark, Norway, and Austria) or use worker councils to work closely with management (as in Belgium, Luxembourg, France, Italy, Ireland, and the Netherlands). Nevertheless, research on German co-determination has found that legislation requiring firms to put employee representatives on their boards lowered dividend payments, led to a more conservative investment policy, and reduced firm values.[72]

Interlocking Directorates

interlocking directorate a situation where organizations have representatives on each other's boards of directors so they become linked

CEOs often nominate chief executives (as well as board members) from other firms to membership on their own boards to create an interlocking directorate. A direct **interlocking directorate** occurs when two firms share a director or when an executive of one firm sits on the board of a second firm. An indirect interlock occurs when two corporations have directors who also serve on the board of a third firm, such as a bank. On average, both inside and outside directors at the large companies serve on three boards. Interlocking occurs because large firms have a big impact on other corporations; these other corporations, in turn, have some control over the firm's inputs and marketplace. For example, most large corporations in the United States, Japan, and Germany are interlocked either directly or indirectly with financial institutions.[73] Interlocking directorates are also a useful method for gaining both inside information about an uncertain environment and objective expertise about potential strategies and tactics. Family-owned corporations, however, are less likely to have interlocking directorates than are corporations with highly dispersed stock ownership, probably because family-owned corporations do not like to dilute their corporate control by adding outsiders to boardroom discussions. Nevertheless, some evidence indicates that well-interlocked corporations are better able to survive in a highly competitive environment.[74]

TRENDS IN CORPORATE GOVERNANCE

The role of the board of directors in the strategic management of the corporation is likely to be more active in the future. The change will probably be evolutionary, however, rather than radical or revolutionary. Different boards are at different levels of maturity and will not be changing in the same direction or at the same speed. Although neither the composition of boards nor the board leadership structure has been consistently linked to firm financial performance, a McKinsey survey reveals that investors are willing to pay 16% more for a corporation's stock if it is known to have good corporate governance. The investors explained that they would pay more because, in their opinion (1) good governance leads to better performance over time, (2) good governance reduces the risk that the company will get into trouble, and (3) governance is a major strategic issue.[75]

Some of today's trends in governance that are likely to continue include the following:[76]

- Boards are getting more involved not only in reviewing and evaluating company strategy, but also in shaping it.
- Institutional investors, such as pension funds, mutual funds, and insurance companies, are becoming active on boards and are putting increasing pressure on top management to improve corporate performance. For example, the California Public Employees'

Retirement System (CalPERS), the largest pension system in the United States, annually publishes a list of poorly performing companies, hoping to embarrass management into remedial action.

- Shareholders are demanding that directors and top managers own more than token amounts of stock in the corporation. Stock is increasingly being used as part of a director's compensation.

- Non-affiliated outside (non-management) directors are increasing their numbers and power in publicly held corporations as CEOs loosen their grip on boards. Outside members are taking charge of annual CEO evaluations.

- Boards are getting smaller, partially because of the reduction in the number of insiders but also because boards desire new directors to have specialized knowledge and expertise instead of general experience.

- Boards continue to take more control of board functions by either splitting the combined chair–CEO role into two separate positions or establishing a lead outside director position.

- As corporations become more global, they are increasingly looking for international experience in their board members.

- Society, in the form of special interest groups, increasingly expects boards of directors to balance the economic goal of profitability with the social needs of society. Issues dealing with workforce diversity and the environment are now reaching the board level. For example, the board of Chase Manhattan Corporation recently questioned top management about its efforts to improve the sparse number of women and minorities in senior management.[77]

As a way to enhance strategic control, corporate governance mechanisms act as a way to minimize agency problems. Increasingly we are seeing organizations developing missions and visions that encompass a broad range of organizational stakeholders, not just shareholders. As a result, many boards of directors are representing the diverse interests of key organizational stakeholders, and as such act as input into the management of the organization. The nature of the corporation forces the separation of its ownership from its day-to-day operations. But as the trends in corporate governance presented earlier suggest, the board is taking an increasingly important role in the management of corporations today, and this trend will likely continue. The result is a closer eye on organizational activities, and a more regular monitoring of how its activities contribute to the achievement of organizational goals and objectives.

10.7 Strategic Incentive Management

To ensure congruence between the needs of the corporation as a whole and the needs of the employees as individuals, management and the board of directors should develop an incentive program that rewards desired performance. This reduces the likelihood of agency problems (when employees act to feather their own nest instead of building shareholder value) mentioned earlier. Incentive plans should be linked in some way to corporate and divisional strategy. For example, a survey of 600 business units indicates that the pay mix associated with a growth strategy emphasizes bonuses and other incentives over salary and benefits, whereas the pay mix associated with a stability strategy has the reverse emphasis.[78] Research does indicate that SBU managers having long-term performance elements in their compensation program favour a long-term perspective and thus greater investments in R & D, capital equipment, and employee training.[79] The typical CEO pay package comprises 21% salary, 27% short-term annual incentives, 16% long-term incentives, and 36% stock options.[80]

The following three approaches are tailored to help match measurements and rewards with explicit strategic objectives and time frames.[81]

1. *Weighted-Factor Method:* This method is particularly appropriate for measuring and rewarding the performance of top SBU managers and group level executives when performance factors and their importance vary from one SBU to another. One corporation's measurements might contain the following variations: the performance of high-growth SBUs is measured in terms of market share, sales growth, designated future payoff, and progress on several future-oriented strategic projects; the performance of low-growth SBUs, in contrast, is measured in terms of ROI and cash generation; and the performance of medium-growth SBUs is measured for a combination of these factors. (Refer to **Table 10–3**.)

2. *Long-Term Evaluation Method:* This method compensates managers for achieving objectives set over a multi-year period. An executive is promised some company stock or "performance units" (convertible into money) in amounts to be based on long-term performance. An executive committee, for example, might set a particular objective in terms of growth in earnings per share during a five-year period. The giving of awards would be contingent on the corporation's meeting that objective within the designated time. Any executive who leaves the corporation before the objective is met receives nothing. The typical emphasis on stock price makes this approach more applicable to top management than to business unit managers. Because rising stock markets tend to raise the stock price of mediocre companies, there is a developing trend to index stock options to competitors or to the Standard & Poor's 500.[82]

3. *Strategic-Funds Method:* This method encourages executives to look at developmental expenses as being different from expenses required for current operations. The accounting statement for a corporate unit enters strategic funds as a separate entry below the current ROI. It is, therefore, possible to distinguish between those expense dollars consumed in the generation of current revenues and those invested in the future of the business. Therefore, the manager can be evaluated on both a short- and a long-term basis and has an incentive to invest strategic funds in the future. (See **Table 10–4**.)

Table 10–3 Weighted-Factor Approach to Strategic Incentive Management

Strategic Business Unit Category	Factor	Weight
High Growth	Return on assets	10%
	Cash flow	0%
	Strategic-funds programs (developmental expenses)	45%
	Market-share increase	45%
	Total	100%
Medium Growth	Return on assets	25%
	Cash flow	25%
	Strategic-funds programs (developmental expenses)	25%
	Market-share increase	25%
	Total	100%
Low Growth	Return on assets	50%
	Cash flow	50%
	Strategic-funds programs (developmental expenses)	0%
	Market-share increase	0%
	Total	100%

Source: Reprinted by permission of the publisher from "The Performance Measurement and Reward System: Critical to Strategic Management," by Paul J. Stonich, from *Organizational Dynamics* (Winter 1984), p. 51. Copyright © 1984 with permission from Elsevier Science.

Table 10–4 Strategic Funds Approach to an SBU's Profit-and-Loss Statement

Sales	$12,300,000
Cost of sales	−6,900,000
Gross margin	$ 5,400,000
General and administrative expenses	−3,700,000
Operating profit (return on sales)	$ 1,700,000
Strategic funds (development expenses)	−1,000,000
Pretax profit	$ 700,000

Source: Reprinted by permission of the publisher from "The Performance Measurement and Reward System: Critical to Strategic Management," by Paul J. Stonich, from *Organizational Dynamics* (Winter 1984), p. 52. Copyright © 1984 with permission from Elsevier Science.

An effective way to achieve the desired strategic results through a reward system is to combine the three approaches:

1. Segregate strategic funds from short-term funds as is done in the strategic-funds method.
2. Develop a weighted-factor chart for each SBU.
3. Measure performance on three bases: The pre-tax profit indicated by the strategic-funds approach, the weighted factors, and the long-term evaluation of the SBUs' and the corporation's performance.

Genentech, General Electric, and Textron are some of the firms in which CEO compensation is contingent upon the company's achieving strategic objectives.[83]

10.8 Impact of the Internet on Evaluation and Control

Privacy is becoming a major issue with the use of the internet. According to the American Management Association, nearly 75% of US companies actively monitored their workers' communications and on-the-job activities in 2000—more than double the number four years earlier. Around 54% tracked individual employees' internet connections and 38% admitted storing and reviewing their employees' email. About 45% of the companies surveyed had disciplined their workers (16% fired them). For example, Xerox fired 40 employees for visiting pornographic websites.[84] New desktop software products now allow anyone—boss, business partner, or spouse—to track a person's internet activities. One software firm advertises, "Secretly record everything your spouse, children, and employees do online." The US Congress was considering in late 2000 several bills regarding computer surveillance, but none would make monitoring illegal.[85] According to Paul Saffo, director of Institute of the Future:

> What will end up happening—and it already is happening—is that privacy becomes an increasingly scarce good that you will pay increasingly more for. That is, if you want an unlisted phone number, you pay for that privilege. If you don't want your transactions tracked.... (you know, theoretically an electronic transaction could be tracked. In fact, the system's so screwed up I don't think anyone can find anything.) But, in theory, if you didn't want your transactions tracked, you would get cash and put up with the inconvenience of doing that....
>
> Well, I think the fact is there's a multiplicity of players in this. And everybody's trying to have their role. The problem is that the boundaries between the roles are not clear. The legislative process is a very heavy club and not a precise tool. On the other hand, high-tech in particular has a dreadful history about protecting privacy. Companies just can't help but put unique serial numbers in chips or unique serial numbers in software. This is an industry that still calls its customers "users." As far as I know, there are only two high-growth industries on this planet that reserve such a scornful term for their customers. The other one's in Colombia.[86]

Privacy is also an issue for companies wanting to safeguard confidential information from unwanted visitors. Computer hackers are seemingly able to get into almost any company through their internet websites. In October 2000, hackers were able to view Microsoft's source code. They entered the giant software company by infecting the company's network with a Trojan horse program. This was probably done by sliding past disabled antivirus programs, static IP addresses at Microsoft (a problem with any site constantly connected to the internet via a T-1, cable, or DSL line), and employee laptops used while telecommuting. With this program, hackers obtained Microsoft IP addresses, user names, and passwords that enabled them to access the corporate network from somewhere in Russia.[87]

Intelligence agencies from America, Britain, Canada, Australia, and New Zealand jointly monitor all international satellite communications traffic via a system called Echelon that can identify specific words or phrases from hundreds of thousand of messages. The National Security Agency (NSA) of the United States and its partners have been accused in the European Parliament of tapping into billions of messages ranging from telephone calls to email. The NSA was said to have used the Echelon system to assist US corporations to win two large business contracts in the mid-1990s.[88]

Even though the US Congress passed a law allowing digital signature in July 2000, many people are still concerned that the internet is not a secure means of communicating important or confidential information. Don't expect the internet to replace FedEx or UPS anytime soon.

Discussion Questions

1. Is **Figure 10–1** a realistic model of the evaluation and control process?

2. What are some examples of behaviour controls? Output controls? Input controls?

3. Is EVA an improvement over ROI, ROE, or EPS?

4. How much faith can a manager place in a transfer price as a substitute for a market price in measuring a profit centre's performance?

5. Is the evaluation and control process appropriate for a corporation that emphasizes creativity? Are control and creativity compatible?

Strategic Practice Exercise

Each year, *Fortune* magazine publishes an article entitled "America's Most Admired Companies." It lists the 10 most admired and the 10 least admired. *Fortune*'s rankings are based on scoring publicly held US companies on what it calls "eight key attributes of reputation": innovativeness, quality of management, employee talent, quality of products or services, long-term investment value, financial soundness, social responsibility, and use of corporate assets. *Fortune* asks Clark, Martire & Bartolomeo to survey more than 10 000 executives, directors, and securities analysts. Respondents are asked to choose the companies they admire most, regardless of industry. *Fortune* has been publishing this list since 1982. The 2000 *Fortune* listing of the top 10 most admired were (starting with #1) GE, Microsoft, Dell Computer, Cisco Systems, Wal-Mart Stores, Southwest Airlines, Berkshire Hathaway, Intel, Home Depot, and Lucent Technologies. The bottom 10 were Humana, Revlon, Trans World Airlines, CKE Restaurants, CHS Electronics, Rite Aid, Trump Resorts, Fruit of the Loom, Amerco, and Caremark Rx (least admired).

Try one of these exercises:

1. Go to the library and find a "Most Admired Companies" article from the 1980s or early 1990s and compare that list with the latest one. Which companies have fallen out of the top 10? Pick one of the companies and investigate why it is no longer "admired."

2. How much of the evaluation is dominated by the profitability of the company? See how many of the top 10 are very profitable and how many of the bottom 10 are losing money. How many of these companies also appear in *Fortune*'s list of the "100 Best Companies to Work For"?

3. Pick one of the least admired companies in any year of the survey (such as Trump Resorts) and find out why that company has such a poor reputation. How many of the least admired had received bad publicity the previous year? How many of the least admired companies were listed in multiple years, compared with the most admired companies?

Notes

1. http://cms.3m.com/cms/CA/en/1-30/cFlieFW/view.jhtml (accessed May 14, 2003).

2. A.J. Morrison and K. Roth, "Developing global subsidiary mandates," *Business Quarterly*, Vol. 57, No. 4, (Summer 1993), pp. 104–110.

3. D. Pickton, M. Starkey, and M. Bradford, "Understand Business Variation for Improved Business Performance," *Long Range Planning* (June 1996), pp. 412–415.

4. R. Muralidharan and R.D. Hamilton III, "Aligning Multinational Control Systems," *Long Range Planning* (June 1999), pp. 352–361. These types are based on W.G. Ouchi, "The Relationship between Organizational Structure and Organizational Control," *Administrative Science Quarterly*, Vol. 20 (1977), pp. 95–113, and W.G. Ouchi, "A Conceptual Framework for the Design of Organizational Control Mechanisms," *Management Science*, Vol. 25 (1979), pp. 833–848. Muralidhara and Hamilton refer to Ouchi's clan control as input control.

5. W.G. Rowe and P.M. Wright, "Related and Unrelated Diversification and Their Effect on Human Resource Management Controls," *Strategic Management Journal* (April 1997), pp. 329–338.

6. Muralidharan and Hamilton, pp. 356–359.

7. F.C. Barnes, "ISO 9000 Myth and Reality: A Reasonable Approach to ISO 9000," *SAM Advanced Management Journal* (Spring 1998), pp. 23–30.

8. M.V. Uzumeri, "ISO 9000 and Other Metastandards: Principles for Management Practice?" *Academy of Management Executive* (February 1997), pp. 21–36.

9. A.M. Hormozi, "Understanding and Implementing ISO 9000: A Manager's Guide," *SAM Advanced Management Journal* (Autumn 1995), pp. 4–11.

10. J.K. Shank and V. Govindarajan, *Strategic Cost Management* (New York: The Free Press, 1993).

11. R. Gruber, "Why You Should Consider Activity-Based Costing," *Small Business Forum* (Spring 1994), pp. 20–36.

12. T.P. Pare, "A New Tool for Managing Costs," *Fortune* (June 14, 1993), pp. 124–129.

13. C.K. Brancato, *New Corporate Performance Measures* (New York: The Conference Board, 1995).

14. C.D. Ittner, D.F. Larcker, and M.V. Rajan, "The Choice of Performance Measures in Annual Bonus Contracts," Working paper reported by K.Z. Andrews in "Executive Bonuses," *Harvard Business Review* (January–February 1996), pp. 8–9; J. Low and T. Siesfeld, "Measures That Matter: Wall Street Considers Non-Financial Performance More Than You Think," *Strategy & Leadership* (March/April 1998), pp. 24–30.

15. P.C. Brewer, G. Chandra, and C.A. Hock, "Economic Value Added (EVA): Its Uses and Limitations," *SAM Advanced Management Journal* (Spring 1999), pp. 4–11.

16. D.J. Skyrme and D.M. Amidon, "New Measures of Success," *Journal of Business Strategy* (January/February 1998), p. 23.

17. G.B. Stewart III, "EVA Works—But Not If You Make These Common Mistakes," *Fortune* (May 1, 1995), pp. 117–118.

18. S. Tully, "The Real Key to Creating Wealth," *Fortune* (September 20, 1993), p. 38.

19. A. Ehrbar, "Using EVA to Measure Performance and Assess Strategy," *Strategy & Leadership* (May/June 1999), pp. 20–24.

20. Brewer, Chandra, and Hock, pp. 7–9.

21. **Pro:** K. Lehn and A.K. Makhija, "EVA & MVA as Performance Measures and Signals for Strategic Change," *Strategy & Leadership* (May/June 1996), pp. 34–38. **Con:** D.I. Goldenberg, "Shareholder Value Debunked," *Strategy & Leadership* (January/February 2000), pp. 30–36.

22. Ehrbar, p. 21.

23. S. Tully, "America's Wealth Creators," *Fortune* (November 22, 1999), pp. 275–284, and A.B. Fisher, "Creating Stockholder Wealth: Market Value Added," *Fortune* (December 11, 1995), pp. 105–116.

24. A.B. Fisher, "Creating Stockholder Wealth: Market Value Added," *Fortune* (December 11, 1995), pp. 105–116.

25. Lehn and Makhija, p. 37.

26. R.S. Kaplan and D.P. Norton, "Using the Balanced Scorecard As a Strategic Management System," *Harvard Business Review* (January–February 1996), pp. 75–85; R.S. Kaplan and D.P. Norton, "The Balanced Scorecard—Measures That Drive Performance," *Harvard Business Review* (January–February, 1992), pp. 71–79.

27. D.I. Goldenberg, p. 34.

28. C.K. Brancato, *New Performance Measures* (New York: The Conference Board, 1995).

29. B.P. Stivers and T. Joyce, "Building a Balanced Performance Management System," *SAM Advanced Management Journal* (Spring 2000), pp. 22–29.

30. H. Threat, "Measurement Is Free," *Strategy & Leadership* (May/June 1999), pp. 16–19.

31. Z.U. Khan, S.K. Chawla, M.F. Smith, and M.F. Sharif, "Transfer Pricing Policy Issues in Europe 1992," *International Journal of Management* (September 1992), pp. 230–241.

32. H. Rothman, "You Need Not Be Big To Benchmark," *Nation's Business* (December 1992), p. 64.

33. C.W. Von Bergen and B. Soper, "A Problem with Benchmarking: Using Shaping As a Solution," *SAM Advanced Management Journal* (Autumn 1995), pp. 16–19.

34. "Tool Usage Rates," *Journal of Business Strategy* (March/April 1995), p. 12.

35. R.J. Kennedy, "Benchmarking and Its Myths," *Competitive Intelligence Magazine* (April–June 2000), pp. 28–33.

36. L. Mann, D. Samson, and D. Dow, "A Field Experiment on the Effects of Benchmarking & Goal Setting on Company Sales Performance," *Journal of Management*, Vol. 24, No. 1 (1998), pp. 73–96.

37. S.A.W. Drew, "From Knowledge to Action: The Impact of Benchmarking on Organizational Performance," *Long Range Planning* (June 1997), pp. 427–441.

38. S.M. Robbins and R.B. Stobaugh, "The Bent Measuring Stick for Foreign Subsidiaries," *Harvard Business Review* (September–October 1973), p. 82.

39. J.D. Daniels and L.H. Radebaugh, *International Business*, 5th edition (Reading, Mass.: Addison-Wesley, 1989), pp. 673–674.

40. W.A. Johnson and R.J. Kirsch, "International Transfer Pricing and Decision Making in United States Multinationals," *International Journal of Management* (June 1991), pp. 554–561.

41. "Global Economy Makes Taxing Harder," *The Futurist* (March–April 2000), p. 11; "Financial Indicators," *The Economist* (August 26, 2000), p. 89.

42. "Fixing the Bottom Line," *Time* (November 23, 1992), p. 20.

43. T.A. Stewart, "The New Face of American Power," *Fortune* (July 26, 1993), p. 72; G.P. Zachary, "Behind Stocks' Surge Is an Economy in Which Big U.S. Firms Thrive," *The Wall Street Journal* (November 22, 1995), pp. A1, A5.

44. J.M.L. Poon, R. Ainuddin, and H. Affrim, "Management Policies and Practices of American, British, European, and Japanese Subsidiaries in Malaysia: A Comparative Study," *International Journal of Management* (December 1990), pp. 467–474.

45. C.W.L. Hill, P. Hwang, and W.C. Kim, "An Eclectic Theory of the Choice of International Entry Mode," *Strategic Management Journal* (February 1990), pp. 117–128; D. Lei, J.W. Slocum, Jr., and R.W. Slater, "Global Strategy and Reward Systems: The Key Roles of Management Development and Corporate Culture," *Organizational Dynamics* (Autumn 1990), pp. 27–41; W.R. Fannin and A.F. Rodriques, "National or Global?—Control vs. Flexibility," *Long Range Planning* (October 1986), pp. 84–88.

46. A.V. Phatak, *International Dimensions of Management*, 2nd edition (Boston: Kent, 1989), pp. 155–157.

47. S. McAlary, "Three Pitfalls in ERP Implementation," *Strategy & Leadership* (October/November/December 1999), pp. 49–50.

48. R.M. Hodgetts and M.S. Wortman, *Administrative Policy*, 2nd edition (New York: John Wiley & Sons, 1980), p. 128.

49. J.R. Wooldridge and C.C. Snow, "Stock Market Reaction to Strategic Investment Decisions," *Strategic Management Journal* (September 1990), pp. 353–363.

50. D.R. Schmidt and K.L. Fowler, "Post-Acquisition Financial Performance and Executive Compensation," *Strategic Management Journal* (November–December 1990), pp. 559–569.

51. D. Jones, "Bad News Can Enrich Executives," *Des Moines Register* (November 26, 1999), p. 8S.

52. J.F. Porac, J.B. Wade, and T.G. Pollock, "Industry Categories and the Politics of the Comparable Firm in CEO Compensation," *Administrative Science Quarterly* (March 1999), pp. 112–144.

53. W. Zellner, E. Schine, and G. Smith, "Trickle-Down Is Trickling Down at Work," *Business Week* (March 18, 1996), p. 34.

54. www.on.ec.gc.ca/announce.cfm?ID=565&Lang=e (accessed May 18, 2003).

55. T.J. Peters and R.H. Waterman, *In Search of Excellence* (New York: HarperCollins, 1982), pp. 75–76.

56. A.G. Monks and N. Minow, *Corporate Governance* (Cambridge, Mass.: Blackwell Business, 1995), pp. 8–32.

57. Ibid., p. 1.

58. A. Demb and F.F. Neubauer, "The Corporate Board: Confronting the Paradoxes," *Long Range Planning* (June 1992), p. 13. These results are supported by a 1995 Korn/Ferry International survey in which chairmen and directors agreed that strategy and management succession, in that order, are the most important issues the board expects to face.

59. L. Light, "Why Outside Directors Have Nightmares," *Business Week* (October 23, 1996), p. 6.

60. W.Q. Judge, Jr., and C.P. Zeithaml, "Institutional and Strategic Choice Perspectives on Board Involvement in the Strategic Choice Process," *Academy of Management Journal* (October 1992), pp. 766–794; J.A. Pearce II and S.A. Zahra, "Effective Power-Sharing Between the Board of Directors and the CEO," *Handbook of Business Strategy*, 1992/93 Yearbook (Boston: Warren, Gorham, and Lamont, 1992), pp. 1.1–1.16.

61. *26th Annual Board of Directors Study*, Korn/Ferry International (1999), p. 7.

62. W.Q. Judge, Jr., and C.P. Zeithaml, "Institutional and Strategic Choice Perspectives on Board Involvement in the Strategic Choice Process," *Academy of Management Journal* (October 1992), pp. 766–794.

63. Statistics on boards of directors are taken from *26th Annual Board of Directors Survey* (New York: Korn/Ferry International, 1999), and *Directors' Compensation and Board Practices in 1999* (New York: Conference Board, 1999).

64. L.L. Carr, "Strategic Determinants of Executive Compensation in Small Publicly Traded Firms," *Journal of Small Business Management* (April 1997), pp. 1–12.

65. *26th Annual Board of Directors Study*, Korn/Ferry International (1999), p. 8.

66. See S. Finkelstein and D.C. Hambrick, *Strategic Leadership: Top Executives and Their Impact on Organizations* (St. Paul, Minn.: West, 1996), p. 213.

67. R.A.G. Monks, "What Will Be the Impact of Acting Shareholders? A Practical Recipe for Constructive Change," *Long Range Planning* (February 1999), p. 20.

68. *Globalizing the Board of Directors: Trends and Strategies* (New York: The Conference Board, 1999).

69. For additional information on average board retainers, fees, and stock compensation, see *Directors' Compensation and Board Practices in 1999* (New York: The Conference Board, 1999).

70. R.W. Pouder and R.S. Cantrell, "Corporate Governance Reform: Influence on Shareholder Wealth," *Journal of Business Strategies* (Spring 1999), pp. 48–66.

71. R.E. Berenbeim, *Corporate Boards: CEO Selection, Evaluation and Succession: A Research Report* (New York: The Conference Board, 1995), p. 15.

72. L.H. Clark, Jr., "What Economists Say about Business—and Baboons," *The Wall Street Journal* (June 7, 1983), p. 33. Article summarizes a research paper presented to the Interlaken Seminar on Analysis and Ideology, Interlaken, Switzerland, 1983.

73. M.L. Gerlach, "The Japanese Corporate Network: A Blockmodel Analysis," *Administrative Science Quarterly* (March 1992), pp. 105–139.

74. J.A.C. Baum and C. Oliver, "Institutional Linkages and Organizational Mortality," *Administrative Science Quarterly* (June 1991) pp. 187–218; J.P. Sheppard, "Strategy and Bankruptcy: An Exploration into Organizational Death," *Journal of Management* (Winter 1994), pp. 795–833.

75. D.R. Dalton, C.M. Daily, A.E. Ellstrand, and J.L. Johnson, "Meta-Analytic Reviews of Board Composition, Leadership Structure, and Financial Performance," *Strategic Management Journal* (March 1998), pp. 269–290; G. Beaver, "Competitive Advantage and Corporate Governance—Shop Soiled and Needing Attention!," *Strategic Change* (September–October 1999), p. 330.

76. For governance trends in Europe, see A. Cadbury, "What Are the Trends in Corporate Governance? How Will They Impact Your Company?" *Long Range Planning* (February 1999), pp. 12–19.

77. J.S. Lublin, "Texaco Case Causes a Stir in Boardrooms," *The Wall Street Journal* (November 22, 1996), p. B1.

78. D.B. Balkin and L.R. Gomez-Mejia, "Matching Compensation and Organizational Strategies," *Strategic Management Journal* (February 1990), pp. 153–169.

79. C.S. Galbraith, "The Effect of Compensation Programs and Structure on SBU Competitive Strategy: A Study of Technology-Intensive Firms," *Strategic Management Journal* (July 1991), pp. 353–370.

80. T.A. Stewart, "CEO Pay: Mom Wouldn't Approve," *Fortune* (March 31, 1997), pp. 119–120.

81. P.J. Stonich, "The Performance Measurement and Reward System: Critical to Strategic Management," *Organizational Dynamics* (Winter 1984), pp. 45–57.

82. A. Rappaport, "New Thinking on How to Link Executive Pay with Performance," *Harvard Business Review* (March–April 1999), pp. 91–101.

83. W. Grossman and R.E. Hoskisson, "CEO Pay at the Crossroads of Wall Street and Main: Toward the Strategic Design of Executive Compensation," *Academy of Management Executive* (February 1998), pp. 43–57.

84. L. Armstrong, "Someone to Watch over You," *Business Week* (July 10, 2000), pp. 189–190.

85. B. Wallace and J. Fenton, "Is Your PC Watching You?" *PC World* (December 2000), pp. 59–63.

86. *The Charlie Rose Show* on PBS, transcript of May 24, 1999.

87. C. Machrone, "Security," *PC Magazine* (February 6, 2001), p. 159.

88. "The Surveillance Society," *The Economist*, May 1, 1999, p. 22.

CHAPTER 11

Strategic Issues in Non-profit Organizations

Learning Objectives

After reading this chapter you should be able to

Identify the characteristics of the Canadian non-profit sector

Explain the effects of sources of revenue on non-profit organizations' strategies

Identify differences in the strategic management of for-profit and non-profit organizations

VHA Home Healthcare is a Toronto-based non-profit organization whose vision is to be the best provider of home and community health support services in the province. Policy reforms undertaken by the Conservative government in the 1990s have solidified the trend toward increased home care over institutional care. In 1995, the Ontario government created a system that would reduce its involvement to that of coordinator and contractor of services in a quasi-competitive market. It did so by creating Community Care Access Centres (CCACs) across the province. The role of these centres was to introduce an element of market efficiency into home care by acting as an information and referral service. VHA is one of the many non-profits contracting for homecare services with CCACs. These non-profits are now in competition with each other, as well as for-profit organizations like ParaMed and Comcare. To receive any home care business paid for by the provincial government, organizations must win a CCAC service contract to get referrals. Because the CCAC is the only way of accessing publicly subsidized services, winning a contract is now critical to the success of these non-profits. VHA has had to devote considerable resources to the preparation of requests for proposals (RFPs). This has required the hiring of additional administrators to prepare these proposals and evaluate the effectiveness of VHA's programs in order to maintain their contracts. Smaller non-profits have already been forced out of operation or into alliances with larger non-profits because these administrative functions cannot be performed (because of a lack of expertise or money, or both). The goal of CCACs was to put downward pressure on prices by introducing competition into the provision of home care. Although competition has been increased, and the process by which contracts are awarded is transparent, the increase in administrative costs has to some extent offset the cost savings experienced as a result of the competitive bidding processes.

As the case of VHA indicates, many non-profit organizations are turning to strategic management and other concepts from business to ensure their survival. This is a significant change because most non-profit managers had traditionally felt that business concepts were not relevant to their situation. According to Peter Drucker:

> Twenty years ago, management was a dirty word for those involved in non-profit organizations. It meant business, and non-profits prided themselves on being free of the taint of commercialism and above such sordid considerations as the bottom line. Now most of them have learned that non-profits need management even more than business does, precisely because they lack the discipline of the bottom line.[1]

The non-profit sector in Canada is often ignored in discussions of strategic management, but this sector is important not only because of its size, but also because of the important benefits it provides society. Organizations like hospitals, universities, social service organizations, arts councils, food banks, social clubs, trade associations, and places of worship are all part of the non-profit sector (sometimes called the voluntary sector). Government cutbacks throughout the 1990s have led to significant reductions in a wide range of community and social services, a trend that has made the contributions of the non-profit sector all the more important.[2] As the example at the beginning of this chapter illustrated, Ontario's Community Care Access Centres channel access to health services in local communities. Provincial governments are therefore using non-profit organizations to create more efficient service delivery systems, relying on the private donations these organizations receive.

Non-profit organizations are an alternative to market-driven firms or government agencies. Their lack of a primary profit motive creates an impression of care, concern, and trustworthiness in the delivery of sensitive public services. They often rely significantly on volunteers, and if incorporated they must be governed by a volunteer board of directors. These directors act as a link to the local communities in which they operate, which gives them legitimacy. The small size of many non-profits makes them more flexible and responsive than bureaucratic governmental agencies. They are also typically able to garner contributions of time and money that governments never could. These benefits show the importance of maintaining a prosperous non-profit sector in Canada and justify the importance of understanding their key strategic issues.

Canadian non-profits can be registered as charities. If they are, they can issue tax receipts for donations that can be used by donors to obtain tax credits. These registered charities must file Public Information Returns with the Canada Customs and Revenue Agency, and these provide a source of data on the non-profit sector. We know little about non-profits that are not registered charities. Based on available data, there were almost 80 000 registered charities in Canada in 1999. There were an estimated 10 000 additional legally incorporated non-profits.[3] The number of registered charities has been growing by approximately 3% a year for the past 10 years, and this trend is expected to continue. **Table 11–1** shows the charity types, numbers, and revenue base. These data show that 36% of Canadian charities are places of worship, the largest category of charity. Social services are the second largest (14%), followed by community benefit organizations (7%). The smallest category is hospitals (1%).

Examining the non-profit sector in terms of revenues paints a very different picture. The Canadian Centre for Philanthropy estimates revenues of $90.5 billion in 1994.[4] Slightly over half of these go to the two smallest categories of non-profits, hospitals and universities. Only 6% of these revenues to go places of worship, despite their large number. Most of the revenue in the non-profit sector comes from the government in the form of grants or transfer payments. **Table 11–2** shows the revenue sources for different types of non-profit organizations. As the example at the beginning of this chapter showed, many non-profits are extremely dependent on government funding, and as such are vulnerable to changes in government spending and policy. Hospitals, universities, libraries, and museums, for example, rely on governments for more than 70% of their revenues.

All of these unique features of non-profit organizations point to the need for unique strategies. In many ways they follow the same strategic management process as a profit-seeking organization would, using a combination of internal and external analysis to generate strategic options that will improve firm performance. Of course, one big difference is that performance in non-profits will not be based on profits, share price, or return on equity. They are concerned with delivering services as efficiently and effectively as possible and operating within their budgets. For these reasons, many non-profit organizations are adopting strategic management principles in increasing numbers.

non-profit organization private corporations or governmental agencies that lack a primary profit motive in their operations

Typically, **non-profit organizations** include private non-profit organizations (such as hospitals, institutes, private colleges, and organized charities) as well as public governmental units or agencies (such as welfare departments, prisons, and state universities). Traditionally studies in strategic management have dealt with profit-making firms to the exclusion of non-profit or governmental organizations. This, however, is changing. Non-profit organizations are adopting strategic management in increasing numbers.

Scholars and practitioners are concluding that many strategic management concepts and techniques can be successfully adapted for non-profit organizations.[5] Although the evidence is not yet conclusive, there appears to be an association between strategic planning efforts and performance measures such as growth.[6] The purpose of this chapter is, therefore, to highlight briefly the major differences between the profit-making and the non-profit organization, so that the effects of their differences on the strategic management process can be understood.

Table 11–1 Types of Charities and Distribution of Revenues

Type of Charity	Number	% of All Charities	Total Revenue	% Total Revenue
Arts and Culture	3 187	4.5	2.0	2.2
Community Benefit (e.g., humane societies, John Howard Society, Meals-on-Wheels)	5 238	7.3	2.5	2.8
Education (e.g., organizations supporting schools and education)	4 158	5.8	3.5	3.9
Health (e.g., organizations supporting medical research, public health)	3 180	4.5	6.4	7.1
Hospitals	978	1.4	27.4	30.4
Libraries and Museums	1 615	2.3	1.3	1.4
Places of Worship (e.g., churches, synagogues, mosques)	25 458	35.6	5.3	5.9
Private Foundation (organizations disbursing private funds)	3 356	4.7	1.5	1.6
Public Foundations (e.g., United Way, Centraide, hospital foundations)	3 466	4.9	4.7	5.2
Recreation	2 753	3.9	0.7	0.7
Religion (e.g., convents, monasteries, missionary organizations)	3 978	5.6	2.8	3.1
Social Services (child, youth, family and disabled welfare and services, international assistance, relief, etc.)	10 317	14.4	8.8	9.7
Teaching Institutions (universities and colleges)	2 642	3.7	23.5	25.9
Other (e.g., service clubs, employee charitable trusts)	1 087	1.5	0.1	0.1
Total	71 413	100.0	90.5	100.0

Note: Revenues expressed in thousands.

Source: M. Hall and K.G. Banting, "The nonprofit sector in Canada: An introduction," in K.G. Banting (ed.) *The Nonprofit Sector in Canada: Roles and Relationships* (Kingston: School of Policy Studies, Queen's University), pp. 1–28.

11.1 Why Non-profit?

public goods goods that many people can consume simultaneously

The non-profit sector of an economy is important for several reasons. First, society desires certain goods and services that profit-making firms cannot or will not provide. These are referred to as **public goods** (sometimes called collective consumption goods) because people who might not have paid for the goods receive benefits from them. Paved roads, police protection,

Table 11–2 Sources of Revenues of Charitable Organizations

Type of Charity	Revenues from Government (%)	Revenues from Earned Income (%)	Revenues from Private Giving (%)
Arts and Culture	50	40	10
Community Benefit	64	24	12
Education	61	31	8
Health	64	20	16
Libraries and Museums	74	17	9
Other	6	28	66
Places of Worship	1	18	81
Private Foundations	11	54	35
Public Foundations	41	22	37
Recreation	27	58	15
Religion	13	46	41
Social Services	64	25	15
Teaching Institution	71	26	3

Source: M. Hall and K.G. Banting, "The nonprofit sector in Canada: An introduction," in K.G. Banting (ed.) *The Nonprofit Sector in Canada: Roles and Relationships* (Kingston: School of Policy Studies, Queen's University), pp. 1–28.

museums, and schools are examples of public goods. A person cannot use a private good unless she or he pays for it. Generally once a public good is provided, however, anyone can use or enjoy it. In other words, it is difficult to exclude somebody from using a public good.

Certain aspects of life do not appear to be served appropriately by profit-making business firms yet are often crucial to the well-being of society. These aspects include areas in which society as a whole benefits from a particular service, but in which a particular individual benefits only indirectly. It is in these areas that non-profit organizations have traditionally been most effective. Libraries and museums are examples. Although most people do not visit libraries or museums very often, they are usually willing to pay taxes and/or donate funds to support their existence. They do so because people believe that these organizations act to uplift the culture and quality of life of the region. To fulfill their mission, entrance fees (if any) must be set low enough to allow everyone admission. These fees, however, are not profitable—they rarely even cover the costs of the service. The same is true of animal shelters managed by the Humane Society. Although few people want abandoned pets running wild through city streets, fees charged from the sale of these animals cannot alone pay the costs of finding and caring for them. Additional revenue is needed, either in the form of donations or public taxation. Such public or collective services cannot generate a profit, yet they are necessary for any successful civilization. Which aspects of society are most suited for being served by non-profit organizations rather than by profit-making business organizations? This is the issue being faced by governments when they privatize what was previously provided by the state. See the **Global Issue** feature to learn more about this development.

A second reason why the non-profit sector is important is that private non-profit organizations tend to receive benefits from society that private profit-making firms cannot obtain. They are exempt from income taxes and other sales taxes. **Registered charities** are also able to provide receipts for donations that donors can use to claim tax credits. These benefits are allowed because private non-profit organizations are typically service organizations, which are expected to use any excess of revenue over costs and expenses (a surplus rather than a profit) either to improve service or to reduce the price of their service. This service orientation is reflected in the fact that non-profit organizations do not use the term "customer" to refer to the recipient of the service. The recipient is typically referred to as a patient, student, client, case, or simply "the public."

registered charities
non-profit organizations providing some kind of social goods or services that are able to issue tax receipts for donations

Global Issue

Which Is Best for Society: Business or Non-profit?

Many nations throughout the world are attempting to privatize state-owned enterprises to balance their budgets. **Privatization** is (1) the selling of state-owned enterprises to private individuals or organizations or (2) the hiring of a private business to provide services previously offered by a state agency. The British government, for example, sold British Airways, its state-owned airline, to private investors. In the United States, many city governments now allow private companies to collect and dispose of trash—something that had previously been done by the city.

Problems can result, however, if privatization goes too far. For example, in converting from a communist-oriented, centrally managed economy to a more democratic, free-market economy, Eastern European countries are finding that profit-making business firms are unable to satisfy all of society's needs. What used to be provided by the state free of charge (tax-supported) in Russia and other countries may now be

provided only for the rich or not at all. The same problem is evident in the United States in the controversies over the provision of health care, retirement benefits, and private versus public education.

Some of the aspects of life that cannot easily be privatized and are often better managed by non-profit organizations are these:

- Religion
- Education
- Charities
- Clubs, interest groups, unions
- Health care
- Government

The privatization of state-owned business enterprises is likely to continue globally because most of these enterprises must expand internationally to survive in the increasingly global environment. They cannot compete successfully if they are forced to follow inefficient, socially oriented policies and regulations (emphasizing employment over efficiency) rather than economically oriented, international practices (emphasizing efficiency over employment). The global trend toward privatization will probably continue until each country reaches the point where the efficiency of business is counterbalanced by the effectiveness of the non-profit sector of the economy. As political motives overcome economic ones, government will likely intervene in that decision.

privatization selling or contracting out state-owned business to private organizations

11.2 Importance of Revenue Source

The feature that best differentiates non-profit organizations from each other as well as from profit-making organizations is their source of revenue.[7] The profit-making firm depends on revenues obtained from the sale of its goods and services to customers, who typically pay for the costs and expenses of providing the product or service plus a profit. The non-profit organization, in contrast, depends heavily on dues, assessments, or donations from its membership, or on funding from a sponsoring agency such as the United Way or government to pay for much of its costs and expenses.

SOURCES OF NON-PROFIT REVENUE

Revenue is generated from a variety of sources—not just from clients receiving the product or service from the non-profit. It can come from people who do not even receive the services they are subsidizing. As **Table 11–2** indicates, charitable organizations display different patterns of revenue sources. In some organizations (for example libraries and museums), most revenues come from the government. In other types of non-profits, however, most revenues come from the members, the people who receive the service (for example, recreation and arts or culture).

In profit-making organizations, there is typically a simple and direct connection between the customer or client and the organization. The organization tends to be totally dependent on sales of its products or services to the customer for revenue and is therefore extremely interested in pleasing the customer. As shown in **Figure 11–1**, the profit-making organization (*organization A*) tries to influence the customer (through advertising and promotion) to continue to buy and use its services. Either by buying or not buying the item offered, the customer, in turn, directly influences the organization's decision-making process. The business is thus market-oriented.

In the case of the typical non-profit organization, however, there is likely to be a very different sort of relationship between the organization providing and the person receiving the service. Because the recipient of the service typically does not pay the entire cost of the service, outside sponsors are required. In most instances, the sponsors receive none of the service but provide partial to total funding for the needed revenues. As indicated earlier, these sponsors can be the government (using taxpayers' money) or charitable organizations, such as the United Way (using voluntary donations). As shown in **Figure 11–1**, the non-profit organization can be partially dependent on sponsors for funding (*organizations B and C*) or totally

Figure 11–1 The Effects of Sources of Revenue on Patterns of Client-Organization Influence

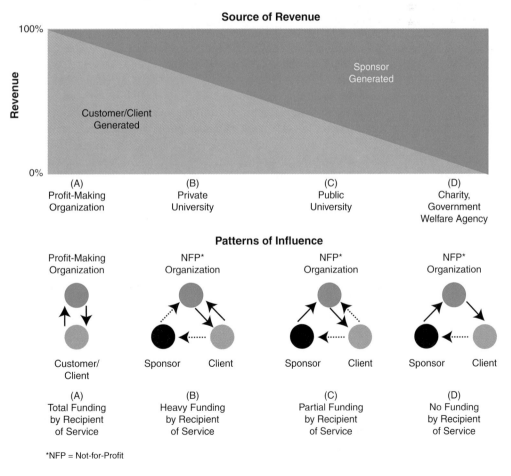

Source: Thomas L. Wheelen and J. David Hunger, "The Effect of Revenue upon Patterns of Client-Organization Influence." Copyright © 1982 by Wheelen and Hunger Associates. Revised 1991. Reprinted by permission.

dependent on the sponsors (*organization D*). The less money it receives from clients receiving the service or product, the less market-oriented is the non-profit organization.

PATTERNS OF INFLUENCE ON STRATEGIC DECISION MAKING

pattern of influence
the relationship
between non-profits and
their sources of funds
(clients and/or sponsors)

The **pattern of influence** on the organization's strategic decision making derives from its sources of revenue.[8] As shown in **Figure 11–1**, a private university (*organization B*) is heavily dependent on student tuition and other client-generated funds for about 70% of its revenue. Therefore, the students' desires are likely to have a stronger influence (as shown by an unbroken line) on the university's decision making than are the desires of the various sponsors such as alumni and private foundations. The sponsors' relatively marginal influence on the organization is reflected by a broken line. In contrast, a public university (*organization C*) is more heavily dependent on outside sponsors such as a state legislature for revenue funding. Student tuition and other client-generated funds form a small percentage (typically less than 40%) of total revenue. Therefore, the university's decision making is heavily influenced by the sponsors (unbroken line) and only marginally influenced directly by the students (broken line).

In the case of *organization D*, however, the client has no direct influence on the organization because the client pays nothing for the services received. In this situation, the organization tends to measure its effectiveness in terms of sponsor satisfaction. It has no real measure of its efficiency other than its ability to carry out its mission and achieve its objectives within the dollar contributions it has received from its sponsors. In contrast to other organizations in which the client contributes a significant proportion of the needed revenue, *organization D* actually might be able to increase its revenue by heavily lobbying its sponsors while reducing the level of its service to its clients.

Regardless of the percentage of total funding that the client generates, the client may attempt to indirectly influence the non-profit organization through the sponsors. This is depicted by the broken lines connecting the client and the sponsor in *organizations B, C, and D* in **Figure 11–1**. Welfare clients or prison inmates, for example, may be able to indirectly improve the services they receive if they pressure government officials by writing to legislators or even by rioting. Students at public universities can lobby state officials for student representation on governing boards.

The key to understanding the management of a non-profit organization is thus learning who pays for the delivered services. If the recipients of the service pay only a small proportion of the total cost of the service, strategic managers are likely to be more concerned with satisfying the needs and desires of the funding sponsors or agency than those of the people receiving the service. The acquisition of resources can become an end in itself.

USEFULNESS OF STRATEGIC MANAGEMENT CONCEPTS AND TECHNIQUES

Some strategic management concepts can be equally applied to business and non-profit organizations, whereas others cannot. The marketplace orientation underlying portfolio analysis, for example, does not translate into situations in which client satisfaction and revenue are only indirectly linked. Industry analysis and competitive strategy are primarily relevant to non-profits that obtain most of their revenue from user fees rather than from donors or taxpayers. For example, as American hospitals find themselves relying increasingly on patient fees for their revenue, they use competitive strategy to gain advantage versus other hospitals. Smaller non-profit hospitals stress the "high touch" of their staff over the "high tech" of competitors having better diagnostic machinery. To pick an example that is closer to home, Canadian universities with MBA programs are less reliant on government funds than other universities. As a result they are more expensive but also more student-focused. Universities can position themselves differently based on the institutional advantage they have, which explains the relative strength of computer science at the University of Waterloo, journalism at Carleton University, law at York University, and so on. The concept of competitive advantage is less useful to the typical non-profit than the related concept of institutional advantage, which sets aside the profit-making objective of competitive advantage. A non-profit can be said to have **institutional advantage** when it performs its tasks more effectively than other comparable organizations.[9]

institutional advantage a non-profit organization's ability to perform tasks more effectively than its rivals

SWOT analysis, mission statements, stakeholder analysis, and governance are, however, just as relevant to a non-profit as they are to a profit-making organization.[10] Portfolio analysis can be helpful but is used very differently. (See the section on strategic piggybacking later in this chapter.) As with any organization, non-profits usually have boards of directors whose job is to ensure that the paid executive director and staff work to fulfill the organization's mission and objectives. Unlike the boards of most business firms, however, non-profit boards are often required to take primary responsibility for strategic planning and fundraising. Many non-profits are finding a well-crafted mission statement helps not only in finding donors, but also in attracting volunteers. Take the example of the mission statement of a local animal shelter:

> *To shelter and care for stray, lost, or abandoned animals and to responsibly place animals in new homes and enforce animal laws. We are also here to better educate people in ways to be solutions to animal problems, not causes.*[11]

Strategic management is difficult to apply when the organization's output is hard to measure objectively, as is the case with most non-profit organizations. Thus, it is very likely that many non-profit organizations have not used strategic management because its concepts, techniques, and prescriptions do not lend themselves to situations where sponsors, rather than the marketplace, determine revenue. The situation, however, is changing. The trend toward privatizing public organizations usually means that the clients/patients pay a larger percentage of the costs. As these non-profits become more market-oriented (and thus client-oriented), strategic management becomes more applicable and is increasingly used.[12] Nevertheless, various constraints on non-profits mean that strategic management concepts and techniques must be modified to be effective.

11.3 Impact of Constraints on Strategic Management

Several characteristics peculiar to the non-profit organization constrain its behaviour and affect its strategic management. Newman and Wallender list the following five constraints on strategic management:[13]

1. **Service is often intangible and hard to measure.** This difficulty is typically compounded by the existence of multiple service objectives developed to satisfy multiple sponsors.

2. **Client influence may be weak.** Often the organization has a local monopoly, and clients' payments may be a very small source of funds.

3. **Strong employee commitments to professions or to a cause may undermine allegiance** to the organization employing them.

4. **Resource contributors may intrude on the organization's internal management.** Such contributors include fund contributors and government.

5. **Restraints on the use of rewards and punishments** may result from constraints 1, 3, and 4.

It is true that several of these characteristics can be found in profit-making as well as in non-profit organizations. Nevertheless, as Newman and Wallender state, the "frequency of strong impact is much higher in non-profit enterprises."[14]

IMPACT ON STRATEGY FORMULATION

The effects of the constraints listed above on long-range planning and decision making add at least four complications to strategy formulation:

1. **Goal conflicts interfere with rational planning.** Because non-profit organizations typically lack a single clear-cut performance criterion (such as profits), divergent goals and objectives are likely, especially with multiple sponsors. Differences in the concerns of various important sponsors can prevent management from stating the organization's mission in anything but very broad terms, if they fear that a sponsor who disagrees with a particular, narrow definition of mission might cancel its funding. For example, a study of 227 public Canadian hospitals found that more than half had very general, ambiguous, and unquantified objectives.[15] "The greater openness within which they are compelled to operate—the fishbowl atmosphere—impedes thorough discussion of issues and discourages long-range plans that might alienate stakeholders."[16] In such organizations, it is the reduced influence of the clients that permits this diversity of values and goals to occur without a clear market check. For example, when a city council considers changing zoning to implement a strategic plan for the city, all sorts of people (including the press) will demand to be heard. A decision might be made based on pressure from a few stakeholders (who make significant contributions or who threaten to stir up trouble) to the detriment of the community as a whole.

2. **An integrated planning focus tends to shift from results to resources.** Because non-profit organizations tend to provide services that are hard to measure, they rarely have a net bottom line. Planning, therefore, becomes more concerned with resource inputs, which can easily be measured, than with service, which cannot. Goal displacement (explained in **Chapter 10**) becomes even more likely than it is in business organizations.[17]

3. **Ambiguous operating objectives create opportunities for internal politics and goal displacement.** The combination of vague objectives and a heavy concern with resources allows managers considerable leeway in their activities. Such leeway makes possible political manoeuvring for personal ends. In addition, because the effectiveness of the non-profit organization hinges on the satisfaction of the sponsoring group, management tends to ignore the needs of the client while focusing on the desires of a powerful sponsor. University administrators commonly say that people will donate money for a new building (which will carry the donor's name), but not for more pressing needs, such as the maintenance of existing buildings. In this situation, powerful department heads might wine and dine the donor, hoping to get the money for their pet projects. This problem is compounded by the common practice of selecting people to boards of trustees or boards of directors not on the basis of their managerial experience, but on the basis of their ability to contribute money, raise funds, and work with politicians. (A major role of the non-profit board is to ensure adequate resources—usually translated to mean fundraising.)[18] Directors usually receive no compensation for serving on the board. Their lack of interest in overseeing management is reflected in an overall non-profit board-meeting attendance rate of only 50%, compared with 90% for boards of directors of business organizations. This is one reason why boards of non-profits tend to be larger than are boards of business organizations. Board members of non-profit organizations tend to ignore the task of determining strategies and policies, often leaving it to the paid (or sometimes unpaid) executive director. The larger the board, the less likely it is to exercise control over top management.[19]

4. **Professionalization simplifies detailed planning but adds rigidity.** In non-profit organizations in which professionals play important roles (as in hospitals or colleges), professional values and traditions can prevent the organization from changing its con-

ventional behaviour patterns to fit new service missions tuned to changing social needs. This rigidity, of course, can occur in any organization that hires professionals. The strong service orientation of most non-profit organizations, however, tends to encourage the development of static professional norms and attitudes. As non-profits attempt to become more businesslike, this may be changing. One study of non-profits revealed that 29% of the program directors and 15% of the staff had degrees or experience in business administration.[20]

IMPACT ON STRATEGY IMPLEMENTATION

The five constraining characteristics also affect how a non-profit organization is organized in both its structure and job design. Three complications to strategy implementation in particular can be highlighted:

1. **Decentralization is complicated.** The difficulty of setting objectives for an intangible, hard-to-measure service mission complicates the delegation of decision-making authority. Because of the heavy dependence on sponsors for revenue support, the top management of a non-profit organization must be always alert to the sponsors' view of an organizational activity. This necessary caution leads to **defensive centralization**, in which top management retains all decision-making authority so that low-level managers cannot take any actions to which the sponsors may object.

2. **Linking pins for external–internal integration become important.** Because of the heavy dependence on outside sponsors, a special need arises for people in buffer roles to relate to both inside and outside groups. This role is especially necessary when the sponsors are diverse (revenue comes from donations, membership fees, and federal funds) and the service is intangible (for instance, a "good" education) with a broad mission and multiple shifting objectives. The job of a "Dean for External Affairs," for example, consists primarily of working with the school's alumni and raising funds.

3. **Job enlargement and executive development can be restrained by professionalism.** In organizations that employ a large number of professionals, managers must design jobs that appeal to prevailing professional norms. Professionals have rather clear ideas about which activities are, and which are not, within their province. Enriching a nurse's job by expanding his or her decision-making authority for drug dosage, for example, can cause conflict with medical doctors who believe that such authority is theirs alone. Because a professional often views managerial jobs as non-professional and merely supportive, promotion into a management position is not always viewed positively.

defensive centralization top management's decision to make decisions it believes will appease sponsors

IMPACT ON EVALUATION AND CONTROL

Special complications to evaluation and control arising from the constraining characteristics affect how behaviour is motivated and performance is controlled. Two problems, in particular, are often noticed:

1. **Rewards and penalties have little or no relation to performance.** When desired results are vague and the judgment of success is subjective, predictable and impersonal feedback cannot be established. Performance is judged either intuitively ("You don't seem to be taking your job seriously") or on the basis of whatever small aspects of a job can be measured ("You were late to work twice last month").

2. **Inputs rather than outputs are heavily controlled.** Because its inputs can be measured much more easily than outputs, the non-profit organization tends to focus more on the

resources going into performance than on the performance itself.[21] The emphasis is thus on setting maximum limits for costs and expenses. Because there is little to no reward for staying under these limits, people usually respond negatively to such controls.

Because of these and other complications, non-profits can waste money in many ways, especially on administrative costs and expenses. Because of this, it is becoming increasingly common to calculate ratios comparing total support and revenue with the amounts spent on specific service activities. For example, analysts become concerned when the total spent on the mission of the organization (community service, for example) is less than 50% of total income received from sponsors and activities. Other rules of thumb are that a non-profit should not spend more than 35% on administrative expenses and that the costs of fundraising should not account for more than 15% of total income.[22]

11.4 Popular Non-profit Strategies

Because of various pressures on non-profit organizations to provide more services than the sponsors and clients can pay for, these organizations are developing strategies to help them meet their desired service objectives. In addition to a heavy use of volunteers to keep costs low, non-profits are choosing the strategies of strategic piggybacking, mergers, and strategic alliances.

STRATEGIC PIGGYBACKING

strategic piggybacking a resource development strategy used by non-profits to fund their core activities

Coined by Nielsen, the term **strategic piggybacking** refers to the development of a new activity for the non-profit organization that would generate the funds needed to make up the difference between revenues and expenses.[23] The new activity is related typically in some manner to the non-profit's mission, but its purpose is to help subsidize the primary service programs. It appears to be a form of concentric diversification, but it is engaged in only for its money-generating value. In an inverted use of portfolio analysis, the organization invests in new, safe cash cows to fund its current cash-hungry stars, question marks, and dogs.

Although this strategy is not new, it has recently become very popular. As early as 1874, for example, New York's Metropolitan Museum of Art retained a professional to photograph its collections and to sell copies of the prints. Profits were used to defray the museum's operating costs. More recently, various income-generating ventures have appeared under a wide range of auspices, from the Girl Scouts to UNICEF, and in numerous forms, from cookies and small gift shops to vast real estate developments. The amount of funds resulting from income-producing activities has significantly increased since the 1970s. Some 70% of American colleges and universities now offer "auxiliary" services, such as bookstores, conference rooms, and computer centres as sources of income.[24] The American Cancer Society earns millions annually from allowing its name to appear on products sold by private drug companies, such as Smith-Kline Beecham's Nicoderm chewing gum. The Metropolitan Museum of Art now has 16 stores outside the main museum and a fast-growing website—all of which generate money.

Although strategic piggybacks can help non-profit organizations self-subsidize their primary missions and better use their resources, according to Nielsen, there are several potential drawbacks.[25] First, the revenue-generating venture could actually lose money, especially in the short run. Second, the venture could subvert, interfere with, or even take over the primary mission. Third, the public, as well as the sponsors, could reduce their contributions because of negative responses to such "money-grubbing activities" or because of a mistaken belief that the organization is becoming self-supporting. Fourth, the venture could interfere with the internal operations of the non-profit organization. To avoid these drawbacks, a non-profit should first carefully evaluate its resources before choosing this strategy. See the boxed feature to see the resources needed for a piggyback.

Resources Needed for Successful Strategic Piggybacking

Based on his experience as a consultant to non-profit organizations, Edward Skloot suggests that a non-profit organization should have five resources before engaging in strategic piggybacking:

1. **Something to Sell:** The organization should assess its resources to see whether people might be willing to pay for goods or services closely related to the organization's primary activity. Repackaging the Boston Symphony into the less formal Boston Pops Orchestra created a way to subsidize the deficit-creating symphony and provide year-round work for the musicians.

2. **Critical Mass of Management Talent:** Enough people must be available to nurture and sustain an income venture over the long haul. This can be very difficult, given that the most competent non-profit professionals often don't want to be managers.

3. **Trustee Support:** If the trustees have strong feelings against earned-income ventures, they could actively or passively resist commercial involvement. When the Children's Television Workshop began licensing its Sesame Street characters to toy companies and theme parks, many people criticized it for joining business in selling more things to children.

4. **Entrepreneurial Attitude:** Management must be able to combine an interest in innovative ideas with businesslike practicality.

5. **Venture Capital:** Because it often takes money to make money, engaging in a joint venture with a business organization can provide the necessary start-up funds as well as the marketing and management support. For example, Massachusetts General Hospital receives $50 million from Hoechst, the German chemical company, for biological research in exchange for exclusive licences to develop commercial products from particular research discoveries.

Source: E. Skloot, "Should Non-profits Go into Business?" *Harvard Business Review* (January–February 1983), pp. 20–24. Copyright © 2001 by the President and Fellows of Harvard College.

MERGERS

Dwindling resources are leading an increasing number of non-profits to consider mergers as a way of reducing costs. For example, two children's mental health service providers in Scarborough, Ontario, merged to form Aisling Discoveries Child and Family Centre. Both organizations catered to children from infancy to age 12 and their families but were experiencing severe financial constraints as a result of reduced government funding. By merging, these organizations were able to eliminate considerable duplication in administration and managerial functions, and maintain a level of service provision suitable to children with special needs through prevention and early intervention programs. The ability to achieve economies of scale and scope provided a powerful incentive for non-profits to merge in order to survive in the context of government retrenchment in Canada during the 1990s.

STRATEGIC ALLIANCES

Strategic alliances involve developing co-operative ties with other organizations. Alliances are often used by non-profit organizations as a way to enhance their capacity to serve clients or to acquire resources while still enabling them to keep their identity.[26] Services can be purchased and provided more efficiently through co-operation with other organizations than if they were done alone. For example, a number of Canadian universities are joining forces to create and operate a range of academic programs. The Alberta Executive MBA is a combined effort of the business schools at the University of Alberta and the University of Calgary. The ability to share teaching faculty and bring together managers from both major cities in Alberta created a program superior to what either university could do on its own. Similarly, Saint Mary's University and the Atlantic School of Theology have collaborated to form the Atlantic Centre for Ethics and Public Affairs. By partnering two organizations with very different academic programs, the centre will encourage collaboration across disciplines and build coalitions with community partners.

Strategic alliances and mergers are becoming commonplace among non-profit organizations. The next logical step is strategic alliances between business firms and non-profits. Already business organizations are forming alliances with universities to fund university research in exchange for options on the results of that research. Business firms find it cheaper to pay universities to do basic research than to do it themselves. Universities are in need of research funds to attract top professors and to maintain expensive labs. Such alliances of convenience are being criticized, but they are likely to continue.

11.5 Impact of the Internet on Non-profit Organizations

The internet is just beginning to have an impact on non-profit organizations. By far the most impact has been on government activities—especially in terms of taxation and the provision of services.

TAXATION

The first impact of the internet on non-profit organizations (especially government) was the issue of taxation. Businesses must collect and pay sales taxes to the government of each province in which they operate. Mail order retailers—both catalogue and internet—generally collect provincial sales tax from consumers only if the company operates a facility in the province where the merchandise is being sent. Because internet companies usually don't have brick-and-mortar operations, they collect little sales tax. Many provincial and municipal government officials fear that as more of the economy shifts online, they will lose tax revenue needed for schools, police officers, and other basic services. These government officials have been supported by traditional retailers fearing that they will not be able to compete with internet rivals who receive special tax advantages. Anti-tax activists and some business leaders have responded that the lack of tax has accelerated the growth of electronic commerce. According to them, a complex tax structure dealing with more than 6000 different tax jurisdictions would stifle the growth of the internet retail industry and hurt the overall economy. The US Congress agreed in 1998 to a three-year moratorium on the taxation of sales by purely internet-based businesses.[27] So far Canada has yet to pass any similar legislation.

The European Union (EU) is also concerned that the internet will reduce its tax revenues. For example, if a German buys a CD from an American internet retailer who delivers it by post, the German escapes paying the 16% value-added tax (VAT) paid at the local shop. In addition, internet businesses can avoid taxes by moving to low-tax countries or to tax havens, just as British gambling firms have done with online gambling. The European Commission has proposed that foreign companies with annual online sales of more than 100 000 euros in the EU should register for VAT in at least one EU country and then collect the tax on all services downloaded from the internet. According to *The Economist*, this tax would be almost impossible to enforce.[28]

IMPROVEMENT OF GOVERNMENT SERVICES

After ecommerce (B2C) and business to business (B2B), the next internet revolution will be in government services (G2C). The internet can play an important role in helping government reduce its costs and improve its services. For example, a pioneering project called ServiceArizona allows the residents of Arizona to conduct transactions on the web, from ordering personalized licence plates for their cars to replacing lost identification cards. Instead of standing in line for hours, people can renew their registrations with the motor vehicle department in just a few minutes any hour or day of the week. The website has been built, maintained, and hosted by IBM in return for 2% of the value of each transaction (about $4 for an auto registration). Because processing an auto registration costs only $1.60 compared with $6.60 in person, the state saves money. With 15% of renewals now being processed by ServiceArizona, the motor vehicles department saves around $17 million annually.

Governments around the world are realizing that they will need to construct internet portals, similar to that of Yahoo!, that can provide one location to satisfy all of their citizens' needs. A central government portal has been launched in Singapore; another is being developed in Austria. In Britain, BT won the contract to build UK Online, a portal to government services. Just as businesses are pushing their suppliers into doing business with them online, so can governments—thus streamlining the activities of government agencies. For example, EDS developed a web-based intranet for the naval airbase at Corpus Christi, Texas, so that its mechanics could have access to spare parts anywhere in the world. IBM worked with Emekli Sandigi, a Turkish government social security organization, to develop an intranet to link 17 000 pharmacies so that they can check the validity of a customer's health card and other factors. The new system reduces the amount of time pharmacists are paid from two months to less than a week. The internet can also improve the quality of the relationship between a government and its citizens. For example, a Democratic Party primary in Arizona in which online voting was allowed boosted voter turnout to six times its usual level.[29]

IMPACT ON OTHER NON-PROFIT ORGANIZATIONS

The internet is also having an impact on non-profits other than government. Although the media tends to talk mostly of dot-coms, three major internet domains have been edu, gov, and org. Along with net, these have been the primary internet domains until the number of domains was increased in 2000 by ICANN. (See the **Internet Issue** feature for who regulates the internet.) Most non-profit organizations now have their own websites to provide services to their members and to interested outsiders.

According to Peter Drucker, the greatest impact of the internet may be on higher education and health care (85% of US hospitals are non-profit).[30] Internet access can enable medical practitioners to access the knowledge of specialists in distant locations. Patients can learn more about their illness by talking in internet chat rooms with other people who have the same illness. Around 75% of US colleges and universities have websites enabling students to access course information (including the syllabus) and download assignments. Such websites are replacing library reserve rooms. Although 1.4 million people were enrolled in distance education courses during the 1997–1998 academic year, that number has risen considerably during the following years.[31] Some universities, such as Athabasca University, are offering complete courses and degree programs over the internet.

Internet Issue

The Non-profit Organizations That Rule the Internet

There is a myth that the internet has grown because of a complete absence of rules or regulations. In reality, the internet is a highly organized place. What is unique about the internet is that its regulation has developed from the bottom up instead of from the top down. The Internet Engineering Task Force (IETF) develops agreed-upon technical standards, such as communication protocols. The Internet Corporation for Assigned Names and Numbers (ICANN) oversees the system of domain names, such as com (business), edu (education), gov (government), and org (non-profit organizations). The World Wide Web Consortium (W3C) also oversees internet standards. Without such global standards, there would be no way to connect modems to computers for internet access or for viewers to read websites, let alone download files or host chat rooms. These non-profit bodies are largely self-created and self-governing. They are open in membership and willing to hear all arguments on an issue. According to David Clark of MIT, a member of IETF, "We reject kings, presidents, and voting. We believe in rough consensus and running code." Anyone can become a member of the IETF simply by going to the task force's website and signing up for a working group's mailing list. Anyone can come to the three meetings held annually by the task force.

These organizations seem to work so well because they comprise like-minded individuals who have common interests, even though they are located in various parts of the world. Very function-oriented, IETF decisions are based on effectiveness and efficiency. Since anyone can access all proposals, the process is very hard to manipulate. In 1999, the IETF argued about how far it should go to help law enforcement conduct wiretaps; eventually it decided not to "consider requirements for wire-tapping." W3C is an organization founded by Tim Berners-Lee, the inventor of the World Wide Web, to develop standards for the web. Most of the 400-plus members are companies paying $50 000 per year for membership. W3C also upholds the consensus principle in decision making. It has developed more than 20 technical specifications, including one on XML (Extensible Markup Language), which may replace HTML as the language used in websites. ICANN wrested monopoly control of internet domain names from Network Solutions and has accredited more than 120 registers who can sell domain names. It recently added a number of new top-level domains to the usual com, edu, gov, org, and net. ICANN also helps resolve conflicts over who has the right to a domain name. The World Intellectual Property Organization, one of four dispute-resolution bodies accredited by ICANN, recently ruled that internet addresses bearing the names of British author Jeanette Winterson and American actress Julia Roberts should be returned to their rightful owners. Both addresses had been registered by internet "squatters" who had argued that the names of living people are not trademarks.

Source: "Regulating the Internet: The Consensus Machine," *The Economist* (June 10, 2000), pp. 73–79. Copyright © 2000. The Economist Newspaper Group, Inc. Reprinted with permission.

Discussion Questions

1. Are non-profit organizations less efficient than profit-making organizations? Why or why not?

2. How does the lack of a clear-cut performance measure, such as profits, affect the strategic management of a non-profit organization?

3. What are the advantages and disadvantages of strategic piggybacking? In what way is it "unfair competition" for non-profits to engage in revenue-generating activity?

4. What are the pros and cons of mergers and strategic alliances? Should non-profits engage in alliances with business firms?

5. Recently, many non-profit organizations in the United States have been converting to profit making. Why would a non-profit organization want to change its status to profit making? What are the pros and cons of doing so?

Strategic Practice Exercise

1. Read the **Global Issue** feature on page 294 of this chapter. It lists six aspects of society that it proposes are better managed by non-profit organizations than by profit-making organizations. Do you agree with this list? Should some aspects be deleted from the list? Should other aspects be added?

2. Examine a local college or university—perhaps the one you may be currently attending. What strategic issues is it facing? Develop a list of strategic factors. Is it attempting to use any strategic management concepts? If so, which ones? What sorts of strategies should it be con-

sidering for continued survival and future growth? Is it currently using strategic piggybacks to obtain additional funding? What sorts of additional piggybacks should it consider? Are strategic alliances with another college or university or business firm a possibility?

Notes

1. P.F. Drucker, "What Business Can Learn from Non-profits," *Harvard Business Review* (July–August 1989), p. 89.
2. M. Hall and K.G. Banting, "The Non-profit Sector in Canada: An Introduction," in K.G. Banting, editor, *The Non-profit Sector in Canada: Roles and Relationships* (Kingston: School of Policy Studies, Queen's University), pp. 1–28.
3. J. Quarter, *Canada's Social Economy* (Toronto: James Lorimer, 1992).
4. M.H. Hall and L.G. Macpherson, "A Provincial Portrait of Canada's Charities," *Research Bulletin,* Vol. 4 (Toronto: Canadian Centre for Philanthropy, 1997).
5. K. Ascher and B. Nare, "Strategic Planning in the Public Sector," *International Review of Strategic Management,* Vol. 1, edited by D.E. Hussey (New York: John Wiley & Sons, 1990), pp. 297–315; I. Unterman and R.H. Davis, *Strategic Management of Non-profit Organizations* (New York: Praeger Press, 1984), p. 2.
6. P.V. Jenster and G.A. Overstreet, "Planning for a Non-Profit Service: A Study of U.S. Credit Unions," *Long Range Planning* (April 1990), pp. 103–111; G. J. Medley, "Strategic Planning for the World Wildlife Fund," *Long Range Planning* (February 1988), pp. 46–54.
7. B.P. Keating and M.O. Keating, *Non-profit* (Glen Ridge, NJ: Thomas Horton & Daughters, 1980), p. 21.
8. J.D. Hunger and T.L. Wheelen, "Is Strategic Management Appropriate for Non-profit Organizations?" in *Handbook of Business Strategy, 1989/90 Yearbook,* edited by H.E. Glass (Boston: Warren, Gorham and Lamont, 1989), pp. 3.1–3.8. The contention that the pattern of environmental influence on the organization's strategic decision making derives from the organization's source(s) of income agrees with the authorities in the field. See R.E. Emerson, "Power-Dependence Relations," *American Sociological Review* (February 1962), pp. 31–41; J.D. Thompson, Organizations in Action (New York: McGraw-Hill, 1967), pp. 30–31; and J. Pfeffer and G.R. Salancik, *The External Control of Organizations: A Resource Dependence Perspective* (New York: HarperCollins, 1978), p. 44.
9. M. Goold, "Institutional Advantage: A Way into Strategic Management in Non-profit Organizations," *Long Range Planning* (April 1997), pp. 291–293.
10. Ascher and Nare, "Strategic Planning in the Public Sector," pp. 297–315; R. McGill, "Planning for Strategic Performance in Local Government," *Long Range Planning* (October 1988), pp. 77–84.
11. Lorna Lavender, Supervisor of Ames (Iowa) Animal Shelter, quoted by K. Petty, "Animal Shelter Cares for Homeless," *ISU Daily* (July 25, 1996), p. 3.
12. E. Ferlie, "The Creation and Evolution of Quasi Markets in the Public Sector: A Problem for Strategic Management," *Strategic Management Journal* (Winter 1992), pp. 79–97. Research has found that for-profit hospitals have more mission statement components dealing with principal services, target customers, and geographic domain than do non-profit hospitals. See R. Subramanian, K. Kumar, and C.C. Yauger, "Mission Statements of Hospitals: An Empirical Analysis of Their Contents and Their Relationship to Organizational Factors," *Journal of Business Strategies* (Spring 1993), pp. 63–78.
13. W.H. Newman and H.W. Wallender III, "Managing Non-profit Enterprises," *Academy of Management Review* (January 1978), p. 26.
14. Ibid., p. 27. The following discussion of the effects of these constraining characteristics is taken from pp. 27–31.
15. J. Denis, A. Langley, and D. Lozeau, "Formal Strategy in Public Hospitals," *Long Range Planning* (February 1991), pp. 71–82.
16. F. Heffron, *Organization Theory and Public Administration* (Upper Saddle River, NJ: Prentice Hall, 1989), p. 132.
17. Heffron, pp. 103–115.
18. R.T. Ingram, *Ten Basic Responsibilities of Non-profit Boards,* 2nd edition (Washington, DC: National Center for Non-profit Boards, 1997), pp. 9–10.
19. I. Unterman and R.H. Davis, *Strategic Management of Non-profit Organizations* (New York: Praeger Press, 1984), p. 174; J.A. Alexander, M.L. Fennell, and M.T. Halpern, "Leadership Instability in Hospitals: The Influence of Board–CEO Relations and Organizational Growth and Decline," *Administrative Science Quarterly* (March 1993), pp. 74–99.
20. Froelich, "Business Management in Non-profit Organizations," p. 9.
21. R.M. Kanter and D.V. Summers, "Doing Well While Doing Good: Dilemmas of Performance Measurement in Non-profit Organizations and the Need for a Multiple-Constituency Approach," in *The Non-profit Sector: A Research Handbook,* edited by W.W. Powell (New Haven: Yale University Press, 1987), p. 163.
22. J.P. Dalsimer, *Understanding Non-profit Financial Statement: A Primer for Board Members,* 2nd edition (Washington, DC: National Center for Non-profit Boards, 1997), p. 17.
23. R.P. Nielsen, "SMR Forum: Strategic Piggybacking: A Self-Subsidizing Strategy for Non-profit Institutions," *Sloan Management Review* (Summer 1982), pp. 65–69; R.P. Nielsen, "Piggybacking for Business and Non-profits: A Strategy for Hard Times," *Long Range Planning* (April 1984), pp. 96–102.
24. D.C. Bacon, "Non-profit Groups: An Unfair Edge?" *Nation's Business* (April 1989), pp. 33–34; "Universities Push Auxiliary Services to Generate More Revenue," *The Wall Street Journal* (April 27, 1995), p. A1.
25. R.P. Nielsen, "Piggybacking Strategies for Non-profits: A Shared Costs Approach," *Strategic Management Journal* (May–June 1986), pp. 209–211.
26. K.G. Provan, "Interorganizational Cooperation and Decision Making Autonomy in a Consortium Multihospital System," *Academy of Management Review* (July 1984), pp. 494–504; R.D. Luke, J.W. Begun, and D.D. Pointer, "Quasi-Firms: Strategic Interorganizational Forms in the Health Care Industry," *Academy of Management Review* (January 1989), pp. 9–19.
27. H. Fineman, "The Tax War Goes Online," *Newsweek* (December 20, 1999), p. 31; R. Chandrasekaran, "Tax Debate Heats Up Over On-line Sales," *International Herald Tribune* (December 14, 1999), p. B2; G.R. Simpson, "Internet Panel Pushes Reform of Sales Taxes," *The Wall Street Journal* (December 16, 1999), p. A3.
28. "The End of Taxes?" *The Economist: A Survey of the New Economy* (Special insert: September 23, 2000), p. 30.
29. "The Next Revolution" and "Quick Fixes," *The Economist: A Survey of Government and the Internet* (Special insert: June 24, 2000), pp. 3–9, 13.
30. M. Williams, "Prophet Sharing," *Red Herring* (January 30, 2001), pp. 100–107.
31. A. Levinson, "Students Attend College Online," *The [Ames, Iowa] Tribune* (January 29, 2001), p. A2.

Disaster Planning

Contingency planning is an important organizational task. As this video explains, the creation of sound continuity and contingency plans is a complex and costly undertaking. For example, the underlying risks and the potential impacts of disaster on an organization must be understood. These form the building blocks upon which a continuity plan or disaster recovery plan can be built. The plan itself must then be created, maintained, updated, and tested to ensure that it remains current. The time and effort required to undertake this type of planning is costly, with no positive effect on revenue. Additionally, most disaster plans require a number of backup systems to be established, further increasing the cost of operations. What makes disaster planning worthwhile?

Significant and unpredictable events like the September 11 terrorist attacks, SARS, mad cow, the blackout that left most of the eastern seaboard of the United States and southern Ontario powerless, and hurricane Juan that crippled the electrical and communications infrastructure of Halifax and many parts of rural Nova Scotia have all had a tremendous impact. Not only did these events directly affect the revenues of many organizations (especially those associated with aerospace and tourism), but there were also many wake-up calls experienced as firms without plans in place attempted to deal with the aftermath of these events.

What is involved in creating these types of contingency plans? The first step is to consider the potential impacts of each type of disaster or event. This is critical because you cannot properly plan for a disaster if you do not know how it will impact your organization. The second step is to create an organizational response to each type of event, regardless of how unlikely that event might be. Part of the reason so many organizations fail to consider the impact of these types of events is their belief that the odds are in their favour. While this may be true, the survival of the organization may be at stake if no thought is given to how an organization will continue operations in the context of certain events. Although these plans may never be acted upon, it is important that they do not fall short when they are needed. The third step is to perform assessments at regular intervals to ensure that the plans remain current.

Like all aspects of the strategic management model discussed in this text, the process of planning for disaster should be an ongoing one. Organizations that take this task seriously should be better able to withstand the harmful short- and long-term effects of disasters. ISO standards require appropriate business continuity and contingency planning. Although compliance with this internationally recognized standard is growing in importance, it seems many organizations devote little attention to this type of planning process.

Concepts Illustrated in the Video

Contingency planning

Strategic control systems

Environmental scanning

Causes of organizational success and failure

Competitive advantage

Organizational change

Study Questions

1. Explain how the competitive advantage of an organization like Magma Communications necessitates a strong emphasis on contingency planning.

2. How is preparing a disaster plan different from preparing a contingency plan as discussed in Chapter 10? Consider differences in objectives, components, and place in the strategic management process.

3. Use the internet to access examples of the recovery plans of the following:

   • Massachusetts Institute of Technology (MIT) **http://web.mit.edu/security/www/pubplan.htm**

   • California Energy Commission **http://www.energy.ca.gov/contingency**

Using these examples, discuss the types of contingencies these plans are able to handle, and assess how effective the plans will likely be.

4. Use a cost/benefit framework to discuss an organization's choice to prepare a disaster plan. Are there certain organizations or certain strategies that seem to suggest a greater need for this type of plan?

5. A history of flooding events in Ontario can be found on Environment Canada's website (www.ec.gc.ca/water/en/manage/floodgen/e_ont.htm). This history of unpreparedness echoes what is stated in the video: without a brush with disaster, human nature is to avoid planning for it. Discuss the ways in which an organization can create the changes necessary to more proactively deal with an uncertain future.

Video Resource: "Disaster Planning," *Venture* #882, June 1, 2003.

307

Case Analysis

1 The Case Method

The analysis and discussion of case problems has been the most popular method of teaching strategic management for many years. The case method provides the opportunity to move from a narrow, specialized view that emphasizes functional techniques to a broader, less precise analysis of the overall organization. Cases present actual business situations and enable you to examine both successful and unsuccessful organizations. In case analysis, you might be asked to critically analyze a situation in which a manager had to make a decision of long-term corporate importance. This approach gives you a feel for what it is like to be faced with making and implementing strategic decisions.

What we refer to as a "case" in university teaching is a story of an organization—facts, events, people, circumstances that describe a situation you would encounter if you were a consultant to, or a member of, that organization. Cases can depict complex, multidimensional business problems and issues so that students can use their knowledge and experience to *diagnose* the root causes of the situation as it is described and then *recommend* a suitable course of action. In other words, case analysis provides students the opportunity to put their skills and knowledge into practice without leaving the classroom. Among the benefits that students can derive from case analysis are these:

- An understanding of the role individuals play in guiding their organizations to success
- Sharpened analytical skills in assessing firm resources or capabilities as well as industry or competitive scenarios
- Practice in identifying key strategic issues and options to address them, and in formulating workable action plans
- An enhanced sense of business judgment and exposure to a range of industries and companies

Strategic management is not the type of discipline you can learn by memorizing a textbook and lecture notes. Knowing facts, theories, and concepts permits you to make good recommendations by providing you with an analytic toolbox. And because students all have different experiences and different values, they do not always see problems in exactly the same way—or the best solutions to them. In a case analysis, there is rarely one "right" answer and a number of "wrong" ones. It is unreasonable to expect that all students agree on what a company should do in the situation described in a case. Nor should we expect reaching a decision about what to do to be straightforward or clear-cut. In the real world, people routinely have to make decisions without knowing whether their decisions are "right." They make their decisions based on a range of factual knowledge, experience and skill, and intuition. How do they know whether their decisions are good? Only the passage of time permits that sort of assessment. The *only* important determinant of decision quality is results. Good decisions result in improved performance, whether that is defined by sales, profits, share price, return on equity, reputation, or some other measure. Doing a good job on a case analysis is not about picking the "right" solution, but rather undergoing a thorough process of identifying issues, diagnosing situations, generating and evaluating options, and preparing implementation plans that will result in improved organizational performance. Your objective is therefore to create a strong argument for a particular course of action, not to investigate what an organization really did in order to prepare an elaborate post hoc justification. Keep in mind that organizations make unwise decisions all the time, not because they are ill-informed or irresponsible, but just because things do not always turn out as expected. In fact, many cases are written about exactly these sorts of situations. So just because an organization did something in real life does not mean that what it did was necessarily the best thing to do. In hindsight, many organizations would do things differently. Do not fall into the trap of using what an organization *actually* did as a starting point and working backward from there to justify or make sense of it. If you do, you will find yourself terribly unprepared to answer questions about the foundations of your recommendation, and unable to learn from the experiences of conducting a strategic analysis.

Your *objective* in case analysis is to prepare a well-justified course of action to improve firm performance. A specific recommendation must be made, and it must be supported by systematic analysis and clear thinking. Consider preparing for a case analysis in the following way:

1. **Read the case twice.** The first time gives you a sense of the context of the case (time, industry, firm, products) and the issues or problems you will have to address. Resist trying to analyze or solve the case at this point. Rather, read it through to get the big picture of the issues presented in the case. The second reading permits you to identify information in the case that you will use in your analysis, to generate ideas about possible solutions, and to prioritize issues or concerns raised in the case.

2. **Examine the content of exhibits.** Often there are interesting bits of information in the organizational charts, process maps, or financial statements at the end of the case. Usually there is something in the exhibits worth using, or else they wouldn't be there.

3. **Identify strategic issues and factors.** Some cases are written in such a way that these are patently obvious. But don't count on this. Until you have identified issues to address or problems to solve, you are not in a position to start analyzing information or making recommendations. As a guide, look to the beginning and/or ending of the case for a statement of issues. If you cannot find them there, you will need to infer from the facts of the case.

4. **Analyze the situation described in the case.** Analysis is not repetition of the facts of the case. It is a process of adding meaning to facts in order to interpret them for later use. Similarly, analysis is not just your opinion (however good it might be). Use tools and techniques from the textbook to produce important insight and understanding of strategic situations. If you find yourself "analyzing" the case by cutting and pasting large chunks of text into your report or reporting on common sense observations, you are not doing an analysis that shows what you know about the concepts of strategic management.

5. **Don't treat the facts of the case as gospel.** Many cases are written from the perspective of people with particular opinions, values, and assumptions. Their view of the situation is therefore not necessarily the same one that you might have, or that others within the organization might have. Similarly, financial statements might be inaccurate or misleading, or projections might be made on dubious assumptions. Feel free to challenge the validity of the data and information provided in the case, because you will not sound convincing justifying your recommendation by saying "but that's what the case said."

6. **Use strong rationale.** Everything you include in your report needs to be explained and justified. Opinions should be avoided, not because they are necessarily wrong, but because they are not supported by any form of evidence. When you use strong rationale, you take away the "Why?" questions that make analysis look thoughtless or incomplete. Including your rationale demonstrates the comprehensiveness and clarity of your thinking, and makes it much easier for a listener or reader to understand how you reached your recommendation.

7. **Prepare a detailed action plan.** The tough part about strategic management is not making a "good" decision based on the facts available, but turning that decision into actions that will produce the desired results. Here is where you can demonstrate your creativity and thoroughness by specifying what needs to be done, by whom, at what time, and at what cost. The more detail you provide here, the more likely you are to be convincing about the overall recommendation you make. Nothing looks worse than a recommendation that is not accompanied by details on how to implement it. It's easy to say "we need to sell more products." But is anyone going to be prepared to act on that sort of recommendation without knowing *how* to do it?

In conclusion, there is a definite skill in preparing case analyses. The case is both a way to introduce a little "real life" to students without leaving the classroom and a way for students to demonstrate their ability to apply concepts from the class to a particular situation. To do well on your cases, you therefore need to be thorough in preparing your analysis and recommendations, have clear reasons for the choices you have made, use evidence to support your reasons, and show a conviction to your course or action. Try not to worry about what actually happened—it is not always a good indicator of what *should* have happened. If you are convincing in your recommendation as described above, you will do well on your case analyses. But do not interpret this as meaning that any case report is as good as the next, or that any case report will receive a top grade. Some analyses, recommendations, and action plans are better than others are. You must be prepared to clarify the process by which your decisions were made. If you do so in a way that most reasonable people can see merit in, then you know you've done a good job. Be worried if you cannot answer "Why?" questions for every piece of advice you give. And be sure you understand how every section of your strategic reports tells the reader something about why, how, when, and by whom firm performance will be improved.

2 Researching the Case Situation

Depending on the type of assignment used by your instructor, you may be required to conduct your own research on the case situation prior to preparing your recommendations. Here you should undertake outside research into the environmental setting. Check the decision date of each case (typically the latest date mentioned in the case) to find out when the situation occurred, and then screen the business periodicals for that time period. Use computerized company and industry information services such as COMPUSTAT, Compact Disclosure, ABI/INFORM Global, CBCA (Canadian Business and Current Affairs), and CD/International, available on CD-ROM or online at many university libraries. On the internet, Hoover's Online Corporate Directory (**www.hoovers.com**), the *Financial Post* (**www.nationalpost.com/ financialpost**), and the CBC (**www.cbc.ca/business**) provide a wide range of business activity and the circumstances at the time a case was written. These sites also have links to company and industry sites, as well as their own archives of stories and reports.

A company's annual report from the year of the case can be very helpful. Annual reports contain not only the usual income statements and balance sheets, but also cash flow statements and notes to the financial statements indicating why certain actions were taken. An understanding of the economy during that period will help you avoid making a serious error in your analysis, for example, suggesting a sale of stock when the stock market is at an all-time low or taking on more debt when the prime interest rate is over 15%. Information on the industry will provide insights on its competitive activities. Some resources available for research into the economy and a corporation's industry are suggested in later in this chapter.

Many instructors, however, want students to work *only* with the facts as provided in the case. This changes the experience of analyzing a case from one of researching and investigating to one of working with a limited amount of information and trying to do the most with it. The reality of decision making in any organizational context is one of incomplete information. But it is both timely and costly to collect and interpret data. Unfortunately, with so much information available through the internet and other computerized sources, decision makers can easily be flooded with information. Do they make better decisions as a result? Not necessarily. Although the cases you will study in a strategic management class contain much less information than a strategic decision maker would like to have, it is good practice to work with the information you have, making judicious assumptions only where necessary and not using a lack of information as an excuse for not making a decision. In other words, use the information that is presented in the case to the best of your abilities. All professionally written cases provide you with more than enough material to conduct a strategic analysis as described in this book. Learn to construct defensible recommendations in the context of imperfect information, and most important, use whatever information you do have at your disposal as support or rationale for the decisions you do make.

3 Financial Analysis: A Place to Begin

ratio analysis the interpretation of financial ratios computed from an organization's financial statements

Once you have read a case, a good place to begin your analysis is with the financial statements. **Ratio analysis** is the calculation of ratios from data in these statements. It is done to identify possible financial strengths or weaknesses. Thus, it is a valuable part of SWOT analysis. A review of key financial ratios can help you assess the company's overall situation and pinpoint some problem areas. Ratios are useful regardless of firm size and enable you to compare a company's ratios with industry averages. **Table 1** on page 312 lists some of the most important financial ratios, which are (1) liquidity ratios, (2) profitability ratios, (3) activity ratios, and (4) leverage ratios. These ratios are usually used in one of two ways: (a) to identify financial trends over time for an organization or one of its divisions; or (b) to make comparisons across companies at a given point in time. Financial ratios in isolation are rarely particularly revealing. Having some basis of comparison allows for analysts to make comparisons that point to improving or deteriorating financial position, suggesting how future performance will be affected by recent changes.

LIQUIDITY RATIOS
Liquidity ratios indicate how easily an organization can complete its operating cycle. In financial terms, an operating cycle is the length of time it takes to produce its product, sell it, and use the proceeds to product more products. Normally, organizations need to finance their production through paying for raw materials and components in cash or on credit. When products are sold, the organization uses cash or creates accounts receivable to meet its accounts payable or replenish inventory levels. The ability to repeat this cycle requires liquidity, a surplus of current assets that can be used to finance operating activities and meet current liabilities. Liquidity analysis, therefore, compares the organization's current asset endowments with its obligations. This suggests a margin of safety provided by the cash and other current assets available to the organization in comparison with its obligations. In reality, no organization liquidates all its current assets. If it did, it would have no inventory to sell and would therefore not be able to operate as a going concern. Liquidity rations need to be interpreted carefully, with the optimal level of liquidity determined by economic and real-world factors. In other words, a current ratio of 2.0 is virtually meaningless out of context. For some organizations it might be very high, while for others it might be dangerously low.

PROFITABILITY RATIOS
An organization's owners are concerned with its ability to generate, sustain, and increase profitability. This is normally measured by examining the organization's net profits and two

Table 1 Financial Ratio Analysis

	Formula	How Expressed	Meaning
1. Liquidity Ratios			
Current ratio	$\dfrac{\text{Current assets}}{\text{Current liabilities}}$	Decimal	A short-term indicator of the company's ability to pay its short-term liabilities from short-term assets; how much of current assets are available to cover each dollar of current liabilities.
Quick ratio	$\dfrac{\text{Current assets} - \text{Inventory}}{\text{Current liabilities}}$	Decimal	Measures the company's ability to pay off its short-term obligations from current assets, excluding inventories.
Inventory to net working capital	$\dfrac{\text{Inventory}}{\text{Current assets} - \text{Current liabilities}}$	Decimal	A measure of inventory balance; measures the extent to which the cushion of excess current assets over current liabilities may be threatened by unfavourable changes in inventory.
Cash ratio	$\dfrac{\text{Cash} + \text{Cash equivalents}}{\text{Current liabilities}}$	Decimal	Measures the extent to which the company's capital is in cash or cash equivalents; shows how much of the current obligations can be paid from cash or near-cash assets.
2. Profitability Ratios			
(a) Return on Sales			
Net profit margin	$\dfrac{\text{Net profit after taxes}}{\text{Net sales}}$	Percentage	Shows how much after-tax profits are generated by each dollar of sales.
Gross profit margin	$\dfrac{\text{Sales} - \text{Cost of goods sold}}{\text{Net sales}}$	Percentage	Indicates the total margin available to cover other expenses beyond cost of goods sold, and still yield a profit.
(b) Return on Investment			
Return on investment (ROI)	$\dfrac{\text{Net profit after taxes}}{\text{Total assets}}$	Percentage	Measures the rate of return on the total assets utilized in the company; a measure of management's efficiency, it shows the return on all the assets under its control regardless of source of financing.
Return on Assets (ROA)	$\dfrac{\text{Net profit after tax}}{\text{Average assets}}$	Percentage	The most basic measure of profit performance, showing profits earned per asset dollar.
Return on equity (ROE)	$\dfrac{\text{Net profit after taxes}}{\text{Shareholders' equity}}$	Percentage	Measures the rate of return on the book value of shareholders' total investment in the company.
3. Activity Ratios			
(a) Short-term (operating)			
Inventory turnover	$\dfrac{\text{Net sales}}{\text{Inventory}}$	Decimal	Measures the number of times that average inventory of finished goods was turned over or sold during a period of time, usually a year.
Days of inventory	$\dfrac{\text{Inventory}}{\text{Cost of goods sold} \div 365}$	Days	Measures the number of one day's worth of inventory that a company has on hand at any given time.
Net working capital turnover	$\dfrac{\text{Net sales}}{\text{Net working capital}}$	Decimal	Measures how effectively the net working capital is used to generate sales.
Average collection period	$\dfrac{\text{Accounts receivable}}{\text{Sales for year} \div 365}$	Days	Indicates the average length of time in days that a company must wait to collect a sale after making it; may be compared to the credit terms offered by the company to its customers.

Table 1   (continued)

	Formula	How Expressed	Meaning
Accounts receivable turnover	$$\frac{\text{Annual credit sales}}{\text{Accounts receivable}}$$	Decimal	Indicates the number of times that accounts receivable are cycled during the period (usually a year).
Accounts payable period	$$\frac{\text{Accounts payable}}{\text{Purchases for year} \div 365}$$	Days	Indicates the average length of time in days that the company takes to pay its credit purchases.
Days of cash	$$\frac{\text{Cash}}{\text{Net sales for year} \div 365}$$	Days	Indicates the number of days of cash on hand, at present sales levels.
(b) Long-term (investment)			
Fixed asset turnover	$$\frac{\text{Sales}}{\text{Fixed assets}}$$	Decimal	Measures the utilization of the company's fixed assets (i.e., plant and equip-ment); measures how many sales are generated by each dollar of fixed assets.
(c) Hybrid			
Asset turnover	$$\frac{\text{Sales}}{\text{Total assets}}$$	Decimal	Measures the utilization of all the com-pany's assets; measures how many sales are generated by each dollar of assets.
4. Leverage Ratios			
Debt to assets	$$\frac{\text{Total debt}}{\text{Total assets}}$$	Percentage	Measures the extent to which borrowed funds have been used to finance the com-pany's assets.
Debt to equity	$$\frac{\text{Total debt}}{\text{Shareholders' equity}}$$	Percentage	Measures the funds provided by creditors versus the funds provided by owners.
Long-term debt to equity	$$\frac{\text{Long--term debt}}{\text{Shareholders' equity}}$$	Percentage	Measures the long-term component of cap-ital structure.
Times interest earned	$$\frac{\text{Profit before taxes} + \text{Interest charges}}{\text{Interest charges}}$$	Decimal	Indicates the ability of the company to meet its annual interest costs.
Coverage of fixed charges	$$\frac{\text{Profit before taxes} + \text{Interest charges} + \text{Lease charges}}{\text{Interest charges} + \text{Lease obligations}}$$	Decimal	A measure of the company's ability to meet all of its fixed-charge obligations.
Current liabilities to equity	$$\frac{\text{Current liabilities}}{\text{Shareholders' equity}}$$	Percentage	Measures the short-term financing portion versus that provided by owners.
5. Other Ratios			
Earnings per share (EPS)	$$\frac{\text{Net profit after taxes} - \text{Preferred stock dividends}}{\text{Average number of common shares}}$$	Dollars per share	Shows the after-tax earnings gener-ated for each share of common stock.
Price/earnings	$$\frac{\text{Market price per share}}{\text{Earnings per share}}$$	Decimal	Shows the current market's evaluation of a stock, based on its earnings; shows how much the investor is willing to pay for each dollar of earnings.
Divided payout	$$\frac{\text{Annual dividends per share}}{\text{Annual earnings per share}}$$	Percentage	Indicates the percentage of profit that is paid out as dividends.
Dividend yield	$$\frac{\text{Annual dividends per share}}{\text{Current market price per share}}$$	Percentage	Indicates the dividend rate of return to common shareholders at the current mar-ket price.

Note: In using ratios for analysis, calculate ratios for the corporation and compare them with the average and quartile ratios for the particular industry. Refer to Standard and Poor's and Robert Morris Associates for average industry data. Special thanks to Dr. Moustafa H. Abdelsamad, Dean, Business School, Texas A&M University–Corpus Christi, Corpus Christi, Texas, for his definitions of these ratios.

interrelated dimensions. First, comparing profits to sales indicates the residual return an organization earns for every dollar of sales revenue. By measuring how well an organization is able to control costs in relation to revenues, return on sales points to the earning power of the organization. Second, comparing profits to the investments required to generate them allows owners to compare the return per dollar invested in the organization with the returns possible in debt or equity markets. Whichever method is used, some form of profitability index is invariably used by management as an assessment of its overall performance. This is particularly important in highly competitive industries, where a firm's above-average levels of profitability will allow it to withstand the downward pressure on prices that occurs as industry profits attract new entrants.

ACTIVITY RATIOS

Activity ratios describe the relationship between an organization's operations (such as manufacturing and selling products, providing services) and the investment in assets required to sustain that level of activity. Whatever the scope of an organization's activities might be, it requires both current assets (e.g., cash, inventory, accounts receivable) and fixed assets (e.g., property, plant, equipment) in order to function. A high activity ratio indicates efficiency in operations because fewer assets are required to produce a certain level of activity. Trends in this ratio can be predictive of changes in profitability, given that inefficient operations tend to put organizations at some level of competitive disadvantage. Activity ratios are also useful in forecasting an organization's capital requirements because they point to the increased investments necessary to support targeted sales increases.

The first set of activity ratios presented in **Table 1** are referred to as short-term or operating activity ratios. They focus on how efficiently current or short-term assets such as cash, inventory, and accounts receivable are used. Low ratios in these areas indicate a drain on current assets based on poor credit policies and/or inventory management. Long-term or investment activity ratios specifically examine the efficiency of fixed assets such as property, plant, and equipment. Larger investments like these are usually made periodically to meet planned increases in sales. So as production levels near capacity, fixed asset turnover appears very good. But as soon as a capacity expansion is made, the ratio declines. Using an aggregate measure of overall investment efficiency such as total asset turnover can, therefore, be helpful.

LEVERAGE RATIOS

Leverage is the term referring to the partial use of debt to finance investments. Leveraged firms can provide superior returns to their shareholders when there is a gap between the cost of debt (the interest rate associated with the debt) and the return on the investments made by it. These benefits, however, come with certain risks. Any time debt financing is used, firms create fixed costs of interest and principal repayment. If demand or profit margins decline, these newly created fixed financing costs can decrease profitability.

A normal amount of financial leverage often varies by industry. Some are very capital-intensive, such as steel production, automobile manufacturing, and oil refining. In these industries it is normal to incur high levels of debt to finance the capital equipment necessary to finance business activity. Generally speaking, debt should be long term to match the useful life of the assets it was used to acquire. Analysts also want to consider the organization's ability to meet current debt obligations, more specifically the interest expense created by incurring debt. Once again matching is what is desired—an ability to meet current interest or principal payments based on current net profit levels.

OTHER RATIOS

A variety of ratios are used for securities valuation. Corporations have common shares that may be publicly or privately traded. Potential investors look to certain measures of firm performance to gauge the desirability of investment in particular organizations, and as such look to its profitability in relation to the number and value of shares outstanding. Earnings per share is the most widely used performance indicator for publicly traded firms. It permits a quick comparison of the profits associated with each dollar of equity invested in the firm. The price earnings ratio is another popular measure, showing the degree to which the market capitalizes a firm's earnings. By showing how much investors are willing to pay per dollar of reported profits, the price earnings ratio indicates the growth prospects for a firm and the associated risks in its operations. A high ratio indicates market perceptions that a firm's operations are less risky than most, that growth prospects are good, or both.

ANALYZING FINANCIAL STATEMENTS

In the preceding section you were introduced to a variety of financial ratios that are commonly used in the analysis of financial statements. These ratios (liquidity, profitability, activity, and leverage) all measure some aspect of an organization's operating, investment, and financing activities. They are intended to give insight into different dimensions of firm performance, both by an organization's managers in their decisions about the future, as well as by potential creditors and investors. In case analysis, the analysis of financial statements forms part of the assessment of the organization's current position and serves as an indicator of its financial resources that may permit further investments associated with changes in firm strategy. Ratio analysis cannot answer all questions about an organization's performance, but it can point to aspects of a firm's operations, investments, and financing that have strategic importance.

How should the financial ratios you calculated be used? In your analysis, do not simply make an exhibit including all the ratios; select and discuss only those ratios that have an impact on the company's problems. For instance, accounts receivable and inventory may provide a source of funds. If receivables and inventories are double the industry average, reducing them may provide needed cash. In this situation, the case report should include not only sources of funds, but also the number of dollars freed for use. Compare these ratios with industry averages to discover whether the company is out of line with others in the industry. A typical financial analysis of a firm would include a study of the operating statements for five or so years, including a trend analysis of sales, profits, earnings per share, debt-to-equity ratio, return on investment, and so on, plus a ratio study comparing the firm under study with industry standards. Developing trends may be revealed through examination of the information obtained through these steps:

- Scrutinize historical income statements and balance sheets. These basic two statements provide most of the data needed for analysis. Statements of cash flow may also be useful.

- Compare historical statements over time if a series of statements is available.

- Calculate changes that occur in individual categories from year to year, as well as the cumulative total change.

- Determine the change as a percentage as well as an absolute amount.

- Adjust for inflation if that was a significant factor.

Compare trends in one category with trends in related categories. For example, an increase in sales of 15% over three years may appear to be satisfactory until you note an increase of 20% in the cost of goods sold during the same period. The outcome of this comparison might suggest that further investigation into the manufacturing process is necessary. If a company is reporting strong net income growth but negative cash flow, this would suggest that the company is relying on something other than operations for earnings growth. Is it selling off assets or cutting R & D? If accounts receivable are growing faster than sales revenues, the company is not getting paid for the products or services it is counting as sold. Is the company dumping product on its distributors at the end of the year to boost its reported annual sales? If so, expect the distributors to return the unordered product the next month—thus drastically cutting the next year's reported sales.

Other "tricks of the trade" need to be examined. Until June 2000, firms growing through acquisition were allowed to account for the cost of the purchased company through the pooling of both companies' stocks. This approach was used in 40% of the value of mergers between 1997 and 1999. The pooling method enabled the acquiring company to disregard the premium it paid for the other firm (the amount above the fair market value of the purchased company often called "goodwill"). Thus, when PepsiCo agreed to purchase Quaker Oats for $13.4 billion in PepsiCo stock, the $13.4 billion was not found on PepsiCo's balance sheet. As of June 2000, merging firms must use the "purchase" accounting rules in which the true purchase price is reflected in the financial statements.[1]

Note that multinational corporations follow the accounting rules for their home country. As a result, their financial statements may be somewhat difficult to understand or to use for comparisons with competitors from other countries. For example, British firms such as British Petroleum and The Body Shop use the term "turnover" rather than sales revenue. In the case of AB Electrolux of Sweden, a footnote to the annual report indicates that the consolidated accounts have been prepared in accordance with Swedish accounting standards, which differ in certain significant respects from generally accepted accounting principles (GAAP) in Canada. For one year, net income of 4830 million SEK (Swedish kronor) approximated 5655 SEK according to GAAP. Total assets for the same period were 84 183 million SEK according to the Swedish principle, but 86 658 according to GAAP.

COMMON-SIZE STATEMENTS

Common-size statements are income statements and balance sheets in which the dollar figures have been converted into percentages. For the income statement, net sales represent 100%: calculate the percentage of each category so that the categories sum to the net sales percentage (100%). For the balance sheet, give the total assets a value of 100% and calculate other asset and liability categories as percentages of the total assets. (Individual asset and liability items, such as accounts receivable and accounts payable, can also be calculated as a percentage of net sales.)

When you convert statements to this form, it is relatively easy to note the percentage that each category represents of the total. Look for trends in specific items, such as cost of goods sold, when compared with the company's historical figures. To get a proper picture, however, make comparisons with industry data, if available, to see if fluctuations are merely reflecting industry-wide trends. If a firm's trends are generally in line with those of the rest of the industry, problems are less likely than if the firm's trends are worse than industry averages. Common-size statements are especially helpful in developing scenarios and pro forma statements because they provide a series of historical relationships (for example, cost of goods sold to sales, interest to sales, and inventories as a percentage of assets) from which you can estimate the future with your scenario assumptions for each year.

Z-VALUE, INDEX OF SUSTAINABLE GROWTH, AND FREE CASH FLOW

Altman's bankruptcy formula a composite index of an organization's financial strength

If the organization being studied appears to be in poor financial condition, use **Altman's bankruptcy formula** to calculate its Z-value. The Z-value formula combines five ratios by weighting them according to their importance to a corporation's financial strength. This is the formula:

$$Z = 1.2x_1 + 1.4x_2 + 3.3x_3 + 0.6x_4 + 1.0x_5$$

where:

$$x_1 = \text{Working capital/Total assets (\%)}$$

$$x_2 = \text{Retained earnings/Total assets (\%)}$$

$$x_3 = \text{Earnings before interest and taxes/Total assets (\%)}$$

$$x_4 = \text{Market value of equity/Total liabilities (\%)}$$

$$x_5 = \text{Sales/Total assets (number of times)}$$

Scores below 1.81 indicate significant credit problems, whereas a score above 3.0 indicates a healthy firm. Scores between 1.81 and 3.0 indicate question marks.[2]

index of sustainable growth a measure of how much of an organization's sales growth can be sustained by internally generated funds

The **index of sustainable growth** is useful to learn if a company embarking on a growth strategy will need to take on debt to fund this growth. The index indicates how much of the growth rate of sales can be sustained by internally generated funds. Here is the formula for it:

$$g^{\star} = \frac{[P(1-D)(1+L)]}{[T - P(1-D)(1+L)]}$$

where:

$P = (\text{Net profit before tax/Net sales}) \times 100$

$D = \text{Target dividends/Profit after tax}$

$L = \text{Total liabilities/Net worth}$

$T = (\text{Total assets/Net sales}) \times 100$

If the planned growth rate calls for a growth rate higher than its $g^{\star}$, external capital will be needed to fund the growth unless management is able to find efficiencies, decrease dividends, increase the debt to equity ratio, or reduce assets by renting or leasing arrangements.

Takeover artists and LBO (leveraged buyout) specialists look at an organization's financial statements for operating cash flow: the amount of money generated by a company before the cost of financing and taxes. This is the company's net income plus depreciation plus depletion, amortization, interest expense, and income tax expense. LBO specialists will take on as much debt as the company's operating cash flow can support.

A similar measure, EBITDA (earnings before interest, taxes, depreciation, and amortization), is sometimes used, but it is *not* determined in accordance with generally accepted accounting principles and is thus subject to varying calculations. Although operating cash flow is a broad measure of a company's funds, some takeover artists look at a much narrower free cash flow: the amount of money a new owner can take out of the firm without harming the business. This is net income plus depreciation, depletion, and amortization less capital expenditures and dividends. The free cash flow ratio is very useful in evaluating the stability of an entrepreneurial venture. The danger in using these instruments is that they appear to be the same as cash flow—which they are not. According to Martin Fridson, chief of high-yield research with Merrill Lynch, "A capital intensive company isn't earning a profit if its assets are wearing down from wear and tear."[3]

constant dollars an adjustment for inflation that permits direct comparison of sales and revenue figures

consumer price index a measure of inflation based on the cost of a basket of items representing typical household expenditures

USEFUL ECONOMIC MEASURES

If you are analyzing a company over many years, you may want to adjust sales and net income for inflation to arrive at "true" financial performance in constant dollars. **Constant dollars** are dollars adjusted for inflation to make them comparable over various years. See the **Global Issue** feature to learn why inflation can be an important issue for multinational corporations. One way to adjust for inflation is to use the **consumer price index** (CPI), as given in **Table 2** on page 319. Dividing sales and net income by the CPI factor for that year will change the figures to 1992 constant dollars (when the CPI was 1.0).

prime interest rate the rate of interest banks charge their preferred customers

Another helpful analytical aid provided in **Table 2** is the **prime interest rate**, the rate of interest banks charge on their lowest-risk loans. For better assessments of strategic decisions, it can be useful to note the level of the prime interest rate at the time of the case. A decision to borrow money to build a new plant would have been a good one in 1993 at 6%, but less practical in 2000 when the rate reached 9.5%.

gross domestic product a country's total output of goods and services

In preparing a scenario for your pro forma financial statements, you may want to use the **gross domestic product** (GDP) from **Table 2**. GDP is used worldwide and measures the total output of goods and services within a country's borders. The amount of change from one year to the next indicates how much that country's economy is growing. Remember that scenarios have to be adjusted for a country's specific conditions.

Global Issue

Why Consider Inflation in Case Analysis?

Inflation has been a recent problem in North America. Between 1800 and 1940, there was no clear trend up or down in the overall cost of living. A moviegoer in the late 1930s watching a drama set in the early 1800s would not notice prices to be unusual. For example, the cost of a loaf of bread in the late 1930s was roughly the same as in 1800. With the minor exceptions of 1949 and 1955, prices have risen every year since 1945. The US consumer price index (a generally used measure of the overall cost of living) increased nine times from 1945 to 1996. (Watch the movie *It's a Wonderful Life* to see how much prices have changed since 1948.) From 1970 to 1980, the CPI more than doubled. After an average rate of 7.1% during the 1970s, inflation slowed to 5.5% in the 1980s, and 3.4% during the 1990s. Inflation seemed to be under control in the United States. Although people complained about the rising price of retail gasoline, the average price in constant dollars in 2000 was the same as in 1970—before the OPEC oil embargo. Nevertheless, economist Milton Friedman warns of an increase in inflation. "We're in a period like the 1960s, when no one paid any attention to the money supply. Then we got inflation," says Friedman.

The rate of inflation in other countries varies and has a significant impact on a multinational organization's profits. Although most countries in the developed parts of the world kept inflation under control during the five-year period from 1994 to 1999, the developing nations did not fare as well. For

example, the average annual inflation rate in Turkey during 1994–1999 was 81%. Supermarkets were forced to list prices on electronic displays rather than on printed labels. Turkey's rate of inflation was high but was a far cry from Bolivia's astounding annual rate during 1985 of 25 000%. During 1994–1999, the countries of the European Union had an inflation rate of around 2%–3%, while Eastern European countries were dealing with higher rates, such as 64% in Russia and 19% in Hungary. During 1997 alone, Romania's annual inflation rate was 170%, while Bulgaria's was 1268%. During the 1994–1999 time period in Latin America, Mexico's annual rate was 24%, Colombia's was 18%, and Brazil's was 17%. Although most Asian countries had a low rate of inflation (Singapore, Taiwan, and Malaysia increased less than 5%), Indonesia's was 20% and India's was 8%.

Before inflation is declared dead by politicians anxious to reduce cost-of-living increases to social insurance payments (to reduce government expenditures and thus government debt), note what happens with a relatively constant 3.4% rate of inflation. Through the working of compound interest, the price level rose about 40% during the 1990s. This means that companies have to be constantly monitoring not only their costs, but also the prices of the products they offer. Unless a company's dollar sales are increasing over 3.5% annually, its sales are actually falling (in constant dollars). The same is true for net income. This point is often overlooked by the chief executive officers of troubled companies who are anxious to keep their jobs by fooling both the board and the shareholders.

Sources: P.W. Boltz, "Is Inflation Dead?" *T. Rowe Price Report* (Winter 1997), pp. 10–11; P. Brimelow with M. Friedman, "Beware the Funny Money," *Forbes* (May 3, 1999), pp. 138–141; "Managing Inflation: Talking Turkey," *The Economist* (October 11, 1997), p. 95; "Emerging Market Indicators," *The Economist* (December 9, 2000), p. 116; J.T. Allen and D. McGraw, "The Gas Crisis That Isn't—Yet," *U.S. News & World Report* (April 3, 1990), p. 22.

Table 2 Economic Indicators

Year	GDP	CPI	Interest Rate
1992	188 708	100.0	7.762
1993	193 124	101.8	5.155
1994	202 504	102.0	5.666
1995	208 034	104.2	5.159
1996	211 289	105.9	3.323
1997	220 684	107.6	2.499
1998	229 750	108.6	3.690
1999	241 912	110.5	3.522
2000	253 266	113.5	4.075
2001	256 717	116.4	3.210

Sources: Adapted from the Statistics Canada CANSIM database, Tables 380-0002 (GDP, expenditure based, computed annual average in millions of dollars), 326-0002 (CPI, 1996 basket content, annual average, 1992 base period), and 176-0048 (Bank of Canada rate, computed annual average).

4 Conducting a Strategic Audit of an Organization[4]

The strategic audit is designed to help students "ask the right questions" to help prepare a case analysis. Through questions based on the content of each chapter of this book, you are provided with a checklist that matches the elements of the strategic decision-making process shown in **Figure 1–6** (in **Chapter 1**). The answers to these questions do not, in and of themselves, give the "answer" to the case. Rather they can assist students to identify the most important aspects of each part of the strategic development process, from environmental scanning to strategy formulation and implementation, and finally evaluation and control. The strategic audit is, therefore, a tool that permits a systematic assessment of the organization and its environment. Use the answers to these questions to complete a SWOT analysis, develop and choose between strategic alternatives, prepare an implementation plan, and create systems of evaluation and control. The strategic audit is only the *starting* point for your strategic analysis, not the end of it. It provides a description of the organization and its environment. By interpreting these facts and events, attaching significance to them, and integrating them into a well-justified course of action to improve organizational performance, you will end up with a comprehensive, well-justified recommendation that is the hallmark of a good case report.

I. CURRENT SITUATION

A. Current Performance See Section 10.2 on pages 257–270

1. How did the organization perform the past year overall in terms of return on investment, market share, and profitability?

B. Strategic Posture See Section 1.4 on pages 12–20

1. What are the organization's current mission, objectives, strategies, and policies? Are they clearly stated or are they merely implied from performance?
2. Mission: What business(es) is the organization in? Is the mission statement appropriate?
3. Objectives: What are the corporate, business, and functional objectives? Are they consistent with each other, with the mission, and with the internal and external environments?
4. Strategies: What are the current corporate, business, and functional strategies? Are they consistent with each other, with the mission and objectives, and with the internal and external environments?

5. Policies: What are they? Are they consistent with each other, with the mission, objectives, and strategies, and with the internal and external environments?

6. Do the current mission, objectives, strategies, and policies reflect the organization's international operations—whether global or multidomestic?

II. ETHICS AND CORPORATE SOCIAL RESPONSIBILITY

A. Business Ethics See Section 2.1 on pages 30–36

1. What is contained in a code of ethics that will guide organizational strategy?
2. Is there a history of ethical behaviour, or the presence of a culture of ethics?
3. How does the organization articulate its broader social responsibility?
4. What are the relevant organizational stakeholders and how does the organization view their claims?

B. Top Management See Sections 2.2–2.4 on pages 36–45

1. What person or group constitutes top management?
2. What are top management's chief characteristics in terms of knowledge, skills, background, and style? If the organization has international operations, does top management have international experience? Are executives from acquired companies considered part of the top management team?
3. Has top management been responsible for the organization's performance over the past few years? How many managers have been in their current position for less than three years? Were they internal promotions or external hires?
4. Has it established a systematic approach to strategic management?
5. What is its level of involvement in the strategic management process?
6. How well does top management interact with lower level managers and with the board of directors?
7. Are strategic decisions made ethically in a socially responsible manner?
8. What role do stock options play in executive compensation?
9. Is top management sufficiently skilled to cope with likely future challenges?

III. EXTERNAL ENVIRONMENT: OPPORTUNITIES AND THREATS (SWOT)

A. Societal Environment See Section 3.1 on pages 51–58

1. What general environmental forces are currently affecting both the organization and the industries in which it competes? Which of these present current or future threats? Opportunities? (See **Table 3–1**.)
   a. Economic
   b. Technological
   c. Political-legal
   d. Socio-cultural
2. Are these forces different in other regions of the world?

B. Task Environment (Industry) See Section 3.2 on pages 62–74

1. What forces drive industry competition? Are these forces the same globally or do they vary from country to country?

a. Threat of new entrants

b. Bargaining power of buyers

c. Threat of substitute products or services

d. Bargaining power of suppliers

e. Rivalry among competing firms

f. Relative power of unions, governments, special interest groups, etc.

2. What key factors in the immediate environment (that is, customers, competitors, suppliers, creditors, labour unions, governments, trade associations, interest groups, local communities, and shareholders) are currently affecting the organization? Which are current or future threats? Opportunities?

C. Summary of External Factors

Which of these forces and factors are the most important to the organization and to the industries in which it competes at the present time? Which will be important in the future?

IV. INTERNAL ENVIRONMENT: STRENGTHS AND WEAKNESSES (SWOT)

A. Organizational Structure See Sections 4.3 and 8.4 on pages 92–94 and 203–218

1. How is the organization currently structured?

a. Is the decision-making authority centralized around one group or decentralized to many units?

b. Is it organized on the basis of functions, projects, geography, or some combination of these?

2. Is the structure clearly understood by everyone in the organization?

3. Is the present structure consistent with current corporate objectives, strategies, policies, and programs as well as with the firm's international operations?

4. In what ways does this structure compare with those of similar corporations?

B. Organizational Culture See Section 4.3 on pages 94–96

1. Is there a well-defined or emerging culture composed of shared beliefs, expectations, and values?

2. Is the culture consistent with the current objectives, strategies, policies, and programs?

3. What is the culture's position on important issues facing the organization (that is, on productivity, quality of performance, adaptability to changing conditions, and internationalization)?

4. Is the culture compatible with the employees' diversity of backgrounds?

5. Does the company take into consideration the values of each nation's culture in which the firm operates?

C. Organizational Resources Marketing See Section 4.3 on pages 96–97

1. What are the organization's current marketing objectives, strategies, policies, and programs?

a. Are they clearly stated, or merely implied from performance and/or budgets?

b. Are they consistent with the organization's mission, objectives, strategies, and policies, and with internal and external environments?

2. How well is the organization performing in terms of analysis of market position and marketing mix (that is, product, price, place, and promotion) in both domestic and international markets? What percentage of sales comes from foreign operations? Where are current products in product life cycle?

    a. What trends emerge from this analysis?

    b. What impact have these trends had on past performance and how will they probably affect future performance?

    c. Does this analysis support the organization's past and pending strategic decisions?

    d. Does marketing provide the company with a competitive advantage?

3. How well does this corporation's marketing performance compare with that of similar corporations?

4. Are marketing managers using accepted marketing concepts and techniques to evaluate and improve product performance? (Consider product life cycle, market segmentation, market research, and product portfolios.)

5. Does marketing adjust to the conditions in each country in which it operates?

6. What is the role of the marketing manager in the strategic management process?

Finance See Sections 4.3 and Appendix on pages 97–98 and 308–319.

1. What are the organization's current financial objectives, strategies, policies, and programs?

    a. Are they clearly stated or merely implied from performance and/or budgets?

    b. Are they consistent with the organization's mission, objectives, strategies, policies, and with internal and external environments?

2. How well is the organization performing in terms of financial analysis? (Consider ratios, common size statements, and capitalization structure.) How balanced, in terms of cash flow, is the company's portfolio of products and businesses?

    a. What trends emerge from this analysis?

    b. Are there any significant differences when statements are calculated in constant versus reported dollars?

    c. What impact have these trends had on past performance and how will they probably affect future performance?

    d. Does this analysis support the organization's past and pending strategic decisions?

    e. Does finance provide the company with a competitive advantage?

3. How well does this corporation's financial performance compare with that of similar corporations?

4. Are financial managers using accepted financial concepts and techniques to evaluate and improve current corporate and divisional performance? (Consider financial leverage, capital budgeting, ratio analysis, and managing foreign currencies.)

5. Does finance adjust to the conditions in each country in which the company operates?

6. What is the role of the financial manager in the strategic management process?

Research and Development (R & D) See Section 4.3 on pages 98–101.

1. What are the organization's current R & D objectives, strategies, policies, and programs?

    a. Are they clearly stated, or merely implied from performance and/or budgets?

    b. Are they consistent with the organization's mission, objectives, strategies, policies, and with internal and external environments?

    c. What is the role of technology in corporate performance?

    d. Is the mix of basic, applied, and engineering research appropriate given the corporate mission and strategies?

e. Does R & D provide the company with a competitive advantage?

2. What return is the organization receiving from its investment in R & D?

3. Is the organization competent in technology transfer? Does it use concurrent engineering and cross-functional work teams in product and process design?

4. What role does technological discontinuity play in the company's products?

5. How well does the organization's investment in R & D compare with the investments of similar corporations?

6. Does R & D adjust to the conditions in each country in which the company operates?

7. What is the role of the R & D manager in the strategic management process?

Operations and Logistics See Section 4.3 on pages 101–102.

1. What are the organization's current manufacturing/service objectives, strategies, policies, and programs?
   a. Are they clearly stated, or merely implied from performance and/or budgets?
   b. Are they consistent with the organization's mission, objectives, strategies, policies, and with internal and external environments?

2. What is the type and extent of operations capabilities of the organization? How much is done domestically versus internationally? Is the amount of outsourcing appropriate to be competitive? Is purchasing being handled appropriately?
   a. If product-oriented, consider plant facilities, type of manufacturing system (continuous mass production, intermittent job shop, or flexible manufacturing), age and type of equipment, degree and role of automation and/or robots, plant capacities and utilization, productivity ratings, availability and type of transportation.
   b. If service-oriented, consider service facilities (hospital, theatre, or school buildings), type of operations systems (continuous service over time to same clientele or intermittent service over time to varied clientele), age and type of supporting equipment, degree and role of automation and/or use of mass communication devices (diagnostic machinery, videotape machines), facility capacities and utilization rates, efficiency ratings of professional/service personnel, availability and type of transportation to bring service staff and clientele together.

3. Are manufacturing or service facilities vulnerable to natural disasters, local or national strikes, reduction or limitation of resources from suppliers, substantial cost increases of materials, or nationalization by governments?

4. Is there an appropriate mix of people and machines in manufacturing firms, or of support staff to professionals in service firms?

5. How well does the organization perform relative to the competition? Is it balancing inventory costs (warehousing) with logistical costs (just-in-time)? Consider costs per unit of labour, material, and overhead; downtime; inventory control management and/or scheduling of service staff; production ratings; facility utilization percentages; and number of clients successfully treated by category (if service firm) or percentage of orders shipped on time (if product firm).
   a. What trends emerge from this analysis?
   b. What impact have these trends had on past performance and how will they probably affect future performance?
   c. Does this analysis support the organization's past and pending strategic decisions?
   d. Does operations provide the company with a competitive advantage?

6. Are operations managers using appropriate concepts and techniques to evaluate and improve current performance? Consider cost systems, quality control and reliability

systems, inventory control management, personnel scheduling, TQM, learning curves, safety programs, and engineering programs that can improve efficiency of manufacturing or of service.

7. Do operations and logistics adjust to the conditions in each country in which the organization has facilities?

8. What is the role of the operations manager in the strategic management process?

Human Resources Management (HRM) See Section 4.3 on pages 103–105

1. What are the organization's current HRM objectives, strategies, policies, and programs?

   a. Are they clearly stated, or merely implied from performance and/or budgets?

   b. Are they consistent with the organization's mission, objectives, strategies, policies, and with internal and external environments?

2. How well is the organization's HRM performing in terms of improving the fit between the individual employee and the job? Consider turnover, grievances, strikes, layoffs, employee training, and quality of work life.

   a. What trends emerge from this analysis?

   b. What impact have these trends had on past performance and how will they probably affect future performance?

   c. Does this analysis support the organization's past and pending strategic decisions?

   d. Does HRM provide the company with a competitive advantage?

   e. Do the company's employees (skills, education, knowledge) provide the company with a competitive advantage?

3. How does this corporation's HRM performance compare with that of similar corporations?

4. Are HRM managers using appropriate concepts and techniques to evaluate and improve corporate performance? Consider the job analysis program, performance appraisal system, up-to-date job descriptions, training and development programs, attitude surveys, job design programs, quality of relationship with unions, and use of autonomous work teams.

5. How well is the company managing the diversity of its workforce? What is the company's position and record on human rights?

6. Does HRM adjust to the conditions in each country in which the company operates? Does the company have a code of conduct for HRM in developing nations? Are employees receiving international assignments to prepare them for managerial positions?

7. What is the role of the HRM manager in the strategic management process?

Information Systems (IS) See Section 4.3 on pages 105–106

1. What are the organization's current IS objectives, strategies, policies, and programs?

   a. Are they clearly stated, or merely implied from performance and/or budgets?

   b. Are they consistent with the organization's mission, objectives, strategies, policies, and with internal and external environments?

2. How well is the organization's IS performing in terms of providing a useful database, offering internet access and websites, automating routine clerical operations, assisting managers in making routine decisions, and providing information necessary for strategic decisions?

   a. What trends emerge from this analysis?

   b. What impact have these trends had on past performance and how will they probably affect future performance?

   c. Does this analysis support the organization's past and pending strategic decisions?

   d. Does IS provide the company with a competitive advantage?

3. How does this corporation's IS performance and stage of development compare with that of similar corporations? Is it appropriately using the internet?

4. Are IS managers using appropriate concepts and techniques to evaluate and improve corporate performance? Do they know how to build and manage a complex database, establish websites with firewalls, conduct system analyses, and implement interactive decision-support systems?

5. Does the company have a global IS and internet presence? Does it have difficulty with getting data across national boundaries?

6. What is the role of the IS manager in the strategic management process?

D. Summary of Internal Factors

Which of these factors are core competencies? Which are distinctive competencies? Which of these factors are the most important to the organization and to the industries in which it competes at the present time? Which of these factors will be important in the future?

V. ANALYSIS OF STRATEGIC FACTORS (SWOT)

A. Situational Analysis See Sections 5.1 and 5.2 on pages 116–118

What are the most important internal and external factors (Strengths, Weaknesses, Opportunities, Threats) that strongly affect the organization's present and future performance? The most important strategic factors?

B. Review of Mission and Objectives See Section 5.2 on page 118

1. Are the current mission and objectives appropriate in light of the key strategic factors and problems?

2. Should the mission and objectives be changed? If so, how?

3. If changed, what will be the effects on the firm?

VI. STRATEGIC ALTERNATIVES AND RECOMMENDED STRATEGY

A. Strategic Alternatives See Sections 5.3, 5.4, 6.2, and 7.1 on pages 119, 120–134, 140–154, 168–181.

1. Can the current or revised objectives be met by the simple, more careful implementation of those strategies presently in use (that is, by fine-tuning the strategies)?

2. What are the major feasible alternative strategies available to this organization? What are the advantages and disadvantages of each? Can corporate scenarios be developed and agreed upon? (Alternatives must fit societal environment, industry, and company for next three to five years.)

   a. Consider cost leadership and differentiation as business strategies.

   b. Consider stability, growth, and retrenchment as corporate strategies.

   c. Consider any functional strategic alternatives that might be needed for reinforcement of an important corporate or business strategic alternative.

B. Recommended Strategy See Sections 7.3 and 7.4 on pages 183–190

1. Specify which of the strategic alternatives you are recommending for the corporate, business, and functional levels of the organization. Do you recommend different business or functional strategies for different units of the organization?

2. Justify your recommendation in terms of its ability to resolve both long- and short-term problems and effectively deal with the strategic factors.

3. What policies should be developed or revised to guide effective implementation?

4. What is the impact of recommended strategy on the company's core and distinctive competencies?

VII. IMPLEMENTATION SEE CHAPTERS 8 AND 9.

A. What kinds of programs (for example, restructuring the organization or instituting TQM) should be developed to implement the recommended strategy?

1. Who should develop these programs?
2. Who should be in charge of these programs?

B. Are the programs financially feasible? Can pro forma budgets be developed and agreed upon? Are priorities and timetables appropriate to individual programs?

C. Will new standard operating procedures need to be developed?

VIII. EVALUATION AND CONTROL SEE CHAPTER 10.

A. Is the current information system capable of providing sufficient feedback on implementation activities and performance? Can it measure strategic factors?

1. Can performance results be pinpointed by area, unit, project, or function?
2. Is the information timely?

B. Are adequate control measures in place to ensure conformance with the recommended strategic plan?

1. Are appropriate standards and measures being used?
2. Are reward systems capable of recognizing and rewarding good performance?
3. Who takes corrective action?

C. Are there adequate governance structures to ensure good strategic control?

1. Who are the directors, and what are their backgrounds?
2. What do they contribute to the organization in terms of knowledge, skills, background, and connections?
3. What stakeholder interests do they represent?
4. What is their level of involvement in the strategic management of the organization?

5 Format for Case Analysis: The Strategic Audit

There is no one best way to analyze or present a case report. Each instructor has personal preferences for format and approach. Nevertheless, we suggest an approach for both written and oral reports later in this appendix, which provides a systematic method for successfully attacking a case. This approach is based on the strategic audit, which is presented at the end of this appendix. We find that this approach provides structure and is very helpful for the typical student who may be a relative novice in case analysis. Regardless of the format chosen, be careful to include a complete analysis of key environmental variables—especially of trends in the industry and of the competition. Look at international developments as well.

If you choose to use the strategic audit as a guide to the analysis of complex strategy cases, you may want to use the strategic audit worksheet in **Figure 1**. This is one example of what a case analysis in outline form may look like.

Case discussion focuses on critical analysis and logical development of thought. A solution is satisfactory if it resolves important problems and is likely to be implemented successfully. How the corporation actually dealt with the case problems has no real bearing on the analysis because management might have analyzed its problems incorrectly or implemented a series of flawed solutions.

Figure 1 Strategic Audit Worksheet

Strategic Audit Heading	Analysis		Comments
	(+) Factors	(−) Factors	
I. Current Situation			
A. Past Corporate Performance Indexes			
B. Strategic Posture: Current Mission Current Objectives Current Strategies Current Policies			
SWOT Analysis Begins:			
II. Corporate Governance			
A. Board of Directors			
B. Top Management			
III. External Environment (EFAS): **Opportunities and Threats (SW<u>OT</u>)**			
A. Societal Environment			
B. Task Environment (Industry Analysis)			
IV. Internal Environment (IFAS): **Strengths and Weaknesses (<u>SW</u>OT)**			
A. Corporate Structure			
B. Corporate Culture			

Figure 1 Strategic Audit Worksheet (continued)

Strategic Audit Heading	Analysis		Comments
	(+) Factors	(−) Factors	
C. Corporate Resources			
1. Marketing			
2. Finance			
3. Research and Development			
4. Operations and Logistics			
5. Human Resources			
6. Information Systems			
V. Analysis of Strategic Factors (SFAS)			
A. Key Internal and External Strategic Factors (SWOT)			
B. Review of Mission and Objectives			
SWOT Analysis Ends. Recommendation Begins:			
VI. Alternatives and Recommendations			
A. Strategic Alternatives—pros and cons			
B. Recommended Strategy			
VII. Implementation			
VIII. Evaluation and Control			

Note: **See the complete Strategic Audit on pages 319–326. It lists the pages in the book that discuss each of the eight headings.**

Source: T. L. Wheelen and J. D. Hunger, "Strategic Audit Worksheet." Copyright © 1989 by Wheelen and Hunger Associates. Revised 1991, 1994, and 1997. Reprinted by permission.

6 Impact of the Internet on Case Analysis

The internet is an excellent source of information about industries as well as individual companies. It can be especially useful if your instructor gives you the assignment to either update a case or to research an industry. To begin, you only need access to the internet and a browser like Netscape Navigator or Microsoft's Internet Explorer. When surfing the net, you will be amazed by the amount of information (much of it worthless) you can find. A word of caution: Beware of getting caught by an online confidence game. (See the **Internet Issue** feature for the top 10 internet scams.)

FINDING A COMPANY'S WEBSITE

If you are looking for information about a particular company, you can first try using a simplified version of the firm's name to directly get to the firm's home (primary) webpage. For example, first type in the protocol, the standard first part of the URL (uniform resource locator)—**http://www**. Don't capitalize any letters in the URL. Then type in a likely name for the firm, such as **maytag**, **ibm**, **toyota**, **hp** (Hewlett-Packard), **ti** (Texas Instruments), or **pearsoned** (Pearson Education Canada). This is referred to as the company's server name. Follow this name with the suffix **.com**. This is called a domain. In the United States, most business URLs still end with the domain name **.com**. Many Canadian organizations end in **.ca**. The same is true for other URLs, such as **.edu** for schools and colleges in America, **.gov** for government agencies, and **.org** for non-profit organizations. Outside the United States each country has its own suffix, such as **.uk** for Great Britain, **.au** for Australia, **.de** for Germany. This string of words and letters usually completes the URL. For example, try typing **http://www.maytag.com** in the location line of your internet browser and tap the Enter key. This takes you directly to Maytag's homepage. In some instances, the URL may also contain a more specific web page beyond the company's homepage. In this case, the **.com** is followed by **/xxxx.html** (**xxxx** can be anything). This indicates that this is another webpage that uses the HTML (hypertext markup language) of the World Wide Web.

USING A SEARCH ENGINE

If typing in an obvious company name doesn't work, use a search engine. This is especially the case if you are investigating a non-US corporation like AB Electrolux of Sweden. Search engines are services that act like a library's card file to help you find information on a topic. Type in **http://www.** followed by the search engine's URL. Some of the common search engines are Yahoo! (**www.yahoo.ca**), Alta Vista (**www.altavista.com**), Lycos (**www.lycos.ca**), Google (**www.google.ca**), Excite (**www.excite.com**) and Copernic (free download from **www.copernic.com**). These URLs will take you to the search engine's webpage where you can type in the name of a company. The search engine finds any references to that firm. One of these references should include the company's URL. Use it to get to the company's homepage.

FINDING MORE INFORMATION

Getting to the company's home webpage does not necessarily mean that you now have access to the firm's financials. If the website does include a link to a webpage containing the company's financials, that page will probably have only financials for the most recent year or two. In that case, try related business directories such as Hoover's Online (**www.hoovers.com**). If the company's stock is publicly traded and listed on one of the major stock exchanges, these business directories should get you to the database containing the latest annual reports and quarterly reports. Here are some other sites offering valuable information relating to business firms:

- Annual Report Gallery (www.reportgallery.com)
- Web 100 (www.w100.com)
- Toronto Stock Exchange (www.tse.com)
- CEO Express (www.ceoexpress.com)
- Wall Street Research Net (www.wsrn.com)
- Companies Online (www.companiesonline.com)
- Corporate Financials Online (www.cfonews.com)
- Corporate Information (www.corporateinformation.com)
- Kompass International (www.kompass.com)
- CorpTech Database of Technology Companies (www.corptech.com)
- ZDNet Company Finder (www.companyfinder.com)

Note that websites constantly change. Just because a particular URL works one time does not mean that it will work a year or two later. If the company is doing a good job of managing its websites, it will leave a message on its abandoned webpage sending you to a new page. If nothing works, simply go to one of the search engines and begin again. Good luck!

Internet Issue

Top 10 Internet Scams

The US Federal Trade Commission reports the following list of most popular internet-related complaints regarding confidence games being played on unsuspecting visitors to the information highway:

- **Auctions** (45%): Buyer pays but gets wrong item or none at all.
- **Internet Access** (21%): Supposedly "free" internet access has hidden charges and high cancellation fees.
- **Credit Card Fraud** (9%): Adult-only sites ask for credit card data to verify age—resulting in unauthorized charges.
- **Personal Website** (5%): Offers free website for 30 days but charges via the phone bill.

- **Modem Scam** (5%): Download a "free" dialler to access adult sites but high charges soon follow.
- **Home Business** (3%): Pay a fee but earn nothing.
- **Travel Bargains** (2%): Inexpensive trip is either not what was promised or is non-existent.
- **Sell Special Products** (2%): Sells product at low price, but there are no buyers.
- **Invest Now** (1%): Promises stock appreciation, but little actually happens after stock purchase.
- **Health Products** (1%): Miracle medicines sold as internet "snake oil" to solve all problems.

The modem scam is especially ingenious. A pornographic website offers to download a special "viewer" or "dialler" program to see nude photos. When the file is downloaded, the internet connection is disconnected and the program makes the computer dial a phone number to a small island in the southwest Pacific called Vanuatu (formerly the New Hebrides) at a rate of $2 to $7 per minute. Few people report this scam because they don't want others to know they were visiting pornographic websites.

Sources: "Top Ten Scams on the Information Highway," *U.S. News & World Report* (November 13, 2000), p. 16; S.S. Woo, "Scam Prompts Surf Warning," *Des Moines Register* (February 17, 2001), pp. D1, D6.

7 Resources for Case Research

COMPANY INFORMATION

1. Annual reports
2. *Moody's Manuals on Investment* (a listing of companies within certain industries that contains a brief history and a five-year financial statement of each company)
3. Securities and Exchange Commission Annual Report Form 10-K (annually) and 10-Q (quarterly)
4. Standard and Poor's *Register of Corporations, Directors, and Executives*
5. Value Line's *Investment Survey*
6. COMPUSTAT, Compact Disclosure, CD/International, and Hoover's Online Corporate Directory (computerized operating and financial information on thousands of publicly held corporations)
7. Shareholders' meeting notices

ECONOMIC INFORMATION

1. Regional statistics and local forecasts from large banks
2. Chase Econometric Associates' publications
3. Canadian census data publications on population, income, education, employment, and culture
4. *Economic Indicators* (from Statistics Canada) on business, construction, manufacturing, national accounts, and prices
5. *Economic Analysis and Statistics of Industries* (by Industry Canada)
6. *Monthly Bulletin of Statistics* (United Nations)
7. *Statistical Yearbook* (United Nations)
8. *World Trade Annual* (United Nations)
9. *Overseas Business Reports* (by country, published by US Department of Commerce)
10. *The World Factbook* (US CIA)

INDUSTRY INFORMATION

1. Analyses of companies and industries by investment brokerage firms
2. Business information by sector and company directories (from Industry Canada)
3. *Business Week* (provides weekly economic and business information, and quarterly profit and sales rankings of corporations)
4. *Fortune* (each April publishes listings of financial information on corporations within certain industries)
5. *Canadian Business Resource* (an interactive source for contact information, officers' and directors' names, brief company descriptions, financial data, SIC codes, direct links to email and website addresses, press releases, stock analysis, and investment information.
6. *Industry Survey* (published quarterly by Standard and Poor's Corporation)
7. *Industry Week* (late March/early April issue provides information on 14 industry groups)
8. *Forbes* (mid-January issue provides performance data on firms in various industries)
9. *Inc.* (May and December issues give information on fast-growing entrepreneurial companies)
10. *The Information Catalogue* (a listing by MarketResearch.com of more than 11 000 studies conducted by leading research firms)

DIRECTORY AND INDEX INFORMATION ON COMPANIES AND INDUSTRIES

1. CBCA (Canadian Business and Current Affairs), available by computer in most university libraries
2. *Directory of National Trade Associations*
3. *Encyclopedia of Associations*
4. Funk and Scott's *Index of Corporations and Industries*
5. Thomas's *Register of American Manufacturers*
6. *Wall Street Journal Index*

RATIO ANALYSIS INFORMATION

1. *Almanac of Business and Industrial Financial Ratios* (Prentice Hall)
2. *Annual Statement Studies* (Robert Morris Associates)

3. *Dun's Review* (Dun and Bradstreet; published annually in September–December issues)
4. *Industry Norms and Key Business Ratios* (Dun and Bradstreet)

ONLINE INFORMATION

1. Hoovers Online—financial statements and profiles of public companies (**www.hoovers.com**)
2. Fortune 500—statistics for largest US corporations (**www.pathfinder.com**)
3. Dun & Bradstreet's Online—short reports on 10 million public and private companies (**www.dbisna.com/dnb/dnbhome.htm**)
4. Ecola's 24-Hour Newsstand—links to websites of 2000 newspapers, journals, and magazines (**www.ecola.com/news**)
5. Competitive Intelligence Guide—information on company resources (**www.fuld.com**)
6. *The Economist*—provides international information and surveys (**www.economist.com**)
7. Web 100—information on 100 largest US and international companies (**www.w100.com**)
8. Bloomberg—information on interest rates, stock prices, currency conversion rates, and other general financial information (**www.bloomberg.com**)
9. The World Factbook—profiles of many countries (**www.odci.gov/cia/publications/factbook/index.html**)
10. Canadian Broadcasting Corporation—national and business stories, backgrounder series and archives of Canadian events (**www.cbc.ca**).
11. Strategis—Canada's Business and Consumer Site (**www.strategis.gc.ca**)

8 Suggested Case Analysis Methodology Using the Strategic Audit

1. READ CASE

First Reading of the Case

- Develop a general overview of the company and its external environment.

- Begin a list of the possible strategic factors facing the company at this time.

- List the research information you may need on the economy, industry, and competitors.

2. READ THE CASE WITH STRATEGIC AUDIT

Second Reading of the Case

- Read the case a second time using the strategic audit as a framework for in-depth analysis. You may want to make a copy of the strategic audit worksheet to use to keep track of your comments as you read the case.

- The questions in the strategic audit parallel the strategic decision making process shown in **Figure 1–6**.

- The audit provides you with a conceptual framework to examine the company's mission, objectives, strategies, and policies as well as problems, symptoms, facts, opinions, and issues.

- Perform a financial analysis of the company using ratio analysis (see **Table 1**) and do the calculations necessary to convert key parts of the financial statements to a common-size basis.

3. DO OUTSIDE RESEARCH (IF REQUIRED BY INSTRUCTOR)

Library and Online Computer Services

- Each case has a decision date indicating when the case actually took place. Your research should be based on the time period for the case.

- Use resources for case research discussed earlier in this appendix. Your research should include information about the environment at the time of the case. Find average industry ratios. You may also want to obtain further information regarding competitors and the company itself (such as annual reports). This information should help you conduct an industry analysis. Check with your instructor to see what kind of outside research is appropriate for your assignment.

- Don't try to learn what actually happened to the company discussed in the case. What management actually decided may not be the best solution. It will certainly bias your analysis and will probably cause your recommendation to lack proper justification.

4. BEGIN SWOT ANALYSIS:

External Environmental Analysis

- Analyze the major societal forces to see what trends are likely to affect the industry or industries in which the company is operating.

- Conduct an industry analysis using Porter's competitive forces from **Chapter 3**.

- Generate a list of external factors. These should be the most important opportunities and threats facing the company at the time of the case.

- **Suggestion:** Rank the external factors from most to least important. Start by grouping the top factors and then the bottom factors.

Internal Organizational Analysis

- Generate a list of internal factors. These should be the most important strengths and weaknesses of the company at the time of the case.

- **Suggestion:** Rank the internal factors from most to least important. Start by grouping the top factors and then the bottom factors.

5. WRITE YOUR STRATEGIC AUDIT (PARTS I TO IV)

First Draft of Your Strategic Audit

- Write Parts I to IV of the strategic audit. Remember to include the factors from your internal and external analysis in your audit.

6. WRITE YOUR STRATEGIC AUDIT (PART V)

Strategic Factor Analysis Summary

- Condense the list of factors from those identified in the previous sections to only the eight to ten most important factors.

- Select the most important external and internal factors.

- Analyze strategic factors from your final list of top internal and external environmental factors. Assess management's performance on each factor.

- This is a good time to re-examine what you wrote earlier in Parts I to IV. You may want to add to or delete some of what you wrote. Ensure that each one of the strategic factors you have included in your analysis is discussed in the appropriate place in Parts I to IV. Part V of the audit is not the place to mention a strategic factor for the first time.

■ Write Part V of your strategic audit. This completes your SWOT analysis.

■ This is the place to suggest a revised mission statement and a better set of objectives for the company. The SWOT analysis and any revised mission and objectives for the company set the stage for the generation of strategic alternatives.

7. WRITE YOUR STRATEGIC AUDIT (PART VI)

Strategic Alternatives and Recommendation

A. Alternatives

■ Develop at least three mutually exclusive strategic alternatives. If appropriate to the case you are analyzing, you might propose one alternative for growth, one for stability, and one for retrenchment. Within each corporate strategy, you should probably propose an appropriate business/competitive strategy. You may also want to include some functional strategies where appropriate.

■ Construct a scenario for each alternative. Use the data from your outside research to project general societal trends (GDP, inflation, etc.) and industry trends. Use these as the basis of your assumptions to write pro forma financial statements (particularly income statements) for each strategic alternative for the next five years.

■ List advantages and disadvantages for each alternative based on your scenarios.

B. Recommendations

■ Specify which one of your alternative strategies you recommend. Justify your choice in terms of dealing with the strategic factors you listed in Part V of the audit.

■ Develop policies to help implement your strategies.

8. WRITE YOUR STRATEGIC AUDIT (PART VII)

Implementation

■ Develop programs to implement your recommended strategy.

■ Specify who is to be responsible for implementing each program and how long each program will take to complete.

■ Refer to the pro forma financial statement you developed earlier for your recommended strategy. Do the numbers still make sense? If not, this may be a good time to rethink the budget numbers to reflect your recommended programs.

9. WRITE YOUR STRATEGIC AUDIT (PART VIII)

Evaluation and Control

■ Specify the type of evaluation and controls that you need to ensure that your recommendation is carried out successfully. Specify who is responsible for monitoring these controls.

■ Indicate whether sufficient information is available to monitor how the strategy is being implemented. If not, suggest a change to the information system.

10. PROOF AND FINE-TUNE YOUR AUDIT

Final Draft of Your Strategic Audit

■ Check to ensure that your audit is within the page limits provided by your instructor. You may need to cut some parts and expand others.

■ Make sure that your recommendation clearly deals with the strategic factors.

■ Attach exhibits such as ratio analysis and pro forma statements. Label them as numbered exhibits and refer to each of them within the body of the audit.

■ Proofread your work for errors. If on a computer, use a spell checker (although this does not catch all errors).

Depending on your assignment, it is relatively easy to use the strategic audit you have just developed to write a written case analysis in essay form or to make an oral presentation. The strategic audit is just a detailed case analysis in an outline form and can be used as the basic framework for any sort of case analysis and presentation.

Strategic Practice Exercise

Nike, Inc. designs, develops, and markets quality footwear, apparel, athletic equipment, and accessories worldwide. The company sells its products to approximately 25 000 retail accounts in North America and through a mix of independent distributors, licensees, and subsidiaries in approximately 110 countries around the world.

Reebok International Ltd. designs and markets sports, fitness, and casual-use footwear and apparel. The company has four major brands: Reebok, Greg Norman (clothing), Rockport (shoes), and the Ralph Lauren Footwear

Company. Financial statements for Nike and Reebok are shown below.

1. Using the information in the financial statements, calculate the following financial ratios for fiscal 1999 for each company. Values for 1998 have already been computed.

2. Use the results of the ratio analysis to identify similarities and differences in the profitability, liquidity, and long-term solvency of the two firms. How would these findings be incorporated into a strategic analysis of these firms?

	1999		1998	
	Nike	Reebok	Nike	Reebok
Current ratio			2.07	2.22
Quick ratio			1.25	1.35
Accounts receivable turnover			5.57	5.97
Days receivables outstanding 61.1				65.5
Inventory turnover			6.84	6.03
Days of inventory			82.2	98.4
Accounts payable turnover			9.63	10.16
Accounts payable period			37.9	35.9
Days of cash			4.15	20.38
Return on assets			9.7%	4.9%
Return on equity			12.25%	4.56%
Times interest earned			11.88	1.59
Long-term debt to assets			7.0%	31.9%
Asset turnover			1.78	1.84

Reebok International Ltd.
Consolidated Statements of Income

(US$ in thousands)	1999	1998	1997
Net sales	$2 899 872	$3 224 592	$3 643 599
Other income (expenses)	(8 635)	(19 167)	(6 158)
	2 891 237	3 205 425	3 637 441
Cost and expenses			
Cost of sales	1 783 914	2 037 465	2 294 049
Selling, general, and administrative expenses	971 945	1 043 199	1 069 433
Special charges	61 625	35 000	58 161
Amortization of intangibles	5 183	3 432	4 157
Minority interest	6 900	1 178	10 476
Interest expense	49 691	60 671	64 366
Interest income	(9 159)	(11 372)	(10 810)
	2 870 099	3 169 573	3 489 832
Income before income taxes	21 138	35 852	147 609
Income taxes	10 093	11 925	12 490
Net income	$ 11 045	$ 23 927	$ 135 119

Nike, Inc.
Consolidated Statements of Income

(US$ in thousands)	1999	1998	1997
Revenues	$8 776 900	$9 553 100	$9 186 500
Cost and expenses			
Cost of sales	5 493 500	6 065 500	5 503 000
Selling and administrative expenses	2 426 600	2 623 800	2 303 700
Interest expense	44 100	60 000	52 300
Other (income) expense (net)	21 500	20 900	32 300
Restructuring charges	45 100	129 900	–0–
	8 030 800	8 900 100	7 891 300
Income before income taxes	746 100	653 000	1 295 200
Income taxes	294 700	253 400	499 400
Net income	$ 451 400	$ 399 600	$ 795 800

Reebok International Ltd.
Consolidated Balance Sheets

(US$ in thousands)	1999	1998
Assets		
Current assets		
Cash and cash equivalents	$ 281 744	$ 180 070
Accounts receivable (net)	417 404	517 830
Inventories	414 616	535 168
Deferred income taxes	88 127	78 419
Prepaid expenses	41 227	50 309
Total current assets	1 243 118	1 361 796
Property and equipment (net)	178 111	172 585
Intangibles (net)	68 892	68 648
Deferred income taxes	43 868	99 212
Other	30 139	37 383
Total assets	$1 564 128	$1 739 624
Liabilities and Stockholders' Equity		
Current liabilities		
Notes payable to bank	$ 27 614	$ 48 070
Current portion of long-term debt	185 167	86 640
Accounts payable	153 998	203 144
Accrued expenses	248 822	191 833
Income taxes payable	8 302	82 597
Total current liabilities	623 903	612 284
Long-term debt (net)	370 302	554 432
Minority interest	41 107	31 972
Outstanding redemption value of equity put options	–0–	16 559
Shareholders' equity		
Common stock	930	933
Retained earnings	1 170 885	1 156 739
Treasury stock	(617 620)	(617 620)
Unearned compensation	–0–	(26)
Accumulated comprehensive income	(25 379)	(15 649)
Total shareholders' equity	528 816	524 377
Total liabilities and shareholders' equity	$1 564 128	$1 739 624

Nike, Inc.
Consolidated Balance Sheets

(US$ in thousands)	1999	1998
Assets		
Current assets		
Cash and cash equivalents	$ 198 100	$ 108 600
Accounts receivable (net)	1 540 100	1 674 400
Inventories	1 199 300	1 396 600
Deferred income taxes	120 600	156 800
Income tax receivable	15 900	–0–
Prepaid expenses	1290 900	196 200
Total current assets	3 264 900	3 532 600
Property and equipment (net)	1 264 800	1 153 100
Identifiable intangible assets and goodwill	426 600	435 800
Deferred income taxes	290 400	275 900
Total assets	$5 247 700	$4 397 400
Liabilities and Stockholders' Equity		
Current liabilities		
Current portion of long-term debt	$ 1 000	$ 1 600
Notes payable	419 100	480 200
Accounts payable	373 200	584 600
Accrued liabilities	653 600	608 500
Income taxes payable	-0-	28 900
Total current liabilities	1 446 900	1 703 800
Long-term debt (net)	386 100	379 400
Deferred income taxes and other liabilities	79 800	52 300
Redeemable preferred stock	300	300
Shareholders' equity		
Common stock, Class A convertible	200	200
Common stock, Class B	2 700	2 700
Capital in excess of stated value	334 100	262 500
Foreign currency translation adjustment	(68 900)	(47 200)
Retained earnings	3 066 500	3 043 400
Total shareholders' equity	3 334 600	3 261 600
Total liabilities and shareholders' equity	$5 247 700	$5 397 400

Notes

1. A.R. Sorking, "New Path on Mergers Could Contain Loopholes," *The [Ames, Iowa] Daily Tribune* (January 9, 2001), p. B7; "Firms Resist Effort To Unveil True Costs of Doing Business," *USA Today* (July 3, 2000), p. 10A.
2. M.S. Fridson, *Financial Statement Analysis* (New York: John Wiley & Sons, 1991), pp. 192–194.
3. H. Greenberg, "EBITDA: Never Trust Anything That You Can't Pronounce," *Fortune* (June 22, 1998), pp. 192–194.
4. T.L. Wheelen and J.D. Hunger, *Strategic Audit of a Corporation.* Copyright © 1982 by Wheelen and Hunger Associates. Reprinted by permission. Revised 1988, 1991, 1994, 1997, and 2001.

Name and Company Index

Subject Index

counterfeiters, 269

crisis of autonomy, 207

crisis of control, 207

crisis of leadership, 205

cross-functional work teams, 103, 213

cross-impact analysis (CIA), 77

cultural integration, 95

cultural intensity, 95

culture. *See* national culture; organizational culture

currency convertibility, 57

customer value, 169

cybersquatting, 43–44

D

debt financing, 175

decentralization, 220, 222

decision making. *See* strategic decision making

declining industries, 127

deculturation, 240–241

defensive centralization, 299

defensive tactics

  defined, 129

  expectation of future profits, 130

  expected retaliation, 130

  goal of, 129

  structural barriers, 129–130

Delphi technique, 77

demography, 54

  see also socio-cultural trends

developed nations, 57

developing nations, 58

devil's advocate, 189

dialectical inquiry, 189

differentiation strategy

  with broad mass-market target, 121

  consolidated industry, 125

  defined, 120

  described, 122

  focused differentiation, 121, 122

directional strategies

  described, 140

growth strategies. *See* growth strategies

  orientations, 140–141

  retrenchment strategies, 151–154

  stability strategies, 149–150

directors. *See* board of directors

disruptive technology, 100

distinctive competencies

  described, 87, 116

  and functional strategy, 17

  identification of, 116

  as key strengths, 169–170

distribution channels

  access to, 64

  international variations, 72

diversification strategies

  concentric diversification, 145–146

  conglomerate diversification, 146

  and financial strategy, 175

  related diversification, 145–146

  synergy, 145

  unrelated diversification, 146

diversity in workforce and markets, 56

divestment, 153

divisional and functional IS support, 271

divisional and functional performance

  benchmarking, 267–268

  responsibility centres, 266–267

  variety of measurement techniques, 266

divisional structures, 93, 207–208

do everything strategy, 182

dogs, 155

downsizing, 232–233

due diligence, 276

durability, 87

dynamic industry expert, 229

dynamic pricing, 191

dynamic service, 191–192

E

e-commerce. *See* electronic commerce

e-marketing, 191

e-marketing software, 191

earnings per share (EPS), 260, 315

EBITDA, 317

echo generation, 55

Economic Espionage Act (U.S.), 75

economic indicators, 317–318

economic value added (EVA), 262, 263

economies of scale, 63, 203

economies of scope, 92, 203

eCRM software, 191

edge-of-heartland businesses, 161

electronic commerce

  see also Internet

  challenges of, 9

  defined, 9

  "eyeballs," 262

  MUUs (monthly unique users), 262

electronic customer relationship management (eCRM) software, 191

electronic networking, 53–54

emerging industries, 127

employee profiles, 103

employee stock ownership plans, 281

employees on board of directors, 281–282

encirclement, 129

enterprise resource planning (ERP) systems, 219, 270–271

entrepreneurial mode of decision making, 23

entry barriers

  capital requirements, 64

  defined, 63

  distribution channel access, 64

  economies of scale, 63

  government policy, 64

  product differentiation, 63–64

  proprietary product technology, 64